Winter Tourism

Trends and Challenges

Winter Tourism

Trends and Challenges

Edited by

Ulrike Pröbstl-Haider, Harold Richins and Stefan Türk

CABI

CABI is a trading name of CAB International

CABI
Nosworthy Way
Wallingford
Oxfordshire OX10 8DE
UK

CABI
745 Atlantic Avenue
8th Floor
Boston, MA 02111
USA

Tel: +44 (0)1491 832111
Fax: +44 (0)1491 833508
E-mail: info@cabi.org
Website: www.cabi.org

Tel: +1 (617)682-9015
E-mail: cabi-nao@cabi.org

© CAB International 2019. All rights reserved. No part of this publication may be reproduced in any form or by any means, electronically, mechanically, by photocopying, recording or otherwise, without the prior permission of the copyright owners.
A catalogue record for this book is available from the British Library, London, UK.

Library of Congress Cataloging-in-Publication Data

Names: Pröbstl, Ulrike, editor. | Richins, Harold, editor. | Türk,
 Stefan, editor. | C.A.B. International.
Title: Winter tourism : trends and challenges / edited by Ulrike
 Pröbstl-Haider, Harold Richins and Stefan Türk.
Other titles: CABI series in tourism management research.
Description: Wallingford, Oxfordshire ; Boston, Massachusetts : CABI,
 [2019] | Series: CABI series in tourism management research | Includes
 bibliographical references and index.
Identifiers: LCCN 2019013223 | ISBN 9781786395207 (Hardback : alk. paper) |
 ISBN 9781786395214 (ePDF) | ISBN 9781786395221 (epub)
Subjects: LCSH: Tourism. | Winter resorts. | Winter sports. | Winter
 festivals.
Classification: LCC G155.A1 W525 2019 | DDC 338.4/791--dc23
LC record available at https://lccn.loc.gov/2019013223

ISBN-13: 978 1 78639 520 7 (hardback)
         978 1 78639 521 4 (ePDF)
         978 1 78639 522 1 (ePub)

Commissioning Editor: Claire Parfitt
Editorial Assistant: Emma McCann
Production Editor: Marta Patino

Typeset by SPi, Pondicherry, India
Printed and bound in the UK by Severn, Gloucester

Dedicated to Wolfgang Haider for his tireless efforts to strengthen international cooperation in outdoor recreation and tourism.

Contents

List of Contributors   xi

Preface   xv

1   Winter Tourism Introduction: Motivation and Scope of the Book   1
Ulrike Pröbstl-Haider, Harold Richins and Stefan Türk

PART I   WINTER TOURISM FORCES AND CHALLENGES   7

2   Winter Tourism Forces and Challenges: Spatial, Socio-Cultural and Economic Issues and Climate Change Adaptation   9
Ulrike Pröbstl-Haider

3   Winter Sport Destinations, Spatial Planning and Protected Areas   24
Gero Nischik, Marius Mayer and Hubert Job

4   Winter Resorts, Indigenous Rights and First Nations Planning for Traditional Territories in British Columbia, Canada   35
Murray B. Rutherford

5   The Different Shades of Snow – An Analysis of Winter Tourism in European Regional Planning and Policy Documents   47
Dorothee Bohn and Cecilia De Bernardi

6   Winter Tourism in the Alps and the Implications of Climate Change   64
Ulrike Pröbstl-Haider

7   Climate Change Risk Perceptions in Nature-Based Tourism Systems: A Case Study from Western Maine   73
Lydia Horne, Sandra De Urioste-Stone, John Daigle, Caroline Noblet, Laura Rickard, Hope Kohtala and Andrew Morgan

8   Alpine Winter Tourists' View on Climate Change and Travel Mobility   82
Bruno Abegg, Leandra Jänicke, Rainer Unger and Markus Mailer

9   Climate Change Adaptation – A New Strategy for a Tourism Community: A Case from the Bavarian Alps   92
Thomas Bausch

10   Economic Relevance of Different Winter Sport Activities Based on Expenditure Behaviour   103
Marius Mayer and Felix Kraus

11   The Knockout Deal – Pricing Strategies in Alpine Ski Resorts   116
Ulrike Pröbstl-Haider and Rainer Flaig

12	Snow Sports in Schools and Their Importance for Winter Tourism – A Descriptive Study in North Rhine-Westphalia *Luca Mariotti*	138
13	The Impact of Commercial Snowmobile Guiding on Local Communities *Iain Stewart-Patterson*	146
14	Sustainable Winter and Summer Mountain Tourism Destinations: Idealism or Possible Reality? The Perception of the Millennial Generation Regarding Achieving Success of Sustainability of Whistler, BC, Canada *Ilse van Ipenburg and Harold Richins*	155

PART II WINTER TOURISM EXPERIENCES   173

15	Winter Tourism Experiences: Visitor Trends, Preferences and Destination Choice; Diversification of Experience Offers; Segments and Marketing *Stefan Türk*	175
16	Winter Recreation Trends in the Swedish Mountains – Challenges and Opportunities *Peter Fredman and Tatiana Chekalina*	183
17	A Matter of Culture: How Cultural Differences Shape Skiing Motivation, Behaviour and Destination Choice *Ulrike Pröbstl-Haider and Nina Mostegl*	192
18	Winter Visitors' Perceptions in Popular Nature Destinations in Iceland *Anna Dóra Sæþórsdóttir and C. Michael Hall*	212
19	Winter Recreationist Motivations: Motorized, Non-Motorized and Hybrids *Jerry J. Vaske and Aubrey D. Miller*	228
20	Alternative Outdoor Activities in Alpine Winter Tourism *Bruno Abegg, Leandra Jänicke, Mike Peters and Alexander Plaikner*	236
21	Winter Tourism Management and Challenges in the Tatra National Park *Karolina Taczanowska, Mikołaj Bielański, Joanna Hibner, Miłosz Jodłowski and Tomasz Zwijacz-Kozica*	246
22	Chinese Guests in Alpine Destinations – What Are They Looking for? A Case Study from Switzerland Regarding Product Preferences and Landscape Perception *Barbara Haller Rupf, Katrin Schillo, Wolfgang G. Arlt and Reto Rupf*	257
23	The 2-Year Tourist: Lifestyle Migration in Whistler, British Columbia *Joe Pavelka*	276

	PART III WINTER TOURISM DEVELOPMENT AND SUSTAINABILITY	289
24	Winter Tourism Development and Sustainability: Regional Development, Ownership and Infrastructure; Environmental Management and Sustainability; Historical and Future Perspectives, Trends and Implications *Harold Richins*	291
25	Development of Downhill Skiing Tourism in Sweden: Past, Present, and Future *O. Cenk Demiroglu, Linda Lundmark and Magnus Strömgren*	305
26	The Challenges of Sustainability in the Management of Ski Resorts: The Experience of the Dolomites *Umberto Martini, Federica Buffa and Serena Lonardi*	324
27	The Role of Cable Cars and Ski Lifts as Key Innovations in the Evolution of Winter Tourism *Marius Mayer*	339
28	Merging of Ski Resorts, Monopolization and Changes in Ownership Structures: The Case of Whistler *Alison M. Gill*	354
29	How to Manage Ski Resorts in an Environmentally Friendly Way – Challenges and Lessons Learnt *Ulrike Pröbstl-Haider and Claudia Hödl*	369
30	Tourism Diversification in the Development of French Ski Resorts *Coralie Achin and Emmanuelle George*	388
31	Preferences for Renewable Energy Sources Among Tourists in the European Alps *Alexandra Jiricka-Pürrer, Johannes Schmied and Ulrike Pröbstl-Haider*	400
32	A Resort Municipality Without Residents? The Case of Jumbo Glacier Resort in the Purcell Mountains of British Columbia, Canada *Cameron E. Owens and Murray B. Rutherford*	425
33	Winter Tourism and Seasonality in Iceland *Þorvardur Árnason and Johannes T. Welling*	442
34	Safety, Risk and Accidents – Experiences from the European Alps *Ulrike Pröbstl-Haider*	461
35	Collaboration and Leadership as Success Factors of a Ski Resort – A Multiple Case Study from Finland *Raija Komppula and Emma Alegria*	476
36	Winter Tourism: Lost in Transition? The Process of Transformation and Inertia of the Ski Industry and Places in the French Alps *Philippe Bourdeau*	493
Index		509

List of Contributors

Bruno Abegg (corresponding author), Institute of Geography, University of Innsbruck, Innsbruck, Austria Institute for Systemic Management and Public Governance, University of St. Gallen, St. Gallen, Switzerland. E-mail: bruno.abegg@uibk.ac.at

Coralie Achin (corresponding author), University of Grenoble-Alpes, Irstea-LESSEM, Grenoble, France. E-mail: coralie.achin@irstea.fr

Emma Alegria, Business School, University of Eastern Finland, Joensuu, Finland

Wolfgang G. Arlt, COTRI China Outbound Tourism Research Institute, Hamburg, Germany and Beijing, China

Þorvarður Árnason (corresponding author), Hornafjörður Research Centre, University of Iceland, Hornafjörður, Iceland. E-mail: thorvarn@hi.is

Thomas Bausch (corresponding author), Competence Centre for Tourism and Mobility, Free University of Bozen-Bolzano, Bolzano, Italy. E-mail: thomas.bausch@unibz.it

Mikołaj Bielański, Faculty of Tourism and Leisure, University of Physical Education in Kraków, Kraków, Poland

Dorothee Bohn (corresponding author), Department of Geography, Umeå University, Umeå, Sweden. E-mail: dorothee.bohn@umu.se

Philippe Bourdeau (corresponding author), UMR PACTE CNRS, LabEx ITEM, University of Grenoble-Alpes, Grenoble, France. E-mail: philippe.bourdeau@univ-grenoble-alpes.fr

Federica Buffa (corresponding author), Department of Economics and Management, University of Trento, Trento, Italy. E-mail: federica.buffa@unitn.it

Tatiana Chekalina, Mid-Sweden University, Östersund, Sweden

John Daigle, University of Maine, Orono, ME, USA

Cecilia De Bernardi, Centre for Tourism and Leisure Research (CeTLeR), School of Technology and Business Studies, Dalarna University, Falun, Sweden

Sandra De Urioste-Stone, University of Maine, Orono, ME, USA

O. Cenk Demiroglu (corresponding author), Department of Geography, Umeå University, Umeå, Sweden. E-mail: cenk.demiroglu@umu.se

Rainer Flaig, Andermatt-Sedrun Sport AG, Andermatt, Switzerland

Peter Fredman (corresponding author), Mid-Sweden University, Östersund, Sweden. E-mail: peter.fredman@miun.se

Emmanuelle George, University of Grenoble-Alpes, Irstea-LESSEM, Grenoble, France

Alison M. Gill (corresponding author), Department of Geography and School of Resource and Environmental Management, Simon Fraser University, Burnaby, BC, Canada. E-mail: agill@sfu.ca

C. Michael Hall, University of Canterbury, Christchurch, New Zealand

Barbara Haller Rupf (corresponding author), Tourism Academy, College of Higher Education Lucerne, Lucerne, Switzerland, Tourism consulting company haller-tournet, Felsberg, Switzerland. E-mail: barbara.haller@haller-tournet.ch

Joanna Hibner, Department of Tourism and Health Resort Management, Institute of Geography and Spatial Management, Jagiellonian University, Kraków, Poland

Claudia Hödl (corresponding author), Institute of Landscape Development, Recreation and Conservation Planning, University of Natural Resources and Life Sciences, Vienna, Austria. E-mail: claudia.hoedl@boku.ac.at

Lydia Horne (corresponding author), University of Maine, Orono, ME, USA. E-mail: lydia.horne@maine.edu

Leandra Jänicke, Institute of Geography, University of Innsbruck, Innsbruck, Austria

Alexandra Jiricka-Pürrer (corresponding author), Institute of Landscape Development, Recreation and Conservation Planning, University of Natural Resources and Life Sciences, Vienna, Austria. E-mail: alexandra.jiricka@boku.ac.at

Hubert Job, Julius-Maximilians-Universität Würzburg, Würzburg, Germany

Miłosz Jodłowski, Department of Physical Geography, Institute of Geography and Spatial Management, Jagiellonian University, Kraków, Poland

Hope Kohtala, University of Maine, Orono, ME, USA

Raija Komppula (corresponding author), Business School, University of Eastern Finland, Joensuu, Finland. E-mail: raija.komppula@uef.fi

Felix Kraus, Julius-Maximilians-Universität Würzburg, Würzburg, Germany

Serena Lonardi, DP Tourism and Leisure in Mountain Regions, University of Innsbruck, Innsbruck, Austria

Linda Lundmark, Department of Geography, Umeå University, Umeå, Sweden

Markus Mailer, Institute of Infrastructure Engineering, University of Innsbruck, Innsbruck, Austria

Luca Mariotti (corresponding author), Institute of Outdoor Sports and Environmental Science, German Sport University Cologne, Cologne, Germany. E-mail: l.mariotti@dshs-koeln.de

Umberto Martini, Department of Economics and Management, University of Trento, Trento, Italy

Marius Mayer (corresponding author), Universität Greifswald, Greifswald, Germany. E-mail: marius.mayer@uni-greifswald.de

Aubrey D. Miller, National School of Surveying, University of Otago, Dunedin, New Zealand

Andrew Morgan, University of Maine, Orono, ME, USA

Nina Mostegl (corresponding author), Institute of Landscape Development, Recreation and Conservation Planning, University of Natural Resources and Life Sciences, Vienna, Austria.

Gero Nischik (corresponding author), Swiss Federal Institute for Forest, Snow and Landscape Research WSL, Birmensdorf, Switzerland. E-mail: gero.nischik@wsl.ch

Caroline Noblet, University of Maine, Orono, ME, USA

Cameron E. Owens, Department of Geography, University of Victoria, Victoria, BC, Canada

Joe Pavelka (corresponding author), Mount Royal University, Calgary, AB, Canada. E-mail: jpavelka@mtroyal.ca

Mike Peters, Department of Strategic Management, Marketing and Tourism, University of Innsbruck, Innsbruck, Austria

Alexander Plaikner, Department of Strategic Management, Marketing and Tourism, University of Innsbruck, Innsbruck, Austria

Ulrike Pröbstl-Haider (corresponding author), Institute of Landscape Development, Recreation and Conservation Planning, University of Natural Resources and Life Sciences, Vienna, Austria. E-mail: ulrike.proebstl@boku.ac.at

Harold Richins (corresponding author), Faculty of Adventure, Culinary Arts and Tourism, Thompson Rivers University, Kamloops, BC, Canada. E-mail: hrichins@tru.ca

Laura Rickard, University of Maine, Orono, ME, USA

Reto Rupf, Institute of Natural Resource Science, Zurich University of Applied Sciences, Wädenswil, Switzerland

Murray B. Rutherford (corresponding author), School of Resource and Environmental Management, Simon Fraser University, Burnaby, BC, Canada. E-mail: murray_rutherford@sfu.ca

Anna Dóra Sæþórsdóttir (corresponding author), University of Iceland, Reykjavík, Iceland. E-mail: annadora@hi.is

Katrin Schillo, Swiss Institute for Entrepreneurship (SIFE), University of Applied Sciences HTW Chur, Chur, Switzerland

Johannes Schmied, Institute of Landscape Development, Recreation and Conservation Planning, University of Natural Resources and Life Sciences, Vienna, Austria

Iain Stewart-Patterson (corresponding author), Thompson Rivers University, Kamloops, BC, Canada. E-mail: spatterson@tru.ca

Magnus Strömgren, Department of Geography, Umeå University, Umeå, Sweden

Karolina Taczanowska (corresponding author), Institute of Landscape Development, Recreation and Conservation Planning, University of Natural Resources and Life Sciences, Vienna, Austria. karolina.taczanowska@boku.ac.at

Stefan Türk (corresponding author), Institute of Outdoor Sports and Environmental Science, German Sport University Cologne, Cologne, Germany. E-mail: tuerk@dshs-koeln.de

Rainer Unger, alpS – Centre for Climate Change Adaptation, Innsbruck, Austria

Ilse van Ipenburg, Faculty of Adventure, Culinary Arts and Tourism, Thompson Rivers University, Kamloops, BC, Canada

Jerry J. Vaske (corresponding author), Human Dimensions of Natural Resources, Colorado State University, Fort Collins, CO, USA. E-mail: jerryv@colostate.edu

Johannes T. Welling, Department of Geography and Tourism Studies, University of Iceland, Reykjavík, Iceland

Tomas Zwijacz-Kozica, Tatra National Park, Zakopane, Poland

Preface

Winter tourism is an important income source in many mountainous regions of the world. The future development of winter and skiing tourism is essential for these often rural and peripheral areas and their socio-cultural and economic wellbeing. The mountainous regions are, on the other hand, sensitive and vulnerable environments characterized by a high biodiversity. Winter tourism development as well as the management of winter destinations need to find a balance between societal needs and the preservation of mountain ecosystems.

With this book, we would like to contribute to increasing the number of specific winter tourism publications and to raise awareness in general for environmentally friendly and resource sparing management in winter sports areas. This publication would not have been realized without the support of a number of partners. Particular thanks in this respect go to the pro natura – pro ski foundation located in Liechtenstein and represented by the Princely Counsel Hans Brunhard for supporting the collection of interesting research findings from the European Alps and to the cooperation between the University of Natural Resources and Life Sciences (Vienna, Austria), the Thompson Rivers University (Kamloops, BC, Canada) and the German Sport University Cologne (Cologne, Germany), which made this joint publication possible. We are grateful to all the contributors and experts from various ski areas that provided image material as well as exemplary solutions and experience.

Special thanks also go to Claudia Hödl for her coordination efforts and meticulous compilation of the manuscript and to Benjamin Seaman for helping with English translations when necessary.

Ulrike Pröbstl-Haider, Harold Richins and Stefan Türk

1 Winter Tourism Introduction: Motivation and Scope of the Book

ULRIKE PRÖBSTL-HAIDER[1]*, HAROLD RICHINS[2] AND STEFAN TÜRK[3]

[1]*Institute of Landscape Development, Recreation and Conservation Planning, University of Natural Resources and Life Sciences, Vienna, Austria; [2]Faculty of Adventure, Culinary Arts and Tourism, Thompson Rivers University, Kamloops, BC, Canada; [3]Institute of Outdoor Sports and Environmental Science, German Sport University Cologne, Cologne, Germany*

Winter tourism is becoming increasingly globalized thanks to international ownership models of ski resorts, innovative pricing systems, and new travel habits and travel experiences, especially in Europe. This phenomenon has been the subject of several conferences, such as the Tourism Naturally Conference in Austria in 2018. This international exchange was the motivation to compile all of the separate experiences into one book and to draw attention to the fact that this development towards globalization also warrants globalized attention through scientific research. The contributions of more than 40 authors from major winter tourism destinations in North America, Scandinavia and Central and Eastern Europe also allow – for the first time – an overarching discussion and comparison of management issues and main drivers.

The book consists of three parts. *Part I Winter Tourism Forces and Challenges* is addressed to current challenges including regional planning, socio-cultural conditions, climate change and economic challenges. *Part II Winter Tourism Experiences* gives an overview of behavioural research in winter tourism. The authors present case studies and methodological concepts for both understanding the preferences and behavioural intentions of current guests as well as the needs and requirements of potential guests in the future. Of high relevance in this context are also the trade-offs between the different attributes of ski resorts and destinations. *Part III Winter Tourism Development and Sustainability* discusses opportunities for future development considering and implementing sustainable development goals. The presented solutions include national concepts as well as solutions for single aspects such as social conflicts, safety or landscape beauty.

The three main book parts and related chapters show two major outcomes:

1. That ski resorts worldwide face many common challenges and can learn from each other.
2. That the respective development concept and related set of socio-economic and cultural conditions has a significant influence on future development and requires adaptation processes.

---

* E-mail: ulrike.proebstl@boku.ac.at

Since these two aspects form the background of the book and are essential for an overall understanding of the presented case studies, they are briefly presented in the following.

1.1 Common Challenges

The international scientific exchange revealed that ski resorts have many challenges in common, despite different geographical locations. For many winter tourism destinations, adapting to climate change and its impact on the range of products offered is currently the biggest challenge. Many contributions to the book, therefore, discuss winter tourism development in this respect, presenting adaptation opportunities and ways of achieving the desired transformation to an all-season destination. Climate change also influences many other management aspects, such as changing demand, short reaction times to changing weather conditions, cost efficiency or the documentation duties in the case of artificial snowmaking (see Fig. 1.1). While European destinations mostly trust in opportunities of adapting to climate change on a technological level (e.g. snowmaking with only −1°C), global warming has also accelerated the discussion of developing new destinations at higher elevations, e.g. in Kyrgyzstan and other currently still remote places of high conservation value.

However, climate change is only one crucial aspect influencing the management strategies and actions in winter tourism destinations. Societal changes and the shift to an international market have also had a significant effect on demand, on its diversification

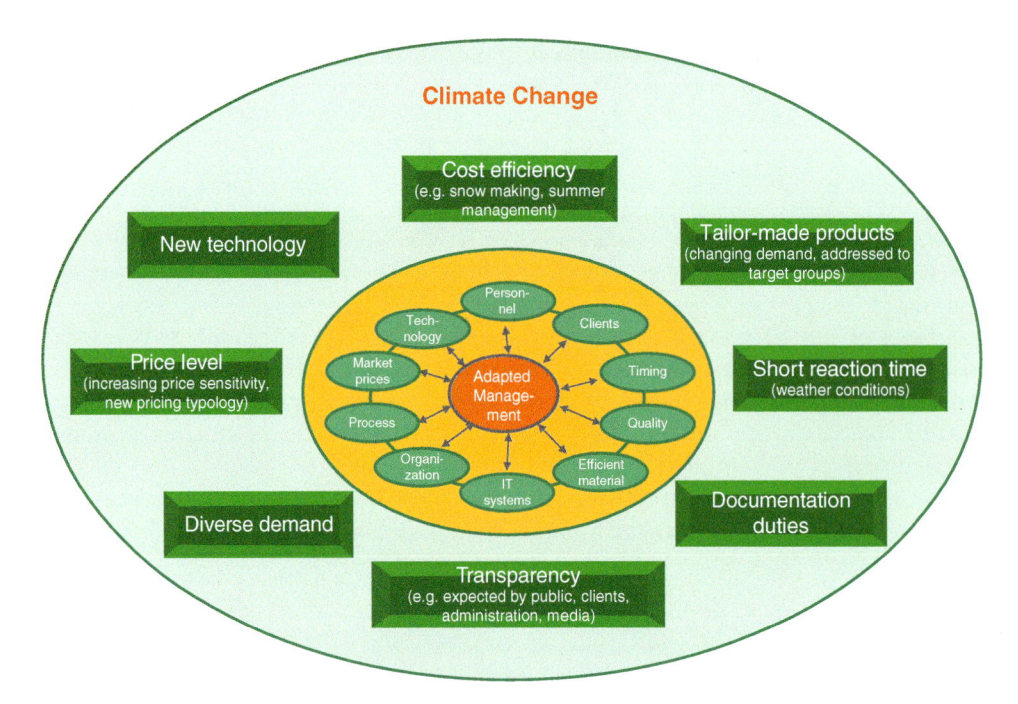

Fig. 1.1. Major challenges and drivers for the development and management of winter tourism destinations worldwide. (After Pröbstl-Haider, 2018.)

and on the development of respective target groups. Part II of the book characterizes the increasing diversity of demand, considers the influence of cultural differences on management and explores the great potential of new emerging demand from Chinese guests. Diverse and changing demand means that ski resorts and winter tourism destinations need to develop adaptation processes consisting of spatial solutions as well as new products, marketing and pricing strategies.

Long-term, resilient, adaptive management must take all these aspects into account. Part III presents these strategies and discusses means to achieve this challenging goal, such as management tools, auditing systems and collaboration, and introduces specific management solutions, e.g. to enhance safety on the slopes.

1.2 The Influence of Development Concepts

For many mountain areas across the world, winter tourism has been the opportunity to gain an attractive source of income, achieve local wealth and further economic development options. However, as the book shows, implementation of winter tourism destinations and ski resorts has been, and still is, diverse. The respective geographical conditions are less of a determining factor in this process than are the differing socio-cultural conditions, histories, forms of land use and ownership structures.

These conditions are strongly related to the respective past developments, but also – as the many case studies in this book show – to the current challenges and opportunities for sustainable development. Two major development processes can be distinguished: the 'incremental model' and the 'business model'.

The incremental model, which is characteristic of many destinations in Austria, Germany and Italy, but also of most Scandinavian resorts, describes a destination development in co-existence with existing settlements, forms of land use and traditions. The triggering of tourism development was based on multiple activities by farmer families or other community members, who started new businesses by providing accommodation, opening ski schools, constructing cable cars or becoming operators of ski lifts. What is more, this model is characterized by an overlap of the agricultural and touristic operations, without spatial discrimination between the two. Initially, the developing tourism infrastructure followed the traditional architectural characteristics and the local style.

The incremental model stands for a rather smooth or soft transition from an agricultural- to a tourism-dominated society. This model succeeds in providing a quality tourism product that is perceived as authentic and highly beneficial for the local population. Positive effects include the significant contribution to maintaining traditional agricultural land use, the creation of new jobs and related deceleration of rural depopulation, and the limited environmental impacts due to dual use.

Very often, incrementally developed resorts are characterized by an attractive, unique atmosphere consisting of traditional architecture, visible elements of former land use traditions, and a high diversity of owners and respective variety of entrepreneurial decisions.

However, this diverse ownership structure, ranging from accommodation to ski instruction to cable car services, may be a weakness when it comes to reacting to the challenges mentioned above. For example, increasing costs for artificial snowmaking are typically covered by the cable car enterprise but not by the whole accommodation industry that profits from the provided snow security on the slopes. On the other hand, the diverse ownership structure, in combination with communal leadership, might make these resorts more resilient in finding new niches or transforming from winter to all-season destinations.

The 'business model', largely applied in the French Alps, the United States and Canada, describes resorts that have been started from scratch. They have been specially constructed for winter tourism purposes without any or only very little link to existing settlements, and are commonly not based on local but rather on external investment. The design of these specific winter tourism destinations is independent from existing socio-cultural and economic structures, but is addressed to the market, to demand and to the expected economic return. These investments are likely to bring external money to the mountains, and they form a new, rather urban development within the mountains, with attractive job opportunities, e.g. management positions. The new resorts are often detached from the traditional communities and are operated by external companies owning several resorts, such as the Compagnie des Alpes in France or Vail Resorts, Inc. based in North America.

In this case, the developer profits from the increasing property value. The economic benefit for the local population is significantly lower than in the incremental model. However, adaptation strategies, such as a strategic shift or the implementation of new, sustainable development goals, are relatively easy to achieve.

Considering these different development approaches is helpful, and is in fact crucial to understanding the challenges and respective strategies that follow in the presented international case studies. However, the discussion of future development and the consideration of sustainable development goals (UNWTO, 2015) should also take further 'waves of development' into account. So, a number of resort communities in Canada and the USA have shown 'incremental development' over many years. Examples clearly include Vail, Aspen, Jackson Hole, Steamboat Springs, Whistler, Squaw Valley and other communities that have uphill capacity and communities attached which have developed in conjunction with them. Further examples of distinctive towns (based on other economic drivers previously, but now having a more prominent focus on winter sports) include, amongst others, Fernie (Fernie Mountain Resort), Rossland (Red Mountain), Revelstoke (Revelstoke Mountain Resort), Ketchum (Sun Valley) and Crested Butte (Crested Butte Mountain Resort). Globalized ownership, engagement of investors outside tourism, new regional cooperations with and without communal initiatives and other drivers will shape and influence the development options in the future.

1.3 Lessons Learnt

We, the editors from Europe and North America, believe that the greatest benefit of this book is the globally integrated view on winter tourism, with contributing authors from 12 different countries and even more destinations. Many aspects underline the need to discuss winter tourism from a global perspective:

- Winter tourism demand has changed from a local to an international focus, including the significant impulse provided by a potential Chinese market.
- The impacts of climate change affect ski resorts worldwide and, therefore, require common actions as well as adaptation strategies in all parts of the world.

- The contributions in this book show that, rather than 're-inventing the wheel', we should learn from each other and transfer best practices, e.g. in the field of pricing, environmental management, security and health issues, and in considering the demand side.
- Finally, the case studies presented in this book illustrate the various solutions, business models, planning tools and governance models applied to achieve sustainable development and a successful business.

References

Pröbstl-Haider, U. (2018) The digital future and its possible influence on winter tourism in the European Alps. In: Dehez, J. (ed.) *Proceedings of the 9th International Conference on Monitoring and Management of Visitors in Recreational and Protected Areas (MMV)*. Bordeaux Sciences Agro and Irstea, Bordeaux, France, pp.192–193.

UNWTO (2015) Tourism and the Sustainable Development Goals. Available at: http://cf.cdn.unwto.org/sites/all/files/pdf/sustainable_development_goals_brochure.pdf (accessed 22 January 2019).

Part I Winter Tourism Forces and Challenges

2 Winter Tourism Forces and Challenges: Spatial, Socio-Cultural and Economic Issues and Climate Change Adaptation

Ulrike Pröbstl-Haider*

Institute of Landscape Development, Recreation and Conservation Planning, University of Natural Resources and Life Sciences, Vienna, Austria

2.1 Introduction

The first part of the book covers chapters that deal with a number of winter tourism dynamics currently influencing tourism planning and development in mountainous areas worldwide. The first chapters also introduce major challenges in the overall development of ski resorts and the consideration of the respective spatial and socio-cultural conditions. Climate change adaptation appears of utmost importance in this context. Finally, economic challenges and drivers towards a sustainable future are presented.

2.1.1 Spatial and socio-cultural challenges

In the European Alps, instruments to steer development and protect valuable habitats have a long tradition. In Chapter 3, Gero Nischik, Marius Mayer and Hubert Job present solutions developed for the Bavarian and Tyrolean Alps. Despite significant political and economic pressure, concepts based both on spatial planning and the development of protected areas have been rather successful. Thus, many valleys of the Alps have remained untouched (see Fig. 2.1) and provide recreationists and tourists the opportunity to experience other forms of winter activities beside downhill skiing, such as ski touring, free-riding, winter hiking or cross-country skiing. These positive European experiences based on a zoning system could serve as a blueprint for the development of winter destinations in other parts of the world, specifically the Carpathians, the Caucasus region, the Ural or East Asian mountain ranges, for the very reason that economic benefits have increased constantly over time despite limited development options due to protected areas and restrictive zoning.

A second major component of long-term winter tourism development – beside spatial planning and the preservation of unspoiled nature – is the adequate consideration

---

* E-mail: ulrike.proebstl@boku.ac.at

Fig. 2.1. Zoning systems support the preservation of unspoiled landscapes, here the Malfontal in Austria. (Photograph courtesy of Lukas Umgeher/REVITAL.)

of socio-cultural aspects. The Canadian case study presented by Murray Rutherford in this book addresses First Nations and their traditional territories in British Columbia and the resulting conflicts with winter tourism development. The reported experiences and lessons learnt can, however, be transferred to other parts of the world. Early consultation of local communities, their involvement in planning processes as well as an open discussion about potential benefits such as direct monetary payments, jobs and job training or business opportunities are essential and may have a positive influence on acceptance. The globally applicable lessons learnt include:

- An avoidance of sites that are of cultural or environmental importance.
- An early consultation and involvement of the affected population claiming rights or territories in the area.
- The development of compensation or impact benefit agreements and a return to Our Common Understanding laid down by the United Nations.

Current discussions about winter tourism development in the Carpathian Alps, in Kyrgyzstan, Kazakhstan or China underline the significant relevance of socio-cultural aspects.

While early planning approaches tried to prevent further impact to sensitive alpine environments, recent planning processes are driven by a multitude of additional challenges. Chapter 5 by Dorothee Bohn and Cecilia De Bernardi discusses whether tourism strategies are aware of these challenges, and provides answers on how to maintain the significant economic benefit of winter tourism for rural and peripheral areas:

- reacting to changing tourism preferences and new communication demands;
- responding to climate change; and
- meeting new expectations regarding sustainable development including product development and marketing.

The European regional planning and policy documents appear to have a clear understanding of key problems and are therefore helpful for destinations. For both alpine and Northern European areas, tourism strategies and policy documents advise transforming the winter season from a distinct season to a versatile umbrella product.

2.1.2 Climate change adaptation

Many chapters in this part address current challenges for winter tourism destinations and the winter tourism industry. Often these challenges are directly or indirectly linked to climate change and necessary adaptation strategies. Adaptation strategies in tourism have been described and discussed in several publications (see Abegg, 1996; Harrer, 1996; Bürki, 2000; Elsasser and Bürki, 2004; Scott and McBoyle, 2007) and can be conveniently summarized in the following four categories:

1. The first adaptation strategy comprises means of reducing CO_2 emissions. In the context of winter tourism, it is especially important to reduce the most significant emissions from travelling.

2. Technical solutions are implemented to maintain the recreation activities and tourism products in their currently existing form. For example, technical solutions in artificial snowmaking are used to maintain snow cover, in order to ensure the continued attractiveness of winter sports destinations. In Finland, skiing tunnels have become popular means for extending the cross-country skiing season.

3. An expansion of services involves maintaining the main tourism product in principle, but compensating for negative effects of climate change with additional product offers or improvements to services. The added value contributed by these improvements should keep the overall tourism product, or destination, attractive. Examples for this adaptation strategy are the expansion into new product components offered by low-lying winter sports destinations, such as horse-sleigh tours, free child care, free use of wellness and spa facilities, or additional services such as special spa treatments (massages, beauty farms, etc.). In the case of lake tourism, new product opportunities present themselves in the form of cultural events and tours and activities around regional themes such as wine, which are intended to balance the negative effects of declining water levels. Basically, these offers should compensate for declining visitor numbers due to the deterioration of the original product or product components (i.e. more days of rainfall and lower levels of snow during winter), while the original product components or concept of tourism and outdoor recreation remain the main selling features.

4. Shifting to new products may be a proactive strategy, or the final adaptation strategy in a reactive sense when it becomes clear that the existing tourism product is no longer viable due to climate change and that it should undergo a major product reorientation. Examples of these strategies are the enhancement of summer tourism in traditional winter sports destinations in Austria, or the branding of destinations around non-regional themes, such as witches in the case of Söll in Tyrol. Similar trends can be observed in Scandinavia, where new tourism products emphasize a unique nature and/or wildlife experience, at least partly with the purpose of compensating for losses during the winter season.

Needless to say, multiple strategies can be applied in combination.

Against this background, Ulrike Pröbstl-Haider explains the implications of climate change for the European Alps. Her contribution covers the significant emphasis on technical adaptation via widespread artificial snowmaking, the increased investment in devices for summer and all-season tourism, and the cooperation between high- and low-lying ski resorts. However, as Fig. 2.2 shows, many European destinations still focus mainly on technical snowmaking. Slowly, investment in nature experience offers is also gaining importance in many destinations to enhance summer tourism and tourism in the shoulder seasons.

Lydia Horne, Sandra De Urioste-Stone, John Daigle, Caroline Noblet, Laura Rickard, Hope Kohtala and Andrew Morgan describe the perception of climate change in western Maine in the United States, focusing on visitors' climate change risk perception and resulting behavioural intentions. Understanding these behavioural intentions may help create suitable summer and year-round attractions. Biking and especially mountain

Fig. 2.2. Many skiing regions rely on the progress of artificial snowmaking technologies, here Lech am Arlberg in Austria. (Photograph courtesy of Michael Manhart.)

biking opportunities (see Fig. 2.3) appear to be offering new and highly accepted solutions for the summer and shoulder seasons.

In the context of climate change adaptation, Bruno Abegg, Leandra Jänicke, Rainer Unger and Markus Mailer focus on tourists' perception of climate change and their willingness to switch from their private cars to coaches and trains. They discuss how convenient the new offer would have to be to make people break with their preferred habits. New impulses may also be possible if various forms of mobility can be tested, including sharing concepts but also innovative e-mobility, and such offers may also have a greater influence on people's behaviour than criticism of their current use of private cars.

Various strategies for climate change adaptation have been tested and implemented in a case study area in the Bavarian Alps that is likely to be significantly affected by global warming in the future. This destination will have to address its products to newly defined target groups in summer, winter and the shoulder seasons. To attract these partly existing but also new target groups, Thomas Bausch proposes a combination of new infrastructure as well as a new positioning of the area, while simultaneously preserving its sensitive habitats and biotopes. Overall, this careful planning procedure ensures a destination development that is tailored to new target groups but which will not harm the sensitive environmental conditions in this valuable Bavarian resort.

2.1.3 Economic challenges

Future destination planning and management also faces the challenge of ensuring economic viability despite changing demand and increasing costs due to climate change

Fig. 2.3. Bike tourism is perceived as an alternative for winter tourism under conditions of climate change and can be tailored to different target groups. (Photograph courtesy of Oliver Schmid-Selig.)

adaptation measures. The two following chapters look at expenditure behaviour and related pricing strategies in winter tourism destinations. Marius Mayer and Felix Kraus illustrate that winter tourists spend more money than summer tourists and are therefore of high economic importance for tourism in many peripheral valleys in mountain regions.

Against this background, Chapter 11 by Ulrike Pröbstl-Haider and Rainer Flaig discusses winter tourists' price sensitivity and various pricing strategies from day tickets to different forms of seasonal tickets, to dynamic models and attempts to turn skiers into 'members'. Detailed information about clients will then be used to develop additional, customized lifestyle-oriented products.

2.1.4 Current and future customers

To secure future demand and the prosperity of destinations in the European Alps, it is crucial that many children are introduced to winter sports activities. In the past, winter sports offers in schools have been an appropriate and successful way of achieving this goal. Participation in winter sports in early life significantly influences later investment in winter tourism. However, winter sports offers at schools are declining. Luca Mariotti discusses the main reasons and concepts for maintaining this offer and making it even more attractive in the future.

The contribution by Iain Stewart-Patterson introduces readers to the increasing conflicts between different user groups in winter tourism destinations, describing the impact of commercial snowmobile offers in British Columbia, Canada. Zoning, training and licensing of guides is perceived as a possible solution for a complex but profitable development.

The chapter shows that resort planning requires the integrative consideration of different user groups with different expected experiences such as peace and quiet, wilderness, landscape and sport experiences, beside ecological and geomorphological aspects. Planning for snowmobiles in this case requires early consideration of those areas that are closed due to caribou recovery management.

The final chapter in this part by Ilse van Ipenburg and Harold Richins integrates several aspects that have been mentioned in previous contributions to arrive at a concept for sustainable winter and summer destinations. While many contributions in this book underline the role of regions, destinations or the industry, the authors highlight the significant influence of the customer by using the millennial generation as an example. They also illustrate that, due to the different structures in ownership and management, the pathways to sustainable development in European and North American resorts are likely to be different.

2.2 Summary of Chapters in Part I Winter Tourism Forces and Challenges

The chapters in this section provide insights into winter tourism challenges from different perspectives. The contributions include analyses of legal frameworks, analyses of strategies and surveys as well as well-documented case studies. The provided collection illustrates that major problems such as climate change adaptation or the consideration of socio-cultural conditions are common challenges that need to be considered worldwide.

2.2.1 Chapter 3. Winter Sport Destinations, Spatial Planning and Protected Areas

Authors: Gero Nischik, Marius Mayer and Hubert Job

The development of winter tourism facilities and destinations in a sensitive environment requires special consideration in spatial planning. Chapter 3 by Gero Nischik, Marius Mayer and Hubert Job discusses why limitations of tourism development are necessary and how these limits have been implemented in regional planning. In doing so, the chapter concentrates on the western part of the European Alps, which is one of the most intensively developed mountain areas in ski tourism globally. Basically, two main instruments exist to steer and limit winter tourism development: spatial planning and regulation by protected areas. The chapter presents and discusses the following cases: the Bavarian 'Alpenplan', the Tyrolean 'Seilbahn- und Skigebietsprogramm' and the Tyrolean 'Ruhegebiete'. All of these planning instruments were implemented many decades ago and have since guided winter tourism development in Tyrol and Bavaria. The 'Alpenplan' defines three zones: 'A' the development zone, 'B' the buffer zone with some restrictions and 'C' the strictly protected zone. The authors show that this strict solution has not led to negative tourism development, since the share of winter overnight stays has increased, as has the share of winter tourism overall. In contrast, expansion in Tyrol has mainly been regulated by a specific class of protected areas called 'Ruhegebiete' (quiet areas). These quiet areas also represent a consistent form of alpine zoning to preserve undeveloped open spaces; however, they are not linked to spatial planning but are anchored in Tyrolean nature conservation law. Again, despite this limitation of ski tourism, in this case by nature conservation law, Tyrol is still one of the most successful winter tourism destinations worldwide. Therefore, the authors conclude that both spatial planning and protected areas can be suitable instruments to steer winter tourism development. However, the chapter's discussion section underlines that these instruments are only successful if the political backing and public support remain as strong as they have been in the past. It is also important to note that spatial planning and regulations based on protected areas should not be perceived as two different instruments but rather as two approaches for an integrated spatial planning. The long-term experience of the presented case studies makes them suitable to also be applied in other alpine winter destinations worldwide.

2.2.2 Chapter 4. Winter Resorts, Indigenous Rights and First Nations Planning for Traditional Territories in British Columbia, Canada

Author: Murray Rutherford

What happens if an internationally well-known ski resort and winter sports destination expands into First Nations land, a 'reserve' area defined in 1862? The chapter by Murray Rutherford presents this interesting case and explains, against its background, the need for a new style of winter resort planning in British Columbia, Canada, including First Nations' rights and an integrative territorial planning. The conflicts at Sun Peaks are not unique in recent BC history, which is characterized by blockades, occupation, protests and preserved spirits on the one hand, and unsuccessful development plans and financial losses on the other. Such events of conflict and confrontation between Indigenous peoples and those who wish to develop or exploit natural resources are taking place in many parts of the world and are also typical for mountainous areas in New Zealand, the Australian Alps or the Sami people in the Swedish mountain ranges. Solutions first require a deeper understanding of the legal system and the evolution of the respective rights. Therefore, this chapter explains the complex colonial history and the evolution of the recognition of Indigenous rights in the Canadian legal system, before discussing alternative planning options and initiatives. In the second part of the chapter, Rutherford explains how further development, including outdoor recreation facilities, could be developed based on land use planning by First Nations including zones for tourism development or co-management arrangements including sustainable small-scale resource development. He also makes clear that any attempt to develop a winter resort in BC without prior free and informed consent of potentially affected First Nations would be unjust and probably fruitless.

2.2.3 Chapter 5. The Different Shades of Snow – A Comparative Analysis of Winter Tourism in European Regional Tourism Strategies

Authors: Dorothee Bohn and Cecilia De Bernardi

This chapter by Dorothee Bohn and Cecilia De Bernardi looks at the challenges and trends in European winter tourism and discusses whether respective tourism-, policy- and regional planning provide adequate answers. According to the scientific literature review, winter tourism planning should address climate change adaptation and the maintenance of a significant economic contribution. The analysis of policy and strategic planning documents across Europe is based on an extended literature review of 21 different regional strategic documents from Austria, Finland, France, Germany, Italy, Norway, Sweden and Switzerland. The applied thematic analysis systematically tries to identify patterns of text that are relevant for distinguishing and understanding the differences between these strategies. The thematic analysis revealed three fields of particular pressure for European winter tourism regions, namely the global economy and regional economic dependency, shifting tourism demand and climate change. The second part of the chapter analyses how regional planning in the different regions responds to these identified trends and challenges. Most of the examined documents provide a vision for the development of tourism in the region in response to economic pressure, shifting customer demand and climate change. On a concrete level, the regional strategies provide recommendations for regional stakeholders, mainly regarding infrastructure marketing and product development. Finally, the strategies perceive cooperation between public and private bodies as a vital precondition for future-oriented, competitive tourism development. There are differences in the perceived relevance and consideration of second home owners, e.g. in the Canton of Valais in Switzerland or in Agder in Norway, and in the emphasis on accessibility and the provided transportation network. Concerning marketing and product development, all regions aim at expanding tourism products relating to culture, wellness and culinary tourism, as well as conference tourism. The promotion of hiking, biking and mountaineering should strengthen products that are not seasonally bound. Overall, the diversification of winter tourism towards non-snow-dependent products supports not only shifting customer demand but also the adaptation to climate change. Therefore, Bohn and De Bernardi conclude that regional policy and planning in winter tourism is advancing development strategies away from the notion of winter as a distinct tourism season dominated by downhill skiing or other snow-related activities. From a tourism and policy perspective, in the traditional European holiday, 'winter' is going to transform from a distinct season to a versatile umbrella product.

2.2.4 Chapter 6. Winter Tourism in the Alps and the Implications of Climate Change

Author: Ulrike Pröbstl-Haider

Ulrike Pröbstl-Haider discusses the influence of climate change on winter tourism development in Chapter 6. Against the high economic relevance of winter tourism and its increasing vulnerability, adaptation strategies are presented and analysed. They encompass technical solutions, indoor offers in winter and new products in summer and in the shoulder seasons. In Austria, technical adaptation options have already reached their limit with a proportion of 80–100% of pistes with artificial snow coverage. Further initiatives therefore aim at achieving a stable, year-round tourism focusing on nature-based experiences, educational offers, cultural products or offers addressed to health and wellbeing. However, these products will not achieve the same value added as winter tourism products. Additionally, the chapter reports on recent strategies by ski resorts to reduce the impact of tourism on climate change. Accommodation currently causes the largest share of CO_2 emissions, accounting for 58%, followed by arrival, departure and feeder traffic at 38%. Cable cars, tow lifts, snow grooming vehicles and snow cannons, meanwhile, accumulatively cause only 4% of emissions linked to snow-based winter tourism. Therefore, beside the use of renewable energy, a shift in the chosen means of transport from private cars to public transport would lead to a significant reduction of energy consumed. Finally, the chapter also highlights the need for new promotional campaigns by the industry, including an appeal to travellers' personal responsibility and highlighting their own adaptation strategies.

2.2.5 Chapter 7. Climate Change Risk Perceptions in Nature-Based Tourism Systems: A Case Study from Western Maine

Authors: Lydia Horne, Sandra De Urioste-Stone, John Daigle, Caroline Noblet, Laura Rickard, Hope Kohtala and Andrew Morgan

Western Maine is a four-season tourism destination in the state of Maine; the area experiences the highest visitation during the winter months. The destination is heavily reliant on weather conditions given that natural resources represent the key tourism assets. The majority of visitors to the area engage in nature-based tourism activities. This chapter reflects and integrates lessons from the application of qualitative and quantitative methodologies to examine climate change perceptions by tourism stakeholders, such as business owners, regional tourism planners and outdoor recreation non-profit organizations engaged in tourism development, and local residents. We describe key findings from a qualitative phenomenological study to understand tourism stakeholder intentions and experiences with the effects of climate change in western Maine. We also present findings from a western Maine resident survey, focusing primarily on outdoor recreation users. Given the importance of natural resources and weather as destination assets, tourism stakeholders are adapting to climate change, though few implement mitigation actions into their business models despite adopting many small-scale pro-environmental behaviours. Limited climate change knowledge specific to western Maine, lack of perceived financial incentives, as well as uncertainty posed barriers to tourism stakeholders engaging more directly on mitigation and adaptation actions. Recreationists in western Maine seem to be generalists and indicated a high likelihood to substitute when they recreate in western Maine and in which activities they participate given changes in weather conditions. Survey results show that tourism stakeholders can take advantage of this substitution behaviour by developing four-season activities to enhance business sustainability during poor winter seasons.

2.2.6 Chapter 8. Alpine Winter Tourists' View on Climate Change and Travel Mobility

Authors: Bruno Abegg, Leandra Jänicke, Rainer Unger and Markus Mailer

Tourism contributes significantly to climate change, especially through transport to and from the respective destination. In Chapter 8, Bruno Abegg, Leandra Jänicke, Rainer Unger and Markus Mailer studied whether Austrian tourists were aware of their responsibility and analysed factors that might support more eco- and climate-friendly modes of transportation. The survey, conducted in the winter of 2016/2017, included 518 respondents mainly from Germany, the UK, Austria and other European countries, and was distributed in the tourism destination Alpbach-Tal-Seenland (Austria). The results show that a clear majority of respondents believe in anthropogenic climate change, perceive climate change as a significant challenge for the tourism industry with negative impacts on winter tourism and understand that tourism contributes to climate change. However, when the respondents were asked about real changes in travel behaviour, they were much more reluctant or unwilling to change. The study therefore underlines that the provision of knowledge alone is not sufficient to influence behavioural change. The chapter also highlights that respondents underestimate the role of accommodation. More energy-efficient accommodation and gastronomy relying on renewable energy would reduce a destination's carbon footprint and could also be used for marketing purposes. Since the study region of Alpbach is not only a well-known winter destination, but also a climate and energy model region and climate change adaptation model region, the region is obligated to improve its energy efficiency and enhance sustainable mobility. The regional engagement should therefore include tourism purposes and address new mobility concepts such as attractive public transport, new forms of automobility, e.g. with electric cars, or new mobility modes based on a sharing economy. Testing eco-friendly mobility onsite is perceived as one opportunity to improve the intra-destination mobility but, what is more, to also introduce new technology to tourists and reduce possible barriers towards new technology. At least the authors believe that this is more efficient than information alone.

2.2.7 Chapter 9. Climate Change Adaptation – A New Strategy for a Tourism Community: A Case from the Bavarian Alps

Author: Thomas Bausch

The German ski resorts and alpine destinations are situated at lower altitudes and are already highly affected by climate change. What is more, as Thomas Bausch explains in his Chapter 9, German winter tourism providers are challenged by new offers promoting winter holidays in warm destinations that are easy to reach by plane at reasonable prices, as well as by an expanding cruise ship industry. Against this background, the author describes the challenging task of developing an adaptation strategy for a small German ski resort, helping it transform into an all-season destination. This adaptation plan consists of a critical SWOT (strengths, weaknesses, opportunities, threats) analysis, a newly formulated strategy, the definition of main guest segments and target groups, and finally an implementation based on a multi-stage planning process. The SWOT analysis included climatic aspects, an ecological inventory and evaluation, but also the consideration of mega-trends such as demographic change and a development towards experience-led tourism. Future product development will be tailored to selected segments of all-season, winter season and summer season guests. The multi-stage planning process included the involvement of a nature conservation agency, to ensure its implementation, and a discussion with the local municipality. Finally, the chapter discusses limitations and lessons learnt from this case study. In contrast to many other publications, the presented process did not follow a bottom-up approach with an early and very broad stakeholder involvement. Planning processes should be tailored to the respective history and local situations. In this case, a top-down process was more suitable. Iterative planning, involving the required expertise at each round of improvement of alternatives, leads to a sustainable solution. The successful planning process was based on a holistic approach focused mainly on the guests' experiences and less on the single interests of local stakeholders. The chapter underlines that climate change adaptation should never consider the perspective of one single interest group but should include the consideration of mega-trends, societal developments and an always-changing tourism market.

2.2.8 Chapter 10. Economic Relevance of Different Winter Sport Activities Based on Expenditure Behaviour

Authors: Marius Mayer and Felix Kraus

Adaptation strategies always argue in favour of year-round tourism and a significant shift from winter to summer and autumn. Marius Mayer and Felix Kraus analyse this suggestion from an economic point of view in Chapter 10, discussing different expenditure behaviours, the economic impact of maintaining winter tourism and the contribution of different winter sports activities from downhill skiing to ski touring in the context of the European Alps. A worldwide review shows that studies presenting winter and summer expenditures in a comparable manner are rare. Based on case study areas in Switzerland and Germany, the authors analysed visitor spending according to the main activities in the summer and winter seasons. The case study conducted in Switzerland revealed that expenditures related to winter sport activities are often, but not for all activities, higher than compared with those related to summer activities.

Infrastructure-based activities like alpine skiing or downhill biking in summer led to higher spending compared with nature-based activities. The German case study conducted in the Black Forest showed that the length of stay was more relevant for expenditure than the activities themselves. Expenditures by walkers (overnight) in summer were even higher than the expenditures by alpine skiers. Day trippers in general spend significantly less in summer and winter. Here, alpine skiing was the most relevant activity. Overall, the study confirms that winter tourists generally spend more money, and it underlines their economic importance for many peripheral areas in mountain regions. However, the comparison of different cases shows that expenditures vary significantly and depend on many other factors beside the season and the outdoor activity, such as the regional price level or the offered infrastructure and quality.

2.2.9 Chapter 11. The Knockout Deal – Pricing Strategies in Alpine Ski Resorts

Authors: Ulrike Pröbstl-Haider and Rainer Flaig

An increasingly international winter tourism market also enhances the exchange and discussion of business models and pricing. Chapter 11 by Ulrike Pröbstl-Haider and Rainer Flaig first describes the winter tourists' price sensibility. Their review shows that pricing is of high relevance and is the main argument against this activity. However, costs are only one factor, and are included in a trade-off with other aspects such as snow security, slope quality or a close connection to the accommodation. For day visitors, the respective price level is more important than for vacationers. Against this background, the chapter illustrates principal pricing strategies and business models in North America and in the European Alps. The comparison reveals significant differences between the European Alps and North American destinations in the past. Furthermore, the chapter presents new concepts and alternative solutions such as a crowdfunding model and a dynamic pricing concept recently applied in Switzerland. The discussion section shows that the new pricing models must be seen in the context of new marketing strategies based on a digital transformation of the market. The authors argue that the cable car enterprises should become digitally integrated providers offering individualized products instead of transportation only. The chapter closes by presenting four main lessons learnt. The authors advise to also discuss pricing systems against the external competition, e.g. the cruise ship industry, to include a year-round perspective, and to involve the local population and tourism industry in the respective destinations in Europe. Second, they argue in favour of more networking and cooperation between the big players and smaller resorts, which are crucial for beginners, and to keep the sport attractive to tourists. Third, any enterprise should invest in customer loyalty. In this context, the price is only one aspect. The product should be adapted, modified, upgraded and changed to meet the changing demands of its future customers and guests. Finally, the authors highlight that, for future successful development, aspects such as the lifestyle character of an activity and its contribution to a meaningful leisure time will be of increasing relevance. A shift towards lifestyle and experience-oriented tourism requires a fundamental rethink including a re-evaluation of the entrepreneurial goals: the number of sold tickets may have to be replaced by customer loyalty as well as capacity utilization as the primary indicators of a healthy business.

2.2.10 Chapter 12. Snow Sports in Schools and Their Importance for Winter Tourism – A Descriptive Study in North Rhine-Westphalia

Author: Luca Mariotti

Chapter 12 by Luca Mariotti analyses the role of snow sports in the German school system based on the situation in North Rhine-Westphalia as an example. Currently, these types of courses have come under significant discussion. Despite the positive effects on health and wellbeing, the higher costs compared with other activities and also the lack of suitable destinations close to home and the influence of climate change have led to a critical discussion mainly with students' parents. Against this background, the German Sport University Cologne conducted a survey including schools with and without snow sport offers. Overall, 34 schools participated in the survey in 2017. Non-participating schools argued that snow sport activities are more expensive and riskier and that the organizational workload for teachers is higher than for other activities such as inline skating. Furthermore, the study revealed a need for more qualified instructors willing to join school trips. On the other hand, these winter sport trips should be perceived as an opportunity for students to understand the development of winter tourism, to learn more about the sensitive environment and to discuss their own responsibility as a tourist. One-third of all schools included in this survey did not offer any activities in the field of 'gliding, driving and sliding' to which winter sport activities belong. These snow sports offers in German schools are crucial for the future development of tourism destinations in the European Alps since about half of the tourists currently come from Germany. If a child once had a positive experience as a student, winter sports might become or remain attractive in later life as an adult.

2.2.11 Chapter 13. Impact of Commercial Snowmobile Guiding on Local Communities

Author: Iain Stewart-Patterson

Chapter 13 by Iain Stewart-Patterson describes the product shift in commercial snowmobiling in British Columbia, Canada. The current development is characterized by significant growth and demand for guided tours. Associated with this growth, the economic impact, the number of operators and the willingness to pay for the desired experiences are increasing. From a tourist's perspective, the guide provides the required local knowledge to find areas with untouched powder, is trained in hazard management and avalanche terrain selection as well as emergency management and incident response. However, as Stewart-Patterson points out, there are many challenges limiting the growth and the desired product development. Land tenure for commercial snowmobile operation is difficult to get since most of the mountainous land base in southern British Columbia has existing winter tenure holders, mainly heli-ski operations. In addition, the current situation is characterized by competition over high-quality wilderness experiences with non-commercial recreational snowmobilers and increasing conflicts with other winter backcountry users such as ski tourers searching for tranquil natural settings. Finally, nature conservation regulations also need to be considered, which limit the accessible terrain. Against this background, the author argues in favour of profound education and training of snowmobile guides and a certification including knowledge in risk-, wildlife- and guest management, technical and riding skills, experiences in terrain assessment, decision making and professional planning. The absence of this kind of snowmobile certification coupled with the challenges in securing land tenure for a commercial operation are dangerous for the guest, the growing market, the environment and the experience of other guests. The great opportunities of a growing market should be used to ensure the quality of the product and enhance its sustainability.

2.2.12 Chapter 14. Sustainable Winter and Summer Mountain Tourism Destinations: Idealism or Possible Reality? The Perception of the Millennial Generation Regarding Achieving Success of Sustainability of Whistler, BC, Canada

Authors: Ilse van Ipenburg and Harold Richins

Chapter 13 by Ilse van Ipenburg and Harold Richins discusses the feasibility of sustainable development in mountain tourism based on the example of Whistler in British Columbia, Canada. The presented understanding of sustainability comprises the avoidance of environmental degradation, long-term and careful planning, limited growth and a respective management framework. Beside these increasingly common goals, the way of planning and developing destinations has also changed. Early involvement of the local community, reciprocal understanding and respect, and the consideration of local needs are important elements to ensure sustainable outcomes in the long run. Furthermore, this chapter analyses the specific role of the millennial generation. For this purpose, the authors set up a survey with respondents below 40 years of age, followed up by semi-structured in-depth interviews with local and regional experts. Concerning sustainability, the respondents stated a different behaviour at home than on holidays, where they act less sustainably. Community involvement is of high relevance for the guests, but less so for the locals. Overall the tourists, especially the millennials, agree that sustainable aspects ought to be implemented in mountain destinations. The chapter specifies the main aspects of their behaviour in detail and also highlights that millennial consumers expect that sustainable behaviour should be easy and facilitated by the resort management or the community. The experts' answers regarding Whistler's sustainability and its development, however, differ significantly, especially in light of the new ownership by Vail Resorts, Inc. The survey results and the interviews show that, according to the authors, first attempts to implement a sustainable concept can be perceived but are not yet a full reality. Despite having a positive impact on sustainable development in Whistler, the respective development model cannot serve directly as a suitable model for European alpine destinations. The survey results underline the fact that sustainability requires more than the respective entrepreneurial management in combination with sustainable community involvement, but should also include and specifically address consumer interest and behaviour within the destination.

References

Abegg, B. (1996) *Klimaänderung und Tourismus: Klimafolgenforschung am Beispiel des Wintertourismus in den Schweizer Alpen*. Schlussbericht NPP 31. Zusammenfassung III. vdf Hochschulverlag AG, Zürich, Switzerland.

Bürki, R. (2000) *Klimaänderung und Anpassungsprozesse in Wintertourismus*. Ostschweizerische Geographische Gesellschaft, St. Gallen, Switzerland.

Elsasser, H. and Bürki, F. (2004) Auswirkungen von Umweltänderungen auf den Tourismus – dargestellt am Beispiel der Klimaänderung im Alpenraum. In: Becker, C., Hopfinger, H. and Steinecke, A. (eds) *Geographie der Freizeit und des Tourismus*. Oldenburg Wissenschaftsverlag GmbH, Munich, Germany, pp. 865–875.

Harrer, B. (1996) *Wirtschaftsgeographische Auswirkungen einer veränderten ökologischen Situation: Konsequenzen für den Wintertourismus in Deutschland*. Verlag des Deutschen Wissenschaftlichen Institut für Fremdenverkehr, Munich, Germany.

Scott, D. and McBoyle, G. (2007) Climate change adaptation in the ski industry. *Mitigation and Adaptation Strategies for Global Change* 12, 1411–1431.

3 Winter Sport Destinations, Spatial Planning and Protected Areas

Gero Nischik[1]*, Marius Mayer[2] and Hubert Job[3]

[1]*Swiss Federal Institute for Forest, Snow and Landscape Research WSL, Birmensdorf, Switzerland;* [2]*Universität Greifswald, Greifswald, Germany;* [3]*Julius-Maximilians-Universität Würzburg, Würzburg, Germany*

3.1 Introduction

Due to the considerable environmental impact of ski tourism, winter sport areas are a prominent example of the manifold and often contradictory land use demands (Mayer and Job, 2014) and are only partially compatible with more traditional human land uses in mountain areas. For this reason, the parallel expansion of winter tourism and protected areas in mountain regions has often been accompanied by strong conflicts between developers, locals and conservationists – and this is still the case today. The competition for the use/non-use of high-alpine areas by either ski tourism or nature protection is a rather new phenomenon of the service society as virtually no economic interests in these 'worthless lands' existed earlier (Mayer and Mose, 2017). However, these conflicts, as well as winter tourism development in general, are regulated by spatial planning authorities.

This contribution discusses therefore why limitations of winter tourism development might be worthwhile and which approaches exist to limit it, focusing on spatial planning and protected areas. In doing so it concentrates on the western part of the European Eastern Alps, which is one of the most intensively developed mountain areas in terms of ski tourism globally (Mayer *et al.*, 2011; Bätzing, 2015).

3.2 Reasons to Limit Winter Tourism Development

Its enormous economic importance notwithstanding (especially for peripheral high-alpine valleys with few economic development alternatives) (Bätzing, 2015), there are several arguments for limitation of winter tourism development: (i) environmental impacts and landscape aesthetics, and (ii) balanced regional economic development.

3.2.1 Environmental aspects

The considerable negative impacts of ski tourism on the environment and landscape features have been analysed and criticized since the 1970s (Cernusca, 1986; ANL,

---

* E-mail: gero.nischik@wsl.ch

1999; Rixen and Rolando, 2013). Ski tourism today usually implies a specific cultural landscape consisting of technical infrastructure like cable cars and ski lifts, snow-making equipment (including artificial lakes), restaurants, half-pipes and fun parks, access roads for construction and maintenance, levelling the ground of the ski runs, removal of rocks and other impediments, illumination for night skiing, etc. (Pröbstl, 2006; Mayer et al., 2011). These installations lead to a considerable landscape change inside the ski resorts, to forest felling, soil compaction, vegetation loss and/or change, higher runoff, water scarcity in the winter season in some catchment areas, fragmentation of habitats, etc. (Meurer, 1988; Dietmann et al., 2005). Furthermore, indirect effects due to functional relationships between the high mountain areas, alpine valleys and main valleys exist: if a ski resort is built on the mountain this also implies the construction of accommodation, gastronomy, retail and entertainment facilities as well as roads and parking lots in the valleys. All these measures entail their own specific environmental consequences (Schindelegger, 2017).

In order to prevent the further development of ecologically highly valuable mountain areas especially in the wake of the potential negative impact of climate change on ski tourism (Steiger et al., 2019) and to preserve areas not impaired by tourism infrastructure for other, non-infrastructure-based recreation activities, the state as the most powerful land use coordinator has to limit the expansion of winter sport tourism and balance its demands with those of other stakeholders (e.g. farmers, environmentalists, other outdoor recreationists). While ski tourism is a commercial land use paying off for investors and landowners, nature protection does not, even though society as a whole often benefits greatly from those areas (e.g. ecosystem services like water purification etc.) (Tschurtschenthaler, 2007).

3.2.2 Economic development

By limiting ski tourism development and thus capping the maximum size of ski areas the competitive pressures between destinations would be reduced to achieve a better balance between weaker and stronger tourism actors. This should enhance the financial viability and thus the economic sustainability of ski destinations and at the same time prevent too strong disparities between intensively developed valleys and the remainder. The latter phenomenon is shown by Bätzing and Lypp (2009) analysing the spatial concentration of overnight stays in the Austrian Alps. Careful planning should also avoid misinvestments and maladaptations by letting only the most suitable areas be developed for ski tourism, in contrast to the infamous 'vineyard lifts' in low altitudes developed due to local pressures (Jülg, 2001).

Two approaches for limiting winter sport tourism exist: spatial planning and protected areas. The first aims at balancing the diverging demands of different land uses, while the latter aim to prevent infrastructure-based tourism, at least in their strict form. We present examples for both. Spatial planning aims at coordinating and weighing up land use demands through the implementation of planning instruments. Due to the large number of actors in tourism with various often conflicting land use demands, a coordinating forum is needed. Spatial planning can fulfil this role to a certain extent, particularly at regional level, and functions as a means of conflict resolution in addition to the regulating of the intended spatial development in general (ARL, 2015). Finally, land use needs to be balanced between the general principle of sustainable development in mountain regions and a not too far-reaching restriction of the local people's scope for action.

3.3 Spatial Planning and Winter Sport Tourism

This chapter briefly describes the most important ideas and backgrounds as well as the development and impact of three spatial planning instruments in the Alps on winter sport tourism: the Bavarian Alpine Plan (Alpenplan), the Tyrolean cable car and ski resort programme (Tiroler Seilbahn- und Schigebietsprogramm) and the Tyrolean Quiet Areas (Ruhegebiete). These instruments are chosen because they have proven themselves over decades and have enabled and guided winter tourism developments through planning.

3.3.1 Alpine Plan in Bavaria, Germany

The Alpine Plan (Alpenplan) regulates mass (winter) tourism infrastructure development through an area-wide zoning of the Bavarian Alps. The 'ski-boom' of the 1960s and early 1970s led to quickly rising numbers of ski areas in the Bavarian Alps, a development that critics said was uncontrolled. Recognizing that the Bavarian Alps could not be protected from mass tourism infrastructure with individual case assessments, the basic idea of the Alpine Plan is that the transport infrastructure serves as a key function concerning spatial development of any kind and hence the usage of different areas (Job *et al.*, 2013, 2014).

Following an initiative of a few actors and nature conservation/mountain sports associations publicized first in 1968, the Bavarian State Government decreed the Alpine Plan in September 1972. As part of the first Bavarian State Development Programme the binding force of spatial planning goals also holds true for the Alpine Plan. The Alpine Plan regulates the transport infrastructure development of the Bavarian Alps concerning roads, cable cars, ski lifts, ski slopes, airports, etc. to balance the spatial needs of the tourism industry while preventing an overuse of landscapes (Karl, 1969; Barker, 1982).

The targets of the Alpine Plan were implemented by a central mechanism, the zoning of the entire Bavarian Alps (4393.3 km^2, excluding lakes) according to pre-existing land uses, environmental sensitivity and a suitable future development (StMFLH, 2018a). Thus, the Bavarian Alps were divided into three zones by institutional regulation (see Fig. 3.1).

Zone A (35%) includes all settlements and most areas with substantial pre-existing land uses, e.g. valley floors and tourism resorts and is earmarked 'generally suitable' (except airports) for further infrastructure development. Zone A provides an area for ski tourism and other mass-market forms of recreational land use (see ski resorts in Fig. 3.1).

Zone B (22%) serves as a buffer zone in which projects are permitted only if they do not conflict with more stringent regional planning requirements. Infrastructure projects require an individual review of potential impacts and are mostly allowed if necessary for forestry and mountain agriculture.

Zone C (43%) is designated as a strictly protected zone in which only traditional agriculture and non-intensive, 'adjusted' nature-based recreational activities such as

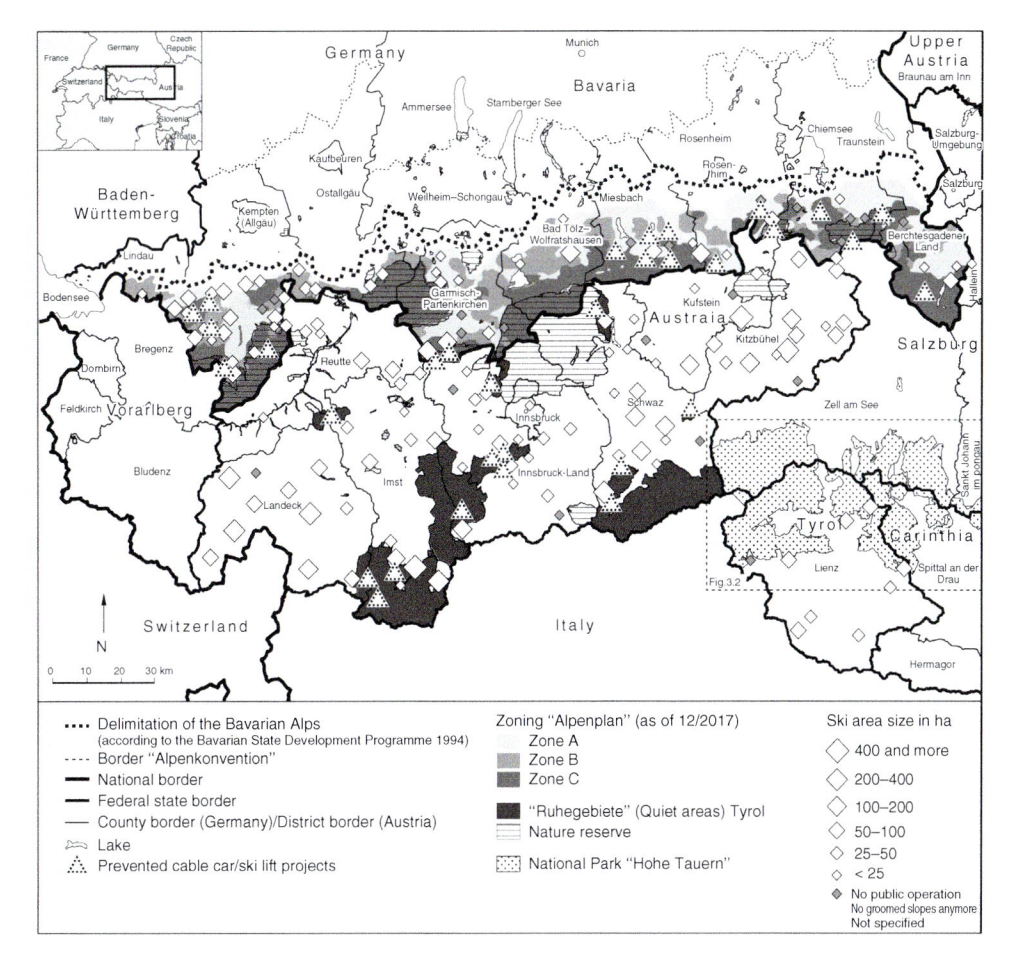

Fig. 3.1. Spatial planning limiting ski tourism in Bavaria, Germany and Tyrol, Austria. (Ski areas and protected areas in Vorarlberg, Salzburg and South Tyrol are not displayed).

hiking and ski touring are acceptable. Zone C is generally not suitable for any infrastructure development (e.g. ski areas), the only exceptions are forest tracks and dirt roads for the management of traditional cultural landscapes, e.g. to reach alpine pastures – these exceptions were necessary to overcome the resistance of the primary sector and water management agencies to the Alpine Plan.

Nineteen intended and still unrealized cable car/ski lift projects could be identified, of which only three are still up-to-date, i.e. actively promoted by supporters (most prominent example: Riedberger Horn). Since 1972 hardly any new developments of cable cars/ski lifts have taken place. The comparison with 46 ski resorts currently in operation in the Bavarian Alps (see Fig. 3.1, Mayer and Steiger, 2013) illustrates the quantitative dimension of development measures, in the prevention of which the Alpine Plan has usually played a central role. Without the Alpine Plan, the Bavarian Alps would have been developed much more intensively than is the case today and regarding the problematic profitability of several cable car companies and ski resorts (11 of a total of 57 ski resorts in the Bavarian Alps are now closed, see Mayer and Steiger,

2013, updated) the competition for visitors would be even stronger today and the probability for investment ruins would be much greater (Job *et al.*, 2017).

Concerning the Alpine Plan's limitations, it must be made clear that the Alpine Plan aims at regulating first and foremost ski tourism. Thus, neither the qualitative infrastructure development in existing resorts e.g. the upgrading of ski lifts, nor the tourism performance in general have been impaired by the Alpine Plan (Job *et al.*, 2013, 2014; Mayer *et al.*, 2016). In 2015, the level of overnight stays equalled that of 1972 almost exactly (–0.06%), whereas the arrivals were 113.5% higher than 1972. Also the cable car and ski lift infrastructure relied on to a considerable extent by winter tourism does not seem to have suffered from the Alpine Plan regulations: the share of winter overnight stays rose from 25.5% in 1969/70 to 28.4% in 1974/75 and 30.1% in 1979/80. In 2015 the share of winter tourism reached 35.4% (Mayer *et al.*, 2016).

In conclusion, there is not another comparable strict instrument of comprehensive as well as innovative spatial planning in the Alps like the Alpine Plan, which illustrates an early implementation of the principles of sustainability in a similarly fragile environment and on a regional scale two decades before the declaration of Rio in 1992 (Job *et al.*, 2014).

3.3.2 Tyrolean cable car and ski resort programme, Austria

In contrast to some public perceptions and despite the high economic importance of ski tourism, spatial planning in the Austrian federal state of Tyrol has limited and regulated the further expansion of ski resorts for quite some time (Haßlacher, 2007). While during the boom phase of ski tourism in the 1960s and early 1970s allegedly only rough sketches on maps were sufficient to obtain permissions to build new cable cars/ski lifts, this is not possible anymore. At that time neither nature protection laws nor spatial planning approaches to govern tourism development existed and the network of protected areas was only in its infancy. Today, it is not per se more difficult to get official authorizations for ski resort expansions, but it is a time-consuming, costly (due to required expert assessments) and highly bureaucratic while nevertheless more transparent process compared with the earlier more hands-on approaches (A. Schindelegger, 2018, personal communication).

Except for the concept of the Quiet Areas (Ruhegebiete) (see Section 3.3.3 in this chapter), spatial planning in Tyrol first tried to balance ski tourism development on a regional level in the early 1980s with the 'Tyrolean recreational areas concept (Tiroler Erholungsraumkonzept)' and the 'Tyrolean cable car and ski slope concept (Tiroler Seilbahn- und Pistenkonzept)' decreed in 1981 followed by the 'Tyrolean tourism concept (Tiroler Fremdenverkehrskonzept)' in 1982. These approaches were followed in 1992 by the 'Cable car principles (Seilbahngrundsätze)', which represented on a non-committal level the first attempt to avoid spatially negative developments caused by overcapacities and not to let only local actors decide about the further development of ski areas. Based on these cable car principles the 'Tyrolean cable car and ski resort programme (Tiroler Seilbahn- und Schigebietsprogramm)' was finally decreed in 2005, revised in 2011 and prolonged to 2018 in 2015 (Schindelegger, 2017; Amt der Tiroler Landesregierung, 2019). Since then it has provided the framework for new developments, connections and extensions of ski areas (Schindelegger, 2017).

However, the Tyrolean cable car and ski resort programme only provides guidelines and is only relevant if other sections relevant to planning like building or nature protection refer to it. The Tyrolean cable car and ski resort programme can be interpreted as a political self-commitment of the Tyrolean government on which ski tourism projects it deems reasonable and supports and thus communicates to the stakeholders in the tourism industry in a transparent way. Compared with the Bavarian Alpine Plan (see Section 3.3.1 in this chapter) the Tyrolean cable car and ski resort programme is much less strict; however, firmer regulations might be unrealistic given the much higher economic importance of ski tourism in Tyrol (Job *et al.*, 2014).

3.3.3 Quiet Areas in Tyrol, Austria

The Tyrolean 'Quiet Areas (Ruhegebiete)' were proposed for the first time in 1972/73 in the 'Landscape Plan' of the Tyrolean Forestry Authority. However, in contrast to the Alpine Plan adopted almost simultaneously in Bavaria, the landscape plan had no legal effect. The legal anchoring of Quiet Areas by way of ordinances has only taken place since their incorporation into the Tyrolean Nature Conservation Act in 1975. The technical foundation of the spatial planning security of the Quiet Areas is guaranteed in the Tyrolean recreational areas concept developed by the Tyrolean state planning in the chapters 'Tourism' and 'Alpine Spatial Planning'. Although anchored in the Nature Conservation Act, the Quiet Areas are a specific planning instrument (Haßlacher, 2016).

According to the Tyrolean Nature Conservation Act, Quiet Areas lie outside built-up areas and are particularly suitable for calm recreation. Their special characteristics consist of very clear prohibitions without exceptions: (i) no establishment of noisy businesses, (ii) no installation of cable cars for public transport or of ski lifts, (iii) no new construction of public roads, (iv) no significant noise emissions and (v) no landings or take-offs of powered aircraft for tourism purposes (with a few exceptions) (Haßlacher, 2007). Due to their clear prohibition regulations and by drawing borders directly on the external borders of ski areas and roads, Quiet Areas are also preferred for the designation of protected areas when it comes to setting final limits to ski areas. Landscape protection areas (see Section 3.4 in this chapter) are not capable of this due to their weaker conservation status. Therefore, Quiet Areas represent a consistent alpine zoning to preserve undeveloped open spaces, which is anchored in the nature conservation planning (Haßlacher, 2007).

In Tyrol, eight Quiet Areas were designated by the state government between 1981 and 2000 (Haßlacher, 2016). With a total area of 1370.94 km², they currently cover 10.84% of Tyrol's territory, mainly in high-alpine locations (the permanent settlement area of Tyrol equals 11.8%). Despite considerable development pressures, the Quiet Areas have not been impaired substantially by ski tourism since their designation. Years of efforts by ski area operators and local communities to implement various projects – especially in the Quiet Area Kalkkögel, which has existed since 1983 – have so far failed (Essl, 2017).

The limiting effect of the Quiet Areas on alpine land use can undoubtedly be demonstrated: 18 ski tourism (cable cars, ski lifts, etc.) and road projects have been documented in planning and publicly discussed. They were not implemented because of the Quiet Areas' regulations. After extensive political and public discussion, they did not even reach the procedural stage due to the clear contents of the ordinance (Job *et al.*, 2017). Despite the limitations of ski tourism through the Quiet Areas, Tyrol is one of the most successful winter tourism destinations worldwide. Since the designation of the Quiet Areas the number of overnight stays in the winter season has risen by more than 120% (1974/75: 11.8 million; 2016/17: 26.5 million) (Amt der Tiroler Landesregierung, 2017).

3.4 Protected Areas and Winter Sport Tourism

A second possibility to limit the expansion of winter sport tourism are protected areas, which in theory should prevent any large-scale infrastructure developments required for today's ski resorts (Bender *et al.*, 2017). However, even if it might sound counterintuitive, protected areas and ski resort development are not mutually exclusive. The legal incompatibility of both land uses depends on the protected areas category and on the national legislation. Usually, weaker protected area categories (like the International Union for Conservation of Nature (IUCN) protected area category V protected landscape) do not impose strong restrictions for infrastructure-based tourism development. For instance, most ski areas in the Bavarian Alps are situated in landscape protection areas (StMFLH, 2018b; own research). Their protection status has not hindered any landscape interventions for ski tourism yet. Nevertheless, stronger protected area categories like national parks or nature reserves usually prevent ski tourism development, at least in the European Alps (see Fig. 3.1).

The notion of 'usually' is crucial here as also in the Alps some exceptions exist where some national parks indeed overlap with ski resorts in the form of glacier ski resorts. This is the case in the French Vanoise and the Italian Stelvio National Parks where summer ski areas are situated in the parks' core zones (Mayer and Mose, 2017). During the boom phase of glacier skiing between the 1960s and 1980s several severe conflicts between ski resort development and existing or projected national parks occurred. In France, the so-called 'Affaire Vanoise' saw a highly publicized antagonism between the national park and ski resort developers between 1969 and 1971 in which finally the French president Pompidou intervened. A compromise solution preserved the integrity of the park and allowed only very moderate development compared with the initial large-scale plans (Laslaz, 2004). The Hohe Tauern National Park (Austria) in particular shows that these protected areas can effectively limit the expansion of ski tourism in fragile high-alpine environments as only two out of nine originally planned glacier ski resorts were finally built (see Fig. 3.2, Mayer and Mose, 2017). However, these experiences cannot simply be transferred to the international level as, for instance, in Canada or New Zealand ski resorts are directly located inside of national parks (Dearden, 2000, referring to the Canadian Banff National Park). Without doubt, protected areas and Quiet Areas lead to opportunity costs for ski resort developers but they also serve as important preconditions for nature-based or soft-tourism approaches. The latter were in part invented and promoted in the Austrian Alps for the first time as a kind of compensation for the municipalities for the forsaking of large-scale ski tourism projects in favour of protected areas (e.g. in the Virgental on the southern slope of the Hohe Tauern; see Fig. 3.2; Mose, 2007). Another good example of soft approaches is the promotion of Austrian mountaineering villages by the alpine club. This branding and certification approach

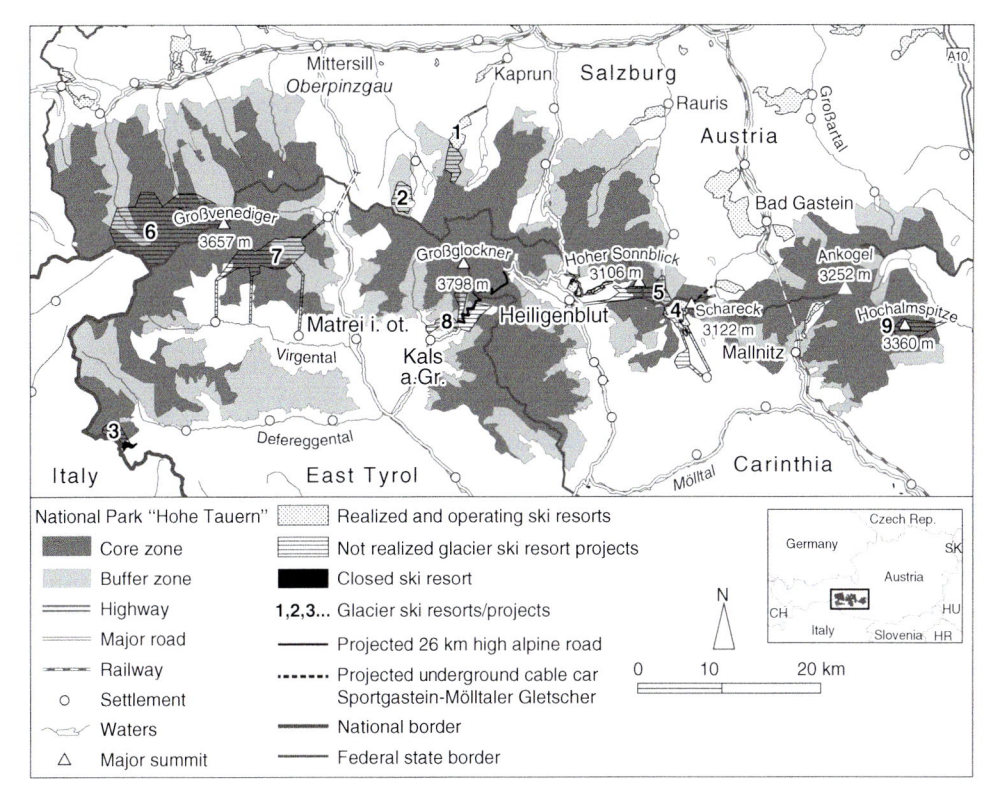

Fig. 3.2. Hohe Tauern National Park, Austria with realized and prevented glacier ski area projects. (Adapted from Mayer and Mose, 2017, p. 41.)

has also been extended recently to the first villages in Germany, Italy and Slovenia (Österreichischer Alpenverein, 2018).

However, Mayer *et al.* (2011) show that at least in Tyrol, protected areas often have been designated in areas less suitable for ski tourism development. In other words, the steep and rocky ranges of the northern limestone Alps are clearly overrepresented in terms of protected areas designations compared with the smoother relief of the greywacke zone in the Kitzbüheler or Tuxer Alps, which are much more suitable for skiing. The same can be observed for the Bavarian Alps and the Alpine Plan where the restrictive zone C also concentrates in the northern limestone Alps (Barnick, 1980). Both observations fit very well to Runte's (1973) worthless land theory.

3.5 Conclusions

Both spatial planning and protected areas can be suitable instruments to limit winter sport tourism. However, this only works out if the political back-up and public support are strong enough and if false compromises are avoided, like ski lifts in national parks' core zones for instance.

Spatial planning and protected areas have been able to hold large areas of the Bavarian and Tyrolean Alps free from infrastructure-based tourism without impairing the profitable further growth of ski tourism in the past few decades. In addition, protected areas and areas kept free from large-scale tourism infrastructure represent tourism destinations in their own right for outdoor activities like ski touring or hiking.

Spatial planning and protected areas designations should not be regarded as two separate approaches but rather constitute two sides of the same coin. Both their functioning and their effects overlap. For instance, the Tyrolean Quiet Areas are the outcome of spatial planning procedures, but they are legally safeguarded by the law on nature protection. Furthermore, the Bavarian Alpine Plan has a stronger protection effect compared with weaker protected area categories. Its core zone C stretches out beyond existing strict protected area categories, covering nearly 10% more of the Bavarian Alps than the ones mentioned first (Mayer *et al.*, 2016).

The Alpine Plan could therefore serve as a best-practice model for emerging mountain tourism markets like the Carpathians, the Caucasus, the Urals or eastern Asian ranges. In these still-growing ski tourism markets an easily understandable, transferable and applicable tool like the Alpine Plan could steer tourism development by limiting development to the areas suitable for ski tourism while at the same time protecting sensitive environments (Job *et al.*, 2014).

However, compared with project developers in tourism, spatial planners and nature protectionists share one clear immanent disadvantage: while project developers can repeatedly submit and slightly change their proposals over the years (until they finally get approved, maybe after a political change), planners and conservationists wanting to limit tourism expansion are not able to concede even once, as if they do the damage to nature, the environment and the landscape will be done (Haßlacher, 2013).

References

Akademie für Raumforschung und Landesplanung (ARL) (2015) *Handwörterbuch der Raumordnung*. ARL, Hannover, Germany.
Amt der Tiroler Landesregierung (2017) Der Tourismus im Winter 2016/17. Available at: https://www.tirol.gv.at/fileadmin/themen/statistik-budget/statistik/downloads/FV_Winter_2017.pdf (accessed 14 July 2018).
Amt der Tiroler Landesregierung (2019) Gesamte Rechtsvorschrift für Seilbahn-und Schigebietsprogramm 2018 -TSSP 2018, Tiroler, Fassung vom 14.01.2019. Available at: https://www.tirol.gv.at/fileadmin/themen/landesentwicklung/raumordnung/ueberoertl_ro/Seilbahnkonzept/TSSP_2018__Fassung_vom_14.01.2019.pdf (accessed 14 April 2019).
Barker, M.L. (1982) Comparison of parks, reserves and landscape protection in three countries of the eastern Alps. *Environmental Conservation* 9(4), 275–285.
Barnick, H. (1980) 'Alpine Raumordnung'. Ein wichtiger Teil der Tiroler Raumplanung. *Berichte zur Raumforschung und Raumordnung* 24(5), 3–7.
Bätzing, W. (2015) *Die Alpen: Geschichte und Zukunft einer europäischen Kulturlandschaft*, 4th edn. Verlag C.H. Beck, Munich, Germany.
Bätzing, W. and Lypp, D. (2009) Verliert der Tourismus in den österreichischen Alpen seinen flächenhaften Charakter? Eine Analyse der Veränderungen der Gästebetten und Übernachtungen auf Gemeindeebene zwischen 1985 und 2005. *Mitteilungen der Fränkischen Geographischen Gesellschaft* 56, 327–356.
Bayerische Akademie für Naturschutz und Landschaftspflege (ANL) (1999) (ed.) *Wintersport und Naturschutz. Ursprung – Gegenwart – Zukunft* (Laufener Seminarbeiträge 6/99). ANL, Laufen, Germany.

Bayerisches Staatsministerium der Finanzen, für Landesentwicklung und Heimat (StMFLH) (2018a) Landesentwicklungsprogramm. Available at: https://www.landesentwicklung-bayern.de/teilfortschreibung-lep (accessed 28 July 2018).

Bayerisches Staatsministerium der Finanzen, für Landesentwicklung und Heimat (StMFLH) (2018b) Bayern Atlas. Available at: https://geoportal.bayern.de/bayernatlas (accessed 20 July 2018).

Bender, O., Roth, C.E. and Job, H. (2017) Protected areas and population development in the Alps. *eco.mont* 9, 5–16. DOI:10.1553/eco.mont-9-sis5

Cernusca, A. (1986) *Ökologische Auswirkungen des Baues und Betriebes von Skipisten und Empfehlungen zur Reduktion der Umweltschäden*. Council of Europe, Strasbourg, France.

Dearden, P. (2000) Tourism, national parks and resource conflicts. In: Butler, R.W. and Boyd, S.W. (eds) *Tourism and National Parks*. Wiley, Chichester, UK, pp. 187–202.

Dietmann, T., Kohler, U. and Lutz, G. (2005) Die Skigebiete in den bayerischen Alpen. Ökologischer Zustand, Konfliktbereiche, Lösungsmöglichkeiten – eine Schlussauswertung der Skipistenuntersuchung Bayern. *Jahrbuch des Vereins zum Schutz der Bergwelt* 70, 45–60.

Essl, J. (2017) Die Kalkkögel kommen nicht zur Ruhe. *Innsbruck Alpin* 1, 36–37.

Haßlacher, P. (2007) Schutzgebiets- und Erholungsraumplanung in Tirol im Wandel der Zeit. Ein Streifzug seit 1960. In: Merlin, F.W., Hellebart, S. and Machatschek, M. (eds) *Bergwelt im Wandel*. Verlag des Kärntner Landesarchivs, Klagenfurt, Austria, pp. 81–90.

Haßlacher, P. (2013) Die Eroberung des Piz Val Gronda – ein umwelt- und raumordnungspolitischer Skandal. *Jahrbuch des Vereins zum Schutz der Bergwelt* 78, 79–82.

Haßlacher, P. (2016) Alpenkonvention muss alpine Raumordnung endlich stärken. *Die Alpenkonvention* 83(2), 7–9.

Job, H., Fröhlich, H., Geiger, A., Kraus, F. and Mayer, M. (2013) Der Alpenplan – eine raumplanerische Erfolgsgeschichte. In: Job, H. and Mayer, M. (eds) *Tourismus und Regionalentwicklung in Bayern* (Arbeitsberichte der ARL Band 9). ARL, Hannover, Germany, pp. 213–242.

Job, H., Mayer, M. and Kraus, F. (2014) Die beste Idee, die Bayern je hatte: der Alpenplan. Raumplanung mit Weitblick. *GAIA* 23 (4), 335–345. DOI:10.14512/gaia.23.4.9

Job, H., Mayer, M., Haßlacher, P., Nischik, G., Knauf, C. *et al*. (2017) *Analyse, Bewertung und Sicherung alpiner Freiräume durch Raumordnung und räumliche Planung* (Forschungsberichte der ARL 7). ARL, Hannover, Germany.

Jülg, F. (2001) *Österreich. Zentrum und Peripherie im Herzen Europas*. Klett-Perthes, Gotha/Stuttgart, Germany.

Karl, H. (1969) Landschaftsordnung und Bergbahnplanung – dringende Anliegen im Alpenraum. In: DAV (ed.) *Jahrbuch des Österreichischen Alpenvereins 1969*. Bergverlag Rudolf Rother, Munich, Germany, pp. 152–165.

Laslaz, L. (2004) *Vanoise. 40 ans de Parc National. Bilan et perspectives*. Harmattan, Paris.

Mayer, M. and Job, H. (2014) Die Bayerischen Alpen als Lebens-und Wirtschaftsraum zwischen Nutzungs-und Schutzansprüchen. In: Chilla, T. (ed.) *Leben in den Alpen. Verstädterung, Entsiedlung und neue Aufwertungen*. Haupt, Bern, Switzerland, pp. 33–49.

Mayer, M. and Mose, I. (2017) The opportunity costs of 'worthless land': the nexus between national parks and glacier ski resorts in the Alps. *eco.mont* 9, 35–45. DOI:10.1553/eco.mont-9-sis35.t

Mayer, M. and Steiger, R. (2013) Skitourismus in den Bayerischen Alpen – Entwicklung und Zukunftsperspektiven. In: Job, H. and Mayer, M. (eds) *Tourismus und Regionalentwicklung in Bayern* (Arbeitsberichte der ARL Band 9). ARL, Hannover, Germany, pp. 164–212.

Mayer, M., Kraus, F. and Job, H. (2011) Tourismus – Treiber des Wandels oder Bewahrer alpiner Kultur und Landschaft? *Mitteilungen der Österreichischen Geographischen Gesellschaft* 153, 31–74. DOI:10.1553/moegg153s31

Mayer, M., Strubelt, N., Kraus, F. and Job, H. (2016) Der bayerische 'Alpenplan' – viele Stärken und wenige Schwächen. *Jahrbuch des Vereins zum Schutz der Bergwelt* 81/82, 177–218.

Meurer, M. (1988) Vergleichende Analysen touristisch bedingter Belastungen des Naturhaushaltes im Südtiroler Grödner- und Villnöß-Tal. *Geographische Rundschau* 40(10), 28–38.

Mose, I. (2007) Hohe Tauern National Park: a model for protected areas in the Alps? In: Mose, I. (ed.) *Protected Areas and Regional Development in Europe. Towards a New Model for the 21st Century*. Routledge, Aldershot, UK, pp. 99–114.

Österreichischer Alpenverein (2018) Die Philosophie der Bergsteigerdörfer. Available at: https://www.bergsteigerdoerfer.org/6-0-Die-Philosphie-der-Bergsteigerdoerfer.html (accessed 12 November 2018).

Pröbstl, U. (2006) *Kunstschnee und Umwelt. Entwicklung und Auswirkungen der technischen Beschneiung*. Haupt, Bern, Switzerland.

Rixen, C. and Rolando, A. (2013) *The Impacts of Skiing and Related Winter Recreational Activities on Mountain Environments*. Bentham Science Publishers, Oak Park, IL.

Runte, A. (1973) 'Worthless' lands – our national parks: the enigmatic past and uncertain future of America's scenic wonderlands. *American West* 10, 4–11.

Schindelegger, A. (2017) Tourismusorte an der Wachstumsgrenze? Lokale und regionale planerische Strategien in Tirol. In: Luger, K. and Rest, F. (eds) *Alpenreisen. Erlebnis. Raumtransformationen. Imagination*. Studien Verlag, Innsbruck, Austria, pp. 295–308.

Steiger, R., Scott, D., Abegg, B., Pons, M. and Aall, C. (2019) A critical review of climate change risk for ski tourism. *Current Issues in Tourism*. 22(11), 1343–1379. DOI:10.1080/13683500.2017.1410110

Tschurtschenthaler, P. (2007) Was hat Ökonomie mit Natur zu tun? *Natur und Landschaft* 82(7), 301–305.

4 Winter Resorts, Indigenous Rights and First Nations Planning for Traditional Territories in British Columbia, Canada

Murray B. Rutherford*

School of Resource and Environmental Management, Simon Fraser University, Burnaby, BC, Canada

4.1 Introduction

On 23 July 2001, four members of the Indigenous Secwepemc Nation were arrested for occupying the 'Skwelkwek'welt Protection Centre', a protest camp established by the Secwepemc at Sun Peaks Ski Resort in south-central British Columbia (BC) (*British Columbia v. Billy, Sauls, Manuel Jr., and Willard*, 2003). Sun Peaks Resort Corporation had obtained approval from the BC provincial government to expand an existing ski area known as Tod Mountain into a major all-season destination resort. The Secwepemc protestors challenged the expansion of the resort, claiming that not only was it within their traditional territory, but that it was also within an area surveyed in 1862 by the British colonial government as a 'reserve' for the Neskonlith peoples (the Neskonlith are one of 17 bands of the Secwepemc Nation) (St. Pierre, n.d.). According to a brochure issued by the Skwelkwek'welt Protection Centre and the Neskonlith Band:

> With ongoing urban and rural encroachment, Skwelkwek'welt is one of the last places in our territory where we can still hunt for food, gather medicines and continue to practice other Secwepemc cultural traditions. This area is particularly important for our children and youth who have been continually learning, practicing and returning to many of our Secwepemc cultural practices, many of which are dependent on our access to and use of our land.
>
> (St. Pierre, n.d., p. 1)

The arrests in 2001 at Sun Peaks did not resolve the dispute, and over the ensuing decade there were further arrests for occupation of the protest camp, blockades of the road to the ski area and conflicts between Indigenous and non-Indigenous people at the resort village (Albinati, 2017). Despite the protests, the expansion of Sun Peaks Resort proceeded.

The conflicts at Sun Peaks are not unique in recent BC history. In Melvin Creek Valley, a remote alpine region north-east of Whistler, members of the St'át'imc Nation

---

* E-mail: murray_rutherford@sfu.ca

established a camp in 2000 to protect their territory and stop a proposed new four-season mountain tourism development called Melvin Creek/Cayoosh Mountain Resort. The proposed resort would have included 14 ski lifts and more than 14,000 bed units (Cole, 2012). The St'át'imc also set up an information blockade that temporarily closed a local highway (CBC News, 2000). Despite this opposition, the BC provincial government issued a Project Approval Certificate for the resort. Five years later, however, the provincial government issued an order prohibiting construction, to allow time for the province to fulfil its legal obligation to consult with the St'át'imc. That order is still in place and the resort has not been built. As recently as 2012, the camp established by the St'át'imc to protect the valley remained in place and was occupied (Cole, 2012).

At Apex Mountain near Penticton, BC, the Penticton Indian Band and the Lower and Upper Similkameen Bands blockaded the main access roads to the Apex Mountain Ski Resort for more than a month in 1994, contesting land ownership and protesting against a CA$20 million expansion programme being undertaken at the resort. The developer was unable to obtain the international financing that it had arranged for the resort expansion, and subsequently went into receivership and the resort was sold. The receiver unsuccessfully sued the province, claiming that the developer's losses arose from the blockaded road and the government's failure to deal quickly with the blockade (*Apex Mountain Resort Ltd. et al. v. HMTQ*, 2000).

In the Purcell Mountains of south-eastern BC, at the proposed location of the Jumbo Glacier Resort, the Ktunaxa First Nation issued a 'Qat'Muk Declaration' in 2010 stating that Jumbo Valley is the home of the Grizzly Bear Spirit, and proclaiming a refuge area 'consisting of the upper part of the Jumbo valley' and a buffer area 'consisting of the remainder of the Jumbo watershed ... so that the Grizzly Bear Spirit, as well as grizzly bears, can thrive within and around Qat'muk' (Ktunaxa Nation, 2010). When the BC government approved the proposed resort, the Ktunaxa petitioned to the Canadian courts to overturn the approval on the grounds that the government had not met its duty to consult and accommodate the Ktunaxa, and that the construction of the resort would violate the constitutionally protected religious rights of the Ktunaxa people (see Owens and Rutherford, Chapter 32 of the present volume, for a detailed discussion of the conflict over the Jumbo Glacier Resort).

Such conflicts between Indigenous people and those who wish to develop or exploit natural resources are taking place in many areas of the world, as Indigenous people assert their rights and ownership in the face of development pressures. The issues for winter resorts are perhaps less widely publicized than those for industrial developments such as logging, mining and dam building, but examples involving winter tourism can be found in places as far removed from BC as New Zealand, where there are mountains sacred to the Māori people (Ruru, 2004), or the Australian Alps, which have been occupied by Aboriginal people for millennia (Walker, n.d.), or the Patagonian resort city of Bariloche in Argentina, where the Mapuche people have ancestral lands and rights (Renaud and Guyot, 2010), or the mountain peaks in Idre, Sweden, where Sami people carry on traditional reindeer herding practices (Engström and Boluk, 2012).

In this chapter I discuss the Indigenous rights of First Nations people in BC, their efforts to assert those rights as they plan for, manage and use their traditional territories, and the implications for winter resort development. Although the provisions of the Canadian constitution that specifically support claims of 'Aboriginal' rights and title (Indigenous rights) are unique to this country, international principles of Indigenous rights, including the right of free, prior and informed consent, are universal.

4.2 First Nations, Colonization and the Canadian Federal and Provincial Governments

The roots of modern conflicts between First Nations and winter resorts in BC can be traced back to European colonization of what is now the province of BC in the 1800s, and the accompanying forced displacement of Indigenous people, along with the denial or restriction of their rights to enjoy and use their territories as they had in the past. Before discussing this colonial history and the evolution of the recognition of Indigenous rights in the Canadian legal system, I begin with two quotes from First Nations leadership groups in BC describing their perspectives on Indigenous rights and the appropriate relationship between First Nations and the Canadian federal and provincial governments. The first quote comes from an 'Aboriginal Title and Rights Position Paper' issued in 1985 by the Union of British Columbia Indian Chiefs (a society formed by leaders of First Nations in BC):

> The sovereignty of our Nations comes from the Great Spirit. It is not granted nor subject to the approval of any other Nation. As First Nations we have the sovereign right to jurisdictional rule within our traditional Territories. Our lands are a sacred gift. The land is provided for the continued use, benefit and enjoyment of our people, and it is our ultimate obligation to the Great Spirit to care for and protect it.
>
> ....
>
> Aboriginal Title and Rights means we as Indian people hold Title and have the right to maintain our sacred connection to Mother Earth by governing our territories through our own forms of Indian Government. Our Nations have a natural and rightful place within the family of Nations of the World. Our political, legal, social and economic systems developed in accordance with the laws of the Creator since time immemorial and continue to this day.
>
> Our power to govern rests with the people and, like our Aboriginal Title and Rights, it comes from within the people and cannot be taken away.
>
> (UBCIC, 1985)

The second quote comes from a 2014 meeting of the BC First Nations Leadership Council and First Nations Leaders, at which they identified four fundamental principles to govern the relationship between Canadian governments and First Nations in BC:

> 1. Acknowledgement that all our relationships are based on recognition and implementation of the existence of indigenous peoples inherent title and rights, and pre-confederation, historic and modern treaties, throughout British Columbia.
> 2. Acknowledgement that indigenous systems of governance and laws are essential to the regulation of lands and resources throughout British Columbia.
> 3. Acknowledgement of the mutual responsibility that all of our government systems shall shift to relationships, negotiations and agreements based on recognition.
> 4. We immediately must move to consent based decision-making and title based fiscal relations, including revenue sharing, in our relationships, negotiations and agreements.
>
> (First Nations Summit, 2015, p. 1)

4.3 Historical Context

Indigenous people lived in the area now known as Canada for thousands of years before European explorers and settlers arrived. As with other Indigenous societies in the world, Indigenous people in Canada developed close relationships with the living and non-living environment, and their cultures and communities included self-governance institutions that cultivated and managed those relationships. The first European explorers reached Vancouver Island and the Pacific Coast in the late 1700s. Early explorers and the settlers that followed them introduced smallpox and other diseases that decimated the populations of local First Nations communities. Colonial laws and government were imposed upon the survivors. The colonial and succeeding Canadian governments also forcibly displaced First Nations people from their lands and territories onto relatively small 'Indian Reserves', freeing up the rest of the land base for settlers and resource development. For most of what is now the province of BC, this displacement took place without treaties with the affected First Nations.

In 1866 the British colonies of Vancouver Island and British Columbia merged to form a new Colony of British Columbia, and in 1871 that new colony joined the confederation of Canada, becoming Canada's westernmost province. Canada is a federal state, with a constitution that allocates distinct, although not always unambiguous, jurisdictional powers to the federal government and the provincial governments. The federal government was allocated authority over 'Indians, and Lands reserved for the Indians' (*Constitution Act*, 1867, s. 91(24)), but other sections of the constitution gave the provincial governments broad powers over natural resources and lands owned by the provinces (Muldoon et al., 2015).

Under the terms of confederation, the province of BC retained ownership of most of the land previously held by the British colonies that had merged to form BC. As a result, more than 90% of the current land area of BC is controlled and managed by the province as provincial 'Crown Land' (BC, n.d.a). Most of this land is claimed by First Nations as unceded traditional territory (areas they occupied, governed or used in the past, and sometimes currently). However, BC has granted resource tenures to these lands to non-First Nation settlers, their descendants and subsequent immigrants, allowing resource extraction, tourism development and other uses. The province has also granted outright ownership of lands to private individuals or corporations.

First Nations in BC have long claimed rights to the lands from which they were displaced, and have contested Crown ownership and grants of tenure to these lands. The provincial and federal governments paid little attention to these claims until the Supreme Court of Canada issued a landmark decision in 1973, in a lawsuit commenced by Nisga'a chief Frank Calder and other Nisga'a elders. The Calder lawsuit asked the court for a declaration that the Nisga'a held Aboriginal title to their 'ancient tribal territory' and that the title had never been extinguished (*Calder et al. v. Attorney-General of British Columbia*, 1973). The lawsuit was partially successful, in that the Supreme Court ruled that Aboriginal title did exist in Canada prior to colonization, but the judges were evenly divided on the question of whether Nisga'a title had been extinguished by colonial laws and the confederation of Canada as a nation.

In 1982, 9 years after the Calder decision, a new provision was added to the Canadian constitution that specifically recognized and affirmed 'existing' Aboriginal rights (*Constitution Act*, 1982, s. 35). Since that amendment, the success of First Nations in pursuing claims of Aboriginal rights and title has improved dramatically. The constitutional amendment opened the door for the courts to revisit the question of Aboriginal rights and to define the nature and extent of those rights.

4.4 Aboriginal Rights and Title Under the Canadian Constitution

The modern era of Indigenous rights in Canada began with the 'patriation' of the Canadian constitution from Britain in 1982. Until that time, Canada's constitution was the *British North America Act*, 1867 (subsequently renamed the *Constitution Act*, 1867), an Act of the British Parliament that joined several British colonies together in 1867 to form the Dominion of Canada. More than 100 years later, in 1982, at the request of the Canadian government, the British Parliament passed legislation that formally transferred to Canada the power to control and amend its own constitution. At the same time, several new provisions were added to the constitution, including a new section concerning the rights of Aboriginal peoples:

> 35. (1) The existing aboriginal and treaty rights of the aboriginal peoples of Canada are hereby recognised and affirmed.
>
> (*Constitution Act*, 1982)

The meaning of the term 'Aboriginal peoples' is defined in s. 35(2) as 'the Indian, Inuit and Métis peoples of Canada'. However, it was left to the Canadian courts to interpret the meaning of 'existing aboriginal and treaty rights' and to determine the legal implications of this constitutional recognition and affirmation of rights. Many of the subsequent court cases that have clarified the meaning of section 35 originated with disputes and lawsuits in BC, because unlike much of the rest of Canada, only a small portion of BC is covered by treaties with First Nations.

The first major legal case to consider s. 35 of the *Constitution Act*, 1982 was *R. v. Sparrow* (1990). In that case, the Supreme Court of Canada ruled that a First Nations fisherman was not bound by Canadian legal restrictions on the length of fishing nets because he had an Aboriginal right to fish that had existed since before contact with settlers, and that right continued to the present day. That right was recognized and affirmed by s.35 of the *Constitution Act*, 1982. The judges in the Sparrow case explained that the Canadian government has a fiduciary (or 'trust') responsibility to Aboriginal people that requires the government to act honourably and in good faith. The nature and extent of this 'honour of the Crown' and the associated fiduciary responsibilities described in the Sparrow case were clarified and expanded upon over the ensuing three decades in a series of judicial decisions involving Aboriginal fishing rights, hunting rights and title to lands.

To briefly summarize the main principles outlined in these cases, Aboriginal rights exist in Canada because Aboriginal people were exercising these rights before contact with colonial settlers. Aboriginal title is a particular form of Aboriginal right that arises from historical occupation of lands and the exclusion of others from using those lands. Canadian governments have the authority to infringe on Aboriginal rights, including Aboriginal title, but only when the infringement is for a legitimate and compelling government objective such as environmental protection or, in some circumstances, economic development. In addition, before making any decision that may infringe on Aboriginal rights, the government must consult with potentially affected Aboriginal people, and may be required to provide appropriate 'accommodation' to compensate for any infringement. The degree of consultation and accommodation that is required varies with the nature and strength of the asserted Aboriginal right and the degree of infringement. The legal principles described above were articulated by the Supreme Court of Canada in the cases of *R. v. Sparrow* (1990), *R. v. Gladstone* (1996), *R. v. Van der Peet* (1996) and *Delgamuukw v. British Columbia* (1997). In 2014, the Supreme Court extended this line of reasoning by declaring that the Tsilhqot'in people have Aboriginal title to a specific portion of their traditional territory (*Tsilhqot'in Nation v. British Columbia*, 2014).

4.5 International and Canadian Principles and Policy Concerning Aboriginal Rights

The Canadian court cases interpreting s. 35 of the *Constitution Act*, 1982 and defining the nature of Aboriginal rights in Canada were decided in the context of evolving international norms concerning the rights of Indigenous people. Together, domestic court cases and international norms are pushing Canadian federal and provincial governments to adopt new approaches and policies in their interactions with First Nations. Internationally, although Canada initially opposed the United Nations Declaration on the Rights of Indigenous Peoples (UNDRIP) when it was adopted in 2007, the country subsequently changed its position and became a supporter of the declaration (United Nations – Indigenous Peoples, n.d.). The Canadian House of Commons has now passed a bill that would require the federal government to ensure that the laws of Canada are 'consistent' with UNDRIP. That bill is currently under consideration by the Senate (CBC News, 2018a).

Many of the articles of UNDRIP are relevant to the issues discussed in this chapter, but several stand out:

Article 10 – Indigenous peoples shall not be forcibly removed from their lands or territories. No relocation shall take place without the free, prior and informed consent of the indigenous peoples concerned and after agreement on just and fair compensation and, where possible, with the option of return.

Article 18: Indigenous peoples have the right to participate in decision-making in matters which would affect their rights, through representatives chosen by themselves in accordance with their own procedures, as well as to maintain and develop their own indigenous decision-making institutions.

Article 19: States shall consult and cooperate in good faith with the indigenous peoples concerned through their own representative institutions in order to obtain their free, prior and informed consent before adopting and implementing legislative or administrative measures that may affect them.

Article 26:

> 1. Indigenous peoples have the right to the lands, territories and resources which they have traditionally owned, occupied or otherwise used or acquired.
> 2. Indigenous peoples have the right to own, use, develop and control the lands, territories and resources that they possess by reason of traditional ownership or other traditional occupation or use, as well as those which they have otherwise acquired.
> 3. States shall give legal recognition and protection to these lands, territories and resources. Such recognition shall be conducted with due respect to the customs, traditions and land tenure systems of the indigenous peoples concerned.

Article 32:
> 1. Indigenous peoples have the right to determine and develop priorities and strategies for the development or use of their lands or territories and other resources.
> 2. States shall consult and cooperate in good faith with the indigenous peoples concerned through their own representative institutions in order to obtain their free and informed consent prior to the approval of any project affecting their lands or territories and other resources, particularly in connection with the development, utilization or exploitation of mineral, water or other resources.
> 3. States shall provide effective mechanisms for just and fair redress for any such activities, and appropriate measures shall be taken to mitigate adverse environmental, economic, social, cultural or spiritual impact.
>
> (United Nations, 2007, Article 10, p. 5; Article 18, p. 6; Article 19, p. 6; Article 26, p. 8; Article 32, p. 9)

In 2017 the Canadian federal government issued a set of ten 'Principles Respecting the Government of Canada's Relationship with Indigenous Peoples' (Department of Justice Canada, 2018) The preamble to these principles declares that they are 'rooted in section 35' and 'guided by' UNDRIP (Department of Justice Canada, 2018, p. 3). Three of the principles are particularly salient for the discussion in this chapter:

> **Principle 6**: The Government of Canada recognizes that meaningful engagement with Indigenous peoples aims to secure their free, prior, and informed consent when Canada proposes to take actions which impact them and their rights, including their lands, territories and resources.
> **Principle 7**: The Government of Canada recognizes that respecting and implementing rights is essential and that any infringement of section 35 rights must by law meet a high threshold of justification which includes Indigenous perspectives and satisfies the Crown's fiduciary obligations.
> **Principle 8**: The Government of Canada recognizes that reconciliation and self-government require a renewed fiscal relationship, developed in collaboration with Indigenous nations, that promotes a mutually supportive climate for economic partnership and resource development.
>
> (Department of Justice Canada, 2018, Principle 6, p. 12; Principle 7, p. 14; Principle 8, p. 15)

In May 2018 the BC provincial government issued its own 'Draft Principles that Guide the Province of British Columbia's Relationship with Indigenous Peoples' (BC, n.d.b). The provincial principles are almost identical to the federal principles, with minor modifications to reflect the provincial context and the role of the provincial government rather than the federal government.

4.6 First Nations Planning Initiatives

Through direct action, court decisions, negotiations with the federal and provincial governments, and government-to-government agreements such as treaties and protocols, First Nations in BC are attaining greater control over their traditional territories. They are also developing comprehensive and specific land use plans for their lands, including federally designated 'reserves', and the much larger territories that First Nations occupied and used before contact with Europeans. Land use planning on First Nation reserves is authorized by the federal *Indian Act* and the *First Nations*

Land Management Act. The latter legislation enables a First Nation to institute a land management regime for a reserve by developing and adopting a land code that includes rules and procedures for use and occupancy as well as rules and procedures for dealing with revenues from natural resources. Although it may be unlikely that areas on reserves in BC would be considered for winter resort development, it is possible that a First Nation could allocate particular sites on a reserve for hotels, housing or other facilities to support winter tourism.

The authority for First Nations to develop more comprehensive land use plans for their traditional territories comes from inherent Aboriginal rights and title, and from treaties and other government-to-government agreements. Many First Nations in BC have developed such land use plans. For example, in 2006 the Líl'wat Nation of the St'át'imc people (whose members established the protection camp in the Melvin Creek Valley discussed in the introduction to this chapter) issued a 'Vision and Plan for the Land and Resources of Líl'wat Nation Traditional Territory' (Líl'wat Nation, 2006). The plan 'focuses on the land and waters of the Traditional Territory at a strategic level, and provides high-level land allocation and resource management direction' (p. 9). The plan begins with a strong declaration of Líl'wat authority:

> The Líl'wat Nation has aboriginal title to, and aboriginal rights throughout, our Traditional Territory, our T'micw. We have never ceded, surrendered or abandoned the rights to our Traditional Territory. Similarly, our aboriginal rights to this Traditional Territory have not been extinguished. As is amply illustrated through the archaeological, ethnographic, and oral history records on the land, we can conclusively demonstrate our aboriginal rights and title interests throughout the area.
> (Líl'wat Nation, 2006, p. 12)

Six land use zones are established under the Líl'wat plan: 'Líl'wat Nt'ákmen (Our Way) Areas, Líl'wat Collaborative Management Areas, Líl'wat Cultural Education Areas, Líl'wat Stewardship Areas, Líl'wat Conditional Economic Development Areas, and Líl'wat Managed Resource Use Areas' (Líl'wat Nation, 2006, pp. 56–57). Among the defined potential uses are 'Low-impact tourism and recreation' and 'Intensive tourism and recreation'. The plan and the accompanying zoning map specify where on the landscape these uses may be permitted and where they will be prohibited.

In addition to and in coordination with such broad land use planning, First Nations in BC have also established specific protected areas in their territories. The 'Qat'Muk Declaration' of the Ktunaxa Nation, establishing a refuge area in the Jumbo Valley and a buffer area around that refuge, is an example of a protected area unilaterally declared by a First Nation. Other examples include 'tribal parks' such as those declared by the Tsilhqot'in Nations and the Tla-oh-qui-aht Nation (Groenewoud, 2018). These protected areas would fit within the International Union for Conservation of Nature's (IUCN) definition of Indigenous Community and Conserved Areas: 'natural and/or modified ecosystems containing significant biodiversity values, ecological services and cultural values, voluntarily conserved by Indigenous peoples and local communities, both sedentary and mobile, through customary laws or other effective means' (IUCN, 2010). The Indigenous Circle of Experts in Canada uses the term 'Indigenous Protected and Conserved Areas' and defines these areas as places where 'Indigenous governments have the primary role in protecting and conserving ecosystems through Indigenous laws, governance and knowledge systems' (ICE, 2018, p. 35). First Nations have also joined with federal and provincial parks agencies in co-management arrangements for protected areas in their traditional territories. One important type of co-managed protected area in BC is the 'Conservancy' designation that was added to the BC *Park Act* in 2006. Conservancies 'are intended not only to achieve conservation goals, but also to accommodate social, ceremonial, and cultural uses of First Nations, and sustainable small-scale resource development' (Stronghill *et al.*, 2015, p. 40).

4.7 Winter Resort Development and First Nations Rights and Territorial Planning

The preceding discussion makes it clear that any attempt to develop a winter resort in BC without the free, prior and informed consent of potentially affected First Nations would be unjust and unlikely to succeed. How Canadian federal and provincial governments will navigate the distance between the Canadian legal doctrine of 'justified infringement' and the international principle of 'free, prior and informed consent' remains to be seen. But several lessons can be drawn from the experiences of winter resorts and First Nations in BC and the evolution of Canadian law concerning Aboriginal rights and title discussed in this chapter. In outlining these lessons, I use the Canadian term 'First Nations', but the lessons are relevant for other settings in the world where non-Indigenous developers of winter resorts interact with Indigenous people.

First, developers should avoid locating proposed winter resorts in areas that are of cultural or environmental importance to First Nations. Avoidance is the preferred mitigation strategy in environmental impact assessment, and the logic applies here as well. This recommendation may seem simplistic and obvious, but the historical record of proposals and projects in BC and elsewhere in the world shows that it is a lesson that developers have been slow to learn. To be fair, sometimes information about the locations of sacred or otherwise important Indigenous sites may not be disclosed to the public and may be known only by Elders or specific knowledge keepers. However, the comprehensive land use plans that First Nations in BC have prepared for their traditional territories typically indicate broad zones or areas where particular types of development and land use may be acceptable or not acceptable. More detailed information may become available with early consultation with the affected First Nation(s).

The second lesson flows from the first: developers should determine which Indigenous people claim rights or territories in the area in which they are considering a project and should contact them at the beginning of the project development process, rather than after initial plans have been formulated. Although First Nations in BC normally receive 'referral notices' from government staff when the government begins to consider an application for approval of a project, the developer should engage with First Nations long before this point. Under Canadian law the ultimate obligation is on the provincial and federal governments to consult and accommodate Aboriginal people before making any decision that may infringe on their rights, but non-governmental proponents should institute their own consultation and collaboration processes before applying for governmental approvals. By doing so they may identify ways to avoid or alleviate the concerns of First Nations, or to provide benefits and compensation for impacts that cannot be avoided but that might be mitigated. Early consultation and discussions may also reveal opportunities for partnerships, joint ventures and other forms of collaboration. Some First Nations may wish to develop winter resort opportunities on their own, but they may still call on the non-Indigenous tourism industry for expertise, investment and other support.

Often, consultations lead to impact benefit agreements between developers and First Nations. For First Nations, potential benefits may include direct monetary payments, jobs and job training, transfers of land, dedicated business opportunities associated with the development, and construction of community facilities and infrastructure. For developers, there are potential benefits beyond simply obtaining consent, including the opportunity to train and work with a local and expert workforce and the possibility of jointly developing and offering cultural tourism products. Several sets of 'best practices' for impact benefit agreements have been published based on the wide body of experience in BC and elsewhere (Cascadden, 2018).

The recently approved Valemount Glacier Destination Resort in the traditional territory of the Simpcw First Nation in eastern BC, near Jasper National Park, provides an interesting contrast to the story of the struggle over the Jumbo Glacier Resort mentioned above and discussed in Chapter 32. For the Valemount project, the developer contacted and began discussions with representatives of the Simpcw Nation soon after the site was first suggested for a resort (Oberti Resort Design and Pheidias Group, 2016). These discussions eventually led to a Memorandum of Understanding and an Impact and Benefits Agreement. The Simpkw will receive revenues from the resort and property within the resort village (BC, 2017; Matthews, 2017). The Master Plan for the resort includes the construction and operation of an interpretive centre devoted to the Simpkw in a prominent location (Oberti Resort Design and Pheidias Group, 2016). In addition, as part of the accommodation for the Valemount Resort development, in 2018 the province transferred Crown land to the Simpkw in another part of their traditional territory (CBC News, 2018b). The transferred land 'includes a historical village site on the banks of the Fraser River, as well as several hunting and fishing camps' (CBC News, 2018b).

As a final lesson, it is imperative that governments and resort developers deal with past and ongoing infringements by existing winter resorts on the rights of First Nations. Article 28 of UNDRIP clearly sets out the rights and responsibilities:

> **Article 28**: 1. Indigenous peoples have the right to redress, by means that can include restitution or, when this is not possible, just, fair and equitable compensation, for the lands, territories and resources which they have traditionally owned or otherwise occupied or used, and which have been confiscated, taken, occupied, used or damaged without their free, prior and informed consent.
> 2. Unless otherwise freely agreed upon by the peoples concerned, compensation shall take the form of lands, territories and resources equal in quality, size and legal status or of monetary compensation or other appropriate redress.
>
> (United Nations, 2007, p. 8)

References

Albinati, C.E.J. (2017) Indigenous blockades and the power to speak the law: from settler colonialism to Indigenous resurgence. LLM Thesis, Osgoode Hall Law School, York University. Available at: http://digitalcommons.osgoode.yorku.ca/llm/25 (accessed 21 September 2018).

BC (British Columbia) (2017) Province approves new all-season mountain resort in Valemount. BC Forests, Lands, Natural Resource Operations and Rural Development News Release. Available at: https://news.gov.bc.ca/releases/2017FLNR0045-000865 (accessed 1 October 2018).

BC (British Columbia) (n.d.a) Accessing and using our natural resources. Available at: https://www2.gov.bc.ca/gov/content/industry/natural-resource-use (accessed 6 January 2019).

BC (British Columbia) (n.d.b) Draft principles that guide the Province of British Columbia's relationship with Indigenous peoples. Available at: https://www2.gov.bc.ca/gov/content/governments/indigenous-people/new-relationship/about-the-ten-principles (accessed 6 January 2019).

Cascadden, M. (2018) Best practices for impact benefit agreements: a case study of the Mary River Project. Master's project. School of Resource and Environmental Management, Simon Fraser University, Burnaby, British Columbia.

CBC News (2000) Natives protest ski development. Available at: https://www.cbc.ca/news/canada/natives-protest-ski-development-1.225947 (accessed 30 September 2018).

CBC News (2018a) Romeo Saganash's Indigenous rights bill passes in the House of Commons. Available at: https://www.cbc.ca/news/politics/saganash-undrip-bill-passes-1.4684889 (accessed 26 September 2018).

CBC News (2018b) Crown land transferred to First Nation as part of B.C. resort deal. Available at: https://www.cbc.ca/news/canada/british-columbia/valemount-resort-land-transfer-simpcw-first-nation-1.4567416 (accessed 26 September 2018).

Cole, Y. (2012) First Nations protest lingers against proposed Melvin Creek ski resort. *The Georgia Straight* newspaper. Available at: https://www.straight.com/news/first-nations-protest-lingers-against-proposed-melvin-creek-ski-resort (accessed 30 September 2018).

Department of Justice Canada (2018) Principles respecting the government of Canada's relationship with Indigenous peoples. Available at: https://www.justice.gc.ca/eng/csj-sjc/principles.pdf (accessed 6 January 2019).

Engström, C. and Boluk, K.A. (2012) The battlefield of the mountain: exploring the conflict of tourism development on the three peaks in Idre, Sweden. *Tourism Planning and Development* 9(4), 411–427.

First Nations Summit (2015) One year later: First Nations continue to wait for government to recognise and implement principles contained in Tsilhqot'in decision. Available at: http://fns.bc.ca/news/tsilhqotin-decision-one-year-later (accessed 21 September 2018).

Groenewoud, T. (2018) Informing Indigenous marine protection in Gitga'at territory. Master's project, School of Resource and Environmental Management, Simon Fraser University, Burnaby, British Columbia.

ICE (Indigenous Circle of Experts) (2018) We rise together: achieving pathway to Canada target 1 through the creation of Indigenous protected and conserved areas in the spirit and practice of reconciliation. Available at: www.conservation2020canada.ca/resources (accessed 30 September 2018).

IUCN (2010) Indigenous and community conserved areas: a bold new frontier for conservation. Available at: https://www.iucn.org/content/indigenous-and-community-conserved-areas-bold-new-frontier-conservation (accessed 1 August 2018).

Ktunaxa Nation (2010) Qat'muk declaration. Available at: www.ktunaxa.org/who-we-are/qatmuk-declaration (accessed 1 August 2018).

Líl'wat Nation (2006) Lil'wat land use plan: phase 1 – the vision and plan for the land and resources of Lil'wat Nation traditional territory. Available at: https://lilwat.ca/wp-content/uploads/2015/03/LLUP-Phase-1-August-2006-FINAL.pdf (accessed 29 September 2018).

Matthews, E. (2017) Valemount resort opening pushed back again: Oberti. *Rocky Mountain Goat* newspaper, 16 June 2017. Available at: https://www.therockymountaingoat.com/2017/06/valemount-resort-opening-pushed-back-again-oberti/ (accessed 26 September 2018).

Muldoon, P., Lucas, A.R., Gibson, R., Pickfield, P. and Williams, J. (2015) *An Introduction to Environmental Law and Policy in Canada*, 2nd edn. Emond Montgomery, Toronto, Canada.

Oberti Resort Design and Pheidias Group (2016) Valemount Glacier Destination master plan. Valemount Glacier Destinations Ltd and Pheidias Project Management Corporation. Available at: http://valemountglaciers.com/master-plan (accessed 26 September 2018).

Renaud, M. and Guyot, S. (2010) Conflicts and cooperation in the mountainous Mapuche territory (Argentina): the case of the Nahuel Huapi National Park. *Revue de Géographie Alpine/Journal of Alpine Research* 98, 138–153.

Ruru, J. (2004) Indigenous peoples' ownership and management of mountains: the Aotearoa/New Zealand experience. *Indigenous Law Journal* 3, 11–137.

St. Pierre, C. (n.d.) Skwelkwek'welt: working together to protect our land, culture and future. Skwelkwek'welt Protection Centre and Neskonlith Band. Available at: http://www.firstnations.de/media/06-3-2-brochure.pdf (accessed 21 September 2018).

Stronghill, J., Rutherford, M.B. and Haider, W. (2015) Conservancies in coastal British Columbia: a new approach to protected areas in the traditional territories of First Nations. *Conservation and Society* 13(1), 39–50.

UBCIC (Union of British Columbia Indian Chiefs) (1985) Aboriginal title and rights position paper. Available at: https://www.ubcic.bc.ca/ubcic_publications (accessed 21 September 2018).

United Nations – Indigenous Peoples (n.d.) United Nations declaration on the rights of Indigenous peoples. Available at: https://www.un.org/development/desa/indigenouspeoples/declaration-on-the-rights-of-indigenous-peoples.html (accessed 6 January 2019).

United Nations (2007) United Nations declaration on the rights of Indigenous peoples. Official resolution text. Available at: https://undocs.org/A/RES/61/295 (accessed 14 May 2019).

Walker, C. (n.d.) Alpine traditional owners re-asserting their rights. *Mountain Journal*. Available at: https://themountainjournal.wordpress.com/indigenous-land/alpine-traditional-owners (accessed 24 September 2018).

Legislation and Legal Cases Cited

Apex Mountain Resort Ltd. et al. v. HMTQ [2000] BCSC 907.
British Columbia v. Billy, Sauls, Manuel Jr., and Willard [2003] BCSC 55.
Calder et al. v. Attorney-General of British Columbia [1973] SCR 313.
Constitution Act, 1867, 30 & 31 Victoria, c. 3 (UK)
Constitution Act, 1982. Schedule B to the Canada Act 1982 (UK), 1982, c 11.
Delgamuukw v. British Columbia [1997] 3 S.C.R. 1010.
First Nations Land Management Act. S.C. 1999, c. 24.
Indian Act. R.S.C., 1985, c. I-5
Park Act. RSBC 1996, Ch. 344.
R. v. Gladstone [1996] 2 SCR 723.
R. v. Sparrow [1990] 1 SCR 1075.
R. v. Van der Peet [1996] 2 S.C.R. 507.
Tsilhqot'in Nation v. British Columbia [2014] SCC 44.

5 The Different Shades of Snow – An Analysis of Winter Tourism in European Regional Planning and Policy Documents

DOROTHEE BOHN[1]* AND CECILIA DE BERNARDI[2]

[1]*Department of Geography, Umeå University, Umeå, Sweden;* [2]*Centre for Tourism and Leisure Research (CeTLeR), School of Technology and Business Studies, Dalarna University, Falun, Sweden*

5.1 Introduction

Snow and ice are the defining elements of winter tourism (König and Abegg, 1997; Elsasser and Messerli, 2001; Franch *et al.*, 2008; Rixen *et al.*, 2011). Glaciers, snow-covered tundra, mountains or Scandinavian fells provide domestic and international tourists alike a wide range of winter holiday experiences. In some regions, winter tourism is centred in resorts that offer downhill skiing, snowboarding and après-ski partying, whereas in others, cross-country skiing and nature-based activities like snow hiking, snowmobiling, ice skating, husky tours and aurora borealis safaris are dominating the market (Tervo, 2008). The Christmas industry also attracts also plenty of travellers during the winter season and is of great significance in Northern and in Central European regions. Locally distinct hospitality cultures contribute to the heterogeneity of the winter travel product as well. Yet, winter tourism is in transformation. In addition to changing trends in consumer demand, global economic fluctuations and intensified competition among European destinations that provoke innovation in the travel sector generally, winter tourism is particularly vulnerable to the effects of climate change (Bank and Wiesner, 2011; Rixen *et al.*, 2011; Landauer *et al.*, 2012; Dawson and Scott, 2013; Bonzanigo, *et al.*, 2016). Research has concentrated therefore much on strategies of how the tourism sector can adapt to global warming (Abegg *et al.*, 2007) since the winter season is of great importance in providing employment and, thus, keeping many rural areas across Europe populated (Pechlaner and Tschurtschenthaler, 2003; Franch *et al.*, 2008). Tranos and Davoudi (2014) observe that those adaptation initiatives in winter tourism destinations are usually initiated as autonomous actions of individual businesses but comprehensive public policy and planning advances are needed in order to foster a resilient tourism economy in European regions. Nonetheless, not many winter tourism studies have paid attention to actual public planning initiatives. This

---

* E-mail: dorothee.bohn@umu.se

chapter addresses this gap and examines tourism policy and planning documents of alpine, Arctic and subarctic regions in terms of:

- the challenges and trends in European winter tourism;
- the planned regional responses to those challenges and trends; and
- the future of European winter tourism from a policy and planning perspective.

The regional level was chosen as the scale of analysis because winter tourism is highly localized. While national policy and planning address tourism development at a fairly general level, regional planning caters more to the place-specific actualities of the tourism sector.

5.2   What is the Raison d'être for Tourism Planning?

The need for tourism policy and planning through public bodies is widely acknowledged in the relevant literature (Inskeep, 1994; Hall, 2008; Harilal *et al.*, 2018). The economic potency of tourism with its multiplier effect is not only attractive for governments in low- and middle-income countries but also in rural areas, where tourism is often seen as a replacement for declining primary production and as a means for regional development (Saarinen, 2007; World Bank, 2017). However, the growing demand and unrestrained supply of tourism entails often grave ecological and socio-cultural consequences as tourism research has diligently pointed out (e.g. Mathieson and Wall, 1982). International, national, regional and local level public bodies are therefore drawn into tourism for steering the sector's development into rendering favourable economic outcomes for local populations while minimizing environmental and social harms as much as possible. The influential position of triple bottom line sustainability in tourism scholarship materializes also in prevailing approaches to define planning. Although there is no universally accepted definition, King and Pearlman (2009, p. 2) state that tourism planning is commonly outlined as 'a strategic decision-making process about the allocation of resources, which aims to derive optimum economic, environmental and socio–cultural outcomes for destinations and their stakeholders'. There is also no common agreement how public policy ought to be defined but Goeldner *et al.* (2000, pp. 514–515) maintain that policies provide the bigger picture of 'what' should be done in long-term tourism development and determine 'the rules of the game' for further planning initiatives. Yet, said rule setting and the concrete implementation of tourism policies evolve along the lines of dominating political, cultural, economic and environmental paradigms of a society (Dredge and Jamal, 2015).

State authorities in Organisation for Economic Co-operation and Development (OECD) countries are usually not planning tourism in an isolated, top-down manner but adopt instead a coordinating role inside a network comprising private sector bodies and community members (Laws *et al.*, 2011). Planning rests therefore frequently upon public–private partnerships and is overall rooted in the concept of governance (Volgger and Pechlaner, 2014). Governments foster tourism commonly through infrastructural development, business subsidies, funding of marketing efforts and the provision of tourism education for a skilled workforce (Hall, 2008, p. 48). Legislation-based statutory policy and planning procedures for tourism relate to visa and entry regulations, labour law, the use of national parks, ownership structures and building regimentations

(King and Pearlman, 2009, p. 8). In addition to statutory planning, many national, regional and local tourism authorities engage in indicative planning that provides a non-binding vision of how the travel and hospitality sector is desired to develop (King and Pearlman, 2009, p. 9). Especially strategic planning is employed nowadays as a dynamic approach to integrate planning and management into a single process rooted inside a governance network (Scott and Marzano, 2015). The goal of strategic planning is to match touristic demand and global trends with local supply while considering the interests of various destination stakeholders (Inskeep, 1994, p. 5). Destination management organizations (DMOs) across Europe, which are often semi-public structures and function traditionally as cooperative marketers and coordinators, engage in this respect increasingly also in strategic destination planning (Flagestad and Hope, 2001).

5.3 What are the Specific Planning Contexts for Winter Tourism?

Winter tourism is an important economic pillar in many rural regions of the European Alps (Elsasser and Bürki, 2002; Soboll and Dingeldey, 2012; Tranos and Davoudi, 2014) as well in the Nordic countries (Tervo, 2008; Brouder and Lundmark, 2011; Tervo-Kankare, 2011). Besides changing trends in consumer demand, global economic fluctuations (Franch et al., 2008; Steiger and Mayer, 2008; Falk and Hagsten, 2016) and intensified competition among European destinations (Müller et al., 2010) that challenge the travel sector in general, demand and supply of winter tourism are especially susceptible to climate change (Bank and Wiesner, 2011; Rixen et al., 2011; Landauer et al., 2012; Dawson and Scott, 2013; Bonzanigo et al., 2016). The predominant body of winter tourism literature seeks therefore to establish an understanding of climate change impacts, mainly at regional and local levels, due to the spatial variability of climatic conditions (Tervo, 2008; Soboll and Dingeldey, 2012).

With respect to planning, tourism research points out possibilities of overcoming climate change vulnerability through adaptation strategies (Müller et al., 2010; Bank and Wiesner, 2011; Landauer et al. 2012; Dawson and Scott, 2013; Bonzanigo et al., 2016). Mitigation strategies, like the reduction of greenhouse gas emissions, are often highlighted as even more vital in terms of counteracting the very cause of global warming (Elsasser and Bürki, 2002), but have received overall less attention in the relevant winter tourism literature. Due to the global nature of climate change, mitigating actions necessitate collective transnational arrangements while adaptation to warmer temperatures and less natural snowfall in addition to changing touristic consumption patterns can be realized at a local level through:

- Technological advancements, like artificial snowmaking, extensions in, or expansion to, higher altitudes and glacier areas, landscaping and slope grooming (Abegg et al., 2007).
- Financial tools like snow insurances and weather derivatives that protect against monetary losses but maintain tour operators' loyalty (Bank and Wieser, 2011).
- Cooperation and mergers between winter tourism operators and resorts (Abegg et al., 2007).
- The development of year-round tourism and a broad product portfolio that is not based on snow (Unbehaun et al., 2008).

However, Tranos and Davoudi (2014) remark that those adaptation initiatives are to date largely undertaken autonomously by individual ski operators and in response to market forces. This perspective reflects also in the predominant focus of winter tourism research on the corporate level with the justification being that knowledge about private sector adaptation determinants enables policy makers to choose appropriate planning instruments and strategies (Hoffmann *et al.*, 2009). Research articles conclude therefore frequently with recommendations for public planning in the light of climate change and alterations in the tourism market place while a small number of papers discuss indicative planning and policy selection explicitly. Adopting a case study approach, Bonzanigo *et al.* (2016) explore the first steps to a collaborative community approach to sustainable winter tourism planning on a municipal level, and Pechlaner and Tschurtschenthaler (2003) outline the role of tourism organizations in providing a policy basis for corporate success and leadership in market adaptation. In this regard, strategic planning and management issues in winter tourism destinations have gained some momentum. Flagestad and Hope (2001) propose a model of a winter tourism destination for strategic management analysis and Müller *et al.* (2010) as well as Pechlaner *et al.* (2009) look at rejuvenating strategies of mature alpine winter tourism destinations. Nonetheless, a recurrent finding, which is also addressed by Pechlaner and Sauerwein (2002) in their case study on South Tyrol, is the difficulties of formulating and implementing strategic plans inside a dynamic multi-stakeholder and multi-interest destination environment.

A conclusion that can be drawn from existing papers is the sentiment that strategic planning and policy in winter tourism destinations should provide a locally specific and enabling business framework for enterprises that facilitates adaptation to economic, environmental and social developments of global scale. Pechlaner and Tschurtschenthaler (2003) stress the significant economic role that small business tourism has had in keeping rural alpine areas populated. In this vein, the purpose of tourism policy and planning is also to provide a sustainable future for local communities. In practice, however, planning implementation and the conduct of tourism enterprises do not easily go hand in hand due to diverging interests and perceptions (Tervo-Kankare, 2011). Amending the largely prescriptive approaches to winter tourism planning, this chapter offers a comparative analysis of strategic planning and policy documents of alpine, Arctic and subarctic regions across Europe.

5.4 Research Framework

5.4.1 Data collection

The purpose of this study is to analyse and compare policy and strategic planning documents of regions relying heavily on winter tourism. The website www.skiresort.info, which is promoted as the largest platform for detailed information on ski resorts (Ski Resort Service International, n.d.), was consulted in order to identify winter tourism regions in Europe. The most common way to classify the size of resorts is based on the number of visitors (Vanat, 2019, pp. 13–14). However, this figure can vary, while a classification according to criteria such as length of slopes and elevation difference of the resorts such as the website employs is not that subject to fluctuations (Size Saalbach Hinterglemm Leogang Fieberbrunn, n.d.).

Data collection proceeded according to the following steps:

- The largest ski resorts in Europe were chosen.
- Results: Italy, Andorra, France, Switzerland, Germany and Austria (Europe: ski resort size, n.d.).
- Andorra was excluded from further investigation due to language constraints.
- The largest ski resorts in Sweden, Finland and Norway were included.
- The regional tourism planning documents where the resorts are located were retrieved in a Google search.

It is important to note that the term 'region' is not universally consistent. It might refer to a subnational spatial entity that possesses a certain degree of jurisdictional autonomy, a loosely defined area that holds some cultural or natural communalities and receives tourism-related funding from central governments or a supranational territory (Church, 2004, p. 555; King and Pearlman, 2009, p. 418). In this study, all three types of region are present. Some touristic regions correspond to federal states and cantons, while the Allgäu region in Germany is located inside two German federal states and in Austria. In the case of Italy, France, Norway and Sweden, all regions have some degree of jurisdictional power. One exception is the region called Vestlandet, which is geographical and encompasses four regional authorities (fylke).

The obtained documents, presented in Table 5.1, differ considerably from each other, both in form and function since different public and private organizations with different objectives are involved in tourism policy and planning. Semi-public DMOs focus usually on marketing, communication and generating a tourism development vision relevant for all stakeholders. Policy and planning strategies put forward by public organizations address also broader issues such as regional development and land use. Most regional tourism strategies are available as PDF files but some are only outlined on a website.

5.4.2 Data analysis

A qualitative analysis approach was selected due to the heterogeneity of the sample documents. Unlike a quantitative word count analysis, which would have remained rather superficial and ambiguous with respect to the different languages of the texts, a qualitative take on the data allows for interpreting the presence, absence or degree of attention given to certain topics. Thematic analysis was chosen because it is a flexible 'method for systematically identifying, organising, and offering insight into patterns of meaning (themes) across a data set' (Clarke and Braun, 2014, p. 57). The aim is to detect implicit and explicit themes that are relevant to the specific research questions of a study (Clarke and Braun, 2014). In this case, the main emphasis is on semantic meanings presented in the planning documents, but the authors paid also attention to latent and omitted issues. A prominent example relates to sustainability and climate change, which are frequently left out entirely or are only superficially addressed subjects in policy documents (Landauer et al., 2017), yet this neglect creates meaning.

The analysis followed a deductive–inductive procedure. Initial themes were formulated based on information from previous studies on winter tourism. While reading through the policy and planning documents, additional categories emerged and were coded respectively. A list of codes was created and relevant contents were classified and summarized several times until a final conceptual map (see Fig. 5.1) was generated.

Table 5.1. Sample of examined regional tourism strategy and policy documents.

Country	Region	Strategy	Responsible organizations
Austria	Salzburg	Salzburg's Tourism. Healthy. Innovative. Sustainable. Strategy Plan Tourism 2020	State of Salzburg, Division 1 Economy, Research and Tourism
	Styria	Strategy 2015–2020. A joint path to the future of the tourism brand Styria	Styria Tourism
	Tyrol	Tyrol's Way 2021 – Core messages of a strategy for Tyrol's tourism	Tirol Werbung GmbH, Tyrolean Regional Government, Tyrol's tourism associations
Finland	Lapland	Lapland's Tourism Strategy 2015–2018	Regional Council of Lapland
France	Provence-Alpes-Côte d'Azur	Actions 2017	Regional Committee of Tourism
	Auvergne-Rhone-Alpes		Auvergne-Rhone-Alpes Tourisme
Germany	Allgäu	Strategy 2018–2020	Allgäu Marketing GmbH
	Bavaria	Destination Strategy Allgäu 2020	Bavarian Ministry of Economic Affairs, Energy and Technology
		Tourism Policy Concept of Bavaria's Federal Government	
Italy	Valle d'Aosta	Regional policy of development 2014/20 – National Strategic Framework	Autonomous Region of Valle d'Aosta
	Trentino Alto Adige	The future of tourism in Alto Adige 2030	EURAC research
	Piemonte	Piedmont and Tourism – International scenarios, market trends and tourism products from Piedmont	Piedmont Region
Norway	Hedmark	Sustainable experiences in Hedmark – Regional plan for the experience industry in Hedmark (2012–2019)	Hedmark County
	Vestlandet	Tourism Strategy for Western Norway 2013–20	Vestland council
	Oppland	Tourism strategy for Oppland county municipality	County council
	Telemark	Regional plan for tourism and experiences	County council
	Agder	Visit Agder 2030	Aust-Agder County
			Vest-Agder County
Sweden	Dalarna	Tourism strategy 2030	Visit Dalarna
	Jämtland Härjedalen	Strategy 2030	Jämtland Härjedalen Tourism (JHT)
Switzerland	Bern	Tourism BE 2025 Working Paper	Economic Directorate of the Canton of Bern
	Grisons	White Paper for Grisons' Tourism 2017	Tourism Council of Grisons
	Valais	Tourism Policy of the Canton of Valais 2016	Canton of Valais

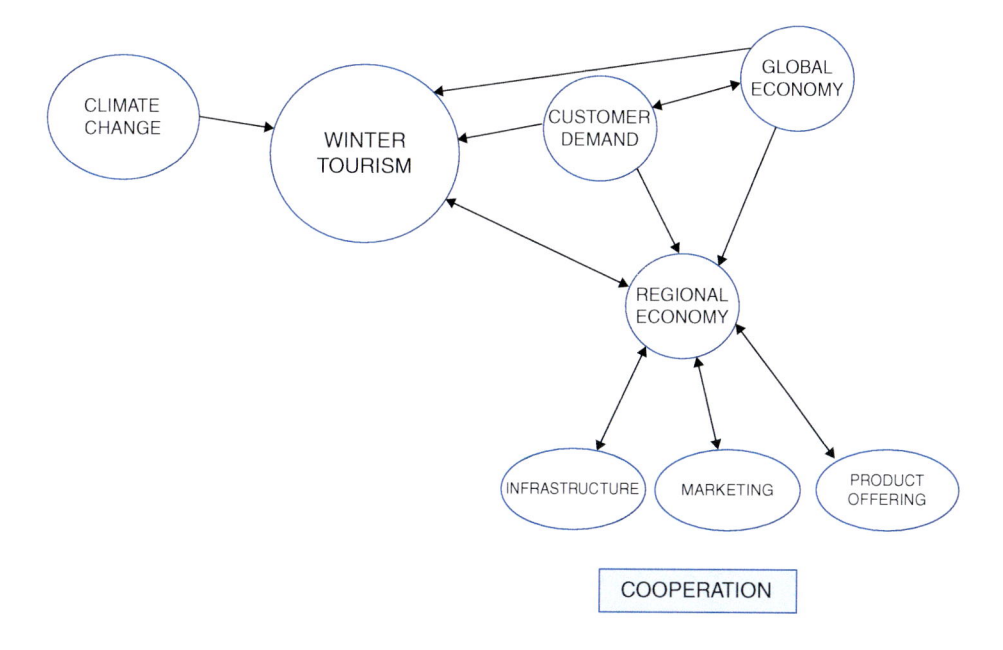

Fig. 5.1. Conceptual map depicting challenges and responses in winter tourism.

This map visualizes the main thematic areas relating to the challenges for European winter tourism and the main areas of regional planning responses. Four particular pressure areas for European winter tourism regions, namely the global economy, regional economic dependency, shifting tourist demand and climate change are discernible. These macro issues force destinations to plan locally. The examined documents recognize economic issues and shifting tourist demand as immediate concerns that are tackled by planning initiatives related to developing infrastructure, marketing and the tourism product offering. Cooperation between a multitude of regional stakeholders is fundamental for implementing planning objectives associated with aforesaid response areas. The situation of the regional economy is a central concern for regional tourism planning and the links to the global economy and customer demand are well addressed. Climate change, however, is described as a major threat to winter tourism, but stands in all examined documents rather isolated with planning responses targeting adaptation and to a lesser degree mitigation.

5.5 What are the Challenges and Development Trends for Winter Tourism in Europe?

This section presents the main challenges for winter tourism identified in the regional policy and planning documents. While national level tourism planning sets the broad framework for tourism development in a country, regional and local tourism planning seek to balance effects and benefits of tourism in a place-specific manner (Inskeep, 1994). In the analysed policy and planning documents, the main pressure on winter tourism stems from three areas, namely economic factors, touristic demand and climate change.

5.5.1 Economic factors

Winter tourism is a major source of income for many regions in the European Alps and in Northern Europe (Unbehaun *et al.*, 2008). Especially in rural areas where economic alternatives to winter tourism are lacking, the sector is important in providing employment for the local population (Grisons, p. 83; Aosta Valley, p. 42). Alpine and Nordic winter tourism is characterized by small to medium-sized enterprises (SMEs) and entrepreneurship is in this respect very important for many regions. Tourism started often as a sideline business for primary producers, but due to structural changes, the provision of hospitality and experience services became a professionalized main occupation. In many regions, family-owned businesses are vital for the attractiveness of the tourism product (Tyrol, p. 25). Coinciding with the main goal of all regional plans to ensure growth of the tourism sector, it is emphasized that tourism companies should be 'economically viable and competitive' (Hedmark, p. 19). Yet, winter tourism is stagnating in many places in the Alps (Müller *et al.*, 2010) and this circumstance is also well recognized in the policy and planning documents. The dominant strategic reaction is to encourage development of the spring, summer and autumn offer with the goal to create year-round tourism and achieve higher capacity utilization, especially for cable cars. Also in Finnish Lapland, where winter tourism is constantly growing, the strategy targets the extension of the summer season in order to stabilize year-round tourism employment and ensure overall sustainable development (pp. 5–6).

Norway and Switzerland as non-members of the European Union (EU) and the Economic and Monetary Union (EMU), face economic difficulties with respect to price levels and unfavourable exchange rates. The respective regions describe themselves in the strategy and planning documents as being expensive. For the Swiss regions, competition with other European winter destinations is portrayed as particularly fierce. The strategy papers of the Norwegian regions also mention the well-paid workforce putting pressure on consumer prices. The UK exit from the EU is highlighted in the tourism strategies of the Provence-Alpes-Côte d'Azur (pp. 30–31) and the Canton of Grisons (p.36) as a question mark for the future in terms of incoming tourists.

Many rural European regions are highly dependent on (winter) tourism due to structural decline of primary production and the lack of economic alternatives. This puts pressure on the regions to maintain a profitable tourism sector. In addition, the situation of the global economy constitutes a strong influence on winter tourism. The predominant strategic planning response in adhering to economic growth is to develop year-round tourism.

5.5.2 Changing tourist demand

Trends in demand and developments in existing and emerging geographical target markets are aspects that all of the documents pay much attention to. Health, longing for nature, interest in regional, authentic products, environmental consciousness and safety are identified as the leading consumer movements that ought to be incorporated into the tourism offering. The ageing traveller, however, receives in the majority of tourism plans particular consideration as a wealthy and quality-conscious customer who is willing to spend more for superior services and facilities (Salzburg, p. 13). This issue relates to the emerging discussion on accessibility for the elderly and people with disabilities in tourism literature. Ambrose (2012) argues that improved accessibility can facilitate more customer-centric products plus a competitive edge in the international market. Nonetheless, only the Italian documents address accessibility for disabled people explicitly (Piedmont, pp. 49, 117–118; Trentino Alto Adige, p. 11). Vestlandet (pp. 8–9), Hedmark (pp. 16–19) and Piedmont (pp. 117–118) write that impairment should not exclude anyone from having safe and memorable holiday experiences. Finnish Lapland adopts an 'accessible hospitality' approach, which emphasizes an accessible destination for everyone (p. 43). Similar advances are undertaken by the Italian, Norwegian and Swedish strategies.

Many policy and planning documents indicate that the European markets are stagnating and the Styrian tourism strategy adds that domestic and German markets are extremely weather- and public holiday-dependent (p. 8). Therefore, further internationalization of target markets is suggested. Grisons prioritizes also geographical segments outside of Europe and hopes to attract customers who are willing to pay more for quality experiences in Switzerland since the amount of guests from neighbouring countries has strongly declined (p. 36). Like in all the other regional policy and planning documents, the Middle East, Brazil, India, China and other Asian countries are pointed out as new promising generating areas.

The internet has become a leading platform for marketing communication and booking. All regions stress the need for approaching the customer online and providing convenient ways to find information about the destination and to make reservations. Social media as well as tourism 4.0, which embraces big data collection in order to create personalized travel experiences (Arctur, 2018), are seen as vital ways for offering products and engaging the consumer emotionally. Packaging and touring products are ways to enhance the value for the traveller while increasing the revenue of the tourist for the region based on digital optimization and are particularly advocated by Grisons (p. 55), Bern (pp. 10–11), the Aosta Valley (p. 42) and Dalarna (p. 14).

Almost all examined plans underline the need for customer research to ensure demand matches regional supply. In order to respond to consumer trends, diversification of the destinations' product portfolio is promoted. The projected implication on winter tourism is that traditional downhill skiing will be of less importance in the future. The ageing tourist and people from non-European countries, who are pointed out as a very important segments, are not seen as downhill skiing enthusiasts in the examined documents. Moreover, a decline in domestic demand is feared if the young people are not actively introduced to skiing as a hobby.

5.5.3 Climate change and sustainability factors

Unique scenery and natural landscapes are the leading marketing images of alpine and Northern European regions. Beside picturesque natural environments, winter tourism is heavily dependent on snow (Elsasser and Messerli, 2001; Franch et al., 2008). Yet, climate change is the major threat to winter tourism in terms of snow insecurity as tourism research has diligently pointed out (Bank and Wiesner, 2011; Falk, 2013). The effects of a warming climate and diminishing snow reliability are well acknowledged for winter tourism in the majority of the documents. The responses to climate change on a regional level vary in the plans. Tyrol aspires to develop a research-based tourism climate strategy in addition to ecological traffic, mobility and spatial planning initiatives (p. 34). Salzburg wants to become a destination with a 'green image' and builds its tourism strategy on sustainable actions such as fostering public transport, education and energy efficiency (p. 39). Similar plans are adopted by the Aosta Valley (pp. 38; 62–68). Nevertheless, the dominant approach to climate change is diversifying the tourism product range. Rising temperatures are frequently perceived as a threat to winter but a benefit for summer and autumn tourism and new products like 'summer mountain retreat' and 'Indian summer' are brought up in the strategy document of Grisons (p. 44). Salzburg plans to develop its winter tourism product portfolio towards non-snow-dependent winter and Christmas experiences (p. 29). The regional strategies of Norway do not even address climate change at all. Styria seeks to achieve a green brand image and declares nature as a core tourism resource but no climate or sustainability policies are presented (p. 18).

Nonetheless, the lack of substance and concrete guidance in policy and planning documents for tourism stakeholders addressing climate change is quite notable and reinforces the findings of Landauer *et al.* (2017). The lack of specificity and clear goals for policies that deal with sustainability is also criticized by Grant *et al.* (2018). An outstanding example of 'greening' mainstream tourism development is the plan for the region Jämtland Härjedalen in Sweden, in which the authors state: 'More and sustainable direct flights need to be established to the region (…)' (p. 7). This statement is an antithesis: the will is to provide 'more sustainable flights', but at the moment there is no alternative to fossil fuel and emissions contribute to global warming. It is also doubtful that direct flights would make any changes in terms of sustainability if the guests have short stays in the region.

Climate change is a force to be reckoned with for winter tourism planning. Yet, it seems difficult for tourism-dependent regions to address climate change in a holistic manner. The predominant adaptation strategy is to diversify the destinations' product portfolio towards snow-independent activities and other seasons. Mitigation efforts in regional planning focus on the improvement of public transportation and energy efficiency. Nonetheless, the economic growth paradigm persists in all regions and attracting more long-haul international travellers leads to greater carbon emissions. Beside the necessity for economic growth, the global nature of climate change makes effective mitigation a challenging task and planning for adaptation on a regional level seems less challenging.

5.6 How Does Regional Planning Respond to Identified Trends and Challenges in Winter Tourism?

Many of the examined documents provide strategies for winter tourism development in the region in response to economic pressures, shifting customer demand and also to climate change. Actions focus concretely on developing infrastructure, marketing and product offerings in a collaborative manner. Indeed, cooperation between public and private bodies is highlighted in all planning papers as a vital precondition to achieve a future-oriented and competitive tourism sector.

5.6.1 Infrastructure

Infrastructure includes all basic systems that are required by a country to be able to function properly (Infrastructure, n.d.) and is an essential constituent in every tourist destination and directly linked to its competitiveness (Akama, 2002, p. 2). Hence, all policy and planning documents single out infrastructure as an area that has to be adapted to shifting consumer demand and climate change so that tourism remains economically profitable. The strategic approaches are either to upgrade, to construct more or to rationalize existing infrastructure and public–private partnerships (Weiermair et al., 2008). For Valais, it is important to create infrastructure that can be cooperatively used by agriculture and tourism (p. 31). In Switzerland and Norway, second home owners are crucial tourism stakeholders for several reasons. Grisons' strategy paper states that second home owners are often forgotten in tourism development, although they are valuable customers for hospitality and tourism services and might play vital roles as regional ambassadors, advisers and investors (p. 71). In the Canton of Valais, two-thirds of the touristic added value derives from second home owners and the strategy seeks to involve those actors much more in the future (p. 11). Regional planning strives on the one hand to adapt winter tourism facilities to the needs of second home owners (p. 28) while, on the other, a tax for second home owners for tourism development and maintenance is considered (p. 17). In the Norwegian region Agder, more than half the tourists stay at private houses (p. 10) and Telemark points out the key role of second home tourists in achieving year-round employment in tourism (Telemark, p. 9).

Convenient accessibility, by plane, train and car is a requirement in all of the examined papers and for Finnish Lapland, ease of access constitutes a section in its overall touristic vision for the year 2025 (p. 5). Travelling by air is rising in popularity and the regions adapt to this trend by encouraging good connectivity to the main airports, such as in Norway (Hedmark, p. 16) and in France (Provence-Alpes-Côte d'Azur, pp. 2–5). The strategy document of Valais aims at short-trip and charter tourists from Europe and targets therefore the extension of the airport in Sion (p. 16). An effective transportation network inside the destination is favoured in Dalarna's strategy (p. 12).

With respect to winter tourism, cable cars, slopes and accommodation facilities are crucial. The production of artificial snow has been one of the most popular infrastructural adaptation strategies to encounter snow insecurity (Elsasser and Messerli, 2001; Unbehaun et al., 2008) although large investments are required and maintenance is costly (Soboll and Dingeldey, 2012). The production of artificial snow is not only very energy-intensive and expensive but also leads to very high water consumption (Rixen et al., 2011). The only region that mentions potential issues regarding water management is the Aosta Valley (p. 42). Slopes are usually privately owned and artificial snowmaking is primarily incumbent on the operating companies rather than being an issue for public tourism authorities. Nevertheless, strict environmental requirements might be imposed on the installation of new equipment as is the case in Bavaria (p. 46). Merging ski resorts to larger areas and enhancing the attractiveness through size for the customer is a viable option for Bavaria (p. 46) and the Canton of Valais (p. 15) if investments are seen as long-term favourable. For small resorts in lower altitudes, which can be strongly affected by climate change, both regions opt for dismantling those facilities (Bavaria, p.46; Canton of Valais, p. 15). The Aosta Valley regional development plan acknowledges the risks for winter tourism operations at lower altitudes as well but without specific recommendations (p. 44). The Bavarian tourism policy paper underlines that there are enough external investors who are willing to spur bigger tourism development projects but the local population opposes such programmes frequently and it is therefore necessary to undertake far-reaching image campaigning for tourism (p. 15). The documents pertaining to the Italian regions highlight EU funds as a viable source of tourism development. The regional development plan for the Aosta Valley is even built around all the EU projects and programmes that can be a benefit for tourism and the region as a whole (Regione autonoma della Valle d'Aosta, 2015).

5.6.2 Marketing and product development

Cooperative marketing and product development is highlighted in all strategies as an important means to match demand and supply. All regions aim at expanding tourism products relating to culture, wellness, food and drink, meetings, incentives, conferences, and exhibitions (MICE), in addition to sports, where the focus is on hiking, biking and mountaineering. The goal is to develop products that are not season-bound. The aspired direction for winter tourism is to diversify the range of activities so that also non-skiers will be attracted. Bavaria seeks to achieve this through a marketing campaign called 'SchneeBayern' (SnowBavaria, author's translation) in order to denote the versatility of the tourism offering beyond downhill skiing (p. 46). While Tyrol is very proud of its leadership role in alpine winter tourism (p. 27), Bern's planning paper states that the traditional winter tourism infrastructure caters more to the 'conventional guest' and the existing product portfolio should be amended by 'superior' experiences offerings, especially in the cultural sector (p. 11). The marketization of culture is also advanced in the Norwegian, French, Swedish and Italian strategies.

Cable cars, which are predominantly utilized during winter, are encouraged to be operated also during the summer months so that the mountains become accessible in Switzerland and the Trentino Alto Adige (p. 53). Through dynamic yield management for skiing slopes Grisons seeks to attract more day trippers (p. 109) and Bavaria supports the combination of slope and public transportation tickets (pp. 44, 46). Winter sports competitions of national and international character are emphasized in the Swiss and Austrian strategy documents as important tourism marketing tools for the region worthy of receiving financial support. In Piedmont, the 2006 Winter Olympics functioned not only as a catalyst in attracting a record number of visitors during the event, but the trend continued also during the following years (pp. 138–144).

Although all regions identify the same global tourism trends, identical target markets and seek to develop similar product offerings, there is a strong emphasis on the idea that that customer value stems from local distinctiveness. Authenticity is a contested concept in tourism scholarship (e.g. Brown, 2013), but the analysed documents strongly accentuate the uniqueness of the regions' nature and culture. The documents of Aosta Valley (p. 43), Vestlandet (p. 8) and Tyrol (p. 25) highlight not only the world-class winter sports landscape, but also the region's authentic and excellent hospitality culture. This kind of local positioning relates strongly to branding, which has become an important communication tool in many examined regions. However, the brands for Tyrol, Finnish Lapland, the Allgäu region, Bern or Styria embrace also other economic and socio-cultural sectors. The goal is to create a holistic regional brand that exerts two functions, namely identification and distinction (Qu *et al.*, 2011). The regional brand identity is quite similar for all the analysed regions: a thriving sphere for locals and tourists alike where wellbeing, innovation and ecological mindfulness are cultivated. Specifically for tourism, an important image conveyed in the brand is year-round attractiveness. The tourism strategy for Lapland mentions in this regard that a too-strong winter image is hindering the development of economically viable summer tourism (p. 17).

5.7 Conclusions: What is the Outlook from a Regional Planning Perspective on the Future of European Winter Tourism?

Given the global nature of tourism, the economy, plus the effects of climate change, the identified challenges for winter tourism are similar across the studied regions. Due to economic structural changes, rural alpine and Northern European regions are heavily dependent on (winter) tourism and the primary duty of planning is to sustain a profitable and competitive tourism sector. Economic growth is the overall strategic objective. Yet, winter tourism is often framed as problematic in the examined policy and planning documents because of stagnating tourist numbers and the future detrimental effects of climate change on snow security. The predominant planning initiatives focus therefore on the development of year-round tourism and product diversification. All planning documents recognize health, longing for nature, demand for regional products, environmental consciousness and safety as leading tourist trends that should be incorporated into the winter tourism offering. Those new products are especially tailored to the older traveller and non-European markets. The diversification of winter tourism towards non-snow-dependent products supports not only shifting customer demand but also the adaptation to climate change. Indeed, diversifying the tourism product is the principal adaptation strategy because it entails economic growth potential and the possibility for many regional tourism stakeholders to participate in the production of tourism. Mitigation strategies for climate change are either half-heartedly addressed or not addressed at all. Those findings are congruent to the existing body of winter tourism research.

The broad conclusion of the examined documents is that regional policy and planning in winter tourism advances development strategies away from winter as a distinct tourism season where downhill skiing or other snow-related outdoor activities dominate. Instead, winter is incorporated into a diverse, year-round product range. This planning approach seeks to encourage economic viability of the tourism sector in the future for many regional actors and buffer the negative effects of climate change in alpine and Northern European areas. Many examined regions pursue also place branding with the goal to convey an image of a destination that is attractive year-round and not just in winter. Thus, from a policy and planning perspective, winter tourism is going to transform from a distinct season to a versatile umbrella product.

References

Abegg, B., Agrawala, S., Crick, F. and de Montfalcon, A. (2007) Climate change impacts and adaptation in winter tourism. In: OECD (ed.) *Climate Change in the European Alps: Adapting Winter Tourism and Natural Hazards Management*. OECD Publishing, Paris, pp. 25–58.

Akama, J.S. (2002) The role of government in the development of tourism in Kenya. *International Journal of Tourism Research* 4(1), 1–14. DOI:10.1002/jtr.318

Allgäu GmbH (n.d.) *Destinations strategie 2020* [Destination strategy 2018–2020]. Available at: https://extranet.allgaeu.de/destinationsstrategie (accessed 29 October 2018).

Ambrose, I. (2012) European policies for accessible tourism. In: Buhalis, D., Darcy, S. and Ambrose, I. (eds) *Best Practice in Accessible Tourism: Inclusion, Disability, Ageing Population and Tourism*. Channel View Publications, Bristol, UK, pp. 19–35.

Arctur (2018) What is tourism 4.0? Available at: https://www.tourism4-0.org/#1_eng (accessed 29 October 2018).

Aust-Agder Fylkeskommune and Vest-Agder Fylkeskommune [Aust-Agder County and Vest-Agder County] (2015) Besøk agder 2030 [Visit Agder 2030]. Available at: http://regionplanagder.no/media/5967743/Besoek-Agder-2030.pdf (accessed 29 October 2018).

Auvergne-Rhône-Alpes Tourisme (2018) *Strategie 2018–2020* [Strategy 2018–2020]. Available at: http://pro.auvergnerhonealpes-tourisme.com/article/plan-d-actions-marketing-2018 (accessed 29 October 2018).

Bank, M. and Wiesner, R. (2011) Determinants of weather derivatives usage in the Austrian winter tourism industry. *Tourism Management* 32(1), 62–68. DOI:10.1016/j.tourman.2009.11.005

Bayerisches Staatsministerium für Wirtschaft, Infrastruktur, Verkehr und Technologie [Bavarian Ministry of Economic Affairs, Energy and Technology] (2010) Tourismuspolitisches Konzept der Bayerischen Staatsregierung [Tourism Policy Concept of Bavaria's Federal Government]. Available at: https://www.stmwi.bayern.de/fileadmin/user_upload/stmwi/Publikationen/2012/Tourismuspolitisches_Konzept.pdf (accessed 26 June 2019).

Bonzanigo, L., Giupponi, C. and Balbi, S. (2016) Sustainable tourism planning and climate change adaptation in the Alps: a case study of winter tourism in mountain communities in the Dolomites. *Journal of Sustainable Tourism*, 24(4), 637–652. DOI:10.1080/09669582.2015.1122013

Brouder, P. and Lundmark, L. (2011) Climate change in northern Sweden: intra-regional perceptions of vulnerability among winter-oriented tourism businesses. *Journal of Sustainable Tourism* 19(8), 919–933. DOI:10.1080/09669582.2011.573073

Brown, L. (2013) Tourism: a catalyst for existential authenticity. *Annals of Tourism Research* 40(1), 176–190. DOI:10.1016/j.annals.2012.08.004

Church, A. (2004) Local and regional tourism policy and power. In: Lew, A., Hall, M.C. and Williams, A.M. (eds.) *A Companion to Tourism*. Blackwell Publishing Ltd, Oxford, UK, pp. 555–568.

Clarke, V. and Braun, V. (2014) Thematic analysis. In: Teo, T. (ed.) *Encyclopedia of Critical Psychology*. Springer, New York, pp. 1947–1952.

Comité Régional de Tourisme – Provence-Alpes-Cote d'Azur Tourisme [Regional Committee of Tourism – Provence-Alpes-Cote d'Azur Tourism] (n.d.) Actions 2017. Available at: https://web.archive.org/web/20170421062251/tourismepaca.fr/portfolio/strategie-et-actions-2017 (accessed 26 June 2019).

Dawson, J. and Scott, D. (2013) Managing for climate change in the alpine ski sector. *Tourism Management* 35, 244–254. DOI:10.1016/j.tourman.2012.07.009

Dredge, D. and Jamal, T. (2015) Progress in tourism planning and policy: a post-structural perspective on knowledge production. *Tourism Management* 51, 285–297. DOI:10.1016/j.tourman.2015.06.002

Elsasser, H. and Bürki, R. (2002) Climate change as a threat to tourism in the Alps. *Climate Research* 20(3), 253–257. DOI:10.3354/cr020253.

Elsasser, H. and Messerli, P. (2001) The vulnerability of the snow industry in the Swiss Alps. *Mountain Research and Development* 21(4), 335–339. DOI:10.1659/0276-4741(2001)021[0335:TVOTSI]2.0.CO;2

EURAC Research (2017) *Il futuro del turismo in Alto Adige 2030* [The future of tourism in Alto Adige 2030]. Available at: http://webfolder.eurac.edu/EURAC/Publications/Institutes/mount/regdev/170526_Report_IT.pdf (accessed 29 October 2018).

Europe: ski resort size – best ski resort size in Europe (n.d.) Available at: www.skiresort.info/best-ski-resorts/europe/sorted/ski-resort-size (accessed 29 October 2018).

Falk, M. and Hagsten, E. (2016) Importance of early snowfall for Swedish ski resorts: evidence based on monthly data. *Tourism Management* 53, 61–73. DOI:10.1016/j.tourman.2015.09.002

Flagestad, A. and Hope, C.A. (2001) Strategic success in winter sports destinations – a sustainable value creation perspective. *Tourism Management* 22, 445–461. DOI:10.1016/S0261-5177(01)00010-3

Franch, M., Martini, U., Buffa, F. and Parisi, G. (2008) 4L tourism (landscape, leisure, learning and limit): responding to new motivations and expectations of tourists to improve the competitiveness of alpine destinations in a sustainable way. *Tourism Review* 63(1), 4–14. DOI:10.1108/16605370810861008

Fylkestinget [County council] (2011) Regional plan for reiseliv og opplevelser [Regional plan for tourism and experiences]. Available at: https://www.telemark.no/Vaare-tjenester/Naeringsutvikling/Reiseliv/Regional-plan-for-reiseliv-og-opplevelser (accessed 29 October 2018).

Goeldner, C.R., Ritchie, J.R.B. and MacIntosh, R.W. (2000) *Tourism. Principles, Practices, Philosophies*, 8th edn. John Wiley and Sons, New York.

Grant, J.L., Beed, T. and Manuel, P.M. (2018) Integrated community sustainability planning in Atlantic Canada: green-washing an infrastructure agenda. *Journal of Planning Education and Research* 38(1), 54–66. DOI:10.1177/0739456X16664788

Hall, C.M. (2008) *Tourism Planning. Policies, Processes and Relationships*, 2nd edn. Pearson Education Ltd, Harlow, UK.

Harilal, V., Tichaawa, T.M. and Saarinen, J. (2018) 'Development Without Policy': Tourism planning and research needs in Cameroon, Central Africa. *Tourism Planning and Development*, 1–10. DOI:10.1080/21568316.2018.1501732

Hedmark Fylkeskommune [Hedmark County] (2011) *Bærekraftige opplevelsesnæringer i Hedmark (2012–2019)* [Sustainable experiences in Hedmark – regional plan for the experience industry in Hedmark (2012–2019)]. Available at: https://www.hedmark.org/globalassets/hedmark/om-fylkeskommunen/planer/regional-plan-for-opplevelsesvaringer-2012-2017.pdf (accessed 29 October 2018).

Hoffmann, V.H., Sprengel, D.C., Ziegler, A., Kolb, M. and Abegg, B. (2009) Determinants of corporate adaptation to climate change in winter tourism: an econometric analysis. *Global Environmental Change* 19(2), 256–264. DOI:10.1016/j.gloenvcha.2008.12.002.

Infrastructure (n.d.) Meaning in the Cambridge English Dictionary. Available at https://dictionary.cambridge.org/dictionary/english/infrastructure (accessed 26 June 2018).

Inskeep, E. (1994) *National and Regional Tourism Planning. Methodologies and Case Studies*. Routledge, London.

Jämtland Härjedalen Tourism (JHT) (2016) Jämtland Härjedalen – Strategy 2030: for the tourism industry – 'Jämtland Härjedalen – leaders in nature based experiences'. Available at: www.mynewsdesk.com/material/document/63068/download?resource_type=resource_document (accessed 29 October 2018).

Kanton Wallis (2016) [Canton of Vallais] *Tourismuspolitik des Kantons Wallis* [Tourism Policy of the Canton of Valais 2016]. Available at: https://www.vs.ch/documents/303730/740705/Walliser+Tourismuspolitik+2016/6d5a0fbf-671f-48b7-9c01-61a2bb5746f7 (accessed 29 October 2018).

King, B. and Pearlman, M. (2009) Planning for tourism at local and regional levels: principles, practices and possibilities. In: Jamal, T. and Robinson, M. (eds) *The SAGE Handbook of Tourism Studies*. Sage, Los Angeles, California.

König, U. and Abegg, B. (1997) Impacts of climate change on winter tourism in the Swiss Alps. *Journal of Sustainable Tourism* 5(1), 46–58.

Land Salzburg (2013) [State of Salzburg, Division 1 Economy, Research and Tourism] *Salzburger Tourismus. Gesund. Innovativ. Nachhaltig. Strategieplan Tourismus 2020*. [Salzburg's Tourism. Healthy. Innovative. Sustainable. Strategy Plan Tourism 2020]. Available at: https://www.salzburg.gv.at/tourismus_/Documents/strategieplan_2020_-_internetversion.pdf (accessed 29 October 2018).

Land Tirol et al. (2015) [Federal State of Tyrol] *Der Tiroler Weg 2021. Kernbotschaft einer Strategie für den Tiroler Tourismus* [Tyrol's Way 2021 – core messages of a strategy for Tyrol's tourism]. Available at: https://www.tirolwerbung.at/wp-content/uploads/2016/06/strategie-tiroler-weg-2021.pdf (accessed 29 October 2018).

Landauer, M., Pröbstl, U. and Haider, W. (2012) Managing cross-country skiing destinations under the conditions of climate change – scenarios for destinations in Austria and Finland. *Tourism Management* 33(4), 741–751. DOI:10.1016/j.tourman.2011.08.007

Landauer, M., Goodsite, M.E. and Juhola, S. (2017) Nordic national climate adaptation and tourism strategies – (how) are they interlinked? *Scandinavian Journal of Hospitality and Tourism* 2250, 1–12. DOI:10.1080/15022250.2017.1340540.

Lapin liitto (2015) Lapin matkailustrategia 2015–2018 [Lapland's tourism strategy 2015–2018]. Available at: www.lappi.fi/lapinliitto/fi/lapin_kehittaminen/strategiat/lapin_matkailustrategia (accessed 29 October 2018).

Laws, E., Richins, H., Agrusa, J. and Scott, N. (2011) *Tourist Destination Governance: Practice. Theory and Issues*. CAB International, Wallingford, UK.

Mathieson, A. and Wall, G. (1982) *Tourism, Economic, Physical and Social Impacts*. Longman, London.

Müller, S., Peters, M. and Blanco, E. (2010) Rejuvenation strategies: a comparison of winter sport destinations in Alpine regions. *Turizam: medunarodni znanstveno-stručni časopis* 58(1), 19–36.

Oppland Fylkeskommune [Oppland county] (2012) *Reiselivsstrategi for Oppland fylkeskommun* [Tourism strategy for Oppland county municipality]. Available at: https://www.oppland.no/Handlers/fh.ashx?MId1=1818&FilId=598 (accessed 26 July 2019).

Pechlaner, H. and Sauerwein, E. (2002) Strategy implementation in the alpine tourism industry. *International Journal of Contemporary Hospitality Management* 14(4), 157–168. DOI:10.1108/09596110210427003

Pechlaner, H. and Tschurtschenthaler, P. (2003) Tourism policy, tourism organisations and change management in alpine regions and destinations: a European perspective. *Current Issues in Tourism* 6(6), 508–539. DOI:10.1080/13683500308667967

Pechlaner, H., Herntrei, M. and Kofink, L. (2009) Growth strategies in mature destinations: linking spatial planning with product development. *Turizam: medunarodni znanstveno-stručni časopis* 57(3), 285–307.

Qu, H., Kim, L.H. and Im, H.H. (2011) A model of destination branding: integrating the concepts of the branding and destination image. *Tourism Management* 32(3), 465–476. DOI:10.1016/j.tourman.2010.03.014

Regione autonoma della Valle d'Aosta [Autonomous Region of Valle d'Aosta] (2015) *Politica regionale di sviluppo 2014/20 – Quadro strategico nazionale* [Regional policy of development 2014/20 – National Strategic Summary]. Available at: www.regione.vda.it/europa/Politica_regionale_di_sviluppo_2014-20 (accessed 29 October 2018).

Regione Piemonte [Piedmont region] (2009) *Piemonte e Turismo – Scenari internazionali, trend dei mercati e prodotti turistici piemontesi* [Piedmont and Tourism – International scenarios, market trends and tourism products from Piedmont]. Available at: https://www.visitpiemonte-dmo.org/wp-content/files/Piemonte_e_Turismo.pdf (accessed 17 July 2019).

Rixen, C., Teich, M., Lardelli, C., Gallati, D., Pohl, M. *et al.* (2011) Winter tourism and climate change in the Alps: an assessment of resource consumption, snow reliability, and future snowmaking potential. *Mountain Research and Development* 31(3), 229–236. DOI:10.1659/MRD-JOURNAL-D-10-00112.1

Saarinen, J. (2007) Contradictions of rural tourism initiatives in rural development contexts: Finnish rural tourism strategy case study. *Current Issues in Tourism* 10(1), 96–105. DOI:10.2167/cit287.0

Scott, N. and Marzano, G. (2015) Governance of tourism in OECD countries. *Tourism Recreation Research* 40(2), 181–193. DOI:10.1080/02508281.2015.1041746

Size Saalbach Hinterglemm Leogang Fieberbrunn (Skicircus) (n.d.) Available at: https://www.skiresort.info/ski-resort/saalbach-hinterglemm-leogang-fieberbrunn-skicircus/test-result/size (accessed 29 October 2018).

Ski Resort Service International (n.d.) Background information regarding the Skiresort online portal. Available at: www.skiresort-service.com/en/portal (accessed 29 October 2018).

Soboll, A. and Dingeldey, A. (2012) The future impact of climate change on Alpine winter tourism: a high-resolution simulation system in the German and Austrian Alps. *Journal of Sustainable Tourism* 20(1), 101–120. DOI:10.1080/09669582.2011.610895

Steiermark Tourismus (2014) [Styria Tourism] *Strategie 2015–2020. Ein gemeinsamer Weg in die Zukunft der Tourismusmarke Steiermark* [Strategy 2015–2020. A joint path to the future of the tourism brand Styria]. Available at: https://www.steiermark.com/de/b2b/unternehmen/strategie (accessed 29 October 2018).

Steiger, R. and Mayer, M. (2008) Snowmaking and climate change: future options for snow production in Tyrolean ski resorts. *Mountain Research and Development* 28(3), 292–298. DOI:10.1659/mrd.0978

Tervo, K. (2008) The operational and regional vulnerability of winter tourism to climate variability and change: the case of the Finnish nature-based tourism entrepreneurs. *Scandinavian Journal of Hospitality and Tourism* 8(4), 317–332. DOI:10.1080/15022250802553696

Tervo-Kankare, K. (2011) The consideration of climate change at the tourism destination level in Finland: coordinated collaboration or talk about weather? *Tourism Planning and Development* 8(4), 399–414. DOI:10.1080/21568316.2011.598180

Tourismusrat [Tourism Council of Grisons] Graubünden (2017) Weissbuch für den Bündner Tourismus [White Paper for Grisons' Tourism 2017]. Available at: https://innovationgr.ch/news/6430/weissbuch-fuer-den-buendner-tourismus (accessed 26 June 2019).

Tranos, E. and Davoudi, S. (2014) The regional impact of climate change on winter tourism in Europe. *Tourism Planning and Development* 11(2), 163–178. DOI:10.1080/21568316.2013.864992

Unbehaun, W., Pröbstl, U. and Haider, W. (2008) Trends in winter sport tourism: challenges for the future. *Tourism Review* 63(1), 36–47. DOI:10.1108/16605370810861035

Vanat, L. (2016) International report on snow and mountain tourism: overview of the key industry figures for ski resorts (Report No. 8). Available at: www.isiaski.org/download/20160408_RM_World_Report_2016.pdf (accessed 29 October 2018).

Vanat, L. (2019) 2019 International report on snow and mountain tourism: overview of the key industry figures for ski resorts (11th edition). Available at: https://www.vanat.ch/international-report-on-snow-mountain-tourism (accessed 26 June 2019).

Vestlandsrådet [Vestland council] (2012) Reiselivsstrategi for Vestlandet 2013–20 [Tourism strategy for western Norway 2013–20 opportunities]. Available at: https://www.hordaland.no/globalassets/for-hfk/naringsutvikling/filer/felles-reiselivsstrategi-for-vestlandet-med-innarbeidde-endringer-etter-behandling-i-vr-radet.pdf (accessed 29 October 2018).

Visit Dalarna (n.d.) Dalarnas Besöksnäringsstrategi 2030 [Dalarna's tourism strategy 2030] – Visit Dalarna AB. Available at: https://www.visitdalarna.se/media/383 (accessed 8 February 2019).

Volgger, M. and Pechlaner, H. (2014) Requirements for destination management organizations in destination governance: understanding DMO success. *Tourism Management* 41, 64–75. DOI:10.1016/j.tourman.2013.09.001

Volkswirtschaftsdirektion des Kantons Bern (2018) *Tourismus BE 2025. Arbeitspapier* [Tourism BE 2025 Working Paper]. Available at: https://mmbe.ch/web/sites/default/files/2018-01-18-tourismus-2025-de.pdf (accessed 29 October 2018).

Weiermair, K., Peters, M. and Frehse, J. (2008) Success factors for public private partnership: cases in alpine tourism development. *Journal of Services Research* 7(February), 7–21.

World Bank Group (2017) *Tourism for Development: 20 Reasons Sustainable Tourism Counts for Development*. The World Bank, Washington, DC.

6 Winter Tourism in the Alps and the Implications of Climate Change

ULRIKE PRÖBSTL-HAIDER*

Institute of Landscape Development, Recreation and Conservation Planning, University of Natural Resources and Life Sciences, Vienna, Austria

6.1 Introduction

Over the past few decades, climate change has markedly increased the vulnerability of the alpine tourism sector. The following trends have been predominantly responsible for these developments (Pröbstl-Haider and Pütz, 2016).

Alpine tourism has come to be characterized by significant geographical and seasonal concentrations. Apart from metropolitan centres, most tourist-intensive municipalities are gathered around skiing regions. Around 54% of overnight stays in Austria, for instance, occur in the districts of Tyrol (~35%) and Salzburg (~19%). Moreover, vulnerability of the sector has intensified due to the increased importance of winter holidays in relation to the summer season, as well as the higher revenue intake during the winter months. Whereas around 70 million overnight stays in 1990 were booked in summer and about 50 million in the winter season, today, these percentages have levelled out at around 70 million each (Statistik Austria, 2018a; see Fig. 6.1).

The daily spending rates among holidaymakers averaged around €152 in the winter of 2015, while those in the summer of the same year only amounted to €125 (WKO, 2016). The greater economic significance of winter tourism compared with summer tourism has also been observed in Switzerland (Mayer *et al.*, 2009; Backhaus *et al.*, 2013).

Alongside the growing vulnerability of the tourist sector, various effects of climate change have already been observed in the Alps over the past years. The rise of temperature in this region has surpassed the global average, and other well-known phenomena include a decrease in snow coverage at lower altitudes, the melting of glaciers and permafrost areas at high altitudes, changes in water resources and an increase in natural hazard events (Jacob *et al.*, 2007; OECD, 2007; Grothmann *et al.*, 2009). An analysis of the frequency of extreme conditions, such as dry spells, thunder storms or heavy rainfall, has, however, shown that seasonal and annual fluctuations have not yet significantly increased over the past 250 years. This observation also holds true for the past three decades most strongly influenced by human intervention (ZAMG, 2012). However, the amount of stressful tropical nights in urban areas increased significantly and increased the risks especially for elderly people (Arnberger *et al.*, 2017).

---

* E-mail: ulrike.proebstl@boku.ac.at

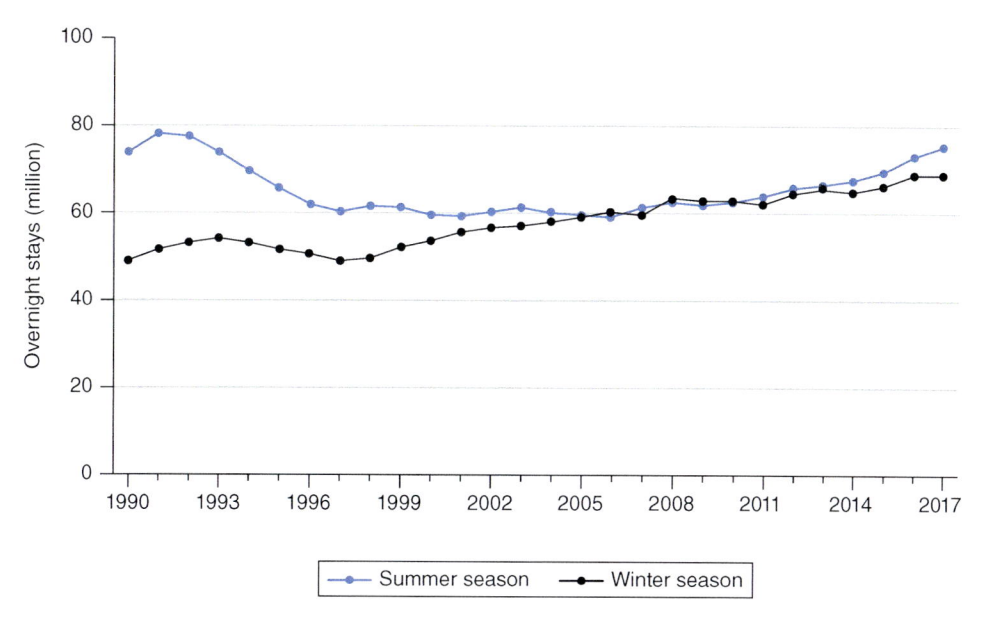

Fig. 6.1. Development of overnight stays in Austria since 1990 in the summer and winter season. (Statistik Austria, 2018a, translated into English.)

6.2 Current Strategies

Climate change is expected to have universally negative effects on snow-dependent alpine winter tourism, though specific impacts will vary depending on region. Technical adaptation strategies involving artificial snowmaking are already extensively in use in the alpine region (Pröbstl, 2006; Pütz *et al.*, 2011). In Austria, about 80% of pistes are already equipped with snowmaking facilities, and it is now commonplace in larger skiing regions to rely on artificial snowmaking to ensure full snow coverage. Contrary to popularized claims made in numerous publications, the conditions required for artificial snowmaking do not solely depend on altitude but are linked to a wider range of local characteristics including the local geomorphology, slope aspect, the frequency of foehn effects, and other microclimatic conditions (Pröbstl *et al.*, 2008a, b). While a few (small-scale) expansions may still occur in existing skiing regions at higher altitudes, Austria's potential for technical adaptation via widespread artificial snowmaking has reached its limits. To this effect, data compiled by the Austrian Tourism Bank (ÖHT, 2012) identified a strong downward trend as early as 2012. However, this does not preclude the replacement of existing facilities as well as an upgrade of terminal devices.

Due to the long regeneration periods following construction projects in high mountain regions (Pröbstl, 2006), small-scale expansion in high altitudes will need to rely on sensitive construction measures adapted to local landscapes, in order to avoid long-term ecological impacts. The districts of Tyrol, Salzburg and Carinthia have implemented specific legal regulations for ecological construction supervision – a step that has already contributed to more sensitive approaches in the past.

Therefore, expansion of artificial snowmaking in existing skiing regions is not likely to lead to significant impacts on protected natural assets in affected areas, nor on Austrian biodiversity overall. This is also due to the fact that areas affected by artificial snowmaking only account for a small percentage of the total alpine region (snowmaking is currently employed in only about 0.3% of Austria's alpine area). Furthermore, if affected areas are properly cared for during the summer months, they can still retain a near-natural character. The use of water reservoirs, meanwhile, ensures that interference with the natural hydrological regime is kept to a minimum.

In low-altitude regions without snowmaking facilities, large investments are no longer economically expedient due to the highly competitive environment of alpine tourism. Recent developments have made this abundantly clear: the past few years have seen an expansion of skiing areas both into and within higher altitudes, as well as numerous mergers of existing skiing regions to larger units. At the same time, the relative proportion of piste areas at lower altitudes (with valley stations under 1200 m) has decreased from 40% to 34% (Peck, 2005), and this trend is continuing (Pröbstl-Haider and Mostegl, 2016).

In the meantime, skiing regions trust in the progress of snowmaking technologies (e.g. snowmaking at −1°C). However, the high energy demand and consistently increasing costs are seen with some concern within the industry. Several businesses have therefore also started to utilize their snowmaking facilities for energy recovery, and employ photovoltaics and geothermal energy to compensate for their increasing energy consumption (see, for example, Zell am See, See in Tyrol and Lech am Arlberg in Austria, and Safiental in Switzerland). On the basis of Lech's ski lifts, a pilot project to calculate the carbon footprint of cableway operators was developed in cooperation with the Environmental Committee of OITAF (The International Organization for Transportation by Rope) (Pröbstl and Jiricka, 2012). The total calculated emissions demonstrated that, aside from the use of renewable energy sources, slope management is the main factor that can contribute to a reduction of greenhouse emissions. Further reductions can, moreover, be achieved through effective snow management, especially by measuring actual snow coverage during preparation, thereby reducing the amount of technical snowmaking to the exact level required. Based on their experience, operators estimate the achievable energy savings to be at least around 15%.[1]

A closer look at the various investments undertaken in these areas reveals that – aside from investments in artificial snowmaking – funds have been increasingly directed towards efforts to boost all-year tourism. This is also reflected in the national subsidies for business-led tourism promotion, awarded by the federal government and distributed by the Austrian Tourism Bank (ÖHT, 2012). The total amount of subsidized investments amounted to approximately €880 million in the year 2011. A total of 85% of loan-based investments went to the hotel industry, 8% to infrastructure (mostly snowmaking facilities) and 7% to gastronomy. A solid 27% of funded investment costs were allocated for measures to extend the tourist seasons (mainly summer and autumn).

The question of how to design communication strategies in relation to climate change and adaptation measures has largely gone unanswered within the industry. Studies have shown that sensationalized – but poorly substantiated – media reports have led to a great deal of uncertainty among consumers. Furthermore, various authors emphasize that decision making within the tourist sector is strongly influenced by the manner in which issues relating to climate change and adaptation strategies are communicated (Stehr and von Storch, 1995; Grothmann and Patt, 2005; Gössling *et al.*, 2012). Pröbstl (1998) demonstrated that holidaymakers who live more than 200 km away from the Alps are more likely to assume that snowmaking has negative effects on the environment than those who live closer to skiing regions and who also visit the area in the summer. MANOVA (2007) also confirm these findings with regard to the perception of climate change in the Austrian context.

Currently, the information consumers can access on websites run by skiing regions and destinations is mostly inadequate. Communication strategies range from promotional campaigns (e.g. the 'Frau Holle Guarantee' or the 'Sound of Snow') to more exact calculations of energy savings or contributions made by renewable energy sources within the respective skiing region (e.g. the Schmittenhöhebahn in Zell am See) based on their environmental auditing. Comparisons with other holiday models, e.g. by drawing attention to the climate impact of long-distance travel compared with a day of skiing in the region (e.g. Fellhornbahn in Oberstdorf, Germany), are a new addition to destinations' communication strategies.

6.3 Discussion of Current Adaptation Strategies

In view of the potential consequences of climate change, international tourism research emphasizes the need to develop proactive and foresighted strategies (Dwyer *et al.*, 2009; Pröbstl-Haider and Haider, 2013) and backs efforts to diversify touristic programmes (Dubois and Ceron, 2006). However, a recent publication on adaptation strategies in the Austrian tourist sector determined that the measures described above are 'largely of an individual and reactive nature in response to already perceptible changes (e.g. the use of snowmaking facilities or the gradual shift of skiing slopes to higher altitudes), and cannot be seen as concerted and foresighted efforts directed at the projected effects of climate change in the future' (Moshammer *et al.*, 2014, p. 969). The report, in conclusion, underscores that there is 'heightened danger with regards to possible maladjustments and conflicts with other sectors and trades'.

Regarding the development of additional tourist products beyond snow-dependent alpine (skiing) tourism, the existing literature on diversification and flexibilization in winter tourism indicates that the potential to diversify the range of offerings is limited, due to a persistent reliance on snow. According to Pröbstl *et al.* (2008b), relaxation and wellness offers, cultural programmes, sports halls and ice rinks, hiking trails and other offers cannot fully compensate for snow-bound activities. A mere 15% of winter tourists stated that a 'perfect' set of alternative activities could fully replace skiing on a 7-day holiday. These findings underscore the fact that visitors choose destinations based on snow-based activities rather than on their range of alternative, snow-independent offerings (Pröbstl *et al.*, 2008b).

Further initiatives, therefore, aim at achieving stable, year-round tourism. Weather- and season-independent activities, e.g. in the educational, cultural or health segment, are considered essential in this respect, to boost off-season tourism. A recent study funded by the Austrian climate change programme 'Startclim' explored the potential of 'nature experience programmes' to improve diversification and combat seasonality in tourism (Pröbstl-Haider and Melzer, 2015). The study looked at programmes that are offered for longer than 8 months a year, and programmes that are offered for 5–8 months a year but could potentially be extended to 8 months a year. A total of 236 natural experience programmes were surveyed with regard to their opening times, overall themes, connection to protected areas, the specific type of experience offered, entrance fees and effect on employment, among other aspects. The analysis concluded that it is generally feasible to develop a tourist sector in Austria that is oriented towards natural experiences, does not depend on weather conditions and is sustainable all year round. However, the research project also found that many programmes were not offered permanently and with sufficient reliability. The findings, moreover, indicated that off-peak seasons in spring and autumn could be further strengthened. The vital importance of protected areas is reflected in the large number of nature experience programmes that are in some way connected to nature reserves (56%). The large share of activities requiring an entrance fee (60%), meanwhile, suggests that these offers already contribute to the added value in the respective regions. Almost all of the overall themes covered by the study (e.g. landscape mise-en-scène, natural environment, culinary offers, geology, links to local land use, and health and sport; see Fig. 6.2) boast relatively high direct employment effects and carry significant potential for further product development.

An increase in seasonal flexibility is considered to provide an – albeit temporary – solution. Flexibilization could be achieved by rearranging holiday periods in order to better spread tourist flows, and by stepping up efforts to attract target groups that are not bound by specific holiday periods (e.g. 50+, seniors and high earners).

As indicated above, tourism not only contributes to climate change through snow-making, wellness and other types of infrastructure, the visitors' means of travel to reach their tourist destinations also plays a significant role. This aspect, however, often remains neglected in the debate on effective adaptation strategies. According to the Tourism Monitor of the Austrian Tourist Office (Österreich Werbung), the vast majority of domestic and international guests in 2013/14 arrived by private car (74%). An

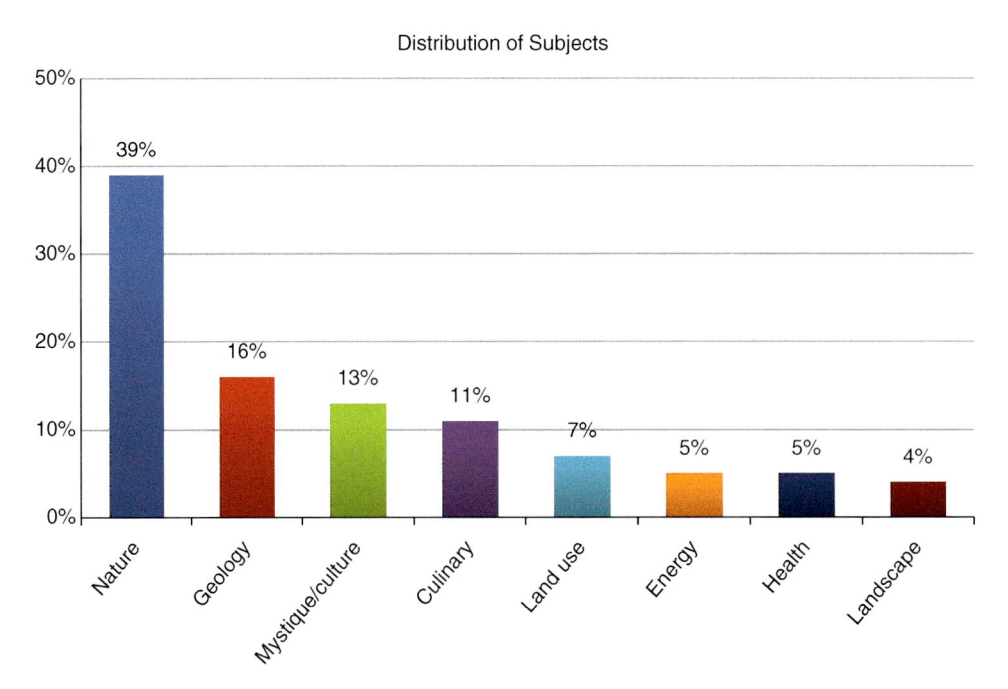

Fig. 6.2. Thematic subjects of 236 natural experience programmes in Austria. (From Pröbstl-Haider and Melzer, 2015.)

additional 9% arrived by plane, while only 8% travelled by train and 6% by bus. Finally, 2% of guests arrived by caravan/camper and 1% by motorcycle (WKO, 2018). Considering Friesenbichler's (2003) findings, which show that arrival, departure and feeder traffic account for 38% of CO_2 emissions produced by snow-based winter tourism, it would appear that a shift in modal share in tourist transportation harbours significant potential for energy savings. He compiled figures for CO_2 emissions of snow-based winter tourism (including accommodation and means of arrival) and revealed that winter sports infrastructure (ski lifts and other ascent systems, snowmaking facilities, snow-grooming machinery, etc.), transport (arrival and departure traffic and traffic within the holiday location), and accommodation and catering collectively accounted for 3.9 million tonnes of CO_2 per winter season or almost 6% of Austria's total CO_2 emissions (Friesenbichler, 2003). Accommodation, according to these results, caused the largest share of CO_2 emissions, accounting for 58%, followed by arrival, departure and feeder traffic at 38%. Cable cars, tow lifts, snow-grooming vehicles and snow cannons, meanwhile, accumulatively caused only 4% of emissions linked to snow-based winter tourism. Studies on Switzerland's alpine tourism have drawn similar conclusions (Zegg *et al.*, 2010). The ski resort Fellhorn in Germany uses these facts in promoting their destination (see Table 6.1) and making the public aware of its daily trade-offs.

In light of these findings, South Tyrol's alpine tourist sector has in recent years increasingly focused its attention on enabling a comfortable arrival by public transport. For this purpose, two key adaptation strategies were combined: First, the range of nearby slopes easily accessible to visitors during their holidays was expanded. Second, the large share of emissions caused by travel to and from the destination was reduced (for the overall strategy, see also Pröbstl-Haider and Mostegl, Chapter 17 in this volume).

Alongside a shift of the chosen means of transport to include more public transport, an increase in the average duration of stay would also lead to a reduction in energy consumption. Current trends in vacation habits, however, point in the opposite direction. For years now, the average duration of stay among tourists in Austria has continuously decreased, dropping from 4.8 days in 1995 to 3.4 days in 2017 (Statistik Austria, 2018b).

Table 6.1. Energy consumption of different activities to enhance the public awareness. (Compilation by Augustin Kröll from the German ski resort Fellhorn, based on data from 2014.)

Activity	Energy consumption, equivalent
1 day skiing in the ski resort Fellhorn in Oberstdorf, Germany, without travelling	15.67 kWh/person/day on average
Trip by private car 7 l/100 km	22 km = 15.67 kWh
Visiting a spa area with auna in Germany per person one day	29 kWh/person/day on average
Flight to and from the Caribbean islands (Munich–Santo Domingo, 200 people on board)	7500 kWh/person Per flight the used energy would enable about 95,700 persons to ski 1 day in the ski resort Fellhorn in Oberstdorf

6.4 Conclusions

The article indicates an increased vulnerability of the winter tourist sector. This development is not only – or even primarily – caused by climate change but is instead linked to the economically lower significance of the summer season, high flexibility among holidaymakers and a considerably higher added value achieved in the winter. Weather conditions that are unfavourable for winter sports therefore have increasingly severe consequences. Although technical adaptation still receives the most attention, the article also highlights innovative projects that reveal the potential of alternative adaptation strategies. Product development in these cases, however, is still in its infancy. Considering the proportion of areas maintained by artificial snowmaking in the alpine region on the one hand, and the considerable impacts caused by travel to and from holiday destinations on the other hand, there is also an urgent need to increasingly appeal to travellers' personal responsibility – even if it may seem most convenient to put the question of adaptation solely to the tourist regions and providers. Naturally, this does not diminish the responsibility carried by Austrian tourist regions and operators to pursue adequate and efficient adaptation strategies.

Note

[1] Estimation based on the experience offered by the Planai cable car operators in 2014 and Pröbstl-Haider *et al.* (2019).

References

Arnberger, A., Allex, B., Eder, R., Ebenberger, M., Wanka, A. *et al.* (2017) Elderly resident's uses of and preferences for urban green spaces during heat periods. *Urban Forestry and Urban Greening* 21, 102–115. DOI:10.1016/j.ufug.2016.11.012

Backhaus, N., Buser, C., Butticaz, M., Jorio, D. and Speich, M. (2013) *Wirtschaftliche Auswirkungen des Sommertourismus im UNESCO Biosphärenreservat Val Müstair Parc Naziunal.* Schriftenreihe Human geography series 27, Department of Geography, University of Zürich. DOI:10.5167/uzh-80488

Dubois, G. and Ceron, J.P. (2006) Tourism and climate change: proposals for a research agenda. *Journal of Sustainable Tourism* 14(4), 399–415. DOI:10.2167/jost539.0

Dwyer, L., Edwards, D., Mistilis, N., Roman, C. and Scott, N. (2009) Destination and enterprise management for a tourism future. *Tourism Management* 30, 63–74. DOI:10.1016/j.tourman.2008.04.002

Friesenbichler, J. (2003) Energieeinsatz und CO_2-Emissionen im Wintertourismus. Diploma Thesis, FH JOANNEUM – University of Applied Sciences, Kapfenberg, Austria.

Gössling, S., Scott, D., Hall, C.M., Ceron, J.-P. and Dubois, G. (2012) Consumer behavior and demand response of tourists to climate change. *Annals of Tourism Research* 39(1), 36–58. DOI:10.1016/j.annals.2011.11.002

Grothmann, T. and Patt, A. (2005) Adaptive capacity and human cognition: the process of individual adaptation to climate change. *Global Environmental Change* 15, 199–213. DOI:10.1016/j.gloenvcha.2005.01.002

Grothmann, T., Nenz, D. and Pütz, M. (2009) Adaptation in vulnerable alpine regions – lessons learnt from regional case studies. In: European Environment Agency (ed.) *Regional Climate Change and Adaptation. The Alps Facing the Challenge of Changing Water Resources*. EEA Technical Report 8/2009. EEA, Copenhagen, pp. 96–108.

Jacob, D., Göttel, H., Kotlarski, S. and Lorenz, P. (2007) Mögliche Klimaänderungen im Alpenraum. In: Bundesumweltministerium für Umwelt, Naturschutz und Reaktorsicherheit (ed.) *Klimawandel in den Alpen: Fakten – Folgen – Anpassung*. BMU, Berlin, pp. 22–27.

MANOVA (2007) Gästeverhalten bei Schneemangel und Klimawandel. *Mountain Manager* 4/2007, 44–45.

Mayer, M., Wasem, K., Gehring, K., Pütz, M., Roschewitz, A. et al. (2009) *Wirtschaftliche Bedeutung des naturnahen Tourismus im Simmental und Diemtigtal. Regionalökonomische Effekte und Erfolgsfaktoren*. Eidgenössische Forschungsanstalt für Wald, Schnee und Landschaft, Birmensdorf, Switzerland.

Moshammer, H., Prettenthaler, F., Damm, A., Hutter, H.P., Jiricka, A. et al. (2014) Kapitel 4: Gesundheit, Tourismus. In: APCC (ed.) *Austrian Assessment Report 2014 (AAR14)*. Verlag der Österreichischen Akademie der Wissenschaften, Vienna, pp. 933–977.

OECD (Organisation for Economic Co-operation and Development) (2007) *Climate Change in the European Alps. Adapting Winter Tourism and Natural Hazards Management*. OECD Publications, Paris. DOI:10.1787/9789264031692-en

ÖHT (Österreichische Hotel- und Tourismusbank Gesellschaft m.b.H.n) (2012) Geschäftsbericht 2012. Available at: https://www.oeht.at/fileadmin/user_upload/Dokumente/Impressum/Geschaeftsbericht2012.pdf (accessed 28 November 2018).

Peck, S. (2005) Die Entwicklung der Wintersportinfrastruktur in Österreich von 1995 bis 2005. Eine Untersuchung der Aufstiegshilfen und Beschneiungsanlagen in Österreich vor dem Hintergrund der Klimavariabilität. Diploma Thesis, TU Vienna, Austria.

Pröbstl, U. (1998) Ist umweltgerechter Skisport möglich? In: Commission Internationale pour la Protection des Alpes (CIPRA) (ed.) *1. Alpenreport: Daten – Fakten – Probleme – Lösungsansätze*. Haupt, Bern, Switzerland, pp. 265–271.

Pröbstl, U. (2006) *Kunstschnee und Umwelt – Entwicklung und Auswirkungen der technischen Beschneiung*. Haupt, Bern, Switzerland.

Pröbstl, U. and Jiricka, A. (2012) Carbon Foot Print Skilifte Lech – Modellprojekt in Zusammenarbeit mit dem OITAF Umweltausschuss. *Internationale Seilbahn-Rundschau* 4, 24–25.

Pröbstl, U., Dallhammer, E., Formayer, H., Grabler, K., Haas, P. et al. (2008b) Strategien zur nachhaltigen Raumentwicklung von Tourismusregionen unter dem Einfluss der globalen Erwärmung am Beispiel der Wintersportregion um Schladming. STRATEGE final project report. University of Natural Resources and Life Science, Vienna, Austria.

Pröbstl, U., Prutsch, A., Formayer, H., Landauer, M., Grabler, K. et al. (2008a) Climate change in winter sport destinations – transdisciplinary research for implementing sustainable tourism. *Tourism and Environment* 69, 85–93. DOI:10.2495/ST080171

Pröbstl-Haider, U. and Haider, W. (2013) Tools to measure the intention for adapting to climate change by winter tourists: some thoughts on consumer behavior research and an empirical example. *Tourism Review* 68(2), 44–55. DOI:10.1108/TR-04-2013-0015

Pröbstl-Haider, U. and Melzer, V. (2015) Witterungsunabhängige Tourismusangebote basierend auf Naturerlebnisangeboten – Bedeutung und innovative Entwicklungen. StartClim2014.E final project report. University of Natural Resources and Life Science, Vienna, Austria. Available at: www.startclim.at/fileadmin/user_upload/StartClim2014_reports/StCl2014E_lang.pdf (accessed 8 January 2019).

Pröbstl-Haider, U. and Mostegl, N.M. (2016) Skigebiete im Vergleich – Macht Größe alleine schon sexy? *FdSnow – Fachzeitschrift für den Skisport* 49, 28–35.

Pröbstl-Haider, U. and Pütz, M. (2016) Großschutzgebiete und Tourismus in den Alpen im Zeichen des Klimawandels. *Natur und Landschaft* 1, 15–19. DOI:10.17433/1.2016.50153375.15-19

Pröbstl-Haider, U., Brom, M., Dorsch, C. and Jiricka-Pürrer, A. (2019) *Environmental Management in Ski Areas: Procedure – Requirements – Exemplary Solutions*. Springer, Berlin. DOI:10.1007/978-3-319-75061-3

Pütz, M., Gallati, D., Kytzia, S., Elsasser, H., Lardelli, C. et al. (2011) Winter tourism, climate change, and snowmaking in the Swiss Alps: tourists' attitudes and regional economic impacts. *Mountain Research and Development* 31(4), 357–362. DOI:10.1659/MRD-JOURNAL-D-11-00039.1

Statistik Austria (2018a) Übernachtungen seit 1990. Available at: www.statistik.at/web_de/statistiken/wirtschaft/tourismus/beherbergung/ankuenfte_naechtigungen/index.html (accessed 28 November 2018).

Statistik Austria (2018b) Ankünfte, Nächtigungen sowie durchschnittliche Aufenthaltsdauer nach Bundesländern (1995 bis 2017). Available at: www.statistik.gv.at/web_de/statistiken/wirtschaft/tourismus/beherbergung/ankuenfte_naechtigungen/index.html (accessed 20 December 2018).

Stehr, N. and von Storch, H. (1995) The social construct of climate and climate change. *Climate Research* 5, 99–105.

Wirtschaftskammer Österreich (WKO) (2016) Tourismus und Freizeitwirtschaft in Zahlen, Österreichische und internationale Tourismus- und Wirtschaftsdaten, 52nd edn. Available at:https://www.wko.at/branchen/tourismus-freizeitwirtschaft/Tourismus-Freizeitwirtschaft-in-Zahlen-Mai-2016_2.pdf (accessed 28 November 2018).

Wirtschaftskammer Österreich (WKO) (2018) Tourismus und Freizeitwirtschaft in Zahlen, Österreichische und internationale Tourismus- und Wirtschaftsdaten, 54th edn. Available at: https://www.wko.at/branchen/tourismus-freizeitwirtschaft/tourismus-freizeitwirtschaft-in-zahlen-2018.pdf (accessed 20 December 2018).

ZAMG (2012) Bringt der Klimawandel mehr Extremereignisse? Available at: https://www.zamg.ac.at/cms/de/klima/news/bringt-der-klimawandel-mehr-wetterextrema (accessed 28 November 2018).

Zegg, R., Küng, T. and Grossrieder, R. (2010) *Energiemanagement Bergbahnen – Studie und Handbuch*. Seilbahnen Schweiz, Bern, Switzerland.

7 Climate Change Risk Perceptions in Nature-Based Tourism Systems: A Case Study from Western Maine

Lydia Horne*, Sandra De Urioste-Stone, John Daigle, Caroline Noblet, Laura Rickard, Hope Kohtala and Andrew Morgan

University of Maine, Orono, ME, USA

7.1 Introduction

Climate change risk perceptions are views directed to processing information and making sense of climate change as an external threat, phenomenon and situation (Shakeela and Becken, 2015). Risk perceptions of climate change can impact the extent to which tourism businesses and destinations implement mitigation and adaptation strategies. The effects of climate change are already being felt worldwide in the tourism industry, especially destinations that rely on nature-based tourism (Bicknell and McManus, 2006; Shakeela and Becken, 2015). In many destinations, local actors and community residents are reliant on tourism as a tool for economic development (UNWTO, 2016). Climate change is likely to change visitor behaviour to and at tourism destinations, while also influencing supply-side management decisions. At the same time that tourism is being impacted by climate change, the industry acknowledges its role in contributing to greenhouse gas emissions (UNWTO, 2016). Therefore, understanding tourism stakeholders' and visitors' climate change risk perceptions and resulting behaviours can have important implications for long-term tourism destination sustainability and mitigation practices.

We begin this chapter by introducing the case study area of Western Maine and its site characteristics, followed by a brief description of the climate change risk perception model and research methodologies utilized with tourism stakeholders and recreation users. Our chapter will then discuss results from our research to identify perceptions of risks and challenges associated with changes in climate, what variables influence perceptions of risk, and tourism stakeholder and recreation user behavioural intention as associated with climate change perceptions. The final section integrates results from both qualitative (tourism stakeholder) and quantitative research (recreation users) approaches to provide a richer understanding of climate change risk perceptions to guide more effective sustainable tourism planning efforts in light of changing conditions in tourism destinations.

---

* E-mail: lydia.horne@maine.edu

7.1.1 Case study description

The state of Maine, located in north-east US, is divided into eight tourism regions, including the Lakes and Mountains Region in Western Maine along the New Hampshire border (see Fig. 7.1). Our case study area of Western Maine is a four-season destination with over half of tourists and recreation users visiting the area to engage primarily in outdoor recreation activities (Maine Office of Tourism, 2012). The region received over 4.8 million visitors in 2017 (2.3 million being day visitors), with the majority of visitors residing in Maine, New Hampshire and Massachusetts (Maine Office of Tourism, 2018). Visitors to the destination spent over $670 million, which supported over 69 million in taxes, $251 million in total earnings and over 13,000 jobs (DPA, 2018).

Fig. 7.1. Location of the state of Maine within North America, and division of the state according to the eight official tourism regions. Highlighted in green is the case study tourism destination in Western Maine, the Maine Lakes and Mountains Region.

The majority of visitors to the region are particularly interested in participating in active nature-based, outdoor activities such as winter activities, outdoor swimming and hiking/backpacking. More popular winter activities in 2017 included alpine skiing or snowboarding, Nordic skiing and snowmobiling. Outdoor recreation activities that are becoming more popular in the area include mountain biking, camping, hiking, exploring parks and outdoor fun centres targeting visitors travelling with children (Maine Office of Tourism, 2018). Top attractions included state parks, ski resorts and trails. Though a four-season destination, visitation is higher during the winter season, making the tourism destination especially vulnerable to changes in climate conditions.

Since 1895, the average annual temperature in Maine has increased by 1.67°C and is expected to increase another 1.67–2.78°C by 2050 (Fernandez *et al.*, 2015). Maine's winter tourism industry faces a shorter season with projected decreases in precipitation and temperature. In Maine, snowfall total has declined by 2.54 cm since 1895 and with rising temperatures, the snow season has decreased by 2 weeks since 1895 (Fernandez *et al.*, 2015). Though overall snowfall is expected to continue to decrease, Maine will likely experience more frequent winter storms and mixed precipitation. Changes in winter snowfall total and season length are jeopardizing winter recreation, especially in mountain regions of Western Maine that rely on ski tourism.

7.2 Research Methodologies and Theoretical Framework

We used a mixed-methods research approach to understand both nature-based tourism stakeholder and recreation user climate change risk perceptions and behavioural intent. Nature-based tourism is a type of tourism that utilizes natural features such as mountains, lakes, beaches, rivers and weather as primary tourism attractions. We first applied a phenomenological research methodology (Moustakas, 1994) via tourism stakeholder in-depth interviews with an embedded pile sort activity (Bernard, 2011). Second, we conducted a mail resident survey (Dillman *et al.*, 2014) to measure recreation use, perceptions of risk and future recreation behaviour in light of changes in resource conditions. Data from interviews, pile sort and survey were integrated for a holistic understanding of the case – Western Maine tourism destination.

Our research employed a modified version of van der Linden's (2015) social-psychological theoretical framework to understand climate change risk perceptions within the nature-based tourism industry. The risk perceptions model we used included van der Linden's proposed constructs of socio-demographics, cognition, experiential processing and social structures, and Mase and colleagues' (2015) trust in climate change communication sources construct.

Socio-demographic factors that influence risk perceptions can include gender, political affiliation, levels of education, income and age. Being female and liberal increases climate change risk perceptions (Safi *et al.*, 2012; van der Linden, 2015), while age may influence risk perceptions of climate change (De Urioste-Stone *et al.*, 2015). Belief in anthropogenic climate change and more knowledge of climate change are associated with increased levels of concern and higher perceived risk (Milfont, 2012; Pidgeon, 2012; Safi *et al.*, 2012; van der Linden, 2015). Experiencing an event first-hand that is the result of climate change usually equates to higher risk perceptions (Milfont, 2012; Pidgeon, 2012; Spence *et al.*, 2012; van der Linden, 2015). Further, the more people act upon the risk of climate change, the more prevalent the issue becomes in society and the more amplified an individual's risk perceptions (van der Linden, 2015). In addition, trust in climate change communicators, such as scientists or media outlets, influences how information is internalized and how information shapes risk perceptions (Johnson, 2012; Mase *et al.*, 2015).

7.3 Stakeholder Perceptions of Challenges and Responses

7.3.1 Experiences, concerns and opportunities

Tourism stakeholders in Western Maine were generally informed of global climate change impacts but lacked knowledge of specific local climate change impacts (Horne *et al.*, 2019). Business owners felt more informed about climate change and more aware of its impacts on the region compared with tourism managers (Horne *et al.*, 2019). This difference in knowledge could be explained by a daily connection to the environment through being nature-based tourism business owners who are constantly in the field, experiencing nature and the natural tourism assets. In contrast, town and regional planners do not work directly with the environment and oftentimes have different tasks in promoting nature-based tourism in the area, hence having more office-based work responsibilities.

Due to limited local climate change knowledge and low trust in climate change information, participants relied on first-hand experiences with impacts to inform their risk perceptions. Participants frequently discussed environmental changes they were observing in the region and how those changes connected back to large-scale environmental and climatic changes. Changes in snowfall, unpredictable winters and shifting seasons were experienced by nearly all tourism stakeholders interviewed (Horne, 2017). Of highest concern were the climate change impacts perceived to be directly connected to winter nature-based tourism (Horne *et al.*, 2019). Changes in temperatures, precipitation, storm frequency and severity, and shifting seasons were especially salient to participants (Horne, 2017).

Most participants were uncertain about future climate change impacts to the region, which posed a challenge as they conceptualized the future of their business or organization (see Table 7.1). Uncertainty of how climatic changes could impact the region poses a problem for mitigation and adaptation behaviours, as did the unpredictability of the winter season, lack of financial resources and difficulty planning long-term. Results from the pile sorts indicated that low perceived control over many climate change causes and impacts was a significant barrier to mitigation and adaptation actions (Horne *et al.*, 2018). With limited resources and knowledge, it can be difficult to invest in long-term adaptation and mitigation strategies. Finding ways to overcome and minimize barriers to climate change action while increasing facilitators to action will be important opportunities for Western Maine's nature-based tourism industry to bolster its regional resilience.

7.3.2 Adaptation

Whether or not participants thought climate change was impacting the region, most participants were employing at least one adaptation strategy in response to observed

Table 7.1. Facilitators and challenges for nature-based tourism stakeholders.

Facilitators	Challenges
Collaboration (i.e. with Chambers of Commerce, other tourism business owners)	Lack of collaboration
Conservation ethic among residents	Competition between tourism businesses
Institutional support, especially at the regional and industry level	Lack of institutional support at the state level
Knowledge of overall climate change	Uncertainty about climate change
Financial incentives	Negative attitudes towards tourism by residents and visitors
Financial resources	Lack of resources (i.e. financial, staffing, space and difficulty reaching target markets)
Natural assets to support nature-based tourism	Winter weather dependence and the unpredictability of the winter seasons
	'Wearing many hats' (juggling many tasks) making it difficult to plan long term
	High socio-economic and environmental diversity of the tourism region, making it difficult to promote, collaborate, etc.

environmental change. Winter businesses were especially likely to implement extensive adaptation strategies focused primarily on product development and modification. Adaptation strategies included snowmaking and adding bike trails for summer use at ski resorts, diversifying product offerings and altering the timing of activities (Horne *et al.*, unpublished results). Many adaptation strategies were motivated primarily by economic decisions and a need to ensure a more certain future for specific nature-based tourism businesses. Our results are similar to Bicknell and McManus's finding that high climate change risk perceptions among ski resort managers in Australia were associated with reliance on snowmaking to overcome the unpredictability of the season (Bicknell and McManus, 2006).

7.3.3 Mitigation and emission reduction

Few participants are adopting business-level mitigation strategies despite generally high awareness of and concern for climate change (Horne *et al.*, 2019). This could be explained by the influence of barriers, such as lack of resources, and facilitators, such as collaboration between tourism businesses and local Chambers of Commerce (see Table 7.1). Economic incentive was a strong motivator to engage in emission mitigation strategies. Participants who talked about economic payoffs, such as increased efficiency or attracting specific high-paying clientele, were more likely to incorporate mitigation strategies into their business models (Horne *et al.*, 2019). This is consistent with other research that found participants were more likely to reduce their emissions if there were financial incentives and a high perceived response-cost (Poussin *et al.*, 2014; Thuy *et al.*, 2014). For those businesses that were actively reducing their carbon emissions, large-scale investments in renewable energy were used, especially solar. In addition to environmental benefits, these businesses also saw green marketing as a means to attract visitors and boost profits. Those who did not include mitigation strategies in their tourism business model perhaps did not perceive any economic benefits or faced other barriers.

Many tourism stakeholders were using individual-level pro-environmental behaviours, such as recycling to reduce their environmental impact, though these behaviours were not often linked to climate change concerns (Horne *et al.*, unpublished results). For most interviewees, social and economic pressures were the primary motivators of small-scale mitigation efforts. While small-scale mitigation efforts were personal measures taken to reduce stakeholders' environmental impact, these actions were not necessarily directly connected to climate change concerns and rarely scaled up to become business-level mitigation strategies (Horne *et al.*, 2019).

7.4 Resident Perceptions and Behaviours

7.4.1 Profile and recreational behaviour

Survey participants were 59.9% male while 39.4% were female (the remaining 0.7% responded 'prefer not to answer') with a total mean age of 55 years. The majority of participants held a bachelor's degree at 30.1%. Further, respondents were 39.7% republicans, 24.5% democrats, 14.2% were independent; 21.6% of participants chose not to identify their political affiliation.

Residents who participated in the survey mentioned engaging in an array of recreational activities throughout the Western Maine tourism destination. The majority of residents engage in sightseeing or driving for pleasure, shopping, pursuing arts and cultural activities, backpacking and hiking. The most popular winter outdoor recreation activities among residents in the region are snowshoeing and snowmobiling.

A total of 32.6% of residents mentioned that they recreate in Western Maine a few times in the year with 18% of people saying that they recreate weekly and 15.9% saying that they recreate every few weeks (see Fig. 7.2). The majority of residents recreate outdoors in the winter a few times in the season (18.2%), every few weeks (17.7%), and weekly (15.5%). This shows that residents in the region are regularly engaging in outdoor recreation activities in the region throughout the year.

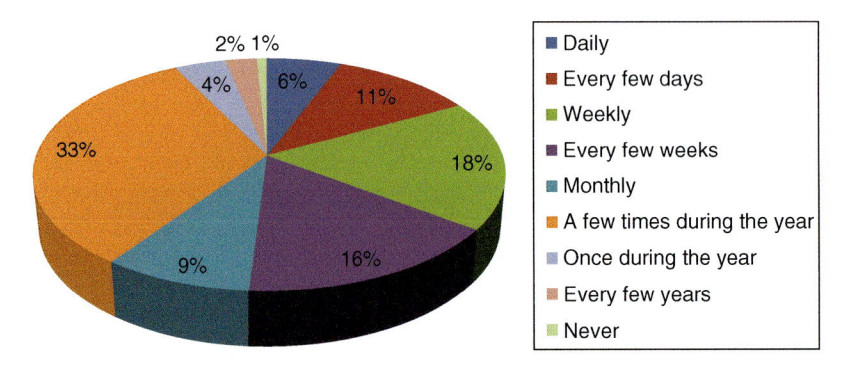

Fig. 7.2. Frequency of participation in outdoor recreation activities among Western Maine survey participants (*n* = 337).

7.4.2 Climate change risk perceptions

In terms of global climate change, the majority of residents believe that air temperature is rising and permanently frozen snow in the Arctic is now thawing. The majority of respondents (88.7%) believe that humans contribute to climate change, with 42.9% strongly agreeing, 29% agreeing and 16.8% somewhat agreeing to the human role in global climate change.

Among the climate change effects that residents expressed personally having experienced included changes in temperature, precipitation, storms and flooding. In the future, residents expect to increasingly experience changes in temperature (including heat waves), changes in precipitation and storms.

In terms of resident perceptions of climate change-related risks to outdoor recreation, residents believed that higher temperatures were more of a threat to the area than colder temperatures. Residents were particularly concerned with an increased amount of ticks and mosquitoes in the area as a result of climate change.

Further, 69% of respondents were concerned that climate change will affect tourism in Western Maine, while 76% of respondents mentioned being concerned that climate change will affect outdoor recreation in Western Maine. Finally, residents agreed that we can all contribute to reducing the effects of climate change (90.6%), most people they care about believe in climate change (77.3%), the government should be in charge of addressing climate change impacts (67.8%) and most people they care about are personally doing something to reduce the risk of climate change (62.5%).

7.4.3 Recreation behaviour

After considering the effects of climate change on the area, people were questioned on whether this would affect their decisions to recreate in the area. The most concerning topics that would influence a person's decision to recreate outdoors in the region were the prevalence of ticks and mosquitoes, extreme weather events, more ice storms, heat waves and reduced snow. Residents shared that the following conditions would be potential threats to Western Maine and its nature-based tourism industry: increased presence of ticks (85%), increased presence of mosquitoes (79%), reduced snow (63%) and extreme weather events (63%).

Finally residents expressed that if Western Maine experienced poor weather conditions, they would likely visit other places in Maine (70%), recreate at another time of year (60%), pursue other outdoor recreation activities (56%), visit another place in the north-east (53%) or visit another place in the US (45%). Participants believed that climate change could have harmful and long-term impacts on Western Maine communities (79%), and affect its outdoor recreation opportunities (76%) and tourism industry in the region (77%).

7.5 Conclusions and Lessons Learnt

Tourism stakeholders perceived the risk of climate change as high and as a result many businesses have already incorporated adaptation responses to observed impacts and challenges, especially among ski resorts. Most stakeholders were employing small-scale pro-environmental behaviours, though these actions were not specifically directed towards reducing their business's carbon footprint. The exceptions were those businesses that had heavily invested in renewable energy systems. Promoting the financial benefits of adopting mitigation behaviours could encourage businesses to make larger investments in renewable energy and other carbon offsetting initiatives. Furthermore, reducing barriers to adaptation and mitigation behaviours, such as providing subsidies and climate change information specific to the Western Maine tourism destination, will help ensure a climate resilient destination.

Outdoor recreationists in this study tended to be generalists, participating in multiple activities. This could explain the high willingness to substitute recreation activities among respondents. Additionally, participants indicated a high likelihood to visit Western Maine at a different time of year if conditions were unacceptable for outdoor recreation. Understanding this outdoor recreation behaviour could help nature-based tourism stakeholders justify investing in alternative winter tourism activities to help businesses sustain themselves during low snow years and draw users during the extending shoulder seasons. For example, several tourism stakeholders and outdoor recreation providers were developing mountain bike opportunities to create a summer market in this traditionally winter tourism destination (Horne, 2017).

Acknowledgements

We would like to thank Ashley Cooper for her assistance with the visitor survey and map making. This project was supported by the USDA National Institute of Food and Agriculture, McIntire Stennis project number ME041504 through the Maine Agricultural and Forest Experiment Station, and by a George J. Mitchell Center for Sustainability Solutions grant.

References

Bernard, H.R. (2011) *Research Methods in Anthropology: Qualitative and Quantitative Approaches*, 5th edn. Altamira Press, Walnut Creek, California.

Bicknell, S. and McManus, P. (2006) The canary in the coalmine: Australian ski resorts and their response to climate change. *Geographical Research* 44(4), 386–400. DOI:10.1111/j.1745-5871.2006.00409.x

De Urioste-Stone, S., Scaccia, M. and Howe-Poteet, D. (2015) Exploring visitor perceptions of the influence of climate change on tourism at Acadia National Park, Maine. *Journal of Outdoor Recreation and Tourism* 11, 34–43. DOI:10.1016/j. jort.2015.07.001

Dillman, D.A., Smyth, J.D. and Christian, L.M. (2014) *Internet, Phone, Mail, and Mixed-Mode Surveys: The Tailored Design Method*, 4th edn. John Wiley & Sons, Inc., Hoboken, New Jersey.

DPA (2018) Maine Lakes and Mountains: 2017 regional tourism impact estimates. Available at: https://9d2d4942db293a72d48a-483d7c2d30991038dc16c042d6541655.ssl.cf2.rackcdn.com/downloads/Maine-Lakes-and-Mountains-2017-Visitation-and-Econ-Impact.pdf (accessed 6 July 2018).

Fernandez, I.J., Schmitt, C.V., Birkel, S.D., Stancioff, E., Pershing, A.J. et al. (2015) *Maine's Climate Future: 2015 Update.* University of Maine, Orono, Maine.

Horne, L. (2017) Risk perceptions of climate change amongst nature-based tourism stakeholders in Western Maine. MSc Thesis, The University of Maine, Maine, USA.

Horne, L., De Urioste-Stone, S., Daigle, J. and Noblet, C. (2019) Climate change resilience in the face of local uncertainty, a phenomenological study. Manuscript submitted for publication.

Horne, L., De Urioste-Stone, S.M., Daigle, J. and Noblet, C. (in press) Using pile sorts to understand perceptions of climate change. *WIT Transactions on Ecology and the Environment* 227, 175–183. DOI:10.2495/ST180171

Johnson, B.B. (2012) Climate change communication: a provocative inquiry into motives, meanings, and means. *Risk Analysis* 32(6), 973–991. DOI:10.1111/j.1539-6924.2011.01731.x

Maine Office of Tourism (2012) Maine Office of Tourism Visitor tracking research 2013 calendar year annual report. Available at: https://www.skowhegan.org/DocumentCenter/View/949/2013-Annual-Report-04-17-14-Final-state-of-maine?bidId= (accessed 29 January 2019).

Maine Office of Tourism (2018) Visitor tracking research 2017 calendar year annual report regional insights: Maine Lakes and mountains. Available at: https://9d2d4942db293a72d48a-483d7c2d30991038dc16c042d6541655.ssl.cf2.rackcdn.com/downloads/Maine-Lakes-Mountains-2017-Regional-Report.pdf (accessed 7 July 2018).

Mase, A.S., Cho, H. and Prokopy, L.S. (2015) Enhancing the Social Amplification of Risk Framework (SARF) by exploring trust, the availability heuristic, and agricultural advisors' belief in climate change. *Journal of Environmental Psychology* 41, 166–176. DOI:10.1016/j.jenvp.2014.12.004

Milfont, T.L. (2012) The interplay between knowledge, perceived efficacy, and concern about global warming and climate change: a one-year longitudinal study. *Risk Analysis* 32(6), 1003–1020. DOI:10.1111/j.1539-6924.2012.01800.x

Moustakas, C. (1994) *Phenomenological Research Methods*. Sage, Thousand Oaks, California.

Pidgeon, N. (2012) Climate change risk perception and communication: addressing a critical moment? *Risk Analysis* 32(6), 951–956. DOI:10.1111/j.1539-6924.2012.01856.x

Poussin, J.K., Botzen, W.J.W. and Aerts, J.C.J.H. (2014) Factors of influence on flood damage mitigation behaviour by households. *Environmental Science and Policy* 40, 69–77. DOI:10.1016/j.envsci.2014.01.013

Safi, S.A., Smith, J.W. and Liu, Z. (2012) Rural Nevada and climate change: vulnerability, beliefs, and risk perception. *Risk Analysis* 32(6), 1041–1059. DOI:10.1111/j.1539-6924.2012.01836.x

Shakeela, A. and Becken, S. (2015) Understanding tourism leaders' perceptions of risks from climate change: an assessment of policy-making processes in the Maldives using the Social Amplification of Risk Framework (SARF). *Journal of Sustainable Tourism* 23(1), 65–84. DOI:10.1080/09669582.2014.918135

Spence, A., Poortinga, W. and Pidgeon, N. (2012) The psychological distance of climate change. *Risk Analysis* 32(6), 957–972. DOI:10.1111/j.1539-6924.2011.01695.x

Thuy, P.T., Moeliono, M., Locatelli, B., Brockhaus, M., Di Gregorio, M. and Mardiah, S. (2014) Integration of adaptation and mitigation in climate change and forest policies in Indonesia and Vietnam. *Forests* 5(8), 2016–2036. DOI:10.3390/f5082016

UNWTO (2016) Climate change and tourism. Available at: http://sdt.unwto.org/en/content/climate-change-tourism (accessed 30 March 2017).

van der Linden, S. (2015) The social-psychological determinants of climate change risk perceptions: towards a comprehensive model. *Journal of Environmental Psychology* 41, 112–124. DOI:10.1016/j.jenvp.2014.11.012

8 Alpine Winter Tourists' View on Climate Change and Travel Mobility

Bruno Abegg[1,2*], Leandra Jänicke[1], Rainer Unger[3] and Markus Mailer[4]

[1]*Institute of Geography, University of Innsbruck, Innsbruck, Austria;* [2]*Institute for Systemic Management and Public Governance, University of St. Gallen, St. Gallen, Switzerland;* [3]*alpS – Centre for Climate Change Adaptation, Innsbruck, Austria;* [4]*Institute of Infrastructure Engineering, University of Innsbruck, Innsbruck, Austria*

8.1 Introduction

Tourism is significantly contributing to climate change with transportation to/from the destination often being recognized as the primary contributor. In 2005, global tourism was responsible for 1.3 $GtCO_2$ – this was approximately 5% of the world's total CO_2 emissions at that time, excluding other greenhouse gases (GHGs) and secondary impacts caused by aviation (UNWTO-UNEP-WMO, 2008). These emissions can be broken down into three categories: transport (75%), accommodation (21%) and activities (4%), with air travel alone being responsible for 40% (UNWTO-UNEP-WMO, 2008; Peeters and Dubois, 2010). A recent study, taking into account direct and indirect GHG emissions etc., found that global tourism is contributing much more to climate change: 4.5 $GtCO_2e$ or about 8% of the global GHG emissions in 2013 (Lenzen *et al.*, 2018). Direct emissions from air transport (absolute numbers) are similar to previous research, however, the relative contribution of air transport to global tourism's overall emissions is much smaller given that the approach is more comprehensive (see Lenzen *et al.*, 2018 – supplementary information).

Different methods have been used to calculate tourism's carbon footprint. Becken *et al.* (2003), for example, calculated the individual energy use (MJ) of domestic and international tourists in New Zealand. They found that transport is responsible for 73% of the domestic and 65% of the international tourist's energy bill. The corresponding figures for the accommodation and attractions/activities sectors are 17%/22%, and 10%/13%, respectively. Notably, international tourists' flights to/from New Zealand were not included in this analysis. Kelly and Williams (2007) calculated the energy consumption and GHG emissions (CO_2e) for Whistler/Canada. Their results show that travel to/from Whistler is responsible for 80% of the total energy consumption and 86% of the total CO_2e emissions in the municipality of Whistler. Air travel alone is responsible for 72% and 78%, respectively. Peeters and

---

* E-mail: bruno.abegg@uibk.ac.at

Schouten (2006) applied the ecological footprint concept to the city destination of Amsterdam. They found that 70% of tourism's footprint is related to transport to/from Amsterdam, 21% to accommodation, 8% to local activities and 1% to local transport. Summarizing existing literature, most studies – independent of applied methodology – highlight the dominant role of transport, in particular of air travel, in contributing to tourism's energy use and GHG emissions.

Energy and emission intensities in tourism, however, can vary significantly. This is due to the different markets (e.g. domestic, short-haul, long-haul), the different products (e.g. bicycle vs. cruise tourism), the distances travelled (which are usually related to a preferred mode of transport), and to the choice of accommodation and activities (e.g. Chenoweth, 2009; Gössling *et al.*, 2015). Filimonau *et al.* (2014), for example, investigated short-haul tourism from the UK to France using life cycle analysis. They confirmed the general finding that travel to/from destination generates the largest carbon footprint, but for tourists arriving by coach and train, and staying longer, the destination-based elements of the vacation, in particular accommodation, can outweigh the transport elements.

Gössling (2010), named five measures to reduce tourism's carbon footprint: (i) develop closer markets, (ii) encourage low-energy transport, (iii) reward visitors staying longer, (iv) encourage low-energy spending and (v) increase high-profit rather than high-turnover spending within the regional economy. Surprisingly little is known in terms of what tourists actually think about such measures. There is one exception: air travel (e.g. Becken, 2002; Cohen and Higham, 2011). Within air travel, it is (voluntary) carbon offsetting that gained particular attention (e.g. McKercher *et al.*, 2010; Mair, 2011). This is related to another body of literature dealing with people's unwillingness to change (air) travel patterns. Many tourists seem to know that their behaviour is harmful to the environment, they also might behave pro-environmentally at home but are reluctant to do so when it comes to travelling, displaying the often-cited awareness/attitude–behaviour gap (e.g. Barr *et al.*, 2010; Hares *et al.*, 2010; Lassen, 2010; Kroesen, 2013). The difference between 'home and away' (Barr *et al.*, 2010) is further substantiated by a representative survey from Germany (Forschungsgemeinschaft Urlaub und Reisen e.V., 2007). The study shows that many people are willing to save energy at home (66% already do, 22% will do in future), to buy locally (and therefore to reduce distances) (37%/28%) and to drive less (31%/25%). The same people, however, are very reluctant when it comes to climate-friendly travel behaviour: the highest values got the option 'one long trip instead of several short trips' (25% already do, 15% will do in future), followed by 'choosing a destination nearby' (22%/16%), 'less travelling in general' (25%/12%), 'less long-haul travel' (26%/8%) and 'train instead of plane/car' (17%/15%). Options related to flying are least accepted: 'voluntary carbon offsetting' (5%/18%) and 'avoid flying' (15%/8%).

This is, briefly, the thematic background of a survey conducted in the alpine destination of Alpbach-Seenland (Province of Tyrol, Austria). Winter tourists ($n = 518$) were asked about the two-way relationship between climate change and tourism, measures to reduce tourism's energy consumption and carbon footprint, and factors that might support more eco-/climate-friendly modes of transport for holiday travel in the future. The aim was to learn more about (i) the tourists' level of knowledge, and (ii) their assessment of measures to reduce tourism's carbon footprint. Results will be presented taking into account socio-demographic characteristics of the sample (age, gender, education, etc.), and implications will be discussed from the destination's point of view.

8.2 Methods

The survey took place in Alpbachtal-Seenland (www.alpbachtal.at/en), a well-known destination in the province of Tyrol, Austria. The destination offers a wide range of winter sport activities in a mountain environment and accounted for 465,000 overnight stays in the winter season of 2016/17 (see www.tirol.gv.at for official tourism statistics). The survey was conducted in January and February of 2016. Tourists were randomly chosen at highly frequented places such as village centres, tourist offices and hotels; however, most tourists willing to fill in the questionnaire were found at the parking lot and in the restaurants and mountain huts of the ski area.

The questionnaire was available in German and English: German, because the majority of guests originate from German-speaking countries (Germany, Austria and Switzerland), and English, because – traditionally – the destination Alpbachtal-Seenland is very popular with tourists from the UK. A preliminary version of the questionnaire was pretested by a number of colleagues and regional tourism stakeholders resulting in minor changes with regard to structure and wording.

The questionnaire was organized in four sections: (i) general travel information (e.g. motives, accommodation, length of stay, etc.); (ii) travel mobility (e.g. transport to/from and within destination); (iii) tourists' knowledge, measures to reduce carbon footprint and factors to facilitate more eco-/climate-friendly mobility in the future; and (iv) socio-demographics (age, gender, education, etc.). In this chapter we focus on section 3. In this section, tourists were asked to answer three questions:

- To judge several statements related to climate change and tourism (e.g. climate change negatively affects snow reliability of alpine ski areas). Answer options included: 'totally agree', 'rather agree', 'rather disagree', 'totally disagree' and 'don't know'. The aim of this question was to learn more about the tourists' basic understanding of the relationship between climate change and tourism.
- To discuss several measures to reduce energy consumption while travelling (e.g. choosing a destination nearby). Answer options included: 'already do', 'will do in the future' (intention), 'will not do in the future' (refusal) and 'don't care'. The aim of this question was to learn more about the tourists' attitudes towards some measures often cited in the literature.
- To judge some prerequisites that must be given to potentially switch to a more eco-friendly mode of transport (e.g. shuttle service from train station to accommodation). Answer options included: 'totally agree', 'rather agree', 'rather disagree' and 'totally disagree'. The aim of this question was to learn about the technical/organizational factors that might influence the willingness to change individual travel mobility behaviour.

Data were analysed using SPSS Statistics. To check whether there are statistically significant differences across socio-demographic groups (age, gender, education, etc.), appropriate tests (Kruskal–Wallis and Mann–Whitney U) were applied. The p values are given in the results section.

8.3 Results

The survey sample (n = 518) is composed of slightly more males than females (51.0% and 49.0%, respectively). Average age is 42 years, with the largest share of respondents falling into the 31–50 age group (54.2%), followed by the respondents older than 50 years (25.3%). The largest number of respondents arrived from Germany (49.8%), followed by the UK (24.8%), Austria (9.9%), The Netherlands (3.7%) and other European countries (11.6%). Only 0.2% of the respondents were of non-European origin. A total of 69.3% of the respondents travelled by car (including rental cars and motor homes), 23.2% by plane, 6.0% by coach, 1.4% by train and the rest by other modes of transport. A total of 86.7% of the respondents spent at least 1 night at the destination, with the majority (71.2%) spending 3–7 nights, the remaining respondents were day visitors. Main reasons to visit the area were sport activities and relaxation, or a combination of both. A comparison with existing tourism data (Rauch *et al.*, 2010; Manova, 2014) suggests that the sample is representative in terms of age structure and countries of origin. However, the day visitors are under-represented.

Figure 8.1 shows the surveyed tourists' consent to several statements related to climate change and tourism. A clear majority of the respondents accepted anthropogenic climate change (76.4% rather or totally disagree with the statement that there is no human-induced climate change). Climate change not only has an impact on tourism; it is considered a big challenge for the tourism industry (42.3% of the respondents totally agree, 37.5% rather agree). Many respondents expect climate change to have negative impacts on winter tourism (= reduction in the number of snow-reliable ski areas) and positive impacts on summer tourism. Tourism also contributes to climate change, with transportation and local activities being regarded as the most important contributors (68.5% and 42.9% of respondents totally or rather agree). These results suggest that most respondents are familiar with some basic relationships between

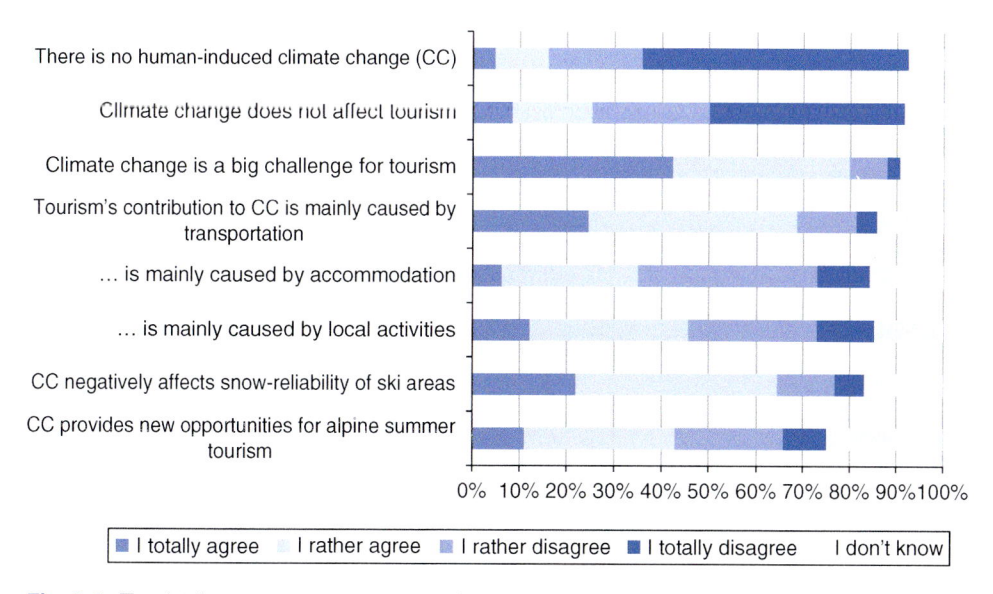

Fig. 8.1. Tourists' consent to statements related to climate change and tourism (n = 482–514).

climate change and tourism. However, consent to specific statements varies among different types of respondents. Females ($p = 0.003$), younger persons (<30 years old; $p = 0.007$) and respondents with higher education ($p = 0.018$), for example, are more willing to accept human-induced climate change.

There are several ways to reduce energy consumption and related GHG emissions while travelling. A selection of measures was used in this survey, and the tourists were asked what they already do, what they might do in the future (intention), what they won't do in the future (refusal) and what they don't care about. Figure 8.2 shows that a majority of respondents already pays attention to reducing energy consumption by turning off lights, saving water etc. (72.1% of respondents) and by buying locally and organically produced goods (58.3%). A large share of respondents is willing to use eco-friendly modes of transport for local activities (34.1% already do, and 36.6% intend to do so in the future). In the future, 42.1% of the respondents might also choose an eco-friendly accommodation relying on renewable energies. When it comes to 'real' changes in travel behaviour (shorter distances, extended length of stay and less flying), respondents are much more reluctant, and many respondents strictly refuse to choose a destination nearby (34.1%), to do fewer but longer trips (instead of more, shorter trips; 36.9%), and to avoid flying (61.6%). Summarizing, many respondents are willing to pick the 'low hanging fruits' as long as it doesn't interfere with the individual freedom to travel. Female respondents are generally more willing to reduce energy consumption and GHG emissions while travelling, in particular to do fewer but longer trips ($p = 0.000$), to buy locally and organically produced goods ($p = 0.021$), and to prefer eco-friendly accommodation ($p = 0.048$). With regard to age and level of education, no statistically significant differences could be found – the only exception refers to the energy-saving measures (e.g. turning off lights etc.), which are more popular for respondents being between 31 and 50 years old than for their younger and older counterparts ($p = 0.001$).

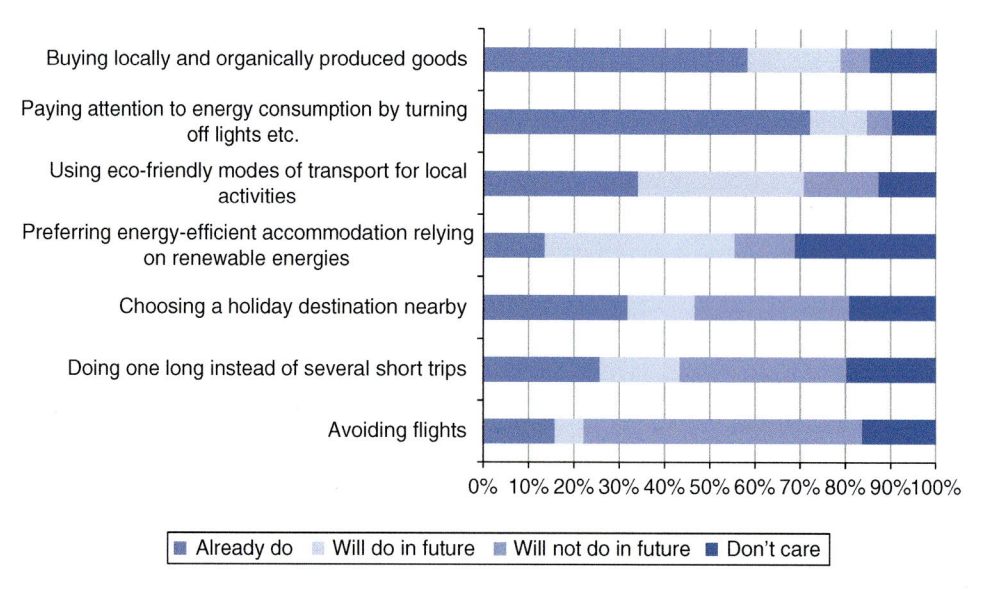

Fig. 8.2. Tourists' willingness to reduce energy consumption and carbon footprint (n = 498–513).

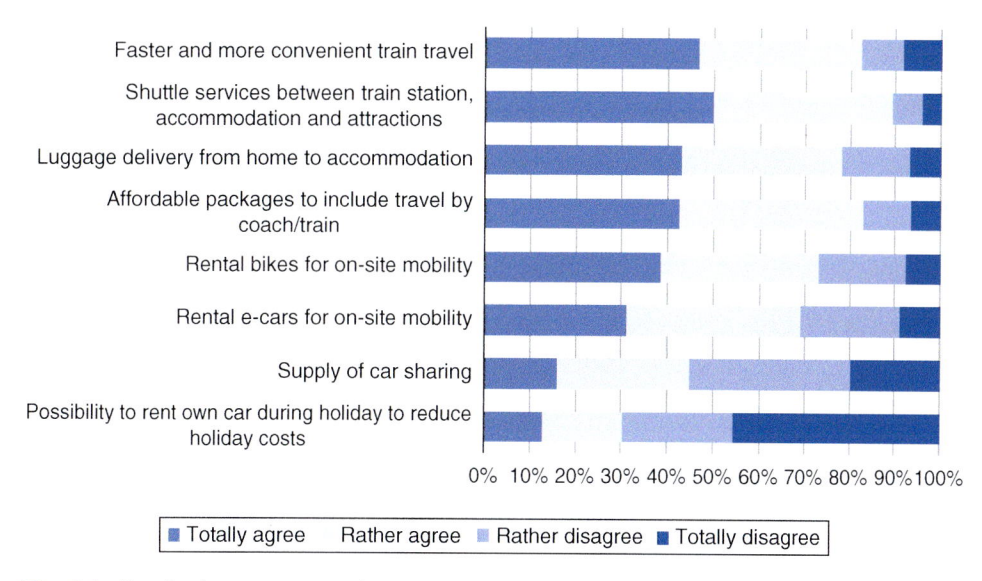

Fig. 8.3. Tourists' assessment of measures to promote more eco-/climate-friendly modes of transport (n = 470–489).

The surveyed tourists were further asked about the necessary framework conditions to go after a more eco-friendly tourism mobility (see Fig. 8.3). A large share of respondents, in particular females (p = 0.001–0.028) and persons being aged between 31 and 50 years (p = 0.002–0.030), expressed high levels of agreement (totally or rather agree) with regard to both the improvement of public transport (i.e. speed, comfort, tariffs) and more eco-friendly on-site mobility (i.e. rental bikes, e-cars). A sharing economy, be it classic car sharing or the possibility to rent out private cars while vacationing (and thereby earning some money), seems to be less favoured. However, respondents with higher education (p = 0.015) are more inclined to potentially do so.

8.4 Discussion

A lot of research has been done with regard to tourists' (non-)reaction to climate change, particularly in the context of flying. Becken (2007), for example, concluded that tourists have very limited knowledge how air travel is affecting global climate change. Apart from that, little is known when it comes to tourists' basic understanding of how climate change impacts tourism, and vice versa. Our survey shows that the winter tourists travelling to Alpbach-Seenland are fairly knowledgeable. On the one hand, it is generally believed that knowledge increases awareness and, subsequently, encourages behavioural change. On the other, there is a lot of scientific evidence that the existence or the provision of knowledge alone is not sufficient to trigger behavioural change. Without knowledge and a basic understanding, however, it is difficult to conceive why people should get involved in any change (Kollmuss and Agyeman, 2002).

The respondents consider transportation the most important contributor to climate change, followed by local activities and accommodation. This is in contrast to existing literature where accommodation is second. Preliminary, yet unpublished results from

Alpbach indicate that travel to/from the destination (including day trips) is responsible for 54% of tourism's total CO_2e emissions, accommodation and gastronomy for 34% and activities for 12%. These figures differ markedly from the ones calculated for Whistler/Canada (Kelly and Williams, 2007). Moreover, in Alpbach it is not planes but cars that are responsible for the highest share of tourism transport's emissions (Unger *et al.*, 2016) and, similar to the work of Filimonau *et al.* (2014), there is a range of holiday settings (e.g. a group of three travelling from Berlin to Alpbach by car, coach or train and spending 5 nights there) where it is not travel to/from the destination but accommodation that contributes most to overall GHG emissions. This is not to downplay transportation's role (in particular the role of international aviation), but to shed light on other contributors. Much of the public and scientific debate seems to concentrate on air travel. Again, from a global perspective, this is more than justified given the annual growth rates in international aviation. However, from a destination point of view, the same discussions are often taken as an excuse to do nothing, arguing that one cannot fight the trends in international aviation. Doing nothing, however, is not an option for a destination like Alpbach that welcomes tourists from relatively nearby source markets. Here, a switch from car to coach/train and more energy-efficient accommodation and gastronomy sectors relying on renewable energies could make a difference and markedly reduce the destination's carbon footprint.

Speaking of measures to reduce energy consumption and GHG emissions in tourism, our findings confirm existing research. Most respondents are willing to pick the 'low hanging fruits' (i.e. use eco-friendly modes of transport for intra-destination mobility) but refuse 'real' changes in travel behaviour (i.e. travel less far and less often). The call for such changes is often perceived as a threat to the individual freedom to travel. There is a lot of evidence that people are unwilling to break with 'dear' habits (e.g. Becken, 2007; Hares *et al.*, 2010; Higham *et al.*, 2013). Cohen *et al.* (2013), summarizing much of the existing literature, identified two gaps: one between attitudes and behaviour, the other between the practices of home and away (see also Barr *et al.*, 2010). People know that (air) travel is harmful but do not respond accordingly (e.g. Hibbert *et al.*, 2013; Juvan and Dolnicar, 2014). This includes people who appear to be very committed to behaving in an environmentally friendly manner at home (Barr *et al.*, 2010; Prillwitz and Barr, 2011). Dickinson *et al.* (2010) added the structures that exist within the travel industry that prevent people – feeling a lack of individual agency to act – from changing their travel habits. As a consequence, little can be expected from tourists in terms of voluntary changes in travel habits.

Eco-friendly on-site mobility is accepted (and wanted) by many tourists. A number of alpine destinations have continuously improved intra-destination mobility. Examples include ski buses, hiking buses and the extension of the existing public transport networks. In some cases, the offers are included in the ski passes and/or the accommodation packages (e.g. access to ski buses and local/regional transport networks), in other cases (e.g. hiking buses), extra must be paid for the services. Challenges include the set-up of these services as they usually have to satisfy both the needs of the locals (e.g. commuters and children going to school) and the tourists, and the financing of the respective services (e.g. Gronau, 2016; Scuttari *et al.*, 2016). Our survey and observations in the destinations show that a lot of tourists (also those arriving by private car) are willing to use these services (and to 'take a holiday from the car') (Böhler *et al.*, 2006). Moreover, an increasing number of people – at least in the European Alps – simply expect these services. Furthermore, a good intra-destination public transport network is often seen as a prerequisite for more eco-friendly travel to/from a destination. However, while such services are definitely important, they are probably not sufficient to induce larger-scale changes in travel to/from a destination.

With regard to travel to/from a destination, coach and train have continuously lost market share and struggle to compete with car and plane. Common arguments against more train travel for holiday purposes include time (e.g. duration of travel), price (e.g. in comparison to current flight tariffs), flexibility (e.g. dependent on schedules) and comfort (e.g. not door-to-door, luggage) (Böhler *et al.*, 2006). A series of measures can help to make train travel more attractive: fast connections, shuttle services from railway station to destination and/or accommodation, luggage service from door-to-door, and attractive all-in packages. Again, improvements in public transport are possible and necessary but probably not sufficient to reach convinced car drivers who see in their vehicles much more than just a means of transportation.

Speaking of improvements: a large number of respondents indicated that they will choose energy-efficient accommodation relying on renewables in the future. However, the question remains: how much intention (will do in future) will translate into real behaviour? Preuss (1991, cited in Kollmuss and Agyeman, 2002, p. 250) distinguished between an 'abstract willingness to act' based on knowledge and values and a 'concrete willingness to act' based on habits. With regard to potential improvements in public transport: being perceived positively does not necessarily mean that people switch from car to coach and train.

There is an ongoing debate about emerging trends in car-based mobility. Apart from e-mobility, an increasing number of people, in particular young adults in urbanized areas, search for new types of mobility, i.e. a 'decreased automobility … characterised by decreasing rates of licensing, vehicle kilometres travelled (VKT) and car ownership' (Hopkins, 2016, p. 371). These changes will also affect travel to/from and within destinations. The respondents signalled interest in e-mobility but are reluctant when it comes to mobility concepts that are related to a sharing economy (see Fig. 8.3). However, much more detailed research is needed to link new types of mobility with tourism mobility. Furthermore, a change in 'auto-mobility' as outlined above does not necessarily mean a reduction in eco-unfriendly tourism mobility as the same people might be very eager to discover the world by plane.

Alpbach is not only a tourism destination but also a Climate and Energy Model region (www.klimafonds.gv.at). As such, the region is not only interested in but obliged to become more energy-efficient and climate-friendly. It is crucial that the tourism industry is part of this process. From a tourism point of view, the destination might focus on energy-efficient accommodation relying on renewable energies. This is one field where governmental support is available, and where tourists indicated that they are willing to prefer such accommodation in the future. Another topic is mobility. Local and tourism mobility are important components in every climate and energy assessment. The calculations by Unger *et al.* (2016) have shown that it is car travel (not air travel) that is responsible for most GHG emissions in Alpbach's tourism. This calls for new mobility concepts: more public transport, but also new forms of auto-mobility (e-cars) and new types of mobility that challenge the current hegemony of private auto-mobility (e.g. sharing economy). So far, it is only an idea, but local policy makers and tourism managers are thinking about establishing an e-mobility park. In such a park, locals and tourists alike could test new forms of e-mobility. This hands-on experience will not change the world but, maybe, will have a bigger impact on people's behaviour than well-intentioned advice.

References

Barr, S., Shaw, G., Coles, T. and Prillwitz, J. (2010) 'A holiday is a holiday': practicing sustainability, home and away. *Journal of Transport Geography* 18, 474–481. DOI:10.1016/j.jtrangeo.2009.08.007

Becken, S. (2002) Analysing international tourist flows to estimate energy use associated with air travel. *Journal of Sustainable Tourism* 10(2), 114–131. DOI:10.1080/0966958020866715

Becken, S. (2007) Tourists' perception of international air travel's impact on the global climate and potential climate change policies. *Journal of Sustainable Tourism* 15(4), 351–368. DOI:10.2167/jost710.0

Becken, S., Simmons, D. and Frampton, C. (2003) Energy use associated with different travel choices. *Tourism Management* 24, 267–277.

Böhler, S., Grischkat, S., Haustein, S. and Hunecke, M. (2006) Encouraging environmentally sustainable holiday travel. *Transportation Research Part A* 40, 652–670. DOI:10.1016/j.tra.2005.12.006

Chenoweth, J. (2009). Is tourism with a low impact on climate possible? *Worldwide Hospitality and Tourism Themes* 1(3), 274–287. DOI:10.1108/17554210910980611

Cohen, S.A. and Higham, J.E.S. (2011) Eyes wide shut? UK consumer perceptions on aviation climate impacts and travel decisions to New Zealand. *Current Issues in Tourism* 14(4), 323–335.

Cohen, S., Higham, J. and Reis, A. (2013) Sociological barriers to developing sustainable discretionary air travel behaviour. *Journal of Sustainable Tourism* 21(7), 982–998. DOI: 10.1080/09669582.2013.809092

Dickinson, J., Robbins, D. and Lumsdon, L. (2010) Holiday travel discourses and climate change. *Journal of Transport Geography* 18, 482–489. DOI:10.1016/j.jtrangeo.2010.01.006

Filimonau, V., Dickinson, J. and Robbins, D. (2014) The carbon impact of short-haul tourism: a case study of UK travel to southern France using life cycle analysis. *Journal of Cleaner Production* 64, 628–638.

Forschungsgemeinschaft Urlaub und Reisen e.V. (2007) *Akzeptanz klimaschonender Verhaltensweisen im Urlaub* [Acceptance of climate-friendly behavior on holiday]. F.U.R., Kiel, Germany.

Gössling, S. (2010) Carbon management: mitigating tourism's contribution to climate change. Routledge, London/New York.

Gössling, S., Scott, D. and Hall, C.M. (2015) Inter-market variability in CO_2 emission-intensities in tourism: implications for destination marketing and carbon management. *Tourism Management* 46, 203–212.

Gronau, W. (2016) Encouraging behavioural change towards sustainable tourism: a German approach to free public transport for tourists. *Journal of Sustainable Tourism* 25(2), 265–275. DOI:10.1080/09669582.2016.1198357

Hares, A., Dickinson, J. and Wilkes, K. (2010) Climate change and the air travel decisions of UK tourists. *Journal of Transport Geography* 18(3), 466–473.

Hibbert, J.F., Dickinson, J.E., Gössling, S. and Curtin, S. (2013) Identity and tourism mobility: an exploration of the attitude–behaviour gap. *Journal of Sustainable Tourism* 21(7), 999–1016. DOI:10.1080/09669582.2013.826232

Higham, J.E.S., Cohen, S.A., Peeters, P. and Gössling, S. (2013) Psychological and behavioural approaches to understanding and governing sustainable mobility. *Journal of Sustainable Tourism* 21(7), 949–967. DOI:10.1080/09669582.2013.828733

Hopkins, D. (2016) Destabilising automobility? The emergent mobilities of generation Y. *Ambio* 46(3), 371–383. DOI:10.1007/s13280-016-0841-2

Juvan, E. and Dolnicar, S. (2014) The attitude-behaviour gap in sustainable tourism. *Annals of Tourism Research* 48, 76–95.

Kelly, J. and Williams, P.W. (2007) Modelling tourism destination energy consumption and greenhouse gas emissions: Whistler, British Columbia, Canada. *Journal of Sustainable Tourism* 15(1), 67–90. DOI:10.2167/jost609.0

Kollmuss, A. and Agyeman, J. (2002) Mind the gap: why do people act environmentally and what are the barriers to pro-environmental behavior? *Environmental Education Research* 8(3), 239–260. DOI:10.1080/1350462022014540 1

Kroesen, M. (2013) Exploring people's viewpoints on air travel and climate change: understanding inconsistencies. *Journal of Sustainable Tourism* 21(2), 271–290. DOI:10.1080/09669582.2012.692686

Lassen, C. (2010) Environmentalist in business class: an analysis of air travel and environmental attitude. *Transport Reviews* 30(6), 733–751.

Lenzen, M., Sun, Y.-Y., Faturay, F., Ting, Y.-P., Geschke, A. and Malik, A. (2018) The carbon footprint of global tourism. *Nature Climate Change* 8, 522–528. DOI:10.1038/s41558-018-0141-x

Mair, J. (2011) Exploring air travellers' voluntary carbon-offsetting behaviour. *Journal of Sustainable Tourism* 19(2), 215–230. DOI:10.1080/09669582.2010.517317

Manova (2014) T-Mona (Tourism Monitor Austria) – Visitor Survey Alpbach, Winter 2013/14. Österreich Werbung, Vienna.

McKercher, B., Prideaux, B., Cheung, C. and Law, R. (2010) Achieving voluntary reductions in the carbon footprint of tourism and climate change. *Journal of Sustainable Tourism* 18(3), 297–317.

Peeters, P. and Dubois, G. (2010) Tourism travel under climate change mitigation constraints. *Journal of Transport Geography* 18, 447–457. DOI:10.1016/j.jtrangeo.2009.09.003

Peeters, P. and Schouten, F. (2006) Reducing the ecological footprint of inbound tourism and transport to Amsterdam. *Journal of Sustainable Tourism* 14(2), 157–171.

Prillwitz, J. and Barr, S. (2011) Moving towards sustainability? Mobility styles, attitudes and individual travel behavior. *Journal of Transport Geography* 19, 1590–1600. DOI:10.1016/j.jtrangeo.2011.06.011

Rauch, F., Peck, S. and Ebner, V. (2010) Zusammenschluß der Skigebiete Alpbach und Wildschönau-Auffach – Verkehrsuntersuchung [Traffic assessment]. Internal report, Innsbruck, Austria.

Scuttari, A., Volgger, M. and Pechlaner, H. (2016) Transition management towards sustainable mobility in alpine destinations: realities and realpolitik in Italy's South Tyrol region. *Journal of Sustainable Tourism* 24(3), 463–483. DOI 10.1080/09669582.2015.1136634

Unger, R., Abegg, B., Mailer, M. and Stampfl, P. (2016) Energy consumption and greenhouse gas emissions resulting from tourism travel in an alpine setting. *Mountain Research and Development* 36(4), 475–483. DOI:10.1659/MRD-JOURNAL-D-16-00058.1

UNWTO-UNEP-WMO (2008) *Climate Change and Tourism: Responding to Global Challenges*. UNWTO, Madrid, Spain.

9 Climate Change Adaptation – A New Strategy for a Tourism Community: A Case from the Bavarian Alps

THOMAS BAUSCH*

Competence Centre for Tourism and Mobility, Free University of Bozen-Bolzano, Bolzano, Italy

9.1 Climate Change Adaptation as a Strategic Field of Destination Development in the Bavarian Alps

9.1.1 Winter tourism in the Bavarian Alps – a multifarious product

Based on the delimitation of the Alpine Convention (*Alpine Convention Reference Guide*, 2010) Germany has a share of about 6% of the alpine region. Thereby half of the German Alps take the form of foothills, while the other half rise up to altitudes mostly between 1000 and 2000 m. Only a few mountains reach a height of more than 2500 m. Compared with other alpine countries the highest summit, the Zugspitze with an altitude of 2964 m, is not extremely high. Furthermore, the level of the settlement areas of most of the tourist centres, for example, Berchtesgaden, Reith im Winkel, Garmisch-Partenkirchen or Oberstdorf, is usually not above 1000 m. Often the relatively flat and wide valley bottoms are located at only 750 m or below. Furthermore, many of the inner alpine mountains are very rocky or the hillsides are covered with steep mountain forest. Considering this topography, the potential for winter sport resorts is very limited compared with other alpine regions. The largest skiing area, the Steinplatte/Winkmoosalm in Reith im Winkl, encompasses slopes with a total length of 42 km, followed by the classic skiing area of Garmisch-Partenkirchen with 40 km (statistics from Skigebiet.de, 2018). In most other skiing areas, the slope network is no more than 20–30 km.

Therefore, the German winter sports resorts in some respects are not competitive on the alpine ski holiday market. For advanced and more athletic skiers, the skiing areas are much too small. Even though they are small, they are often too challenging for beginners and intermediate skiers. Nevertheless, all the skiing areas are very attractive for day trippers as well as short stay guests. The large metropolitan area of Munich with about 2.5 million inhabitants is only 100–150 km away from most Bavarian skiing areas and therefore plays an important role on the day trip market. During winter weekends ski enthusiasts regularly make use of the facilities on 1-day skiing

---

* E-mail: thomas.bausch@unibz.it

excursions. The regional railway companies cover this demand by offering packages combining the railway ticket and an all-day ski-pass.

As most winter holiday areas in Bavaria are competitively limited compared with the large ski areas in Austria, France, Italy and Switzerland, especially on the 1-week skiing vacation market, the product has developed into a multi-recreational winter holiday option: taking walks in a winter wonderland, visiting cosy mountain huts with typical regional dishes, doing some sports like cross-country skiing, alpine skiing, sledging or ice-skating, taking a cable car up a mountain and sitting in the sun, enjoying spa and wellness facilities or visiting cultural or sports events. Within this setting, smaller ski areas play an important role as part of a multi-optional product – in the case of sunny weather and nice snow conditions some of the guests might want to choose the option of skiing and visiting the mountain huts in the ski area for 1–2 days. This is the segment of winter tourists who do not ski every day and who require multi-optional products from which they can chose various options day by day.

9.1.2 General need for adaptation of winter products – not only a matter of climate change

Due to the low altitude of Germany's alpine destinations they are highly affected by climate change. In winter the number of ice days, which are days with a highest temperature not above 0°Celsius, will decline in the next 30 years by 12% to nearly 30% (Potsdam Institut für Klimafolgenforschung [PIK], 2018) (see Table 9.1).

Not only will the ice days decrease – all other snow security-relevant parameters are already showing a significant decline compared with the past 30 years: the first date in autumn with frost, the date of the first 3-day ice period, which is important for artificial snow production, the date of the first natural snowfall, the number of frost days (days with at least one temperature below zero), the amount of natural snowfall and the number of days with natural snow coverage (Bausch *et al.*, 2017a). This leads to a change in the perception of snow security, but also in the general quality of winter holidays in German alpine destinations for skiers (Berghammer and Schmude, 2014). Therefore, climate change has a strong impact on the general framework conditions of the winter product in these tourism regions. Even though in Germany skiing is only a part of the multi-optional product, the guests nevertheless expect a snow-covered landscape with a real winter atmosphere as the central element of their holidays.

Table 9.1. Ice days in Germany. (Based on Potsdam Institut für Klimafolgenforschung [PIK], 2018.)

Region	Ice days 2017	Trend of decrease within 30 years	Trend decrease (%)
Allgäu	36.2	−8.4	−23.2
Alpenregion Tegernsee-Schliersee	38.9	−7.1	−18.3
Berchtesgadener Land	40.5	−7.2	−17.8
Chiemgau	32.1	−7.9	−24.6
Chiemsee-Alpenland	33.0	−9.6	−29.1
Tölzer Land	35.8	−4.6	−12.8
Zugspitz-Region	35.5	−4.7	−13.2

Furthermore, other factors have changed the winter tourism market. First of all, there is the huge volume of warm winter destinations easy to reach by plane and available for a reasonable price. The Canaries, Caribbean, Maldives, Middle East and Persian Gulf, Red Sea region, South Africa, Seychelles, Thailand and Vietnam are attractive and popular winter destinations. In the past 10 years the prices of long-haul flights have decreased, meaning that these destinations can be reached at low cost, yet still enjoy high prestige. Second, the cruise ship sector has developed over the past 20 years very dynamically. While in 1995 only 309,000 German passengers went on cruise holidays, in 2017 the number increased to 2.7 million, which is a growth of 870% (Deutscher Reiseverband e.V., 2019). The fleet of cruise ships and their capacity for travel all year round grew globally in the same way. In the years 2014 to 2017 globally about 27 large new cruise ships with 76,000 new berths and a total capacity of ~24 million overnight stays entered the market (Bosneagu et al., 2015). This continuous growth put enormous pressure on the ship-owning companies to sell these capacities not only in the summer but all year round. Reasonably priced packages entered the market using all available distribution channels and professionally promoted by targeted communication campaigns. As a third factor demographic change has to be mentioned. More and more skiers from the baby boom generation are reaching an age at which physical and health conditions reduce sports activities and, therefore, also winter sports. On the other hand, today, in German families, children do not learn skiing automatically anymore. The reasons for this reduced number of winter sports beginners are manifold: the lack of snow in the mid-range mountains, skiing is not part of school sports anymore, skiing is only rarely part of sports reporting in the programmes of the large TV channels, but also the costs of ski holidays are too high for many middle-class families.

These changed framework conditions have forced winter destinations in the German Alps, but also in other traditional winter holiday regions, to innovate and adapt their products, as otherwise they would enter into the decline phase of the tourist area life cycle (Butler, 2006). Therefore, climate change is one among several factors necessitating adaptation.

9.2 The Case of the Ski and Mountain Recreation Area of Hoher Kranzberg in Mittenwald, Upper Bavaria

9.2.1 General characteristics of tourism and initial cause for adaptation

Mittenwald is a traditional touristically developed alpine village in the district of Garmisch-Partenkirchen to the south of Munich on the border with Austria. The village is located at an altitude of 850 m in the upper valley of the river Isar and surrounded by the massifs of the Karwendel, the Wetterstein and Ester. Together with its two neighbouring villages, Krün and Wallgau, they form the destination known as Alpenwelt Karwendel with about 1.4 million overnight stays and 400,000 guest arrivals annually. Furthermore at least 1.2 million day trip visitors make an excursion to the destination every year, as it can be reached easily by car, train and long-haul buses, making access fast and easy compared with the central alpine areas.

The wide and relatively flat bottom of the valley provides perfect conditions for hiking and cycling in summer as well as cross-country skiing in winter. Several lakes with smaller public bathing beaches provide options for swimming and relaxing in summer. These elements are embedded in a cultural landscape of outstanding quality as well as pure alpine natural scenery formed by the three massifs with several summits above 2000 m as well as by the river Isar, which in most sections of the valley still has the character of a torrential stream. In the north-western part of the village of Mittenwald a mid-range mountain, the Hoher Kranzberg, nestles as a kind of foothill to the Wetterstein massif. With just one single funicular travelling up to the western Karwendelspitz, this is the only touristically developed area within a largely still untouched alpine landscape. One chairlift (all-year) and six cable car lifts (only winter) provide transport up to several typical mountain huts, enabling visitors to go hiking as well as in winter to ski. Therefore, this mountain is a central supply component as an experience and recreation area for guests expecting an unforgettable stay in the Upper Bavarian Alps.

While larger ski resorts in the neighbouring region of Tyrol have shown a yearly stable increase of guests, overnight stays and day trip visitors in the winter season, the Alpenwelt Karwendel destination and especially the village of Mittenwald have been faced with a constant decrease. While in commercial accommodation (establishments with ten or more beds) in 2006 about 73,500 overnight stays were counted in Mittenwald between November and March, in the years 2015 to 2017 the level declined to volumes around 57,500 (Landesamt für Statistik Bayern, 2018). This decline in winter could not be compensated by the summer season, which for years has remained at a stable but not growing level. The number of commercial accommodation establishments decreased within 10 years from 74 to 51, which is a loss of nearly one-third. This crisis in tourism led to a shrinking of the local economy in general: restaurants, retailers, sport and event agencies, the real estate market as well as the local building business. As the village has a remote location in the south of Upper Bavaria a transition of the economic system from tourism to other business sectors is not a realistic option. Therefore, the municipality council mandated the mayor and the destination management to submit a proposal to adapt and innovate the infrastructure and related services at the Hoher Kranzberg as a central element of the tourism product.

9.2.2 SWOT analysis as a basis for adaptation strategy

SWOT analysis is a well-established method in the field of regional as well as destination development (Veser, 2014). First, a list of strengths and weaknesses (SW) of the current tourism system was set up by a local working group consisting of some members of the destination management organization (DMO), the head of the cable car company and four external experts from tourism and infrastructure planning. The SWs they found were then analysed by concentrating on a few mega trends: climate change, demographic change, expectation for experience raising, individualization and digitalization. Each strength and each weakness was analysed in light of each mega trend and their future development and related opportunities or threats (OT) derived.

In general, the area of the Hoher Kranzberg is an example of outstanding nature and scenery created by human cultivation over many centuries, especially its meadows with a surface dotted with humps, the so-called Buckelwiesen. These meadows stand out with their incomparable richness of diversity of alpine flora and related fauna, especially butterflies and dragonflies. Therefore, more than 60% of the area is protected under the Council Directive 92/43/EEC on the conservation of natural habitats and of wild fauna and flora, a so-called Natura2000 reserve (Pröbstl-Haider and Dorsch, 2016). In addition, a large number of protected biotopes are officially mapped and part of the Bavarian biotope mapping of the Alps. On the one hand, this underlines the potential of unspoiled nature as part of the unique selling proposition for visitors in that area. On the other, it obviously sets very strict limitations for adaptation measures, which in any case would require at least small interventions in the natural structure. Furthermore the impacts of additional tourist attractions to the natural environment which might be caused by a higher visitor pressure and the sporting activities of these visitors must be anticipated and weighed up (Pröbstl-Haider and Pütz, 2016).

Concerning winter tourism, climate change was a key field of discussion in the SWOT analysis. As the area of Hoher Kranzberg is located at an altitude between 850 m in the valley and only 1397 m at the summit it is already being affected by climate change today. Analysing the series of weather data between 1985 and 2015 it becomes apparent that all the parameters linked to natural snow security, but also linked to required conditions for artificial snowmaking, have degraded heavily. The number of ice days, which are days with 24 h at a temperature below 0°Celsius, decreased for the period first of November to the end of March from mostly between 40 and 30 days in the past century to often below 10 in the past decade. The first ice day shifted from usually mid or end of November to the end of December; sometimes it did not happen until January. The number of periods with 3 consecutive ice days, which are needed as good conditions for artificial snowmaking, decreased from three to four periods to only one. The maximum number of consecutive ice days in November and December also shrank from usually 10–12 to now 3–5. As the daily average temperature also increased by about 1–1.5°Celsius, rain instead of snow as precipitation can be frequently observed these days during the winter period.

The following climate change-related opportunities and threats were identified:

- Declining average number of days with natural snow coverage in the valley.
- Reduced snow security for cross-country skiing and winter hiking in a snow-covered landscape.
- Shift of first period with minimum 3 consecutive ice days to end of the year/beginning of new year, leading to a need for improvement of the capacity of the artificial snow-making facilities with higher capacity to allow basic snow coverage of 30–50 cm within 3 days.
- Declining average number of days with good to very good skiing conditions from 100 to 80 in combination with later start of the skiing season.
- Longer late autumn periods with relatively warm and sunny weather and good conditions for hiking and mountain biking – more often until the beginning or middle of December.
- Currently existing natural sledge run in future only usable for a very small number of days – need for relocation to the north side of the mountain near to the slopes with snowmaking facilities.
- Because of the wide and flat topography of the Kanzberg summit there is an opportunity to create a winter hiking round trip on the top with long snow security in combination with a large number of days with sun.

A further factor considered by the SWOT analysis was demographic change. The main findings here were in general opportunities coming along with barrier-free access for elderly or handicapped guests as well as families with small children transported in baby buggies or in winter on childsledges. In winter in addition a modern and competitive beginner's area at the valley station offering not only skiing lessons, but also a snow playground for non-skiing children, was judged as a further opportunity.

In general, the discussion of the current strengths and weaknesses and anticipated related opportunities and threats leads to a revision of the former strategy. While in the past the future development of the area of Hoher Kranzberg was always only seen from the perspective of the winter season and alpine skiing, now the approach has widened. First, not only the winter but also the summer are seen as seasons of equal importance. Second, in summer the outstanding unspoiled nature and scenery were moved to the centre of the future product development. While many competitors in the neighbourhood focus on sports and action-oriented, hard tourism development approaches, the positioning of Hoher Kranzberg has moved exactly in the opposite direction: an area for calm, slow and nature-based tourism offering the guests an insight into and experiences from the natural alpine environment. In winter the focus was also changed. To underline the approach of nature-based tourism it was decided not to enlarge the range of slopes with artificial snow. Only those already equipped in the past with snow guns became part of the adaptation. All other slopes were kept as natural snow skiing areas, which were operated only during those periods where natural snow precipitation offered a minimum snow cover of 20–30 cm. In addition, new products were to offer non-skiers genuine alpine winter experiences during the winter season. This is a further new positioning element of the destination, which addresses a market that is not interesting for many competitors with large ski resorts. The target is to increase the share of winter guests from the non-skier segment.

9.2.3 Adaptation plan considering all-season utilization and resolving ecological conflicts

The general strategy decisions were concretized for nine tourist groups:

1. All-season groups:
   a. Real mountain hut experiences with authentic Bavarian cosiness.
   b. Mountain experiences for the handicapped.
   c. Hoher Kranzberg as an area for all-day activities in pure natural surroundings.
2. Winter guests:
   a. The enjoyment of the natural environment – 'slow motion' in winter landscapes.
   b. The exploration of the natural environment – detecting and understanding the mysteries of winter nature.
   c. Family and kids snow fun (0–10 years, parents and grandparents).
3. Summer (including late spring and autumn) guests:
   a. Alpine natural experience for families and kids (0–10 years, parents and grandparents).
   b. Culture and landscape in the alpine space of Upper Bavaria.
   c. The enjoyment of the natural environment – 'slow motion' in the summer mountain world.

For each of the listed nine guest groups a product development project was launched. The status of the infrastructure was ascertained by means of a concrete mapping and evaluation of the status quo of the existing attractions, their location and accessibility and the currently available services. By comparing the status quo and the envisaged future ideal product, a list of development measures and the required stakeholders was drawn up. Finally, all the infrastructure in the area was assessed concerning its current status and the future requirements needed to fulfil the function for the nine guest groups. In this step again, especially for the winter season, climate change scenarios were considered when an adaptation of existing infrastructure was rated as necessary.

Of course, a central concern of the adaptation discussion was the existing and partially obsolete winter tourism infrastructure. A one-seat chair lift, which originally was installed in 1950 and partially adapted in 1973, obviously had to be rated as no longer viable, as well as the fact that the cable lifts are nowhere near the standards adhered to by the competitors in the neighbouring destinations. The small cabin cable car connecting the end station of the chair lift halfway up the mountain with the summit has been out of order for several years. Therefore, the summit cannot be reached by non-skiers via cable car. The beginner's area is currently crossed by one of the main slopes, creating conflicts and risk of accidents. The capacity of the artificial snowmaking facilities is insufficient to produce the needed amount of snow within 3 days of good snowmaking conditions. The toboggan run, partially located on the south side, is separated from the ski run areas and therefore cannot use the artificial snowmaking facilities of the slopes. This means that it is only available for a few winter days when there is sufficient natural snow cover. The parking near the valley station also does not adhere to modern standards – the public buses have problems parking and turning and this is not possible near the valley station. This systematic analysis contrasting the demand of each of the nine groups above with the current infrastructure showed very clearly that the only solution resolving the long list of deficits would be a new two-section detachable cable car lift, each detachable cabin with 12 seats and enough space for wheelchairs or child buggies. The old chair lift, an old and longer cable lift, as well as the summit cabin cable car, are to be dismantled to make way for the construction of the new lift.

The options for the location of the technical buildings of the cable car lift in the valley, the halfway station and the summit station were very limited as the old infrastructure, constructed back in the 1960s and 1970s, was partially located in the Natura2000 reserve. The same problem arose with the routes of the roads and car parking facilities in the valley. In a close dialogue with the nature protection and conservation authorities of the district, the region and the federal state of Bavaria, a solution was found that, on the one hand, embraces the regulative framework of national and European environmental legislation, and, on the other, fulfils the needs of the guests and offers further development options in future within the framework of the tourism strategy.

The most challenging and sensitive elements of the adaptation concept concerning the resolving of potential conflicts with protected nature elements, local property owners or potential criticisms from the public and NGOs were:

- The new route of the two-section detachable cable car lift, especially the location of the three stations and its ropeway pylons, avoiding forest clearance or intervention in highly sensitive biotopes.
- The route of the new round hiking trail at the summit, offering, on the one hand, spectacular views of the surrounding mountain massifs and the alpine natural environment but, on the other, avoiding the disturbance of sensitive and endangered species, especially the grouse in this area.

- The innovation of the artificial snowmaking facilities, especially the provision of a larger water buffer repository without the creation of an artificial pond as well as the hauling traces for the new water pump pipes.
- The relocation of the toboggan run, which in future is to connect the halfway station with the valley, on a route that does not cross slopes, hiking trails or connecting paths to mountain huts.

A multi-stage planning process was selected to find for each element a solution that considers the ecological constraints, technical needs and the functional objectives for the future guest groups. In a first step based on field walking and existing mappings of biotopes, several alternatives for the route and stations were developed. These alternatives were assessed by an external expert concerning their impacts on biotopes or nearby sensitive areas as well as future potential visitor pressure. Based on this expertise, a revision of the alternatives took place until a final best suitable proposal was found. This proposal was then presented to and discussed with the regional nature conservation and protection authority, which finally made several suggestions on the need for further improvements or the possibility of potential minor conflicts – all with the aim of finding detailed solutions. In a further step the owners of the land where building measures or future touristic activities are to take place were informed and agreement was secured. Finally, a presentation of the best suitable solutions took place in a confidential municipality council meeting. This led to an iterative process in which a proposal was developed that, in general, could be rated as ready for detailed planning and later approval (Bausch *et al.*, 2017b).

9.2.4 Planning process and limitations of public participation

Climate change adaptation, as with all kinds of adaptation processes of community relevant infrastructure or services, can be steered between two opposite approaches: top-down or bottom-up. Several publications (Lidskog and Elander, 2009; Amaru and Chhetri, 2013) argue that only by the bottom-up approach can a long-term local resilience of the adaptation measures be reached, as only early participation will guarantee a high level of acceptance of the finally proposed adaptation strategy. These publications therefore suggest starting adaptation from the very beginning on the basis of broad participation of all kinds of stakeholders and interest groups, not only informing them about objectives and the status of the adaptation plans, but also offering them the opportunity to propose further adaptation measures and to take the decision making (Müller *et al.*, 2014) on the final adaptation strategy.

The present case did not follow a bottom-up approach as recommended in many publications. This was a conscious decision after having analysed the history of the former discussion, the local governance structure as well as the general debate about skiing facility adaptation measures in Bavaria in the year 2016. In 1999 a first attempt had already been made to renovate the existing lift and cable car infrastructure in the Hoher Kranzberg area. The municipality council at that time commissioned an engineering expertise project that only considered the question of winter sports and the needs of the tourism stakeholders in the area as well as the village of Mittenwald. This was a mixed process of a top-down approach by the municipality council, but also with low-level participation of the tourism sector. The resulting plan was presented and discussed in a public meeting of the municipality council and became an object of general public debate. This plan was never able to be implemented as during the planning process one group of stakeholders was never informed and asked for their agreement, i.e. the owners of the plots of land needed for adaptation in the area. They blocked all further development as they felt they had been ignored. The fact that other people discussed what was to happen with their property without asking them was unacceptable from their perspective. Their understanding was that they must be involved as owners and must agree before a general public debate can be opened.

A further reason for a confidential planning process was the general political atmosphere concerning skiing area adaptations in Bavaria. In the 1970s and 1980s the very dynamic development of the tourist infrastructure in the Bavarian Alps ignited the fear that the natural environment of the mountains would be irretrievably destroyed. This led to the government adopting a protected areas zoning plan for the Bavarian Alps that declared large parts of the mountains as areas excluded from any further development. Furthermore, the clearing of mountain forest areas larger than 1 ha in general was prohibited by a decision of the Bavarian parliament. With the signature of the Alpine Convention, as well as the nomination of many parts of the Alps as Natura2000 protected areas, the share of protected areas was increased in the 1990s. Later in the first decade of the new century more and more local policy makers, cable car companies and destination managers intervened to abolish the protection measures or at least to allow exceptions to be made. This provoked a backlash from the environmental NGOs. The first exceptions for the necessary adaptations for the 2011 FIS world championships held in Garmisch-Partenkirchen opened the door for more and more projects, each in itself not very large, but in total a gradual undermining of the existing legislation. A point of culmination was the attempt to construct a new cable car installation as well as a new slope at the Riedberger Horn in the western Bavarian Alps, which led to a public debate, both national as well as international, on the conflict brought about by the innovation of skiing resorts and the protection of the alpine natural environment in Bavaria. The project in Mittenwald had just started when the general debate was in full swing. It was very likely at this point that an open public discussion about a new cable car at the Hoher Kranzberg would be interpreted as the next case of protecting the sensitive alpine natural habitat. Subsequently the environmental NGOs wanted to move the discussion from the very beginning from the local to the state level. This was a further reason to desist from a public participation at the beginning of the planning process.

9.3 Lessons to be Learnt from the Case

The present case of climate change adaptation in the area of Hoher Kranzberg underlines that adaptation processes can never be seen only from the perspective of one single factor. Climate change is an issue forcing many alpine regions to develop adaptation strategies to stay competitive or to re-establish themselves as competitive. An adaptation strategy, however, must always consider further relevant mega trends and factors changing the framework conditions of the tourism system as well as related changes in the market. The change in winter travel behaviour of consumers must be considered, but so too must changed expectations and preferences in the summer season be included in the strategy. Second, the change in the competition as a result of new destinations, products and distribution channels cannot be ignored. Factors such as demographic change, global cheap transport or digitalization in many cases can play a more important role than climate change. Therefore, a solid SWOT analysis as the basis for adaptation strategy development is essential.

Concerning the planning process, the literature also promotes bottom-up and participatory processes, embracing the history, culture of the area and the general public debate. Stakeholder groups with a strategic key role and personal concerns for their property – groups that are able to block a process – should always be involved before a public debate is opened. Iterative planning, involving the necessary expertise in each round of the improvement talks, leads to both a suitable and, in this case, sustainable result. Putting sustainability at the centre of the future positioning of the destination and the further development of Hoher Kranzberg as a key feature of guest attractions created a holistic perspective during the planning. Furthermore, the dialogue at an early stage with the nature conservation authorities that are later responsible for the approval of construction permits helps to detect hidden obstacles at an early stage.

References

Alpine Convention Reference Guide (2010) Alpine Signals 1st–2nd edition. Permanent Secretariat of the Alpine Convention, Innsbruck/Bolzano, Austria/Italy. Available at: www.alpconv.org/en/publications/alpine/Documents/AS1_EN.pdf (accessed 29 January 2019).

Amaru, S. and Chhetri, N.B. (2013) Climate adaptation: institutional response to environmental constraints, and the need for increased flexibility, participation, and integration of approaches. *Applied Geography* 39, 128–139. DOI:10.1016/j.apgeog.2012.12.006

Bausch, T., Ludwigs, R. and Meier, S. (2017a) Winter tourism and climate change – impacts and adaptation strategies. Munich University of Applied Sciences, Department of Tourism. Available at: https://www.researchgate.net/publication/313892568_Winter_Tourism_and_Climate_Change_-_Impacts_and_adaptation_strategies (accessed 5 March 2017).

Bausch, T., Koziol, K., Ludwigs, R. *et al*. (2017b) Prozessgestaltung und Steuerung von Klimawandelanpassung in kleinen bayerischen Gemeinden (TUF01UF-66836) Teilprojekt Mittenwald. Abschlussbericht. Munich/Axams: Hochschule Munich, Fakultät für Tourismus in Zusammenarbeit mit Klenkhart & Partner Consulting ZT GmbH.

Berghammer, A. and Schmude, J. (2014) The Christmas–Easter shift: simulating alpine ski resorts' future development under climate change conditions using the parameter 'optimal ski day'. *Tourism Economics* 20(2), 323–336. DOI:10.5367/te.2013.0272

Bosneagu, R., Coca, C.E. and Sorescu, F. (2015) Management and Marketing elements in maritime cruises industry. European cruise market. EIRP Proceedings 10(0). Available at: www.proceedings.univ-danubius.ro/index.php/eirp/article/view/1621 (accessed 26 July 2018).

Butler, R.W. (ed.) (2006) *The Tourism Area Life Cycle. Aspects of Tourism 28*. Channel View Publications, Clevedon, UK.

Deutscher Reiseverband e.V. (2018) Der Deutsche Reisemarkt. Zahlen und Fakten 2018. Available at: https://www.drv.de/fachthemen/statistik-und-marktforschung/detail/reisemarkt-2018-zahlen-und-fakten-liegen-in-neuer-auflage-vor.html (accessed 17 July 2019).

Landesamt für Statistik Bayern (2018) Official tourism statistics Bavaria: establishments, beds, arrivals and overnight stays in commercial establishments. Genesis Online Datenbank, Monatserhebungen im Tourismus. Available at: https://www.statistikdaten.bayern.de/genesis/online/data?operation=statistikAbruftabellen&levelindex=0&levelid=1534507812057&index=2 (accessed 29 January 2019).

Lidskog, R. and Elander, I. (2009) Addressing climate change democratically. Multi-level governance, transnational networks and governmental structures. *Sustainable Development* 18(1), 32–41. DOI:10.1002/sd.395

Müller, E., Durrer Eggerschwiler, B. and Stotten, R. (2014) Awareness rising for demographic change: the need for a participatory approach. In: Bausch, T., Koch, M. and Veser, A. (eds) *Coping with Demographic Change in the Alpine Regions – Actions and Strategies for Spatial and Regional Development*. Springer, Berlin, pp. 37–42.

Potsdam Institut für Klimafolgenforschung (PIK) (2018) Klima in den Deutschen Tourismusregionen: 1961–2017. Karten und Tabellen zu dem Klimawandel in Deutschen Reisegebieten. Available at: www.pik-potsdam.de/~peterh/tourismus/tourismus.html (accessed 29 January 2019).

Pröbstl-Haider, U. and Dorsch, C. (2016) Verträglichkeitsuntersuchung für das Erholungs- und Bergerlebnisgebiet Kranzberg, Markt Mittenwald. Arbeitsgruppe für Landnutzungsplanung Institut für ökologische Forschung, Etting-Polling, Germany.

Pröbstl-Haider, U. and Pütz, M. (2016) Großschutzgebiete und Tourismus in den Alpen im Zeichen des Klimawandels. *Natur und Landschaft* 91(1), 15–19. DOI:10.17433/1.2016.50153375.15-19

Skigebiet.de (2018) Skigebiete – Ranking nach Länge der Piste in Deutschland 2017 Statistik. Available at: https://de.statista.com/statistik/daten/studie/320631/umfrage/skigebiete-anzahl-in-ausgewaehlten-europaeischen-laendern (accessed 17 August 2018).

Veser, A. (2014) Regional SWOT analyses for demographic change issues: tools and experiences. In: Bausch, T. et al. (eds) *Coping with Demographic Change in the Alpine Regions*. Springer, Berlin, pp. 29–36.

10 Economic Relevance of Different Winter Sport Activities Based on Expenditure Behaviour

Marius Mayer[1]* and Felix Kraus[2]

[1]*Universität Greifswald, Greifswald, Germany;* [2]*Julius-Maximilians-Universität Würzburg, Würzburg, Germany*

10.1 Introduction

The economic importance of winter and ski tourism for regional economic development is often used as an argument in favour of infrastructure development in land use planning decisions or when administrative authorizations are needed (Seilbahn.net, 2016; Bundesverwaltungsgericht Republik Österreich, 2018). This is especially relevant as winter and ski tourism activities face considerable challenges: impacts of global warming could reduce the snow-reliability in the future even when artificial snow is taken into account (Soboll *et al.*, 2012; Steiger *et al.*, 2019), while at the same time less snow-dependent alternatives are promoted by environmentalists (CIPRA, 2017) even though their economic viability has yet to be proven (Siegrist and Gessner, 2011). Kleissner (2012, p. 19) even concludes: 'There is no economic alternative to winter sports!' Therefore, it is crucial to assess the economic importance of different winter sport activities to address the following questions:

- What are the differences in the expenditure behaviour between winter tourists and visitors during the rest of the year (mainly the summer season)?
- What are the potential losses if winter sport activities eventually become impossible due to climate change-induced lack of snow?
- Which economic impact of winter sport activities can be maintained by technical adaptation measures to climate change like snowmaking or snow farming?
- Which opportunity costs of ski tourism need to be covered if less infrastructure-intensive activities should be promoted (e.g. in a protected area setting)?
- How much does the economic relevance of several winter sport activities vary (e.g. alpine skiing, cross-country skiing, winter hiking/walking, ski touring, snowshoe walking, tobogganing)?

This chapter addresses the economic relevance of winter tourism based on two case studies in Switzerland and Germany which provide the opportunity to compare the expenditure behaviour and economic impact of different segments of winter tourists from alpine skiers on groomed slopes to eco-tourist snowshoe hikers. Both studies also allow comparisons with the spending behaviour of non-winter tourists.

---

* E-mail: marius.mayer@uni-greifswald.de

10.2 Expenditure Studies in Winter Tourism: An Overview

The main drivers of the economic impact/benefits of tourism are the frequentation, expenditure patterns and the economic structure of the destination/region. The local economy determines the multiplier effect of tourism by the share of leakages and the amount of money spent there again for investments and daily living by businesses and tourism staff alike (Mayer and Vogt, 2016a). This illustrates the central role of spending for the analysis of the economic relevance of tourism, which has been recognized by a number of studies in the past 15 years (see Brida and Scuderi, 2013 and Mayer and Vogt, 2016a for recent overviews).

In the following, we provide a short overview of existing studies on the expenditures of winter tourists and identify research gaps. Even though many publications about mountain and winter tourism in general depict winter tourism as generating more economic impact due to higher spending (Leitner, 1984; Jülg, 2007; StMWIVT, 2007; Feichtner, 2017), there are surprisingly few peer-reviewed studies providing empirical evidence. The problem seems to be a general lack of comparative expenditure and/or economic impact studies for winter and summer activities based on the same base population or the same destinations. For instance, MANOVA (2016) undertook a compelling economic impact analysis of the Austrian cable car and ski lift industry including the visitor spending but there is no counterpart for the summer season. The German Cable Car Association also published an economic impact analysis but does not differentiate between winter and summer season (VDS, 2015).

For Austria, where the economic relevance of winter tourism is widely acknowledged (Kleissner, 2012; Feichtner, 2017), representative market research data are available for 2013/14 differing between the seasons: excluding transport to the destinations, winter tourists on average spend €120.0 per person and day, compared with €98.0 in the summer (+29.6%). The most important differences in absolute terms stem from the expenditure on transport in the destination (winter €21.0 vs. summer €5.0), most likely for lift tickets as well as in the amount of money spent on accommodation (winter €54.0 vs. summer €45.0, +20%) (own calculations based on WKO, 2018).

In Switzerland, BAK Basel (2012) refers to the representative 'Tourism monitor Switzerland' from 2010, which reveals that the share of high-spending guests in the winter season is considerably higher compared with the summer: 27.2% spend more than CHF250 per day in winter, in summer only 17%. Conversely, 22% of winter guests spend less than CHF100 per day, in contrast to 36.2% in the summer. Also in Switzerland, several economic impact studies allow calculations of a winter–summer expenditure gap: in Berner Oberland (10.3%), Valais (9.5%), Engelberg (10.2%) and Nidwalden (10.2%) overnight guests spend more in winter than in summer, while day trippers spend more in summer in both Berner Oberland (1.9%) and Valais (4.3%) and more in winter in Engelberg (15.4%) and Nidwalden (6.4%) (Rütter *et al.*, 1995, 2001, 2004).

A shortcoming of many international studies is the focus on just one winter sport activity, resulting in a lack of comparisons with other alternatives. If leisure activities are differentiated, then the methodological problem arises as to which activities are clearly winter-related. Hiking and walking, as well as hunting, nature observation, driving or fishing could technically be done all year around. The study by Mehmetoglu (2007) is an example with rather vaguely defined activity groups: it is unclear whether his 'challenging nature-based activities' refer to winter or summer activities. Nevertheless, on the international level the following studies provide some indications about the expenditure patterns of winter activities.

Pouta *et al.* (2006) found out that nature trips related to cross-country skiing in Finland were more likely to be high-expenditure trips than trips taken for other purposes, while backpacking, in contrast, was more often related to low-expenditure trips. The availability of alpine skiing facilities was related to higher-expenditure trips.

Fredman (2008) shows that alpine skiers in the Swedish mountains spend on average 3.1 times more per trip in the destination compared with backpackers and even 1.5 times more than snowmobilers.

White and Stynes' (2008) detailed study about spending patterns of different outdoor recreation activities best allows differentiation between winter and summer seasons. Three out of five activity segments showing statistically significant higher per trip expenditures in US National Forests are winter activities (alpine and cross-country skiing, snowmobiling), while hiking/biking is related to significantly lower spending compared with the overall average. The authors stress that it is crucial to analyse the spending of visitors differentiated by trip type (e.g. day trippers vs. overnight visitors) because this 'can mask important differences in the spending of visitors engaged in the activity but participating in different types of recreation trips' (p. 21). Non-local alpine skiing day trippers for instance spend 117% more per trip than hikers/bikers, while for non-local overnight visitors the deviation between both activities still reaches 39.2%.

If one compiles the total average per party per trip spending of the 12 recreation activity groups reported by White (2017) for the US National Forest 2010–2015 expenditure data, rank them in descending order for the four visitor types (non-local and local day trippers, non-local and local overnight visitors) and averages the ranks, it is evident that explicit winter activities (alpine and cross-country skiing, snowshoeing, snowmobiling) reach the best average rank places (2.8), while activities neither attributed solely to winter nor summer reach 6.5 and explicit summer activities rank lowest (10.1). Snowmobiling and alpine skiing/snowboarding achieve the highest expenditure averages for all visitor types, while cross-country skiing/snowshoeing ranks seventh for the day trips and fourth for overnight trips. Alpine skiers spend between 98.5 and 146.9% more than hikers (for day trips), respectively, 52.1–86.6% more per overnight trip. For cross-country skiers the deviations vary from 22.8–50.0% for day trips and from 19.4–46.4% for overnight visits. Thus, White's (2017) results provide further evidence for the higher spending of winter tourists.

The following reasons are given for the higher spending in the winter season (Leitner, 1984; Jülg, 2007):

- Operating costs in winter are higher, especially for energy due to heating and electricity needs of lighting, cable car, ski lifts and snowmaking facilities.
- Winter guests are to some extent more affluent than summer guests and must be able to afford the higher prices for accommodation[1] (partly due to higher costs, partly due to the higher demand with fewer substitution possibilities in the winter season) and equipment.
- Alpine skiers must buy lift passes, which cost more than €50 per day in the biggest and most prominent resorts. In addition, ski school fees have to be paid for children, other beginners or to improve technique.
- The relatively short daylight time leads to long evenings motivating additional spending for food, drinks and entertainment ('après ski').

Finally, the high importance of spending notwithstanding, we must consider also the frequentation in winter and other seasons and the length of stay. Especially in the high mountain regions of the Central Alps more overnight stays are recorded in winter than in summer (Mayer et al., 2011). Evidence from Austria shows that winter guests (in regions with strong ski tourism) stay longer on average (4.5 nights in winter vs. 3.6 nights in summer for Tyrol in 2017; 4.23 vs. 3.45 Salzburg 2015/16; 4.17 vs. 3.24 Vorarlberg 2015/16) (Statistik Austria, 2016; Amt der Tiroler Landesregierung, 2017), which additionally increases the importance of the winter season.

Despite not being representative for winter tourism in all its variations of course, both case studies in sections 10.3 and 10.4 share the advantage of featuring comparable methodologies for several winter as well as summer activities sampled in the same survey areas thus providing unbiased possibilities for comparisons.

10.3 Expenditure Determinants of Nature-Based Tourists in Simmental and Diemtigtal, Switzerland

The first case study analyses visitor spending and economic impact of nature-based tourists in the Simmental and Diemtigtal, two alpine valleys in the Berner Oberland, Switzerland, where 291 respondents in winter and 1009 in summer were asked about their spending, trip characteristics, motivations and activities. The survey area is quite representative for the Alps as it provides all relevant outdoor activities in winter, including several ski resorts of differing size and quality standards as well as purist nature tourism opportunities (Mayer et al., 2009). In addition to descriptive statistics and analyses of variance (ANOVAs), we built several multiple linear regression models (see Mayer and Vogt, 2016b for details).

Visitor spending was analysed according to the main activity respondents named (see Table 10.1). The results are differentiated into winter and summer season and day trippers and overnight visitors. In the summer season, ANOVA post-hoc tests reveal no significant differences in vacationers' expenditures varying between CHF47.0 and 66.9. However, expenses of day trippers vary statistically significantly between downhill mountain bikers (MTB, CHF38.2) and hikers and walkers, who spend only half (CHF19.0 and 21.7, respectively). This is mainly because downhill bikers have to buy lift passes.

In the winter season no significant differences were found for vacationists (between CHF47.6 and 85.8) according to their activity, besides that the spending level generally was significantly higher than in summer (+36.8%). Indicatively, cross-country skiers had the highest daily expenditure per person for vacationers (CHF85.8), whereas alpine skiing/snowboarding took only the third rank (CHF72.6) following winter hikers (CHF85.7).

Among the day trippers, alpine skiers and snowboarders spent by far the most per person and day (CHF46.2). Explicit ecotourism activities, such as snowshoe walking (CHF11.0) or ski touring (CHF13.5) had the lowest spending for day trippers in winter and differ statistically significantly from the alpine skiers. Cross-country skiers and winter hikers spend only a third or a bit more than a third compared with the alpine skiers. However, we also need to treat these results with caution as the sample size of the activity groups is fairly small for some groups.

Table 10.1. Mean daily expenditure per person of visitors to Simmental and Diemtigtal in 2005/06 differentiated by main activities. (Own calculations, data based on Mayer et al., 2009.)

Winter	Day trippers CHF	SD	n	Overnight visitors CHF	SD	n
Winter hiking	16.9	18.7	30	85.7	95.8	64
Snowshoeing	11.0[d]	11.9	9	55.5	35.6	7
Cross-country skiing	13.7	14.5	11	85.8	61.1	27
Alpine skiing/snowboarding	46.2[d,e]	76.6	47	72.6	76.7	47
Ski touring	13.5[e]	16.6	28	47.6	56.4	9
Tobogganing	29.8	28.3	8	60.7	39.6	4
Total	26.7	49.7	133	77.7[f]	80.0	158

Summer	Day trippers CHF	SD	n	Overnight visitors CHF	SD	n
Summer hiking	19.0[a]	20.1	361	53.2	46.2	200
Walking	21.7[b]	25.1	131	66.9	75.0	120
Mountain biking	38.2[a,b,c]	24.5	66	57.2	41.1	13
Summer Other	25.4[c]	32.0	67	47.0	66.0	51
Total	22.3	23.9	625	56.8[f]	59.4	384

Exchange rates (1 August 2006): 1 CHF = €0.64 resp. US$0.82.
Two values sharing the same superscript differ on a statistically significant level according to ANOVA Tamhane test (a, b: $p < 0.001$; c, d, e: $p < 0.1$) and t-test (f: t-value −3.031, $p < 0.01$).

The results of the regression models are more generalizable because they control for the influences of the diverse survey points and make comparisons possible with all other variables treated as being equal. Table 10.2 shows the results of the overall model, which explains about half of the variance of mean daily expenditure in the winter and summer seasons. All winter and summer activity types, with MTB and tobogganing not being different at 0.05 level, spent considerably less than the reference category alpine skiing/snowboarding. The spending of hikers in summer (−75%) and winter (−60%) differed greatly. If one compares the beta values of summer and winter activities, it is obvious that winter activities tend to differ less from the reference category (−0.79 average beta vs. −1.09 for summer activities), which indicates higher expenditure in the winter.

Day trippers spent 58% less per person and day than overnight visitors. At Lenk, the most developed and most important location in the survey area (site type 1 s/w), the daily expenditure was highest. All other sites apart from Erlenbach (site type 2 s) show significantly less mean daily expenditure. At Chiley (−96%) and Meniggrund (−83%), both situated in Diemtigtal on popular ski touring trailheads (site type 4 w) where there is no infrastructure to spend any money, expenditure was especially low. At Grimmialp (−59%, site type 4 s/3 w) and Jaunpass (−69%, site type 3 s/w), which have both only small-scale ski areas in winter with even less infrastructure in summer, visitors also spent less.

Table 10.2. Multiple linear regression model of the spending behaviour of nature-based tourists in Simmental and Diemtigtal (all seasons, all visitors, all survey locations). (From Mayer and Vogt, 2016b, p. 107.)

		Model 1 total	
	Independent variables	β-coefficients	Standardized β-coefficients (*t*-values)
Travel-based variables	Ln group size	−0.175**	−0.074 (−2.807)
	Number of visits (2–5)	−0.383**	−0.111 (−3.379)
	(6–10)	−0.359*	−0.067 (−2.381)
	(>10)	−0.160	−0.057 (−1.558)
	[first time]		
	Activities (hiking/trekking summer)	−1.381***	−0.399 (−11.381)
	(walking summer)	−1.323***	−0.258 (−9.078)
	(mountain biking)	−0.240	−0.029 (−0.896)
	(summer other)	−1.428***	−0.194 (−7.252)
	(winter hiking/walking)	−0.912***	−0.267 (−8.244)
	(snowshoe walking)	−1.226***	−0.174 (−6.597)
	(cross-country skiing)	−0.471**	−0.098 (−3.384)
	(ski touring)	−0.909***	−0.194 (−5.837)
	(tobogganing)	−0.262	−0.030 (−1.132)
	(other winter activities)	−0.968*	−0.060 (−2.370)
	[alpine skiing, snowboarding]		
	Visitor type (day tripper)	−0.869***	−0.314 (−9.767)
	[vacationers]		
Destination-based variables	Ln distance (km)	0.096*	0.095 (2.419)
	Weather (fair)	0.200*	0.071 (2.021)
	(cloudy)	0.257*	0.066 (2.147)
	(overcast)	0.364**	0.083 (2.807)
	(rainy)	0.195	0.049 (1.603)
	[cloudless]		
	Site characteristics*	−3.121***	−0.179 (−7.077)
	(4 w Chiley)		
	(4 w Meniggrund)	−1.772***	−0.167 (−5.844)
	(3 w/4 s Grimmialp)	−0.883***	−0.295 (−8.262)
	(3 s/w Jaunpass)	−1.179***	−0.347 (−10.670)
	(2 s Wiriehorn)	−0.466*	−0.081 (−2.439)
	(2 s Erlenbach)	0.457**	0.080 (2.678)
	(2 s/w Sparenmoos)	−0.044	−0.009 (−0.306)
	[1 s/w Lenk]		
	Numbers of observations	1314	
	R² adjusted	0.480	
	F-values	22.626***	

Level of significance: ***$p < 0.1\%$, **$p < 1\%$, *$p < 5\%$.
*ranking of site characteristics (1–4): tourism infrastructure, price and quality level of accommodation and gastronomy, 1 most, 4 least.
Significant variables in bold letters, variables in square bracket: reference category.
s: summer season; w: winter season.

Table 10.3. Multiple linear regression model of the spending behaviour of nature-based tourists in Simmental and Diemtigtal (winter, all visitors, all sampling locations). (Own calculations, data based on Mayer et al., 2009 and Mayer and Vogt, 2016b.)

		Model 3 winter-only	
	Independent variables	β-coefficients	Standardized β-coefficients (t-values)
Tourist-based variables	(Constant)	4.112	
	Number of visits (2–5)	−0.577*	−0.166 (−2.209)
	(6–10)	−0.393	−0.072 (−1.152)
	(>10)	−0.215	−0.079 (−0.945)
	[first time]		
	Activities (winter hiking/walking)	−0.849***	−0.302 (−4.419)
	(snowshoe walking)	−1.037**	−0.190 (−3.244)
	(cross-country skiing)	−0.352	−0.094 (−1.469)
	(ski touring)	−0.990***	−0.269 (−3.652)
	(tobogganing)	−0.313	−0.046 (−0.767)
	(other winter activities)	−0.653	−0.053 (−0.884)
	[alpine skiing, snowboarding]		
	Visitor type (day tripper)	−0.661**	−0.247 (−3.316)
	[vacationists]	–	
Destination-based variables	Ln distance (km)	0.242*	0.200 (2.061)
	Site characteristics* (4 w Chiley)	−3.110***	−0.233 (−4.114)
	(4 w Meniggrund)	−1.415*	−0.173 (−2.607)
	(3 w/4 s Grimmialp)	−0.689**	−0.254 (−2.976)
	(3 s/w Jaunpass)	−1.217***	−0.395 (−5.168)
	(2 s/w Sparenmoos)	−0.045	−0.009 (−0.134)
	[1 s/w Lenk]		
	Numbers of observations	297	
	R² adjusted	0.499	
	F-values	6.716***	

For explanations see Table 10.2.

The winter-only model (see Table 10.3) produced quite similar results achieving a slightly better fit (approx. 50% of variance explained). All activities deviate negatively from the reference category alpine skiing, especially snowshoeing (−64.5%), ski touring (−62.8%) and winter hiking (−57.2%), with cross-country skiers and tobogganers showing the smallest deviations and no statistical significance (day trippers spend −48.4%). All survey sites (except Sparenmoos where the relatively high-spending tobogganers were sampled) differ negatively from Lenk with the largest ski area and the best tourism offer in terms of quality. Again, especially the ski touring and snowshoeing trailheads (Chiley, Meniggrund) are particularly negative (−95.5% and −75.7%).

Thus, our analyses show that expenditures related to winter sport activities in the two Swiss alpine valleys are often, but not in every case higher compared with those related to summer activities. Infrastructure-based activities like alpine skiing in winter or downhill MTB in summer lead to higher spending compared with more purist activities like ski touring. The latter are also often related to day trippers who spend significantly less compared with overnight visitors. However, the example of the vacationers also shows that high spending is not per se dependent on the main outdoor activity but on the chosen destination, its scope, quality and price level of the accommodation, gastronomy and retail offers. Nevertheless, there seems to be a correlation of these offer elements and characteristics with the state of development of tourism infrastructure like ski areas/cable cars. If one relates the expenditure data analysed here to the estimated annual frequentation of each activity group to derive the gross turnover and finally the economic impact, which was done by Mayer *et al.* (2009), it is obvious that the domination of the infrastructure-based winter activities is even stronger. Alpine skiing is a mass tourism activity related to mostly high daily expenditure (88% share of the regional economic impact in the winter season), while ski touring (0.13%) and snowshoeing (0.17%) are small niche activities with relatively low expenditures and a high share of day trippers. The second largest economic impact was generated by winter hiking/walking (9.2%); cross-country skiing accounted for 1.1%.

10.4 Winter vs. Summer Activities in Black Forest National Park, Germany

The Black Forest National Park designated in 2014 in south-western Germany provides an interesting case as it allows the direct comparison of the expenditure behaviour and economic relevance of alpine skiers in small-scale resorts, cross-country skiers and other less infrastructure-related nature tourism activities in the protected area. The Black Forest is an important winter sport destination for the surrounding areas of the Rhine valley and the agglomeration of Stuttgart. In the National Park region, 12 small-scale ski areas/lifts are situated. Cross-country skiing has a long tradition in the region. Thus, the National Park took over the management of 154 km of tracks (Job and Kraus, 2015).

The case study is based on 2020 interviews (year-round) with 507 visitors conducted during the winter season including 215 interviews with alpine skiers (in five ski areas) and 84 with cross-country skiers. The detailed surveys not only give insights into the spending but also into the trip characteristics, motivation and the role of the National Park for the trip decision. The methodology is based on the standard procedure for economic impact analysis in protected areas in Germany by Job *et al.* (2016). Parallel visitor counting and extrapolation allow the estimation of the economic impact of the different activity groups. The first entries of eight ski areas/lifts were derived from interviews with the operators; one was covered by own counting while the remaining three were estimated in relation to number of lifts, their lengths, capacity and opening time based on the revealed data of the other areas. Cross-country skier frequentation was conservatively extrapolated based on counting from two important trailheads (Job and Kraus, 2015).

Overall, the at-that-time newly established National Park recorded 1.041 million visitor days, among them 142,500 by alpine skiers (13.7%) and 50,000 by cross-country skiers (4.8%) in a very good season in terms of snow conditions (Job and Kraus, 2015). Black Forest National Park is dominated by day trippers (local day trippers[2] 30.7%, non-local day trippers 29.5%), while overnight visitors account for only 39.8% of the visitor days (Mayer and Woltering, 2018). Alpine skiing in the Black Forest is even more strongly characterized by day trippers (81%), with only 19% overnight skiers. This distribution is even more extreme for the cross-country skiers with 91% to 9%. These one-sided distributions of the winter visitors are due to the nearby agglomerations of the Rhine valley. Winter recreationists' demand reacts strongly to recent snowfalls and the weather conditions, which motivate them to visit the small ski areas close by, leading to congestion on weekends with good weather and snow conditions (Job and Kraus, 2015).

Table 10.4 provides an overview of the spending of the different activity groups in Black Forest National Park differentiated by the three main visitor types. Alpine and cross-country skiers as well as hikers show statistically significant differences in the mean daily expenditures per person for overnight guests, non-local day trippers and local day trippers, while for the walkers only local day trippers and overnight visitors and non-local day trippers and overnight visitors differ.

Among local and non-local day trippers the winter activities and especially alpine skiing lead to the highest per person and day spending (though cross-country skiing not for the local visitors). For both visitor types, alpine skiers differ statistically significantly from all other activity groups. This is not the case for overnight visitors where only walkers and hikers differ significantly. Alpine skiers rank only third.

Interestingly, activity groups also reveal inter-seasonal differences: the walkers staying overnight spend on average €122.9 in the winter season compared with only €89.2 (summer), €91.7 (autumn) and €95.5 (spring). These differences are statistically significant for the first three groups ($p < 0.05$, ANOVA tamhane post-hoc test). A converse effect holds true for day tripping walkers, who spend significantly less in winter

Table 10.4. Mean daily expenditure per person and National Park affinity of Black Forest National Park visitor activity groups in 2014/15. (Own calculations, data based on Job and Kraus, 2015.)

	Local day trippers			Non-local day trippers			Overnight visitors			Visitors with a high National Park affinity
	EUR	SD	N	EUR	SD	n	EUR	SD	n	%
Alpine skiers	20.8[a,b,c,d]	12.9	41	30.5[a,b,c,d,e]	25.2	152	88.5	56.6	17	2.8
Cross-country skiers	7.2[a]	11.6	20	17.6[a]	24.4	56	75.3	42.6	7	11.9
Walkers	12.1[b]	17.1	138	15.4[b]	18.9	467	95.4[a]	67.8	359	9.3
(Winter) Hikers	8.3[c]	7.9	50	13.6[c]	13.7	261	71.9[a]	40.6	189	13.7
Bikers	5.4[d]	9.4	15	13.7[d]	7.0	9			2	0.0
Motorcyclists			2	15.1[e]	14.0	22	103.0	52.4	10	2.6
Overall (mean)	12.1	14.9	266	17.4	19.8	967	87.4	60.3	584	9.7

Two values sharing the same superscript differ on a statistically significant level according to ANOVA Tamhane test (at minimum $p < 0.05$).

(€11.0) compared with spring (€15.4) and autumn (€16.8, $p < 0.05$). For hikers, these effects could not be found. Thus, winter guests do not automatically spend more in any case compared with other seasons.

The National Park affinity varies significantly between the activity groups: alpine skiers (2.8%), motorcyclists (2.6%) and bikers (0%) do not care much about the protected area status of the region, which comes as no surprise given that the dependence on infrastructure of alpine skiers is not compatible with the National Park idea; walkers (9.3%) nearly reach the overall mean (9.7%); cross-country skiers (11.9%) and (winter) hikers (13.7%) surpass this threshold. This reflects the strong relatedness to nature of cross-country skiers.

Extrapolated to the overall number of visitor days, alpine skiers generate €5.692 million gross turnover in the park region (12.7%) leading to a regional income of €3.016 million, which translates to 109 income equivalents. Cross-country skiers reach €1.120 million (2.5%) and €0.561 million, respectively (20 income equivalents) (Job and Kraus, 2015). Thus, explicit winter sport activities account for 15.7% of the National Park's regional economic impact. These results underline that winter tourism activities balance the tourism demand over the year, which contributes considerably to a better utilization of the tourism infrastructure.

10.5 Conclusions

Winter tourism is highly diverse and thus so also are visitor spending and their economic impact. There seems to be a tendency for higher spending in the winter season in mountain settings compared with the other seasons in addition to remarkably high expenditures in the home regions for equipment like skis (which we did not show in our two case studies). As expected, visitors pursuing infrastructure-related outdoor activities like alpine skiing spend the most. Important drivers for their higher spending are the high costs associated with lift passes, outdoor equipment and services like ski schools. In contrast, more purist and nature-related activities lead most often to lower expenditures and only relatively few respondents pursue them, which hints at a 'sustainability-profitability-gap' (Moeller et al., 2011). In addition to this rather low regional economic impact the ecological footprint of these activities due to the dominance of car access should not be neglected. The comparison between these extremes in terms of environmental impact, spending and visitor numbers also reminds us that we should not only take expenditure into consideration but also the frequentation, length of stay and multipliers. At the end of the day, it is the economic impact of outdoor activities that is the most relevant, but visitor spending is without doubt an important influencing factor.

However, our case studies show that alpine skiing does not necessarily lead to higher expenditures compared with other activities. This is because visitor spending depends on the region, its price level, tourism offer like the size of ski areas or retail quality but also on personal preferences, willingness to pay, etc. In this way, hybrid visitors might be another reason for diversity in expenditure, like for example ski tourers residing in costly luxury accommodation or alpine skiers staying in basic self-service huts. This underlines that visitor spending is not determined by the leisure activities alone (White and Stynes, 2008) but is influenced by a complex bundle of factors (see Table 10.2 and Table 10.3). As our first case study shows, multiple linear regression models are suitable to control for these various influencing factors. Therefore, specific onsite surveys taking local/regional characteristics into account are required. However, this leads to the methodological problem of very large sample sizes being necessary to enable coverage of niche activities with an adequate sub-sample size, which is an issue with both of our case studies (though the first one more than the other).

All in all, compared with the summer season, winter tourists in general spend more money, which underlines the high economic importance of winter tourism for many peripheral valleys in mountain regions. Thus, high investments in snowmaking and quality improvements of cable cars and ski lifts can still be justified by the argument of economic importance. However, it is because of this importance that threats to winter tourism by climate change and other influencing factors should be taken seriously, and diversification strategies for the winter season be fostered as well as the non-snow-dependent seasons strengthened.

Notes

[1] BAK Basel (2012) compared the prices of circa 4700 three-star hotels (standard double rooms) in the Alps for 2011 in the winter and summer high seasons. In the Alps hotel prices in winter are 17% higher compared with the summer.

[2] Defined as coming from all municipalities that share a part of the park area and/or directly bordering the protected area.

References

Amt der Tiroler Landesregierung (2017) Der Tourismus im Winter 2016/17. Available at: https://www.tirol.gv.at/fileadmin/themen/statistik-budget/statistik/downloads/FV_Winter_2017.pdf (accessed 14 July 2018).

BAK Basel (2012) Bedeutung, Entwicklungen und Herausforderungen im Schweizer Sommertourismus. Basel. Available at: https://www.seco.admin.ch/dam/seco/de/dokumente/Standortfoerderung/Tourismus/Archiv/Studio_Sommertourismus_2012.pdf.download.pdf/Schweizer%20Sommertourismus_2012.pdf (accessed 7 September 2018).

Bayerisches Staatsministerium für Wirtschaft, Infrastruktur, Verkehr und Technologie (StMWIVT) (2007) *Seilbahnen in Bayern*. StMWIVT, Munich, Germany.

Brida, J.G. and Scuderi, R. (2013) Determinants of tourist expenditure: a review of microeconometric models. *Tourism Management Perspectives* 6, 28–40. DOI:10.1016/j.tmp.2012.10.006

Bundesverwaltungsgericht Republik Österreich (2018) Decision 'Schigebietserweiterung Hochsonnberg'. Geschäftszahl (GZ): W225 2014492-1/128E. Vienna, Austria.

CIPRA (2017) Sonnenwende im Wintertourismus. Positionspapier. Available at: https://www.cipra.org/de/positionen/wintertourismus/CIPRA%20Positionspapier_Sonnenwende%20im%20Wintertourismus.pdf/inline-download (accessed 27 September 2018).

Feichtner, D. (2017) Kompetenz, die sich bezahlt macht. *Saison* 05/17, 8–10.

Fredman, P. (2008) Determinants of visitor expenditures in mountain tourism. *Tourism Economics* 14(2), 297–311.

Job, H. and Kraus, F. (2015) Regionalökonomische Effekte des Tourismus im Nationalpark Schwarzwald. Unpublished report, Munich, Germany.

Job, H., Merlin, C., Metzler, D., Schamel, J. and Woltering, M. (2016) *Regionalwirtschaftliche Effekte durch Naturtourismus in deutschen Nationalparken als Beitrag zum Integrativen*

Monitoring-Programm für Großschutzgebiete. Bundesamt für Naturschutz, Bonn-Bad Godesberg, Germany.

Jülg, F. (2007) Wintersporttourismus. In: Becker, C. et al. (eds) *Geographie der Freizeit und des Tourismus. Bilanz und Ausblick*, 3rd edn. Oldenbourg, Munich, Germany, pp. 249–258.

Kleissner, A. (2012). Die gesamtwirtschaftliche Bedeutung des Wintersports in Österreich. Forum Zukunft Winter. Kaprun, 5 November 2012. Available at: https://docplayer.org/37831878-Die-gesamtwirtschaftliche-bedeutung-des-wintersports-in-oesterreich-anna-kleissner-sportseconaustria.html (accessed 27 September 2018).

Leitner, W. (1984) Winterfremdenverkehr. Entwicklung, Erfahrungen, Kritik, Anregungen. Bundesland Salzburg 1955/56-1980/81. Amt der Salzburger Landesregierung, Salzburg, Austria.

MANOVA (2016) Wertschöpfung durch österreichische Seilbahnen. Wertschöpfung im Winter. Endbericht Oktober 2016, Wien, Austria. Available at: https://www.wko.at/branchen/transport-verkehr/seilbahnen/Wertschoepfung-durch-Oesterreichische-Seilbahnen.pdf (accessed 25 August 2018).

Mayer, M. and Vogt, L. (2016a) The economic effects of tourism and its influencing factors. An overview focusing on the spending determinants of visitors. *Zeitschrift für Tourismuswissenschaft* 8(2), 169–198. DOI:10.1515/tw-2016-0017

Mayer, M. and Vogt, L. (2016b) Bestimmungsfaktoren des Ausgabeverhaltens von Naturtouristen in den Alpen – das Fallbeispiel Simmental und Diemtigtal, Schweiz. In: Mayer, M. and Job, H. (eds) *Naturtourismus – Chancen und Herausforderungen* (=Studien zur Freizeit- und Tourismusforschung 12). MetaGIS, Mannheim, Germany, pp. 99–111.

Mayer, M. and Woltering, M. (2018) Assessing and valuing the recreational ecosystem services of Germany's national parks using travel cost models. *Ecosystem Services* 31(Part C), 371–386. DOI:10.1016/j.ecoser.2017.12.009

Mayer, M., Kraus, F. and Job, H. (2011) Tourismus – Treiber des Wandels oder Bewahrer alpiner Kultur und Landschaft? *Mitteilungen der Österreichischen Geographischen Gesellschaft* 153, 31–74. DOI:10.1553/moegg153s31

Mayer, M., Wasem, K., Gehring, K., Pütz, M., Roschewitz, A. and Siegrist, D. (2009) *Wirtschaftliche Bedeutung des naturnahen Tourismus im Simmental und Diemtigtal – Regionalökonomische Effekte und Erfolgsfaktoren*. Eidg. Forschungsanstalt für Wald, Schnee und Landschaft WSL, Birmensdorf, Switzerland.

Mehmetoglu, M. (2007) Nature-based tourists: the relationship between their trip expenditures and activities. *Journal of Sustainable Tourism* 15(2), 200–215. DOI:10.2167/jost642.0

Moeller, T., Dolnicar, S. and Leisch, F. (2011) The sustainability–profitability trade-off in tourism: can it be overcome? *Journal of Sustainable Tourism* 19(2), 155–169. DOI:10.1080/09669582.2010.518762

Pouta, E., Neuvonen, M. and Sievänen, T. (2006) Determinants of nature trip expenditures in Southern Finland – implications for nature tourism development. *Scandinavian Journal of Hospitality and Tourism* 6(2), 118–135. DOI:10.1080/15022250600658937

Rütter, H., Müller, H., Guhl, D. and Stettler, J. (1995) Tourismus im Kanton Bern. Wertschöpfungsstudie. FIF, Bern/Rüschlikon, Switzerland.

Rütter, H., Berwert, A., Rütter-Fischbacher, U. and Landolt, M. (2001) Der Tourismus im Wallis. Wertschöpfungsstudie. Rüschlikon/Siders, Switzerland.

Rütter, H., Rütter-Fischbacher, U. and Berwert, A. (2004) Der Tourismus im Kanton Nidwalden und in Engelberg. Wertschöpfungsstudie. Rüschlikon, Switzerland.

Seilbahn.net (2016) Sölden-Pitztal: Erster Schritt in gemeinsame Zukunft. 18.07.2016. Available at: www.seilbahn.net/sn/index.php?i=60&kat=1&j=1&news=7238 (accessed 27 September 2018).

Siegrist, D. and Gessner, S. (2011) Klimawandel: Anpassungsstrategien im Alpentourismus. Ergebnisse einer alpenweiten Delphi-Befragung. *Zeitschrift für Tourismuswissenschaft* 3(2), 179–194. DOI:10.1515/tw-2011-0207

Soboll, A., Klier, T. and Heumann, S. (2012) The prospective impact of climate change on tourism and regional economic development: a simulation study for Bavaria. *Tourism Economics* 18(1), 139–157.

Statistik Austria (2016) Beherbergungsstatistik ab 1974 nach Saison. Available at: http://statcube.at/superwebguest/login.do?guest=guest&db=detouextsai (accessed 27 September 2018).

Steiger, R., Scott, D., Abegg, B., Pons, M. and Aall, C. (2019) A critical review of climate change risk for ski tourism. *Current Issues in Tourism* 22(11), 1343–1379. DOI:10.1080/13683500.2017.1410110

Verband Deutscher Seilbahnen und Schlepplifte e.V. (VDS) (2015) *Wirtschaftliche Effekte durch Seilbahnen in Deutschland*. VDS, Munich, Germany.

White, E.M. (2017) Spending patterns of outdoor recreation visitors to national forests. General Technical Report PNW-GTR-961. US Department of Agriculture, Forest Service, Pacific Northwest Research Station, Portland, Oregon.

White, E.M. and Stynes, D.J. (2008) National Forest visitor spending averages and the influence of trip-type and recreation activity. *Journal of Forestry* 106(1), 17–24.

Wirtschaftskammer Österreich (WKO) (2018) *Tourismus und Freizeitwirtschaft in Zahlen. Österreichische und internationale Tourismus- und Wirtschaftsdaten 54. Ausgabe, Juni 2018.* Vienna, Austria. Available at: https://www.wko.at/branchen/tourismus-freizeitwirtschaft/tourismus-freizeitwirtschaft-in-zahlen-2018.pdf (accessed 25 August 2018).

11 The Knockout Deal – Pricing Strategies in Alpine Ski Resorts

ULRIKE PRÖBSTL-HAIDER[1]* AND RAINER FLAIG[2]

[1]*Institute of Landscape Development, Recreation and Conservation Planning, University of Natural Resources and Life Sciences, Vienna, Austria;* [2]*Andermatt-Sedrun Sport AG, Andermatt, Switzerland*

11.1 Introduction

For several years, the price level for a daily or weekly ski pass in the alpine region has been on the rise. The price increase over the past 5 years has been higher than the inflation rate in the European Alps (DerStandard, 2017). According to the German ski resort association, the Austrian Chamber of Economics and the alpine tourism industry, the main reason for this increase lies in rising expenditures as a result of growing energy costs, the employment of a highly skilled workforce, costs of artificial snowmaking, as well as the construction of additional infrastructure such as halfpipes, fun parks and special facilities, e.g. for kids (N-TV, 2011). Furthermore, long-term investments are necessary in order to improve service quality and need to be financed (Münchener Zeitungs-Verlag, 2016; WKO, 2018).

However, many ski resorts in the alpine area achieve a good turnover, thereby contributing to the wealth of formerly economically disadvantaged mountainous regions. The turnover rates in French ski areas in the year 2015 (specified in million €/area) show that the Chamonix/Les Houches ski resort achieved a turnover of over €74 million, followed by La Plagne (€70 million) and Val Thorens (€67 million) (Statista Inc., 2016). In Italy, the skiing season is worth a total of approximately €10 billion. In 2016, this number included €4.45 billion for the hospitality industry, €4.39 billion for services connected to sports activities (e.g. equipment rental, skiing instructors, ski passes, ski lifts, etc.) and €1.13 billion for food services, shopping and recreational activities. Overall, mountain tourism adds up to 11.3% of Italy's entire tourist sector (Chierchia, 2016). In Austria, cableway operators' multiplier effect (net) contributed to a turnover of €3.63 billion in the winter season of 2015/16, based on the total value added (direct + indirect). The multiplier effect is considered to be about 1 to 7 (MANOVA, 2016).

Considering this high turnover in all alpine countries, as well as the expected profits and significant amount of investments in the alpine tourist sector, the continuously rising price level has been heavily criticized by the media, political parties and consumer associations. Especially in Austria and Switzerland, critics have argued that the formerly traditional 'national sport' of the local alpine population has turned into a luxury product that is no longer affordable, especially for families (DiePresse, 2013). Many

---

* E-mail: ulrike.proebstl@boku.ac.at

schools in Germany and Austria have already ended the tradition of a 'winter sport week', which included skiing and snowboarding lessons, due to the high costs of equipment and accommodation. Several experts have also warned that the decline in affordability for families and the discontinuation of school courses will intensify the anticipated negative effects of demographic change on winter tourism (Roth et al., 2018a).

This chapter will examine blueprints for new pricing systems and new payments strategies, before concluding with an analysis of key implications for destination development and consumer loyalty.

11.2 Winter Tourists' Price Sensitivity

This section provides an overview of recent findings on tourists' price sensitivity and its possible consequences. In general, income and relative prices are considered the most important determinants of tourism demand (Song and Li, 2008; Falk, 2015; Pröbstl-Haider and Mostegl, 2016; Pröbstl-Haider et al., 2017). However, studies on tourism demand focusing on winter sport destinations find mixed evidence concerning the extent of income elasticities (e.g. Falk, 2010, 2013; Töglhofer et al., 2011). In their analysis of 28 ski resorts in Austria, Töglhofer et al. (2011) report no significant income elasticities. Falk (2013), meanwhile, calculates an elasticity of 0.19 for domestic overnight stays in relation to the domestic GDP, also indicating that domestic winter tourism only marginally increases when there is an improvement in general economic conditions in a given country. These findings show that pricing is certainly relevant, but that income elasticity likely depends on ski resorts' characteristics and the range of offers available.[1] In his investigation of winter tourism demand in six ski areas in France belonging to the Compagnie des Alpes group, Falk (2015) found that relative prices, real income and snow depth are significant long-term determinants of visitor figures. Among these three factors, changes in relative prices had the largest effect on winter tourism demand.

Moreover, these findings are contextualized and substantiated by Roth and Siller (2018). The survey conducted by the German Sport University in Cologne revealed that 40% of alpine ski tourists from Germany have a gross income of less than €2500 per month. In light of this, the authors estimated that many families who want to spend their winter holidays in the Alps must invest more than their monthly income for a 4-day trip. Alongside analyses of visitor figures and guests' preferences, several studies have looked into the preferences revealed by potential tourists in their destination choice. An example from South Tyrol, Italy, illustrates the current overall expenditures of a family skiing holiday. In the 2016/17 season, ski tourists in Italy paid an average of €1015 per person for a week in a domestic mountain resort, corresponding to € 2450 for a household consisting of two adults and one child below the age of 8. The average expenditure per person for a weekend in the mountains amounted to about €350. These figures highlight current challenges, especially concerning families. Based on these results, it does not come as a surprise that 70% of ski tourists live in a partnership without children (Becker, 2015; Tietjen, 2015).

In addition, another survey conducted in 2018 by the German Sport University in Cologne reported that the high costs of skiing are the main argument German winter sport enthusiasts cite for not booking a ski or winter holiday (Roth et al., 2018b).

A recent survey examining the preferences of German and Austrian tourists interested in skiing in the Tyrolian Alps (Pröbstl-Haider and Mostegl, 2016) analysed the relevance of ticket price in relation to ten other attributes in a choice experiment on destination choice. The results of this representative online survey conducted in Germany and Austria showed that vacationer and day visitor segments each have different priorities. For vacationers, cost, snow security and having ski slopes within easy reach of their accommodation are crucial and more important than the size of the resort. Price is a decisive factor for day visitors.

Increasing interest in Eastern European ski resorts can also be explained by their cost advantage over resorts in the European Alps and the improved quality standards in many Eastern European countries (Momondo, 2017). Apart from cheaper ski passes, destinations such as Bansko in Bulgaria also offer significantly cheaper accommodation and opportunities for second homes.

MANOVA (2016), a market research firm specializing in winter tourism, analysed the effects of increasing costs in skiing tourism. In their survey, 18% of respondents cited the high prices of ski passes as a reason for giving up the sport. However, younger respondents under the age of 21 mentioned this reason significantly more often (23%) than older respondents. Overall, MANOVA argues that rising costs for winter sport activities generally reduce

- the likelihood of new people taking up skiing;
- the frequency of winter sports related activities; and
- the number of people who carry on with the sport.

They conclude that, without new approaches to product development, a reduced price level and new communication strategies, the number of active skiers will decline in the future.

11.3 Principal Pricing Strategies and Business Models

A comparison of different pricing strategies reveals that pricing strategy is primarily influenced by the overall economic situation and the various business segments involved in the US, the ski resort industry consists of over 300 companies, generating roughly $4 billion in annual revenue. Apart from selling lift tickets and season passes, ski resorts generate revenue through their affiliated hotels, restaurants, bars and other attractions. Figure 11.1 presents an example from the ski resort Vail in the United States. Aside from lift ticket sales, ski resorts in North America – in contrast to most of the European resorts – are able to generate substantial revenue through their on-mountain rental programmes, food and beverage outlets, retail stores and other attractions.

In addition, two enterprises, Vail Resorts, Inc. and Alterra/Aspen Snowmass, cover about 30% of the whole market. In Europe, the situation is markedly different. With the exception of large enterprises in France such as resorts belonging to the 'Compagnie des Alpes', ownership at most alpine ski resorts is distributed among several different businesses. Rather than one large business running the resort, the situation in Austria, Germany and Switzerland is, therefore, characterized by multi-faceted and diverse decision making processes. Many North American ski resorts, such as Vail and Whistler, claim that they are considerably more profitable than

Tickets ■ **Retail/rental** ■ **Ski school** ■ **Other** ■ **Dining**

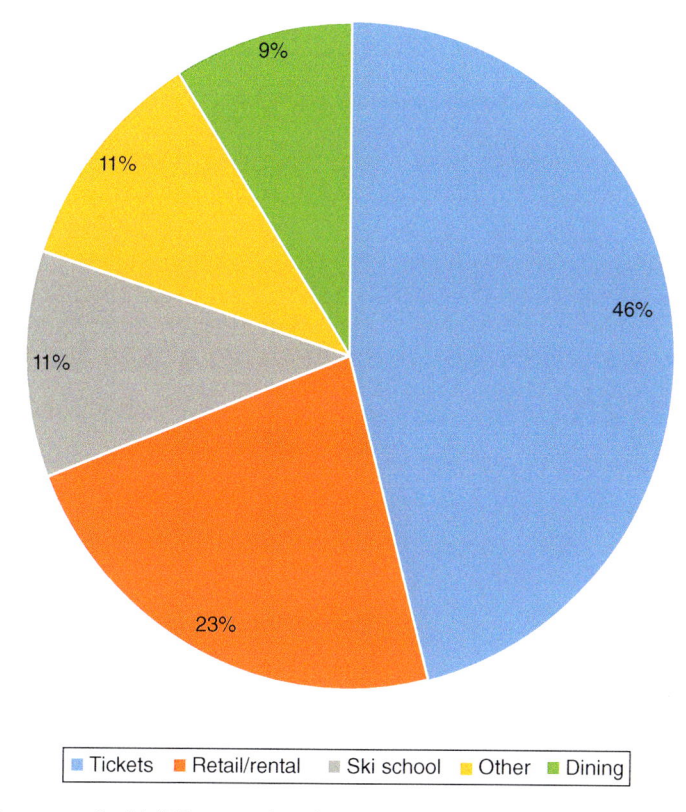

Fig. 11.1. Revenues for Vail Resorts, Inc. (2012) demonstrating that tickets are only one source of income for the enterprise. (After Thompson, 2012.)

large ski resorts in Europe, precisely because they have embraced monopolization. Thompson (2012) argues that, from a North American perspective, the European mountain resembles a 'strip mall', with restaurants, rental shops and service centres mostly owned by different companies renting space. By contrast, at Whistler and Vail, the mountain can be likened to an amusement park, where vertical integration has been realized in its simplest form; i.e. from village to peak, Vail and Whistler own all key businesses including equipment rentals, food and beverage outlets, and ski schools.

In the European Alps, tourism associations were established to take the lead on a common development plan. These associations were called upon to introduce new ideas and coordinate joint marketing strategies. However, a critical review in the context of climate change adaptation revealed that these associations were successful in their marketing efforts, but less so in steering overall development (Pröbstl, 2008). In contrast to the envisioned concept, in most cases cable car enterprises take on the most crucial leadership roles. A detailed network analysis revealed that, at least in the case of Austrian resorts, the decisions made by cable car enterprises have consequences for hotel owners, ski schools, restaurants and other businesses at the skiing destination, as early investments in artificial snowmaking have allowed hotel owners to also re-invest in their range of offers. Especially in winter seasons with little snowfall and high costs of artificial snowmaking, cable car enterprises, however, often complain in the media of the unfairness of having to cover the entire cost of artificial snowmaking, rather than sharing it with other related businesses in the resort. This uneven distribution of maintenance costs required to ensure good skiing conditions has also contributed to the rise in ticket prices in the past decade.

Aside from these structural differences, a closer look at pricing strategies also uncovers significant differences between most of the European and the North American resorts. The following analysis will focus on strategies for managing the revenue generated by ski lift ticket and season pass sales.

Pricing systems can consider different user groups, such as children, elderly people, students or local residents. Furthermore, the validity period of tickets may vary (ranging from daily to seasonal tickets). Finally, tickets may be valid in different areas of the resort.

Most ski resorts specify exact timings on their tickets due to the limited operating hours of ski lifts, which are usually open only during daylight (with the exception of resorts equipped with night time lighting). In addition, many ski resorts also offer season passes that allow unlimited access to the slopes during operating hours. Upon closer inspection, this basic concept seems to have been repeatedly customized and adapted over time to suit different local requirements.

Lift tickets are typically sold in the following formats: for an entire day (8 h); for multiple consecutive days; a half-day; or on an hourly basis. This model still dominates the European market. Prices for a day pass and a discounted 1-week pass are ordinarily announced in early winter. These prices can be easily viewed and compared on dedicated websites.[2] While it may still be possible to take advantage of reduced offers, these are often linked to so-called packages (e.g. Junior Weekend Discount in Zauchensee – Radstadt; group tickets for buses) or available only in combination with a hotel key-card.

Some resorts in North America also offer more flexible tickets, e.g. 4-hour passes that take the time the customer boards the first lift as their starting point (e.g. Holiday Valley).

While North America in principle applies the same pricing system as Europe, seasonal passes play a different, much more significant role. Moreover, a closer look reveals several further variations. Many North American resorts now offer passes that can only be used on certain days, or for a specified number of days per season (see Table 11.1).

In addition, other North American pricing strategies take the date of purchase into account. For instance, a season pass bought in April for the next season can be much cheaper than a season pass purchased in October (in many cases the price nearly doubles). The price differences between a 1-week ski pass and a seasonal ticket are – compared with Europe – not that substantial. Therefore, season passes play a major role in North America. This pricing scheme is feasible because ski resorts make about half of their money from lodgings, rentals, ski schools and catering (see Fig. 11.1). Even when avid skiing and snowboarding enthusiasts are given the occasional free pass to the slopes, they still contribute to the resorts' overall income, as they spend money on accommodation and meals.

Spatial explicit solutions are mainly provided for beginners who are not able to make use of the full range of slopes available. In order to increase demand, many resorts also offer reduced rates for beginners. These tickets are only valid on a limited number of lifts servicing beginners' slopes.

Table 11.1. The example shows the variety of season passes available in Killington (2012/13).

	Unlimited pass	Blackout pass	Midweek pass	College pass	Express card
Price	Adult (19–64 years) $1049 Youth (7–18 years) $699 Senior (65 years+) $699 Child (0–6 years) $39 Age determined by passholder's age as of 1/11/12	All ages $729	All ages $429	Full time college student $309	Purchase card for one-time to-be-determined fee then receive 50% off midweek and 25% off weekend/peak window rate all season long
Price details	Pricing through 26/4/12	Pricing through 4/26/12	Pricing through 4/26/12	Pricing through 8/30/12	TBD
Blackout dates	None	Valid any 3 out of 17 blackout dates: 24/12/12, 31/12/12, 19/1–20/1/13, 16/2–22/2/13	Saturdays, Sundays and blackout dates: 24/12–31/12/12, 18/2–22/2/13	None	None

11.4 New Trends and Innovation – The Cases of the Vail Epic Pass, the WinterCARD in Saas-Fee and the New Pricing System in Andermatt-Sedrun

Statistics show that booking behaviour has significantly changed over the past decade. This behavioural change is referred to as the 'standby tourist', relating to the current trend of booking late or last minute and travelling more frequently. In fact, many winter destinations have come to understand that a high number of tourists nowadays book their destination only after the weather forecast has predicted good conditions for their winter activities. Winter tourists have also become more and more flexible in terms of their preferred destination. This flexibility – combined with increasing price sensitivity – has led to major losses in Switzerland and a significant rise in the number of Swiss guests in Austrian resorts (Lütolf, 2017) (see Fig. 11.2). However, this added pressure has led to the development of innovative ideas, especially in Switzerland (Schegg and Engeler, 2018), as the following examples will show.

The following case studies illustrate how new strategies – at various scales – attempt to address an altered context characterized by behavioural changes, changing environmental conditions and climate change, as well as changes in demand. We will

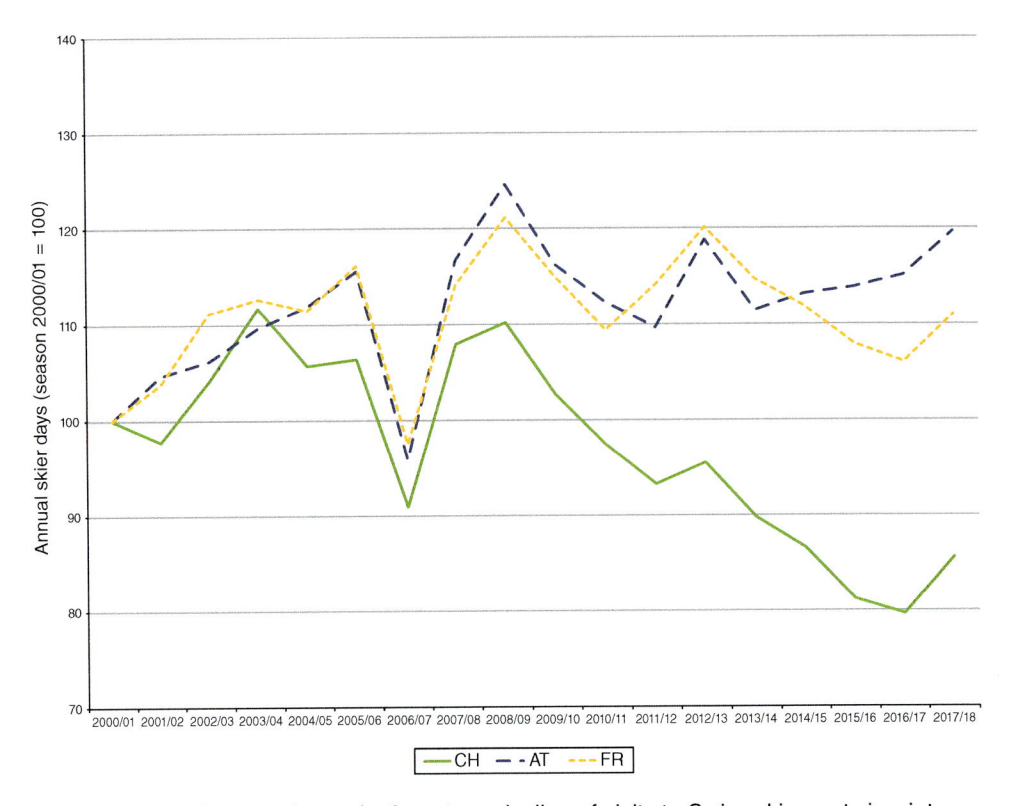

Fig. 11.2. The diagram shows the long-term decline of visits to Swiss ski resorts in winter seasons in comparison to Austria and France (first entries, in million €). (From Lütolf, 2017, translated into English.)

present solutions implemented by Vail Resort Mountains in the USA, and the Saastal Bergbahnen AG and the SkiArena Andermatt-Sedrun in Switzerland.

11.4.1 The Vail Epic Pass

The Vail Epic Pass is a season pass that not only includes the premium destination of Vail, but also a range of other premium destinations, namely Beaver Creek, Whistler Blackcomb, Breckenridge, Keystone, Park City, Heavenly, Northstar, Kirkwood, Wilmot, Afton Alps, Mt. Brighton, Perisher, Grand Teton Lodge Company and Stowe. The season pass not only offers fair prices but also a high degree of flexibility. The international network covered by the Vail Epic Pass has, for example, boosted the number of international guests in Whistler Blackcomb.

Thompson (2012) argues that the best analogy for these ski resorts is the casino: 'There's a core gambler like there's a core skier. Some people hate gambling, like some just want to keep their boots on. The job of the casino or ski resort is to give these people a reason to come, anyway.'

Skiing enthusiasts buying their Vail Epic Pass in April won't know how the snow and weather conditions will develop. However, the fact that they can visit a whole range of resorts significantly reduces the risk they are taking. A season pass bought in Vermont is, for instance, also valid in big resorts in Vail or Whistler. The Vail Epic Pass, thereby, stimulates tourism and boosts visitor figures, since all these resorts are open to season pass holders.

The experiences of these resorts also show that early purchases (in spring or summer) have further implications. By the time winter comes around, the money spent on the ski pass is somewhat 'forgotten'. Skiers report feeling like they are skiing at no cost. This positive sensation often results in additional visits, holidays or weekend trips. Furthermore, season pass holders are likely to convince their friends to join them for skiing trips at the respective resort(s). Both side effects economically benefit the destination. Currently, Vail Resorts, Inc. generates 40% of its overall ticket turnover from the Epic Pass. A similar system – featuring a moderate price for the season pass and a relatively high price level for daily tickets – is also used in Alterra/Aspen Snowmass, which is part of a season pass scheme called 'Icon Pass' spanning 23 resorts (Zegg, 2018).

The positive impact of such schemes can be seen in the ongoing increase of effective ticket prices in US resorts shown in Fig. 11.3.

11.4.2 The WinterCard in Saas-Fee

In contrast to the Vail Epic Pass, the concept of the Saas-Fee/Saas-Almagell WinterCard was perceived as a major gamble, especially because it deviates from the systems used in all of its neighbouring resorts and does not follow any of the traditional European models. The concept consists of several stages as described below.

Promoted by a creative and provocative marketing campaign worth around CHF5 million (see Fig. 11.4), the scheme offered skiers in the Swiss resort of Saas-Fee a season pass for the winter of 2016/17 for only CHF222 ($223), – subject to one condition: enough people had to take up the offer. Based on the crowdfunding principle, the popular alpine resort offered the low-cost season passes on the condition that advance reservations needed to reach 99,999.

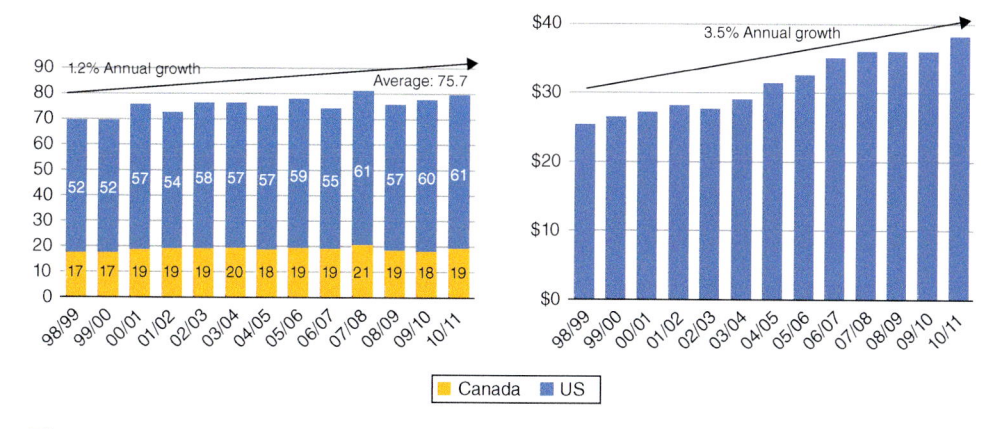

Fig. 11.3. Increasing number of skier visits (in millions) and significant annual growth of ticket prices (in US$). (After Thompson, 2012.)

Fig. 11.4. Marketing campaign, the knockout deal in the year 2016. (Image courtesy of Saastal Tourismus AG.)

Winter sports enthusiasts could book their discounted Saas-Fee WinterCard online, on a dedicated website: 'we-make-it-happen.ch'. They were informed that the 'deal' would come into force once the target had been reached. If sales failed to reach the announced number, passes would be sold at normal prices. The offer represented an 80% discount on regular season passes for Saas-Fee/Saas-Almagell (typically priced at CHF1050) and was even cheaper than a 4-day ski pass for the area. In a statement, the resort explained the initiative as follows (Saastal Tourismus AG, 2016): 'Alpine tourism is facing a challenge due to an imbalance of supply and demand. In many areas, the surplus of resorts means that costs can no longer be covered. Saas-Fee wants to solve the problem by introducing a revolutionary price concept.'

Since the majority of guests in Saas-Fee stay for an average of 4 days, the destination wanted to ensure that the offer's price would represent an attractive alternative to a 4-day ski pass. In 2016, a 4-day pass cost CHF259. With the Saas-Fee WinterCard, loyal customers could pay less than that and, more importantly, ski throughout the entire winter season.

The deal proved successful and was repeated the following year for the 2017/18 season. The passes were again sold for CHF222 and the targeted number (77,777 this time around) was again reached before the deadline. The pass included an additional 40 km of slopes, so that the WinterCard holder could now enjoy 150 km of slopes from November 2017 up to April 2018. Skiing enthusiasts were even given the option of buying passes for subsequent years (from 3 up to 15 seasons).[3]

According to the Saas-Fee tourism association, the resort normally sells around 120,000 ski passes during the winter season, ranging from 1-day passes to full-season passes. This figure demonstrates that the initiative was a well-planned move, widespread in the media (Coffey, 2016).

Indeed, the destination has since declared that the risk they took in proposing such a bold deal involving a crowdfunding concept has paid off. In the winter season 2016/17, visitor figures at the ski resort soared compared with the previous year: the number of overnight stays increased by 15% and new arrivals by 22%. While skier days in neighbouring resorts and other parts of Switzerland stagnated, Saas-Fee reported a significant increase of 50%. Both the resort and the local community claim that the whole Saas-Valley has profited from the new pricing concept. This includes hotel owners, food and beverage outlets and other businesses. The popularity of the second deal in the 2017/18 season has been interpreted as proof of the initiative's successful implementation.

The next step aimed at increasing the offer's appeal as well as its focus on the lifestyle segment saw the introduction of the new WinterCard Gold, which includes a number of additional services (worth around CHF1000) making a stay in Saas-Fee even more attractive (see Fig. 11.5). Incentives for instance include free transportation of luggage, special dining experiences, skiing activities (e.g. 'moonshine skiing' or 'virgin skiing'), as well as various summer packages.

When buying a WinterCard or a WinterCard Gold, clients can also contribute to sustainability and climate protection. The customer can choose to pay an additional €2, which will then be doubled by the enterprise and added to a sustainability fund that supports international and local projects run by myclimate – 'Cause We Care'.[4]

The amount of addresses and customer details collected through this online booking campaign has significant implications for future communication strategies, as it can be used for direct marketing and to forge a closer relationship with clients. This kind of data is invaluable and considered key to innovative and tailored customer relationship management. The concept developed by Sass-Fee also includes full and independent data ownership.

Fig. 11.5. To enhance the offer's lifestyle-oriented focus an additional WinterCard Gold was developed for the season 2017/18. (Image courtesy of Saastal Tourismus AG.)

11.4.3 Dynamic pricing in the SkiArena Andermatt-Sedrun

The third new model discussed in this section was implemented by the SkiArena Andermatt-Sedrun and Ticketcorner, a specialized company in online ski tickets. In the season 2017/18, a flexible pricing model for ski tickets was introduced. The SkiArena announced that there would be no more fixed prices for the day pass and simultaneously launched a joint booking platform with flexible prices. The basic principle of the new pricing system is simple: the earlier you book, the cheaper the ticket. The starting price of the offered day passes lies at CHF37 for adults and CHF13 for children. Prices are continuously adjusted depending on the season, day of the week, weather conditions and booking date. The technical partner, Ticketcorner, is well acquainted with these dynamics, as it runs a booking platform for more than 70 Swiss ski lift operators. The company especially developed this new, flexible pricing tool that takes account of key driving forces while also ensuring that the needs of guests and ski lift operators are met. The new system was launched in the winter season 2017/18 in cooperation with SkiArena Andermatt-Sedrun. Figures 11.6 and 11.7 show the offers available in February and March, 2018. By way of example, a client inquiring on 22 February 2018 can view a comparison of ticket prices over a 2-week period. The compilation suggests it would be cheapest to buy at the 22 February 2018 tickets for mid-March (13–15 March 2018).

Similar to airline and hotel prices, effective sales prices vary every day and depend on a large number of determining factors, including the season, the day of the week, the booking date and the weather. The partnered companies argue that this solution

Fig. 11.6. Screen shot of the booking website illustrating the information it provides. (From Ticketcorner AG, 2018.)

Fig. 11.7. A website check on 22 February 2018 shows the price level in March to be significantly cheaper than other upcoming dates. The strategic concept expects that clients' decision making will be influenced by this kind of information. (From Ticketcorner AG, 2018.)

differs from other pricing models in the market, as it benefits all parties involved – skiers can take advantage of lower prices, while ski lift operators enjoy an increase in demand during week days and profit more on peak days. They also highlight that the system empowers customers, who can now finally influence the price of their ski passes. Overall, skiing will become cheaper for families and those who book early. Guests at SkiArena Andermatt-Sedrun will also benefit from significantly lower prices on weekdays and during the off-peak season. Clearly, the new low entry-level prices available at SkiArena Andermatt-Sedrun are aimed at encouraging greater demand during traditionally quieter periods. Furthermore, the cable car enterprise wants to motivate its guests to book online to avoid long waiting times and to improve their service. There will, however, be no price changes for annual passes which are currently (in 2018) available for CHF875 for adults.

According to SkiArena CEO Silvio Schmid, the wide range of promotions offered in other areas in the past were aimed at reducing the prices of season passes and were generally tied to specific conditions, such as poor weather or minimum sale quantities. The new model launched by SkiArena Andermatt-Sedrun and Ticketcorner works very differently. In the new system, prices are continuously readjusted depending on supply and demand. These offers could be booked from 30 October 2017 onwards for a 7-month season lasting from November to May, 2018.[5]

Other destinations have also installed flexible pricing systems. For instance, the flexible pricing and booking system called 'Skinow' is currently used in the skiing regions Bellwald, Lauchernalp and Aletsch Arena (Skinow GmbH, 2019).

11.5 Discussion

11.5.1 The digital future of cable car enterprises

Any discussion of pricing systems needs to be conducted in the context of a significant shift towards 'digitalization'.[6] One crucial part of the 'digital transformation' is that cable car enterprises will be able to answer the question 'Who is my client?' in great detail. However, it remains unclear whether this additional knowledge will fundamentally impact their overall business model, since the understanding of digitalization and the main benefits differ significantly within the branch (Schegg and Engeler, 2018). Currently projections cover a wide range of possible developments, including:

- improved communication with the client;
- a more tailored and target group-specific marketing and marketing strategy;
- a tool for influencing booking behaviour;
- greater individualization of offers linked with tailor-made product development;
- opportunities for new products such as the 'ski movie' (video) and the 'speed check' (including a finish line photo);
- an economic benefit derived from an increasing automatization of internal processes;
- a tool to optimize cable car maintenance and spatial management; and
- significant support for controlling and monitoring, especially concerning energy efficiency and checking for wear.

Among Europe's alpine destinations, current implementations and future visions of digitalization already exhibit significant differences. While, in Switzerland, all the above-mentioned opportunities are being explored (e.g. in Laax), Austrian entrepreneurs tend to focus predominantly on marketing and communication opportunities.

Many experts argue that the tasks performed by cable car enterprises in winter tourism have changed. Originally providing mainly transportation services, they have transformed into fully integrated local tourism enterprises offering a range of touristic 'experiences'. And they may change yet again to become digitally integrated providers offering individualized products (Schegg and Engeler, 2018).

11.5.2 Critical evaluation of the different pricing strategies

Each of the presented pricing concepts and new initiatives has been critically discussed in the media, by experts and in the related literature. At least in Austria, the discussion was even covered on primetime television (ORF, 2018).

In the case of Vail Resort Inc., the pricing system itself was not the topic of discussion, rather the size of the enterprise and its new dimension. For an enterprise of this size, one particular destination is of little relevance as long as an average amount of season passes has been sold. In Whistler, which has only recently been added to the enterprise group, members of the local community have expressed their apprehensions that this kind of approach to marketing and pricing and the way it views resorts as interchangeable may allow corporations to reduce their engagement with the destination itself, and its local community. Asked for an example a respondent in Whistler pointed to diminished efforts to establish stable year-round tourism and the dissolution of plans to create new incentives to visit Whistler (such as a large spa facility).

Saas-Fee, which introduced a variation of the North American concept to its alpine network, was initially heavily criticized in the media, experts and members of the branch (Eiselin, 2016; Seilbahn.net, 2017). 'Is Saas-Fee destroying Winter tourism?', 'Is Saas-Fee very clever or very desperate?' and 'Saas-Fee fights to survive' were typical comments heard at the time. The new pricing concept was – and still is – labelled a 'dumping offer', 'entrepreneurial cannibalism' and something of an 'unsustainable marketing gag', mainly by other cable car enterprises in Switzerland and their Austrian counterparts. However, in 2017, 1 year after its first introduction, the media already reported on the 'miracle of Saas-Fee', highlighting its positive effects (Blick.ch, 2017; Walliser Bote, 2017; Wild, 2017). Nevertheless, scientific experts and consultants in the tourism sector remain somewhat sceptical. A critical argument concerns the target group this kind of offer reaches, and its further implications. Many commentators in the tourism industry compared the concept of Saas-Fee and its effects with low-cost supermarket chains that primarily target highly price-conscious customers and need to compensate this by increasing their sales volume. In other words, it has been argued that such a crowdfunding strategy chooses quantity over quality. This assessment is supported by recent findings on guest expenditures.

For the Austrian context, MANOVA (2016) argues that economical guests (e.g. who stay in private guesthouses) spend around 15–20% less than the average guest. If these findings are transferrable to the Swiss context, the increase of economical guests in Saas-Fee attracted by the new WinterCard will have rather limited additional benefits.

Haimayer (2016) argues that this pricing concept is not sustainable, because skiers are highly flexible and no skier would want to keep visiting the same resort. He maintains that regional cards are much more effective, as they enhance digital marketing without relying on this kind of price reduction, rather applying a moderate price increase instead. Other tourism experts, on the other hand, acknowledge the initiative's substantial marketing effect and applaud the innovative concept. However, Martin Vincenz, a tourism expert from Graubünden, considers it to be a 'unique campaign' that should not be copied (Van der Elst, 2016).

Forays into more dynamic pricing systems have also received strong criticism. In an interview, the president of the industry association of transportation enterprises in central Switzerland (TUZ), Sepp Odermatt, raises the question how clients will deal with daily changing price levels. Transparency and accountability, he argues, may be undermined by highly fluctuating ticket prices – a ticket going for CHF37 on 1 day and for CHF68 on another (Küttel, 2018). Other professionals in the field have been debating whether changing prices may also give customers the impression that ski resorts have been overcharging them in previous years and that earlier prices were not justified. Should the ticket prices in Switzerland go down any further (Fettner, 2018; Zegg, 2018), the discussion about justifiable price levels is likely to start up in Austria and Germany as well.

11.6 Lessons Learnt? The Case of Saas-Fee

What lessons have we learnt? In our view, there are four main aspects that need to be considered to ensure an integrated approach in the future: vertical engagement and networking; increasing customer loyalty; products aimed at the lifestyle segment; and, last but not least, a strategy that actively addresses increasing price levels.

11.6.1 Actively confronting the risk of increasing prices

Prospects for European winter tourism are not exactly bright. Aside from rising temperatures, experts predict an increasing frequency of snow-scarce winter seasons as well as rising energy prices (Unbehaun *et al.*, 2008; Damm *et al.*, 2014; and see other chapters in this book). These trends raise questions about future profitability, particularly concerning low-altitude ski resorts. A cost–revenue analysis of artificial snowmaking in a case study site in Austria – based on projected daily snowmaking hours and visitor numbers up until 2050 – revealed that lift operators are at risk of facing a substantial increase in total energy expenses due to the expected rise in electricity costs. This risk persists, even though the total number of hours of snowmaking is projected to slightly decrease in the future, as – on the basis of current snowmaking technologies – the time periods in which snowmaking is feasible are expected to shorten (Damm et al., 2014). Overall, this profitability analysis shows that ticket prices will need to further increase in the future, a little higher than observed in the recent past, in order to keep skiing operations profitable.

Against this background, new strategies need to be considered, especially concerning price level and affordability. However, the competitive landscape of the tourist sector has to be addressed in this context as well. If flying to a beach holiday destination is cheaper, it may affect the development of the winter tourism industry. Here, especially the cruise industry has become an increasingly relevant competitor having grown by a staggering 49% since 2008. In 2015, as many as 123 cruise ships from 39 cruise lines operated in European waters, carrying a total of 6.6 million passengers (+3% on the previous year). The cruise industry provides a significant boost to local economies: in 2015, it generated almost €41 billion output (+2% on the previous year); direct industry spending in Europe was at €16.89 billion (Ship2Shore, 2016).

To confront these trends, the winter tourism industry ought to turn to joint marketing initiatives, particularly targeting the domestic market by highlighting the advantage of having tourist destinations close by, and fostering prosperity in the alpine valleys, which have no other alternative than tourism. As suggested by several other authors, year-round tourism should also be strengthened by focusing more on offers promoting health, wellbeing and the enjoyment of natural, unspoiled environments. Even concepts emphasizing the unique character of the national or alpine landscape that appeal to customers' emotional attachment could be included.

In the case of Saas-Fee, the enterprise has already begun its work on strengthening summer and shoulder seasons. The 'Bürger Pass' (citizen pass) – offering an unlimited number of cable car rides in summer – has had a significantly positive effect on the resort's popularity and the number of overnight stays.

In this context, a stronger involvement of local populations and enterprises (hotels, gastronomy, clothing stores, etc.) has also been discussed, making the future of a ski resort to everybody's challenge.

11.6.2 Vertical engagement and networking

There is no doubt that the WinterCARD in Saas-Fee cannot be considered a blueprint for every other ski resort in Switzerland or Austria. First of all, the concept requires a high degree of snow security (Saas-Fee benefits in this respect from its proximity to the glacier). Saas-Fee could, moreover, capitalize on its peripheral location – far, but not too far, from urban centres such as Bern and Zürich. Therefore, the risk of bad weather and snow conditions is negligible and the likelihood of getting 'good value for money' during a long season is relatively high. This unique geographical constellation allows this concept to be feasible and attractive to a wide range of customers. For low-altitude resorts, it could be too risky to implement a similar scheme, because of potential snow scarcity. Moreover, in resorts located overly close to urban settlements, this kind of comparatively cheap offer (were the concept to be directly replicated) would lead to significant overcrowding on popular days. This would certainly adversely affect the overall quality of services and maintenance.

In terms of the financial risks faced by relatively snow-secure, high-altitude destinations in the Alps, the season pass system seems to be a better fit than flexible pricing systems, because it allows enterprises to achieve a significant level of income even before the season has started, thereby enabling them to plan investments without exposing themselves to substantial economic uncertainties. The overall profits generated by a flexible pricing system are more likely to be affected by unfavourable weather conditions and climate change-related risks.

One could argue that, if more ski resorts in high altitudes were to apply the WinterCard system, it would create 'winners' and 'losers' within the sector. Here, a look at the North American system may be of help. Ski resorts like Saas-Fee can only survive in the long run, if there are enough skiers interested in the range of activities they offer. Ski resorts in high altitudes depend on collaborations with partnering resorts that introduce winter sport activities to the wider public, e.g. destinations close to urban areas and small ski resorts for beginners, families and those coming back to the sport. In this respect, the strategy pursued by the Vail Epic Pass may serve as a suitable blueprint, because its season pass also helps promote smaller resorts.

Therefore, it would be wise to build up a network of ski resorts of different scopes and market positioning with the common goal of attracting as many people as possible to this fascinating sport and to offer a joint flat rate. This would require extensive conversations about support, cooperation and financial contributions. This network would be informed by a basic recognition that both sides (large-scale/high-altitude as well as small-scale businesses) are set to profit from close cooperation and that a product such as the WinterCard can work in a positive, 'non-cannibalistic' manner as an added value for all partnering companies.

Applying the WinterCard concept long term will eventually force ski resorts to think about increasing vertical engagement. Certainly, the situation in Europe is very different from the North American resort concept; however, European cable car enterprises also have opportunities to invest in and profit from their own infrastructure, such as shops, restaurants or ski rentals. An excellent example in this respect is Laax in Switzerland. In addition, further expansions into other businesses – either directly or indirectly through cooperation and networking – may need to be undertaken to meet future demands. In this respect, the above-mentioned Bürgerkarte (Citizen Card) in Saas-Fee provides a positive example, alongside other regional card systems that strengthen the cooperation between key stakeholders. Cable car operators may again be asked to take the lead in such schemes, but, unlike past experiences, this leadership role will need to foster partnerships and networking.

11.6.3 Price dumping or customer loyalty 4.0

Vocal detractors of the season pass concept, as applied in North America or in Saas-Fee, have overlooked several aspects. First of all, since it does not replace existing pricing models such as daily tickets, the season pass is only one option among many for the customer. Comparing the pricing system in Saas-Fee with those in Vail or Whistler, it does, however, become evident that the price level for regular daily tickets in Canada/BC and in ski resorts in the US is significantly higher. The prices for daily tickets in Saas-Fee correspond to the general price level of ski resorts of a similar scale in Switzerland and Austria. Dynamic pricing systems, on the other hand, have been found to be in conflict with existing systems. Consequently, season pass concepts contribute less to price dumping than dynamic pricing concepts.

Those criticizing pricing concepts with a strong focus on season passes also ignore the fact that such models are not about short-term discounts but mark the start of a long-term engagement with the customer. The overarching goal of introducing the Vail Epic Pass, the dynamic pricing concepts or the WinterCard is customer loyalty, as well as a deeper understanding of customer characteristics, including the customer's needs, expectations and main habits.

The literature shows that investments to increase customer loyalty are likely to generate positive returns in the future in a number of ways (Griffin, 2002; Parviainen *et al.*, 2017). In the case of ski resorts, these may include:

- reduced marketing costs;
- reduced customer turnover expenses (fewer lost customers to replace);
- increased cross-selling success leading to a larger share of customers; and
- a positive effect of word-of-mouth advertising.

The detailed personalized information gathered by the WinterCard initiative can be used to develop new products and offers, and can help boost word-of-mouth recommendations including social media. In this regard, tourism experts agree that this kind of impact should be considered the ultimate goal of any campaign, and interpret it as evidence of customer loyalty 4.0.

The Saas-Fee case study faithfully followed crucial steps in the development of a successful customer loyalty strategy – starting off by successfully capturing the public's attention of the offer. The memorable 'knockout deal' campaign (see Fig. 11.4) positioned the product uniquely within the market and increased its popularity among prospective customers. In announcing the deal and its limited conditions, the enterprise capitalized on customers' predilection for initial purchases. The following post-purchase evaluation, which received significant media coverage, resulted in an overall very positive assessment, regarding both the feedback of tourists themselves, as well as that of suppliers, hotels and other partners in the destination. The next challenge is to influence the decision to repurchase. Recent evaluations conducted in Saas-Fee have shown that this is no easy task. Currently, the enterprise estimates that only every second customer will buy the WinterCard again in the next winter season. Since the decision to repurchase is influenced by the customer's emotional ties with the product, the key to customer loyalty lies in the use of digital data to promote and call to mind exceptional winter experiences, thereby strengthening the emotional bond. Digital campaigns should enhance this process by addressing customers' individual preferences.

The development of the WinterCard and the WinterCard Gold is also an attempt to create something akin to premium loyalty in winter tourism, i.e. a situation in which customers are proud of discovering and using the product and take pleasure in sharing their experience with peers and family. Especially the additional offers are designed to make skiers feel like upgraded customers. Additional products rewarding premium loyalty have been part of the new pricing system from its initial conception. However, the specific volume and configuration of incentives included in the WinterCard and the WinterCard Gold will be adapted in the future, based on newly gained insights on visitor preferences and behaviour. To maintain a high degree of customer loyalty over time, the team in Saas-Fee is aware that it will need to modify, upgrade and change the current offer to meet the changing demands of its future customers and guests.

11.6.4 Lifestyle and meaningful leisure time

In western societies, meaningful leisure time has become increasingly important (Zellmann and Mayrhofer, 2012). Furthermore, tourism research underlines the relevance of 'experiences' as the key to future booking behaviour. Therefore, modern cable car operators should promote a shift away from a cost-based pricing system towards demand- and/or behaviour-oriented pricing. This would also entail a change of perspective, calling on modern cable car operators to no longer perceive themselves as transportation enterprises but as companies offering leisure and recreational activities. Consequently, the price level can no longer be linked to haulage capacity but needs to reflect the offered experiences. According to this school of thought, high prices stand for very intense and appealing experiences. Taking the shift towards lifestyle- and experience-oriented tourism seriously requires a fundamental rethink including a re-evaluation of entrepreneurial goals: the number of sold tickets may have to be replaced by customer loyalty as well as capacity utilization as the primary indicators of a healthy business.

However, recent research has underlined that there is no 'one uniform client', rather there are different customer segments with different interests and behavioural preferences (Pröbstl-Haider *et al.*, 2017; Pröbstl-Haider and Mostegl, Chapter 17 in this book). One can easily imagine a scenario in which, in addition to the basic transportation flat rate included in the two WinterCard options, customers are given the opportunity to select further 'components' to customize their winter holidays (e.g. five out of ten). Current research may offer several suggestions as to which target groups should be addressed by such initiatives and what kind of additional products should be listed. From a scientific perspective, the current concept leaves plenty of room for adaptation and improvement.

Currently, the WinterCard can be seen as a product targeting the younger generation of digitally savvy, lifestyle-oriented skiers. In this target group, the experience of being among the first on the slopes, enjoying powder snow and early opening times, at an affordable price level is considered a priority.

The WinterCard Gold is not yet well positioned in the market. To an outsider, it is not immediately obvious who the main target group for this card is. In order to differentiate it more clearly from the regular WinterCard, the Gold Card could increase its appeal for convenience-oriented customers, similar to the business or first-class categories offered by airlines. Leitmotifs for this direction could include 'experience', 'deceleration', 'health benefits', 'service quality' and 'reliability'. The targeted customer segment is presumed to be much more demanding than others, while the price level does not constitute a crucial factor in their decision making. Instead, they want to enjoy certain privileges and extra service. Therefore, instead of offering reduced entrance fees, further extras could be added, such as separate dining opportunities, changing rooms, reserved parking space, etc.

Since any loyalty-based system must be continuously modified, the ongoing adaptation of the WinterCard – its efforts to reach different target groups and adjust to customers' lifestyles – will afford many opportunities for further innovation in the future.

11.7 Conclusions

Today's winter sports tourists demand a modern lift infrastructure and a snow guarantee despite changing environmental conditions. In many alpine countries, the ski industry feels compelled to undertake significant investments irrespective of declining visitor numbers. The introduction of new pricing strategies is seen as an urgent necessity within the industry at least in Switzerland. This chapter illustrated various concepts underlying these different strategies.

Most innovative new concepts are characterized by a common principle: They all want to turn skiers into 'members'. With the help of digital data, they aim to better understand their clients and address their individual preferences. This kind of information about their customers can be used to boost overall revenues per skier, primarily by increasing the frequency and length of stays. Detailed information – utilized to develop additional and customized products – is likely to enhance the desired lifestyle-orientation within winter tourism and may, thereby, attract new guests. However, maintaining this appeal in the long term may prove the real challenge.

Saas-Fee has decided to follow this difficult, yet innovative new path. However, the challenges they face are substantial. An investment of about CHF40 million alone will be needed until 2025 to improve their snowmaking facilities, restaurants and chair lifts.

Notes

[1] See also the findings from Pröbstl-Haider and Mostegl, Chapter 17 in this book.
[2] For Austria, see for example https://www.bergfex.at/oesterreich/suchen or https://at.skiinfo.com/oesterreich/skipaesse.html (both accessed 9 January 2019).
[3] This so-called 'knockout deal' was also repeated for the season 2018/19 with a targeted threshold of 66,666 WinterCard holders.
[4] Myclimate 'Cause We Care' is an initiative for climate protection and sustainable tourism in Switzerland. For further information, see their website www.causewecare.ch. Myclimate is also a partner organization of the 2017 International Year of Sustainable Tourism for Development (see www.tourism4development2017.org) (both accessed 9 January 2019).
[5] For more information on the SkiArena Andermatt-Sedrun, see www.skiarena.ch or www.ticketcorner.ch/ski (both accessed 9 January 2019).
[6] Digitalization and digital transformation are often used interchangeably as the changes in processes, roles, work methods and business offering caused by the adoption of digital technology in an organization or an organization's operation environment, affecting every aspect of an organization. These aspects include, for example, operational processes, business models, user experience, customer interaction and digital capabilities (Parviainen et al., 2017).

References

Becker, T. (2015) Der Alpenraum muss aufpassen, dass Skifahren nicht zu exklusiv wird. Available at: https://www.ispo.com/people/id_76264296/-aufpassen-dass-skifahren-nicht-zu-exklusiv-wird-.html (accessed 7 March 2018).

Blick.ch (2017) Bilanz der Saas Fee-Crowdfunding-Aktion: War der Hammer-Deal behämmert? Available at: https://www.blick.ch/news/wirtschaft/bilanz-der-saas-fee-crowdfunding-aktion-war-der-hammer-deal-behaemmert-id6526391.html (accessed 9 January 2019).

Chierchia, V. (2016) Winter season hits €10 billion turnover. Available at: www.italy24.ilsole24ore.com/art/business-and-economy/2016-10-24/winter-season-hits-10-billion-turnover--114403.php?uuid=ADcl5DiB (accessed 9 January 2018).

Coffey, H. (2016) Skiing in Switzerland could be about to get a whole lot cheaper with crowd-funded lift passes. Available at: https://www.telegraph.co.uk/travel/ski/news/saas-fee-is-crowdfunding-for-season-ski-list-pass/ (accessed 16 July 2019).

Damm, A., Köberl, J. and Prettenthaler, F. (2014) Does artificial snow production pay under future climate conditions? – A case study for a vulnerable ski area in Austria. *Tourism Management* 43, 8–21. DOI:10.1016/j.tourman.2014.01.009

DiePresse (2013) Österreicher können sich Skifahren nicht mehr leisten. Available at: https://diepresse.com/home/meingeld/verbraucher/1471119/Oesterreicher-koennen-sich-Skifahren-nicht-mehr-leisten (accessed 9 January 2019).

Eiselin, S. (2016) Macht Saas-Fee den Wintertourismus kaputt? Available at: https://www.tagesanzeiger.ch/wirtschaft/unternehmen-und-konjunktur/Macht-SaasFee-den-Wintertourismus-kaputt/story/10056999#overlay (accessed 9 January 2019).

Falk, M. (2010) A dynamic panel data analysis of snow depth and winter tourism. *Tourism Management* 31, 912–924. DOI:10.1016/j.tourman.2009.11.010

Falk, M. (2013) Impact of long-term weather on domestic and foreign winter tourism demand. *International Journal of Tourism Research* 15, 1–17. DOI:10.1002/jtr.865

Falk, M. (2015) The demand for winter sports: empirical evidence for the largest French ski-lift operator. *Tourism Economics* 21(3), 561–580. DOI:10.5367/te.2013.0366

Fettner, F. (2018) Schweiz/Österreich: Liftpasspreise im Vergleich. *Tourismus Wissen – quarterly* 11, 3.

Griffin, J. (2002) *Customer Loyalty: How to Earn It, How to Keep It*. Jossey-Bass, San Francisco, CA.

Haimayer, P. (2016) #digitalisierungimtourismus #winterCARD #SaasFee. Available at: https://www.tp-blog.at/innovationen/digitalisierungimtourismus-wintercard-saasfee (accessed 7 March 2018).

Küttel, K. (2017) Tourismus: Streit um Billig-Skibillette in Andermatt-Sedrun. Available at: https://www.luzernerzeitung.ch/zentralschweiz/tourismus-streit-um-billig-skibillette-in-andermatt-sedrun-ld.92583 (accessed 9 January 2019).

Lütolf, P. (2017) OTC-X Research, Branchenanalyse Bergbahnen – Für die Ausflugsbahnen geht es weiter aufwärts. Available at: https://www.schweizeraktien.net/wp-content/uploads/2017/10/OTC-X-Research_Bergbahnen-2017.pdf (accessed 7 March 2018).

MANOVA (2016) Wertschöpfung durch österreichische Seilbahnen im Winter. Available at: https://www.wko.at/branchen/transport-verkehr/seilbahnen/Wertschoepfung-durch-Oesterreichische-Seilbahnen.pdf (accessed 7 March 2018).

Momondo (2017) Günstig Skifahren: 9 Orte, die den Alpen Konkurrenz machen. Available at: https://www.momondo.at/entdecken/artikel/gunstige-skigebiete (accessed 9 January 2019).

Münchener Zeitungs-Verlag (2016) Höhere Liftpreise: Skifahren wird teurer. Available at: https://www.merkur.de/outdoor/skifahren-wird-teurer-hoehere-liftpreise-durch-hohe-energiekosten-zr-3198653.html (accessed 9 January 2019).

N-TV (2011) Wintersport teurer: Energiekosten treiben Liftpreise. Available at: https://www.n-tv.de/ticker/Reise/Wintersport-teurer-Energiekosten-treiben-Liftpreise-article5102711.html (accessed 9 January 2019).

ORF (2018) Themenmontag: Ski-Schnäppchen in Österreich. Available at: https://tv.orf.at/orf3/stories/2890462 (accessed 9 January 2019).

Parviainen, P. Kääriäninen, J., Tihinen, M. and Teppola, S. (2017) Tackling the digitalization challenge: how to benefit from digitalization in practice. *International Journal of Information Systems and Project Management* 5(1), 63–77. DOI:10.12821/ijispm050104

Pröbstl, U. (2008) Stratege: Klimawandel und Wintersport. *RAUM* 72, 44–49.

Pröbstl-Haider, U. and Mostegl, N. (2016) Skigebiete im Vergleich – Macht Größe alleine schon sexy?. *FdSnow – Fachzeitschrift für den Skisport* 49, 28–35.

Pröbstl-Haider, U., Mostegl, N. and Haider, W. (2017) Panoramablick versus Pistenkilometer – Wichtige Kriterien bei der Buchung eines Skigebietes in Österreich. *Tourismus Wissen – Quarterly* 7, 34–40.

Roth, R. and Siller, H. (2018) Zukunft Wintersport Alpen. *Tourismus Wissen – Quarterly* 11, 16–19.

Roth, R., Schiefer, D., Siller, H.J., Beyer, J., Fehringer, A. *et al.* (2018a) The future of winter travelling in the Alps. Available at: https://www.deinwinterdeinsport.de/files/dwds2015/media/stories/events/FM2016_theAlps2016_ExecutiveSummary_02_03_17.pdf (accessed 7 March 2018).

Roth, R., Krämer, A. and Severins, J. (2018b) *Nationale Grundlagenstudie Wintersport Deutschland 2018.* Stiftung Sicherheit im Skisport e.V., Cologne, Germany.

Saastal Tourismus AG (2016) Saas-Fee launches season pass for just CHF 222. Available at: https://www.saas-fee.ch/en/media/saas-fee-launches-season-pass-for-just-chf-222/ (accessed 9 January 2019).

Schegg, R. and Engeler, M. (2018) Bergbahnen Geschäftsmodelle, Kooperationen und Digitalisierung. Available at: https://www.pwc.ch/de/publications/2018/PwC%20Studie-Bergbahnen-Hoch%20hinaus-DE.pdf (accessed 7 March 2018).

Seilbahn.net (2017) Clever oder verzweifelt? Saas-Fee nimmt beim TFA erstmals Stellung zur WinterCARD-Kampagne. Available at: http://seilbahn.net/sn/index.php?i=60&news=7805&zurueck=1&titel=Clever%20oder%20verzweifelt?%20Saas-Fee%20nimmt%20beim%20TFA%20erstmals%20Stellung%20zur%20WinterCARD-Kampagne (accessed 9 January 2019).

Ship2Shore (2016) Continued growth of the cruise industry in Europe. Available at: http://www.ship2shore.it/en/shipping/continued-growth-of-the-cruise-industry-in-europe_62992.htm (accessed 9 January 2019).

Skinow GmbH (2019) Your price – your ticket – your day. Bestimme deinen eigenen Preis. Buche dein Skiticket jetzt einfach und bequem. Available at: https://skinow.ch (accessed 9 January 2019).

Song, H. and Li, G. (2008) Tourism demand modelling and forecasting: a review of recent research. *Tourism Management* 29(2), 203–220. DOI:10.1016/j.tourman.2007.07.016

DerStandard (2017) Skipässe in Wintersportorten heuer zum Teil massiv teurer. Available at: https://derstandard.at/2000068621903/Skipaesse-in-Wintersportorten-heuer-zum-Teil-massiv-teurer (accessed 9 January 2019).

Statista Inc. (2016) Ranking of the ten ski areas with the highest turnover in France in 2015 (in million euros). Available at: https://www.statista.com/statistics/764865/figure-business-areas-skiable-la-france (accessed 9 January 2019).

Thompson, D. (2012) No business like snow business: the economics of big ski resorts. Available at: https://www.theatlantic.com/business/archive/2012/02/no-business-like-snow-business-the-economics-of-big-ski-resorts/252180 (accessed 7 March 2018).

Ticketcorner AG (2018) SkiArena Andermatt-Sedrun Preisentwicklung. Available at: https://ski.ticketcorner.ch (accessed 22 February 2018).

Tietjen, F. (2015) Herausforderung Nachwuchs – Ralf-Dieter Roth mit Zahlen zum Wintersport. Available at: www.netzathleten.de/lifestyle/reise-freizeit/item/5913-herausforderung-nachwuchs-ralf-dieter-roth-mit-zahlen-zum-wintersport (accessed 7 March 2018).

Töglhofer, C., Eigner, F. and Prettenthaler, F. (2011) Impacts of snow conditions on tourism demand in Austrian ski areas. *Climate Research* 46(1), 1–14. DOI:10.3354/cr00939

Unbehaun, W., Pröbstl, U. and Haider, W. (2008) Trends in winter sport tourism: challenges for the future. *Tourism Review* 63, 36–47. DOI:10.1108/16605370810861035

Vail Resorts, Inc. (2012) Vail Resorts Reports Fiscal 2012 First quarter results and early season indicators. Available at: http://investors.vailresorts.com/news-releases/news-release-details/vail-resorts-reports-fiscal-2012-first-quarter-results-and-early (accessed 7 March 2018).

Van der Elst, R. (2016) Skifahren für 222. – auch bei uns? Available at: https://www.grheute.ch/2016/11/04/skifahren-fur-222-auch-bei-uns (accessed 20 December 2018).

Walliser Bote (2017) 222-Franken-Saisonabo neu auch für die Bergbahnen Hohsaas im Angebot. Available at: https://www.1815.ch/news/wallis/aktuell/saastal (accessed 9 January 2019).

Wild, K. (2017) Das Wunder von Saas-Fee: Der Skipass für 222 Franken hat im Saastal eine Euphorie ausgelöst – und übertüncht ein paar Probleme. Available at: https://www.tagesanzeiger.ch/reisen/standard/Das-Wunder-von-SaasFee/story/20080054 (accessed 9 January 2019).

WKO (2018) Schigebiete in Österreich: Winter am Berg. Aktuelles rund um das Skifahren in Österreich. Available at: https://www.wko.at/branchen/transport-verkehr/seilbahnen/schigebiete-oesterreich.html (accessed 9 January 2019).

Zegg, R. (2018) Bergansichten – the American way. *Internationale Seilbahn – Rundschau* 1/2018, 19.

Zellmann, P. and Mayrhofer, S. (2012) Die Bedeutung einzelner Bereiche für das Leben: Eine Analyse nach Bevölkerungsgruppen. *Forschungstelegramm* 10/2012. Available at: www.freizeitforschung.at/data/forschungsarchiv/2012/110.%20FT%2010-2012_Lebensbereiche.pdf (accessed 7 March 2018).

12 Snow Sports in Schools and Their Importance for Winter Tourism – A Descriptive Study in North Rhine-Westphalia

Luca Mariotti*

Institute of Outdoor Sports and Environmental Science, German Sport University Cologne, Germany

12.1 Introduction

Snow sports are popular activities in Germany. According to a recent study (Roth *et al.*, 2018) that surveyed the winter sports habits of the German population about 60% of Germans practise sport actively. Among those, 63.4% have practised any sort of winter sports at least once. These results suggest that about 27 million people in Germany have been involved in winter sports at least once in their lives. However, there is a general agreement among the media and the winter sports community that snow sports in schools have witnessed a constant decline over the past two decades (Prommer, 2016; Steinlein, 2016). This is one of the reasons that has led to the development of many initiatives aimed at bolstering the winter sports segment of the market.[1] Among these initiatives, for instance, the website www.wintersportschule.de has been developed. Its purpose is to provide school teachers with readily accessible information for organizing winter sports activities. It is believed that by bolstering snow sports early in life, participation in adult life might be positively influenced (see Müllner, 2013).

There are no studies at the moment that might support the assumption of a decline of snow sports in German schools. Similarly, no information could be found about the distribution, or motives for or against winter sports in German schools.

The purpose of this article is to present the first results of a pilot study aimed at identifying the main reason for undertaking or not undertaking a snow sports school trip in Germany. To fulfil this purpose a questionnaire was developed and a small sample of schools in the German state of North Rhine-Westphalia (NRW) was interviewed.

In a first step a short overview will be given about snow sports in the German school system. In a second step the questionnaire and the methods used for this research will be presented followed by the most important results. Finally, the results will be discussed and suggestions for further research and future policies will be given.

---

* E-mail: l.mariotti@dshs-koeln.de

12.2 Snow Sports and the German School System

Müllner (2013) in his article about the importance of skiing in Austria states that one of the key elements in the development of ski sport in Austria as an economic and cultural factor was skiing in schools. According to Müllner (2013) the introduction of snow sports in Austrian schools after the First World War contributed to the establishment of a strong domestic winter tourism. Two key elements of the political debate at that time are considered by Müllner as crucial – and can be still considered relevant at the moment: on the one hand the idea that skiing should be accessible to all and not only to a privileged few; on the other hand, the wish that school teachers should be responsible for teaching skiing to their pupils, a concept that implies a snowball principle and that can enable as many people as possible to learn this sport (Müllner, 2013).

These two key elements can easily be applied to the actual German school system and can be determining factors in the successful development of a healthy snow sports tourism.

In Germany each federal state is responsible for school policies. This being the case each federal state provides the guidelines and the curricula for the implementation of sport in schools. In NRW for example (which is the state where this study had been carried out) snow sports are included in the curriculum under the more general title 'Gleiten, Fahren, Rollen – Rollsport/Bootsport/Wintersport' (MfSW, 2014), an umbrella term that covers not only skiing but also many other disciplines. According to this, on the one hand snow sports are legitimized and to some extent compulsory. On the other hand, there are also other similar sport activities (such as all kinds of watersports and cycling disciplines, inline skating, ice skating, etc.) that could be chosen as an alternative. According to the ministry of school in NRW school trips are a welcome activity and are encouraged. Furthermore, official guidelines are provided by the ministry for organizing school trips. These guidelines state that school trips should be affordable, so that the costs should never be a reason for exclusion (MfSW, 1997). In the interviews conducted by Link (2017) school teachers reported that the main reasons for not organizing snow sports trips are in the first instance the higher costs compared with other activities or destinations. Other reasons are the organizational complexity, the equipment costs and the lack of qualified snow sports teachers to accompany the pupils.

Thus, although encouraged by the ministry, snow sports activities face some obstacles, which even if not yet scientifically surveyed are still perceived as such by the involved actors.

Since no data about the distribution and composition of snow sports trips in Germany are available, the abovementioned issues are based mainly on assumptions rather than reliable sources. In order to overcome this lack of information and in order to provide schools and policy makers with a better instrument to organize and implement snow sports, a questionnaire was developed (see Link, 2017) and subsequently a pilot study was conducted in 2017 in NRW (see Brill, 2018).

12.3 Methods

A first quantitative questionnaire was developed and tested by Bartz (2008), who interviewed 21 schools in NRW that had organized snow sports trips in the previous year. Link (2017) took the questionnaire from Bartz and after conducting qualitative interviews, developed a new version by adding a part addressed to those schools with no winter sports activities at all. The new questionnaire fulfils a dual purpose: on the one hand it attempts to describe the characteristics and the distribution of snow sports in NRW as Bartz did in 2008. This part of the questionnaire is addressed to those schools that have snow sports in their curriculum. On the other hand, it surveys the reasons for not undertaking winter sports activities. To this purpose the second part of the questionnaire aims to highlight the reasons and then provide solutions.

The new questionnaire consists of 46 questions that are divided as follows: 8 general questions addressed to all schools, 25 questions for snow sports-active schools and finally 13 questions for non-snow sports-active schools. The questions are for the most part multiple choice with a few open questions. The final questionnaire was digitalized using the research provider Unipark[2] and submitted to the recipients as a link via e-mail.

The chosen sample comprises 147 schools of all types[3] in three main cities and two counties in NRW.[4] The schools were contacted via e-mail and asked to forward the questionnaire to the sport teacher in charge of organizing sport trips. The questionnaires were submitted to the schools between November and December 2017. A reminder was sent to all school about 2 weeks after the first contact.

The results of Brill's survey (2018) will be presented and discussed in the next section.

12.4 Results

A total of 34 schools, representing 23% of the sample, successfully completed the questionnaire. Among them 21 (61.8%) reported that they organized snow sports trips, whereas 13 did not. For those winter sports-active schools, some interesting findings can be presented. All schools reported that they organized snow sports activities regularly every year and had done so on average for 12.4 years (SD = 6.7). The destination for nearly all schools (95.2%) was the Alps, with Austria as the most popular winter sports destination.

Snow sports were also implemented in the normal school curriculum before the organized trip. More than half (60%) of the snow sports-active schools included ski gymnastics in normal sport lessons. Some schools (25%) went to an indoor ski slope for more practice and about 30% of them included snow sports-related topics in normal school lessons (i.e. in science, politics, etc.).

Beside skiing, which was provided by all snow sports-active schools, snowboarding was the second most common discipline (57.1%), followed by snowshoeing (9.5%) and to a minor extent Nordic skiing and tobogganing (both with <5%). Furthermore, it is interesting to notice that 14.3% of these schools used short skis to facilitate learning. The results are reported in Fig. 12.1.

A total of 65% of the schools relied on a travel agency, whereas the remaining schools did it autonomously. An average cost of €399 per person (SD = 44.5) for an average of 7.5 days was reported. Included in the costs were accommodation, food, transfers and a ski pass. Most of the schools (88.9%) rented the equipment at their destination, with only few schools having their own equipment.

Another interesting aspect is the composition of the classes and the instructor's team. On average there were about 7 school teachers and 1.4 external instructors in the teams, with an average group size of about 9 pupils for each instructor. Among the external instructors 30% were actual sport students and 40.7% were former pupils of the same school, these two groups being the most actively engaged in supporting snow sports trips in schools.

Even more interesting is the part of the questionnaire that deals with those schools that do not offer snow sports at all: there are many arguments against snow sports, but only a few can be defined as being common to all schools. When asked about the most important factors that prevent them from organizing a snow sports trip, 46% responded the high costs and 30% the difficulty of finding qualified instructors.

More than half (53%) of these schools offered alternatives to snow sports trips in the form of adventure education camps or similar activities. When asked to compare snow sports and adventure camps, all of the schools reported perceived higher costs, higher organizational workload for the teachers, higher risk of injuries and the need for more qualified instructors/teachers for winter sports. The results are shown in Fig. 12.2.

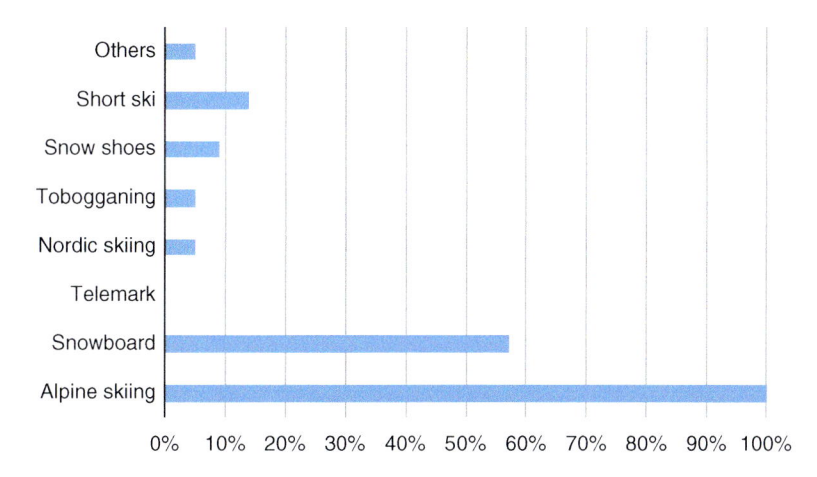

Fig. 12.1. Distribution of snow sport disciplines in winter sport-active schools.

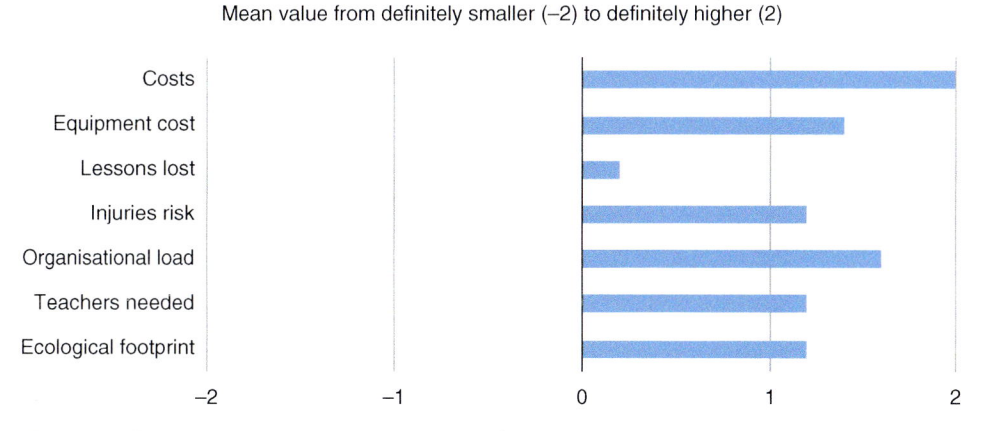

Fig. 12.2. Comparison between snow sports trips and adventure education camps (or similar activities).

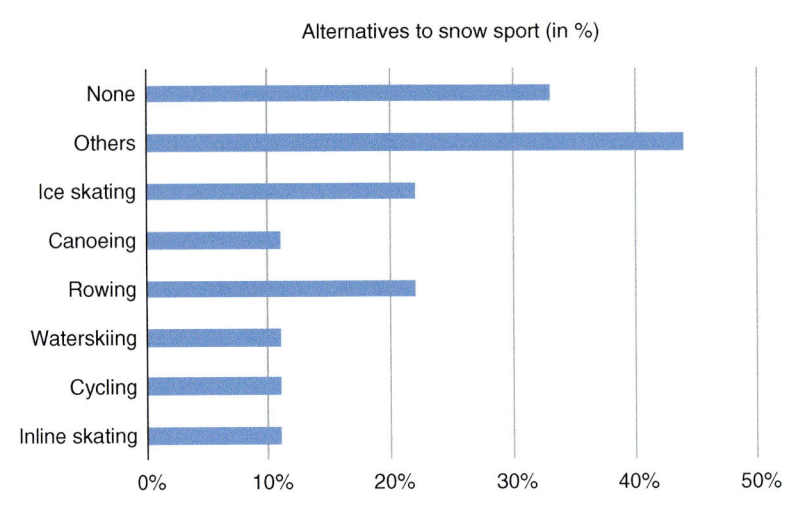

Fig. 12.3. Alternative disciplines to snow sports in non-active schools.

For these reasons ~67% of the schools reported providing alternative sport disciplines to snow sports. So in the field 'Gleiten, Rollen, Fahren – Rollsport/Bootsport/Wintersport' the most common alternatives were water sports, followed by cycling and inline skating. The remaining 33% of the schools were not able to cover this field of activity at all. An overview is given in Fig. 12.3.

The last part of the questionnaire was addressed to all schools (snow sports-active and non-active schools) and asked about the snow sports qualifications of the teachers and future intention to organize snow sports trips.

To the former questions (multiple answers were possible) the majority of schools responded that most of their teachers (70.4%) were qualified as snow sports instructors as part of their university studies and 37% held a commercial licence.

The last question asked whether they were willing to continue to practise snow sports or if they were planning to introduce it in the following years. Among the active schools 80% responded positively, whereas the remaining 20% responded that they were not sure. Even more interesting were the responses of the non-active schools: 20% of them were actively planning to introduce snow sports in the future, 20% were not and the remaining 60% were not sure.

12.5 Discussion

The results suggest the need to tackle the following issues in order to make snow sports in schools more appealing and affordable.

As stated by Müllner (2013) snow sports in school can be considered a milestone in the development and sustainment of successful winter sports tourism. The more children are familiarized with snow sports, the higher is the chance that they will become someday snow sports tourists. The history of winter sports in Austria as depicted by Müllner (2013) is an example. Besides that, snow sports in school are not only a valuable resource for the tourism market, but also have a positive impact on the pupils' socio-psychological and physiological health. For instance, Künzell *et al.*

(2008) provide information about the positive aspects of snow sports for the health, personal skills and social competencies of the pupils. Similarly, Luthe (2007) sees snow sports as an important instrument for developing awareness about the sustainability of winter tourism and the ecological aspects of this sport.

Although this study is not representative of the whole German population, it can be said that more than half of the participating schools include snow sports in their curriculum. Among the remaining schools about 20% were planning a snow sports trip in the next few years. Since no school seems to be about to abandon this practice we can cautiously conclude that the number of schools organizing winter sports trips in this sample is not diminishing as reported in the media (Prommer, 2016; Steinlein, 2016).

However, there is a need for more qualified instructors who may be willing to join school trips. More training courses for instructors should be organized in order to fulfil the demand of the market. As Müllner (2013) stated, with a large base of instructors the snowball effect should achieve the goal of making snow sports accessible to the masses. As a consequence, snow sports might become more attractive later in adult life. Since many of the external instructors that participate in snow sports trips are sport science students or former pupils, more efforts should be made to make training possibilities for those groups more accessible and attractive. Furthermore, most of the teachers qualify as snow sports instructors at university during their studies. This result suggests again the importance of a university curriculum that includes the possibility of qualifying in this field. The role of universities should not be understated and more affordable conditions should be offered to the students perhaps in cooperation with winter sports destinations. As snow sports destinations we should consider not just the German market, but rather have a more global approach to the matter. According to recent studies (e.g. Roth *et al.*, 2018) German winter sports tourists more frequently spend their holidays abroad (Austria, Switzerland, Italy and France) than in Germany. Since more than 40% of the German winter tourists have been on holiday to Austria (Roth *et al.*, 2018, p. 60), Austrian destinations and tourism association should be interested in supporting snow sports in German schools and the qualification of snow sport instructors. If we believe in the assumptions of Müller (2013), a win–win situation would arise and both actors would benefit from this cooperation.

The general perception among the non-participating schools is that snow sports are more expensive, riskier and demand a higher organizational workload for the teachers than other activities. Whether true or not these perceptions are widespread and in many cases they contribute to the discarding of the idea of organizing winter sports trips at an early stage of planning. Something could be done to tackle these obstacles.

First of all, more information should be provided to those interested in organizing snow sports activities about the costs and any subvention programmes. This could be done by providing average costs for example based on representative survey data. These data should be regularly collected from a representative sample with the support of governmental organizations. Only in this way can real and actual information not based on simple assumptions be provided to the public. Unfortunately, at the moment no official statistics can be found.

Second, school teachers should be helped with the organization. In 2016 a website was developed for this purpose. The website www.wintersportschule.de[5] provides much important information for the organization of a winter sports trip, including background information about the positive aspects of snow sports for the health, personal skills and social competencies of the pupils, legal aspects, documents and even tips for planning snow sports lessons. However, more can be done. Since most of the winter sports-active schools use specialized travel agencies, more easily accessible information could be made available by providing an online platform where travel agencies are able to promote their offers. This would reduce the searching time and surely contribute to reducing the organizational workload of the school teachers.

12.6 Conclusions

This pilot study has provided an interesting insight in a very real and discussed, but yet unknown, field of research. According to the results shown above, snow sports are still very present in school sport although many schools might need more support, skilled teachers and accessible information. However, the results have unfortunately many limitations. Due to the small sample size the results are far from representative. The low participation rate might be due to two interconnected issues. On the one hand the questionnaires were sent to the official school e-mail addresses, which in most cases are managed by school secretaries and not directly to sports teachers. We assume that in many cases, and although a remainder was sent, many emails were not forwarded or landed in spam folders. On the other hand, there is a general agreement in the academic community that schools are overloaded with requests to participate in scientific studies. This might be also a reason for the reluctance to participate in this study. Another criticism of the representativeness is that it is likely that those who participated were schools (or sport teachers) that are personally interested in snow sports.

All in all, the questionnaire has provided interesting information about the topic and should be used for a representative study all over Germany. On the basis of reliable information, new policies and interventions can be planned and thus help to preserve the future of snow sports in schools.

Notes

[1] See for instance the campaign 'Dein Winter, dein Sport' started in 2015. Available at: https://www.deinwinterdeinsport.de (accessed 29 January 2019).
[2] Unipark is an online survey software from Questback. More information is available at: www.unipark.com (accessed 29 January 2019).
[3] The interviewed school types were: Gymnasium, Realschule, Gesamtschule, Hauptschule and Berufsschule.
[4] The surveyed cities are: Duisburg, Oberhausen and Krefeld. The two surveyed counties are: Kleve and Wesel.
[5] For more information, visit the website www.wintersportschule.de (accessed 29 January).

References

Bartz, C. (2008) Schneesport an Schulen im Ruhrgebiet. Bachelor's Thesis. Ruhr-Universität Bochum, Bochum, Germany.
Brill, C. (2018) Deskriptive Grundlagenforschung zur Untersuchung der Motive für und gegen die Durchführung einer Schneesportfahrt in der Schule. Master's Thesis. Deutsche Sporthochschule Köln, Cologne, Germany.

Künzell, S., Szymanski, B. and Theis, R. (2008) Warum Schneesport unterrichten? In: Bach, I. (ed.) *Skilauf und Snowboard in Lehre und Forschung*. Czwalina, Hamburg, Germany, pp. 9–19.

Link, M. (2017) Entwicklung eines Fragebogens zur Untersuchung von Motiven für und gegen die Durchführung einer Schneesportfahrt in der Schule. Master's Thesis. Deutsche Sporthochschule Köln, Cologne, Germany.

Luthe, T. (2007) *Schneesport und Bildung für eine nachhaltige Entwicklung*. DSV/SIS Umweltreihe, Band 9. Stiftung Sicherheit im Skisport/DSV-Umweltbeirat, Planegg, Germany.

MfSW – Ministerium für Schule und Weiterbildung des Landes NRW (1997) Richtlinie für Schulfahrten. Available at: https://www.schulministerium.nrw.de/docs/Recht/Schulrecht/Schulfahrten/Fragen-und-Antworten/Richtlinien-fuer-Schulfahrten.pdf (accessed 6 July 2018).

MfSW – Ministerium für Schule und Weiterbildung des Landes NRW (2014) Rahmenvorgaben für den Schulsport Nordrhein-Westfalen. Available at: https://www.schulentwicklung.nrw.de/lehrplaene/upload/klp_SI/HS/sp/Rahmenvorgaben_Schulsport_Endfassung.pdf (accessed 6 July 2018).

Müllner, R. (2013) The importance of skiing in Austria. *The International Journal of the History of Sport* 30(6), 659–673.

Prommer, F. (2016) Schulen verzichten immer öfter auf Skilager. Available at: https://www.merkur.de/bayern/schulen-verzichten-immer-oefter-auf-skilager-7146754.html (accessed 6 July 2018).

Roth, R., Krämer, A. and Severines, J. (2018) Zweite Nationale Grundlagestudie Wintersport Deutschland 2018. Schriftenreihe SIS, Planegg, Germany.

Steinlein, E. (2016) Die Schneelose Generation. Available at: https://www.zeit.de/entdecken/reisen/2015-12/skilager-uebernachtung-umwelt-kosten (accessed 6 July 2018).

13 The Impact of Commercial Snowmobile Guiding on Local Communities

Iain Stewart-Patterson

Thompson Rivers University, Kamloops, BC, Canada

13.1 Introduction

Many mountain towns in British Columbia are filled with snowmobilers for much of the winter season. A growing element is the availability of snowmobile guiding operations that offer more than just 'cabin tours'. Demand for untouched powder snow is driving the need for all-inclusive snowmobile tour operations that employ highly skilled guides who possess not only intimate localized terrain knowledge, but also excellent avalanche risk management skills and exceptional client care.

13.2 Literature Review

Commercial operators will benefit from knowing what their potential clients are looking for so that meaningful experiences can be constructed. The motivation of skilled riders to engage in mountain snowmobiling may be based in the concept of rush – the combination of a flow experience with the thrill of adrenaline – risk-based activity. Buckley (2012) defines rush as the excitement that a highly skilled athlete experiences when a difficult skill is performed well. Conditions are optimal and there is an inherent level of risk associated with the activity. It all comes together. Participants want to find the optimal balance of rush and risk. Participants experience flow (Csikszentmihalyi and Csikszentmihalyi, 1990) in achieving a peak experience (Maslow, 1968). This is described as a form of flow experienced by someone with some level of expertise. It is not just a thrill, or adrenaline-based experience that is not related to expertise.

Levels of acceptable risk need to be negotiated. Entry-level clients typically want the perception of risk without the reality of potential injury or death, whereas clients with advanced skills may be motivated by the rush experience (Buckley, 2012). It can be difficult to describe rush to someone who has not experienced it (Williams and Soutar, 2009).

Exploring the push and pull motivation of a mountain snowmobiler may provide greater understanding as to the growth of mountain snowmobile guiding. The push motivation for a mountain snowmobiler is likely stimulated by a desire for challenge and the need for arousal (Caber and Albayrak, 2016). The pull motivation that brings

---

[1] E-mail: spatterson@tru.ca

Fig. 13.1. Snowmobiling in fresh powder snow. (Photograph courtesy of Iain Stewart-Patterson.)

a snowmobile tourist to British Columbian mountain towns such as Revelstoke or Golden includes the copious amounts of dry powder snow (see Fig. 13.1) and an infrastructure within the regions that supports access to terrain.

13.2.1 Snowmobile industry growth

Previous economic impact studies have attempted to measure the spending habits of recreational snowmobilers. This has included: road travel, food, alcohol, accommodation, fuel, repairs, equipment and trail fees. The most recent study in North America is a 2018 Utah study. In this study, Utah residents who owned registered snowmobiles were surveyed as to their frequency of trips and the amount that they spent on snowmobile activities. Snowmobile registration is required by Utah state law. Of the owners of the 22,803 registered snowmobiles, 13% responded to the survey. The study did not include out-of-state residents. Guide services were lumped in with snowmobile rentals and tour packages. Only 2% of the typical cost of day trips (representing 79% of the total trips) was spent on guide services and rentals. On overnight trips (representing 21% of the total trips), which were on average 3 days long, only 1% was spent on guide services and rentals. There were many limitations to this study. Out-of-state tourism, both inbound and outbound, was not included. In addition, the assumption was made that all snowmobiles would be registered, as per the legal requirements. Total value of the economic impact including direct effects, indirect effects and induced effects was estimated to be US$138 million.

Table 13.1. Spending per person per day – Revelstoke.

	CA$ spent
Accommodation	114.89
Food and beverage	92.36
Retail shopping	34.90
Snowmobile costs	102.81
Entertainment	67.29
Miscellaneous	63.06
Total	444.31

A recent study conducted for the Canadian Council of Snowmobile Organizations estimated a nation-wide contribution of 41,000 jobs and CA$8 billion of snowmobile-related economic activity in 2015 (Harry Cummings & Associates, 2016). However, the data for British Columbia were based on a 2004 study focused on the potential impact of licensing and registration of off-road vehicles. Adjustments were made to account for the 12% increase in population in BC, but no adjustments were made to account for the increase in popularity of snowmobiling, or the increase in snowmobile tourism due to a massive influx of Albertan snowmobilers. The direct economic impact in BC was estimated at $200 million, with the total economic activity at $398 million. The BC Snowmobile Federation commissioned a new study to be completed in 2018.

The British Columbia Snowmobile Federation (BCSF) was founded in 1965 as a volunteer-driven non-profit organization. The federation's objectives are stated as 'dedicated to safety, the growth of the sport, protection of the environment and securing access to public lands for all' (British Columbia Snowmobile Federation, 2018). By 2018, the BCSF was the voice for British Columbian snowmobilers, representing the interests of its 60 clubs and 6993 members. A conservative estimate puts only 10% of BC snowmobilers as club members.

A recent economic impact study produced by the Revelstoke Snowmobile Club (RSC) suggests that snowmobile tourism generates about $11 million per year for the local economy, with a per person per day spend of $444.31 (see Table 13.1) (Revelstoke Snowmobile Club, 2011).

The RSC lists 11 riding areas on its webpage. Two of the areas have groomed access trails (Boulder and Frisby). Trail passes are collected and accurate rider numbers are recorded. In 1990–1991, just over 2000 riders used the Boulder and Frisby staging areas (Streeter, 2002). This grew to 12,000 riders by 2001–2002. From 2015–2018, the RSC has recorded about 30,000 rider visits per year. Just over 50% of the riders came from Alberta and Saskatchewan, whereas locals represented only 17% of the recorded visits.

13.3 Why Hire a Guide?

A downside of the increasingly popular snowmobile destinations like Revelstoke is that the most well known and easily accessible areas such as Boulder and Frisby become quickly tracked out. A snowmobile tourist is likely lacking the local knowledge to find

Fig. 13.2. Untouched powder is attractive to snowmobilers, but without local knowledge often hard to find. (Photograph courtesy of Iain Stewart-Patterson.)

the secret stashes of untouched powder (see Fig. 13.2). The evolving solution is to hire a guide with local knowledge. The challenge is to find a guide who can safely lead a tourist in complex mountainous terrain complicated by an ever-changing avalanche hazard.

As of June 2018, 24 snowmobile guiding and tour companies had web profiles in British Columbia. Some of these companies have their own tenures, some have joint use agreements with tenure holders, while others do not have tenures. Anecdotal evidence suggests that there are many more sole proprietor businesses that operate by word of mouth. It is likely that these smaller operators do not have tenures and are conducting business on the fringe of legitimacy.

Snowmobile guiding operations offer three distinct types of experiences:

- 'Cabin tours' use groomed trails to access treeline locations. Many of the operators have cabins that are used for warming up and/or eating lunch. Often a trail snowmobile is used that has seating for two people. Two guides can manage a group size of up to 10–12 guests. The goal of the tour is to experience winter. Due to the higher guide to guest ratio, these tours often have a better profit margin for the operators. The guides need intermediate-level technical snowmobile skills and group management skills.
- Backcountry tours go beyond the groomed access trails into ungroomed avalanche terrain. Mountain snowmobiles are used. A single guide will manage a group of up to six guests. The goal of the tour is to build snowmobile skills. The guides need extensive avalanche terrain management skills.
- Avalanche skills training courses (AST).

An examination of the guiding companies' websites found the following statements used to attract guests.

Would you like to find the deepest pockets of powder right now? Would you like to get to the best spots in the sledding area without having to guess your way around where they are?

Stop wasting fuel and daylight searching for Powder. Allow our highly trained, knowledgeable and certified guide lead you to the best snow and terrain imaginable. Our guides will teach you back-country safety and riding tips that will allow you to get to that next level and ride another day.

We know the secret, back areas of our sledding playground. We will show you around the sledding paradise – on your timeline! We promise to find you fresh snow EVERY TIME – as long as you can ride!

We guarantee you won't be bored!!

Let our guides show you the best terrain in a safe environment.

Like we said; if you can handle it, we'll ride it.

AST is a curriculum that has been developed by Avalanche Canada. Two levels are offered. Level 1 is a 2-day course ($350) and Level 2 is a 4–5-day course ($700). Level 1 uses simple mountainous terrain, while Level 2 will move into more complex terrain. The instructor skill set and avalanche certification needs to be correspondingly higher for the Level 2 course. The curriculum is delivered across Canada, but the majority of courses are offered in the mountainous regions of BC and Alberta. An average of 1250 snowmobilers per year have taken courses over the past 3 years. The bulk of these courses have been the 2-day Level 1 course. This generates a conservative estimate of $475,000. Although there are 37 companies listed with Avalanche Canada as offering avalanche training for snowmobilers, the bulk of the training courses are delivered by five or six providers.

13.4 Challenges for Snowmobile Guiding Operations

13.4.1 Land tenure

The greatest challenge for commercial snowmobile operations is access to terrain. The British Columbia government has an Adventure Tourism – Land Use Operational Policy that defines how commercial operators will access land. The application process for a tenure is extensive. The policy includes the obligation to consult with Aboriginal groups who have rights and title to the applicable area. A key consideration for new tenure applications is that most of the mountainous land base in southern British Columbia has existing winter tenure holders. Just over 106,000 km^2 are under tenure agreements. Most of these tenures are helicopter ski operations. To overlap on an existing tenure holder, new applicants must demonstrate the compatibility of the two business models. Mountain snowmobiling is not a compatible activity with heli skiing. If the proposed activity has the potential to negatively impact the existing activity, then a joint use agreement must be negotiated. The only joint use agreements in place are for valley bottom snowmobile trails.

For example, there are nine snowmobile tenure holders in the Whistler region with tenures ranging in size from 24 km^2 up to 703 km^2. Some of these tenures are overlapping with each other. In contrast, the two helicopter ski operations in the area have tenures in the range of 2700–2800 km^2 and they are exclusive.

13.4.2 Conflict with other user groups

Snowmobile guiding operations seek to provide high-quality wilderness experiences, with the emphasis on finding untracked snow. As commercial snowmobile operators use the same terrain as recreational snowmobilers, 'getting to the goods' first is an ongoing battle. Guiding operations have a limited number of secret spots to take their guests. Inherent within the problem is that today's guest may become tomorrow's competition.

The three primary backcountry user groups are snowmobiling, ski touring and mechanized skiing (heli skiing and cat skiing). In the quest for untracked powder, snowmobiling is the dominant force within the 'hierarchy of conflict' among winter backcountry users (Cooper, 1995). Overlapping or joint use of terrain has been recognized to place a disproportionate negative impact on non-motorized users, whereas the reverse is not true (Erlandson, 2008). When skiers and snowmobilers meet, the conflict is often perceived as one-sided, as the skiers are not only seeking fresh snow, but also a tranquil, natural setting (Gilden, 2001). Ski touring is potentially the most disadvantaged usage (Webster, 2013), but cat skiing is also at a potential disadvantage, as the groomed access roads created by the snowcats are also a beautiful 'paved' highway for snowmobiles.

In the past, helicopter skiing had the greatest advantage. Some helicopter ski terrain was accessible by snowmobile, but large areas were retained for exclusive use, simply due to the difficulty of access. However, current and evolving snowmobile technology has virtually eliminated this advantage. Expert mountain snowmobilers on state-of-the-art machines can access most of the terrain used by helicopter ski operations. Cat ski operations represent low hanging fruit as groomed cat roads provide easy access to alpine bowls. Due to speed of access, snowmobilers can easily beat ski tourers to untracked snow. Steep trees, once the exclusive domain of skiers, are now being accessed by snow bikes. An emerging trend is the use of snowmobiles by ski tourers (sled skiing) to access terrain more quickly and to access terrain further from the road. Increasing numbers of mountain snowmobilers have exacerbated the conflicts, in the never-ending quest for untracked snow. Informal agreements to share or restrict user groups to specific areas have been based on voluntary compliance. The major hurdle to this is communication of these agreements to all users as many areas experience large influxes of non-local users (Erlandson, 2008). In a study of adventure tourism operations offering ski programmes, 100% of guests complained of a reduction in their satisfaction and the quality of their experience due to interactions with snowmobiles (Webster, 2013). Possible effective strategies to manage conflict include education, zoning and enforcement.

13.4.3 Cariboo closures

One of the greatest challenges for both recreational and commercial snowmobiling is the loss of areas that are closed due to the provincial caribou recovery management plans. Mountain caribou have been identified as a threatened species in Canada (Simpson and Terry, 2000). Mountain snowmobiling has been identified as a contributor to the ease of access for predators such as wolves (Apps et al., 2013). Areas that are closed to snowmobiling rely largely on voluntary compliance from the snowmobile community. Closures are generally well respected, however snowmobile tourists may be unaware of or unwilling to comply with closures resulting in negative public perception of snowmobilers and increased area closures enforced by government compliance officers.

13.4.4 Availability of guides

The industry currently lacks a unified guide training and certification process. This has been identified as a major shortcoming. The British Columbia Commercial Snowmobile Operators Association (BCCSOA) was created in 2005 'to unify, represent and support member owners and operators in the areas of marketing, operations, government regulations and responsible tourism (including safety and the environment)'. Attempts were made to build a training and certification stream, but never came to fruition. As of June 2018 there were 12 member companies listed on the BCCSOA website.

The objectives of the BCCSOA are:

- To promote and enhance professional commercial snowmobiling, to promote our code of ethics and standards in safety operating methods, procedures and protocol for the industry.
- To act as environment stewards and promote backcountry ethics and awareness within the commercial snowmobile industry, to represent the industry as a collective voice in co-operation with government and non-government agencies.
- To strengthen co-operation and promote working relations between its members and sponsors, to act as a governing body to ensure that all members of the association conduct themselves within the standards set out by the association.

As of January 2018, efforts were underway to create a new certifying association. Currently the only requirements to become a snowmobile guide are certification as a Canadian Avalanche Association Level 1, and an 80-h first aid certification.

The exam criteria for a snowmobile guide certification would include:

- Risk management – hazard recognition and analysis, minimization of risk, emergency response.
- Wildlife Management – closures.
- Guest management – client care, finding untracked snow.
- Technical systems – rescue, evacuation, snowmobile field repair.
- Professionalism – equipment, planning, preparation.
- Riding skills.
- Terrain assessment – navigation, route selection, route finding.
- Application – use of the appropriate technique.
- Mountain sense – judgement, decision making, error correction.

The current certifications of first aid and CAA Avalanche Level 1 would be the prerequisites to entry into the guide certification process. CAA Level 2 Avalanche Training would be required for lead guides. The barriers to higher levels of CAA avalanche training are a lack of mentors and opportunities for operational experience.

13.5 Opportunities

There are numerous opportunities for the growth and development of commercial snowmobile guiding in British Columbia. The growth in recreational numbers has led to an increase in the demand for guides. Recreational snowmobilers (see Fig. 13.3) seeking untracked powder are becoming increasingly challenged to find areas that have fewer riders. This has led to an increased willingness to pay for professional services. It is no longer good enough to rely on a friend of a friend's local knowledge. These professional guides do far more than just find the untracked snow. They are increasingly adept at hazard management and avalanche terrain selection. Not only are guided groups less likely to have an accident, the professionally trained guides have skills in emergency management and incident response.

As the demand for professional guiding services rises, so does the willingness to pay. This leads to increasing wages for guides with higher levels of training and certification. Snowmobile guiding operations are beginning to recognize that full service operations which provide guiding, food, accommodation and equipment have the greatest financial opportunities. The 2018–2019 costs of a 5-day all-inclusive backcountry snowmobile excursion is approximately $4500. This compares favourably to a 5-day heli ski trip at $5575 and a 4-day cat ski trip at $4950. Guided snowmobile trips are coming of age.

Fig. 13.3. Snowmobiler heading home at the end of the day. (Photograph courtesy of Iain Stewart-Patterson.)

13.6 Conclusions

Commercial snowmobile guiding is at a crux transition in its evolution into long-term viability as a contributor to local economies. Recreational mountain snowmobiling is growing. The demand is placing strains on small mountain towns to provide both infrastructure and commercial guiding. The absence of snowmobile guiding certification coupled with the challenges in securing land tenure for a commercial operation are channelling guests toward uncertified, unlicensed and uninsured guides.

References

Apps, C.D., McLellan, B.N., Kinley, T.A., Serrouya, R., Seip, D.R. and Wittmer, H.U. (2013) Spatial factors related to mortality and population decline of endangered mountain caribou. *Journal of Wildlife Management* 77(7), 1409–1419. DOI:10.1002/jwmg.601

British Columbia Snowmobile Federation. (2018) History of the BCSF. Available at: https://www.bcsf.org/cpages/history (accessed 29 January 2019).

Buckley, R. (2012) Rush as a key motivation in skilled adventure tourism: resolving the risk recreation paradox. *Tourism Management* 33(4), 961–970. DOI:10.1016/j.tourman.2011.10.002

Caber, M. and Albayrak, T. (2016) Push or pull? Identifying rock climbing tourists' motivations. *Tourism Management* 55, 74–84. DOI:10.1016/j.tourman.2016.02.003

Cooper, L.A. (1995) Evaluating the susceptibility to conflict of outdoor recreation activities: a case study of backcountry skiing, helicopter skiing and snowmobiling in the Revelstoke region of British Columbia. Master's Thesis, University of British Columbia, Vancouver, Canada.

Csikszentmihalyi, M. and Csikszentmihalyi, I.S. (1990) Adventure and the flow experience. In: Miles, J.C. and Priest, S. (eds) *Adventure Education*. Venture Publishing, State College, PA, pp. 149–156.

Erlandson, G. (2008) Recommendations for the management of winter backcountry recreation in the Lillooet River drainage and the sea-to-sky LRMP area. Victoria, BC, Canada. Available at: https://www.ubc-voc.com/mediawiki/images/c/c4/Erlandson_Report.pdf (accessed 29 January 2019).

Gilden, J. (2001) *Solitude, Silence and 'The Freedom to Ride': Real and Perceived Conflicts in Winter Recreation at Mount St. Helens*. Institute for Culture and Ecology, Portland, OR.

Harry Cummings & Associates (2016) The economic impact of snowmobiling in Canada. Available at: www.ccso-ccom.ca/en/homepage (accessed 29 January 2019).

Maslow, A.H. (1968) *Towards a Psychology of Being*, 2nd edn. Van Nostrand, New York.

Revelstoke Snowmobile Club (2011) Revelstoke Snowmobiling Survey 2011. Revelstoke, BC, Canada.

Simpson, K. and Terry, E.L. (2000) Impacts of backcountry recreation activities on mountain caribou: management concerns, interim management guidelines and research needs. Ministry of Environment, Lands and Parks – Wildlife Branch, Victoria, BC, Canada.

Streeter, L. (2002) Revelstoke snowmobile strategy. Available at: http://cmiae.org/wp-content/uploads/reference142.doc (accessed 29 January 2019).

Webster, D. (2013) Adventure tourism operators and snowmobilers: managing interactions. Master's Thesis, Royal Roads University, Victoria, BC, Canada.

Williams, P. and Soutar, G.N. (2009) Value, satisfaction and behavioral intentions in a tourism context. *Annals of Tourism Research* 36(3), 413–438. DOI:10.1016/j.annals.2009.02.002

14 Sustainable Winter and Summer Mountain Tourism Destinations: Idealism or Possible Reality? The Perception of the Millennial Generation Regarding Achieving Success of Sustainability of Whistler, BC, Canada

Ilse van Ipenburg and Harold Richins*

Faculty of Adventure, Culinary Arts and Tourism, Thompson Rivers University, Kamloops, BC, Canada

14.1 Introduction and Literature Review

In contemporary society, sustainability is a much-discussed topic. Especially in the past two decades, literature has expounded upon tourism in mountain areas and the importance of a sustainable focus (Price and Kim, 1999; Gill, 2000; Scott and Del Matto, 2008; Hudson and Hudson, 2016; Hull and Richins, 2016).

Though sustainability might, according to Slaper and Hall (2011), have gained more importance within the tourism sector, the negative impacts are still increasing. This could be explained by the paradox that comes with sustainable development, which is especially applicable for destinations. Namely, to be able to control the market and thus gain a competitive advantage, destinations are forced to continue implementing innovative aspects and, in most cases, increasing their capacity (Price and Kim, 1999; Gill, 2000; Williams and Ponsford, 2008).

Previously, such developments have allowed environmental degradations to certain (unacceptable) levels, seen primarily as 'side-effects', and these have only resulted in sustainability measures when resources upon which the destination was dependent tended to diminish (Arrow *et al.*, 1995). A shift towards long-term planning has therefore allowed destinations to consider possible impacts, thus often resulting in more careful planning. This is especially applicable on the environmental side, as the finiteness of natural resources has been recognized and acknowledged (Gill, 2000; Williams and Ponsford, 2008; George-Marcelpoil and François, 2016).

Over the years, the importance of sustainable mountain development has increased and herewith, policies slowly established. In addition to broader levels of sustainability

---

* E-mail: hrichins@tru.ca

approaches, Del Matto and Scott (2009) attempted to describe sustainability practices on a more specific level: the mountain ski resort areas. The 'ideal' state of mountain destinations was moreover described by principles proposed by Gibson *et al.* (2006), which are referred to as the 'Gibson's principles'. These principles, including inter alia limits to growth, could, according to the authors, provide a viable example of a framework with effective guidelines (Del Matto and Scott, 2009).

Involving the local community in longer-term strategies and plans is a crucial factor towards success of destination sustainability; reciprocal understanding and respect between the tourist and the local community is key for a good relationship and cooperation with the tourism industry and the local community (George *et al.*, 2002; Fraser *et al.*, 2005; Beritelli *et al.*, 2007; Murphy, 2008; Wisansing, n.d.). Furthermore, mountain policies, planning and development strategies are most efficient when specified on a local level; meeting the local needs and based on the availability and capacity of local resources (Murphy, 1987; Price and Kim, 1999; Del Matto and Scott, 2009; Hull and Richins, 2016; Kogler and Boksberger, 2016).

The community of Whistler (see Fig. 14.1), which is home to Whistler Blackcomb the largest ski resort in Canada, is located in British Columbia, and developed an Integrated Comprehensive Sustainability Plan, the 'Whistler 2020 plan', which was based on community involvement with a focus on sustainable practices within the resort (Gill, 2000; Gill and Williams, 2011). The Resort Municipality of Whistler (RMOW), has introduced a shift from primarily growth management towards this

Fig. 14.1. Community of Whistler. (Photograph courtesy of Ilse van Ipenburg.)

Whistler 2020 plan, as the increasing need for community involvement as well as sustainability practices in Whistler was identified and responded to (Gill, 2000; Gill and Williams, 2011). The sustainability practices of Whistler are highly monitored, results are examined, evaluated and turned into specific recommendations and actions to further improve and implement (Gill and Williams, 2011). With the purchase of Whistler Blackcomb mountain operations by the large corporation Vail Resorts, Inc. in 2016 (Lee, 2016), these sustainability practices have had some scrutiny and further consideration and may have a long-term influence on the Whistler Resort Municipality.

In contrast to Whistler, mountain destinations in the European Alps seem to struggle with developing sustainable, innovative models (George-Marcelpoil and François, 2016; Hudson and Hudson, 2016; Zehrer *et al.*, 2016). It is moreover remarkable that despite the importance of community involvement in tourism planning, as has been researched and acknowledged by multiple authors (Murphy, 1987; Gill, 2000; George *et al.*, 2002; Hall, 2008; Gill and Williams, 2011; Wisansing, n.d.), due to a different structure only a few European alpine destinations (e.g. Serfaus-Fis-Ladis in Austria and Laax, Switzerland) involve communities in their tourism planning (Beritelli *et al.*, 2007; Zehrer *et al.*, 2016).

Taking into consideration the apparent challenges for sustainable mountain development, the aim of the study in this chapter is to explore whether mountain tourism destinations can be fully sustainable, or if sustainability within the destinations remains more of an idealized state. The study focused on the development of Whistler by exploring whether its sustainable practices could serve as a potential framework for future implementations of practices within other destinations, in particular the European Alps.

14.1.1 The millennial generation

A critical analysis of Whistler's development model has led to the aspect of consumer interest and behaviour, being of significant value to a mountain destination, with an influence on the success of sustainability performances (Sheth *et al.*, 2010). For this study, the millennial generation, roughly born in 1980 and after, was a further area of emphasis, since this generation is broadly described as the most educated generation in sustainability, while also showing characteristics such as impatience and self-focus (Sinek, 2016). Nevertheless, this generation is, according to Ng *et al.* (2010), willing to pay for 'greener products' in the interest of the environment. However, the question is whether they also act accordingly.

Both Gaudelli (2009) and Hanks *et al.* (2008) argue that, despite the knowledge and awareness of the contemporary issues that exist around the debate of sustainability, the millennial generation does not seem to translate its awareness into more sustainable behaviour. Therefore, it can be argued that this generation is aware of the 'why', but unsure of the 'how' (Hanks *et al.*, 2008; Gaudelli, 2009; Ng *et al.*, 2010). What is more, since the millennial generation is very sensitive to innovations and trends, products or services are likely to lose value quickly (Hanks *et al.*, 2008). The price tag of a product or service is of importance, and even though millennials indicate a willingness to pay for products contributing to a more sustainable future, millennials also want instant gratification (Gaudelli, 2009).

Sustainability is a process that cannot be obtained from one day to another; it requires patience, a characteristic that is not necessarily associated with this generation

(Hanks *et al.*, 2008; Gaudelli, 2009; Ng *et al.*, 2010; Sinek, 2016). Therefore, one of the probable reasons the millennial generation is not (yet) leading the 'green movement' is due to the lack of instant gratification. In addition, since they do not notice the impact of their behaviour on the environment, they argue their involvement and contributions will not make a difference (Gaudelli, 2009).

14.1.2 Whistler: Winter and summer mountain destination resort

The destination of focus for this study, the mountain resort destination Whistler, is regarded as having a competitive advantage in comparison with other Canadian ski resorts (Hudson *et al.*, 2010). Having measured the destination competitiveness of Canadian ski resorts using the Destination Competitiveness Model of Crouch and Ritchie (1999) (see Fig. 14.2), it is not surprising that Whistler was ranked as the top destination, since key indicators of this model have been implemented in the Whistler 2020 plan. However, being ranked as a top destination does not necessarily mean that the destination is doing perfectly well, especially from a sustainability best-practice standpoint (Del Matto and Scott, 2009; Hudson *et al.*, 2010).

In consideration of the context in which Whistler has transitioned from a small summer recreation area with difficult access during non-summer periods, through its early and significant development stages, to the mega winter and summer resort destination and community we see today. Table 14.1 provides a general timeline of significant activities and outcomes over close to a 70-year period.

With the implementation of the Whistler 2020 plan, Whistler commits its focus to 'move towards a sustainable future' and encompasses a long-term vision and a strategic plan as to how its vision can be achieved (Resort Municipality of Whistler, Whistler 2020, 2007). Tasks and responsibilities regarding planning and development have been clearly defined, and additionally, the Whistler 2020 plan has served as a decision making guide in Whistler as it has been 'providing a framework for all involved individuals and organisations for aligning their activities with the resort community's shared vision, strategies and sustainability objectives' (Resort Municipality of Whistler, 2007, p. 3). This plan has been established in response to a need for more community involvement in the planning and development process, as well as the urge for a shift from growth management towards sustainable development (Gill, 2000; Gill and Williams, 2011).

When critically analysing the Whistler 2020 plan, a crucial aspect of sustainability seems to not be included in the plan; namely consumer (visitor) interest and behaviour. Despite Whistler stressing the importance of sustainability practices, a destination cannot be regarded as fully sustainable if the visitor, being a great part in the entire picture, is not acting in a sustainable way (Weaver and Lawton, 1999; Sheth *et al.*, 2010). The visitor is regarded to have a significant impact on a destination's sustainability performance as certain behaviours could lead to unsustainable practices.

14.1.3 Destination sustainability in Europe

Although a direct comparison is very challenging, it may be worth investigating whether Whistler's framework could serve as an example for European alpine destinations.

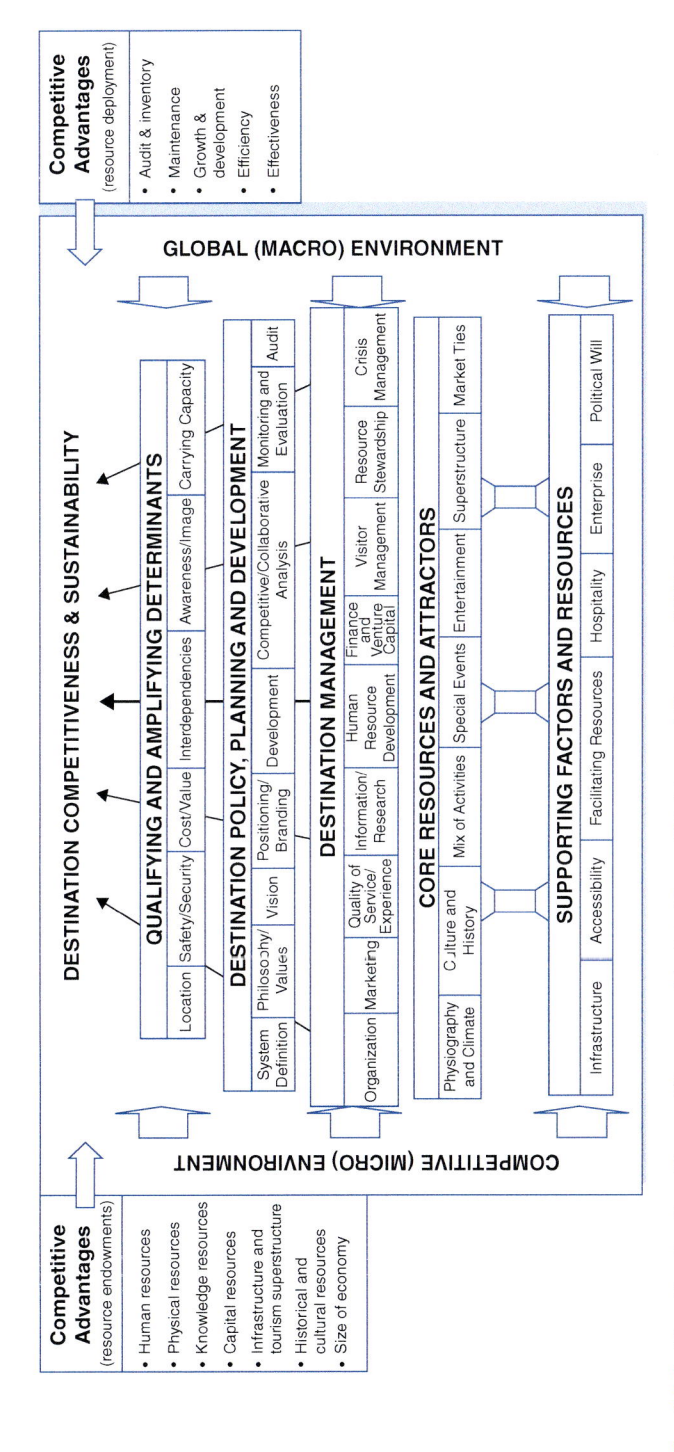

Fig. 14.2. The Destination Competitiveness Model. (From Ritchie and Crouch, 2003.)

Table 14.1. The development story of Whistler as a winter and summer mountain destination. (From Gill and Williams, 2011; International Olympic Committee, 2014; Resort Municipality of Whistler, 2012, n.d.; Vail Resorts, Inc., 2016.)

Whistler as summer resort	Early 1950s	Whistler was considered a local summer resort, before roads were carved to help access during the winter season
Potential host of 1968 Olympics	Early 1960s	Garibaldi Olympic Development Association formed with the intention to develop Whistler as a site to host the Olympic Winter Games of 1968
Whistler opens	1966	Whistler officially opened for skiing
Town centre and municipality formed	1970s	Involved the construction of a town centre, now known as Whistler Village and development of Resort Municipality of Whistler
Second mountain opened (Blackcomb)	1980	Blackcomb mountain opened for skiing, and with expansion of terrain Whistler became the largest and number one ski resort of North America
Development conflicts	1990s	Challenges with development and growth pressures and conflicting community needs
Community plan	1990s+	Official Community Plan (OCP), containing policies regarding land use, development and protection of the natural and community environments
Pro-development and growth management	1996	Pro-community council was introduced together with the adoption of a growth management governance system
Whistler and Blackcomb mountain merged	1997	Whistler and Blackcomb mountain merged under Intrawest Corporation, and summer activities were expanded
Olympic bid	2000s	Whistler shortlisted for hosting the Olympic Winter Games of 2010
Growth challenges	2000s+	Costs of infrastructure and ecosystem stresses indicated a malfunctioning of the Whistler growth management model
Whistler 2020 plan	2007	RMOW's Comprehensive Sustainability Plan (CSP), forming the basis of the Whistler 2020 plan, which was published in 2007
Olympics in BC	2010	Vancouver/Whistler Olympics
Whistler and Vail Resorts	2017	Vail Resorts, Inc. and Whistler Blackcomb Holdings Inc. (the primary enterprise and employer responsible for alpine operations within RMOW) have joined Whistler Blackcomb with Vail Resorts

The challenge is mainly apparent in the different structures of Canadian and European destinations. Whistler has embraced mountain monopolies and owns the ski school, rental, and a significant number of the lodgings and restaurants. This likely results in more profitability compared with the large European resorts, where the destinations mainly consist of privately owned businesses renting a space, causing a greater competition not only between destinations but also within (Price and Kim, 1999; Murphy, 2008; Hudson *et al.*, 2010; Thompson, 2012).

In addition, for the European resorts, tourism policies are often within the purview of the ministries of economy, and a winter-oriented ski resort is normally part of an already existing town or village in a ski area. With further challenges in building consensus and limited land for expansion, the potential for conflicts of interest is present when developing a single overall (sustainable tourism) strategy (Murphy, 2008; Alpine Convention, 2013; Mill and Morrison, 2013; Tomsett and Shaw, 2015; George-Marcelpoil and François, 2016; Volgger *et al.*, 2016).

Nevertheless, significant attempts have been made in addressing sustainability within the Alps. These have resulted in developments including, for example: the European 'Convention on the Protection of the Alps', a ski lift certification programme – meeting the environmental requirements of ISO 14001 – guaranteeing environmental management systems, as well as the development of a number of destination management models (Alpine Convention, 2013; Beritelli *et al.*, 2015; George-Marcelpoil and François, 2016; Volgger *et al.*, 2016). The main purpose of the Alpine Convention is to ensure efficient use of limited resources while preserving culture and nature; thus, minimum requirements were developed. These requirements include, among others, the contribution and involvement of local communities in tourism planning, tourist operators promoting natural heritage and diversifying tourism activities by environmental and socio-economic diversity and demand (Alpine Convention, 2013). These approaches, however, do not include all aspects considered necessary for a realizable sustainable development (Weaver and Lawton, 1999; UNEP and WTO, 2005; Slaper and Hall, 2011). To illustrate, only relatively few European alpine destinations to date have incorporated community involvement or consumer interest and behaviour into their tourism planning (Beritelli *et al.*, 2007; Gill and Williams, 2011; Zehrer *et al.*, 2016).

14.1.4 Mountain sustainability as an idealistic concept or a real concept?

It can be questioned whether mountain sustainability is an idealistic concept or whether it is real and achievable. Especially with regard to a millennial visitor tending to act in a self-oriented manner, it is highly unlikely that a destination will become truly sustainable if the consumer is not willing to change their (unsustainable) consumption pattern (Twenge *et al.*, 2008; Choi and Ng, 2010).

The awareness of the possible impact consumer behaviour can have on destinations has not yet been specifically linked to and implemented in sustainable destination development models. Since the objective of the study is to explore whether mountain tourism destinations can be truly sustainable, the study focused on the following key questions:

- How does the consumer interest and behaviour of the millennial generation influence the sustainability performance of a winter and summer mountain destination, such as Whistler in BC, Canada?
- To what extent can the development framework of Whistler contribute to real sustainability success?

14.2 Methodology

An exploratory mixed-method approach was chosen for this study, as the aim was to elaborate on the perspective towards sustainability of the millennial generation, in relation to their awareness and their actual behaviour, within winter and summer mountain destinations with a focus on Whistler.

Quantitative data were collected through survey research among the millennial generation. Purposive sampling, a non-probability sampling method, was used for the survey as the method is regarded to be time-effective (Bryman, 2012; Denscombe, 2014). The survey was distributed among several Facebook groups linked to Whistler, which were moreover widely used by the millennial generation. The pilot-tested survey included both open-ended and closed-ended questions in which participants were inter alia asked to indicate their (dis)agreement with given statements (based on a 5-point Likert scale). The survey included demographic profile questions, as well as questions related to their commitment to sustainability and personal responsibility, and participants were moreover asked for their views about Whistler's sustainability practices. In addition, the participants were provided a scenario in which they were given an ethical dilemma: would they take the offer of an affordable holiday that is less sustainable? A dilemma to reflect whether the participants would indeed act according to their ideals.

The survey was completed by 123 respondents, between 19 and 40 years of age; the age restriction of 40 years can be explained by the frame of this generation (Gaudelli, 2009; Sinek, 2016). The data were analysed using a combination of the analysis reports of the survey programme Qualtrics, as well as SPSS.

The data of the surveys provided input for the semi-structured in-depth interviews conducted with experts in the field. These experts involved Mr Mathews, CEO of Ecosign Whistler and experienced consultant to ski areas worldwide; Mr Nicolson, CEO of the Canada West Ski Areas Association (CWSAA) and former president of Tourism Sun Peaks; and Mr Raine, former consultant to the British Columbia Ministry of Lands (Provincial Ski Area Coordination), being responsible for the planning, development and implementation of BC's ski area policies, and currently mayor of Sun Peaks, BC, Canada.

14.3 Results

14.3.1 Profile of the respondents

Most of the respondents ($n = 123$) were female (61.8%) and when looking at the different age groups within the millennial generation, a larger part (77.2%) belonged to the younger group (aged 19–29 years) as compared with the second age group (30–40 years). The study included Canadian (55.3%) and international (44.7%) respondents. The level of education varied from high school to postgraduate education, with a bachelor's degree or equivalent being most common (69.9%).

Based on the accepted definition of tourism (UNWTO, 2014) the first-time visitor, returning visitor, as well as the seasonal visitor/worker are regarded as tourists in this study. Therefore, the survey was completed from two perspectives: the millennial tourist perspective ($n = 82$, 66.7%) and the millennial Whistler resident perspective ($n = 41$, 33.3%).

The results provide an insight into the behaviour of the respondents with regard to their transportation choices, their attitude towards sustainability and to what extent the respondents would consider themselves acting sustainably at home compared with their practices while on holiday. The main motivation for visiting Whistler involved winter sports; however, it should be noted that this is possibly skewed since the survey took place during the winter months. Additional motivations included summer activities, the village experience and events, festivals and meetings/conferences.

14.3.2 Sustainable attitude at home and on holiday

Respondents were first asked if they would consider themselves acting sustainably at home (see Table 14.2). Most indicated they do, by recycling, minding the type of packaging, separating waste and limiting water and energy use. They feel responsible towards their environment and would therefore act sustainably: 'It is my responsibility to reduce my negative impact on the environment'. Barriers to doing so include high costs of sustainable products, high energy use and the use of and dependence on a car. Of note, 80% with a high school education level consider themselves acting sustainably compared with 93% of respondents with bachelor's degrees and 94.1% of postgraduate respondents.

While being on holiday, 77% of the respondents indicated they still care about sustainability practices (see Table 14.3). Respondents who consider themselves as acting differently on holiday, or less sustainably, indicated that acting sustainably on holiday is not always possible, due to lack of knowledge or lack of options. Respondents for instance indicated the following: 'There is a lack of education of local resources', 'Unfamiliar environment means you may not seek out sustainable options' and 'Wherever I visit, often there is no infrastructure in place for me to continue good sustainable practices'. Other reasons for not acting sustainably could be summarized by the term 'vacation mode': 'On holidays, I want to relax' and 'Carefree attitude towards sustainability whilst on holiday'.

Table 14.2. Results of respondents acting sustainably at home.

			n	%
Total	I act sustainably at home	Total:	123	91
Tourist versus resident	I act sustainably at home	Tourists	81	90
		Residents	42	93
Gender	I act sustainably at home	Males	47	87
		Females	76	93

Table 14.3. Results of respondents acting sustainably on holiday.

			n	%
Total	I act sustainably on holiday	Total:	123	77
Tourist versus resident	I act sustainably on holiday	Tourist	81	76
		Resident	42	80
Gender	I act sustainably on holiday	Male	47	75
		Female	76	79

14.3.3 Valuing sustainability

Respondents were asked about their perspectives on sustainability practices and their role in attaining sustainability within a (mountain) destination, as well as their role in protection of the environment and involvement of the local community in sustainability aspects. Additional questions were asked regarding how they would value accessibility and affordability regarding mountain destination holiday choice. The protection of the natural environment was ranked as the most important practice (57.7%) out of seven proposed sustainability practices. The least important practices included the use of renewable energy sources ($n = 36$, 29.3%) and businesses and accommodations having green labels or certifications ($n = 26$, 21.1%). Community involvement was, in relation to other statements, ranked as being of high importance and the Chi-square test indicated a significant difference between the perceived importance of the inclusion of community involvement between the tourist and the resident. Interestingly, the tourist perceived the inclusion of community involvement as more important compared with the resident of Whistler.

In addition, the respondents indicated that a sustainable tourism industry is fundamental for the future (with a mean of 4.59, where 5 = Extremely important and 1 = Extremely unimportant). A difference was identified between the tourist and resident perspective, as the tourist would agree to a larger extent (97.4%) that a sustainable tourism industry is fundamental for the future, compared with the resident (84.6%). Most respondents (82.9%) would change their behaviour if their current behaviour is of any harm to their environment ($M = 4.28$, $SD = 1.03$) and 90% of the respondents state that sustainability is their responsibility.

Sustainable practices, including protection of the natural environment and involvement of local communities are thus regarded important (see Table 14.4; $M = 4.17$, $SD = 0.94$). Affordability of a holiday destination ($M = 4.17$, $SD = 1.00$) is perceived to be significantly more important by the tourist respondents compared with the resident respondents.

14.3.4 The millennial perspective on sustainable mountain practices

Multiple questions focused on the millennial perspective on sustainability. The respondents were asked to indicate which practices, according to them, should be implemented in a mountain destination for it to be sustainable. Figure 14.3 shows which sustainable

Table 14.4. Perceived importance of respondents regarding sustainable practices and affordability (1 = Extremely unimportant, 5 = Extremely important).

		n	Mean
Sustainable practices at the destination	Tourist	81	4.24
	Resident	42	4.02
	Total	123	4.17
Affordable holiday at the destination	Tourist	81	4.30
	Resident	42	3.90
	Total	123	4.17

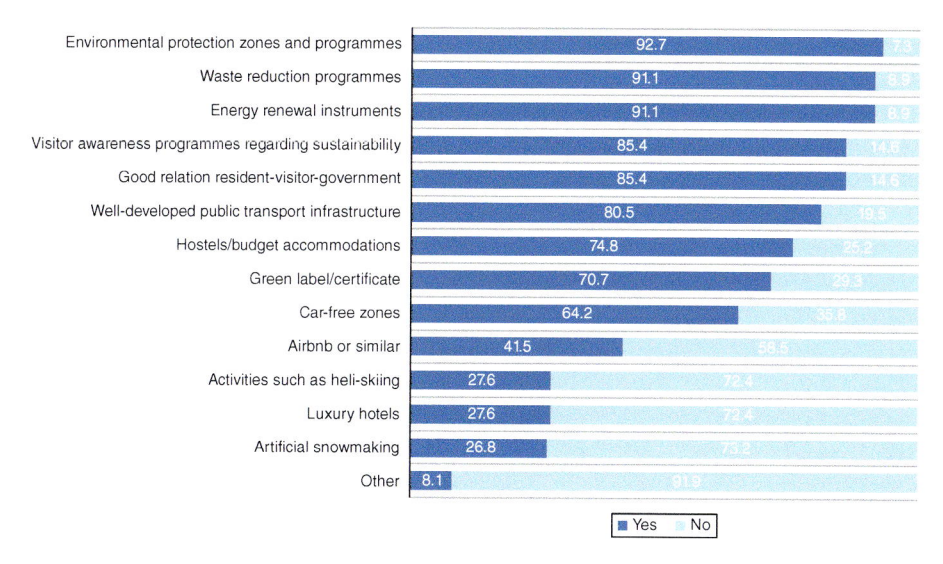

Practice	Yes	No
Environmental protection zones and programmes	92.7	7.3
Waste reduction programmes	91.1	8.9
Energy renewal instruments	91.1	8.9
Visitor awareness programmes regarding sustainability	85.4	14.6
Good relation resident-visitor-government	85.4	14.6
Well-developed public transport infrastructure	80.5	19.5
Hostels/budget accommodations	74.8	25.2
Green label/certificate	70.7	29.3
Car-free zones	64.2	35.8
Airbnb or similar	41.5	58.5
Activities such as heli-skiing	27.6	72.4
Luxury hotels	27.6	72.4
Artificial snowmaking	26.8	73.2
Other	8.1	91.9

Fig. 14.3. Practices needed for a sustainable mountain destination according to millennial respondents (*n* = 123, results in percentages).

aspects ought to be implemented in a sustainable mountain destination, according to this generation.

14.3.5 Is the millennial generation acting in accordance with their sustainability values?

The answer to this question can be summarized by referring to the survey, which provided a question where the respondents were given an imaginary offer: an affordable stay at an attractive destination, when they are aware that the destination is not doing well in terms of sustainable practices. The respondents were asked if they would or would not take the offer. The purpose of this question was to test whether the literature corresponds with the behaviour of the millennial respondents of the survey: would they act sustainably and in accordance with their values? A total of 69.9% (*n* = 78) of the respondents *would* take the offer.

14.4 Discussion

The results of the survey have shown that, indeed, the behaviour of the millennial visitors and residents of Whistler comply with the characteristics of this generation as described in the literature. They value sustainability, which they show by indicating that they feel responsible for their behaviour, are willing to pay more for products contributing to a sustainable future and are moreover willing to change their behaviour if their current behaviour is of negative impact. They certainly have the knowledge of the 'why' and are aware that a sustainable tourism industry is fundamental for the future. However, the results suggest that millennials are not yet fully committed to sustainability. A summary of the findings from the study can be found in Table 14.5.

Table 14.5. Summary of findings.

Acting sustainably:	The millennial generation indicates they act sustainably at home (91%) as well as on holiday, however, to a lesser extent (77%)
Sustainability fundamental for the future:	The millennial tourist perceives sustainable tourism to be fundamental for the future continuation of tourism (97%)
Responsibility and willingness for behavioural change:	The millennials feel responsible for sustainability (90%) and are willing to change their behaviour if their consumer behaviour is of harm to their (social and environmental) environment (92%)
Sustainability vs. affordability:	Even though the millennial consumer indicates they are willing to pay more for a product or service contributing to a sustainable environment (88%), most of the respondents (96%) indicating that they would take the imaginary offer state that an affordable holiday is important to them
Awareness vs. commitment:	As confirmed by expert interviews and in line with the survey results, the millennial generation is aware of the 'why', and in contrast to suggestions made in the literature also aware of the 'how' to contribute to sustainable tourism; however, is not yet taking responsibility or acting accordingly
Consumer interest and behaviour is important:	The inclusion of consumer interest and behaviour is imperative for a destination to be truly sustainable. The results of the interviews and surveys have moreover confirmed this need
Incomplete planning for success:	In contrast with the literature, the Whistler 2020 plan is not considered as complete and perfect as the literature suggests. The value of community involvement within Whistler however, is confirmed by the experts
Importance of community involvement:	The aspect of community involvement as is implemented in Whistler could serve as a valuable example to destinations within the European Alps
Sustainable mountain tourism – not yet achieved:	Sustainable mountain tourism destinations are not yet achieved. However, this study aims to contribute to destinations' sustainability performances by the provision of recommendations based upon the results of the research

As indicated in the literature, the millennial generation tends to be a rather self-interested and impatient generation. Results indicating that roughly 70% of the respondents would accept an offer made by a travel agency that involves a cheap holiday that is not adhering to sustainability practices suggest that this generation is not (even though they indicated differently) taking their responsibility seriously. However, the results of the study indicate that if options are present, and awareness is raised, the millennial consumer is willing to adapt and contribute to sustainability. Hence, destinations could facilitate sustainable behaviour: 'It should not be difficult for people to do the "right" thing for this earth'.

In addition, the study has shown that Whistler, in contrast to what is suggested by the literature, still has a way to go to improve its sustainability practices. Survey respondents and expert views reflect that, though attempting to act responsibly, Whistler's practices seem better on paper than in practice: 'In Whistler I would say on the environmental side, they have pushed the limit already'. In addition, one of the experts expressed his concerns about the emergence of Vail: 'The bigger you get [the destination], the bigger the corporation that is driving your destiny. I don't know the answers of how you would do it, but I don't believe that Vail buying Whistler, is good for Whistler.' The experts consider the Whistler 2020 plan as an idealized written document: '(…) nothing you can implement quite frankly'. It is believed to be written according to rules and procedures, but not necessarily site-specific for Whistler and it is regarded as hard to implement effectively.

Despite the criticisms that have been expressed regarding the performance of Whistler as a destination, certain sustainable practices could serve as an example to destinations within the European Alps. Even though it seems that the European model would suggest that cooperation between the businesses, tourism boards and governments are present, the structure of the European alpine destinations challenges sustainable development: 'The Alps, I don't know what you can do, everything has been owned for centuries and centuries'. 'I don't think you would ever see … the openness that you have in Whistler…'.

Whistler is doing well on social sustainability, especially in terms of community involvement. The following statements confirm Whistlers' performances in the area of community involvement: 'Yes, very good. Excellent. I would say Whistler definitely has been, from day one, very open-minded, very democratic. They go to the community. (…) They give you every opportunity to say your piece and to participate in the whole process.'

Not only does the inclusion of community involvement bring social sustainability, it can moreover lead to economic sustainability: 'They [tourists] are coming back because they enjoyed the community, they enjoyed the people and the vibe and the atmosphere that has been created'. Being innovative within a social context, by for instance developing good relationships between the consumer and the resident, will give the destination a competitive advantage, while also enhancing the interests and needs of the community.

14.5 Conclusions

The aim of the study was to explore whether sustainability performances of mountain destinations such as Whistler (see Fig. 14.4 and 14.5) are being idealized or if they can truly be sustainable. As can be derived from the literature as well as the surveys and interviews, sustainable mountain tourism destinations are not yet a full reality. Referring to the main research question – how does the consumer interest and behaviour of the millennial generation influence the sustainability performance of a winter and summer mountain destination, such as Whistler – it can be concluded that the consumer can have a significant influence on the destination in their practices and outcomes. The millennial generation is willing to contribute towards sustainability, but is not yet acting according to these values and does not intend to make a significant effort to do so. Incentives and actions of a destination to take responsibility and implement measures that will deal with (unsustainable) consumer interest and behaviour may therefore be valuable.

In addition, current development models do not include complete practices that would render a mountain destination truly sustainable. As can be seen in the case of Whistler, even a seemingly well-developed model, following ideal attempts described

Fig. 14.4. Peak to Peak Gondola at Whistler Blackcomb. (Photograph courtesy of Harold Richins.)

in the literature and planning guides, does not guarantee unflawed sustainable performance. As one of the experts indicated, sustainability within a winter and summer mountain destination might not be something that can be fully achieved, but it is certainly an important strategic goal worth pursuing and implementing.

Additionally, it can be suggested that a framework model of one destination, such as the Whistler 2020 plan, may not be directly suitable for European alpine destinations due to multiple differences in policy, environmental settings and circumstances. However, destinations might certainly benefit from successful sustainable practices implemented elsewhere. Nevertheless, even if practices of other destinations are useful, they should be carefully implemented as per site-specific needs, priorities and interests of each mountain destination.

As the literature and exploratory analysis on the Whistler 2020 plan show diverse perspectives, the performance and effectiveness of the Whistler 2020 plan could be further investigated. To illustrate, questions worth investigating include: Are the objectives set in the Whistler 2020 plan implementable? To what extent have they been implemented? Which adaptations are needed to successfully implement objectives that have not yet been implemented? Also, is the plan truly contributing towards the improvement of Whistler's sustainability practices (including social, physical, economic)?

It may be considered useful for Whistler as a destination to be taking the responsibility in fostering sustainable community (resident and visitor) involvement, consumer

Fig. 14.5. Whistler lodging. (Photograph courtesy of Harold Richins.)

interest and behaviour within the destination. This might also include consumer encouragement to more directly contribute to sustainability practices in Whistler and in winter and summer mountain destinations elsewhere.

References

Alpine Convention (2013) *Sustainable Tourism in the Alps, Report on the State of the Alps*. Permanent Secretariat of the Alpine Convention, Innsbruck, Austria.
Arrow, K., Bolin, B., Costanza, R., Dasgupta, P., Folke, C. *et al.* (1995) Economic growth, carrying capacity, and the environment. *Science* 268, 520–521.
Beritelli, P., Bieger, T. and Laesser, C. (2007) Destination governance: using corporate governance theories as a foundation for effective destination management. *Journal of Travel Research* 46(1), 96–107.
Beritelli, P., Reinhold, S., Laesser, C. and Bieger, T. (2015) *The St. Gallen Model for Destination Management*. Institute for Systematic Management and Public Governance, St. Gallen, Switzerland.
Bryman, A. (2012) *Social Research Methods*. Oxford University Press, Oxford, UK.
Choi, S. and Ng, A. (2010) Environmental and economic dimensions of sustainability and price effects on consumer responses. *Journal of Business Ethics* 104, 269–282. DOI:10.1007/s10551-011-0908-8
Crouch, G. and Ritchie, J. (1999). Tourism, competitiveness, and social prosperity. *Journal of Business Research* 44, 137–152.

Del Matto, T. and Scott, D. (2009) Sustainable ski resort principles, an uphill journey. In: Gössling, S., Hall, C.M. and Weaver, D. (eds) *Sustainable Tourism Futures: Perspectives on Systems, Restructuring and Innovations*. Taylor & Francis, London, pp. 131–151.

Denscombe, M. (2014) *The Good Research Guide: For Small-Scale Research Projects*, 5th edn. McGraw-Hill Education Open University Press, Maidenhead, UK.

Fraser, E.D.G., Doubill, A.J., Mabee, W.E., Reed, M. and McAlpine, P. (2005) Bottom up and top down: analysis of participatory processes for sustainability indicator identification as a pathway to community empowerment and sustainable environmental management. *Journal of Environmental Management* 78, 114–127. DOI:10.1016/j.jenvman.2005.04.009

Gaudelli, J. (2009) The greenest generation: the truth behind millennials and the green movement. Available at: https://adage.com/article/goodworks/truth-millennials-green-movement/136331 (accessed 29 January 2019).

George, E., Mair, H., Reid, D. and Taylor, J. (2002) Towards a democratic process for planning community tourism development: a participant action research approach. Available at: www.academia.edu/443469/Towards_A_Democratic_Process_For_Planning_Community_Tourism_Development_A_Participant_Action_Research_Approach (accessed 29 January 2019).

George-Marcelpoil, E. and François, H. (2016) Governance of French ski resorts: will the historic economic development model work for the future? In: Richins, H. and Hull, J.S. (eds) *Mountain Tourism: Experiences, Communities, Environments and Sustainable Futures*. CAB International, Wallingford, UK, pp. 319–330.

Gibson, R.B., Hassan, S., Holtz, S., Tansey, J. and Whitelaw, G. (2006) Sustainability assessment – criteria and processes. *Journal of Environmental Assessment Policy and Management* 8(3), 399–401.

Gill, A. (2000) From growth machine to growth management: the dynamics of resort development in Whistler, British Columbia. *Environment and Planning A* 32, 1083–1103. DOI:10.1068/a32160

Gill, A. and Williams, P. (2011) Rethinking resort growth: understanding evolving governance strategies in Whistler, British Columbia. *Journal of Sustainable Tourism* 19(4–5), 629–648. DOI:10.1080/09669582.2011.558626

Hall, C. (2008) *Tourism Planning. Policies, Processes and Relationships*, 2nd edn. Pearson Education Limited, Harlow, UK.

Hanks, K., Odom, W., Roedl, D. and Blevis, E. (2008) Sustainable millennials: attitudes towards sustainability and the material effects of interactive technologies. Conference Proceedings of the 2008 Conference on Human Factors in Computing Systems, CHI 2008, Florence, Italy, 5–10 April 2008. Available at: https://www.researchgate.net/publication/221518968_Sustainable_millennials_Attitudes_towards_sustainability_and_the_material_effects_of_interactive_technologies (accessed 29 January 2019).

Hudson, S. and Hudson, L. (2016) The Development and design of ski resorts: from theory to practice. In: Richins, H. and Hull, J.S. (eds) *Mountain Tourism: Experiences, Communities, Environments and Sustainable Futures*. CAB International, Wallingford, UK, pp. 331–340.

Hudson, S., Ritchie, B. and Timur, S. (2010) Measuring destination competitiveness: an empirical study of Canadian ski resorts. *Tourism Hospitality Planning and Development* 1(1), 79–94. DOI:10.1080/1479053042000187810

Hull, J. and Richins, H. (2016) Development, planning and governance in mountain tourism: overview, contextual development and areas of focus. In: Richins, H. and Hull, J.S. (eds) *Mountain Tourism: Experiences, Communities, Environments and Sustainable Futures*. CAB International, Wallingford, UK, pp. 290–298.

International Olympic Committee (2014) Whistler used Vancouver 2010 'As a catalyst' for Community Goals [Press Release]. Available at: https://www.olympic.org/news/whistler-used-vancouver-2010-as-a-catalyst-for-community-goals (accessed 29 January 2019).

Kogler, A. and Boksberger, P. (2016) Leisure living in the Alps. In: Richins, H. and Hull, J.S. (eds) *Mountain Tourism: Experiences, Communities, Environments and Sustainable Futures*. CAB International, Wallingford, UK, pp. 141–146.

Lee, J. (2016) New Whistler resort owner aims to make skiing more affordable. Vancouver Sun. Available at: https://vancouversun.com/business/local-business/vail-resorts-makes-1-4-billion-takeover-offer-for-whistler-blackcomb (accessed 29 January 2019).

Mill, R. and Morrison, A.M. (2013) *The Tourism System*, 7th edn. Kendall Hunt Publishing, Dubuque, Iowa.

Murphy, P. (1987) Community driven tourism planning. *Tourism Management* 9(2), 96–104. DOI:10.1016/0261-5177(88)90019-2

Murphy, P. (2008) *The Business of Resort Management*. Butterworth- Heinemann, London.

Ng, E.S.W., Schweitzer, L. and Lyons, S.T. (2010) New generation, great expectations: a field study of the millennial generation. *Journal of Business and Psychology* 25, 281–292. DOI:10.1007/s10869-010-9159-4

Price, M.F. and Kim, E.G. (1999) Priorities for sustainable mountain development in Europe. *International Journal of Sustainable Development and World Ecology* 6, 203–219.

Resort Municipality of Whistler (2007) Whistler 2020. Moving toward a sustainable future, 2nd edn. Available at: www.whistlercentre.ca/sumiredesign/wp-content/uploads/2014/02/Whistler2020-Vision.pdf (accessed 29 January 2019).

Resort Municipality of Whistler (2012) Official Community Plan (Official com Amendment Bylaw No. 1021). Available at: https://www.whistler.ca/sites/default/files/related/ocp_-_text_-_oct_2012.pdf (accessed 29 January 2019).

Resort Municipality of Whistler (n.d.) Community monitoring. Available at: https://www.whistler.ca/municipal-gov/community-monitoring (accessed 21 January 2017).

Ritchie, J. and Crouch, G. (2003) *Destination Competitiveness and Sustainability*. CAB International, Cambridge, Massachusetts.

Scott, D. and Del Matto, T. (2008) Sustainable ski resort principles. In: Weaver, D.B., Hall, C.M. and Gössling, S. (eds) *Sustainable Tourism Futures: Perspectives on Systems, Restructuring and Innovations*. Routledge, New York, pp. 131–151.

Sheth, J.N., Sethia, N.K. and Srinivas, S. (2010) Mindful consumption: a customer-centric approach to sustainability. *Journal of the Academy of Marketing Science* 39, 21–39. DOI:10.1007/s11747-010-0216-3

Sinek, S. (2016) Simon Sinek on millennials in the workplace [Video file]. Available at: https://www.youtube.com/watch?v=hER0Qp6QJNU (accessed 29 January 2019).

Slaper, T.F. and Hall, T.J. (2011) The triple bottom line: what is it and how does it work? *Indiana Business Review* 86, 4–8.

Thompson, D. (2012) No business like snow business: the economics of big ski resorts. Available at: www.theatlantic.com/business/archive/2012/02/no-business-like-snow-business-the-economics-of-big-ski-resorts/252180 (accessed 18 January 2017).

Tomsett, P. and Shaw, M. (2015) Developing a new typology for a behavioural classification of stakeholders using the case of tourism public policy planning in the snow sports industry. *European Journal of Tourism Research* 9, 115–128.

Tourism Whistler (n.d.) Whistler Visitor Centre. Available at: https://www.whistler.com/whistler-visitor-centre (accessed 21 January 2019).

Twenge, J.M., Konrath, S., Foster, J.D., Campbell, W.K. and Bushman, B.J. (2008) Egos inflating over time: a cross-temporal meta-analysis of the narcissistic personality inventory. *Journal of Personality* 76(4), 875–901. DOI:10.1111/j.1467-6494.2008.00507.x

UNEP and WTO (2005) Making tourism more sustainable. A guide for policy makers. Available at: www.unep.fr/shared/publications/pdf/DTIx0592xPA-TourismPolicyEN.pdf (accessed 29 January 2019).

Vail Resorts, Inc. (2016) Vail Resorts and Whistler Blackcomb agree to strategic combination [Press Release]. Available at: http://investors.vailresorts.com/news-releases/news-release-details/vail-resorts-and-whistler-blackcomb-agree-strategic-combination (accessed 29 January 2019).

Volgger, M., Lun, L. and Pechlaner, H. (2016) Protected areas in the Alps: governance and contributions to regional development. In: Richins, H. and Hull, J.S. (eds) *Mountain Tourism: Experiences, Communities, Environments and Sustainable Futures*. CAB International, Wallingford, UK, pp. 299–309.

Weaver, D. and Lawton, L. (1999) Sustainable tourism: a critical analysis. Report no. 1. RC for Sustainable Tourism Pty Ltd. Available at: http://citeseerx.ist.psu.edu/viewdoc/download?doi=10.1.1.606.327&rep=rep1&type=pdf (accessed 29 January 2019).

Williams, P. and Ponsford, I. (2008) Confronting tourism's environmental paradox: transitioning for sustainable tourism. *Futures* 41(6), 396–404. DOI:10.1016/j.futures.2008.11.019

Wisansing, J. (n.d.) Towards community driven tourism planning: a critical review of theoretical demands and practical issues. Available at: www.academia.edu/2272490/towards_community_driven_tourism_planning_a_critical_review_of_theoritical_demands_and_practical_ssues (accessed 29 January 2019).

Zehrer, A., Raich, F., Siller, H. and Tschiderer, F. (2016) Development and governance of a family destination in the Alps: the case of Serfaus-Fiss-Ladis. In: Richins, H. and Hull, J.S. (eds) *Mountain Tourism: Experiences, Communities, Environments and Sustainable Futures*. CAB International, Wallingford, UK, pp. 353–362.

Part II Winter Tourism Experiences

15 Winter Tourism Experiences: Visitor Trends, Preferences and Destination Choice; Diversification of Experience Offers; Segments and Marketing

STEFAN TÜRK*

Institute of Outdoor Sports and Environmental Science, German Sport University Cologne, Cologne, Germany

15.1 Introduction

There are many reasons why a traveller chooses a particular destination (Crompton and Ankomah, 1993). Nevertheless, it is of immense importance for decision makers in the destinations to know as much as possible about destination choice and behavioural intentions. This knowledge is a precondition to address, attract and satisfy guests.

But what are the reasons for a guest to travel to a certain area in winter? First and foremost, it is the option to practise winter sports. Therefore, one has to find a suitable landscape with the perfect climate (Henschel, 2002) for an acceptable price/performance ratio. Of course, cultural or culinary preferences are also of interest to tourists, but the appropriate selection is often made on-site (DiePresse.com, 2017). Thus, it is of great importance to deal with the sportive offers and to see whether there are any particular preferences with regard to the types of sports and the options for exercising them. For tourism destinations, it is important to consider that these preferences might change over time. Preferences for certain activities are also related to the respective socio-demographic but also cultural background of the guests. With marketing initiatives, events and special offers, many destinations try to influence their perceived image, to attract a certain market segment and to establish a relationship with their clients.

Finally, in addition to the sport offers, the surroundings have to fit and fulfil customers' needs. The atmosphere should be harmonious. These are the special stimuli that act as pull factors to attract a guest to a particular destination (Hannich, 2007). The presented studies in this section show that there actually are national- or region-specific requirements that winter sports resorts should ideally follow in order to position themselves successfully. Of course, certain regions stand for defined guest wishes simply because of their name or their specific location. And differences between snow-covered regions such as the Austrian Alps or Iceland quickly become

---

* E-mail: tuerk@dshs-koeln.de

apparent. For example, in one place the slope must be perfectly prepared, in the second place ideal off-piste offers must be found and in the third place a well-cleared road or a functioning rescue service is the decisive criterion for the choice of travel. Choosing a destination still depends on whether its image matches the travel motives (Moutinho, 1987) and/or whether the relevant holiday motives are fulfilled (Crompton, 1979).

These different interests and expectations may lead to conflicts in winter destinations. Such problems are often based on a different understanding of sport (Jacob and Schreyer, 1980; Adelman et al., 1982). If for one group the use of motorized sports equipment is an absolute no-go, it is precisely this motor support that is the reason why others are active in winter landscapes. While the first group combines sports-related performances with peace, quietness and the experience of nature, the second group obviously sees action and speed as important motivators for a stay in a snowy landscape. Even if the free use of motorized sports equipment in snow-covered landscapes is more of a North American than an alpine phenomenon, it is generally valid that such a different motivation, especially in outdoor activities, often causes significant conflicts. Solving these conflicts is always a great challenge for tourism experts. In large areas, spatial solutions such as zoning concepts might be applicable; in addition, the destination may also think about redesigning the offer to satisfy different expectations. If spatial solutions or redesigns are not feasible, the destination has to decide on their desired and most suitable target group(s). In addition to the primary interests that have to be fulfilled, further attractions and activities should be considered to underline a certain profile or image attracting a specific clientele.

In this context, the role of nature reserves or national parks should also be considered. On the one hand, a destination within or close to a protected area is perceived as a sign for attractive and unspoiled landscapes and the opportunity for diverse nature experiences (Pröbstl et al., 2014). On the other hand, the sensitive environmental conditions in protected areas may require restrictions for winter tourism and the right balance between tourism activities and conservation goals. However, this challenging trade-off offers opportunities to combine different interests and to promote mutual acceptance and respect for environmental issues in the long run. In this context one may ask for whom if not for visitors do we protect and conserve the environment (Leslie, 1986).

Conflicts between environmental goals and tourism development are a common issue in many destinations. However, quite new are conflicts caused by significant socio-cultural differences due to guests from other continents or different cultures, such as the arrival of Chinese tourists in Switzerland. How do you meet each other, how do you communicate and how can you ensure mutual understanding? Of course, it seems crucial to find the right answers to these questions in order to reach new target groups (ETC, 2014). But it seems just as important not to lose one's independence and local identity despite the adaptation to new target groups, because authentic and different experiences are the main argument for travelling.

Part II should not end without taking a look at employment in winter tourism. Especially for young people who are enthusiastic about snow sports, winter destinations are attractive workplaces. And exactly these people are needed by touristic enterprises, because guests want to be instructed by good and inspiring teachers. However, living in such places is expensive and these jobs are usually modestly paid. These conditions often lead to an increasing amount of seasonal workers and short-term employment in winter destinations with negative consequences for the social structure in the respective towns and villages. Therefore, it should be a main goal to understand the demand and the behavioural intentions of the workforce in tourism and to provide working and living conditions that allow people to stay in the destination full-time and to actively participate in the political, social and economic development of the destination.

15.2 Summary of Chapters in Part II: Winter Tourism Experiences

The chapters in Part II deal with visitor trends, preferences and destination choice. The authors also deal with experience offers as well as marketing concepts. Downhill skiing, cross-country skiing and snowmobiling are under investigation to identify trends in winter recreation activities. Working with different target groups requires knowledge on their preferences, as well as about their sensitivity. Conflicts between different user groups have to be taken into account when planning winter sports areas. And to know what the guests really want is the best basis for good marketing and corresponding offers. In this context Visitor Monitoring Systems will help to find out which activities lead to which conflicts. New markets and target groups must also be examined, as the benefits might be associated with new challenges. Special offers are an expression of the necessary diversification in ski resorts. Solutions for special problems must also be found in the context of those working in the destinations in order to make winter tourism attractive for the future.

The chapters are described further below.

15.2.1 Chapter 16. Winter Recreation Trends in the Swedish Mountains – Challenges and Opportunities

Authors: Peter Fredman and Tatiana Chekalina

A total of 10% of Sweden is covered by an alpine area. And the Swedish mountain region is of great interest for both summer and winter tourism. In Chapter 16, Peter Fredman and Tatiana Chekalina examine the outstanding significance of winter recreation activities for this mountain region. They discuss the identified trends in downhill skiing, cross-country skiing and snowmobiling in connection with regional as well as with global development.

For their study of possible changes over the period from 1985–2013, they used three previous surveys of domestic visitors in the Swedish mountains. Based on these data they found significant changes. Regarding the development in downhill skiing one can see that the number of skiers significantly increased into the 1990s and has remained stable since then. Nowadays, most people go downhill skiing only once up to a maximum of five times a year, and not more often. The observation of motorized snowmobiling shows a similar development to downhill skiing. But the situation is somewhat different regarding cross-country skiing: one can also observe a declining frequency but in addition one can see that the activity per se is less attractive.

This development in different sectors of winter sports is discussed by the authors under the consideration of a number of overarching influencing factors, e.g. physical demands, work patterns, value seeking or available income. Climate change is also addressed in the discussion. The reasons for the observed development could be a sign of activity diversification, place substitution and/or decrease in loyalty.

15.2.2 Chapter 17. A Matter of Culture: How Cultural Differences Shape Skiing Motivation, Behaviour and Destination Choice

Authors: Ulrike Pröbstl-Haider and Nina Mostegl

It seems to be a matter of fact that our culture determines which sport we practise and how often. Also in tourism our culture may influence our actions. For this reason, Ulrike Pröbstl-Haider and Nina Mostegl examine motives and expectations as well as their influence on the choice and attractiveness of a destination. In Chapter 17, the authors examine the three important target groups of German, Austrian and Italian skiers and snowboarders to test new development and marketing opportunities for South Tyrol, an enchanting alpine winter destination.

German, Austrian and Italian winter sports tourists were questioned with a comprehensive survey in order to obtain information on their winter sports activities, the skiing days and the skiing locations, their perception of the chosen ski resorts, and on some future aspects (e.g. climate change and destination development). The survey included a discrete choice experiment to understand preferences and intended behaviour. Finally, a decision support tool was used to depict the choices of the three different target groups.

Regarding the main motivations, preferences and destination choices, the authors found significant differences among the tourists from the three different countries. Italian tourists seem to be interested in social experiences, preferring to ski within the family and enjoying the time together, while Austrians are more interested in being active and prefer extended winter tourism facilities. These findings may lead to new ideas for marketing and product placement. For tailored marketing strategies it is also of interest that German and Austrian tourists in South Tyrol are also looking for local food and the atmosphere in the typical small restaurants.

15.2.3 Chapter 18. Winter Visitors' Perceptions in Popular Nature Destinations in Iceland

Authors: Anna Dóra Sæþórsdóttir and C. Michael Hall

An important goal of Icelandic tourism is to promote the country as a year-round tourist destination to minimize seasonal fluctuations especially in international visitor arrivals. Especially winter tourism seems to be currently promoted, whereas summer tourism is already showing the first crowding effects. As an all-season destination, Iceland seems to be the solution for sustainable growth/development.

To examine the tourists' perception of crowding as well as their satisfaction, the authors Anna Dóra Sæþórsdóttir and C. Michael Hall conducted a survey in seven popular nature destinations in the south and south-west of Iceland. The questionnaire was divided into three categories: participant background questions, questions about activities, behaviour and preferences, and finally questions about attitude, experience and catalyst/motivation. Of special interest for the study is the fact that the selected destinations differ in their tourism-relevant development. The authors' findings are provided in Chapter 18.

Most of the interviewed persons were visiting Iceland for the first time, coming from all over the world. The natural attractions led to a high level of satisfaction at all the locations surveyed, although the ratings for recreation rooms, services and parking areas at the seven destinations are quite different. However, the survey already revealed some overcrowding effects at certain sites. Assuming a further growth in tourism development, it will be necessary to address crowding effects and to improve the offer, including snow-ploughed roads or organized rescue services. In that case, winter offers the opportunity to promote extraordinary nature-based experiences in Iceland.

15.2.4   Chapter 19. Winter Recreationist Motivations: Motorized, Non-Motorized and Hybrids

Authors: Jerry J. Vaske and Aubrey D. Miller

In Chapter 19, the authors Jerry J. Vaske and Aubrey D. Miller examine whether motorized snowmobilers, non-motorized recreationists such as skiers, backcountry skiers, snowboarders, cross-country skiers and snowshoe walkers, or hybrid participants (e.g. snowmobile-assisted skiers) differ in their motivations for solitude, social interaction, physical fitness and/or thrill seeking. The study was conducted in Vail Pass Recreation Area in Colorado, USA, visited by approximately 35,000 visitors per year. On the basis of more than 20 years of cooperation, the research area has been zoned in order to be able to offer both motorized and non-motorized users a high-quality recreation area. Nearly half of the area is used by non-motorized winter sports enthusiasts and motorized winter sports enthusiasts, respectively. Only a small part of the area is designated for hybrid use.

Data were obtained from online surveys for the backcountry huts and on-site surveys distributed at the parking area to all visitors after their recreation experience. The data were tested for the above-mentioned four different motivation statements and respective statistical differences. The authors show that the motorized visitors ranked the motivations solitude, social and physical fitness significantly lower than the non-motorized recreationists, who consider these motivations most important. The means for the hybrid group were always in between the two other groups, and only thrills were most important for the hybrid group.

A major reason for the interpersonal conflict seems to be the result of noise and exhaust from snowmobiles. However, the differences in motivation between the three groups may also contribute. And finally, a social value conflict is likely to cause the visible differences. In order to regulate these problems effectively, it will be necessary to develop management tools, including signage and messaging. The identified differences should determine management decisions of the Vail Pass Recreation Area for the future.

15.2.5   Chapter 20. Alternative Outdoor Activities in Alpine Winter Tourism

Authors: Bruno Abegg, Leandra Jänicke, Mike Peters and Alexander Plaikner

Chapter 20 by Bruno Abegg, Leandra Jänicke, Mike Peters and Alexander Plaikner describes other activities in alpine tourism besides skiing and snowboarding.

They show that an increasing number of guests practise more and more winter activities such as winter hiking, tobogganing, cross-country skiing and snowshoeing. Consequently, the authors focus their interest on the six most popular 'alternative' winter sport activities in Tyrol, including backcountry skiing and ski touring on slopes. The study analyses people's activity profiles and their satisfaction with the existing offer in Tyrol. Special attention is given to the motivation to practise alternative winter sport activities.

The results section describes the socio-demographic profiles as well as the motives of outdoor recreationists in Tyrol. Most of the alternative activities are of a high importance as secondary or tertiary choices. For example, the tourists state that they like the opportunity for tobogganing but they are not visiting Tyrol for this activity explicitly. The study revealed noticeable differences between overnight guests and day visitors. In order to tailor their respective marketing campaigns and offers, it will be of great importance for the destinations whether their guests are looking for quietness, health improvement or physical achievement. Only then can the destinations perfect their marketing and offers. Although the study can only highlight a few interesting aspects, it clearly shows the importance of alternative winter sports for the future. Considering such alternatives will be of increasing importance also in the context of climate change and demographic development.

15.2.6 Chapter 21. Winter Tourism Management and Challenges in the Tatra National Park

Authors: Karolina Taczanowska, Mikołaj Bielański, Joanna Hibner, Miłosz Jodłowski and Tomasz Zwijacz-Kozica

In Chapter 21, Karolina Taczanowska, Mikołaj Bielański, Joanna Hibner, Miłosz Jodłowski and Tomasz Zwijacz-Kozica examine winter tourism offers in the Tatra National Park in Poland. Even if the winter season lasts more than 4 months, only a relatively small amount of the annual tourists come during this time. Hiking and downhill skiing as well as ski touring seem to be the most popular outdoor recreation activities during winter time in the Tatra National Park. Since the visitor profile is much more heterogeneous than in summer, the national park management is confronted with a number of significant challenges.

The current needs as well as the ongoing expectations challenge the existing recreational system in the nature conservation area. Until now useful distribution studies have been lacking, especially for the winter season. To obtain more information about its visitors the Tatra National Park is currently setting up a visitor monitoring system. Easy access, the possibility of using horse sledges, or the opportunity of consuming warm food and cold drinks explain the likelihood of high visitor numbers. In particular finding the right balance between concentrating versus dispersing recreational use has a high significance in the Tatra National Park. It is also of importance to find out which kind of activity is practised where and which conflicts are related to the respective activity.

For the future the management of the nature protected area needs a mixture of ecological methods and social science approaches to learn more about the necessary operations. The managers need also more knowledge on environmental awareness, the actual behaviour of the different tourist groups and the interests of the locals in the Tatra National Park. This information is needed to maintain the unique natural value of the highest part of the Carpathian Mountains.

15.2.7 Chapter 22. Chinese Guests in Alpine Destinations – What are They Looking for? A Case Study from Switzerland Regarding Product Preferences and Landscape Perception

Authors: Barbara Haller Rupf, Katrin Schillo, Wolfgang G. Arlt and Reto Rupf

There is no question that China appears to be one of the most important tourist markets of the future, not only in Switzerland. But little is known about the behaviour of Chinese tourists. In consequence, a number of questions arise if one really wants to address and benefit from such a growing tourism market. But it is important that a growing market not only brings more tourists into the country, but also leads to an additional income. In this context, the Chinese market seems to be quite difficult.

Therefore, the authors Barbara Haller Rupf, Katrin Schillo, Wolfgang G. Arlt and Reto Rupf study the Chinese guests as well as the special product and destination development in Grisons/Switzerland addressed to this growing market. The authors try to analyse the expectations and the behavioural intentions of the potential Chinese guests. In addition they discuss whether there are already special products and services attracting Chinese guests in the alpine destinations. It is also of great interest whether the service providers and their employees are well informed and trained to welcome the new guests. The experiences may also be transferred to guests from other new target regions such as India or the Gulf States. The presented findings include expert interviews and are based on a survey of visitors from the People's Republic of China, Hong Kong and Taiwan in Grisons/Switzerland and potential guests in Beijing/China. The results are presented in Chapter 22.

The Chinese guests highlighted the different experience Switzerland gave them. Switzerland seems to be more natural and less anthropogenically influenced than their home country. However, the Chinese guests are not getting what they really want. Food and information flow are criticized. It may be a lack of understanding of the culture, but one can see that the destinations try to adapt to this new target group. An important first step is the employment of Chinese-speaking staff. Overall, the study reveals that the Chinese tourism market is still not well-known and diverse. Therefore, destinations need support to achieve satisfying results for both guests and hosts. This makes it all the more important to accompany the destinations as well as the service providers when considering the Chinese market.

15.2.8 Chapter 23. The 2-Year Tourist: Lifestyle Migration in Whistler, British Columbia

Author: Joe Pavelka

Whistler is considered a Mecca for winter tourism, which also means that many people, especially young people, are needed here as seasonal workers. A small amount of them would like to stay in Whistler permanently. The author Joe Pavelka deals with this special group of migrants in Chapter 23. He points out the difficulties, but also the importance of this group of workers for a tourist resort such as Whistler.

Although he uses the term *2-Year Tourist* in the title, the author deals in his study with people who have been living and working in Whistler for at least 2 years. Using qualitative interviews and a multiple analytical iteration of the transcribed interviews he describes the motivations as well as the challenges for a life in Whistler and analyses why some stay and others leave the ski resort.

Most of the people surveyed say that 'Whistler is the place to be' when you are considering a career in the field of snow sports. And it's more than attractive to be surrounded by a lot of people with the same mind-set. However, the quest for an ideal quality of life confronts them with actual reality such as low income, inconsistent jobs and expensive housing. Normally, you have to be rich to live in a ski resort such as Whistler. But teaching skiing is not the way to get rich and often physical injuries lead to having to leave the resort again because of the inability to earn any money. So they hope to make a career quickly and find better jobs in the touristic structure that will stabilize the life they live. And it seems that this hope depends more on the role of the ski resorts company than on that of the community. In this context, the community obviously forgets that this is of particular importance for its future development, as potential future leaders of the community must be seen within this group of migrants.

References

Adelman, B.J.E., Heberlein, T.A. and Bonnicksen, T.M. (1982) Social psychological explanations for the persistence of a conflict between paddling canoeists and motorcraft users in the boundary waters canoe area. *Leisure Sciences* 5 (1), 45–61.

Crompton J.L. (1979) Motivations for pleasure vacation. *Annals of Tourism Research* 6 (4), 408–424.

Crompton J.L. and Ankomah, P.K. (1993) Choice set propositions in destination decisions. *Annals of Tourism Research* 20 (3), 461–476.

DiePresse.com (2017) Reiseströme: Wer warum wohin will. Available at: https://diepresse.com/home/schaufenster/reise/5236041/Reisestroeme_Wer-warum-wohin-will (accessed 17 January 2019).

ETC (European Travel Commission) (2014) Target market – China. Marketing strategies for tourism destinations, a competitive analysis. European Travel Commission, Brussels, Belgium.

Hannich, F.M. (2007) *Destinationsmarken im Special Interest Tourismus*. Gabler Verlag, Wiesbaden, Germany.

Henschel, K. (2002) *Internationaler Tourismus*. Oldenbourg Verlag, Munich/Vienna, Germany/Austria.

Jacob, G.R. and Schreyer, R. (1980) Conflict in outdoor recreation: a theoretical perspective. *Journal of Leisure Research* 12 (4), 368–380.

Leslie, D. (1986) Tourism and conservation in national parks. *Tourism Management* 7(1), 52–56.

Moutinho, L. (1987) Consumer behaviour in tourism. *European Journal of Marketing* 21, 5–44.

Pröbstl, U., Wirth, V. and Haider, W. (2014) Wie viel 'Natur' suchen deutsche Urlauberinnen und Urlauber in den Alpen? Eine Quellgebietsstudie bezogen auf den Sommertourismus. *Natur und Landschaft* 89(1), 26–32.

16 Winter Recreation Trends in the Swedish Mountains – Challenges and Opportunities

PETER FREDMAN* AND TATIANA CHEKALINA

Mid-Sweden University, Östersund, Sweden

16.1 Introduction

The Swedish mountain region is an attractive recreation landscape and tourism is an increasingly important use of the area, despite it being a sparsely populated area far from the more urbanized regions further south (Heberlein *et al.*, 2002; Lundmark, 2005; Fredman *et al.*, 2016). The alpine area above the tree line covers about 10% of the country, while the mountain municipalities have less than 2% of the Swedish population. Besides a handful of larger alpine ski resorts, a few areas have more developed hut-to-hut systems for hiking and cross-country skiing, while most places are less accessible with limited services for tourism. Hence, most of the mountain tourism in Sweden is small-scale, dispersed and features strong seasonality patterns (Lundmark, 2006). The proportion of protected areas is significantly higher than the average for Sweden, providing opportunities for more nature- and culture-oriented tourism, while motorized and extractive activities are typically more restricted in such areas. Whereas summer tourism dominates in the north, winter tourism dominates in the southern parts of the mountain region (Heberlein *et al.*, 2002).

Most of the visitation to the Swedish mountains takes place during the winter season. Fredman *et al.* (2016) estimate that 50% of all domestic visits take place between January and April (main winter season), while 30% take place in the summer (May–August) and 20% in the September–December period. The most popular activities in the winter season are downhill skiing, cross-country skiing, picnicking, sledging and snowmobiling, while in the summer and autumn different forms of hiking dominates. Relaxation, being with family and friends, being close to nature and physical activity are the main motivations to visit the mountains in wintertime (Fredman *et al.*, 2016). The average expenditure for a visit to the mountain region is approximately €950, and winter visitors spend about 10% more compared with summer visitors. A major driver in this context is the downhill ski industry, which in the 2016/17 season reported SEK1.46 billion in ski pass sales (SLAO, 2017). The economic significance is probably also the reason why most of the scientific literature on winter tourism has circled around alpine skiing.

Hudson (2003) estimated the ski market to include some 70 million skiers worldwide, primarily within Europe, North America and Japan. While skiing continues to

---

* E-mail: peter.fredman@miun.se

grow in regions such as Eastern Europe and South-east Asia, the markets in Europe and North America have matured and participation levels have stabilized. However, economic progress in China and Eastern Europe has led to new emerging markets with high growth rates (Vanat, 2019). Looking into the more recent skiing literature it is obvious that more attention is given to impact from climate change than any other issues involving this winter activity. Steiger *et al.* (2019) reviewed 119 publications that examined the climate change risk to ski tourism and made several noteworthy observations. They found decreased reliability of slopes dependent on natural snow, increased snowmaking requirements, shortened and more variable ski seasons, a contraction in the number of operating ski areas, altered competitiveness among and within regional ski markets, and attendant implications for ski tourism employment and values of vacation property real estate values.

These findings are interesting, also beyond the topic of climate change, since they point to the many relationships there are between environmental, economic, technological and social factors affecting tourism in general, and winter tourism in particular. Mega trends, such as climate change or new technology, produce drivers of change that impact conditions at local, regional and national levels (Elmahdy *et al.*, 2017), such as recreation motivations and constraints (Fredman and Heberlein, 2005) and the restructuring of local economies (Lundmark, 2005). They will also play a significant role when it comes to participation in typical mountain recreation activities such as hiking and skiing. Hence, the aim of this chapter is to review trends in some of the main winter recreation activities in the Swedish mountains in order to discuss associated challenges and opportunities through the lens of such mega trends. To do so, we take advantage of previous studies of mountain recreation in Sweden (Naturvårdsverket, 1985; Fredman and Heberlein, 2003) and analyse participation trends with a special focus on downhill skiing, cross-country skiing and snowmobiling.

16.2 Method

Data for this chapter come from three different surveys. The first and original survey (SEPA, 1985) was carried out by the Swedish Environmental Protection Agency in the mid-1980s in order to study participation in mountain recreation for environmental management purposes (Naturvårdsverket, 1985). Questions asked concerned region visited, participation in key activities and choice of lodging. This survey was replicated twice by the European Tourism Research Institute at Mid-Sweden University (ETOUR, 2000 and ETOUR, 2013), providing an opportunity to study trends in Swedish mountain tourism (Fredman and Heberlein, 2003; Fredman *et al.*, 2016). This chapter reports trends among domestic visitors to the Swedish mountains based on these three surveys. Table 16.1 provides an overview of survey methodologies and response rates. In order to study changes over time, the selection of activities and framing of the questions had to rely on the original design from 1985. This survey was administered through regular post to a sample of 2500 individuals living in Sweden. The latter surveys also included a postal questionnaire, but with some methodological variations. The ETOUR (2000) survey used a telephone screener, which identified visitors to the mountain region who later received a follow-up postal questionnaire. Postal survey is a well-established method for a self-administered survey distribution, which is an effective and rather inexpensive approach to reach a specific sample (Finn *et al.*, 2000).

Table 16.1. Survey methodologies and response rates.

Study	Study period	Method	Responses	Response rate
SEPA 1984	1980–1984	Postal survey	1886	75%
ETOUR 2000	1995–1999[a]	Telephone screener + follow-up postal survey	1384	64%
ETOUR 2013	2009–2013	Online panel survey	1000	35%[b]
		Postal survey	355	

[a]May 1995 – April 2000; [b]Response rate of postal survey.

However, due to declining response rates and lower response rates for the younger generation cohorts, the ETOUR (2013) survey had two separate approaches. One online panel survey with 1000 participants complemented a traditional postal survey sent to 1000 individuals. Leisure and tourism research increasingly utilizes online panels as the data collection method (Hung and Petrick, 2012). A mixed data collection strategy is a way to overcome the exclusion of non-internet users from the sample, which is the main disadvantage of online panel surveys (Callegaro et al., 2014). The 2009–2013 figures reported here combine data from the online and postal surveys.

The population surveyed was individuals living in Sweden of age 15–70 years, which grew from 5.9 million in year 1984 to 6.2 million in year 2000 and 6.8 million in year 2013. Although data collection procedures did differ between the surveys, they all applied a random sampling frame to reach the target population. The question asked was: 'Think about your visits to the Swedish mountains the last five years. How many times have you participated in the following activities?'. The frequency of participation was measured on a 5-point scale with the categories: 'Never', '1–2 times', '3–5 times', '6–10 times' and 'More than 10 times'. For the purpose of this study, we report the number of people, and proportion of the population, participating at least once, one to five times, and more than five times during each 5-year period, which means the two latter measures can also be interpreted as people participating on average 'once a year or less' and 'more often than once a year'.

16.3 Winter Recreation Trends 1980–2013

Figures 16.1 to 16.4 show participation trends of the winter recreation activities studied among domestic visitors to the Swedish mountain region between 1980 and 2013. Each figure reports both the proportion of the population participating (in per cent) and the total number of participants (proportion times the surveyed population). Significant changes between the periods studied are estimated with a z-test for the difference of proportions and reported at $p < 0.05$ or better.

The most popular activity, downhill skiing, increased dramatically from the early 1980s to the late 1990s, but has since then been quite stable. Our data show that the early increase in this activity accounts for those participating one to five times, while for the latter period there is a significant drop in participation among people skiing more than once a year. Hence, in this case the trend is quite clear: alpine ski areas increasingly attract less frequent skiers (those skiing no more than once a year on average), while they have lost the more frequent skiers (those skiing more than once a year on average).

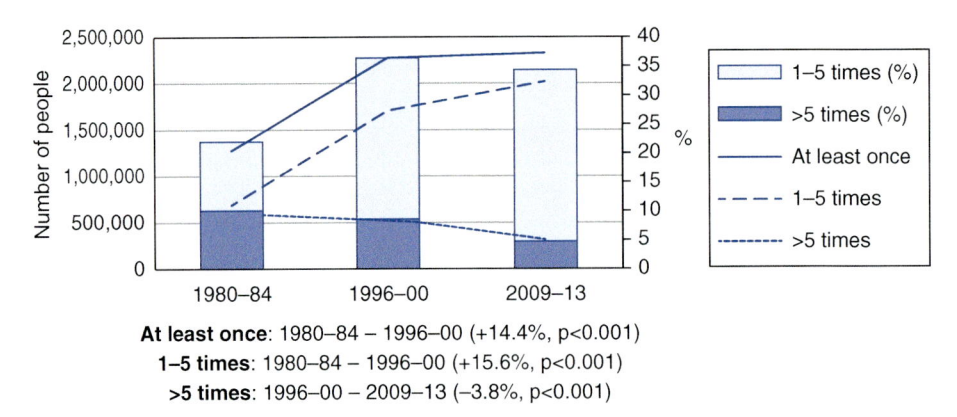

At least once: 1980–84 – 1996–00 (+14.4%, p<0.001)
1–5 times: 1980–84 – 1996–00 (+15.6%, p<0.001)
>5 times: 1996–00 – 2009–13 (−3.8%, p<0.001)

Fig. 16.1. Downhill skiing: changes in participation 1980–2013.

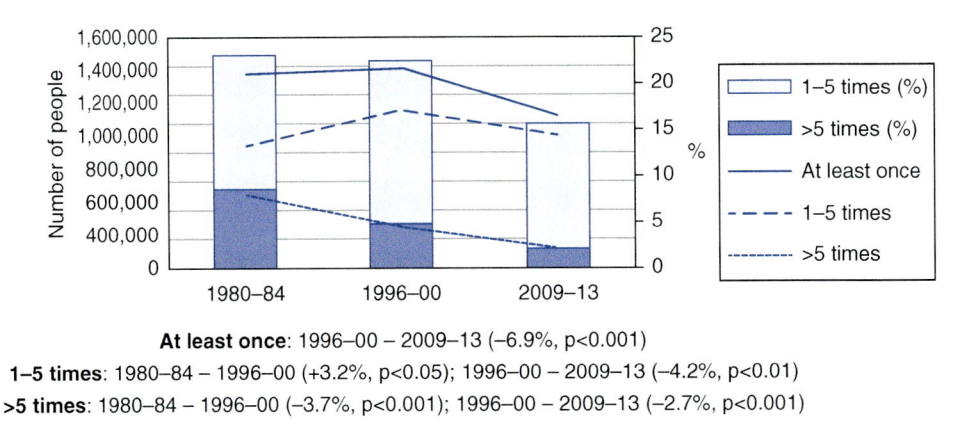

At least once: 1996–00 – 2009–13 (−6.9%, p<0.001)
1–5 times: 1980–84 – 1996–00 (+3.2%, p<0.05); 1996–00 – 2009–13 (−4.2%, p<0.01)
>5 times: 1980–84 – 1996–00 (−3.7%, p<0.001); 1996–00 – 2009–13 (−2.7%, p<0.001)

Fig. 16.2. Cross-country skiing (day): changes in participation 1980–2013.

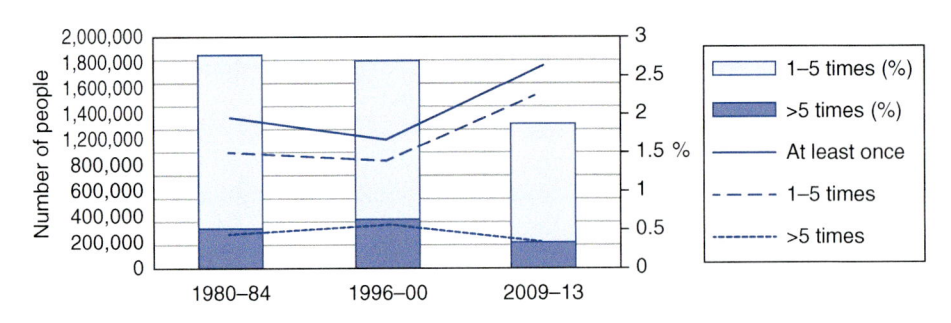

Fig. 16.3. Cross-country skiing (overnight): changes in participation 1980–2013.

The second most popular recreation activity, cross-country skiing, was measured both as 1-day and overnight tours (see Figs 16.2 and 16.3). One-day tours are considerably more common than the overnight tours and feature several significant changes in participation over time. While the proportion of the population that did 1-day tours one to five times during a 5-year period increased from the early 1980s to the

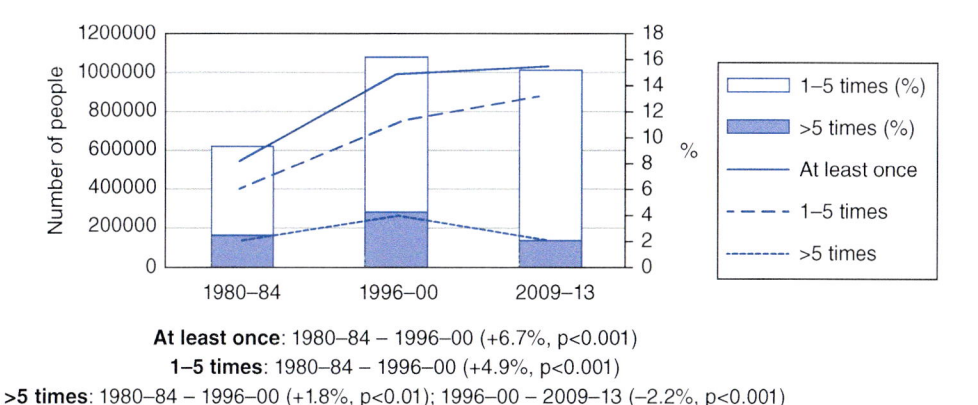

At least once: 1980–84 – 1996–00 (+6.7%, p<0.001)
1–5 times: 1980–84 – 1996–00 (+4.9%, p<0.001)
>5 times: 1980–84 – 1996–00 (+1.8%, p<0.01); 1996–00 – 2009–13 (–2.2%, p<0.001)

Fig. 16.4. Snowmobiling: changes in participation 1980–2013.

late 1990s, those who did ski more than five times decreased. Hence, the number of people participating in 1-day cross-country skiing tours at least once hardly changed at all between the first two periods studied. For the later most recent period, the story is quite different. In this case, total participation decreased significantly, and figures are negative for both the more and less frequent participants.

Looking at the overnight cross-country skiers, statistical analyses did not reveal any significant differences between the periods studied (see Fig. 16.3). The number of people participating in this activity did increase in the 2009–2013 period compared with the two earlier periods, but the small number of observations make conclusions uncertain. With this in mind, the pattern follows the two previous activities with increases among less frequent participants and decreases among the more frequent participants.

Finally, the only motorized activity studied, snowmobiling, features patterns similar to downhill skiing. Participation increased significantly between the early 1980s and late 1990s for all three measures, while the most frequent snowmobilers decreased between late 1990s and the early 2010s (see Fig. 16.4). Hence, overall snowmobiling has increased significantly during the past few decades, but the increase accounts for the less frequent participants, e.g. those doing snowmobiling no more than once a year on average.

16.4 Social, Technological, Economic and Environmental Change 1980–2013

While the trends identified above provide useful information to better understand winter recreation patterns, they certainly do not operate in isolation. Winter tourism, being a subsector of the broader tourism field, is highly affected by several drivers or mega trends (Dwyer *et al.*, 2008). In a literature review, Elmahdy *et al.* (2017) identified 22 different drivers within the social, technological, economic, environmental and political domains of relevance to the nature-based tourism sector. Population growth, urbanization, changing work patterns, lifestyles, high-tech equipment, ICT, economic development and climate change are among those drivers that perhaps have the greatest impact on winter recreation in a mountain context.

Looking at the 33-year timespan of this study, the population studied increased by 15% and the proportion of Swedes living in urban areas (tätort) increased from 83% to 87% (Statistics Sweden, 2018). A reduction in physically demanding employment and more flexible work patterns increase the demand for physical activity during leisure time (Dickinson and Peeters, 2014). Consumers of today are more individualistic, and choices are driven by a desire to define oneself by the products and services consumed. People are increasingly seeking value for money, not necessarily low prices (Dwyer *et al.*, 2008; Enger *et al.*, 2014).

The development of high-tech outdoor recreation equipment and clothing provide opportunities for people to go further and stay longer, even in harsh winter conditions. Smartphones and GPS-based equipment can add safety and enhance the experience of visiting mountains. According to Buckley (2000), this is a key driver behind the immense growth of the outdoor recreation sector. More niche activities (e.g. various forms of skiing such as skate, classic, jibbing, powder) requiring specialized equipment add to this development, which is of course also driven by higher personal incomes. Economic growth in both developed and emerging economies, the increase in disposable income and the emergence of sharing economies have major impacts on the tourism industry (Elmahdy *et al.*, 2017). In Sweden, the median of the disposable income among all households increased by 34% between 1991 and 2013, and the average income from work increased by 61% between 1980 and 2013 (Statistics Sweden, 2018). Today, people can afford to pay their way out in the mountains, through better equipment, guided services and more comfortable lodging, to a larger extent than in the early 1980s.

Finally, the natural environment and climate conditions are crucial in determining the attractiveness and viability of a region as a tourist destination (Elmahdy *et al.*, 2017). In this context, climate change is likely to have major impacts on opportunities for winter recreation in mountain regions in the future. Climate change is not only affecting natural tourist attractions, but also impacts the profitability of the industry through higher energy costs. Climate change will have a negative impact on winter tourism in Northern Europe and North America, where warmer and wetter conditions are expected to shorten the season. In Sweden, the average winter temperature (measured at 35 stations throughout the country) was below average in 11 years and above average in 22 years between 1980 and 2013 (SMHI, 2018). Moen and Fredman (2007) examined 30 years of climate parameters (1970–2000) relevant to alpine winter tourism in Sweden to predict effects on the number of skiing days in order to estimate the monetary impact for the skiing industry. This study show predicted losses larger than ski ticket sales and recommended that ski destinations should implement year-round activities as an adaptation strategy.

16.5 Challenges and Opportunities

The impact from climate change on winter tourism is perhaps the most significant challenge the industry is facing for the future (Steiger *et al.*, 2019). The growing awareness of climate change is, however, mainly limited to perceiving the issue as a global phenomenon, while awareness of regional and branch-specific consequences that will lead to actions is not identified (Trawöger, 2014). Whether the decline in skiing recognized in this study is because of less favourable conditions due to climate change or not is difficult to say. It could just as well be an indication of Swedish skiers substituting the Swedish mountains with other destinations in the European Alps, North America and/or Japan in the vein of increased global travel. One observation, however, is that the capacity for snowmaking has increased considerable during the study period, which is typically identified as a measure to adapt to the negative effects from climate change (Scott, 2006).

One interesting finding from this study is that people appear to participate less frequently in the activities studied. Both alpine skiing and snowmobiling increasingly attract less frequent participants (those participating no more than once a year on average), while they have lost the more frequent participants (those participating more than once a year on average). This could be a sign of activity diversification (people substituting one type of skiing for another), place substitution (people go to different places to ski) and/or decrease in loyalty (people try out skiing once and then do something else). From a business standpoint, a growing market of less frequent participants is probably preferred over the more frequent participants, as the former group is likely to consume more services (rentals, guided tours, etc.) and view a visit to the mountains as relatively more exclusive vis-à-vis the more frequent visitors.

According to Mehmetoglu (2007), nature-based tourism involves mainly affluent tourists from developed countries in relatively high-income groups. Winter tourism is no exception, typically being both equipment- and transportation-dependent. White *et al.* (2016) argue that attracting visitors from high-income groups is particularly important for destinations that focus on outdoor activities that involve high expenditure levels such as developed skiing (snowboarding, downhill) and motorized activities. One approach to target such high-income groups is to look for the international visitors (Fredman, 2008). Since the current study included only domestic visitors, it left out the growing segment of international travellers. According to the Swedish Agency for Economic and Regional Growth (2014), the consumption by foreign tourists in Sweden more than doubled between year 2000 and 2014. While no reliable data exist on foreign visitation to the Swedish mountain region, there are good reasons to believe it is an increasing segment, as shown in, for example, overnight statistics, and may outweigh the negative trend in domestic tourism identified in this study.

As a final remark, we would also like to highlight the methodological challenges in this kind of research. Perhaps the most striking observations are the decreasing response rates reported in Table 16.1. This is a general trend in the social sciences, not unique to these surveys, but nevertheless very problematic for the reliability of this kind of research. One approach to deal with this issue is to switch to other data collection methods, such as online panel surveys (Callegaro *et al.*, 2014). While the validity of such panels is under debate, they are cost-effective and the survey instrument becomes more flexible compared with traditional telephone or paper surveys. Any change in data collection method is. however, a challenge to trend analysis as comparisons across surveys become less reliable.

References

Buckley, R. (2000) Neat trends: current issues in nature, eco- and adventure tourism. *International Journal of Tourism Research* 2(6), 437–444. DOI:10.1002/1522-1970(200011/12)2:6<437::AID-JTR245>3.0.CO;2-#

Callegaro, M., Baker, R., Bethlehem, J., Göritz, A.S., Krosnick, J.A. et al. (2014) Online panel research. In: Callegaro, M., Baker, R., Bethlehem, J., Göritz, A.S., Krosnick, J.A. et al. (eds) *Online Panel Research: A Data Quality Perspective*. John Wiley & Sons, Chichester, UK, pp. 1–22.

Dickinson, J.E. and Peeters, P. (2014) Time, tourism consumption and sustainable development. *International Journal of Tourism Research* 16(1), 11–21. DOI:10.1002/jtr.1893

Dwyer, L., Edwards, D., Mistilis, N., Scott, N., Roman, C. et al. (2008) *Trends Underpinning Tourism to 2020: An Analysis of Key Drivers for Change*. CRC for Sustainable Tourism, Gold Coast, Australia.

Elmahdy, Y.M., Haukeland, J.V. and Fredman, P. (2017) *Tourism Megatrends, a Literature Review Focused on Nature-Based Tourism*. Norwegian University of Life Sciences, Faculty of Environmental Sciences and Natural Resource Management. MINA fagrapport 42.

Enger, A., Sandvik, K. and Kildal Iversen, E. (2014) Developing scenarios for the Norwegian travel industry 2025. *Journal of Tourism Futures* 1(1), 4–17. DOI:10.1108/JTF-12-2014-0018

Finn, M., Walton, M. and Elliott-White, M. (2000) *Tourism and Leisure Research Methods: Data Collection, Analysis, and Interpretation*. Pearson Education, Harlow, UK.

Fredman, P. 2008. Determinants of visitor expenditures in mountain tourism. *Tourism Economics* 14(2), 297–311. DOI:10.5367/000000008784460418

Fredman, P. and Heberlein, T.A. (2003) Changes in skiing and snowmobiling in Swedish mountains. *Annals of Tourism Research* 30(2), 485–488. DOI:10.1016/S0160-7383(02)00110-X

Fredman, P. and Heberlein, T.A. (2005) Visits to the Swedish mountains: constraints and motivations. *Scandinavian Journal of Hospitality and Tourism* 5(3), 177–192. DOI:10.1080/15022250500266583

Fredman, P., Wolf-Watz, D., Sandell, K., Wall-Reinius, S., Lexhagen, M. et al. (2016) *Dagens miljömål och framtidens fjällupplevelser – Iakttagelser av aktivitetsmönster, landskapsrelationer och kommunikationsformer*. Mid-Sweden University, ETOUR, rapport 2016:3.

Heberlein, T.A., Fredman, P. and Vuorio, T. (2002) Current tourism patterns in the Swedish mountain region. *Mountain Research and Development* 22(2), 142–149. DOI:10.1659/0276-4741(2002)022[0142:CTPITS]2.0.CO;2

Hudson, S. (2003) Winter sport tourism. In: Hudson, S. (ed.) *Sport and Adventure Tourism*. Haworth Hospitality Press, New York, pp. 89–123.

Hung, K. and Petrick, J.F. (2012) Testing the effects of congruity, travel constraints, and self-efficacy on travel intentions: An alternative decision-making model. *Tourism Management* 33(4), 855–867. DOI:10.1016/j.tourman.2011.09.007

Lundmark, L. (2005) Economic restructuring into tourism in the Swedish mountain range. *Scandinavian Journal of Hospitality and Tourism* 5, 23–45. DOI:10.1080/15022250510014273

Lundmark, L. (2006) Mobility, migration and seasonal tourism employment: evidence from Swedish mountain municipalities. *Scandinavian Journal of Hospitality and Tourism* 6(3), 197–213. DOI:10.1080/15022250600866282

Mehmetoglu, M. (2007) Nature-based tourists: the relationship between their trip expenditures and activities. *Journal of Sustainable Tourism* 15(2), 200–215. DOI:10.2167/jost642.0

Moen, J. and Fredman, P. (2007) Effects of climate change on alpine skiing in Sweden. *Journal of Sustainable Tourism* 15(4), 418–437. DOI:10.2167/jost624.0

Naturvårdsverket (1985) *Svenskarnas Fjällvanor*. Rapport 3019.

Scott, D. (2006) US ski industry adaptation to climate change: hard, soft and policy strategies. In: Hall, C.M. and Gössling, S. (eds) *Tourism and Global Environmental Change*. Routledge, London, pp. 262–285.

SLAO (2017) *Branschrapport 2016–17*. Svenska liftanläggningars organization, Östersund, Sweden.

SMHI (2018) Klimatindikator – temperatur. Available at: www.smhi.se/klimatdata (accessed 12 November 2018).

Statistics Sweden (2018) Statistikdatabasen. Available at: www.scb.se (accessed 12 November 2018).

Steiger, R., Scott, D., Abegg, B., Pons, M. and Aall, C. (2019) A critical review of climate change risk for ski tourism. *Current Issues in Tourism*, 22(11), 1343–1379. DOI:10.1080/13683500.2017.1410110

Swedish Agency for Economic and Regional Growth (2014) *Results from the Swedish Border Survey IBIS 2014, Foreign visitors in Sweden*. Rapport 0188 Rev A, Stockholm, Sweden.

Trawöger, L. (2014) Convinced, ambivalent or annoyed: Tyrolean ski tourism stakeholders and their perceptions of climate change. *Tourism Management* 40, 338–351. DOI:10.1016/j.tourman.2013.07.010

Vanat, L. (2019) 2019 International report on snow and mountain tourism: overview of the key industry figures for ski resorts. Available at: https://www.vanat.ch/RM-world-report-2019.pdf (accessed 17 July 2019).

White, E.M., Bowker, J.M., Askew, A.E., Langner, L.L., Arnold, J.R. *et al*. (2016) Federal outdoor recreation trends: Effects on Economic Opportunities. USDA, General Technical Report, PNW-GTR-945. US Department of Agriculture, Pacific Northwest Research Station, Portland, Oregon.

17 A Matter of Culture: How Cultural Differences Shape Skiing Motivation, Behaviour and Destination Choice

ULRIKE PRÖBSTL-HAIDER* AND NINA MOSTEGL

Institute of Landscape Development, Recreation and Conservation Planning, University of Natural Resources and Life Sciences, Vienna, Austria

17.1 Introduction and Background

Ski resorts in South Tyrol, the most northern part of Italy, are frontrunners in destination planning and management. Located at the geographical heart of the Alps and on their southern side, South Tyrol is an attractive destination for tourists from many countries in different target markets. However, to maintain this success it is necessary to continuously analyse new trends and to understand the motivations and behavioural intentions of guests – at least of those belonging to the main target groups. In addition, research findings show that today's customers – especially in winter tourism – are less loyal than they used to be in the past (ÖHV, 2012). Hence, it will be vital to respond to new trends and emerging preferences, such as vegan cuisine, internet access on slopes and cosy mountain hut restaurants (as potential replacements for self-service cantinas). Therefore, the region of Sexten, in cooperation with the University of Natural Resources and Life Sciences, Vienna, and local stakeholders, decided to examine future trends in more detail in order to be better prepared for future tourists. In the first meetings, practitioners involved in the field stated that in their opinion 'cultural differences' are key to an understanding of current and future decision making and constituted a major driver accounting for differences in demand. We based a crucial hypothesis for the following research on this practical expertise and tried to verify and understand the concept of cultural differences in the context of winter tourism.

Although tourism research has for decades explored cultural effects, they are still perceived as a complex multidimensional phenomenon that is difficult to define (for an extended discussion of terminology, see Reisinger and Turner, 2003). In tourism research, 'culture' is commonly defined as the set of customs, values, norms, beliefs, habits, arts and lifestyle patterns shared within a group or society (Hall, 1976; Reisinger and Turner, 2003; Kang and Moscardo, 2006). In addition, Reisinger and Turner (2002) point out that culture refers to the stable and dominant character of a society shared by most of its individuals and remaining constant over long periods of time. The concept of 'culture' may also be regarded as a helpful guide to behavioural

---

* E-mail: ulrike.proebstl@boku.ac.at

interpretation in various contexts (Kim and Gudykunst, 1988; Burdge, 1996). The term 'cross-cultural' describes relationships between different cultures (Gibbs, 2001). Cross-cultural differences are perceived as particularly important in tourism planning and management (Turner *et al.*, 2002; Kang and Moscardo, 2006). The research on differences in values, rules of social behaviour, perception and social interaction has contributed to three main fields of interest: the cultural background of tourists and its relevance for the experiences they seek out (Reisinger and Turner, 2002; Ng *et al.*, 2007), the clients' cultural background as the basis for successful marketing strategies (Ooi, 2002; Funk and Bruun, 2006) and, finally, the need for cross-cultural understanding to improve tourism management and to deal with clients from diverse cultural backgrounds (see, for example, Weiermair, 2000; Turner *et al.*, 2002; Moscardo, 2004; Ortega and Rodriguez, 2007). In the context of a South Tyrolian ski resort, we are mainly interested in the experiences the various target groups are looking for.

Studies on outdoor recreation and nature-based tourism in Europe (Bell *et al.*, 2007, 2009; Pröbstl *et al.*, 2010; Landauer *et al.*, 2012, 2013) document the importance of studying cross-continental differences: the popularity of many outdoor recreation and sports activities differs across European regions as a result of deviations in the availability of physical resources as well as the different status they hold in various cultures. All these studies confirm that culture strongly influences participation and non-participation in certain sports and that culture should, therefore, be taken into account when researching behaviour in leisure activities, outdoor recreation and tourism. This view is also reflected in tourism and business research (Hofstede, 1980). Research conducted by Triandis (1972) and Hofstede (1980, 1997) has presented ample evidence of differences and similarities among cultures. Recent literature has covered cultural differences in winter tourism only in the context of climate change disregarding the issue of destination choice and experiences desired by tourists in their winter holidays (Gössling *et al.*, 2012; Landauer *et al.*, 2012, 2013). Reisinger and Turner (2003) as well as Landis and Brislin (1983) report the relevance of cultural differences to an understanding of interpersonal interactions and product development, especially in tourism, as these cultural differences may influence behaviour, motivation and destination choice. Our main research questions, therefore, focus on the following aspects:

- Do the main motives and expectations concerning winter holidays in South Tyrol differ among the main target regions (Germany, Austria and Italy)?
- Are these expectations likely to influence destination choice?
- Do cultural experiences – such as regional specialities, the atmosphere in the provided infrastructure and the southern alpine ambience – contribute to a 'special' holiday experience and increase a region's attractiveness?

17.2 Methods

17.2.1 Study area

Sexten, located in the holiday region 'Drei Zinnen', is well known as a summer and winter tourism destination and hosts around 7% of all yearly overnight stays in South

Tyrol (IDM Südtirol, 2018). In order to investigate future tourism trends based on cultural differences, a rather large study area was selected, which allowed us to consider travel flow effects as well as the overall attractiveness of the region compared with similarly situated destinations.

17.2.2 Data collection

In order to deepen our understanding of and knowledge about how cultural differences shape skiing motivation, behaviour and destination choice, the study applied an online questionnaire that targeted German, Italian and Austrian skiers or snowboarders who had already visited the study area for skiing or snowboarding day trips or vacations over the past 5 years. The survey consisted of 22 open- and closed-ended questions (i.e. multiple choice, dichotomous, rating scale [Likert scale questions (Likert, 1977)], and ordinal scale questions). In addition, a stated preference tool (a discrete choice experiment) was applied, which measured preferences on the basis of intended behaviour. The survey opened with questions relating to winter sports activities, the type of trips undertaken and regional preferences, followed by questions concerning the perception of ski resorts and important factors for their selection, the choice experiment, and future aspects including climate change and destination development. The questionnaire concluded with socio-demographic questions.

17.2.3 The discrete choice experiment

In survey-based choice experiments, respondents are asked to indicate which option they prefer the most out of multiple alternatives (i.e. their preferred ski resort). By systematically varying the levels of attributes out of which the different alternatives are comprised, it becomes possible to determine their influence on the stated choices (Auspurg and Liebe, 2011). This approach enables a more direct testing of causal relations than 'common' methods such as Likert scale questions allow. Choice experiments have been applied in nature-based tourism research for a range of purposes (e.g. Arnberger and Haider, 2005; Hunt *et al.*, 2005; Lindberg and Fredman, 2005; Sorice *et al.*, 2005; Brau and Cao, 2006; Unbehaun *et al.*, 2008, Pröbstl-Haider and Haider, 2014). Several publications have further demonstrated the suitability of discrete choice experiments for cross-cultural contexts (Rose *et al.*, 2009; Landauer *et al.*, 2012). The method has been deemed highly useful in forecasting likely behaviour changes in reaction to changed circumstances or the hypothetical availability of certain consumer goods (Louviere *et al.*, 2000; Landauer *et al.*, 2013). Both the complexity of tourist destinations and the fact that many offers do not currently exist (such as vegan cuisine options) suggest perfect conditions for the application of a discrete choice experiment.

Choice experiments rely on multivariate hypothetical scenarios (composed of several relevant attributes), which, in this case, described two skiing destinations. Respondents are repeatedly asked to choose one out of these two destinations. Assuming that these responses are consistent with random utility theory (RUT), they can be analysed with a multinomial logit model (MNL) (McFadden, 1974), or a related logistic choice model. RUT, formalized by Manski (1977), posits that any individual will try to maximize utility when making choices. For the analysis, the total utility is decomposed into a deterministic component (observable) and a random component (McFadden, 1974; Ben-Akiva and Lerman, 1985; Louviere et al., 2000). The probability of selecting one alternative over another can then be described as the exponent of all measurable elements of the selected alternative over the sum of the exponents of all measurable elements of the second alternative. On the basis of this correlation, a use-value for every attribute and its levels can be calculated, which subsequently allows for a depiction of the acceptance of every contingent alternative with the help of a decision support tool. This tool also allows for a depiction of choices of different target groups (i.e. Germans, Austrians, Italians), which are directly based on the participants' preferences indicated in the choice experiment. The interface of the decision support tool mirrors the choice experiment. Each level of every attribute can be altered individually, thereby 'creating' different hypothetical ski resorts. The results can provide significant information for decision makers based on participants' actual preferences.

The choice experiment applied in this survey was framed as follows: 'Like any tourist destination, alpine ski regions must regularly take a critical look at the future development of their services. The wishes and needs of their guests constitute an important basis for this development. In the following, we ask you to evaluate the attractiveness of alpine ski resorts for your winter holidays. To do this, you will need to choose six times between two ski areas. Please select the more attractive ski resort "A" or "B". If you do not like either of the two ski areas, choose "a different ski area".'

Figure 17.1 shows the choice experiment, which contains 12 attributes divided into three blocks. The first block describes the framing conditions such as the resorts' cross-border skiing opportunities, proximity to protected areas, distance and type of connection from the hotel to the cable car, and connectivity to other resorts (by ski circuit or train). The attributes in the second block ('slope characteristics') describe the main characteristic of each resort including the percentage of snow secure areas above 1500 m, the total length of slopes, the distribution of slopes according to their difficulty levels and its location within the European Alps (north or south). The last block ('catering and costs') includes culinary offers in the resort, the range of dishes, the costs of ski passes and the discounts available for children between 8 and 15 years of age.

The hypothetical scenarios of the choice experiment were created and combined into choice sets through an orthogonal fractional factorial design produced in SAS using a 'mktex' macro (Deff 88.2824, Aeff 74.8455, Geff 94.423, APSE 0.9071). The design plan contained 96 choice sets. Out of those, a respondent evaluated six randomly chosen choice sets. The opt-out alternative was omitted to establish realistic scenarios and trade-offs.

Collected data were analysed in IBM SPSS Statistics 21. A Latent Gold choice model was executed with the choice experiment data in Latent Gold 5.0. In order to investigate cultural differences, the German, Austrian and Italian samples were analysed separately and were used to design a decision support tool.

The online questionnaire was made available between 1 and 25 July 2017. German, Austrian and Italian panels were purchased from renowned providers. The following sections give an overview of the results of the surveyed winter tourists and the particular responses of Austrian, German and Italian skiing and snowboarding vacationers.

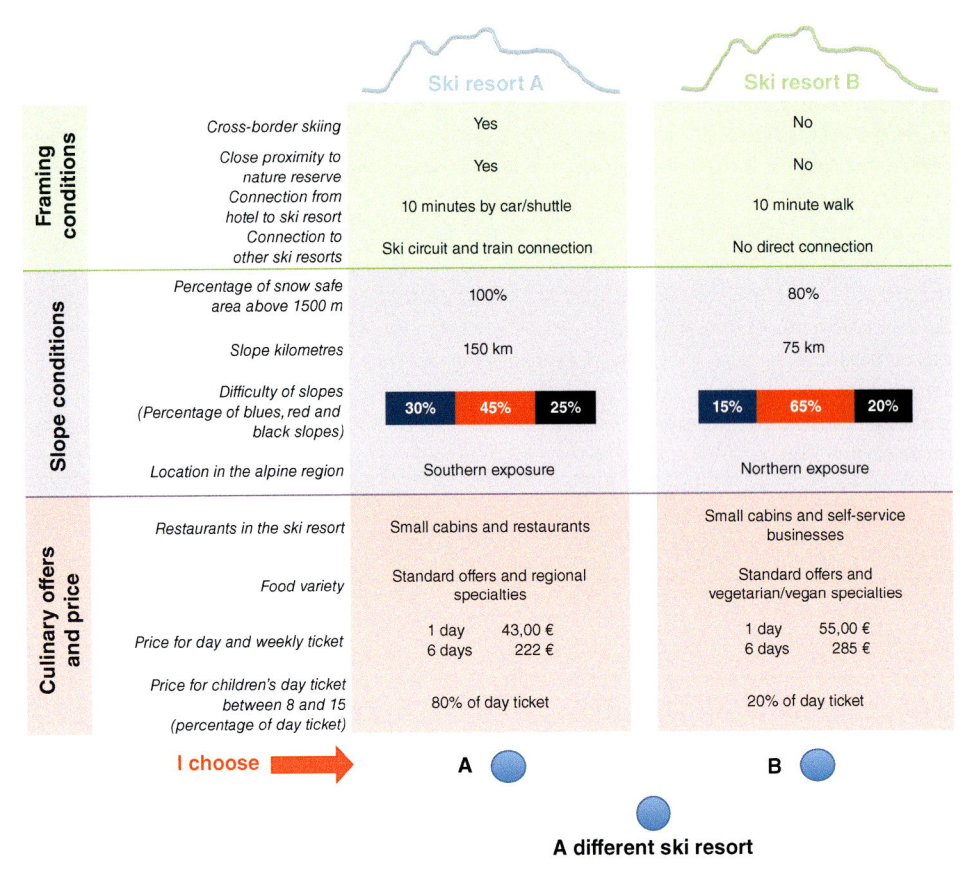

		Ski resort A	Ski resort B
Framing conditions	Cross-border skiing	Yes	No
	Close proximity to nature reserve	Yes	No
	Connection from hotel to ski resort	10 minutes by car/shuttle	10 minute walk
	Connection to other ski resorts	Ski circuit and train connection	No direct connection
Slope conditions	Percentage of snow safe area above 1500 m	100%	80%
	Slope kilometres	150 km	75 km
	Difficulty of slopes (Percentage of blues, red and black slopes)	30% / 45% / 25%	15% / 65% / 20%
	Location in the alpine region	Southern exposure	Northern exposure
Culinary offers and price	Restaurants in the ski resort	Small cabins and restaurants	Small cabins and self-service businesses
	Food variety	Standard offers and regional specialties	Standard offers and vegetarian/vegan specialties
	Price for day and weekly ticket	1 day 43,00 € / 6 days 222 €	1 day 55,00 € / 6 days 285 €
	Price for children's day ticket between 8 and 15 (percentage of day ticket)	80% of day ticket	20% of day ticket
I choose		A	B
		A different ski resort	

Fig. 17.1. Example of a discrete choice experiment depicting the three attribute blocks with a total of 12 attributes: framing conditions, slope conditions, culinary offer and price.

17.3 Results

17.3.1 Sample description

Overall, 2400 participants (800 from each country) responded to the questionnaire: 75% were skiing or snowboarding vacationers, while 25% were classified as day visitors or season ticket holders. The respondents were between 17 and 75 years old (42.44 average age) and displayed an equal gender distribution (48% female, 52% male). The sample featured a high education level but represented all income classes. The three main activities of winter vacations were skiing (66%), winter hiking (11%) and cross-country skiing (8%). The self-evaluation of respondents revealed that about a third classified themselves as advanced skiers/snowboarders. However, the sample also included all kind of experiences: less experienced skiers/snowboarders (beginners 19%, those returning to the sport 26%, advanced 33%, experienced 20%, professional 2%).

From here on out, the presented results refer only to skiing or snowboarding vacationers from the three target countries.

17.3.2 Winter sports activities, company, experience and frequency

The first evident differences emerge from the samples' responses on the activities they planned for their winter vacations. While Austrian participants mainly planned to ski (70%), tourists from Italy and Germany – to a significantly higher percentage – also enjoyed winter hiking and cross-country skiing. Simultaneously, the Austrian sample evaluated itself as more experienced (30% experienced and 3% experts) than German (16% and 1%) and Italian (7% and 0.3%) visitors. About one-third of Italian participants saw themselves as beginners, which corresponds with a low percentage of Italians choosing to ski during their vacations. The results also revealed differences concerning the social aspect of skiing/snowboarding among the different samples. While 46% of German visitors skied with their partner, Austrian and Italian vacationers displayed different social patterns. Among Italian guests, skiing with the whole family seems to be much more common (30%) than among the other two nationalities. This also applies to skiing with friends. The results show that in Italy vacations are considered much more of a 'social event' than in the other two countries. Italian participants were, moreover, the most active in terms of short-term and recreational stays. Just over one-third of all day visitors made regular 1–2-day skiing trips.

The self-owned car constituted the primary means of transport among participants of all three countries. While the particular combination of car and public transport used to reach a holiday destination could potentially offer valuable insights, public transport by itself played a subordinate role, in particular among Austrian participants. Italians used their own cars significantly less often and were more willing to switch to other modes of transport, while Austrian and German participants predominantly drove to their skiing/snowboarding destinations. Over the past decade, South Tyrol has made an effort to improve local train connections in order to pursue two goals: (i) to expand opportunities for the public to reach resorts, and (ii) to connect settlements to ski resorts, thereby offering a new ski circuit of local trains directly connected to cable car stations. While German and Italian guests appeared to be somewhat attracted by this offer, Austrian guests were significantly less interested in train services.

Finally, respondents were asked about their perception of climate change. Awareness of the issue was high among all three nationalities, as the majority believed that first signs of a change in climate are already visible. However, the number of Italian guests stating their uncertainty or arguing that the effects of climate change will occur at a later stage was discernibly higher compared with the other two samples.

17.3.3 Main motivation for and aspects of winter sports activities

Respondents were asked to rate different aspects of winter sports activities on a scale from 1 (unimportant) to 4 (very important). Overall, the most important aspects all participants cited were 'being outdoors and being active in fresh air', 'enjoying nature', and 'experiencing the winter landscape'. A closer look at the three different nationalities reveals a number of significant differences.

As mentioned in the introduction, it is likely that cultural differences will be expressed in different motivations and expectations. The following figure (see Fig. 17.2) shows that Italian respondents in particular rated social experiences as very important

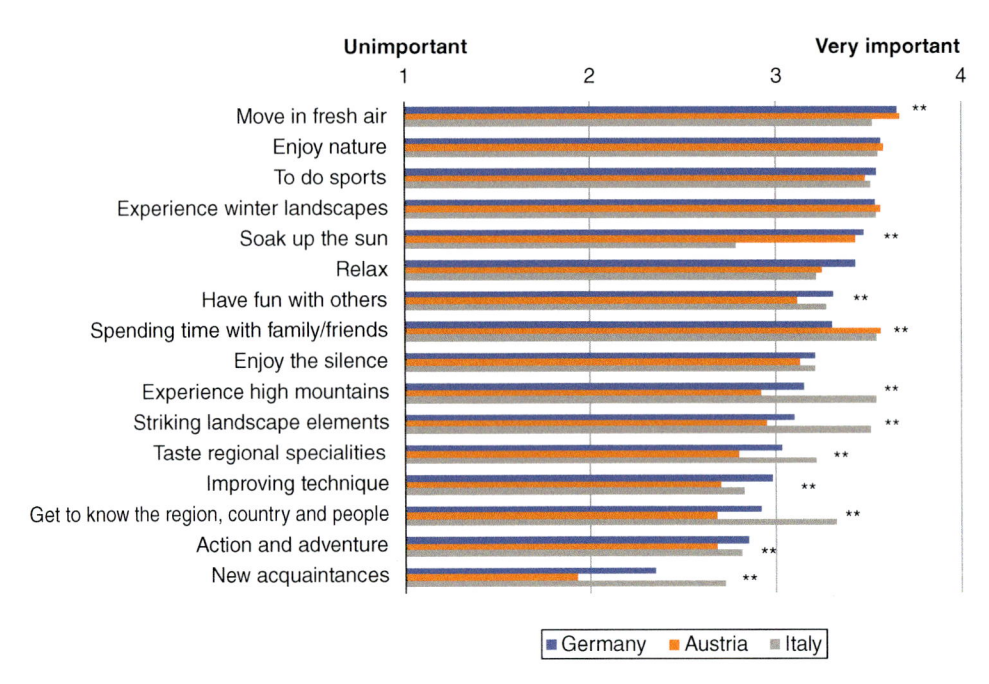

Fig. 17.2. Motivation for and important aspects of winter sports activities; ** indicates significance at a 5% level among the three countries.

(e.g. 'having fun with others', 'spending time with family and friends', 'making new acquaintances', and 'getting to know the region, country and people'). Social and regional aspects were significantly more important for Italian tourists and day visitors than for Austrian and German participants.

For German guests, the pursuit of outdoor activities surrounded by nature was much more important (e.g. 'being active in fresh air', 'experiencing high mountain regions', 'witnessing striking landscape elements'). Furthermore, 'enjoying the sunshine' was much more important to them than to Italian guests.

As for Austrian respondents, the chance to practise their chosen outdoor sport and to improve their technique were considered the most important aspects.

17.3.4 Ski resort selection criteria

When it comes to selection criteria for the choice of a ski resort, the range of influencing factors was similar among all participants, yet they differed in the way they prioritized different aspects. For German and Austrian skiers/snowboarders, the price–performance ratio was the most important criterion, while Italian participants considered the beauty of the winter landscape to be the most crucial factor. In accordance with the main findings concerning motivational factors (see Fig. 17.2), all respondents highlighted the relevance of the 'nature experience and view', the 'beautiful winter landscape' and the availability of 'different slopes'. The least important features when selecting a ski resort were a WiFi connection on slopes and technical infrastructure such as half-pipes (see Fig. 17.3).

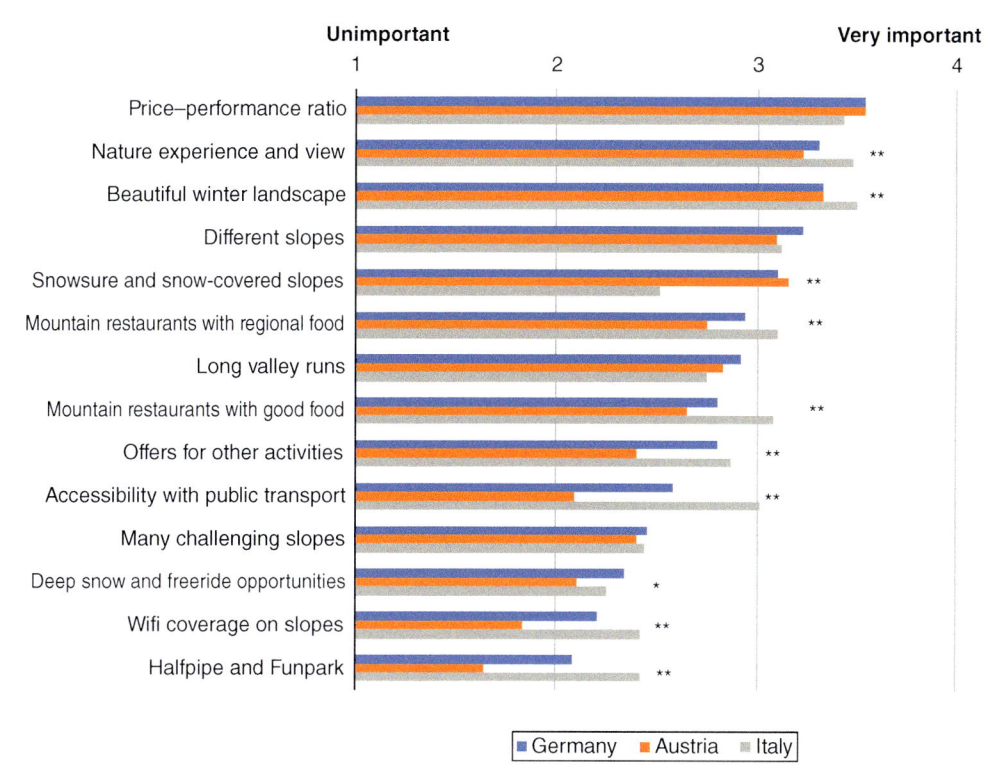

Fig. 17.3. Important criteria when selecting a ski resort for a vacation; ** indicates significance at a 5% level; * indicates significance at the 10% level among the three countries.

With minor exceptions, we again observed significant differences among the three nationalities confirming previous findings. For the Austrian sample, the quality of slopes and the level of snow security was of utmost interest, which differs significantly from the other samples. Public transportation, on the other hand, was perceived as unimportant by this sample, which complies with the findings presented in Fig. 17.2. Italian tourists further reiterated their interest in 'nature experience', the 'winter landscape', 'regional food', 'good mountain restaurants' and 'accessibility via public transport'. Aside from a common interest in 'nature experience', it seems that German vacationers most appreciated diversity and a high variety of recreational offers ('different slopes', 'long ski runs', 'many challenging slopes' and 'free ride opportunities').

17.3.5 Preferences stated in the choice experiment

Cultural experiences and proximity to a nature reserve emerged as particularly important in the overall analysis. In addition, all respondents preferred smaller ski huts and restaurants compared with large-scale self-service cantinas. In general, regional specialities were preferred over vegetarian or vegan offers. The distance from the hotel to the ski resort was preferred to be short and mode of travel should be comfortable; walking distance was deemed ideal. The attractiveness of a resort increased with size – but not indefinitely (up to 80 km). The choice experiment again underlined the crucial importance of the price level: most vacationers were price-sensitive as evidenced by the way a resort's appeal decreased with an increase in pricing. However, a discounted skiing pass for children was only considered relevant by Italian respondents.

The following examples describe the effects of potential management strategies pursued by the cable car enterprise in Sexten. They clearly demonstrate the trade-offs tourists are willing to make as well as their preferences among the proposed strategies.

Access to other ski resorts by train

As Sexten has in the past invested extensively in the improvement of its local train infrastructure, the question arises as to whether additional investments in train services are economically expedient. Linking the platforms of train stations directly to cable car stations, as well as connecting skiing resorts with each other via train will significantly improve accessibility and expand the entire ski circuit for both guests and locals. However, it was unclear whether customers recognized this benefit.

The decision support tool revealed that respondents were well aware of this new strategy. Figure 17.4 shows two ski resorts (A and B) that differ only in size and the train connection they offer to other ski resorts (highlighted in red). Results indicate that the majority in all countries preferred the smaller ski resort 'A', which features a train connection, in spite of the fact that larger resorts are generally preferred. Even vacationers from Austria and Germany, who include more experienced skiers usually aiming for larger resorts, were highly attracted by this offer, despite resort 'A' being only half the size of resort 'B'. This trade-off – 'connectivity in return for size' – supports the strategy pursued by the South Tyrolean cooperation of ski resorts, which Sexten is a part of.

Implications of a resort's location within the Alps

Sexten's proximity to the Austrian border and other Italian regions affords unique opportunities: cross-border skiing and the experience of different lifestyles, regional specialities and landscapes. As a unique feature, this effect has not been investigated before; hence, the question arises if this kind of offer would be of particular interest to vacationers. In addition, testing the economic advantages of a southern alpine exposure as well as of culinary offers provided in attractive smaller establishments such as mountain cabins and restaurants could be of central interest to management in the tourist sector. To this end, a southern resort featuring cross-border skiing opportunities, small restaurants and regional delicacies was contrasted in the decision support tool with a ski resort in the northern part of the Alps with larger infrastructure, no regional food offers, but a significantly lower price for day tickets (see Fig. 17.5). The result revealed that Austrian and German respondents preferred the cross-border experience in the southern part of the Alps despite the higher total costs, which are ordinarily rejected. Italian tourists, on the other hand, were attracted by the resort in the northern part of the Alps, which could be attributed to a desire to experience something new and different rather than the southern parts of the Alps and their familiar lifestyle. However, all things considered, location and a lower price level were not able to fully compensate for other aspects such as culinary experiences.

	Ski resort A	Ski resort B
Cross-border skiing	No	No
Close proximity to nature reserve	No	No
Connection from hotel ski resort	10 minute walk	10 minute walk
Connection to other ski resorts	Ski circuit and train connection	No direct connection
Percentage of snowsafe area above 1500 m	100%	100%
Slope kilometres	50 km	100 km
Difficulty Blue	20%	50%
Difficulty Red	55%	25%
Difficulty Black	25%	25%
Location in the alpine region	Southern exposure	Southern exposure
Restaurants in the ski resort	Self-service businesses	Self-service businesses
Food variety	Standard offers and vegetarian/vegan specialities	Standard offers and vegetarian/vegan specialities
Price for day ticket	€ 40.00	€ 40.00
Price for weekly pass	€ 207	€ 207
Savings for children between 8 and 15 years	100%	100%

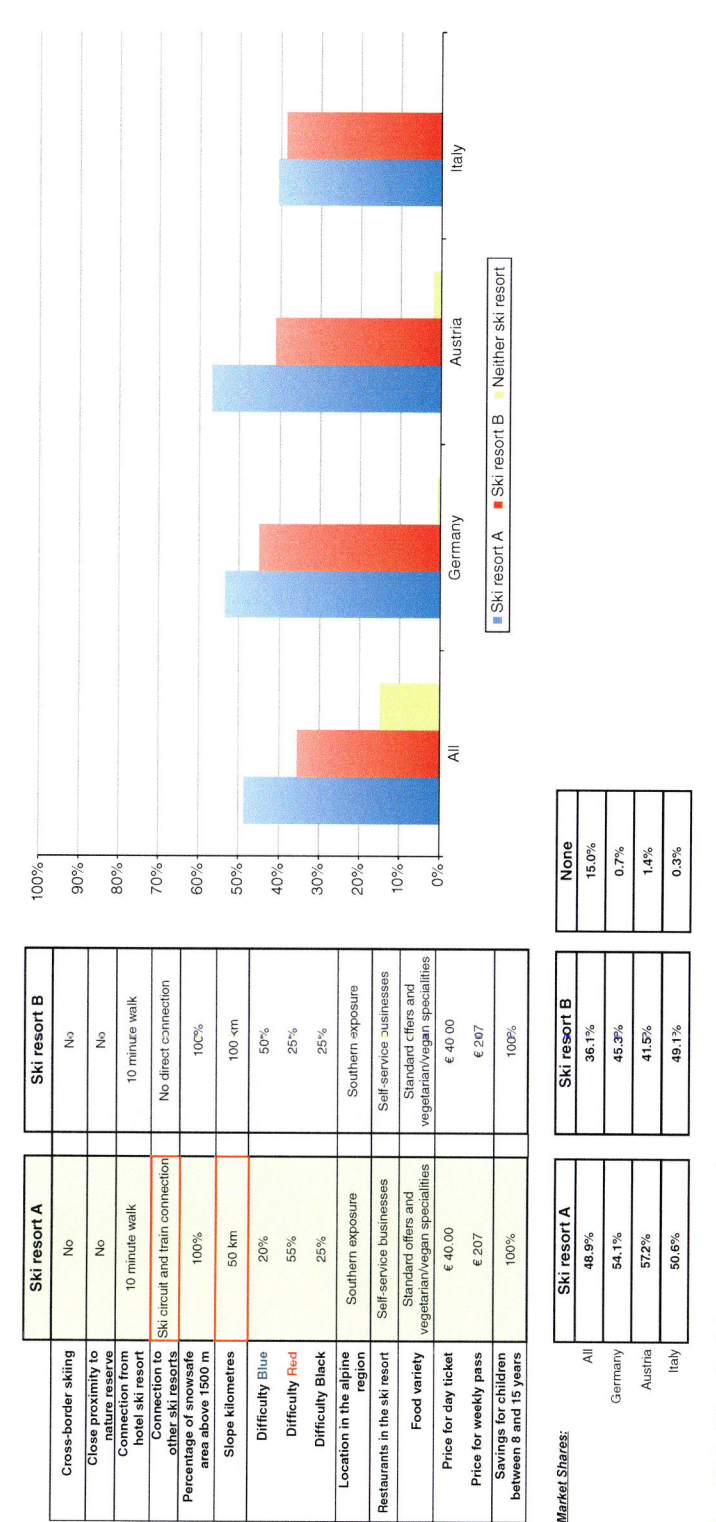

Market Shares:

	Ski resort A	Ski resort B	None
All	48.9%	36.1%	15.0%
Germany	54.1%	45.3%	0.7%
Austria	57.2%	41.5%	1.4%
Italy	50.6%	49.1%	0.3%

Fig. 17.4. The decision support tool shows the relevance of size and train connection to other ski resorts by country. Differences between the ski resorts 'A' and 'B' are highlighted in red.

A Matter of Culture

201

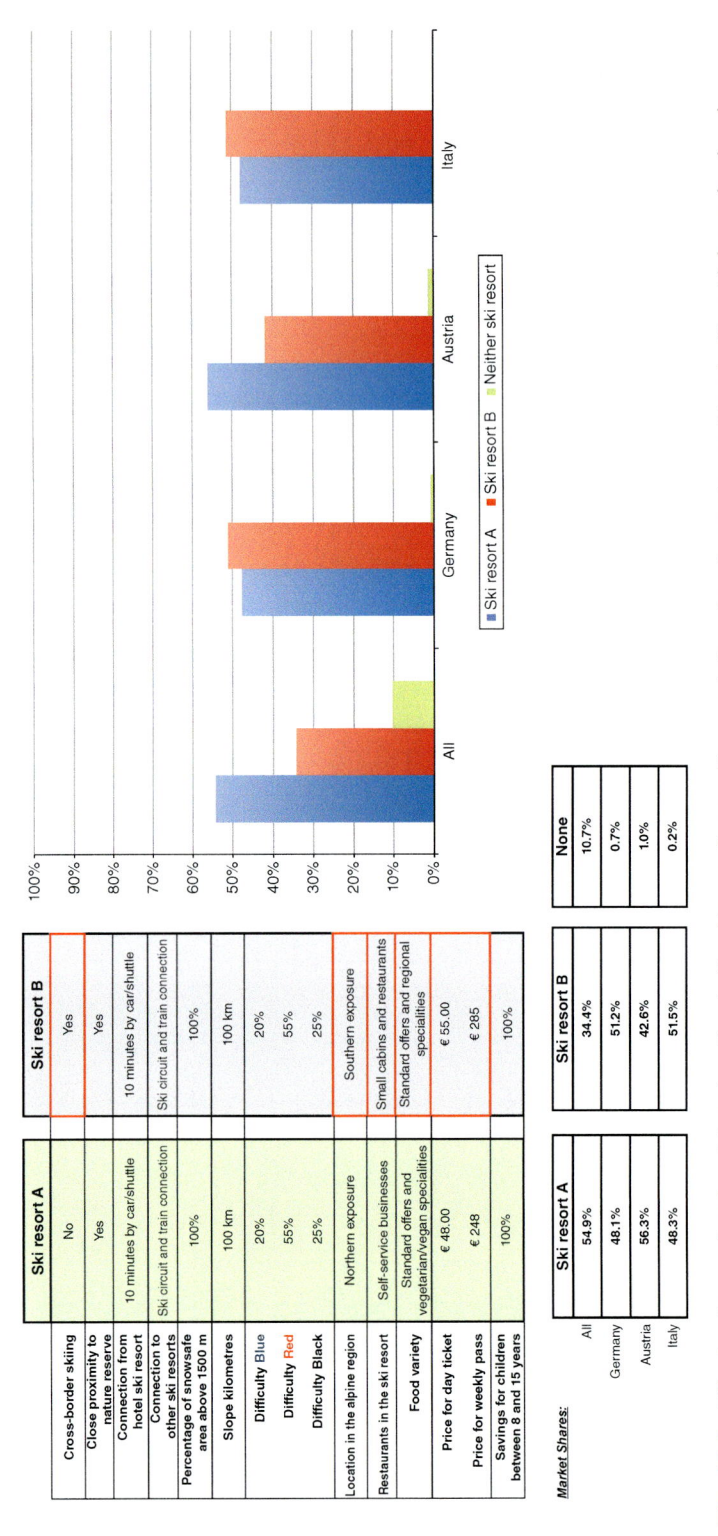

	Ski resort A	Ski resort B
Cross-border skiing	No	Yes
Close proximity to nature reserve	Yes	Yes
Connection from hotel ski resort	10 minutes by car/shuttle	10 minutes by car/shuttle
Connection to other ski resorts	Ski circuit and train connection	Ski circuit and train connection
Percentage of snowsafe area above 1500 m	100%	100%
Slope kilometres	100 km	100 km
Difficulty Blue	20%	20%
Difficulty Red	55%	55%
Difficulty Black	25%	25%
Location in the alpine region	Northern exposure	Southern exposure
Restaurants in the ski resort	Self-service businesses	Small cabins and restaurants
Food variety	Standard offers and vegetarian/vegan specialities	Standard offers and regional specialities
Price for day ticket	€ 48.00	€ 55.00
Price for weekly pass	€ 248	€ 285
Savings for children between 8 and 15 years	100%	100%

Market Shares:

	Ski resort A	Ski resort B	None
All	54.9%	34.4%	10.7%
Germany	48.1%	51.2%	0.7%
Austria	56.3%	42.6%	1.0%
Italy	48.3%	51.5%	0.2%

Fig. 17.5. Effects of cross-border skiing, location in the Alps, culinary offers and size of restaurants combined with a higher price level.

Singling out preferences by country

In light of the discussion on the relevance of cultural differences, the question arose whether it is possible to generate a hypothetical ski resort that is highly appreciated by one nationality but dismissed by the others. In order to test this aspect, one choice set was designed to reflect the values, motivations and preferences of the Italian sample. The aim was to determine whether this resort would be preferred by Italian respondents but disliked by German and Austrian tourists. Figure 17.6 depicts a relevant example. Ski resort 'B' was characterized by attractive natural conditions, convenient connections from the hotel to the ski resort, a comparatively smaller size without connections to other resorts, slopes of a low difficulty level (50% blue and only 5% black) and a 100% discount for children. Despite resort 'B' being more expensive than the alternative resort 'A', all needs and demands of the Italian target group were clearly met, as they significantly preferred resort 'B'. Figure 17.6 also projects typical preferences cited by Austrian and German tourists, who clearly focus on the skiing aspect when selecting their favoured resorts. The latter preferred the more reasonably priced resort 'A' featuring more challenging slopes as well as more kilometres of slopes and a link to other resorts (via ski circuit and train).

17.4 Discussion

17.4.1 Cultural differences

Our first research question asked whether the main motives and expectations for winter holidays in South Tyrol differed between the main target nationalities (Germany, Austria and Italy). The presented results clearly show significant differences between Italian and Austrian, as well as Austrian and German tourists with regard to their main motivations, values, needs and, especially, in their destination choices. The social aspect of skiing was of greater importance to the Italian sample, as the findings shown in Figs 17.2 and 17.3 illustrate, which is most likely a result of different cultural values. Being with family and friends, skiing in family units and enjoying their time together were of significantly higher value to Italian vacationers, which was also reflected in the company they usually go skiing with. These differences were clearly evident in the respondents' selection of resorts in the choice experiment. For their 'socially focused' skiing holidays, Italians did not require long and intricate slopes or connections to other resorts. Italian respondents instead sought readily accessible and easy slopes, which they could ski with family members with different levels of experience, and appreciated pricing systems that offered discounted day tickets for their children. These findings confirm our second research question demonstrating that different values, motivations and expectations are likely to influence destination choice. The results can be interpreted as evidence of cultural inclinations, which is further corroborated by the outcome of the motivation and resort selection analyses. The importance of additional offers and services, such as WiFi on slopes, halfpipes and other sporting activities, highlights another set of differences based around cultural beliefs and values. By comparison, the Austrian sample expressed demands centred around different prerequisites from the others. While being with friends and family constituted an important motivation, the choice experiment clearly demonstrated

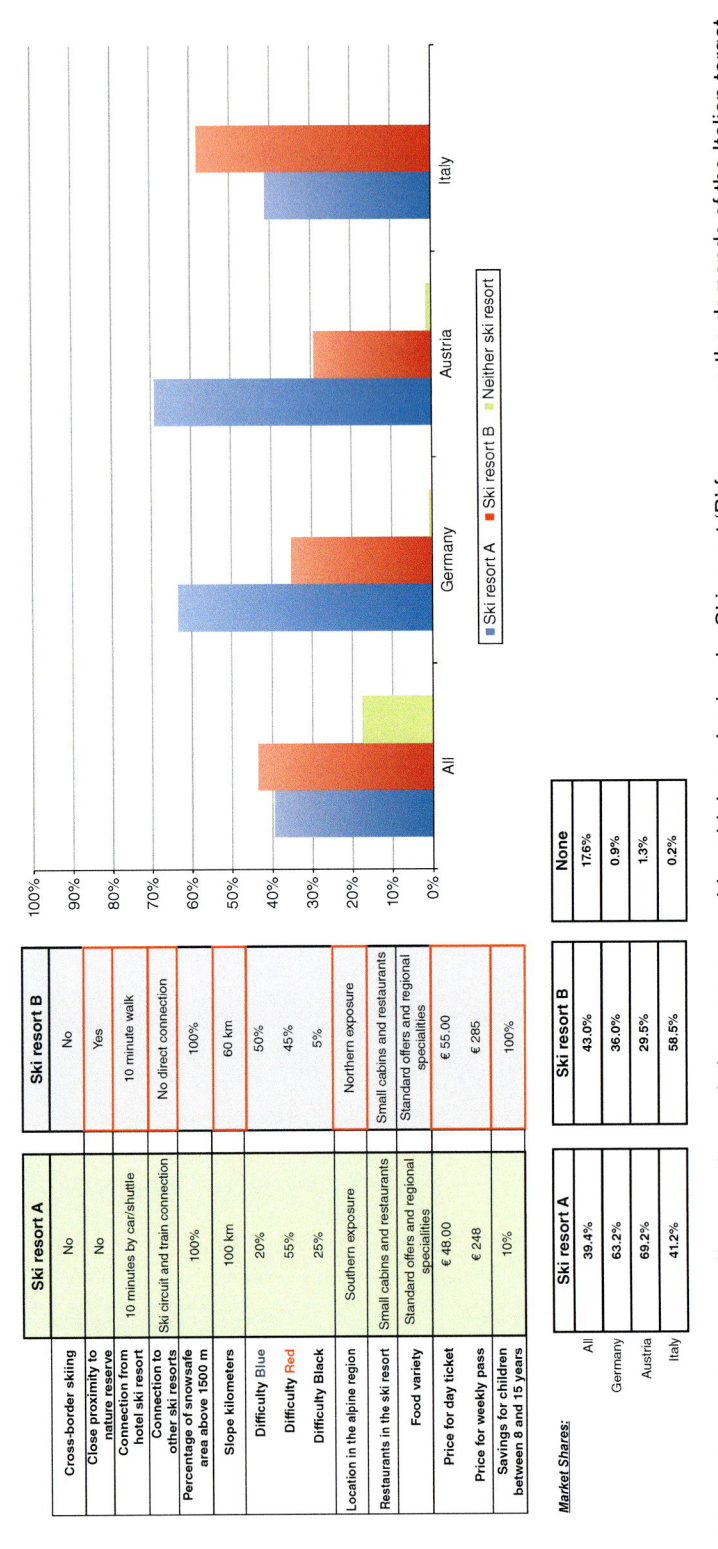

	Ski resort A	Ski resort B
Cross-border skiing	No	No
Close proximity to nature reserve	No	Yes
Connection from hotel ski resort	10 minutes by car/shuttle	10 minute walk
Connection to other ski resorts	Ski circuit and train connection	No direct connection
Percentage of snowsafe area above 1500 m	100%	100%
Slope kilometers	100 km	60 km
Difficulty Blue	20%	50%
Difficulty Red	55%	45%
Difficulty Black	25%	5%
Location in the alpine region	Southern exposure	Northern exposure
Restaurants in the ski resort	Small cabins and restaurants	Small cabins and restaurants
Food variety	Standard offers and regional specialities	Standard offers and regional specialities
Price for day ticket	€ 48.00	€ 55.00
Price for weekly pass	€ 248	€ 285
Savings for children between 8 and 15 years	10%	100%

Market Shares:

	Ski resort A	Ski resort B	None
All	39.4%	43.0%	17.6%
Germany	63.2%	36.0%	0.9%
Austria	69.2%	29.5%	1.3%
Italy	41.2%	58.5%	0.2%

Fig. 17.6. A tailor-made offer covering main interests can achieve higher price levels. Ski resort 'B' focuses on the demands of the Italian target group.

U. Pröbstl-Haider and N. Mostegl

the crucial significance of technical aspects within this target group. Austrians are skilled skiers, who want to improve their abilities and seek out different demanding experiences to test their boundaries. Hence, Austrian participants evidently selected resorts according to their particular values and motivations. Finally, German participants displayed both tendencies yet seemed to veer towards Austrian preferences. However, Germans celebrate their winter vacation and are less driven by technical motivations. Landscape (e.g. proximity to protected areas) and typical 'regional' experiences (e.g. regional cuisine) motivated this sample.

The conclusion that these differences are the result of diverging cultural values and motivations is not only in line with findings by other authors in this research field (e.g. Landis and Brislin, 1983; Reisinger and Turner, 2003), but is also supported by local stakeholders in Sexten, who were able to identify this relationship in the pre-study. With that in mind, we want to further emphasize the urgent need to improve the capacities of those working in the tourism sector to understand cultural differences and to translate this understanding into effective target group communication, tailor-made marketing campaigns, appropriate management and strategic development (Reisinger and Turner 2002; Turner *et al.* 2002).

In this context, the experience of cultural differences, such as regional specialities, atmosphere in the provided infrastructure and the southern or northern alpine ambience, have also been shown to increase a resort's appeal. For German and Austrian tourists, the region around Sexten provides a desired southern alpine ambience, while in a similar manner northern alpine destinations with their distinctive atmosphere prove more attractive to Italians. Resort managers need to carefully address the specific preferences of their desired target group and adjust the respective marketing strategies accordingly, including the introduction of special offers.

17.4.2 Methodological benefits of applying a choice experiment

Using a discrete choice experiment to investigate cultural differences is a fairly unique approach. Consistent with Landauer *et al.* (2012), this study demonstrated that the choice experiment and the subsequent decision support tool are excellent means to analyse data and communicate the complex findings to local stakeholders.

Interpreted with a view to differences in values and motivations, the highly divergent preferences that emerged in the choice experiment underline the importance of cultural differences for tourist holiday experiences, customer satisfaction and, ultimately, continued bookings.

In contrast to other methodologies such as the theory of planned behaviour, this modelling approach focuses on intended behaviour, which has become possible with the advent of more sophisticated multivariate statistical techniques (e.g. the multinomial logit model). Surveys based on a choice experiment also avoid the risk of a strategic response and, thereby, increase the reliability of responses (van Beukering *et al.*, 2007). In addition, choice experiments allow for a consideration of hypothetical attributes such as tourism offers and, more importantly, 'non-use values' (Adamowicz *et al.*, 1998a, b; van Beukering *et al.*, 2007; Pröbstl-Haider and Haider, 2013; Pröbstl-Haider *et al.*, 2015). The presented results once more underline the suitability of this approach for complex and challenging research questions.

The design of a choice experiment typically involves trade-offs between completeness and complexity. The presented choice experiment strives to be as inclusive as possible and, therefore, includes a large number of attributes (12 attributes with two to eight levels each). This is perceived as a cognitively demanding task for respondents. Although there is no golden rule as to the maximum number of attributes and levels that can be included in a choice experiment, the relevant literature generally tends to suggest between four and eight attributes (Curry, 1997; Ryan and Gerard, 2003), while keeping the number of levels to a minimum. According to these authors, scaling up complexity may lead to potential structural biases such as an increased preference for a 'status quo alternative' (see Boxall *et al.*, 2009) or to an increased likelihood of non- or irrational responses (Louviere *et al.*, 2000). However, there is little consensus and even less empirical data available regarding the optimum level of complexity. In addition, multiple studies have shown that choice experiments exceeding the eight-attribute threshold still produce reliable and meaningful results (e.g. Zweifel and Haegeli, 2014; Pröbstl-Haider *et al.*, 2015; Rupf, 2015; Mostegl *et al.*, 2019). Nevertheless, the high number of alternatives included in the choice experiment used in this study certainly increased the complexity of the choice task. Yet, none of the effects mentioned above could be observed. Three reasons may have helped avoid potential biases:

1. Market realism: Louviere *et al.* (2000) use the phrase 'market realism' to describe the degree to which a choice experiment matches the actual environment framing respondents' real life decision making processes. The authors argue that the more closely the experiment resembles the actual market, the higher the content validity. The pursuit of a high degree of market realism obviously has an additional positive effect on the acceptability of more complex choice tasks. As the choice experiment in this study has been thoroughly discussed and refined with the help of practitioners and local stakeholders, it achieves a very high degree of market realism.
2. Presentation and design: The choice sets were diligently designed and pre-tested. The grouping of attributes, as well as the colour coding, were helpful in introducing a clear structure to the choice set. Furthermore, the design reduced the cognitive challenge for respondents.
3. Panel involvement: All respondents were recruited through country-specific panels. These respondents are highly motivated to participate in surveys and have most likely been exposed to complex survey questions in the past.

All things considered, the overall findings significantly benefited from the use of a complex choice experiment, as it is very likely that all crucial aspects were taken into account. The inclusion of additional attributes allowed for a better understanding of the trade-offs respondents are willing to make when choosing a ski resort. This advantage is further illustrated by the following two examples comparing findings from the choice model and conclusions drawn by other studies:

- The size of ski resorts – recently highlighted as the most important criterion for destination choice (Grabler, 2008, 2017) – is less relevant than expected. For resorts, size only constitutes a vital competitive advantage up to 80 km of slope length. If the size exceeds this threshold, the advantage is outweighed by other attributes. This finding indicates that size is interlinked with other factors and also depends on additional attributes, such as connectivity, technical skills of the target

group (see, for example, the Italian sample) and the resort's accessibility. Similar findings have been reported by Pröbstl-Haider *et al.* (2017) and Steiger *et al.* (2017).
- Another example can be found in the importance of day ticket prices. The literature is divided on this issue. While some studies and the media (e.g. Die Presse, 2013; Oe24 GmbH, 2017) highlight the relevance of price levels, others argue that they are irrelevant (Grabler, 2017). Based on the choice experiment, our study found that the overall price level of ski passes, as well as the perceived price–performance ratio play an important role; however, the results also show that the price level can be counterbalanced by other attributes. The decision support tool clearly indicates that suitable culinary offers, cross-border skiing and other cultural experiences can in fact compensate for a higher price. Nevertheless, caution must be exercised, as trade-off effects were shown to impact the national samples differently.

17.4.3 Climate change adaptation

The study reveals that awareness of climate change is equally high in all three countries. However, the willingness to adapt seems to differ according to nationality. Other studies point out that climate change adaptation in the tourism sector needs to take different national cultures into account (Gössling *et al.*, 2012; Landauer *et al.*, 2013). Acknowledging a diverse range of challenges, approaches and capabilities in the debate on climate change adaptation runs counter to widely spread assumptions of homogenous tourist behaviour and preferences dominating research and policy or management recommendations. This assumption implies that any perceptual or behavioural insight gained in one place is – either directly or at least under similar socio-economic and socio-cultural conditions – transferable to another (e.g. Simpson *et al.*, 2008). The findings of this study caution against such unquestioned transfers of climate change adaptation strategies – even within Europe. The results are also in line with research published by Bell *et al.* (2009), Pröbstl *et al.* (2010) and Landauer *et al.* (2013), who detect strong cultural differences across Europe in outdoor recreation and nature-based tourism.

In the case of Sexten, cultural differences related to climate change can, moreover, be identified in the use of public transport. Culturally different attitudes towards self-owned cars and car use in general are clearly reflected in respondents' take on the use of public transport for skiing vacations. From a management perspective, significant investments in regional train connections and current negotiations to link local train services to the pan-European railway network may indeed prove effective in attracting new guests. However, these new customers will most likely be Italian, as this sample group stated they use public transport more often. Austrians and Germans, who clearly indicated their limited interest in public transport, will not be especially attracted by the offer. These findings strongly underline the difficulties efforts to convince Austrian and German skiers to switch to other, more sustainable means of transportation face. Yet, a better understanding of factors influencing destination choice may aid the development of new and customized products (e.g. travel packages), which may be able to increase the appeal of 'alternative' access to winter sports destinations in the Alps. While currently long-distance travellers are not likely to make significant use of train services, train networks have, nonetheless, already greatly contributed to climate change adaptation in the region. Train services have been positively received by locals and day trippers and a trickle-down effect has become evident. Trains reduce local traffic, create additional infrastructure for the local population to use and can generate added value by enabling a more sophisticated winter tourism product (e.g. integration in a ski circuit).

Given the ageing societies in all three countries, it may become necessary to promote winter holidays rather than skiing holidays, which allow vacationers to experience winter landscapes through a variety of activities (potentially involving less snow). The presented data, in this respect, demonstrate that other winter activities, such as winter hiking and cross-country skiing, are already highly relevant and will become even more so in the future due to decreasing snow reliability. Similar findings have been reported by Roth *et al.* (2018) for Germany.

Finally, even in the face of climate change and its effects on winter tourism, the alpine region has a clear advantage. The results of the study show that interest in visiting the region in summer is increasing. This opportunity should be made use of and further enhanced by forward-looking cross-marketing activities.

17.5 Conclusions

This research cooperation between Sexten, a skiing destination in South Tyrol, and the University of Natural Resources and Life Sciences in Vienna aimed to understand and address cultural differences in the demands of German, Austrian and Italian skiers and snowboarders in the region. The project was, moreover, designed to test new development and marketing opportunities. The results show that German, Austrian and Italian respondents differ significantly in their overall skiing motivations, values, the prerequisites they impose, as well as their specific destination choices. These differences were found to be even more relevant for segmentation than any other sampling criterion or combination of criteria (e.g. based on a Latent Gold segmentation). The performed analysis concluded that these differences can be reliably described as cultural differences, which were, furthermore, found to be crucial for marketing and product development. Since development options are limited, management strategies should put an emphasis on communicating specific touristic experiences. Hereby, cross-border experiences and local culinary delicacies offered in small restaurants can come into play, as they are especially in line with German and Austrian preferences, which welcome a special 'southern alpine atmosphere'. Finally, the study highlighted that climate change adaptation will also need to take cultural differences into account.

References

Adamowicz, W., Boxall, P., Williams, M. and Louviere, J. (1998a) Stated preference approaches for measuring passive use values: choice experiments and contingent valuation. *American Journal of Agricultural Economics*. 80(1), 64–75.

Adamowicz, W., Louviere, J. and Swait, J. (1998b) Introduction to attribute-based stated choice methods. Final report to NOAA, US Department of Commerce. Advanis, Edmonton, Canada.

Arnberger, A. and Haider, W. (2005) Social effects on crowding preferences of urban forest visitors. *Urban Forestry and Urban Greening* 3(3–4), 125–136.

Auspurg, K. and Liebe, U. (2011) Choice-Experimente und die Messung von Handlungsentscheidungen in der Soziologie. *Kölner Zeitschrift für Soziologie und Sozialpsychologie* 6(2), 301–314.

Bell, S., Tyrväinen, L., Sievänen, T., Pröbstl, U. and Simpson, M. (2007) Outdoor recreation and nature tourism: a European perspective. *Living Reviews in Landscape Research* 1 (2007-2), 1–46.

Bell, S., Simpson, M., Tyrväinen, L., Sievänen, T. and Pröbstl, U. (2009) *European Forest Recreation and Tourism – a Handbook*. Taylor & Francis, London.

Ben-Akiva, M. and Lerman, S. (1985) *Discrete Choice Analysis. Theory and Application to Travel Demand*. MIT Press, Cambridge, Massachusetts.

Boxall, P., Adamowicz, W.L. and Moon, A. (2009) Complexity in choice experiments: choice of the status quo alternative and implications for welfare measurement. *The Australian Journal of Agricultural and Resource Economics* 53(4), 503–519.

Brau, R. and Cao, D. (2006) Uncovering the macrostructure of tourists' preferences. A choice experiment analysis of tourism demand to Sardinia. *FEEM Working Paper* 33/2006.

Burdge, R. (1996) Introduction: cultural diversity in natural resource use – case studies in cultural definitions of resource sustainability. *Society and Natural Resources* 9(4), 337–338.

Curry, J. (1997) After the basics: keeping key issues in mind makes conjoint analysis easier to apply. *Marketing Research* 9(1), 6–11.

Die Presse (2013) Austrians can't afford to ski any more. Available at: https://diepresse.com/home/meingeld/verbraucher/1471119/Oesterreicher-koennen-sich-Skifahren-nicht-mehr-leisten (accessed 15 July 2018).

Funk, D. and Bruun, J. (2006) The role of socio-psychological and culture-education motives in marketing international sport tourism: a cross-cultural perspective. *Tourism Management* 28(3), 806–819.

Gibbs, M. (2001) Toward a strategy for undertaking cross-cultural collaborative research. *Society and Natural Resources* 14(8), 673–687.

Gössling, S., Scott, D., Hall, C.M., Ceron, J.-P. and Dubois, G. (2012) Consumer behavior and demand response of tourists to climate change. *Annals of Tourism Research* 39(1), 36–58.

Grabler, K. (2008) Kundenzufriedenheit als Schlüssel für den langfristigen Unternehmenserfolg. *Mountain Manager* 6, 44–45.

Grabler, K. (2017) Wahrnehmung, Bedeutung und Stellenwert ökologischer Aspekte für den Kunden. Available at: http://bergumwelt.boku.ac.at/wp-content/uploads/2017/08/Bergumwelt_2017_Grabler.pdf (accessed 15 July 2018).

Hall, E. T. (1976) *Beyond Culture*. Doubleday Anchor Press, New York.

Hofstede, G. (1980) *Culture's Consequences: International Differences in Work-Related Values*. Sage, Beverly Hills, California.

Hofstede, G. (1997) *Cultures and Organizations: Software of the Mind*. McGraw-Hill, New York.

Hunt, L., Haider, W. and Bottan, B. (2005) Accounting for varying setting preferences among moose hunters. *Leisure Sciences* 27(4), 297–314.

IDM Südtirol – Alto Adige (2018) Touristische Zahlen und Fakten : Die Destination Südtirol im Jahr 2017. Available at: https://issuu.com/idm_suedtirol_altoadige/docs/broschu__re-de_rz_issue (accessed 10 January 2019).

Kang, M. and Moscardo, G. (2006) Exploring cross-cultural differences in attitudes towards responsible tourist behaviour: a comparison of Korean, British and Australian Tourists. *Asia Pacific Journal of Travel Research* 11(40), 303–320.

Kim, Y. and Gudykunst, W. (1988) *Theories in Intercultural Communication*. Sage, London.

Landauer, M., Haider, W. and Pröbstl-Haider, U. (2013) The influence of culture on climate change adaptation strategies. *Journal of Travel Research* 53(1), 96–110.

Landauer, M., Pröbstl, U. and Haider, W. (2012) Managing cross-country skiing destinations under the conditions of climate change – scenarios for destinations in Austria and Finland. *Tourism Management* 33(4), 741–751.

Landis, D. and Brislin, R.W. (1983) *Handbook of Intercultural Training: Issues in Theory and Design*. Pergamon Press, New York.

Likert, R. (1977) A technique for the measurement of attitudes. In: Summer, G.F. (ed.) *Attitude measurement*. Kershaw, London, pp. 149–158.

Lindberg, K. and Fredman, P. (2005) Using choice experiments to evaluate destination attributes: the case of snowmobilers and cross-country skiers. *Tourism* 53(2), 127–140.

Louviere, J., Hensher, D.A. and Swait, J. (2000) *Stated Choice Methods*. Cambridge University Press, Cambridge, UK.

Manski, C. (1977) The Structure of random utility models. *Theory and Decision* 8(3), 229–254.

McFadden, D. (1974) Conditional logit analysis of qualitative choice behaviour. In: Zahembka, P. (ed.) *Frontiers in Econometrics*. New York Academic Press, New York, pp.105–142.

Moscardo, G. (2004) East versus west: a useful distinction or misleading myth? *Tourism* 52(1), 7–20.

Mostegl, N.M., Pröbstl-Haider, U., Jandl, R. and Haider, W. (2019) Targeting climate change adaptation strategies to small-scale private forest owners. *Forest Policy and Economics* 99, 83–99 . DOI:10.1016/j.forpol.2017.10.001

Ng, S.I., Lee, J.A. and Soutar, G.N. (2007) Tourists' intention to visit a country: the impact of cultural distance. *Tourism Management* 28(6), 1497–1506.

Oe24 GmbH (2017) Price shock, skiing will be more expensive this year. Available at: www.oe24.at/businesslive/oesterreich/Preis-Schock-Skifahren-wird-heuer-noch-teurer/303704875 (accessed 15 July 2018).

ÖHV – Österreichische Hoteliervereinigung (2012) *Österreichs Destinationen im Vergleich: Entwicklung 2005 bis 2010*. Destinationsstudie und -karte der Österreichischen Hotelierverenigung. ÖHV, Vienna, Austria.

Ooi, C.-S. (2002). Contrasting strategies. Tourism in Denmark and Singapore. *Annals of Tourism Research* 29(3), 689–706.

Ortega, E. and Rodríguez, B. (2007) Information at tourism destinations. Importance and cross-cultural differences between international and domestic tourists. *Journal of Business Research* 60(2), 146–152.

Pröbstl, U., Wirth, V., Elands, B.H.M. and Bell, S. (2010) *Management of Recreation and Nature-Based Tourism in European Forests*. Springer, Berlin.

Pröbstl-Haider, U. and Haider, W. (2013) Tools for measuring the intention for adapting to climate change by winter tourists: some thoughts on consumer behavior research and an empirical example. *Tourism Review* 68(2), 44–55.

Pröbstl-Haider, U. and Haider, W. (2014) The Role of Protected Areas in Destination Choice in the European Alps. *Zeitschrift für Wirtschaftsgeographie* 58(2–3), 144–163.

Pröbstl-Haider, U., Mostegl, N.M. and Haider, W. (2015) Einfluss von Skigebietsverbindungen im Bereich Stubai/westliches Mittelgebirge auf die regionale und deutsche Nachfrage durch Wintersportler. Final Report. Available at: https://www.brueckenschlag-tirol.com/ (accessed 20 December 2018).

Pröbstl-Haider, U., Mostegl, N.M. and Haider, W. (2017) Panoramablick versus Pistenkilometer. Wichtige Kriterien bei der Buchung eines Skigebietes in Österreich. *Tourismus Wissen – Quarterly* 7, 34–40.

Reisinger, Y. and Turner, K. (2002) Cultural differences between Asian tourist markets and Australian hosts, Part 1. *Journal of Travel Research* 40(3), 295–315.

Reisinger, Y. and Turner, K. (2003) *Cross-Cultural Behavior in Tourism*. Butterworth-Heinemann, Oxford, UK.

Rose, J.M., Hensher, D.A., Caussade, S., de Dios Ortùzar, J. and Jou, R.-C. (2009) Identifying differences in willingness to pay due to dimensionality in stated choice experiments: a cross country analysis. *Journal of Transport Geography* 17(1), 21–29.

Roth, R., Krämer, A. and Severins, J. (2018) *Nationale Grundlagenstudie Wintersport Deutschland 2018*. Stiftung Sicherheit im Skisport e.V., Cologne, Germany.

Rupf, R. (2015) *Planungsinstrumente für Wandern und Mountainbiking in Berggebieten. Unter besonderer Berücksichtigung der Biosfera Val Müstair*. Haupt, Bern, Switzerland.

Ryan, M. and Gerard, K. (2003) Using discrete choice experiments to value health care programmes: current practice and future research reflections. *Applied Health Economics and Health Policy* 2(1), 55–64.

Simpson, M.C., Gössling, S., Scott, D., Hall, C.M. and Gladin, E. (2008) *Climate Change Adaptation and Mitigation in the Tourism Sector: Frameworks, Tools and Practices*. UNEP, Paris.

Sorice, M.G., Oh, C.-O. and Ditton, R.B. (2005) Using stated preference discrete choice experiment to analyze scuba divers' preferences for coral reef conservation. Final report prepared for the Coral Reef Competitive Grants Program of the National Fish and Wildlife Foundation. Available at: https://core.ac.uk/download/pdf/19540869.pdf (accessed 20 December 2018).

Steiger, R., Posch, E., Pons-Pons, M. and Vilella, M. (2017) Climate change impacts on skier behaviour and spatial distribution of skiers in Austria. Available at: https://www.ccca.ac.at/fileadmin/00_DokumenteHauptmenue/03_Aktivitaeten/Klimatag/Klimatag2017/Vortr%C3%A4ge/V48_Steiger.pdf (accessed 10 January 2019).

Triandis, H.C. (1972) *The Analysis of Subjective Culture*. Wiley-Interscience, Oxford, UK.

Turner, L.W., Reisinger, Y.V. and McQuilken, L. (2002) How cultural differences cause dimensions of tourism satisfaction. *Journal of Travel and Tourism Marketing* 11(1), 79–101.

Unbehaun, W., Haider, W. and Pröbstl, U. (2008) Trends in winter sport tourism: challenges for the future. *Tourism Review* 63(1), 36–47.

van Beukering, P., Haider, W., Longland, M., Cesar, H., Sablan, J. *et al*. (2007) The economic value of Guam's coral reefs. University of Guam Marine Laboratory Technical Report No. 116. Available at: https://pdfs.semanticscholar.org/5519/843c40d0400afc958a2c163da7b518c68a36.pdf (10 January 2019).

Weiermair, K. (2000) Tourists' perceptions towards and satisfaction with service quality in the cross-cultural service encounter: implications for hospitality and tourism management. *Managing Service Quality* 10(6), 397–409.

Zweifel, B. and Haegeli, P. (2014) A qualitative analysis of group formation, leadership and decision making in recreation groups traveling in avalanche terrain. *Journal of Outdoor Recreation and Tourism* 5–6, 17–26.

18 Winter Visitors' Perceptions in Popular Nature Destinations in Iceland

Anna Dóra Sæþórsdóttir[1]* and C. Michael Hall[2]

[1]*University of Iceland, Reykjavík, Iceland;* [2]*University of Canterbury, New Zealand*

18.1 Introduction

By virtue of its name, Iceland, located just south of the Arctic Circle in the North Atlantic, does not immediately conjure up an image of an attractive tourist winter destination. However, although not having the friendliest climate in the world because of its variability, the climate is actually more temperate than what many might expect for its location – and name – thanks to the warming influence of the Gulf Stream and the Irminger Current (Einarsson, 1984; Ingólfsson, 2008).

Being surrounded by the ocean, summers on the island are cool and the winters relatively mild for its latitude. In the southern part of the country the average temperature in July, is about 10–13°C (50–55°F), although summer days can reach 20–25°C (68–77°F), and about around 0°C (32°F) in winter, while the north is a little cooler. The Highlands of Iceland tend to average around –10°C (14°F) in winter (Einarsson, 1984; Ingólfsson, 2008). According to the Köppen climate classification the climate along the southern coast, along with some coastal valleys in the north, is mainly subarctic while the rest of the country is regarded as tundra. Nevertheless, while the country's name may imply to many people that it is covered in ice, many of the coastal regions are covered in grasslands, and trees grow in some areas that have not been overgrazed. Only about 11% of the country is ice-covered year-round and these are glaciers and ice caps, which also serve as significant tourist attractions (Welling and Árnason, 2016). The largest of which by far is Vatnajökull, covering an area of approximately 8300 km^2, and which is also one of the coldest areas on the island. However, Iceland's glaciers are increasingly affected by climate change and are in retreat, which will affect the glacier tourism industry in the near future (Welling *et al.*, 2017).

Iceland has continuous daylight during the high summer and the midnight sun can be experienced on the island of Grimsey off the north coast through which the Arctic Circle currently passes. In contrast, the shortest days in winter only have 5–6 hours of daylight. From autumn through to spring the darker evenings have made the northern lights an important feature of the island's tourist offerings. Sea temperatures can rise to over 10°C at the south and west coasts of Iceland during

---

* E-mail: annadora@hi.is

the summer, and slightly over +8°C at the north coast, but summer sea temperatures remain below +8°C on the east coast (Einarsson, 1984; Ingólfsson, 2008). It should be noted that Iceland has a nascent surfing community with the period between October and March when heavy storms hit the island being regarded as having the best wave conditions (Ólafsson, 2018). The island is generally wet and windy, with May, June and July being the three driest months, and October and March the wettest. The mean precipitation for Reykjavík by month ranges from means of approximately 43.8 mm and 9.8 precipitation days in May through to 85.6 mm and 14.5 precipitation days in October (Ingólfsson, 2008). However, there is substantial variation in precipitation over the island with it ranging from a high of >4000 mm a year in the south-west of Iceland over Vatnajökull as well as other higher areas to lows of <600 mm in some of the northern and central regions (Icelandic Met Office, 2018). This is because the large low pressure cyclonic events come from the south-west travelling just south of the country, meaning that the dominant wind direction is easterly. Most importantly from a weather experience perspective, the conditions are extremely variable and can fluctuate from calm and beautiful sunny weather to extreme conditions within a few hours, which provides an important dimension for outdoor recreation and tourism activity.

Mainly due to its particular climatic conditions, tourism in Iceland has been very seasonal with, historically, over half of international visitors arriving in the three summer months (June, July and August). Consequently, the principal aim of Icelandic tourism policy ever since the inception of the first national tourism policy in Iceland in 1975 has been to minimize seasonal fluctuations in international visitor arrivals (Pham et al., 1975). However, success in shifting seasonality was limited until after the global financial crisis in 2007–10, when there was a huge increase in international visitors arriving in the off-season, so much so that it can barely be called the off-season anymore. Significantly, these changes were due not so much to developments in Iceland's urban tourism offerings, but to the growing attraction of the Icelandic environment as an all-season attraction.

Nature is the main reason international tourists visit Iceland. The most popular nature destinations are within a daytrip from Reykjavík and there are some destinations that are visited by a great many tourists leading to increased concerns over tourism growth for both the environment and the quality of the visitor experience. Negative experience of crowding has long been recognized as a consequence of visitor satisfaction and the quality of the visitor experience (Stewart and Cole, 2001; Simón et al., 2004). However, research regarding attitudes and satisfaction of travellers due to seasonality in natural areas is limited (Koenig-Lewis and Bischoff, 2005; Palang et al., 2007; Hall et al., 2011). Various studies conducted among summer visitors in the Icelandic Highlands indicate that some destinations already show indications that crowding is a problem (Sæþórsdóttir, 2013; Sæþórsdóttir and Ólafsdóttir, 2017). As winter used to be the low season in tourism in Iceland the increased winter tourism in Iceland raises fundamental questions with respect to how tourists perceive nature destinations in the winter.

This chapter provides an examination of tourist perception of crowding and satisfaction in seven popular nature destinations in the south and south-west of Iceland. The chapter concludes with a discussion regarding the future of winter tourism in Iceland.

18.2 Winter Tourism in Iceland

Iceland has been among the countries in the world with the fastest growth in international tourist arrivals for the past few years, with an annual average increase of about 26% for the period 2010–2017. A two-fold increase in arrivals took place between 2014 and 2017; in 2014 the number of international visitors to Iceland was approximately 1.4 million, while in 2017 it reached approximately 2.2 million. The 2017 arrivals figure is almost seven times the number of residents in Iceland. Significantly, while growth has occurred over all seasons, the greatest growth has been in the winter months (November, December, January, February and March) with an average annual increase of 33% in arrivals (Icelandic Tourist Board, 2018) (see Fig. 18.1).

The largest increases in monthly visits have taken place outside of the summer months (see Fig. 18.2). For instance, between 2016 and 2017 there was a 75% increase in visitors in January and 62% in April, compared with a 17% increase in the summer

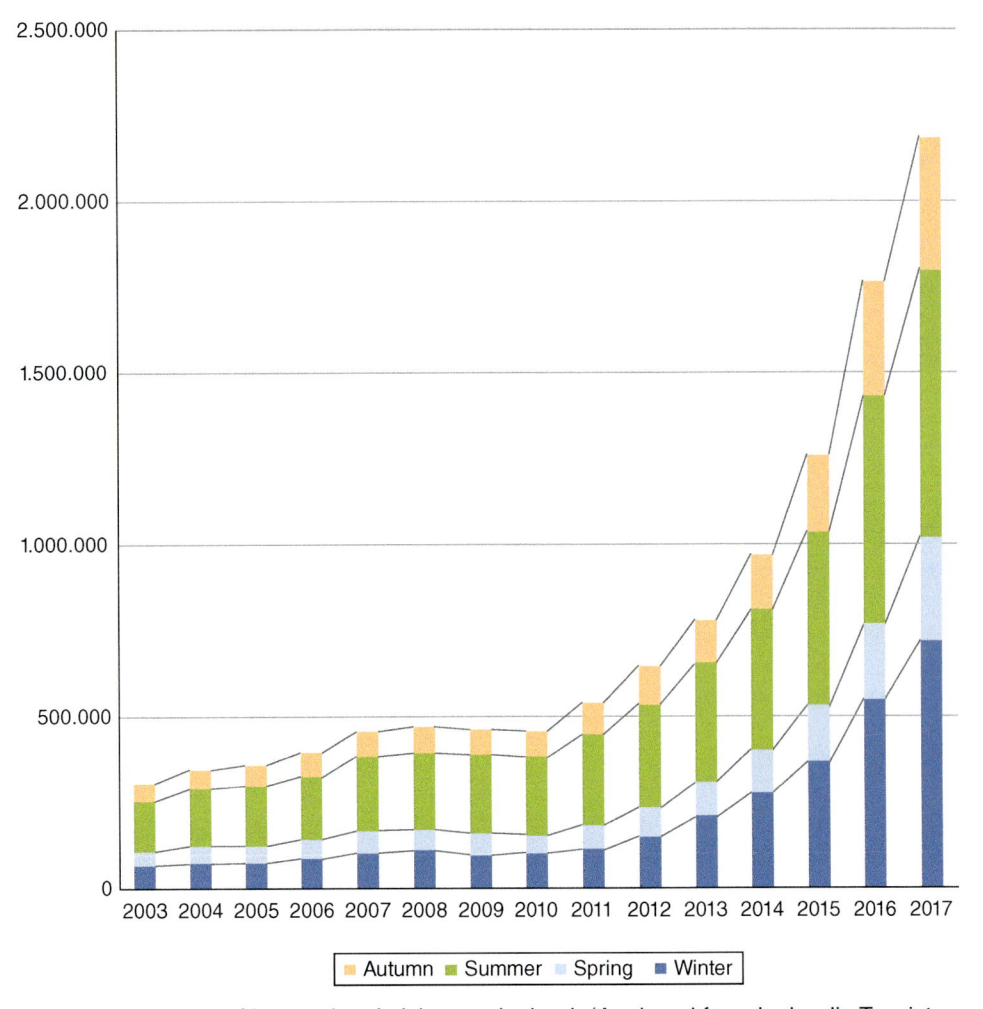

Fig. 18.1. Number of international visitors to Iceland. (Analysed from Icelandic Tourist Board, 2018.)

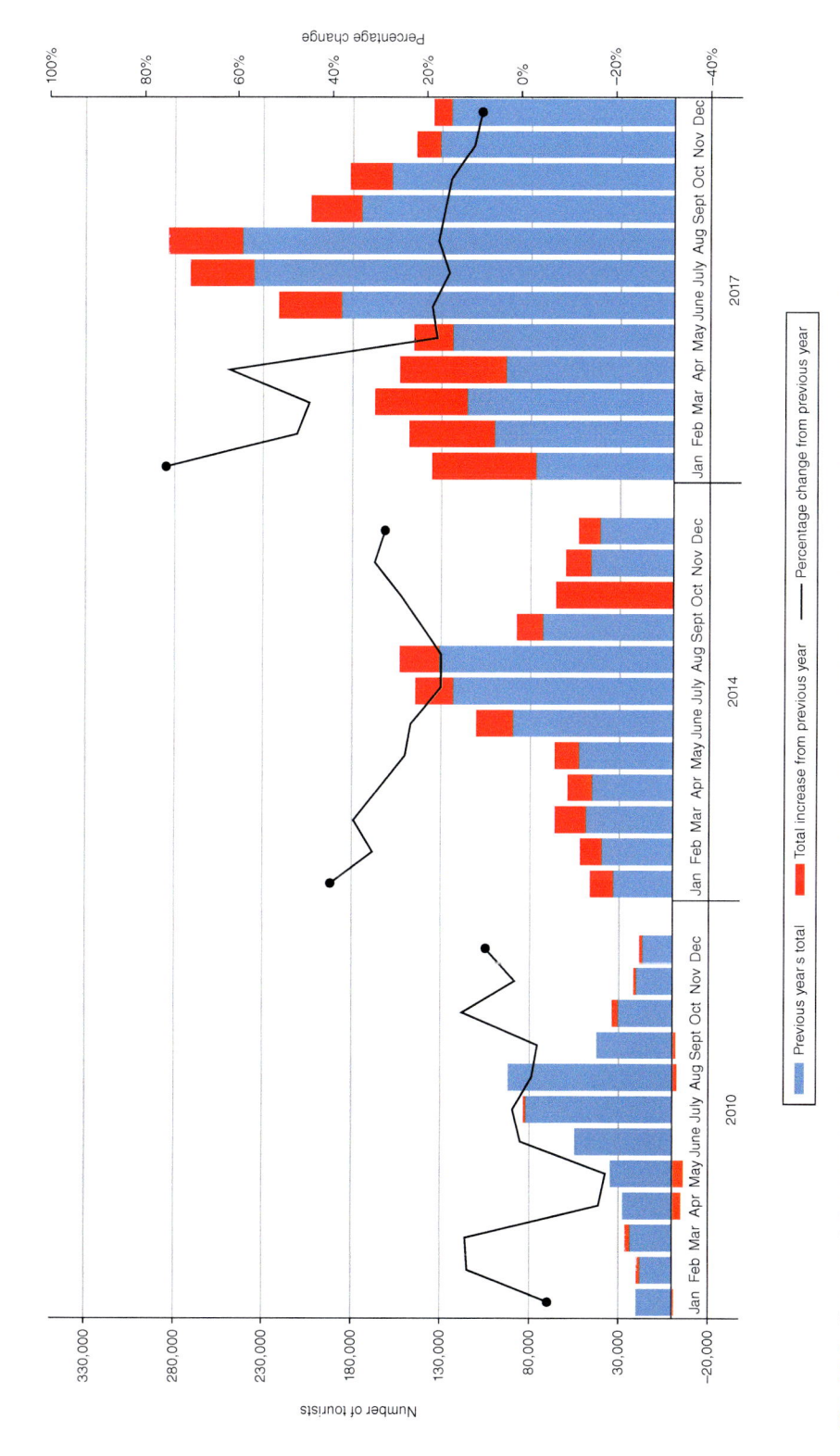

Fig. 18.2. Seasonal changes in international visitor arrivals 2010, 2014 and 2017. (Analysed from Icelandic Tourist Board, 2018.)

Popular Nature Destinations in Iceland 215

months. Only about 4% of international visitors came in January in 2010, with around 20% coming in August. Seasonal changes in arrivals and overall growth meant that by 2017 in terms of the pattern of seasonal visitation about 6% came in January and 13% in August (Icelandic Tourist Board, 2018).

There are also significant differences in the nature of the tourist market by season. Visitors from the USA are by far the largest market in summer. However, about 28% of visitors in January 2017 were from the UK. Travellers from Central and South Europe were prominent during the summer months, while travellers from the Nordic countries, Canada and from countries categorized as 'elsewhere' were distributed more evenly over the year. In 2016, 53% of Central and Southern European visitors came during the summer, as did 42% of North American visitors, 38% of Nordic visitors, 16% of UK visitors and 35% of those categorized as from 'elsewhere'. Travellers from the UK clearly had the greatest seasonal variance in visitation by season, as around half of these visitors came during the winter months. Some 40% of Nordic visitors came in the spring or autumn, as did 28% of UK visitors and 23% of North American visitors (Icelandic Tourist Board, 2018).

At the national level on average international visitors in winter have substantially shorter stays (4.16 nights) than summer visitors (10.33 nights) (Icelandic Tourist Board, 2016). In winter the roads outside the capital are frequently covered by snow or ice, hindering many travellers' capacity to self-drive. Nevertheless, some of them still do while other choose bus transfers or tour companies. As a result of more limited time budgets and the travel conditions, the overnight stays of winter tourists are more concentrated in Reykjavík than other parts of the country compared with the summer months when overnight stays are more evenly distributed throughout the country. However, the geographical location of Keflavík, Iceland's main international airport, on the Reykjanes peninsula in the south-west corner of the country and approximately a 40-min drive to Reykjavík's city centre, has a tremendous year-round effect on seasonality. Close to 99% of all visitors to Iceland arrive through Keflavík airport and hence an overwhelming majority, or 97%, visit the capital area (Icelandic Tourist Board, 2016). In 2010 about 50% of overnight stays in Reykjavík and the surrounding municipalities took place between May and August, while other regions received 87% of their total overnight stays within the same period. Six years later there had been a somewhat positive trend in reducing the peaks of overnight seasonality, with 39% of total overnight stays in the capital area being between May and August and 65% in other regions. Nevertheless, concentrations in overnight stays in Iceland have been diminishing at a far lower rate outside of the capital area (see Fig. 18.3). Accordingly, the great increase in international visitors in the off-season has not benefited all areas equally and those at the greatest distance from the south-west gateway corner still suffer considerable seasonality (Statistics Iceland, 2018). However, such a situation with respect to the spatial intensity of tourism around Keflavík and Reykjavík is similar to that of other high-latitude gateway cities with short visitor stays (Hall, 2015).

The occupancy rate of hotels has increased in accordance with higher numbers of visitors to the country. As an example, the total occupancy rate in January has increased from 25% in 2010 to 62% in 2017. In January, the capital region occupancy rate has grown from 34% in 2010 to 83% in 2017 (see Fig. 18.4). The south-west, the area where the international airport is located, has also had a huge growth in its occupancy rate and has an occupancy rate of over 78% at this time of year. The occupancy rate in the south has also increased and was 45% in January 2017. As may be expected given the spatial distribution of tourists with restricted time budgets the east and the north of Iceland, the

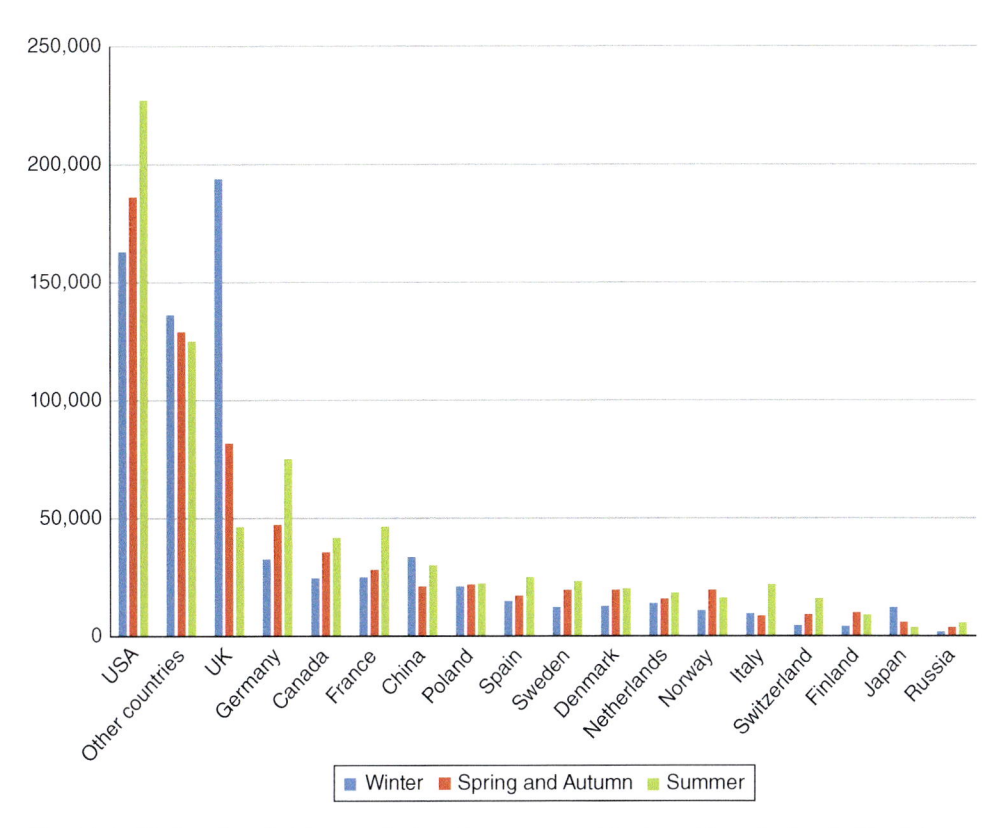

Fig. 18.3. Nationality of visitors to Iceland by seasons. (Analysed from Icelandic Tourist Board, 2018.)

areas furthest from the capital region, continue to have their lowest occupancy rates in January, about 10% and 17% respectively, although even these figures represent increases since 2010. However, the change in the occupancy rate in the summer has not altered much. In August all regions had an occupancy rate of around or over 80% in 2017, although growth from 2010 to 2017 has been greatest in the capital region and in the south-west, where there has been an increase from 78% to 89% and 66% to 78% occupancy, respectively (Statistics Iceland, 2018).

Icelandic nature is by far the most important attraction for international visitors. According to research by the Icelandic Tourist Board (2016), 74% of visitors in the winter and 83% in the summer, rate nature as the most important factor behind their decision to visit the country. However, this figure suggests that a substantial shift in visitor motivations has occurred within a 20-year period. For example, in 1998/99 only 47% of international tourists arriving in winter stated that nature was the principal reason for their visit. Significantly, over the same period, the figures have barely changed for summer tourists (Icelandic Tourist Board, 2004).

The vast majority of all international visitors visit Reykjavík, the capital city of Iceland. The south coast is visited by over 70% in the summer and 55% in winter but other areas are visited far less in winter (see Fig. 18.5). With respect to specific destinations, 48% of all international visitors in winter visited the hot spring area of Geysir, 41% Þingvellir national park and 31% Jökulsárlón glacial lagoon (Icelandic Tourist Board, 2016).

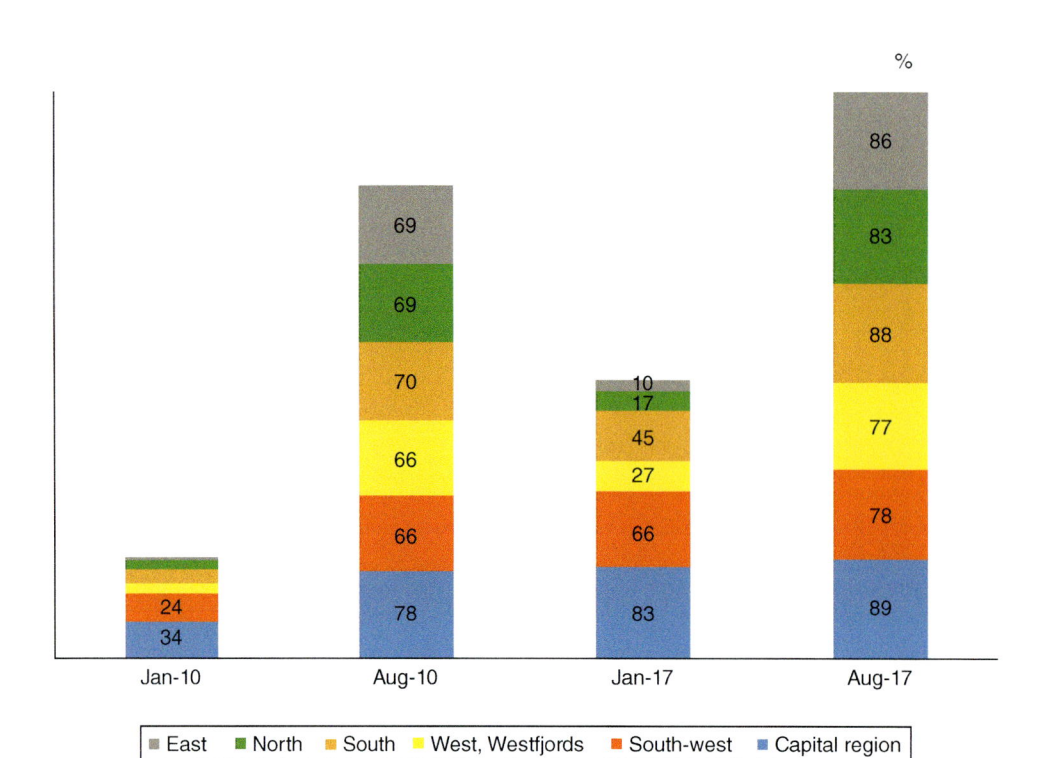

Fig. 18.4. Occupancy rate in January and August in 2010 and 2017. (Analysed from Statistics Iceland, 2018.)

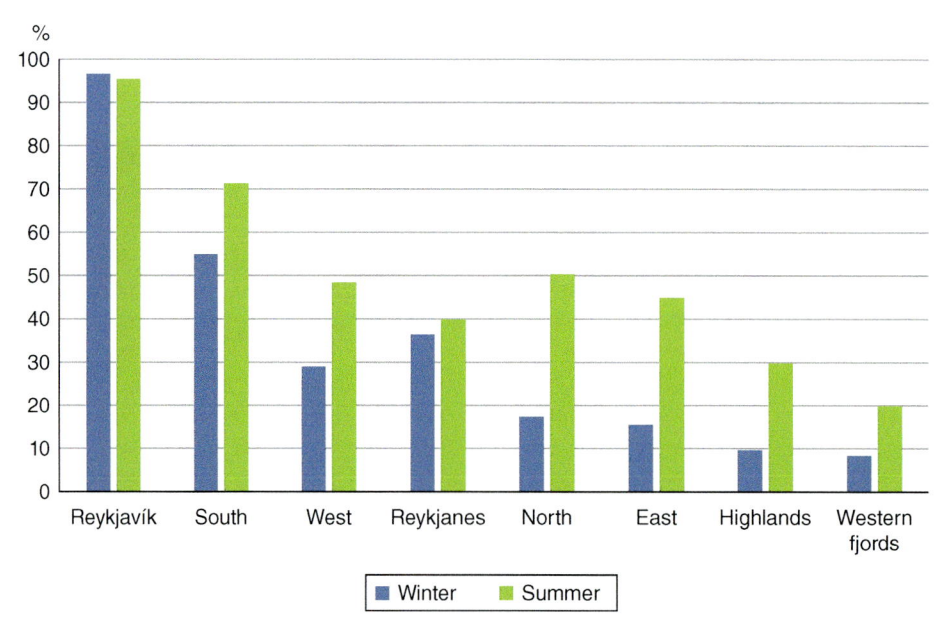

Fig. 18.5. Areas visited by international visitors while in Iceland. (Analysed from Icelandic Tourist Board, 2016.)

Given this situation it therefore becomes important for research to better understand the perceptions and attitudes of tourists to Iceland with respect to the natural environment, especially given the substantial increase in tourist arrivals overall and the growth of visitation to natural areas at times of the year where anthropogenic pressures have historically been much lower.

The massive and exponential surge in international visitors to Iceland resulted in interest from the Icelandic Tourist Board in financing a questionnaire survey on the experiences of tourists at popular nature tourist destinations. The study was conducted in the summer of 2014 and winter of 2015 but in this chapter the focus is on the winter results. Seven popular nature-based tourism destinations (Icelandic Tourist Board, 2014) in the south and south-west of Iceland were selected for study (see Fig. 18.6):

- Geysir – a geothermal area in the south-west.
- Þingvellir – a United Nations Educational, Scientific and Cultural Organization (UNESCO) World Heritage site in the south-west and a national park.
- Jökulsárlón – a large proglacial lake on the edge of Vatnajökull National Park in the south-east.
- Djúpalónssandur – a beach in the Snæfellsnes peninsula in Snæfellsjökull National Park.
- Hraunfossar – waterfalls in the Reykholt area.
- Seltún – geothermal area in the vicinity of the Blue Lagoon, Keflavík and the Reykjanes peninsula.
- Sólheimajökull – an accessible glacier in the south.

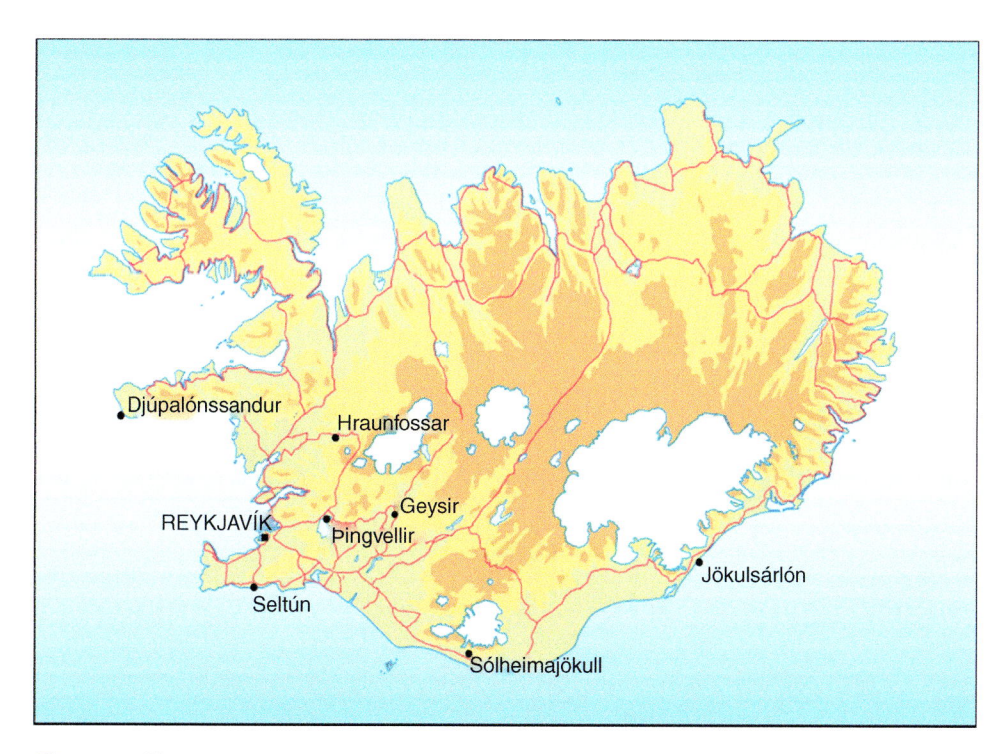

Fig. 18.6. The seven research areas and Reykjavík, the capital city of Iceland.

Popular Nature Destinations in Iceland

The research areas all form a part of popular day tours from the capital area and are among the most visited tourist destinations in Iceland, although Djúpalónssandur and Jökulsárlón (379 km distance from Reykjavík) are mostly a part of overnight tours in the winter.

The research locations' infrastructure is quite dissimilar although all the areas, except Sólheimajökull, are protected areas of various kinds. There is also a lack of coherence between the nature of the infrastructure and the amount of visitation each site receives. For instance, the infrastructure at Jökulsárlón, in spite of being among the most visited nature tourist destinations in Iceland, is rather rudimentary and minimal, while the Geysir area contains various restaurant and accommodation options. The infrastructure at Þingvellir has also developed in recent years although aesthetic issues created by the facilities are relatively contained since they are placed at the national park's entrance making them hardly visible from most of its area. There is very limited service at the other four locations. All have restroom services though some lack these year-round. There are small cafés at Hraunfossar and Seltún in summer but these are closed in winter.

Data were collected by one to five interviewers, depending on the amount of traffic each site receives, who attempted to approach as many visitors as possible. Data were gathered at each destination for a week, and a self-completion survey was given out during the day between approximately 9/10 am and 5/7 pm. The questionnaires were available in English, German, French and Icelandic. A total of 6758 questionnaires were collected at the seven destinations in the winter, with the smallest sample of 132 and largest of 2421 (see Table 18.1).

The questionnaire contained about 30 questions with some sub-questions. Respondents typically completed the questionnaire in <20 min. The questions can be divided into three categories:

1. Participant background questions. Regarding age, nationality, gender, travel companions, and other socio-demographic information.
2. Activities/behaviour/preferences. Previous visits, visit duration, mode of travel, accommodation type, activities in the research area, travel time, time spent on site, duration of hiking and recreational use patterns.
3. Attitude/experience/catalyst. Thoughts on the destination's attractiveness, naturalness and facilities, attitude and expectations on visitor and vehicle numbers, contentment (with previously mentioned elements) and the motivation behind the visit.

Table 18.1. Dates of data collection, sample size and response rate.

Research areas	Data collection	Sample size (*n*)
Djúpalónssandur	2–8 March	132
Geysir	2–8 Feb	2421
Hraunfossar	17–23 March	360
Jökulsárlón	23 Feb – 1 Mar	474
Seltún	17–24 March	529
Sólheimajökull	17–23 Feb	921
Þingvellir	9–15 Feb	1921
Total		6758

The attitude and experience questions were introduced through a 5-point Likert scale. The answers could range from, for example, 1 = very unsatisfied and 5 = very satisfied, from which means for each location were calculated.

18.3 Results

18.3.1 Demographics

The questionnaire sample is nearly exclusively composed of international visitors, and the majority are on their first visit to Iceland. The largest group of visitors in the seven research areas in winter are British (43%) and North Americans (15%), as well as the French and Germans (about 8% each) and the Asian market (6%). Other nationalities are in smaller numbers. These numbers coincide with the seasonal division of international visitors to Iceland (Icelandic Tourist Board, 2018). Icelanders comprise less than 3% of the total sample.

Buses are the most common mode of transport in the winter period (64%), reflecting the issues associated with weather conditions in winter noted in the introduction to the chapter. Rental cars are the second commonly used travel mode, used by 28%. Approximately 19% of visitors choose organized group travel in the winter. Hotels are by far the preferred/most accessible accommodation type as 84% of visitors stay in hotels in the winter. The remaining tourists stay in guesthouses, farmhouse accommodation and at camping sites, as well as in Airbnb and similar apartment rentals.

18.3.2 Satisfaction

The northern lights and nature greatly influenced travellers' decision to visit the area in the winter. On a 5-point Likert scale where 5 is very much influence and 1 is very little influence, nature scored over 4 at all locations. Two destinations dominate when it comes to northern lights tours: the glacial lagoon Jökulsárlón and Geysir hot spring area, which both scored over 4 on the Likert scale (see Table 18.2).

The respondents were very satisfied with the quality of nature at all the destinations, with the greatest satisfaction at Jökulsárlón and Hraunfossar and the least at Geysir, although it was still quite high with 4.57 on the Likert scale (see Table 18.3). Paths were

Table 18.2. The influence of nature and northern lights on tourists' visits to the area.

	Nature	Northern lights
Djúpalónssandur	4.34	3.69
Geysir	4.06	4.07
Hraunfossar	4.27	3.79
Jökulsárlón	4.51	4.27
Seltún	4.14	3.54
Sólheimajökull	4.21	3.85
Þingvellir	4.01	3.83
All locations	4.13	3.92

Calculated from a 5-point Likert scale where 1 = very little influence and 5 = very much influence.

also rated quite highly, which is an important consideration given winter conditions. Tourists were least satisfied with the quality of the restroom facilities. The lowest levels of satisfaction were at the places where restroom facilities were non-existent or limited, i.e. Djúpalónssandur, Seltún and Sólheimajökull, while the greatest satisfaction was at Geysir. Satisfaction with service was also the highest at Geysir, although there the satisfaction with parking and paths was the lowest. Signs and parking had the lowest score at Sólheimajökull. Parking facilities also had a low score at the very busy destinations Þingvellir and Geysir, although they have multiplied in size in recent years.

Visitors to the seven destinations do not perceive much negative impact from tourism on the environment whether the erosion of foot paths, litter, damaged geological formations or damaged vegetation (see Table 18.4). The most significant issue is footpath erosion (mean of 1.82, where 1 is equal to not at all). Noticeably, the best situation is at Þingvellir, one of the most visited destinations.

18.3.3 Perception of the number of travellers

The perception of overcrowding exists in a few places; the most noticeable are Geysir, Jökulsárlón, Þingvellir and Sólheimajökull (see Table 18.5). That goes for visitors in general, tour groups and buses. Private cars are not perceived as being overly numerous.

Table 18.3. Visitors' satisfaction with nature and facilities in the research areas.

Research areas	Nature	Paths	Parking	Service	Signs	Restrooms
Djúpalónssandur	4.73	4.02	4.16	3.65	4.04	3.10
Geysir	4.57	3.99	3.96	4.17	3.85	4.18
Hraunfossar	4.80	4.24	4.33	3.67	3.98	3.69
Jökulsárlón	4.80	4.01	4.15	3.99	3.81	3.92
Seltún	4.67	4.15	4.15	3.53	3.98	3.12
Sólheimajökull	4.78	4.27	3.97	3.89	3.74	3.14
Þingvellir	4.68	4.27	3.99	3.96	3.83	3.55
All locations	4.67	4.14	4.02	3.98	3.85	3.72

Calculated from a 5-point Likert scale where 1 = very unsatisfied and 5 = very satisfied.

Table 18.4. Visitors' perception of the impact of tourism on the environment.

	Erosion of paths	Litter	Damaged geological formations	Damaged vegetation
Djúpalónssandur	1.67	1.42	1.34	1.44
Geysir	1.80	1.53	1.47	1.47
Hraunfossar	2.01	1.36	1.43	1.55
Jökulsárlón	1.80	1.58	1.50	1.50
Seltún	2.15	1.55	1.47	1.59
Sólheimajökull	2.11	1.42	1.56	1.47
Þingvellir	1.57	1.35	1.28	1.29
All locations	1.82	1.46	1.43	1.43

Calculated from a 5-point Likert scale where 1 = not at all and 5 = very much.

Other destinations are perceived as less crowded with an average of below 3 on the Likert scale, the exception being tour groups in Djúpalónssandur, which is just above the mean.

The British are the most numerous geographical market segment at the destinations where visitors mainly experience overcrowding (refer to the size of the circles on Figs 18.7–18.10), followed by North Americans, while the distribution of other nationalities varies considerably between the four destinations. The Jökulsárlón glacial lagoon attracts the Asian market, as well as Germans, the French, Netherlanders and Belgians. Icelanders rarely visit those places in the winter, however some can be found at Þingvellir and Geysir.

There is also a great difference between the various nationalities regarding their satisfaction and whether they perceive too many visitors in the areas (see Figs 18.7–18.10). The Swiss, Austrians, Germans, the French, as well as Icelanders are more sensitive towards the number of visitors than other nationalities, while Asians and the UK market are less sensitive when it comes to crowding. The Asian market and Icelanders also seem less satisfied than others.

Table 18.5. Visitors' attitudes towards number of visitors and vehicles.

	Visitors in general	Tour groups	Cars	Buses
Djúpalónssandur	2.94	3.03	2.89	2.94
Geysir	3.17	3.29	2.99	3.27
Hraunfossar	2.79	2.81	2.82	2.74
Jökulsárlón	3.13	3.33	3.01	3.17
Seltún	2.93	2.98	2.91	3.00
Sólheimajökull	3.07	3.30	2.91	3.19
Þingvellir	3.10	3.26	2.91	3.19
All locations	3.09	3.23	2.94	3.17

Calculated from a 5-point Likert scale where 1 = too few visitors/vehicles and 5 = too many visitors/vehicles.

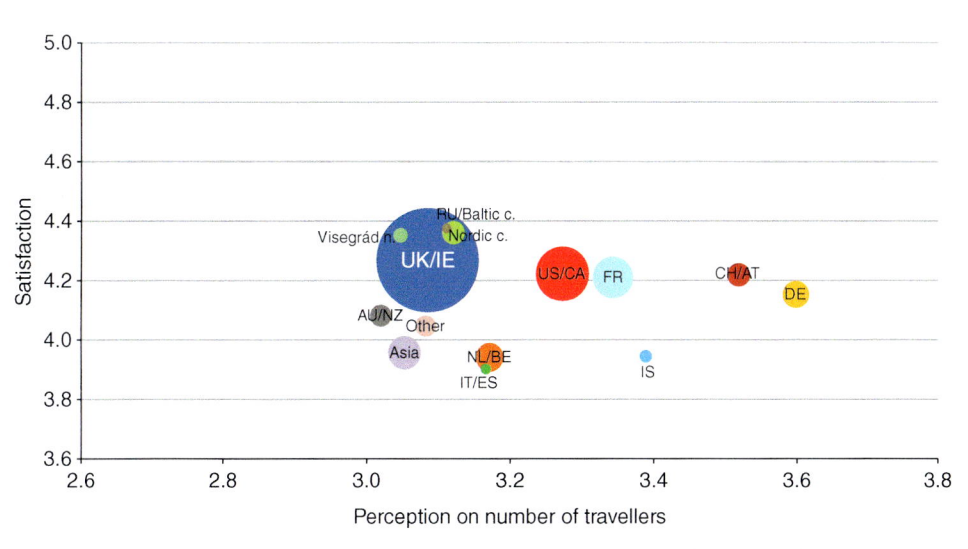

Fig. 18.7. Visitors' perception of the number of travellers and satisfaction at Geysir in winter.

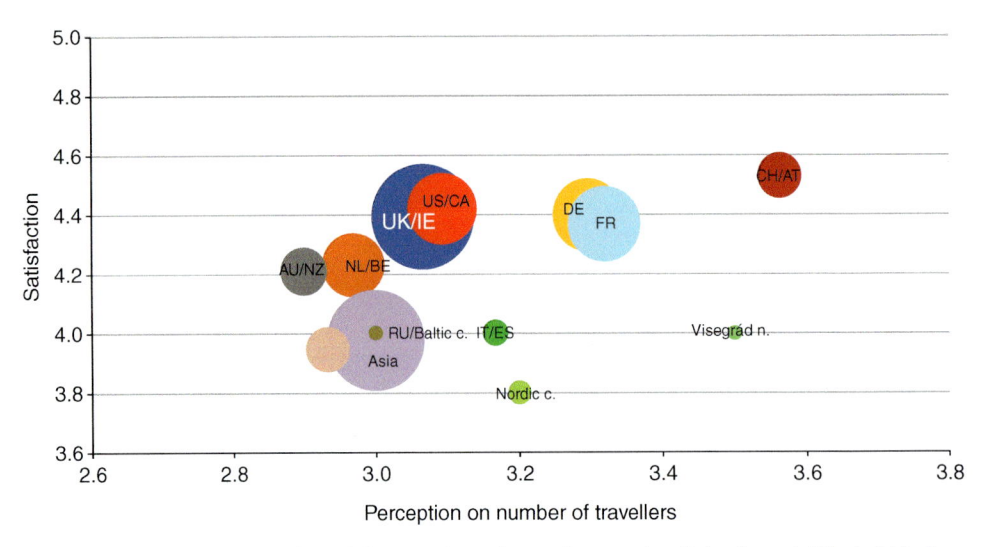

Fig. 18.8. Visitors' perception of the number of travellers and satisfaction at Jökulsárlón in winter.

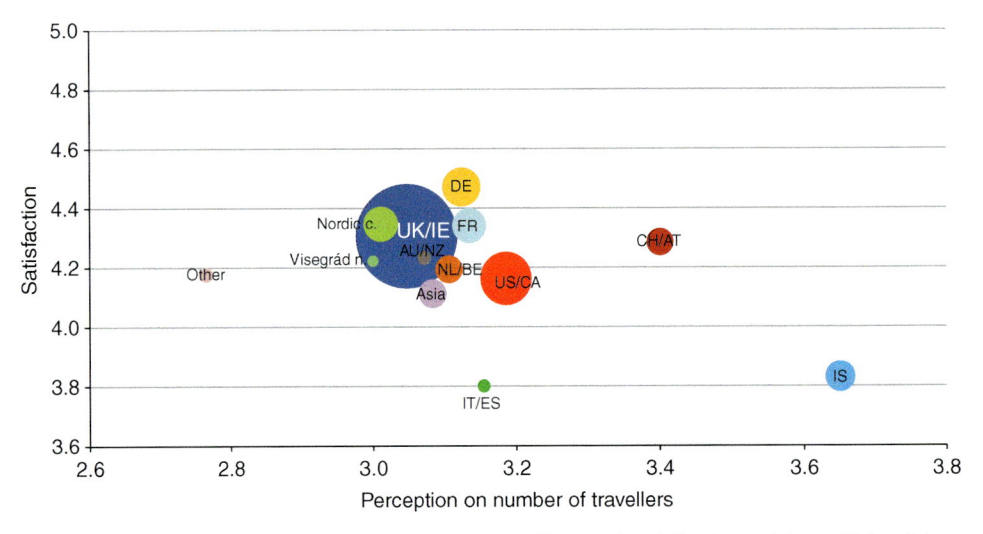

Fig. 18.9. Visitors' perception of the number of travellers and satisfaction at Þingvellir in winter.

18.4 Conclusions

The results of this study indicate that the enormous growth in winter tourism in Iceland has created new challenges. Even in wintertime nature remains Iceland's main attraction. As trips in winter are usually shorter than in summer and road conditions in the countryside are often challenging, winter tourism is highly geographically concentrated in the south-west of the island, close to Reykjavík and the international airport. This leads to a concentration of visitors in a limited number of nature destinations. The results of this study show that despite high satisfaction with nature at the

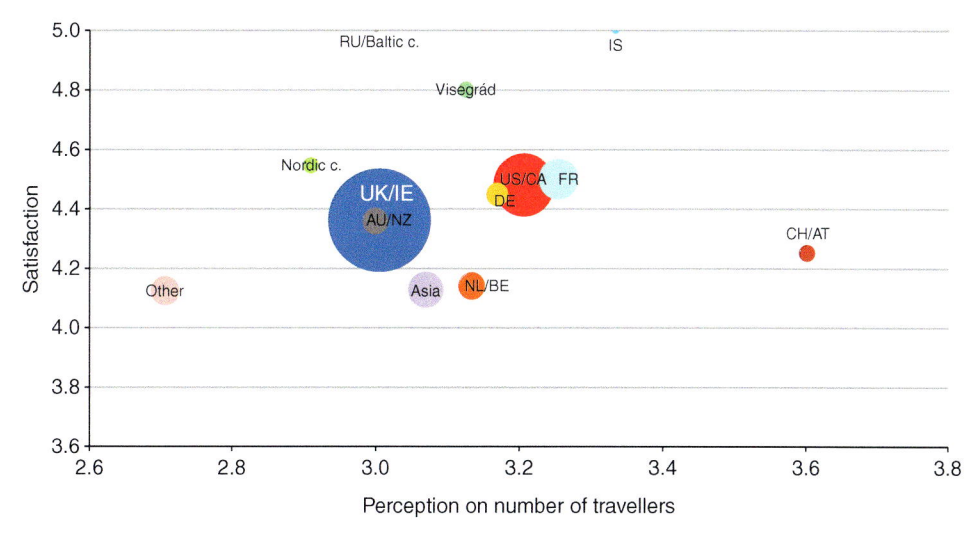

Fig. 18.10. Visitors' perception of the number of travellers and satisfaction at Sólheimajökull in winter.

destinations, service needs to be better, especially regarding restroom facilities. Environmental damage is not recognized, although the perception of overcrowding exists in the most popular destinations. The traditional European market seems to be more sensitive towards high numbers of visitors along with Icelanders, while the Asian and UK market are less sensitive towards crowding. The results have implications for both tourism marketing and site management, especially given the rapid growth in winter visitation to key sites in Iceland in recent years. Given the desire to maintain satisfaction with the winter tourism experience site managers may need to pay more attention to seasonal infrastructure requirements as well as different notions of crowding.

However, the study's results may also be significant for tourism use of winter landscapes beyond the Icelandic experience. Importantly, different marketing and management regimes may be required for the different seasonal landscapes. Increased winter visitation can put extra pressures on site quality not only during the winter period but can also have implications for other seasons given problems of site recovery. In addition, there is a clear management need to provide appropriate all-season infrastructure for walking tracks, toilets and shelters, although considerable debate may ensue as to who should pay for such facilities. Growing winter tourism in Iceland requires different road services, such as more frequent snow ploughing. There is also increased pressure on the organization of rescue services, which has so far been built on volunteer associations. Volunteers are relatively few in rural Iceland as it is sparsely populated and now, due to the huge pressure of increased winter tourism and travellers running into problems in often difficult conditions, the system is under great pressure.

A positive dimension of the study is that, despite issues related to the weather, nature-based tourism can be a viable option for winter tourism beyond the usual focus on skiing and snowmobiles. Indeed, the weather arguably becomes an extremely important part of the winter tourism experience in Iceland and serves to reinforce the role of nature in the country's tourism offerings. Although further research is required, snow on the ground may serve to hide some anthropogenic influences on the landscape and help reinforce the social construction of the Icelandic landscape as a wilderness for many tourists (Sæþórsdóttir *et al.*, 2011). Such findings therefore suggest that there may be new opportunities for developing the tourist attractiveness of some currently highly seasonal attractions in the Arctic and subarctic in a manner following the Icelandic experience. Nevertheless, a significant long-term question for tourism in Iceland is the extent of the impact of tourist concentrations, especially in the winter season, in nature-based destinations on perceptions of the relative naturalness of the Icelandic landscape and the associated management and marketing response.

References

Einarsson, M.Á. (1984) Climate of Iceland. In: van Loon H. (ed.) *World Survey of Climatology: 15: Climates of the Oceans*. Elsevier, Amsterdam, pp. 673–697.

Hall, C.M. (2015) Polar gateway cities: issues and challenges. *Polar Journal* 5(2), 257–277. DOI: 10.1080/2154896X.2015.1080511

Hall, C.M., James, M. and Baird, T. (2011) Forests and trees as charismatic mega-flora: implications for heritage tourism and conservation. *Journal of Heritage Tourism* 6(4), 309–323. DOI:10.1080/1743873X.2011.620116

Icelandic Met Office (2018) Veðurfarsyfirlit. Available at: www.vedur.is/vedur/vedurfar/manadayfirlitIcelandic (accessed 25 October 2018).

Icelandic Tourist Board (2004) Könnun Ferðamálaráðs Íslands meðal erlendra ferðamanna. Niðurstöður fyrir tímabilið júní – ágúst 2004. Available at: https://www.ferdamalastofa.is/static/files/konnun2004/konnun04.html (accessed 25 October 2018).

Icelandic Tourist Board (2016) Research and statistics. Tourism in Iceland in Figures. Visitor surveys. International Visitors in Iceland – Visitor Survey Summer 2016. Available at: https://www.ferdamalastofa.is/static/files/ferdamalastofa/Frettamyndir/2017/januar/sunarkonnun/sumar-2016-islensk.pdf (accessed 25 October 2018).

Icelandic Tourist Board (2018) Research and statistics. Number of foreign visitors. Visitors to Iceland through Keflavik Airport, 2003–2018. Available at: https://www.ferdamalastofa.is/en/research-and-statistics/numbers-of-foreign-visitors (accessed 25 October 2018).

Ingólfsson, O. (2008) The dynamic climate of Iceland. Available at: https://notendur.hi.is/oi/climate_in_iceland.htm (accessed 25 October 2018).

Koenig-Lewis, N. and Bischoff, E.E. (2005) Seasonality research: the state of the art. *International Journal of Tourism Research* 7(4–5), 201–219. DOI:10.1002/jtr.531

Ólafsson, M. (2018) Surfing in Iceland. Guide to Iceland. Available at: https://guidetoiceland.is/travel-info/surfing-in-iceland (accessed 25 October 2018).

Palang, H., Sooväli, H. and Printsmann, A.E. (2007) *Seasonal Landscapes*. Springer, Dordrecht, The Netherlands.

Pham, J., Velayo, N. and Kopecki, S. (1975) *Tourism in Iceland: Phase 2*. Checchi and Company, Washington, DC.

Sæþórsdóttir A.D. (2013) Managing popularity: changes in tourist attitudes to a wilderness destination. *Tourism Management Perspectives* 7, 47–58. DOI:10.1016/j.tmp.2013.04.005.

Sæþórsdóttir A.D. and Ólafsdóttir, R. (2017) Planning the wild: in times of tourist invasion. *Journal of Tourism Research and Hospitality* 6(1), 1–7. DOI:10.4172/2324-8807.1000169

Sæþórsdóttir, A.D., Hall, C.M. and Saarinen, J. (2011) Making wilderness: tourism and the history of the wilderness idea in Iceland. *Polar Geography* 34(4), 249–273. DOI:10.1080/1088937X.2011.643928

Simón, F.J.G., Narangajavana, Y. and Marqués, D.P. (2004) Carrying capacity in the tourism industry: a case study of Hengistbury Head. *Tourism Management* 25(2), 275–283. DOI:10.1016/S0261-5177(03)00089-X

Statistics Iceland (2018) Business sectors. Tourism. Accommodation. Hotels and guesthouses. Occupancy rate of rooms and beds in hotels 2000–2018. Available at: http://px.hagstofa.is/pxis/pxweb/is/Atvinnuvegir/Atvinnuvegir__ferdathjonusta__Gisting__1_hotelgistiheimili/SAM01104.px/table/tableViewLayout1/?rxid=47cb90af-3920-477c-9012-5bf0d2e8b555 (accessed 26 October 2018).

Stewart, W.P. and Cole, D.N. (2001) Number of encounters and experience quality in Grand Canyon backcountry: consistently negative and weak relationships. *Journal of Leisure Research* 33(1), 106–120. DOI:10.1080/00222216.2001.11949933

Welling, J.T. and Árnason, Þ. (2016) External and internal challenges of glacier tourism development in Iceland. In: Richins H. and Hull, J.S. (eds) *Mountain Tourism: Experiences, Communities, Environments and Sustainable Futures*. CAB International, Wallingford, UK, pp. 174–183.

Welling, J.T., Árnason, Þ. and Ólafsdóttir, R. (2017) Glacier tourism: a scoping review. *Tourism Geographies* 17(5), 635–662. DOI:10.1080/14616688.2015.1084529

19 Winter Recreationist Motivations: Motorized, Non-Motorized and Hybrids

JERRY J. VASKE[1]* AND AUBREY D. MILLER[2]

[1]*Human Dimensions of Natural Resources, Colorado State University, Fort Collins, CO, USA;* [2]*National School of Surveying, University of Otago, Dunedin, New Zealand*

19.1 Introduction

Substantial research has sought to understand recreationists' motivations for participation in an activity (Manning, 2011). Motivation theory suggests that people are driven (motivated) to take actions to achieve particular goals (i.e. seek certain outcomes from their experiences). Recreationists, for example, may seek outcomes such as solitude, being outdoors, or socializing with friends and family (Alexandris *et al.*, 2007). Driver and his associates (see Driver *et al.*, 1991, for review) emphasized the importance of understanding the bundle of 'desired psychological outcomes' derived from recreation participation. Recreation was proposed as a way of achieving certain outcomes (e.g. achievement, stress release, family togetherness). The Recreation Experience Preference (REP) scales (i.e. concepts) and the survey items (i.e. variables) used to measure these outcomes were selected based upon a review of the personality trait and motivation literature. In >30 studies, these concepts and variables have demonstrated their usefulness in helping to understand the nature of outdoor recreation experiences and recreationists themselves (Manfredo *et al.*, 1996).

Overall, motivation approaches have contributed in several areas. First, motivation theory has identified the benefits of leisure, such as determining the worth of a particular recreation programme. Knowing the value of recreation helps prioritize budgeting and policy planning. Second, identifying the types of motivations provided in different environments and activities can help improve service delivery. This is particularly the case in market segmentation research that has advocated an experience-based approach to recreation management. Third, motivations can help identify the causes for conflict among the public.

Two types of conflict have been identified in the literature (Vaske *et al.*, 1995). First, interpersonal conflict occurs when the physical presence or behaviour of an individual or group interferes with the goals of another individual or group (Jacob and Schreyer, 1980; Graefe and Thapa, 2004). Research shows interpersonal conflict often occurs between non-motorized and motorized recreation groups, for example, between cross-country skiers and snowmobilers (Knopp and Tyger, 1973; Jackson and Wong, 1982; Vaske *et al.*, 2007), between backcountry skiers and helicopter-assisted skiers (Gibbons and Ruddell, 1995), and between canoers and motorboaters (Adelman *et al.*, 1982).

---

* E-mail: jerryv@colostate.edu

Second, social values conflict occurs between groups who may not share similar norms or values about an activity (Ruddell and Gramann, 1994; Vaske *et al.*, 1995; Needham *et al.*, 2011). Social values conflict can occur between recreationists even with no direct contact between the groups (Carothers *et al.*, 2001; Vaske *et al.*, 2007). One group of recreationists may philosophically disagree about allowing another recreationist activity in the area (e.g. Blahna *et al.*, 1995; Vaske *et al.*, 1995). Long-term education efforts are used to target the commonly held norms a group may have. For example, a Colorado Parks and Wildlife education programme focused on the benefits of a regulation (C.R.S. 25-12-110) that limited off-highway vehicle noise pollution. Snowmobile noise pollution is often a source of animosity from non-motorized recreationists towards motorized recreationists (Vittersø *et al.*, 2004; Lindberg *et al.*, 2009). The education programme on the noise regulation attempted to minimize social values conflict by demonstrating that snowmobiles are quieter now compared with the past.

Decades of research on recreation conflict have focused on two common strategies for limiting conflict between recreationists (Graefe and Thapa, 2004; Lindberg *et al.*, 2009; Miller *et al.*, 2017). First, managers can limit the amount of interaction between groups by zoning recreation into areas open to a particular recreation activity while closed to another (Leung and Marion, 1999). Zoning separates activities and reduces interpersonal conflict. Second, managers use an active management approach to visitor education and enforcement of zoning boundaries. A primary aim of active management is to limit social values conflict (Vaske *et al.*, 2007; Miller and Vaske, 2016).

Miller and Vaske (2016) examined changes in reported interpersonal and social values conflict over a 10-year plus period at the Vail Pass Winter Recreation Area (VPWRA) in central Colorado, USA. The results showed interpersonal conflict decreased over the period for both non-motorized and motorized recreationists. Both groups, however, continued to report interpersonal conflict even with an established zoning system. Despite an active management approach at the VPWRA, social values conflict among non-motorized recreationists *increased* over the period. Even with the zoning system at VPWRA, there were areas with both non-motorized and motorized recreationists present. These mixed-use areas may have been responsible for the lingering interpersonal and social values conflict.

This chapter builds on previous research (Miller and Vaske, 2016; Miller *et al.*, 2017) by examining motivations associated with winter recreation at Vail Pass reported by motorized recreationists (i.e. snowmobiler), non-motorized recreationists (e.g. backcountry skier) and a hybrid group (i.e. snowmobile-assisted skier). Hybrid participants are towed by a snowmobile to a high point on the landscape and then ski down the mountain. The following research questions were addressed: do snowmobilers, skiers and hybrid participants differ relative to their desire for the following?

1. Solitude?
2. Social interaction?
3. Physical fitness?
4. Thrill-seeking?

19.2 Study Site

The VPWRA encompasses 20,240 ha of sub-alpine and alpine terrain ranging from 2652 to 3869 m and is managed by the White River National Forest (WRNF). The area is located immediately south of Vail Mountain resort, west of the Eagles Nest Wilderness Area, and north of the Copper Mountain ski resort (see Fig. 19.1). Both Vail Mountain resort and Copper Mountain ski area hold special-use permits from the WRNF for ski operations on public land. Interstate 70 crosses through the eastern portion of the VPWRA, which is a 1 h 30 min drive to population centres along the Colorado Front Range, including the Denver Metro Area. US Highway 24 forms the western boundary of the VPWRA connecting the mountain communities of Leadville and Minturn.

Visitors to the VPWRA are required to pay an entrance fee (currently $6 per person per day); of which 95% is given to the WRNF to be used for trail grooming and full-time paid rangers who provide active management in the form of parking lot management, enforcement of regulations and public education. The VPWRA sees approximately 35,000 visitors per winter season (USDA Forest Service, 2015). The majority of visitors access the VPWRA from four primary portals, the busiest adjacent to Interstate 70, and three along the west side of the VPWRA (see Fig. 19.1).

The current zoning boundaries at the VPWRA reflect >20 years of collaboration between the WRNF and local stakeholders to provide access to high-quality non-motorized and motorized backcountry terrain (USDA Forest Service, 2015; Miller and Vaske, 2016). Approximately 47% of the winter recreation area is closed to motorized use, while 45% is open to motorized use. There are 1338 ha (7%) of terrain designated for hybrid use. These areas allow motorized use along designated routes to provide access to skiers and snowboarders.

Backcountry hut users account for approximately 11,000 users annually (USDA Forest Service, 2015). There are six backcountry huts located within the VPWRA, which are either operated privately with special-use permits from the WRNF on public lands, or located on private inholdings (see Fig. 19.1). Hut users are predominately non-motorized recreationists, as motorized use is not permitted at most huts. The majority of recreationists access the huts from the main VPWRA portals; however, some visitors travel directly between huts, including from huts located outside the VPWRA.

19.3 Methods

Data were obtained from a survey of both non-motorized and motorized recreationists at the VPWRA during the winter of 2014. Both an on-site and an online version of the survey were used. On-site surveys were distributed at the Vail Pass parking area to all recreationists after their recreation experience. Non-motorized activities include backcountry skiing and snowboarding, cross-country or Nordic skiing, and snowshoeing.

On-site surveys were distributed on weekend days: most VPWRA visitation occurs on weekends. An online version of the survey was also created to capture visitation to the backcountry huts located in the VPWRA. Some hut users do not access the VPWRA though the primary portals, entering instead from Copper Mountain or on a route from other backcountry huts outside of the VPWRA. The online survey was necessary to reach these respondents. Hut users were provided the non-motorized survey because motorized use is not allowed at huts where respondents were staying. Surveys from hut users were collected on weekdays in addition to weekends. Trip leaders were e-mailed information about the survey and a link to complete it online within 3 days of their visit to the VPWRA.

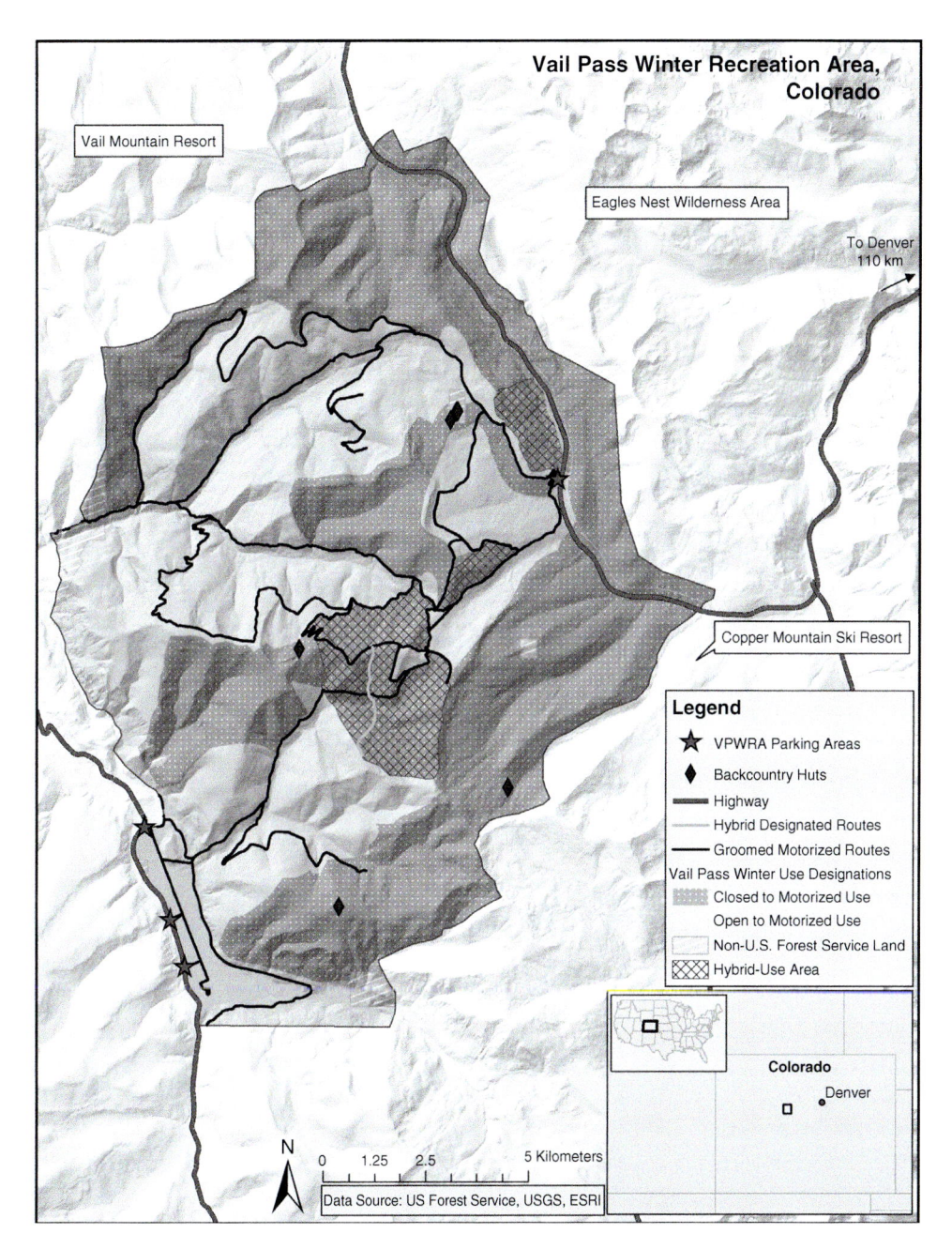

Fig. 19.1. The Vail Pass Winter Recreation Area (VPWRA) and recreation zoning designations and established groomed routes. The six backcountry huts (diamonds) and four primary access portals (stars) are also shown.

Completed surveys were obtained from 2071 respondents. Of these, 1560 (75%) were from the online survey (response rate = 71%), compared with 511 (25%) from the on-site survey (response rate = 88%). Preliminary analyses indicated no statistical difference between the online and on-site response for variables of interest to this chapter.

19.3.1 Variables

The independent variable (type of recreationist) had three categories: motorized recreationists (i.e. snowmobilers, $n = 200$), non-motorized recreationists (e.g. backcountry skiers, $n = 1660$) and a hybrid group (i.e. a snowmobile-assisted skier, $n = 211$). Four dependent motivational indices measured the desire for solitude (three items), social interaction (four items), physical fitness (two items) and thrills (three items). Question wording for each of the motivation items is shown in Table 19.1. All motivation statements were measured on 7-point scales: 'not at all important' (1) to 'extremely important' (7).

Reliability analyses were conducted for the items comprising the four dependent variable indices. Four one-way ANOVAs were run to examine differences between the three levels of the independent variable on each of the dependent indices. Tahmane's T2 posteriori comparisons were also used to detect specific differences in mean scores. A relationship was considered statistically significant at $p < 0.05$. Eta (η) was used to indicate the strength of a relationship. An eta (or effect size) of 0.10 was considered a 'minimal' relationship, 0.243 represented a 'typical' relationship and an $\eta > 0.371$ reflected a 'substantial' relationship (Vaske, 2008).

19.4 Results

The means for solitude (three items), social (four items) and physical fitness (two items) motivations ranged from 5.03 (important) to 6.20 (extremely important) (see Table 19.1). The three means for the thrills concept ranged from 3.13 to 3.62 (slightly

Table 19.1. Reliability analyses of four motivation concepts

I came to Vail Pass to:	Mean	Item total correlation	Alpha if item deleted	Cronbach alpha
Solitude				0.86
be close to nature	6.20	0.68	0.85	
experience tranquillity	5.87	0.85	0.67	
experience solitude	5.46	0.71	0.84	
Social				0.84
be with friends	5.73	0.64	0.81	
meet new people	5.03	0.71	0.78	
be with similar people	5.26	0.77	0.76	
be with my family	5.40	0.58	0.83	
Physical fitness				0.95
get exercise	5.98	0.91	NA	
keep physically fit	5.85	0.91	NA	
Thrills				0.95
experience excitement	3.53	0.91	0.91	
have thrills	3.13	0.92	0.90	
feel exhilaration	3.62	0.84	0.95	

NA = not applicable.

Table 19.2. Motivations reported by motorized, hybrid and non-motorized visitors

Index	Motorized (M)	Hybrid (M)	Non-motorized (M)	F	p	Eta η
Solitude	4.74[a]	5.17[b]	6.05[c]	139.78	<0.001	0.345
Social	3.91[a]	4.53[b]	5.63[c]	236.56	<0.001	0.431
Physical fitness	5.25[a]	5.59[b]	6.05[c]	49.56	<0.001	0.214
Thrills	4.94[a]	5.93[b]	2.93[c]	450.11	<0.001	0.551

Means (M) with different superscripts differ statistically at $p < 0.05$ based on the Tamhane's T2 posteriori comparison.

important). The Cronbach alphas for the four motivation concepts ranged from 0.84 (social) to 0.95 (physical fitness and thrills). The item total correlations within each construct were consistently larger than 0.57. Deleting any motivation item from the associated construct did not improve the overall alpha. For these reasons, indices were computed for each of the four motivation concepts.

One-way ANOVAs indicated statistically significant differences between each of the three independent variable's categories on each of the four motivation indices ($F \geq 49.56$, $p < 0.001$, in all cases, see Table 19.2). Two eta effect sizes were 'substantial' (social η = 0.431, thrills, η = 0.551), and two were 'typical' (solitude η = 0.345, physical fitness η = 0.214). The pattern of the means was identical for solitude, social and physical fitness. Motorized visitors ranked these motivations lowest and non-motorized recreationists considered these motivations most important. The means for the hybrid group for these three motivations were always in between the motorized and non-motorized visitors. The hybrid group considered 'thrills' most important, followed by motorized visitors and then non-motorized visitors.

19.5 Discussion

Findings here indicated that different types of recreationists (i.e. motorized, non-motorized, hybrid) are motivated to visit the VPWRA for different reasons. Non-motorized recreationists considered solitude, social interaction and physical fitness to be most important, while motorized visitors ranked these motivations lowest. The means for the hybrid group, previously unmeasured in a winter recreation study, were always in between the motorized and non-motorized visitors for solitude, social interaction and physical fitness, further clarifying the divide between motivations of motorized and non-motorized recreationists. Finally, thrills were considered most important for the hybrid group followed by motorized visitors and then non-motorized visitors.

As discussed in the introduction, differences in motivations can influence management decisions. For example, the zoning system at VPWRA has been in place for >10 years. Interpersonal conflict among non-motorized respondents decreased significantly between 2003 (Vaske et al., 2007) and 2014 (Miller and Vaske, 2016; Miller et al., 2017). Conversely, social values conflict among non-motorized respondents actually *increased* significantly between 2003 and 2014. For motorized respondents, the results were less mixed. Respondents reported less interpersonal conflict, and social values conflict was not evident either in 2003 or in 2014.

These results have three implications. First, the asymmetrical pattern of reported conflict among non-motorized and motorized recreationists at the VPWRA was consistent with previous research, for example among skiers and snowmobilers (Knopp and Tyger, 1973; Jackson and Wong, 1982), backcountry helicopter-assisted skiers and other skiers (Gibbons and Ruddell, 1995) and between non-motorized and motorized watercraft (Shelby, 1980; Adelman et al., 1982). Such differences between non-motorized and motorized recreationist interpersonal conflict are likely attributable to the noise and exhaust from snowmobiles (Vittersø et al., 2004; Lindberg et al., 2009).

Second, using zoning to reduce interpersonal conflict has become increasingly popular (e.g. Adams and McCool, 2010). Results from VPWRA show that interpersonal conflict among non-motorized recreationists did decrease over time (Miller and Vaske, 2016; Miller et al., 2017). Compared with the interactions between non-motorized and motorized recreationists in the 1990s (Hughes, 1997), such interactions are less contentious now. Despite the decrease, interpersonal conflict was reported by nearly one-third of non-motorized recreationists at the VPWRA in 2014. Managers interested in providing high-quality winter recreation experiences for all visitors must understand the factors that contribute to the persistent interpersonal conflict. Findings here suggest that motivational differences (e.g. desire for solitude vs. thrill-seeking) may be partially responsible.

Third, the results from VPWRA show that social values conflict increased significantly from 2003 to 2014 among non-motorized recreationists (Miller and Vaske, 2016; Miller et al., 2017). Efforts to improve public education and active management at the VPWRA over the past decade have apparently failed. Social values conflict is rooted in shared norms and values of non-motorized recreationists; simple existence of motorized users is problematic for them. Education can help change this sentiment, but education programmes addressing social values conflict (e.g. signage designed to show the benefits of zoning, or regulations limiting noise pollution of snowmobiles) need to be targeted to commonly held norms and are unlikely to fully address underlying conflict on their own (Hidalgo and Harshaw, 2010). Management efforts should focus specifically on norms held by non-motorized recreationists. Research is needed on the effectiveness of management tools such as collaborative planning efforts and the best design and placement of signage and messaging on non-motorized recreationists.

References

Adams, J.C. and McCool, S.F. (2010) Finite recreation opportunities: the Forest Service, the Bureau of Land Management, and off-road vehicle management. *Natural Resources Journal* 49, 45–116.

Adelman, B.J., Heberlein, T.A. and Bonnicksen, T.M. (1982) Social psychological explanations for the persistence of a conflict between paddling canoeists and motorcraft users in the Boundary Waters Canoe Area. *Leisure Sciences* 5, 45–61.

Alexandris, K., Kouthouris, A. and Girgolas, G. (2007) Investigating the relationships among motivation, negotiation, and alpine skiing participation. *Journal of Leisure Research* 39(4), 648–667.

Blahna, J.D., Smith, S.K. and Anderson, A.J. (1995) Backcountry llama packing: visitor perceptions of acceptability and conflict. *Leisure Sciences* 17, 185–204.

Carothers, P., Vaske, J.J. and Donnelly, M.P. (2001) Social values versus interpersonal conflict among hikers and mountain bikers. *Leisure Sciences* 23, 47–61.

Driver, B.L., Brown, P.J. and Peterson, G.L. (eds) (1991) *Benefits of Leisure*. Venture Publishing, Inc., State College, Pennsylvania.

Gibbons, S. and Ruddell, E.J. (1995) The effect of goal orientation and place dependence on select goal interferences among winter backcountry users. *Leisure Sciences* 17, 171–183.

Graefe, A.E. and Thapa, B. (2004) Conflict in natural resource recreation. In: Manfredo, M.J., Vaske, J.J., Bruyere, B.L., Field, D.R. and Brown, P.J. (eds) *Society and Natural Resources: A Summary of Knowledge*. Modern Litho, Jefferson, Missouri, pp. 209–224.

Hidalgo, A.E.R. and Harshaw, H. (2010) Managing outdoor recreation conflict on the Squamish, British Columbia trail network. In: LeBlanc Fisher, C. and Watts, C.E. Jr (eds) *Proceedings of the 2010 Northeastern Recreation Research Symposium, GTR-NRS-P-94*. US Forest Service, Northern Research Station, Newtown, Pennsylvania, pp. 134–140.

Hughes, J. (1997) Vail Pass chill-seekers ending cold war? *The Denver Post* (29 December 1997), pp. A-01. Article ID: 700752.

Jackson, E.L. and Wong, R. (1982) Perceived conflict between urban cross-country skiers and snowmobilers in Alberta. *Journal of Leisure Research* 14, 47–62.

Jacob, G.R. and Schreyer, R. (1980) Conflict in outdoor recreation: a theoretical perspective. *Journal of Leisure Research* 12, 368–380.

Knopp, T.B. and Tyger, J.D. (1973) A study of conflict in recreational land use: snowmobiling versus ski touring. *Journal of Leisure Research* 5, 6–17.

Leung, Y. and Marion, J.L. (1999) Spatial strategies for managing visitor impacts in National Parks. *Journal of Park and Recreation Administration* 17(4), 20–38.

Lindberg, K., Fredman, P. and Heldt, T. (2009) Facilitating integrated recreation management: assessing conflict reduction benefits in a common metric. *Forest Science* 55, 201–209.

Manfredo, M.J., Driver, B.L. and Tarrant, M.A. (1996) Measuring leisure motivation: a meta-analysis of the recreation experience preference scales. *Journal of Leisure Research* 28(3), 188–213.

Manning, R.E. (2011) *Studies in Outdoor Recreation: Search and Research for Satisfaction*, 3rd edn. Oregon State University Press, Corvallis, Oregon.

Miller, A.D. and Vaske, J.J. (2016) Winter recreationist conflict and management approaches at Vail Pass, Colorado. *Journal of Park and Recreation Administration* 34(2), 1–11.

Miller, A.D., Vaske, J.J., Squires, J.R., Olson, L.E. and Roberts, E.K. (2017) Does zoning winter recreationists reduce recreation conflict. *Environmental Management* 59(1), 50–67.

Needham, M.D., Rollins, R.B., Ceurvorst, R.L., Wood, C.J.B., Grimm, K.E. and Dearden, P. (2011) Motivations and normative evaluations of summer visitors at an alpine ski area. *Journal of Travel Research* 50(6), 669–684.

Ruddell, E.J. and Gramann, J.H. (1994) Goal orientation, norms, and noise-induced conflict among recreation area users. *Leisure Sciences* 16, 93–104.

Shelby, B. (1980) Contrasting recreational experiences: motors and oars in the Grand Canyon. *Journal of Soil and Water Conservation* 35, 129–131.

USDA Forest Service (2015, March) White River National Forest official webpage on Vail Pass Winter Recreation Area. Available at: www.fs.usda.gov/recarea/whiteriver/recreation/recarea/?recid=41445&actid=92 (accessed 30 January 2019).

Vaske, J.J. (2008) *Survey Research and Analysis: Applications in Parks, Recreation and Human Dimensions*. Venture Publishing, State College, Pennsylvania.

Vaske, J.J., Donnelly, M.P., Wittmann, K. and Laidlaw, S. (1995) Interpersonal versus social value conflict. *Leisure Sciences* 17, 205–222.

Vaske, J.J., Needham, M.D. and Cline, R.C. (2007) Clarifying interpersonal and social values conflict among recreationists. *Journal of Leisure Research* 39, 182–195.

Vittersø, J., Chipeniuk, R., Skår, M. and Vistad, O.I. (2004) Recreational conflict is affective: the case study of cross country skiers and snowmobiles. *Leisure Sciences* 26, 227–243.

20 Alternative Outdoor Activities in Alpine Winter Tourism

Bruno Abegg[1,2]*, Leandra Jänicke[1], Mike Peters[3] and Alexander Plaikner[3]

[1]*Institute of Geography, University of Innsbruck, Innsbruck, Austria;* [2]*Institute for Systemic Management and Public Governance, University of St. Gallen, St. Gallen, Switzerland;* [3]*Department of Strategic Management, Marketing and Tourism, University of Innsbruck, Innsbruck, Austria*

20.1 Introduction

Downhill skiing and snowboarding are the most popular winter sport activities in the European Alps. However, there is growing interest in activities other than skiing and snowboarding such as ski touring, snowshoeing and tobogganing. An increasing number of winter tourists combine skiing/snowboarding with these activities, or do not ski/snowboard at all (e.g. Dolnicar and Leisch, 2003; Bausch and Unseld, 2017). Winter sport destinations are investing significant amounts of money to diversify the snow-based offer and to appeal to people practising different activities.

There is an abundance of scientific literature on outdoor recreation in general, and on winter sport activities in particular (mostly focusing on skiing; e.g. Hudson *et al.*, 2004; Matzler *et al.*, 2007; Steiger *et al.*, 2017), but little is known about winter sport activities other than skiing. Most of the existing literature on alternative activities focuses on medical and physiological aspects including, for example, biomechanics (e.g. Pellegrini *et al.*, 2013) and injuries (e.g. Ruedl *et al.*, 2017). In addition, there is some literature on risk, for example the risk of avalanches (e.g. Techel *et al.*, 2015) or the risk propensity of outdoor recreationists (e.g. Marengo *et al.*, 2017), and on the impact of alternative outdoor activities on nature and wildlife in protected or non-protected areas (e.g. Sato *et al.*, 2013; Cremer-Schulte *et al.*, 2017). Potential impacts of climate change on alternative winter sport activities, in particular cross-country skiing, have been researched as well (e.g. Pouta *et al.*, 2009; Landauer *et al.*, 2012; Neuvonen *et al.*, 2015). Finally, there is scattered scientific information on topics such as the economic effects of alternative winter sport activities (e.g. McCollum *et al.*, 1990; Filippini *et al.*, 2017) and the potential conflicts between different types of alternative outdoor activities (e.g. Jackson and Wong, 1982; Vittersø *et al.*, 2004).

The same is true when it comes to the question of the motivation to engage in outdoor activities: there is a wealth of information on tourists' motivation in general, there are some studies dealing with the motivation of skiers and snowboarders (e.g. Unbehaun *et al.*, 2008; Alexandris *et al.*, 2009), but little is known about the motivation

---

* E-mail: bruno.abegg@uibk.ac.at

of the people practising alternative winter sport activities. Beier (2002), for instance, named 'experiencing nature', 'improvement of health, fitness and/or performance' and 'social aspects' as the most important motives for practising outdoor activities in Germany. Similarly, 'experiencing scenic beauty and nature', 'recreation/relaxation' and 'wellness/fitness' are most important for outdoor recreationists in Switzerland (Zeidenitz et al., 2007). However, these findings refer to a series of different outdoor activities that are neither restricted to winter nor to mountain activities. A closer look at specific activities, however, reveals some details. A comparison between two totally different activity groups, free-riders (off-piste skiers and snowboarders) and picnickers, shows a similar structure of motives: the top-ranked motives including recreation, nature, health/fitness and socializing, etc. are the same (although in a slightly different order) – the only exception being 'adventure and thrill', which is, unsurprisingly, significantly more important for free-riders than picnickers (Zeidenitz et al., 2007). Perrin-Malterre and Chanteloup (2018) focus on two selected alternative winter sport activities, backcountry skiing and snowshoeing, in the Hautes-Bauges region of Savoy (France). They mention a number of motives to practise these activities, namely 'contact with nature', 'recharge one's batteries' and 'escape from ski resorts', and identify – based on multiple factor analysis – practitioner profiles ranging from 'performers' to 'spiritualists' (with most practitioners being somewhere in between). Finally, there are studies focusing on single activities only, for example on cross-country skiing or ski touring on slopes. Landauer et al. (2009) looked at the motivation of Finnish cross-country skiers. They applied principal component analysis to group the nine motives considered into three factors including 'skiing environment' (e.g. nature experience), 'social features' (e.g. time with family and friends) and 'technical skills and fitness' (e.g. keeping fit). Pröbstl-Haider and Lampl (2017), focusing on ski touring on slopes, surveyed outdoor recreationists from Austria and Germany and found 'sport and exercise', the 'improvement of general health' and the 'escape from the daily routine' to be the most important motives (among 12 motives in total).

In Tyrol (Austria), skiing and snowboarding are given top priority. But like elsewhere in the European Alps, winter activities other than skiing/snowboarding are gaining in importance, as are the numbers of people practising these activities. However, little is known about these people and their activities. For this book chapter, we focus on the six most popular alternative winter sport activities in Tyrol: backcountry skiing, ski touring on slopes (i.e. skiing up the hill on the fringe of groomed ski slopes), winter hiking, tobogganing, cross-country skiing and snowshoeing. More precisely, we want to explore the people's activity profiles and their satisfaction with the existing offer in Tyrol. Special attention is given to the motivation to practise alternative winter sport activities.

20.2 Methods

To investigate this topic a standardized questionnaire was developed. The main focus of the questionnaire was on the performance of alternative winter sport activities (e.g. what kind of activities are performed, how frequent and with whom) and on the motivation to do so. Participants were asked what information sources they consulted to plan the activity, and what infrastructure they used to perform the activity. Experiences while performing the activity were another topic (e.g. satisfaction with the existing offer in Tyrol, suggestions to improve the existing offer and conflicts between different activities). Finally, general information such as gender, age, place of residence and guest type (day visitor or overnight guest) was collected. For the chapter at hand, we focus on the activities practised, the satisfaction and the motivation.

Besides multiple choice questions, 4- and 5-point Likert scales were used to measure the respondent's satisfaction with the supply of alternative winter sport activities in Tyrol (1 'unsatisfied' – 4 'satisfied') and to evaluate the importance of motivational factors to perform these activities (1 'unimportant' – 5 'important'). The motivation to perform alternative winter sport activities was measured with different items. The literature review (see above) revealed a high number of potentially important items. After a consultation process with several experienced winter sport enthusiasts, and after taking into account some practicability issues (i.e. items should be clearly distinguishable from each other; items should be relevant for all alternative winter sport activities investigated; survey participants cannot be asked to evaluate an infinite number of items), the number of items was reduced to 20.

Data collection took place at highly frequented locations (e.g. a parking lot at the starting of the cross-country network) in several Tyrolean destinations from mid-December 2017 to the end of March 2018. People were asked (if not obvious) whether they perform alternative winter sport activities and if they would like to participate in a research project. If they were willing, they were given a brief introduction to the project (content, methods and aims) and were asked for their e-mail addresses. Subsequently, the link to the online questionnaire (available in both German and English) was e-mailed to the participants. To boost participation in the survey, three gift vouchers were drawn among respondents who filled in the questionnaire completely.

A total of 1056 questionnaires were collected. After excluding incomplete questionnaires, a sample of 909 questionnaires remained for further analyses. Descriptive and analytical statistics were applied to explore the profile of the sample and to identify differences between subgroups (e.g. age, gender, guest and activity types). To further analyse the motivational items, a principal component analysis, using the varimax rotation with Kaiser normalization (Field, 2011; Tabachnick and Fidell, 2013), was conducted (see Landauer et al., 2009 and Konu et al., 2011 for similar applications of principal component analysis in snow-based tourism). As a cut-off point, a loading factor of 0.4 was set. To assess the internal reliability of each factor, Cronbach's alpha was computed (Cortina, 1993). All statistical calculations were made in IBM SPSS 24 software.

20.3 Results

There are slightly more male (52.5%) than female respondents in the sample. The average age is 39.2 years (median: 37 years) with the majority of respondents (61.1%) being between 31 and 60 years old. A total of 31.7% of the respondents are younger, 7.2% are older; 61.3% of the respondents are day visitors, 38.7% are overnight guests. Most respondents live in Austria (46.4%; thereof 39% in Tyrol), followed by Germany (43.5%), Switzerland (2.8%), The Netherlands (2.7%), the UK (2.1%) and Italy (0.7%).

Most respondents practise more than one winter sport activity. It is common to combine alternative winter sport activities with downhill skiing/snowboarding (76.5% of respondents) – although the time spent for each of the two categories varies greatly: 28.5% of the respondents indicate that they spend <20% of their

Table 20.1. Alternative outdoor activities practised (first, second and third choice) (n = 909).

Activity	Choice 1	Choice 2	Choice 3	Sum
Backcountry skiing (%)	38.8	12.0	7.5	58.3
Ski touring on slopes (%)	15.8	21.7	9.8	47.3
Winter hiking (%)	13.2	16.8	12.9	42.9
Tobogganing (%)	12.5	19.5	19.3	51.3
Cross-country skiing (%)	11.4	8.9	10.6	30.9
Snowshoeing (%)	8.1	9.8	10.2	28.1
None (%)		11.3	29.8	

overall winter sport time on skiing/snowboarding, whereas 25.5% of the respondents say that they spend >80% of their overall winter sport time on skiing/snowboarding. The percentage of respondents doing alternative winter sport activities only is therefore comparatively small (23.5%). The most popular alternative winter sport activities are backcountry skiing, followed by ski touring on slopes and winter hiking (first choice only, see Table 20.1).

The respondents like companionship, most preferably with friends and partner/family including kids; only 9.5% of the respondents practise on their own. Many respondents seem to be rather experienced: 77% of the respondents have been practising for >3 years, and more than half of the respondents (55.4%) spend at least 10 days per season performing the respective activities. In terms of activity choice, no differences can be detected between female and male respondents. Backcountry skiing, ski touring on slopes and tobogganing become less popular with increasing age; winter hiking, though, becomes more popular ($p = 0.000$). Snowshoeing and cross-country skiing are most popular with respondents aged between 31 and 60 years ($p = 0.000$). Day visitors predominantly practise backcountry skiing (and to lesser extent ski touring on slopes), overnight guests significantly more often choose winter hiking, cross-country skiing, tobogganing and snowshoeing ($p = 0.000$).

20.3.1 Satisfaction

In general, the respondents seem to be very pleased with the existing offer (see Table 20.2). Even the lowest mean score is close to 3, which is remarkable given the scale from 1 (unsatisfied) to 4 (satisfied). Consequently, there are only a small number of respondents suggesting improvement measures. The highest number of respondents doing so ($n = 266$; 29.8%) call for better accessibility by public transport, followed by 183 respondents asking for larger parking lots. Notably, there are 245 respondents making no suggestions at all. With regard to the age of the respondents, no differences in the level of satisfaction can be detected. Female respondents are generally more satisfied with the existing offer than male respondents, particularly with the family-friendliness ($p = 0.000$), the available information material ($p = 0.002$), the night-time activities ($p = 0.005$), the rental services ($p = 0.013$) and the accessibility by public transport ($p = 0.047$). Day visitors are more satisfied with the variety of activities/tours, the information material and the night-time activities (all $p = 0.000$), overnight guests

Table 20.2. Level of satisfaction with existing offer ($n = 255–861^a$).

	Mean	SD	Median
Variety of activities/tours	3.69	0.530	4
Information material	3.42	0.680	4
Signposting	3.38	0.690	3
Rental services	3.37	0.530	4
Connectivity (to lifts, huts, etc.)	3.37	0.642	3
Night-time activities	3.32	0.764	3
Family-friendliness	3.21	0.771	3
Guided tours	3.11	0.778	3
Parking facilities	3.07	0.809	3
Access by public transport	2.89	0.926	3

[a]Not all aspects (e.g. guided tours or rental services) are relevant to all respondents. Only answers from respondents claiming the respective aspects to be relevant (ticking boxes 1–4 in the survey) were considered. Answers from respondents ticking box 0 (= not relevant) were excluded.

with the parking facilities, the accessibility by public transport (both $p = 0.000$) and the rental services ($p = 0.001$). Backcountry skiers are more satisfied with the variety of activities/tours ($p = 0.000$) and the information material ($p = 0.009$) than others (in particular than toboggan riders and cross-country skiers) but less satisfied with the parking facilities ($p = 0.011$) and the accessibility by public transport ($p = 0.000$). However, irrespective of the statistically significant differences between subgroups, the general satisfaction level is high.

20.3.2 Motivation

Table 20.3 shows the ranking of the motivational items for the whole sample. Focusing on single activities, statistically significant differences in the importance can be found for almost all items (except for relieving stress and low cost). For the activity 'ski touring on slopes', for example, the item 'belongs to individual training/workout schedule' is more important than for all other activities ($p = 0.000$). And for toboggan riders, the items 'experiencing action/adventure' and 'Hüttengaudi – fun in mountain huts' are more important than for all others (both $p = 0.000$). In some cases, however, the differences in the importance of single items – although statistically significant – are rather small. For example, the mean value for 'enjoying/experiencing nature' varies only between 4.85 (highest for backcountry skiing) and 4.39 (lowest for tobogganing).

The principal component analysis produced a five-factor solution (see Table 20.4) with eigenvalues >1 representing 55.0% of the total variance of the variables. All items showed factor loadings >0.4, none of them loaded on multiple factors, therefore no item had to be removed. The internal consistency of the factors, measured with Cronbach's alpha, showed good reliability with scores ranging from 0.557 to 0.693. The five factors can be described as follows:

- Factor 1 is made up of five items. It is about stress release and relaxation. Practising alternative winter sport activities (and simply being outdoors) contributes to physical and mental wellbeing. Therefore, this factor is called 'health'.

Table 20.3. The ranking of the 20 motives (n = 909).

Motive	Important[a]	Mean	SD	Median
Being outdoors	712	4.76	0.489	5
Having fun	705	4.72	0.597	5
Enjoying/experiencing nature	691	4.70	0.610	5
Enhancing physical/mental wellbeing	667	4.67	0.637	5
Relaxing	470	4.32	0.848	5
Spending time with family/friends	420	4.19	0.957	4
Being far from 'civilization'	419	4.03	1.125	4
Feeling free	401	4.10	1.029	4
Relieving stress	343	3.98	1.051	4
Enhancing physical performance	335	3.95	1.064	4
Improving skills/technique	329	3.89	1.092	4
Contributing to individual health care	291	3.69	1.197	4
Alternative to skiing/snowboarding	216	3.21	1.363	3
Experiencing action/adventure	196	3.29	1.281	3
(Relatively) low cost	117	3.11	1.140	3
Belongs to training/workout schedule	76	2.46	1.291	2
(Relatively) low time expenditure	64	2.72	1,152	3
Little previous knowledge required	60	2.60	1.179	3
'Hüttengaudi' – fun in mountain huts	57	2.26	1.244	2
Practising a trendy activity	18	1.66	0.942	1

[a]Number of respondents who deemed the motive to be important – scale from 1 'unimportant' to 5 'important'.

- Factor 2 is made up of three items. It corresponds to physical exertion, fitness and skill; moreover, practising alternative winter sport activities is part of an individual training/workout schedule. Therefore, this factor is called 'achievement'.
- Factor 3 is made up of four items. It is about the relatively 'low barriers' related to the performance of these activities: it is relatively low cost (at least in comparison to downhill skiing and snowboarding), it can be done in a relatively short period of time (i.e. it doesn't take the whole day), and at least a few of the respective activities can be enjoyed with no/little previous knowledge and skill. Furthermore, it is trendy. Referring (mainly) to the first three items, this factor is called 'convenience'.
- Factor 4 is made up of four items. It is about 'feelings', to be away from it all (i.e. 'civilization'), to feel free and to enjoy nature. In addition, it is seen as an alternative to skiing and snowboarding on (crowded) slopes. Therefore, this factor is called 'peace and quiet'.
- Factor 5 is made up of four items as well. It refers to fun and action/adventure, and to social aspects such as being with friends and family and having a good time in mountain huts. Therefore, this factor is called 'sociability'.

These factors ('bundle of motives') are significantly more important to female respondents ($p = 0.000–0.020$), the exception being 'sociability' (not significant). The importance of 'sociability' ($p = 0.000$) and 'peace and quiet' ($p = 0.026$) decreases with increasing age. 'Health' is most important for respondents aged between 31 and 60 years ($p = 0.000$). 'Health', 'achievement' and 'peace and quiet' are deemed to be more important for day

Table 20.4. Principal component analysis of the motives to practise alternative winter sport activities.

	Health	Achievement	Convenience	Peace and quiet	Sociability
Being outdoors	0.71				
Relaxing	0.70				
Enhancing physical/mental wellbeing	0.66				
Relieving stress	0.50				
Contributing to individual health care	0.49				
Enhancing physical performance		0.75			
Belongs to training/workout schedule		0.72			
Improving skills/technique		0.68			
Little previous knowledge required			0.72		
(Relatively) low time expenditure			0.69		
(Relatively) low cost			0.66		
Practising a trendy activity			0.49		
Being far from 'civilization'				0.75	
Feeling free				0.60	
Enjoying/experiencing nature				0.52	
Alternative to skiing/snowboarding				0.41	
'Hüttengaudi' – fun in mountain huts					0.69
Spending time with family/friends					0.63
Having fun					0.61
Experiencing action/adventure					0.56
Eigenvalue	4.0	2.4	1.8	1.7	1.1
Cumulative % of variance explained	20.2	32.1	41.1	49.4	55.0

visitors, and 'convenience' and 'sociability' to be more important for overnight guests (all $p = 0.000$). Focusing on activities: 'health' is most important to winter hikers (least to toboggan riders), 'achievement' and 'convenience' to people ski touring on slopes (least to toboggan riders and backcountry skiers, respectively), 'peace and quiet' to backcountry skiers (least to cross-country skiers) and 'sociability' to toboggan riders (least to cross-country skiers) (all $p = 0.000$).

20.4 Conclusions and Outlook

This research produced new insights: (i) ski touring on slopes is a relatively new phenomenon but it seems that the activity has become firmly established in Tyrol;

(ii) outdoor recreationists are happy with the existing offer – this is definitely good news for the Tyrolean destinations; and (iii) the ranking of the motives (see Table 20.3) as well as the factors resulting from the principal component analysis (see Table 20.4) are not very surprising and confirm existing knowledge. Contrary to previous research, however, this analysis focuses on multiple activities, and the relatively large sample allows for a detailed analysis of different subgroups, be it, for example, activity types or visitor types. We can confirm that motives vary between activities, and we can characterize both the socio-demographic profile and the motives of outdoor recreationists practising particular activities. Tobogganing, for example, is not the favourite first choice activity but it is important as a secondary or tertiary activity. It is most popular with younger overnight guests seeking action and fun. Furthermore, there are significant differences between day visitors and overnight guests. Day visitors, for example, prefer backcountry skiing and ski touring on slopes, and they are driven by 'peace and quiet', 'health' and 'achievement'. This is valuable information for destinations seeking to better understand their visitors, and it can be used for product offering, positioning and marketing.

The results presented here are an excerpt only. The dataset allows for further analysis, for example, by including the education of the respondents. Besides day visitors and overnight guests we could also distinguish between recreationists combining downhill skiing/snowboarding with alternative activities and recreationists practising alternative activities only. Moreover, it can be hypothesized that there are distinct outdoor types such as the 'fitness freaks' or the 'pleasure seekers', and a cluster analysis should be conducted to detect such outdoor types. This would contribute to an even clearer picture of the outdoor recreationists in Tyrol.

This research, however, is also subject to limitations. One limitation refers to the representativeness of the sample. Some aspects of the sample (e.g. age distribution and place of residence of the respondents) are in accordance with available data from Tyrol. Other aspects of the sample are more challenging: as there is no reliable information about, for example, the number of day visitors and the share of recreationists practising particular outdoor activities, it is difficult to assess the representativeness. Furthermore, the analysis is restricted to six popular alternative outdoor activities in Tyrol. There are additional activities such as snowmobiling, dog sledding and ice fishing. These activities are of less interest in Tyrol (and the European Alps) but much more important in North America and Scandinavia.

Most of the existing research on snow-based tourism focuses on downhill skiing. This is understandable given the past and current importance of skiing for many winter destinations. Downhill skiing, however, is challenged by climate change, demographics and competition from non-snow-based destinations. To investigate alternative outdoor activities in winter tourism is an important and promising scientific endeavour: it is under-researched, and it can be assumed that the topic will further gain in importance. Many winter sport destinations understand that there is much more to future winter tourism than downhill skiing.

Acknowledgements

The authors would like to thank Steve Borchardt and Alina Kuthe for their support in collecting the e-mail addresses (Steve) and conducting the principal component analysis (Alina). This research was funded by the Tourism Research Centre of Tyrol.

References

Alexandris, K., Kouthouris, C., Funk, D. and Giovani, C. (2009) Segmenting winter sport tourists by motivation: the case of recreational skiers. *Journal of Hospitality Marketing and Management* 18(5), 480–499. DOI:10.1080/19368620902950048

Bausch, T. and Unseld, C. (2017) Winter tourism in Germany is much more than skiing! Consumer motives and implications to alpine destination marketing. *Journal of Vacation Marketing* 24(3), 1–15. DOI:10.1177/1356766717691806

Beier, K. (2002) Was reizt Menschen an sportlicher Aktivität in der Natur? Zu den Anreizstrukturen von Outdoor-Aktivitäten. In: Dreyer A. (ed.) *Tourismus und Sport*. Harzer wirtschaftswissenschaftliche Schriften. Deutscher Universitätsverlag, Wiesbaden, Germany, pp. 81–92.

Cortina, J. (1993) What is coefficient alpha? An examination of theory and applications. *Journal of Applied Psychology* 78(1), 98–104.

Cremer-Schulte, D., Rehnus, M., Duparc, A., Perrin-Malterre, C. and Arneodo, L. (2017) Wildlife disturbance and winter recreational activities in alpine protected areas: recommendations for successful management. *eco-mont* 9(2), 66–73.

Dolnicar, S. and Leisch, F. (2003) Winter tourist segments in Austria – identifying stable vacation styles using bagged clustering techniques. *Journal of Travel Research* 41(3), 281–292.

Field, A. (2013) *Discovering Statistics Using IBM SPSS Statistics*, 4th edn. Sage, Los Angeles, California.

Filippini, M., Greene, W. and Martinez-Cruz, A.L. (2017) Non-market value of winter outdoor recreation in the Swiss Alps: The case of Val Bedretto. *Environmental and Resource Economics* 71(3), 729–754. DOI:10.1007/s10640-017-0181-0

Hudson, S., Ritchie, B. and Timur, S. (2004) Measuring destination competitiveness: an empirical study of Canadian ski resorts. *Tourism and Hospitality Planning and Development* 1(1), 79–94. DOI:10.1080/1479053042000187810

Jackson, E.L. and Wong, R.A.G. (1982) Perceived conflict between urban cross-country skiers and snowmobilers in Alberta. *Journal of Leisure Research* 14(1), 47–62. DOI:10.1080/00222216.1982.11969504

Konu, H., Laukkanen, T. and Komppula, R. (2011) Using ski destination choice criteria to segment Finnish ski resort customers. *Tourism Management* 32(5), 1096–1105. DOI:10.1016/j.tourman.2010.09.010

Landauer, M., Sievänen, T. and Neuvonen, M. (2009) Adaptation of Finnish cross-country skiers to climate change. *Fennia* 187(2), 99–113.

Landauer, M., Pröbstl, U. and Haider, W. (2012) Managing cross-country skiing destinations under the conditions of climate change – scenarios for destinations in Austria and Finland. *Tourism Management* 33(4), 741–751. DOI:10.1016/j.tourman.2011.08.007

Marengo, D., Monaci, M.G. and Miceli, R. (2017) Winter recreationists' self-reported likelihood of skiing backcountry slopes: investigating the role of situational factors, personal experiences with avalanches and sensation-seeking. *Journal of Environmental Psychology* 49, 78–85. DOI:10.1016/j.jenvp.2016.12.005

Matzler, K., Füller, J. and Faullant, R. (2007) Customer satisfaction and loyalty to alpine ski resorts: the moderating effect of lifestyle, spending and customers' skiing skills. *International Journal of Tourism Research* 9(6), 409–421. DOI:10.1002/jtr.613

McCollum, D.W., Gilbert, A.H. and Peterson, G.L. (1990) The net economic value of day use cross country skiing in Vermont: a dichotomous choice contingent valuation approach. *Journal of Leisure Research* 22(4), 341–352. DOI:10.1080/00222216.1990.11969839

Neuvonen, M., Sievänen, T., Fronzek, S., Lahtinen, I., Veijalainen, N. and Carter, T.R. (2015) Vulnerability of cross-country skiing to climate change in Finland – an interactive mapping tool. *Journal of Outdoor Recreation and Tourism* 11, 64–79. DOI:10.1016/j.jort.2015.06.010

Pellegrini, B., Zoppirolli, C., Bortolan, L., Holmberg, H.C., Zamparo, P. and Schena, F. (2013) Biomechanical and energetic determinants of technique selection in classical cross-country skiing. *Human Movement Science* 32(6), 1415–1429. DOI:10.1016/j.humov.2013.07.010

Perrin-Malterre, C. and Chanteloup, L. (2018) Ski touring and snowshoeing in the Hautes-Bauges (Savoie, France): a study of various sports practices and ways of experiencing nature. *Journal of Alpine Research/Revue de géographie alpine* 106-4. DOI:10.4000/rga.3934

Pouta, E., Neuvonen, M. and Sievänen, T. (2009) Participation in cross-country skiing in Finland under climate change: application of multiple hierarchy stratification perspective. *Journal of Leisure Research* 41(1), 92–109.

Pröbstl-Haider, U. and Lampl, R. (2017) Skitourengeher auf Pisten – Überlegungen zur Produktentwicklung für eine neue touristische Zielgruppe. In: Roth, R. and Schwark, J. (eds) *Wirtschaftfaktor Sporttourismus*. Erich Schmidt Verlag, Berlin, Germany, pp. 207–214.

Ruedl, G., Pocecco, E., Raas, C., Brucker, P.U., Greier, K. and Burtscher, M. (2017) Unfallursachen und Risikofaktoren bei erwachsenen Rodlern: eine retrospektive Studie (Causes of accidents and risk factors among adults during recreational sledging (tobogganing): a retrospective study). *Sportverletzung Sportschaden* 31(1), 45–49.

Sato, C.F., Wood, J.T. and Lindenmayer, D.B. (2013) The effects of winter recreation on alpine and subalpine fauna: a systematic review and meta-analysis. *PLoS ONE* 8(5), e64282. DOI:10.1371/journal.pone.0064282

Steiger, R., Scott, D., Abegg, B., Pons, M. and Aall, C. (2017) A critical review of climate change risk for ski tourism. *Current Issues in Tourism*, 1–37. DOI:10.1080/13683500.2017.1410110

Tabachnick, B.G. and Fidell, L.S. (2013) *Using Multivariate Statistics*, 6th edn. Pearson, Harlow, UK.

Techel, F., Zweifel, B. and Winkler, K. (2015) Analysis of avalanche risk factors in backcountry terrain based on usage frequency and accident data in Switzerland. *Natural Hazards and Earth System Sciences* 15, 1985–1997. DOI:10.5194/nhess-15-1985-2015

Unbehaun, W., Pröbstl, U. and Haider, W. (2008) Trends in winter sport tourism: challenges for the future. *Tourism Review* 63(1), 36–47.

Vittersø, J., Chipeniuk, R., Skår, M. and Vistad, O.I. (2004) Recreational conflict is affective: the case of cross-country skiers and snowmobiles. *Leisure Sciences* 26(3), 227–243. DOI:10.1080/01490400490461378

Zeidenitz, C., Mosler, H.J. and Hunziker, M. (2007) Outdoor recreation: from analysing motivations to furthering ecologically responsible behaviour. *Forest Snow and Landscape Research* 81(1/2), 175–190.

21 Winter Tourism Management and Challenges in the Tatra National Park

KAROLINA TACZANOWSKA[1]*, MIKOŁAJ BIELAŃSKI[2], JOANNA HIBNER[3], MIŁOSZ JODŁOWSKI[4] AND TOMASZ ZWIJACZ-KOZICA[5]

[1]*Institute of Landscape Development, Recreation and Conservation Planning, University of Natural Resources and Life Sciences, Vienna, Austria;* [2]*Faculty of Tourism and Leisure, University of Physical Education in Kraków, Kraków, Poland;* [3]*Department of Tourism and Health Resort Management, Institute of Geography and Spatial Management, Jagiellonian University, Kraków, Poland;* [4]*Department of Physical Geography, Institute of Geography and Spatial Management, Jagiellonian University, Kraków, Poland;* [5]*Tatra National Park, Zakopane, Poland*

21.1 Introduction and Study Area

The Tatra Mountains belong to the list of the most popular tourist destinations in the Carpathian Mountains and attract large numbers of visitors throughout the year. Although most of the visitors arrive here in the summer months, the winter season attracts a more heterogeneous visitor profile, which on the one hand contributes to the diversification of tourist offerings, but on the other, poses multiple challenges to area management.

This chapter is based upon studies carried out in the Tatra National Park (TNP) located in Poland, Central Eastern Europe. The national park was established in 1954 (TNP, 2018) and belongs to International Union for Conservation of Nature (IUCN) management category II, which implies nature conservation along with provisioning a foundation for environmentally and culturally compatible recreation opportunities (Dudley, 2013). Visits to TNP, in the past 5 years, ranged from 2.9 to 3.8 million tourist visits a year (TNP, 2018), which considering the rather small area of the national park (212 km^2) resulted in a visitor density of 137–179 visits/ha/year. Winter season typically lasts from the beginning of December till the end of April and accounts for approximately 14% of the total annual visitor load (TNP, 2018). Recreational use is permitted only in designated areas (see Fig. 21.1). The most popular outdoor recreation activities in winter are hiking and downhill skiing. Climbing and caving, in spite of having a long tradition in the area, are less fashionable winter activities. Ski touring, which was quite popular in the first half of the 20th century, now is rapidly developing after

---

* E-mail: karolina.taczanowska@boku.ac.at

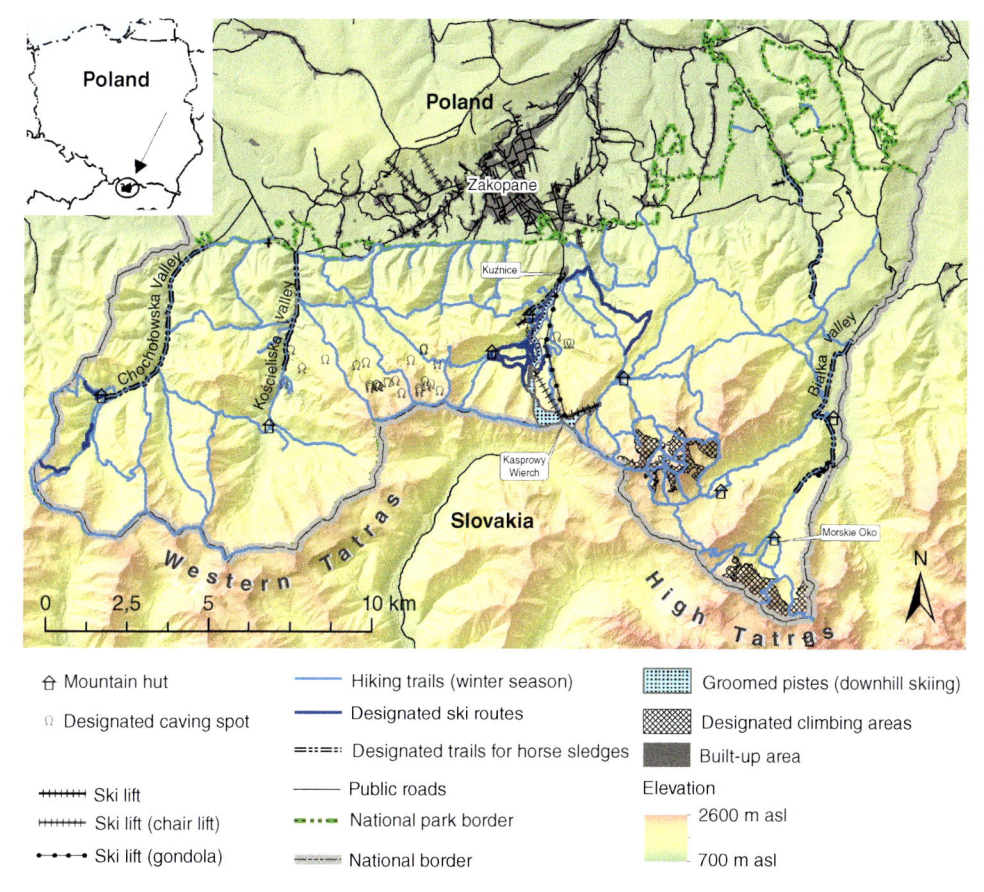

Fig. 21.1. Areas designated for winter outdoor recreation located within the border of the Tatra National Park.

several decades of being almost absent from the TNP. Figure 21.2 illustrates frequencies and shares of outdoor activities performed in the winter season in TNP (TNP, 2018).

21.2 Management Challenges

21.2.1 Zoning of winter recreation

Provisioning environmentally compatible recreation opportunities in popular mountain destinations is one of the major managerial issues in many protected areas worldwide (Manning and Anderson, 2012; Newsome *et al.* 2012; Dudley, 2013; Richins and Hull, 2016). Recreation zoning, accompanied by strategic allocation of tourist infrastructure and sustainable tourism marketing are required management measures in protected areas (Eagles *et al.* 2002; Manning and Anderson, 2012; Newsome *et al.*, 2012). This strategy applies also to the TNP, where general usage rules (see Fig. 21.1), which are supposed to be an integral part of the national park conservation plan (in TPN's case still under preparation) and detailed regulations considering specific

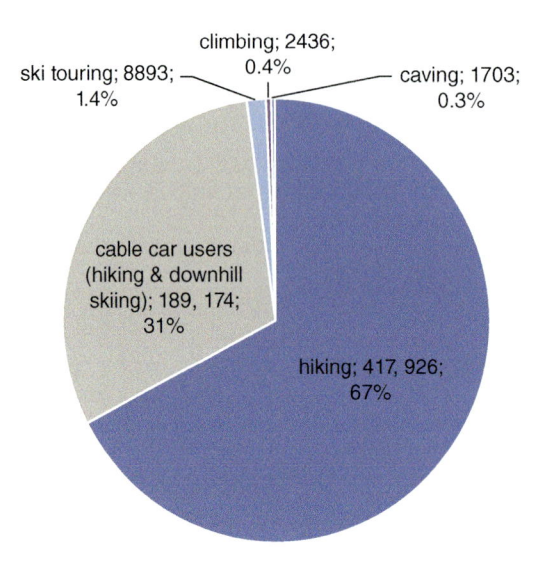

Fig. 21.2. Outdoor recreation activities performed in the Tatra National Park in the winter months of 2017 (January, February, March, April and December 2017). (Chart based on data obtained from TNP, 2018.)

recreational activities are created by decrees issued by the director of the Tatra National Park (TNP, 2017). According to the Polish Nature Conservation Act 2004 (Sejm of the Republic of Poland, 2004), the major goal of a national park is nature protection, and such a protected area can be used for tourism and recreation only in ways that do not pose a threat to its natural resources. However, the system of recreational infrastructure and recreational use in the Tatra Mountains has a longer usage history than the protected area itself. The earliest marked trails and mountain huts dedicated to tourists originated in the 19th century and have developed over subsequent years. The first ski tours were documented in 1894. Ski competitions in the Tatras have taken place since 1907 (Paryski and Paryska, 1995). A cable car from Kuźnice to Kasprowy Wierch was constructed in 1936 (18 years before the formal designation of the Tatra National Park as a national park). The cable car project initiated by the Polish Ski Association and Ministry of Transportation was a topic of severe debate and at that time the National Nature Conservation Council (Państwowa Rada Ochrony Przyrody) along with 94 scientific institutions and tourist associations were against cable car infrastructure being located in the Tatra Mountains. This development attracted further investments, such as the construction of the meteorological observatory at Kasprowy Wierch and a hotel at Kalatówki near Kuźnice.

In the first decades after designation of the Tatra National Park (1954) several zones, located in the most ecologically precious parts of the park, were closed to recreational use. Also, in the 1980s, limestone cliffs, with diverse vegetation, were excluded from climbing use. Currently, in the winter season 259 km of marked trails are open for hiking and ski touring. Ski tourers can also legally use several additional routes dedicated to skiing (see Fig. 21.1). Most granite cliffs are open for climbing and 21 caves are accessible in the winter season. In 2018, several routes in the high-mountain zone within the cliffs and along gullies were additionally designated for ski-alpinism (extreme downhill skiing). Moreover, the ski resort Kasprowy Wierch (1027–1959 masl) offers a cable car and two ski lifts accompanied by 14.1 km of groomed ski pistes and two groomed slopes above the timberline. A few more small ski lifts operate on short pistes on the periphery of the TPN.

Finding the right balance between concentrating versus dispersing recreational use is a topical theme in the ongoing protected area management discourse.

21.2.2 Visitor monitoring

Delineating recreation areas and designing rules for protected areas should be accompanied by systematic visitor monitoring (Cessford and Muhar, 2003; Arnberger *et al.*, 2005). Comprehensive data on recreational use allow us to better assess compliance with nature protection objectives and to gauge the social function of protected areas. Systematically acquired data on visitation level, type of activities, spatial distribution and also socio-demographic profiles of visitors can greatly support management decisions. Long-term monitoring strategies are especially valuable. Thus, changing politics, societies, lifestyles and environmental conditions may contribute to changes in visitor preferences and behaviour.

In the TNP a systematic register of visits, based on tickets sold at major national park trailheads has been conducted since 1993. Additionally, data on cable car transfers are shared with TNP management by the cable car operator. Moreover, climbing and caving activities are reported to the TNP by participating visitors (self-registration in a dedicated website or in a traditional climbing ascent book). As mentioned before, ski touring is a growing outdoor activity in the Tatras. A rapid increase in ski touring has been observed within the past decade. Systematic counting of ski tourers (done at ticket points located at major entries to the national park) was introduced in 2013. Visitor counting data are aggregated by day, month and year. Annual statistics comprise the period between January and December. So far, there is no routine reporting on an entire winter season (stretched over 2 calendar years), which makes comparisons between winter seasons in the TNP more difficult. However, in future, monthly figures could be aggregated also by season.

In addition to systematic visitor counting, studies concerning more detailed tourism aspects are being carried out. They comprise: visitor counting and/or surveys at specific locations of interest, e.g. the areas of highest visitation levels such as Morskie Oko, Kasprowy Wierch, Hala Gąsienicowa, etc. (Ziemilski and Marchlewski, 1964; Czochański and Szydarowski, 2000; Czochański, 2002; Taczanowska *et al.*, 2016); or other current management issues, e.g. a TNP visitor survey concerning the potential inclusion of an insurance fee within a national park entry ticket price. The spatial distribution of visitors within the trail network and outside of the designated areas is being studied within the framework of dedicated research projects, e.g. a study on ski touring (Bielański, 2013; Bielański *et al.*, 2018).

Currently, neither systematic visitor surveys, nor spatio-temporal distribution studies are being carried out in the TNP. Notably, field studies concerning the winter season are more difficult to carry out, due to the demanding outdoor conditions.

Constructed infrastructure and recreational use

Outdoor recreation activities over the winter largely depend on constructed infrastructure, such as the cable car and ski lifts in the Kuźnice-Kasprowy Wierch area, or maintained access roads to mountain huts, e.g. the trail to Morskie Oko in the Białka Valley, the trail to Kalatówki or Kościeliska Valley. Easy access, and huts with warm food and drinks, encourage a high concentration of visitors at specific locations. The most frequently used starting point of winter trips to the TNP is Kuźnice, with multiple attracting outdoor activities: downhill skiing, hiking, climbing and ski touring. Kuźnice attracts 42% of the total winter visits to the TNP, whereas visits by cable car to Kasprowy Wierch account for nearly one-third (31%) of the total winter tourism traffic in the TNP (TNP, 2018a). Interestingly, groomed pistes, originally dedicated to downhill skiing, appeal also to other user groups. Recent studies showed an increased interest in using groomed ski slopes by ski tourers for both ascents and descents (Bielański et al., 2018). In winter 2013, 68% of ski tours started at the Kuźnice trailhead and the highest concentration of ski touring routes was observed on the groomed ski pistes (Bielański et al., 2018).

The second most heavily used TNP destination in the winter season is Białka Valley. A 9-km-long broad and rather easy trail, leading to a picturesque (frozen and snow-covered) lake 'Morskie Oko', attracts a large number of winter strollers and hikers (23% of the total winter visitor load). Additional motivation for some visitors might be the possibility of using traditional horse sledges (or horse carriages in case of insufficient snow cover) to shorten the hike. Similar opportunities are being offered in the frequently visited Kościeliska and Chochołowska valleys. The Chochołowska Valley is mostly private land so night sleigh rides with torches, forbidden on state lands, are becoming more and more popular every year here (so far they are not properly monitored by national park authorities).

Although the Tatra Mountains are acknowledged for their natural value, the visitor numbers indicate the dependence of winter tourism on constructed infrastructure. Therefore, decisions concerning further development of tourist infrastructure inside the protected area should be carefully considered. Existing built objects may require further renovation or development in the future, which may result in an increase of visitation level and concomitant impact on the natural environment. In the TNP there is an ongoing discussion concerning the development of the ski resort. Regularly, ideas suggesting constructing new tunnels, lifts, a water reservoir for artificial snowmaking, and increasing the cable car and ski lifts capacities are being posed by tourism and the ski industry.

Recreation 'off the beaten track'

Although, the large majority of winter tourists in the TNP choose infrastructure-dependent destinations and activities, there are also visitors seeking contact with 'pure' mountain environments. Hiking along marked trails in upper elevations, winter climbing and caving belong to traditional winter outdoor activities in the Tatra Mountains. Within the past 15 years, the rapid increase of ski touring has been noticed in the Tatras, reaching approximately 10,000 visits per year (Bielański, 2013). This activity, although very popular in the European Alps, Scandinavia and North America, has arrived rather late to the Carpathian Mountains and has spread out promptly bringing new challenges to mountain protected areas. Only recently have clear regulations concerning ski touring and monitoring of ski touring entries been introduced by the TNP management (TNP, 2017).

Among the major challenges concerning the management of the spatially unconstrained winter outdoor activities is usage outside of the designated recreation zones. In contrast to infrastructure-dependent outdoor activities, which allow wildlife habituation (Yarmoloy et al., 1988; Miller et al., 2001), faunal species cannot easily adapt to unexpected human disturbances occurring off-trail (Geist, 1978; Miller et al., 2001). Especially in the case of ski touring, the freedom of movement in snow-covered terrain encourages off-trail use. A recent GPS tracking study shows that, on average, 15% of the registered ski tourers' GPS trackpoints were located off-trail (Bielański et al., 2018) and the off-trail behaviour varies among different locations in TNP. For instance, in the surroundings of the Chochołowska and Kościeliska Valleys, off-trail usage was significantly higher than in the Kuźnice–Kasprowy Wierch region (Bielański et al., 2018). Also, in the surroundings of the ski resort Kasprowy Wierch, side-country recreation outside ski field boundaries among downhill skiers and snowboarders is being observed. Between 2001 and 2007 the area intensively used by skiers outside of designated pistes expanded from 53 ha to 130 ha (Zwijacz-Kozica, 2007). This may be attributed not only to the higher popularity of powder skiing, but also to advances in equipment technology – the most popular skis have become shorter, wider and lighter, thus more suitable for off-piste skiing. Illegal climbing activity upon the limestone cliffs is also under observation. The number of climbers depends on weather and snow conditions, but usually does not exceed a few dozen ascents (Jodłowski, 2015). During the winter season, protection of several sensitive species of wildlife, including chamois (*Rupicapra rupicapra tatrica*), marmot (*Marmota marmota latirostris*) and black grouse (*Tetrao tetrix*) has become an important objective for the park management. Similar problems have been reported in other winter tourism destinations worldwide (Sterl et al., 2006; Freuler and Hunziker, 2007; Braunisch et al., 2011; Rupf et al., 2011; Coppes and Braunisch, 2013; Arlettaz et al., 2015).

21.2.3 User conflicts

High concentrations of tourism at specific destinations can cause conflicts among visitors – especially, when recreation activities on offer and visitor expectations differ. There are many examples showing conflicting visitor expectations in winter tourism worldwide (Olson et al., 2017; Pröbstl-Haider and Lampl, 2017). Also in the Tatra Mountains user conflicts exist, however they are not sufficiently investigated. One potential source of conflict might be overcrowding in popular TNP destinations (e.g. Morskie Oko, Kasprowy Wierch and the Kościeliska Valley). Additional problematic cases arise with the spatial co-existence of multiple activity types. Several designated trails may be used by diverse user groups such as hikers, ski tourers and tourists travelling by horse sledge. Groomed ski pistes are being used by some ski tourers while ascending. Different speeds of movement and user expectations may contribute to the dissatisfaction of some visitors and may also pose a safety issue. Figure 21.3 illustrates the movement directions of ski tourers in the surroundings of the Kasprowy Wierch Ski Resort. Map B (see Fig. 21.3) exposes opposing movement directions of visitors within the border of the groomed ski piste, which may be a cause of user conflicts. This issue should be carefully investigated in the future, as the number of ski tourers is growing and Kuźnice is the most popular starting point of winter outdoor activities in the TNP.

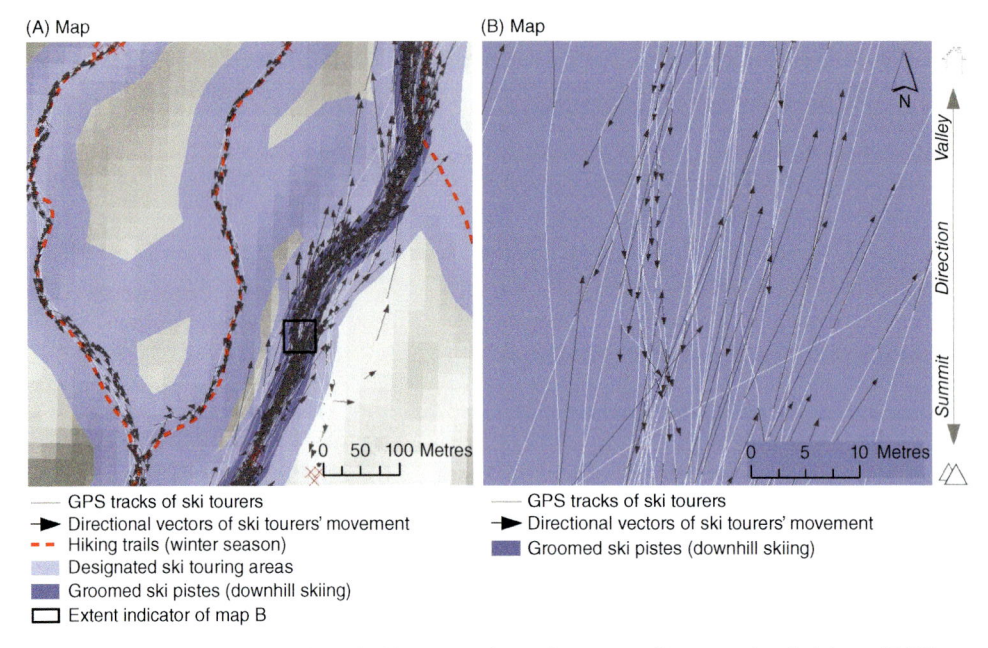

Fig. 21.3. Movement direction of ski tourers, based on a smaller sample of visitors (GPS tracks collected on 16 March 2013). (A) Selected extent of Kuźnice–Kasprowy Wierch region showing ski touring ascents along hiking trails and most of the descents on the groomed downhill ski pistes. (B) Opposing movement directions as potential user conflict on the groomed ski pistes. (Reprinted from Bielański *et al.*, (2018) Application of GPS tracking for monitoring spatially unconstrained outdoor recreational activities in protected areas – a case study of ski touring in the Tatra National Park, Poland. *Applied Geography* 96, 51–65, with permission from Elsevier.)

21.2.4 Risk and safety

Risk and safety management is one of the major issues in mountain outdoor recreation management (Stethem *et al.*, 2003; Höller, 2017; Pfeifer *et al.*, 2018). Polish law designates that the director of the national park is the body responsible for implementing safety rules and regulations within the park (Sejm of the Republic of Poland, 2004). Thence, according to the TNP regulations, visitors take responsibility for their own actions and need to assess the conditions and are culpable for their decisions. Moreover, 15% of the yearly TNP income from ticket sales is redirected to subsidize the Tatra Mountain Rescue Service (Tatrzańskie Ochotnicze Pogotowie Ratunkowe (TOPR). TOPR is responsible for preparing and announcing daily avalanche reports. (TOPR, 2018a). Moreover, TOPR's duties include mountain rescue within the TNP, including the ski resort Kasprowy Wierch. In 2017 there were 848 tourists rescued in the Tatra National Park, which accounts for 0.02% of the annual visitor load. Among rescued visitors there were 749 hikers, 60 downhill skiers, 6 snowboarders, 3 freeriders, 29 ski tourers, 30 climbers and 2 cavers. In 2017 TOPR reported 14 fatal accidents (2%), 36% serious injuries and 63% light injuries among visitor rescues. In 2017 there were 5 accidents caused by an avalanche, which affected 3 hikers, 1 ski tourer and 1 climber; there were no fatal avalanche accidents (TOPR, 2018b, 2018c).

One of the important aims of the TNP management is raising the awareness and safety of visitors concerning risks and safety issues related to winter outdoor activities. Therefore, since 2011 the TNP has organized the information campaign 'Avalanche ABC'. At the weekends TNP visitors can participate in avalanche safety training (free of charge) and also use avalanche safety equipment at the Kalatówki Mountain Hotel, located near Kuźnice. Additionally, there are regular demonstrations of an avalanche airbag system, thematic lectures and meetings. In the winter season 2016/17 more than 400 tourists participated in training offered within the programme. Moreover, the TNP offered educational trips to students of local schools (24 guided trips in the winter season 2016/17). The initiative was also active on social media and the internet, promoting the programme and avalanche safety quizzes, where eight winners took part in an extensive avalanche safety training (Lawinowe ABC, 2017). The information campaign included the distribution of paper flyers with basic avalanche safety information. Moreover, at major trailheads of the TNP (Kuźnice, Hala Gąsienicowa, Palenica Białczańska, Huciska) avalanche transceiver 'checkpoints' have been installed, in order to test the functionality of visitors' own devices.

To increase the safety of winter visitors the avalanche warning signs are placed along the trails where the trail enters a higher avalanche risk zone (e.g. couloir crossings, or at entry points to steeper terrain). Furthermore, avalanche risk information and the current warning level is displayed at each entry point and at the mountain huts.

Interestingly, participation in commercial trainings related to winter tourism and avalanche safety (offered by TOPR, the Polish Mountaineering Association, mountain guides, etc.) has significantly increased in recent years and currently reaches about 1000 participants per year.

As the Tatra Mountains are the only alpine area in Poland, the general public's awareness of mountain risks is rather low. Therefore, further, continuous information campaigns highlighting mountain risks and promoting responsible behaviour in winter conditions are necessary to raise awareness among TNP visitors.

21.2.5 Cooperation for nature conservation

Protected areas try to fulfil the challenging mission of protecting nature and at the same time getting societal support for their actions (Dudley, 2013). Sometimes nature protection objectives and measures do not go along with the expectations of local inhabitants, interest groups or visitors to sites of exceptional natural value (Eagles *et al.*, 2002). The TNP is facing a similar problem trying to balance the needs of people and site capacities. One of the major challenges of the national park is a lack of a significant formal buffer zone, allowing local land owners and municipality intensive urban or tourist infrastructure development along most of the border to the protected area. This creates a certain tension and conflicts of interest. Recently, also larger ideas, potentially having a severe impact on nature, were discussed. The Polish Olympic Committee posed the idea of holding the 2022 Winter Olympics in Kraków, with the majority of sport facilities located in the Tatras and its surroundings. In 2014 the inhabitants of Kraków voted to withdraw the bid in a binding referendum. However, similar initiatives of local and/or national authorities appear regularly and pose serious threats for nature conservation.

Over many years the TNP has run numerous educational and PR campaigns promoting the idea and necessity of nature protection among local inhabitants (mostly school children) and tourists. However, the attitudes towards nature protection vary quite a lot between people. A recent study on travel motives of tourists in the most popular TNP winter destination – Kasprowy Wierch – showed large heterogeneity in motives for visiting (Hibner and Taczanowska, 2016). Cluster analysis conducted among the ski slope users has shown that more than half of the respondents were more sport- or fun-oriented than nature-oriented. Furthermore, a large percentage of visitors expressed their negative opinions on the functioning of the ski resort. Most of them related to the lack of artificial snow or the limited number of ski pistes in the TNP. It is worth educating these segments of skiers in terms of nature-friendly behaviour and explaining the necessity of the introduced limitations. About one-third of ski slope users (28%) belong to the nature-oriented segment. This group of visitors appreciated contact with nature and mountain scenery and was reluctant to see new ski infrastructure in the TNP (Hibner and Taczanowska, 2016).

There is a need for further studies concerning environmental awareness and the actual behaviour of all visitor groups, local inhabitants and key stakeholders. Especially desirable would be the application of participatory methods allowing direct contact with interest groups and other stakeholders.

21.3 Conclusions and Outlook

Winter season in the Tatra National Park, despite smaller visitor numbers due to a more heterogeneous visitor profile, poses many management challenges. Recreational systems that have been developed over decades since the 19th century need to be confronted with the current needs and expectations of visitors and the objectives of nature protection. The TNP has developed the systematic monitoring of visitor entries; however, in order to have a full picture of use within the protected area and social characteristics of visitors, additional regular studies are desirable. Especially, interdisciplinary approaches to recreation ecology linking founded ecological methods with social science approaches could be beneficial for protected area management. There is additionally a need to extend knowledge on inhabitants' and tourists' environmental awareness, awareness of mountain risks and knowledge of safety rules in winter mountainous environments. Regular information campaigns, cooperation with various user groups such as representatives of new activity trends while co-designing the TNP regulations are best-practice examples of protected area management. Current development trends need to be carefully observed in order to support proactive decision making to maintain the unique natural value of the highest part of the Carpathian Mountains.

References

Arlettaz, R., Nusslé, S., Baltic, M., Vogel, P., Palme, R. *et al.* (2015) Disturbance of wildlife by outdoor winter recreation: allostatic stress response and altered activity-energy budgets. *Ecological Applications: A Publication of the Ecological Society of America* 25(5), 1197–1212.

Arnberger, A., Haider, W. and Brandenburg, C. (2005) Evaluating visitor-monitoring techniques: a comparison of counting and video observation data. *Environmental Management* 36(2), 317–327.

Bielański, M. (2013) Skitouring in Tatra National Park and its environmental impacts. PhD Thesis, University School of Physical Education, Kraków, Poland.

Bielański, M., Taczanowska, K., Muhar, A., Adamski, P., González, L.-M. *et al.* (2018). Application of GPS tracking for monitoring spatially unconstrained outdoor recreational activities in protected areas – a case study of ski touring in the Tatra National Park, Poland. *Applied Geography* 96, 51–65. DOI:10.1016/j.apgeog.2018.05.008

Braunisch, V., Patthey, P. and Arlettaz, R. (2011) Spatially explicit modeling of conflict zones between wildlife and snow sports: prioritizing areas for winter refuges. *Ecological Applications* 21(3), 955–967. DOI:10.1890/09-2167.1

Cessford, G. and Muhar, A. (2003) Monitoring options for visitor numbers in national parks and natural areas. *Journal for Nature Conservation* 11(4), 240–250. DOI:10.1078/1617-1381-00055

Coppes, J. and Braunisch, V. (2013) Managing visitors in nature areas: where do they leave the trails? A spatial model. *Wildlife Biology* 19(1), 1–11. DOI:10.2981/12-054

Czochański, J. (2002) Ruch turystyczny w Tatrzańskim Parku Narodowym. In: Partyka, J. (ed.) *Użytkowanie turystyczne parków narodowych*. Ojców, Poland, pp. 385–403.

Czochański, J. and Szydarowski, W. (2000) Diagnoza stanu i zróżnicowanie przestrzenno-czasowe użytkowania szlaków turystycznych w TPN. In: Borowiak, D. and Czochański, J. (eds) *Z badań geograficznych w Tatrach Polskich*. Wyd. UG, Gdańsk, Poland, pp. 207–228.

Dudley, N. (2013) *Guidelines for Applying Protected Area Management Categories* (IUCN). IUCN, Gland, Switzerland. Available at: https://www.iucn.org/sites/dev/files/import/downloads/iucn_assignment_1.pdf (accessed 30 January 2019).

Eagles, P.F.J., McCool, S.F. and Haynes, C.D. (2002) *Sustainable Tourism in Protected Areas: Guidelines for Planning and Management*. IUCN, Gland, Switzerland.

Freuler, B. and Hunziker, M. (2007) Recreation activities in protected areas: bridging the gap between the attitudes and behaviour of snowshoe walkers. *Forest Snow and Landscape Research* 81(1–2), 191–206.

Geist, V. (1978) Behavior. In: Schmidt, J.L. and Gilbert, D.L. (eds) *Big Game of North America: Ecology and Management*. Stackpole Books, Harrisburg, Pennsylvania, pp. 283–296.

Hibner, J. and Taczanowska, K. (2016) Segmentation of alpine downhill skiers and snowboarders in mountain protected areas based on motivation factors: a comparison between two skiing areas: Kasprowy Wierch area (TPN, Poland) and Skalnaté Pleso area (TANAP, Slovakia). In: Vasiljevic, D. (ed.) *MMV 8 Abstract Book*. Faculty of Sciences, Department of Geography, Tourism and Hotel Management, Novi Sad, Serbia, pp. 366–368.

Höller, P. (2017) Avalanche accidents and fatalities in Austria since 1946/47 with special regard to tourist avalanches in the period 1981/82 to 2015/16. *Cold Regions Science and Technology* 144, 89–95. DOI:10.1016/j.coldregions.2017.06.006

Jodłowski, M. (2015) Nowa koncepcja zarządzania ruchem wspinaczkowym w Tatrzańskim Parku Narodowym jako sposób ograniczenia wpływu taternictwa na środowisko. In: *Przyroda Tatrzańskiego Parku Narodowego a Człowiek. Tom III Człowiek i środowisko*. Wydawnictwa Tatrzańskiego Parku Narodowego, Zakopane, Poland, pp. 63–72.

Lawinowe ABC (2017) *Lawinowe ABC (Avalanche ABC)*. Available at: www.lawinoweabc.pl (accessed 30 January 2019).

Manning, R.E. and Anderson, L.E. (eds) (2012) *Managing Outdoor Recreation: Case Studies in the National Parks*. CAB International, Wallingford, UK. DOI:10.1079/9781845939311.0000

Miller, S.G., Knight, R.L. and Miller, C.K. (2001) Wildlife Responses to Pedestrians and Dogs. *Wildlife Society Bulletin (1973-2006)* 29(1), 124–132.

Newsome, D., Moore, S.A. and Dowling, R.K. (2012) *Natural Area Tourism: Ecology, Impacts and Management*. Channel View Publications, Clevedon, UK.

Olson, L.E., Squires, J.R., Roberts, E.K., Miller, A.D., Ivan, J.S. *et al.* (2017) Modeling large-scale winter recreation terrain selection with implications for recreation management and wildlife. *Applied Geography* 86, 66–91. DOI:10.1016/j.apgeog.2017.06.023

Paryski, W.H. and Paryska, Z. (1995) *Wielka Encyklopedia Tatrzańska*. Wydawnictwo Górskie, Poronin, Poland.

Pfeifer, C., Höller, P. and Zeileis, A. (2018) Spatial and temporal analysis of fatal off-piste and backcountry avalanche accidents in Austria with a comparison of results in Switzerland, France, Italy and the US. *Natural Hazards and Earth System Sciences* 18(2), 571–582. DOI:10.5194/nhess-18-571-2018

Pröbstl-Haider, U. and Lampl, R. (2017) From conflict to co-creation: ski-touring on groomed slopes in Austria. In: Correia, A., Kozak, M., Gnoth, J. and Fyall, A. (eds) *Co-Creation and Well-Being in Tourism*. Springer, Cham, Switzerland, pp. 69–82. DOI:10.1007/978-3-319-44108-5_6

Richins, H. and Hull, J. (eds) (2016) *Mountain Tourism: Experiences, Communities, Environments and Sustainable Futures*. CAB International, Wallingford, UK.

Rupf, R., Wyttenbach, M., Köchli, D., Hediger, M., Lauber, S. *et al.* (2011) Assessing the spatio-temporal pattern of winter sports activities to minimize disturbance in capercaillie habitats. *eco.mont* 3(2), 23–32. DOI:10.1553/eco.mont-3-2s23

Sejm of the Republic of Poland (2004) Nature Conservation Act [Ustawa z dnia 16 kwietnia 2004 r. o ochronie przyrody], Pub. L. No. Dz.U. 2004 nr 92 poz. 880. Available at: http://prawo.sejm.gov.pl/isap.nsf/DocDetails.xsp?id=WDU20040920880 (accessed 30 January 2019).

Sterl, P., Eder, R. and Arnberger, A. (2006) Exploring factors in influencing the attitude of on-site ski mountaineers towards the ski touring management measures of the Gesäuse National Park. *eco.mont* 2(1), 31–38. DOI:10.1553/eco.mont-2-1s31

Stethem, C., Jamieson, B., Schaerer, P., Liverman, D., Germain, D. *et al.* (2003) Snow avalanche hazard in Canada – a review. *Natural Hazards* 28(2–3), 487–515. DOI:10.1023/A:1022998512227

Taczanowska, K., Zięba, A., Brandenburg, C., Muhar, A., Preisel, H. *et al.* (2016) *Visitor Monitoring in the Tatra National Park – a Pilot Study – Kasprowy Wierch [Monitorig ruchu turystycznego w Tatrzańskim Parku Narodowym – Studium pilotażowe – Kasprowy Wierch 2014]*. Research Report. Institute of Landscape Development, Recreation and Conservation Planning, University of Natural Resources and Life Sciences, Vienna, Austria.

Tatra National Park (TNP) (2017) Decree Nr 3/2017 of the Tatra National Park Director from 23.02.2017 on hiking, bicycling and skiing in the area of the Tatra National Park [Zarządzenie nr 3/2017 Dyrektora Tatrzańskiego Parku Narodowego z dnia 23 lutego 2017 roku w sprawie ruchu pieszego, rowerowego oraz uprawiania narciarstwa na terenie Tatrzańskiego Parku Narodowego]. Available at: http://tpn.pl/upload/filemanager/Danka/Zarzadzenie_3_2017_w_spr_ruchu_pieszego_rowerowego_itp.pdf (accessed 30 January 2019).

Tatra National Park (TNP) (2018) Tatra National Park. Available at: http://tpn.pl/poznaj (accessed 30 January 2019).

TOPR (2018a) *Komunikat Lawinowy – Tatry Polskie*. Available at: http://lawiny.topr.pl (accessed 30 January 2019).

TOPR (2018b) *Sprawozdanie z działalności ratowniczej TOPR w Zorganizowanych Terenach Narciarskich*. Unpublished report. Zakopane, Poland.

TOPR (2018c) *Zestawienie statystyczne działań TOPR w ramach Ratownictwa Górskiego*. Unpublished report. Zakopane, Poland.

Yarmoloy, C., Bayer, M. and Geist, V. (1988) Behavior responses and reproduction of mule deer (*Odocoileus hemionus*), does following experimental harassment with an all-terrain vehicle. *Canadian Field Naturalist* 102(3), 425–429.

Ziemilski, A. and Marchlewski, A. (1964) Zwiad socjologiczny w Tatrach. Badania nad ruchem turystycznym w rejonie Hali Gąsienicowej. *Wierchy* 33, 51–76.

Zwijacz-Kozica, T. (2007) Tokowiska cietrzewi w centralnej części Tatrzańskiego Parku Narodowego i ich potencjalne zagrożenie ze strony narciarstwa. Presented at the I Międzynarodowa Konferencja Ochrona Kuraków Leśnych, Janow Lubelski, Poland, pp. 145–152.

22 Chinese Guests in Alpine Destinations – What Are They Looking for? A Case Study from Switzerland Regarding Product Preferences and Landscape Perception

Barbara Haller Rupf[1,2]*, Katrin Schillo[3], Wolfgang G. Arlt[4] and Reto Rupf[5]

[1]Tourism Academy, College of Higher Education Lucerne, Lucerne, Switzerland; [2]Tourism consulting company haller-tournet, Felsberg, Switzerland; [3]Swiss Institute for Entrepreneurship (SIFE), University of Applied Sciences HTW, Chur, Switzerland; [4]COTRI China Outbound Tourism Research Institute, Hamburg, Germany and Beijing, China; [5]Institute of Natural Resource Science, Zurich University of Applied Sciences, Wädenswil, Switzerland

22.1 Introduction

Tourism is a globally fast-growing industry and in particular new guests from Asia boost the annual growth rates up to 6% (UNWTO, 2018). This growth is being pushed by the Chinese market, the largest international outgoing market in terms of frequencies and expenses (WTO, 2017). Some questions arise in this context: Who benefits from this growth? How can destinations and service providers realize added value from these new guests? How do Chinese guests perceive landscapes? Are they interested in winter experiences?

The average increase of Chinese guests to Switzerland from 2005 to 2016 was 17% annually (Bundesamt für Statistik, 2016). Arlt (2017) predicts a future annual growth rate of Chinese guests to Europe of 6–8%. Switzerland is considered to be a dream destination for the Chinese (Hu *et al.*, 2014), known as a safe country in the middle of Europe, home to snowy mountains and photogenic landscapes and towns, expensive and ideally suited to shopping for luxury items such as watches.

With only 2% market share, the tourist destinations of Grisons, a mountainous province in the east of Switzerland, whose regional economy is overall based 30% on tourism and whose valleys are reliant on tourism for up to 70% of the economy

---

* E-mail: barbara.haller@haller-tournet.ch

(Bühler and Minsch, 2004), hardly participates in the Chinese tourism market (Plaz and Bösch, 2015). However, in the past few years Chinese guests' overnight stays have been rising steadily, in 2016 by 28%.

Grisons' small market share is, among other reasons, a consequence of Chinese trip planning as large groups bypass the region normally. Therefore, the destination's focus on small groups and individual travellers could be a good strategy with future potential bearing in mind the current discussion about over-tourism in some destinations. Furthermore, 'insight travelling', visiting one or two countries in 10 days and not up to four countries in 5–7 days, is considered as the most important tourist trend in China (Arlt, 2018).

However, the market is only interesting if it brings not just increased numbers, but also income and added value to the regional economy. In many places Chinese first-time travellers are considered less lucrative due to their low spending on tourism services (Keating and Kriz, 2008).

This article presents two studies: 'China Inbound Service' a project to investigate the needs in alpine destinations to host Chinese guests and a pilot study regarding nature perception of tourism students in Shanghai.

22.2 'China Inbound Service' (Case Study)

In order to achieve the goal of adding value, it is crucial to develop local competencies regarding the Chinese market. In particular, knowledge of the customers' expectations and motives (Laesser *et al.*, 2013), the ability to develop and adapt new and existing tourism products (Keating and Kriz, 2008), and the sensitization and training of the service providers and their employees focusing on the new customer group.

22.2.1 Project objectives

Due to these requirements, the project 'China Inbound Service' focuses on the following objectives:

1. Analysis of current and potential customers, especially their expectations and behaviour.
2. Organizational development in the destinations and in market cultivation.
3. Development of customized products and services for Chinese guests in alpine destinations.
4. Awareness raising and education of the service providers and their employees to the new customer group.
5. Transfer of the project's results to other long-distance markets, such as India or the Gulf States. Furthermore, to distribute them to other destinations in Grisons.

22.2.2 Theoretical background – the touristic value chain

Bieger and Beritelli (2013) adapted the idea of Porter's value chain for the specific situation of touristic destinations and created their 'touristic value chain'. Porter introduced the value chain concept back in 1985 (Porter, 1985). This describes the necessary activities for the production of goods and services within a manufacturing enterprise as a sequence of processes, starting from the primary material and ending with the finished product. As the processes occur, value is created while resources are consumed (Porter, 1985). In later years, this concept was also adapted by him and other authors to the creation of services (e.g. Benkenstein *et al.*, 2007). In the planning of tourism offerings of a region/destination, such a value chain can be used as a tool to ensure the compatibility of individual travel modules and to mediate between the service providers (hotels, transport companies, etc.) and other participating organizations (Koch, 2006).

Figure 22.1 shows the service chain of a destination in alpine tourism and is adapted from Bieger and Beritelli (2013). The upper part depicts the supporting processes with personnel, management, control and marketing functions. The lower part illustrates the processes of the customer experience cycle, from information and booking to the actual journey and the after-sales services.

22.2.3 Methodology

In order to gain specific insights into the Chinese guests as well as product and destination development, three different investigations were carried out; one expert, guest and focus group survey each. Initially, ten expert interviews were conducted with European and Chinese experts from national marketing, tour operating, customer perspective, science, etc. On the one hand, these discussions served as a basis for the guest survey, on the other hand, a first glimpse into the travel motivation of the largely unknown group of FIT (foreign independent tourist) travellers from China was offered. In the winter season 2015/16, Chinese-speaking guests from the People's Republic of China, Hong Kong and Taiwan were questioned in the participating destinations by survey. At the same time, research partners from China interviewed the focus group of potential guests in Beijing. The focus of the 'on-site interviews' was on the effective behaviour of the guests. In Beijing, the expectations of potential customers were in the foreground. The tourism monitor Switzerland 2013 TMS (Schweiz Tourismus, 2012) as well as a Scandinavian survey of Chinese guests (Wonderful Copenhagen, 2013) form the basis for the visitor survey in the alpine destinations.

In order to reach only Chinese overnight guests, the questionnaires in Chinese and English were laid out in the hotels of the destinations and the guests were made aware

Fig. 22.1. Value chain in alpine tourism. (Own figure based on Bieger and Beritelli, 2013.)

of them. With 106 useable questionnaires, the return was satisfactory. Although about one-third of respondents said they had good English skills, almost all questionnaires were completed in Chinese and then translated into English. The focus group survey was conducted by Chinese research colleagues in Beijing with eight people, four men and four women, aged between 26 and 64 years. The participants were recruited via Weibo and WeChat. Requirements for participation were an elevated economic background and travel experience in Europe (six of the respondents had already been to Switzerland). The first part of the focus group survey addressed the expectations of potential guests. In the second part of the interview, the focus group commented on summer and winter activities in the Alps and assessed a concrete multi-day offer. The entire survey was recorded and transcribed and finally translated into English for further analysis.

The results from the above three surveys are summarized below. The results of the customer survey show the status quo in retrospect; from expert and focus group surveys, future-oriented findings are then derived.

Limitations

The return rate of the surveys was dominated by two hotels, one from each destination. Due to this dominance, the sample cannot be considered generally representative of FIT guests in alpine destinations.

22.2.4 Results 'China Inbound Services'

The typical questioned Chinese guest

The results of our survey give a good insight into the needs and behaviour of Chinese guests in alpine destinations in Switzerland, which are focused on one matter, e.g. skiing. Our typical questioned Chinese guest is well educated (80% hold a university degree), belongs to the financial upper class and comes from Beijing, Shanghai, the coastal areas or lives as an expatriate in Europe. The English language skills of most of the guests surveyed (besides those from Hong Kong) are rated as relatively low. Most of the guests travelled on individual travel plans (FIT travellers) with family and/or friends. Online information was obtained mainly through TripAdvisor, WeChat, Weibo and Baidu, and to some extent Google. Forty per cent of the bookings of (partial) offers were made online.

Only one-third of the guests were visiting Europe for the first time, nearly 50% were visiting Europe for the second to fifth time and almost 20% had already visited the continent more than five times. For two-thirds of the guests it was the first trip to Switzerland, the specific destination was unknown to almost all respondents.

Importance and satisfaction

In order to gain better insights into the needs and behaviour of Chinese guests, we asked for their perceived importance of and satisfaction levels with various criteria (see Fig. 22.2), on a Likert scale of 1–5 (1 = not important/not satisfied, 5 = very important/very satisfied), analogous to the TMS 2013.

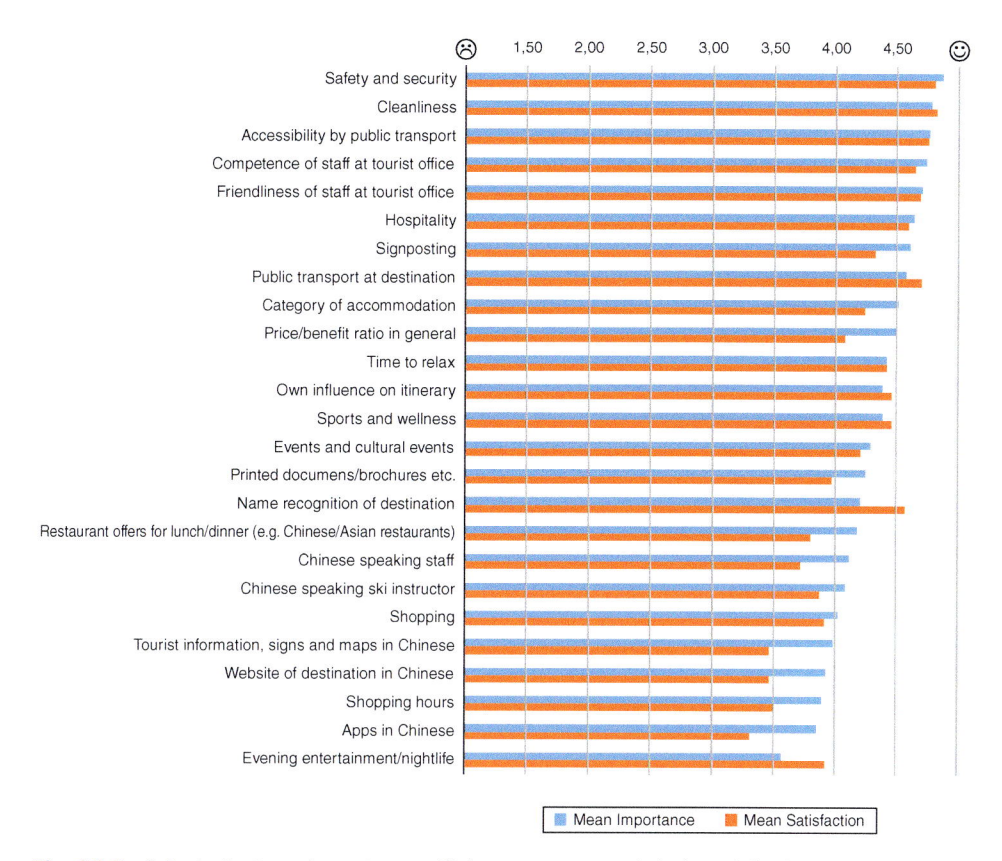

Fig. 22.2. Criteria that are important to Chinese guests and their satisfaction levels.

According to the assessed importance attributed by the Chinese guests, safety and cleanliness are paramount, followed by accessibility by public transport as well as the competence and friendliness of the employees in the destinations. Importance and satisfaction correspond for most of the criteria. Sometimes, satisfaction is even higher rated than importance. Only for 'signposting', is importance much higher rated than satisfaction. In general, it can be stated that the criteria that were important to the Chinese guests also had the highest satisfaction levels. The highest rating of 'safety and security' applies to physical security, security in activities, e.g. skiing, as well as to reliability in offers and prices. According to the customer survey, guests were the least satisfied with shop opening hours, food offerings and the provision of information in Chinese – specifically, apps, tourism information, signs and maps, the destination website and Chinese-speaking staff. In all these cases, the importance was rated much higher, in some cases the corresponding mean value is >0.5 points above the satisfaction value.

Positive and negative customer experiences

The results above are reflected in the open questions about best (positive, see Fig. 22.3) and worst (negative, see Fig. 22.4) experiences during the stay: the best responses were

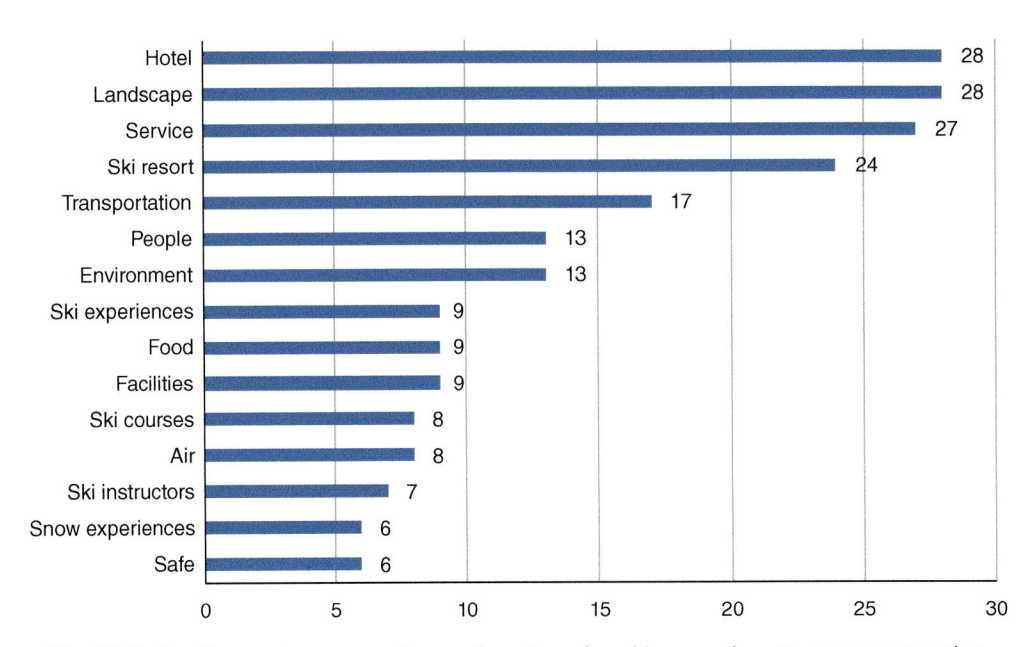

Fig. 22.3. Positive customer experiences (number of positive mentions to an open question, max. three answers possible, *n* = 94).

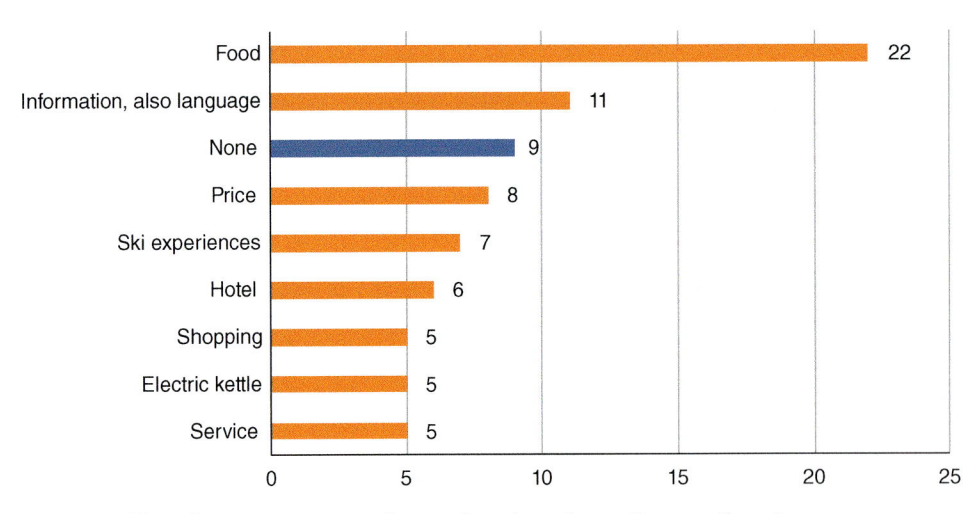

Hotel	28
Landscape	28
Service	27
Ski resort	24
Transportation	17
People	13
Environment	13
Ski experiences	9
Food	9
Facilities	9
Ski courses	8
Air	8
Ski instructors	7
Snow experiences	6
Safe	6

Fig. 22.4. Negative customer experiences (number of negative mentions to an open question, max. three answers possible, *n* = 71).

Food	22
Information, also language	11
None	9
Price	8
Ski experiences	7
Hotel	6
Shopping	5
Electric kettle	5
Service	5

for hotel, landscape, service in general and the ski resort (28 to 24 times), followed by transportation (17), people and environment (both 13). Food was negatively mentioned (22 times), from the relatively low variability, the unfamiliar taste, the lack of Asian food, to the lack of information about the food. The second major criticism was lack of information in Chinese or at least in English (about food, accommodation, excursions, etc.).

The pure and clean appearance of the landscape in Switzerland was mentioned as very different from Chinese cities, as it is 'natural' and little influenced by humankind (see also Section 22.3 in this chapter).

To overcome the criticism in the areas of 'food' and 'information', simple adaptations could be made. For instance, the possibility of sharing food or taking souvenirs could be actively supported by the hosts, and hence the recommendations could be increased. By offering the information materials in Chinese, the destinations could express special respect for the guests from this market. For smaller service providers, the offer of English information (e.g. menus) would be an aid. These findings are largely consistent with the studies of Li *et al.* (2011), ETC and WTO (2012) or McKinsey & Company (2016). Li regards the food and service quality as well as an understanding of Chinese culture as the basis for good tourism services. In the ETC and WTO (2012) study, high prices, lack of Chinese information and food receive the worst ratings.

Activities

According to the survey, the activities most frequently mentioned by the Chinese winter guests were trips on mountain railways (84%), the enjoyment of local food (46%) as well visits to natural attractions and nature parks (41%).

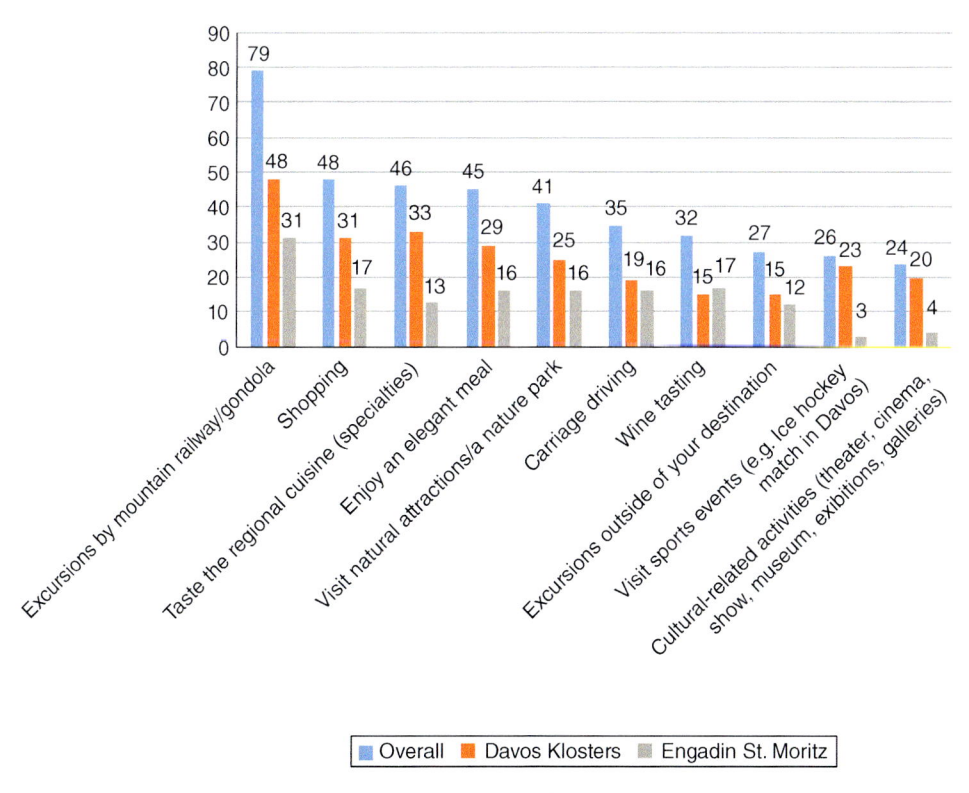

Fig. 22.5. Top ten non-sporting activities (number of mentions, multiple answers possible, *n* = 101).

Owing to the special ski offers from the hotels, from a sporting point of view, skiing (86%), short winter hikes (57%) and other winter activities (33%) such as snowshoeing or sledging were very popular. Snow sports lessons were popular in the destination with a Chinese-speaking ski instructor at 27%, versus 3% without a corresponding offer. Similarly, swimming was mentioned by 55% due to the indoor pool at the hotel.

As expected, shopping was important: interestingly, shopping activities in alpine destinations focused on chocolate (72%), ski and winter sports equipment (68%), souvenirs (62%) and local design (57%). Watches (34%) and luxury items (25%) were not much in demand.

The expert and focus group survey on product and organizational development brought interesting results: in order to meet the need for security and lack of time, modular packages should be available. For guests from China, travelling always includes a 'learning component' – explanations of landscapes, customs and food are therefore asked for in the offers and 'study visits' would also be an attractive offer for FIT guests. Winter sports are experiencing a major boom, especially because of the 2022 Winter Olympics in (North) China.

22.2.5 Management consequences

Generally, it can be stated that while there are numerous studies looking at Chinese outbound tourism and consumer behaviour (Tsang and Hsu, 2011), theory-based implementation concepts in the alpine region are almost completely lacking in product development and service adaptation (Andreu *et al.*, 2013). In order to fill this gap, the participating destinations were given a concept to coordinate their engagement in the Chinese market. The value chain in Fig. 22.6 illustrates the interaction and responsibilities of all parties involved, thus simplifying the coordination and increasing the clarity of activities.

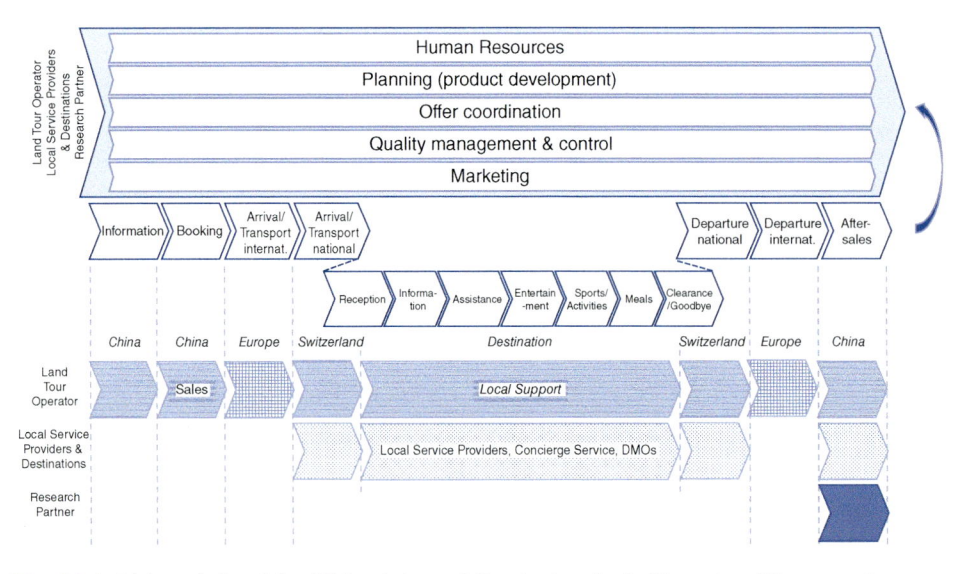

Fig. 22.6. Value chain of the 'China Inbound Service' project. (Based on Bieger and Beritelli, 2013.)

To meet the needs of the new group of guests and the needs of the destinations, a land tour operator (LTO) was established. Based in Switzerland, the LTO has sales offices in China and there takes the role of a Chinese tour operator by offering tailor-made products. Due to the local knowledge and the direct contact with the Swiss service providers and destinations, the guests' needs can be served optimally. Additionally, there is a Chinese-speaking concierge (guest relations manager) in the destinations to support the service providers, the LTO as well as the Chinese guests.

In the upper part of the value chain, the so-called support processes, there is close cooperation between all participants: the LTO, the service providers and destinations as well as the research partners. Important activities include, for example, offer development, planning and bundling as well as employee training.

In addition to the organizational changes, the project results were used to launch further measures with regard to the Chinese market:

- A cross-destination database that lists services and tourism products adapted to the needs and expectations of Chinese FIT guests. The aim of this database is to facilitate the cross-destination collaboration.
- A criteria catalogue for service providers to review the suitability of their products for the Chinese market. This catalogue is based on studies such as Li *et al.* (2011), as well as on various 'tool kits' for service providers to serve Chinese guests (Tourism New Zealand, 2013; Tourism and Events Queensland, 2013; Edinburgh Tourism AG, 2016).
- Furthermore, workshops and individual counselling sessions were offered to the service providers to support them in product development.

It is planned to bundle the offers and products that are adapted to the Chinese market to use them for a common market presence. Therefore, based on the criteria catalogue, the requirements for the service providers who are interested in the collective sales activities as well as the destination organization will be defined. Due to the size and diversity of the Chinese outbound tourism market it is hardly possible for individual service providers and even destinations to develop the necessary market knowledge and an active sales network on their own. Finally, with the power of the common market cash outflow should be avoided.

It is widely known and also recognized in the project 'China Inbound Service', that Chinese guests expect partly different products and services to guests from Europe or North America. From the criticism of the guests regarding food, information and lack of understanding of their culture, the destinations took first initiatives. The Asian eating habits could be catered for in hotel kitchens, restaurants or by third-party providers (catering) at low cost and with little extra effort. In addition, design and translation services were provided on-site and online to meet the need for information, be it for menus or offer descriptions. Due to Switzerland's restrictive immigration policy towards third countries, a higher hurdle is the requirement for Chinese-speaking employees at the destinations. A first step is a Chinese-speaking 'guest relations manager' (concierge) at the destinations. It can be assumed with an increasing number of Chinese guests, there will be a demand for Chinese-speaking employees from the service providers themselves.

Adapting tourism services to guest expectations is crucial (Chang *et al.*, 2010; Andreu *et al.*, 2013; Laesser *et al.*, 2013), as linguistic barriers in particular could discourage potential FIT guests from travelling to alpine destinations. Despite the above criticism, Fig. 22.2 shows that the criteria of safety, cleanliness, accessibility, etc., which are considered very important, meet the expectations of the guests. The existing general and tourist infrastructure of Switzerland forms a promising basis for the development of incoming tourism from China. Investing in the Chinese market could become lucrative for alpine regions: in addition to the large potential due to the market volume, Chinese guests also travel anti-cyclically to the existing travel times. This could help to reduce the negative effects of seasonality in alpine tourism.

22.3 Nature and Landscape Perception of Chinese Students as a Basis for Tourism Product Development in the Alps

22.3.1 The Chinese and nature

Nowadays a stay in the Alps is usually associated with nature experiences. Therefore, the interest of Chinese guests in winter holidays in the Alps depends, among other factors, on their perception of nature.

First, it should be stated that Chinese guests differ a lot in the way they travel, their travel expectations and motivation as well as in their perception of nature. When it comes to Chinese ethical positions in relation to nature, ancient traditions, cultural values, religious and philosophical beliefs – Taoism, Buddhism and Confucianism – each have profoundly impacted the way Chinese people view nature (Gao *et al.*, 2018).

Within these philosophical beliefs, there is often not a unity regarding nature perception. On the one hand, there is the 'Tian ren he yi' [oneness of nature with humans or unity of humans and heaven] thinking; on the other, pragmatic utilitarianism appears to be of more relevance and importance to Chinese people in everyday life (Gao *et al.*, 2018). Many scholars label the Chinese view as anthropocentrism (Bruun, 1995).

As the culture in mainland China is widely based on Confucian values, there are good reasons for investigating fengshui as a key element in the Chinese approach to nature (Bruun, 1995). From a European perspective it is important to understand that among Confucian values nature by itself is not perfect, but can be changed and harmonized by humans and their culture to improve fortunes (Han, 2006). Whereas in the West, nature is able to exist without human beings, in China they are considered to be as a never beginning or ending part of nature (Bruun, 1995). Traditionally in China there exist great concerns for nature, and how to bring it to bear positively on human fortune, whereas the distant, the unimportant, the invisible or even other people's nature are not included in fengshui concerns. Chinese culture optimizes the use of natural powers, even to a degree where the 'Qi' – universal energy – is regarded as a limited resource subject to human competition (Bruun, 1995).

Feng Han (2006, p. 231) in his thesis 'The Chinese view of nature: tourism in China's scenic and historic interest areas' supports the above-mentioned statements with propositions such as 'nature is shaped by high culture' or 'nature is a place of cultivation'. At the same time, nature is seen as an 'ideal place' and a retreat, expressed by 'nature is a symbol of great beauty and morals', 'nature is embedded with the meaning of ideal life' or 'nature is a place for retreat from worldly society'. However, statements such as 'artistic re-built nature is more beautiful than original nature' and 'the eternal value of nature is for a harmonious and artistic human life' show the different views of nature in China compared with the West in an exemplary way.

After the industrialization period, in Europe in the early 20th century and in the US in the 1970s, the protection of nature and cultural landscape gained in importance based on an alienation from nature in daily life (Bätzing, 2015). Forster and Rupf (2007) see the 'longing for compensation of nature experiences' as the starting point on the one hand, for nature conservation and the establishment of protected areas, and, on the other hand, for the demand for tourism and leisure activities in nature or in the wild. In Europe and America this consumer demand was the basis for the development of the outdoor industry with tourist offers including guiding, infrastructure and equipment.

Similarly in China, with the increase in population and urbanization since 1990, natural, historical and cultural landscapes and wilderness increased in acceptance and attractiveness and became a symbol of wealth and power for the privileged new elite urban class. Since the urbanization rate in mainland China rose from 28% in 1993 to 56% in 2017 (Hsu, 2016), the attractiveness of 'Scenic and historic interest areas' has increased as well, as they are expected to provide primarily 'Outstanding natural beauty' as mountains and lakes and 'Excellent ecological qualities' (Han, 2006, p.127).

In addition to pristine nature, cultural features, e.g. to be mentioned in history or poems, are very important tourism areas to attract visitors and to gain recognition. Therefore, newly discovered beautiful landscapes such as Jiuzhaigou or Wulingyuan, which are denigrated for their lack of culture, try to gain a cultural identity, for example, by naming all the peaks, valleys and streams.

Culture is always emphasized if managers want a site to be seen as high class (Han, 2006) and also for commercial reasons. In China, the average entrance fee to National Level Scenic and Historic Interest Areas or World Heritage Sites is nearly 1% of the average GDP per person, about ten times more than that of other countries. This reflects the three characteristics of being expensive, controlled and elitist. Gao (2013) expresses the important price–benefit ratio for landscape visiting slightly differently in her master's thesis. She states that if touristic sights in the Alps consist mainly of nature and sport activities, they might not be attractive enough for Chinese visitors (Gao, 2013).

In the context of urbanization, population growth and landscape loss in China, Gao *et al.* (2018) address an interesting phenomenon related to tourism: people born before 1980 have a stronger connection to nature and are more aware of China's landscape change than those born after 1980. People above the age of 40 years seem to be more concerned about the loss of nature and the pollution of the environment. Therefore, they are more interested in learning about natural phenomena, and are more likely to support nature protection in the Western sense, unlike the younger generation, who are mainly interested in management issues regarding natural areas.

One common feature of many nature tourism studies in China is that customers' safety, accessibility and convenience are top priorities (Li *et al.*, 2011; Zhang *et al.*,

2013). In particular, if the security aspect is not satisfactory, nature attractions are not visited and products not booked.

The principle of 'safety first' from the customer's point of view is also reflected in the results of the following study on the perception of nature and in the customer surveys of the 'China Inbound Service' project.

As alpine tourism products are based on nature to a large extent, it is crucial for service providers and destinations to know about the attitude towards nature of the (new) Chinese guests. On the one hand, this is based on traditional cultural values such as Confucianism; on the other hand it is related to the newest history and development of China. Due to urbanization and economic growth combined with environmental degradation, modern life in China's cities – the target regions for outbound trips – is far from nature. Therefore, tourists from China are increasingly longing for nature experiences, but at the same time, they are often not used to it and therefore more anxious and worried about safety than tourists to the Alps so far.

22.3.2 Landscape perception of Shanghai tourism students

To gain an insight into how young, tourism-related Chinese people rate different alpine landscapes in terms of their their attractiveness for tourism or leisure reasons, a survey among tourism students was conducted. In January 2018, 31 students from the Shanghai University of Engineering Science were asked in a short questionnaire to rate three pictures of the summer season and two pictures of the winter season according to the following questions:

1. Would you refer to the landscape as 'nature'? Answers: yes/no

2. a) Would you like to spend time there as a tourist? Answers: yes/no
   b) What are the reasons for your answer to Question 2a? (Open question).

The answers to the open question 2b were classified in the areas of 'Safety', 'Landscape', 'Convenience' and 'Entertainment' (see Table 22.1).

Whereas pictures A–D are significantly rated as nature ($p < 0.02$), for picture E the nature rating was not clear ($p = 0.215$). Regarding the question of whether participants were likely to spend leisure time in the shown landscape, pictures A and C were rated as significantly positive ($p < 0.02$), whereas acceptance of pictures B, D and E wasn't significant for the reasons 'too dangerous' or 'too cultivated'.

For the students in Shanghai safety reasons were most important; if safety is in doubt, participants are not likely to spend leisure time in a specific landscape, even if the landscape was unique to them as in picture 4. Additionally, it should be mentioned that one person criticized nearly each picture for the lack of culture and several participants rated the shown landscapes as beautiful, appealing, etc. but boring.

In matters of winter holidays, it can be stated that winter experiences such as playing in the snow, enjoying the landscape or a cable car ride were mentioned. Furthermore, skiing was mentioned by about half of the respondents. Skiing is a trend in China and the Olympic Winter Games 2022 in Beijing support it even more, which of course for alpine regions is a potential market.

Table 22.1. Landscape perception, Shanghai 2018.

Picture	1 Rated as nature	2a Attractive for leisure time	2b Reasons for answer regarding attractiveness for leisure time *directly cited mentions*
Picture A: Cultural landscape Heinzenberg, Switzerland (©demateo.com/Viamala Tourismus)	100% ***	90% ***	No safety concerns. Landscape and convenience were mostly positively rated with terms as beautiful, natural environment, good scenery, green, sunshine or fresh air. Furthermore, the picture was rated as quiet, relaxed, peaceful or comfortable
Picture B: Val Cluozza, Switzerland (©Swiss National Park)	94% ***	38% $p > 0.05$	Concerns regarding safety and lack of convenience dominate: no people, dangerous, steep mountains, desolate, too many trees, beasts, one might get lost etc. Furthermore: no food, no shower, no place to reside, hard to be there, insects, difficult to walk, etc. Regarding the landscape there are positive and negative mentions: fresh air, wide, beautiful, green trees, natural environment, etc. but also: ordinary, deserted, no lakes Regarding entertainment, negative mentions dominate as boring, nothing to do, empty

Continued

Table 22.1. Continued.

Picture	1 Rated as nature	2a Attractive for leisure time	2b Reasons for answer regarding attractiveness for leisure time *directly cited mentions*
Picture C: Alp Trida, Austria (©Ischgl.com)	71% *	71% *	Only four people mentioned safety concerns and the majority would like to spend leisure time mainly skiing, playing in the snow, riding a cable car and enjoying the scenery Regarding the landscape especially, snow is attractive to most of the respondents, but also the beautiful, white landscape Regarding convenience there are some concerns because of the cold and crowdedness, but most responses were positive because of the safe, warm house to relax in and get food
Picture D: Winter landscape, Montafon, Austria (©Silvretta Montafon)	94% ***	35% $p > 0.05$	Similar to picture 2 concerns regarding safety and convenience dominate, therefore respondents are not likely to spend leisure time here. Statements such as: No people, dangerous, steep mountains, too much snow, unknown environment, high altitude, one might get lost Furthermore: cold, no facilities, no food, sun too dazzling The landscape appeals to most of the respondents: white, beautiful, snow, snowy mountains, blue sky, fresh air, sunshine Regarding entertainment the answers are both positive and negative: To build an ice-house, climb snow mountains, challenge myself but also nothing, no activities, not inspired, boring

	63%	Not for safety reasons but because of the landscape, lack of entertainment and lack of convenience, the majority of the respondents didn't want to spend leisure time here: agricultural land, farm, man-made, not special
	$p > 0.05$	
	44%	Furthermore: boring, no activities, no infrastructure (food, sanitary, entertainment), insects
	$p > 0.05$	But there are also positive quotes, such as: fresh air, idyllic, green, wide, pick grapes, good for relaxing

Picture E: Vineyard in Bardolino, Italy
(©iStock.com/precinbe)

Statistics: binomial test results, ***$p < 0.001$, **$p < 0.01$, *$p < 0.05$.

22.3.3 Summary

The perception of nature by Chinese people and therefore Chinese tourists varies according to generation, living standard and cultural background. However, pristine nature can still be regarded as imperfect and therefore as not worth visiting. Therefore, lights, ornamentations or signposts add value to natural sites rather than disturb them. Furthermore, as soon as a landscape has a cultural or historical identity its attractiveness increases.

As described, the sample of this study consists of 35 tourism students. Therefore, it gives valuable insights into the landscape perception of potential Chinese guests, but it cannot be used to generalize, e.g. for experienced travellers.

Safety is crucial to all tourism products and landscapes and should be guaranteed and proved. Wilderness, steep and inaccessible terrain, and unknown environmental factors such as snow or wild animals are primarily scary for guests from China. Tourism products dealing with such aspects need to offer comprehensive information and guidelines, included guiding for reasonable prices. Likewise, aspects tourism infrastructure such as accommodation, restaurants and equipment shops or renting stations are expected.

Based on these insights it can be recognized that experiences such as a blue sky or stars, fresh air, drinking water from the tap, green meadows, walking barefoot or snowy mountains and powder snow are highlights for many Chinese guests, but for frequent tourists to the Alps are a matter of course. For Chinese guests the attractiveness of the products increases if they include fun, new learning experiences and can be shared on social media. It can be assumed that the more experienced those guests become, the closer their consumption patterns regarding alpine tourism products will be to those of other guests.

22.4 Conclusions and Outlook

Although the alpine region has only been visited by Chinese guests to a limited extent until now, for example in Chamonix, Interlaken or Lucerne (Bundesamt für Statistik, 2016), the expert and focus group survey as well as different studies, such as a study by the company Kairos Future for the European Commission (European Commission, 2016), indicate a great potential for the alpine regions for second-time or multiple-visit travellers. These guests are increasingly interested in nature as well as in sporting activities, offerings that are among the strengths of the alpine region. In addition, the interest in winter sports in China is growing on the one hand because of the economic and social development (Wu and Wei, 2015), and on the other because of the upcoming Olympic Winter Games in Beijing in 2022. The desire of Chinese guests to experience the winter and corresponding winter sports in their place of origin in the Alps offers great potential. Even more so, when products are adapted to the cultural-based expectations of the Chinese guests regarding safety, convenience and entertainment. Moreover, especially for winter sport offers, fun and experience should dominate.

To exploit the potential of the Chinese tourism market in the alpine region, it is important to be aware of the fast-changing travel behaviour and differentiate among consumer groups. Especially regarding the Beijing 2022 Olympic Games, the demand for winter sport activities will rise. At the same time, it is important to gain a foothold by bundling marketing resources in the huge Chinese market.

In conclusion it should be pointed out that the growing Chinese market in general and the FIT market in particular continue to pose new challenges to destinations and their service providers. Different concepts and tools, such as the value chain, criteria catalogue, offer databases, etc., can help to summarize and coordinate activities. Likewise, the experience from the Chinese market can be exploited for the development of further remote markets such as India, the Gulf States or Brazil.

In the field of nature and landscape perception combined with Chinese behaviour as winter tourists, hardly any research exists. In order to develop their awareness as potential target destinations, alpine regions in particular should be interested in this information.

Acknowledgements

We thank the two destinations Engadin St. Moritz and Davos Klosters for their cooperation and the Economic Development and Tourism Agency of Grison for enabling the project 'China Inbound Service'. Furthermore, we thank the tourism faculty of Shanghai University of Engineering Science for their support of the nature perception survey.

References

Andreu, R., Claver, E. and Quer, D. (2013) Chinese outbound tourism: new challenges for European tourism. *Enlightening Tourism* 3(1), 44–58.
Arlt, W. (2017) *COTRI Market Report*. COTRI: China Outbound Tourism Research Institute, Hamburg/Beijing, Germany/China.
Arlt, W. (2018) *COTRI Market Report*. COTRI: China Outbound Tourism Research Institute, Hamburg/Beijing, Germany/China.
Bätzing, W. (2015) *Die Alpen: Geschichte und Zukunft einer europäischen Kulturlandschaft*. CH Beck Verlag, Munich, Germany.
Bieger, T. and Beritelli, P. (eds) *Management von Destinationen*. Oldenbourg Verlag, Munich, Germany.
Benkenstein, M., Steiner, S. and Spiegel, T. (2007) Die Wertkette in Dienstleistungsunternehmen. In: Bieger, T. and Beritelli, P. (eds) *Management von Destinationen*. Oldenbourg Verlag, Munich, Germany, pp. 51–70.
Bruun, O. (1995) Fengshui and the Chinese perception of nature. In: Bruun, O. (ed.) *Asian Perceptions of Nature: A Critical Approach*. Curzon Press, London, pp. 173–188.
Bühler, D. and Minsch, R. (2004) Der Tourismus im Kanton Graubünden. Wertschöpfungsstudie. HTW Chur, Chur, Switzerland.
Bundesamt für Statistik (BfS) (2016) Beherbergungsstatistik HESTA. BfS, Neuenburg, Switzerland.
Chang, R.C., Kivela, J. and Mak, A.H. (2010) Food preferences of Chinese tourists. *Annals of Tourism Research* 37(4), 989–1011.
Edinburgh Tourism AG (2016) Edinburgh China-ready business opportunities guide. Available at: https://www.etag.org.uk/wp-content/uploads/2016/02/ETAG-China-Ready-Business-Opportunity-Guide.pdf (accessed 31 January 2019).

ETC and WTO (2012) Understanding Chinese outbound tourism – what the Chinese Blogosphere is saying about Europe. UNWTO, Madrid, Spain.

European Commission (2016) Tourism flows from China to the European Union – current state and future developments. European Commission, Brussels, Belgium.

Forster, S. and Rupf, R. (2007) Parkkonzepte – Gratwanderung zwischen Naturschutz und Tourismus, Newsletter – Zernezer Tage. Schweizerischer Nationalpark, Zernez, Switzerland.

Gao, J., Zhang, C. and Huang, Z. (Joy) (2018) Chinese tourists' views of nature and natural landscape interpretation: a generational perspective. *Journal of Sustainable Tourism* 26(4), 668–684. DOI:10.1080/09669582.2017.1377722

Gao, L. (2013) Mainland Chinese tourists and the Swiss alps an ethnographic exploration. Master's Thesis, HTW Chur, University of Applied Science, Chur, Switzerland.

Han, F. (2006) The Chinese view of nature: tourism in China's scenic and historic interest areas. PhD Thesis, Queensland University of Technology, Brisbane, Australia.

Hsu, S. (2016) China's urbanization plans need to move faster in 2017. Available at: https://www.forbes.com/sites/sarahsu/2016/12/28/chinas-urbanization-plans-need-to-move-faster-in-2017/#4e90a19b74db (accessed 31 January 2019).

Hu, T., Marchiori, E., Kalbaska, N. and Cantoni, L. (2014) Online representation of Switzerland as a tourism destination: an exploratory research on a Chinese microblogging platform. *Studies in Communication Sciences* 14(2), 136–143.

Keating, B. and Kriz, A. (2008) Outbound tourism from China: literature review and research agenda. *Journal of Hospitality and Tourism Management* 15(1), 32–41.

Koch, W. (2006) *Zur Wertschöpfungstiefe von Unternehmen: Die strategische Logik der Integration*. Deutscher Universitäts-Verlag, Wiesbaden, Germany.

Laesser, C., Bazzi, D. and Riegler, B. (2013) Tourismus 2020 – Nutzbarmachung von internationalen Tourismuspotentialen durch den Bündner Tourismus: Entwicklungen, Potentiale, Handlungsempfehlungen. Universität St. Gallen – Institut für Systematisches Management und Public Governance, St. Gallen, Switzerland.

Li, X.R., Lai, C., Harrill, R., Kline, S. and Wang, L. (2011) When east meets west: an exploratory study on Chinese outbound tourists' travel expectations. *Tourism Management* 32(4), 741–749.

McKinsey & Company (2016) What's driving the Chinese consumer. Podcast from April 2016. Available at: https://www.mckinsey.com/featured-insights/china/whats-driving-the-chinese-consumer (accessed 31 January 2019).

Plaz, P. and Bösch, I. (2015) Sommergeschäft durch Touringgäste aus Asien beleben. Vertiefungsbericht(V2)im Rahmen des Projekts 'Strategien für Bündner Tourismusorte'. Wirtschaftsforum Graubünden, Chur, Switzerland.

Porter, M.E. (1985) *Competitive Advantage: Creating and Sustaining Superior Performance*. Free Press, New York.

Schweiz Tourismus (2012) Tourismusmonitor Schweiz 2013. Available at: https://www.stnet.ch/de/dienstleistungen/tourismus-monitor-schweiz.html (accessed 8 February 2019).

Tourism and Events Queensland (2013) Meeting the expectations of your Chinese visitors and making them feel welcome. Available at: https://cdn-teq.queensland.com/~/media/15c4dcb13eb643f0b1eb0931a9cb3eae.ashx?la=en-au&vs=1&d=20140515T115458 (accessed 1 April 2017).

Tourism New Zealand (2013) China toolkit. Available at: www.chinatoolkit.co.nz (accessed 1 April 2017).

Tsang, N. and Hsu, C. (2011) Thirty years of research on tourism and hospitality management in China: a review and analysis of journal publications. *International Journal of Hospitality Management* 30(4), 886–896.

UNWTO (2018) 2017 international tourism results: the highest in seven years. Press release from 15 January 2018. Available at: http://media.unwto.org/press-release/2018-01-15/2017-international-tourism-results-highest-seven-years (accessed 31 January 2019).

Wonderful Copenhagen (2013) Survey of Chinese visitors to Scandinavia. Available at: www.visitcopenhagen.com/sites/default/files/asp/visitcopenhagen/Corporate/PDF-filer/Analyser/Chinavia/chinavia_-_survey_of_chinese_visitors_to_scandinavia_-_final.pdf (accessed 15 March 2015).

WTO (2017) Penetrating the Chinese outbound tourism market – successful practices and solutions. UNWTO, Madrid, Spain.

Wu, B. and Wei, Q. (2015) China ski industry white book. Available at: www.fierabolzano.it/alpitecchina/mod_moduli_files/2015%20China%20Ski%20Industry%20White%20Book%20(20160505).pdf (accessed 31 January 2019).

Zhang, H., Chen, B., Sun, Z. and Bao, Z. (2013) Landscape perception and recreation needs in urban green space in Fuyang, Hangzhou, China. *Urban Forestry and Urban Greening* 12(1), 44–52.

23 The 2-Year Tourist: Lifestyle Migration in Whistler, British Columbia

Joe Pavelka*

Mount Royal University, Calgary, AB, Canada

23.1 Introduction

The purpose of this chapter is to describe the landed negotiation dynamic of a particular group of lifestyle migrants in Whistler, British Columbia, Canada. The Resort Municipality of Whistler, BC is a tourism mecca anchored by the Vail Resorts Ltd's Whistler Blackcomb Mountain ski operation, which consistently ranks globally as one of the best winter tourism destinations (Tourism Whistler, 2018). Whistler operates year-round and requires a small army of seasonal, part-time and full-time employees. Thousands of transient young people come from around the world each year to work a season in Whistler and leave; they are not the focus of this research. There is a smaller group of relatively young people who migrate to Whistler to make it their permanent home. They are not retirees, remote tech workers, trust fund babies or second homeowners. They are lifestyle migrants seeking to participate in Whistler's winter mountain recreation, but they also need to work. Their sustained commitment to Whistler means they have gained valuable year-over-year experience in the ski or tourism industry, and often occupy supervisory and leadership positions. This makes them a lifestyle migrant group and an important labour cohort in a winter resort destination that consistently struggles with staffing issues (Dupuis, 2015).

The reality is that many in this cohort who arrive intent on living the 'Whistler Dream' encounter consistent and often profound struggles with structural elements such as housing, cost of living, low wages, etc., and end up determining that the cost of living the dream outweighs the benefits, and so they opt to leave. The '2-year tourist' is a local term that was used initially to describe Australians and New Zealanders on a working visa. However, it is now often applied to lifestyle migrants who do not make it past the 2 years. This research explores the landed negotiation of this cohort, including motivation for migration, landed challenges, perceived differences in those who stay to work through the trade-offs and those who leave. The value of this research is to shed light on an under-represented subgroup of lifestyle migrants who also represent an important labour cohort in resort communities where there is often labour instability.

---

* E-mail: jpavelka@mtroyal.ca

23.2 Study Area: Whistler and Vail Resorts

The Resort Municipality of Whistler is located 120 km north of Vancouver, BC. It includes a myriad of outdoor and touristic amenities, with the primary attraction being Whistler Mountain and Blackcomb Mountain. In 1966, Whistler Mountain was known as London Mountain, a ski operation in the midst of a failed Olympic bid. By the mid-1970s, it was recognized as a premium ski area. In 1980, Blackcomb Mountain opened next to Whistler's ski operation. The two remained separate until they were purchased by Intrawest in 1997. They merged in 2003 and became central to Whistler's 2010 hosting of the Winter Olympics and Para-Olympics. In 2015, Intrawest sold its share of Whistler Blackcomb to Vail Resorts Incorporated. By August 2016, Vail Resorts Inc. owned all of Whistler Blackcomb Mountain (Vail Resorts Fact Sheet, 2018). In 2017, the Resort Municipality of Whistler generated CA$1.44 billion in revenue and recorded over 3 million visitors (40% of those visitors come for winter recreation). There are just over 12,000 full-time residents in the community. Whistler Mountain alone requires 4692 staff to operate, and there are just over 15,000 people employed in tourism overall. The average daily population of Whistler is 30,000 people, with tourists making up over 60% of that crowd (Resort Municipality of Whistler, 2018). Whistler is mainly a tourism destination, but it certainly attracts those who want to make it their home.

Amenity and lifestyle migration have been central features of Whistler for decades (Gripton, 2009). It is easy to see the attraction of Whistler as a lifestyle migration destination. It exists in an outdoor recreation mecca with amenities for people of all abilities and tastes. It is situated in a stable country, and is close to a major city and the Vancouver International Airport. Forty-four per cent of Whistler's 10,000 private dwellings are occupied by 'usual residents'. The 56% of temporarily occupied dwellings imply that it is a second home economy. As well, just over 80% of Whistler's population is between 15 and 64 years, the average age is 36 and just over 60% have a university degree (Statistics Canada, 2016), which reflects strong in-migration.

23.3 Literature Review

There has been much written about amenity migration in the past decades dating back to the back-to-the-land movement of the 1960s (Gosnell and Adrams, 2011). It is projected that amenity migration will increase globally (Cohen *et al.*, 2015). Amenity migration is considered a part of the larger phenomenon of lifestyle migration (Benson and O'Reilly, 2009). Motivations for lifestyle migration can be understood in contrast to those of economic migration, which is an older and more clearly understood phenomenon (Waltert and Schlapfer, 2007). Though most dimensions of lifestyle migration are relevant in Whistler, the aim of this section is to define lifestyle migration and its motivations, and situate the sample of this research in the broader context of lifestyle migrants.

Lifestyle migration is defined as 'The movement of people based on the draw of natural and/or cultural amenities' (Gosnell and Abrams, 2011, p. 3). It is further characterized as 'a constant negotiating and re-negotiating of a path amidst the complex, chaotic and constantly changing socio-economic conditions…' (McIntyre, 2009, p. 230). Individuals are attracted to a particular destination based on a variety of factors, such as one's personal traits, the motivation to travel and for leisure, all of which can be grounded within a broad conceptual push–pull scenario (Suvantola, 2002). For example, the push to 'escape from where I was' and the pull of a mountain recreation lifestyle can fit well within the push and pull framework. Cohen (1979) suggests that the push and pull is due to alienation in one's home place and the search for authenticity in the other. The push–pull aspect of lifestyle migration cannot be overstated given that the chosen destination must offer potential for a lifestyle that is not present in the previous.

A common explanation of amenity migration is the counter-urban movement, which Gosnell and Abrams (2011) claim is based on decades of economic restructuring and job loss/instability, which leads to the rejection and an 'opting out' of the American Dream. It is also argued to be inextricably linked to identity and identity seeking (Williams and McIntyre, 2002; Torkington, 2012). Leisure motivation and negotiation is central to amenity migration (Sherlock, 2001; Pavelka and Draper, 2015), although less attention has been paid to the leisure negotiation process for amenity migrants. Other factors understood to contribute to amenity migration include increased flexibility of work schedules, a desire for healthy lifestyles, improved quality and access to recreation and leisure resources, growth in the leisure and tourism sector, increased marketing and advertising, and growth in leisure and travel technology that make mobility more accessible (Gartner and Lime, 2000). Torkington (2010) argues that the motives underlying such migration includes a better family environment, a lower cost of living, rising affluence, the rise of enabling technologies and the breakdown of social roles that allow for mobility. In essence, lifestyle migration occurs when people seek to reside in a place where they believe they can achieve a lifestyle that is preferable to what they thought possible in their previous residence.

Lifestyle migrants are not a homogeneous group and the lines separating the tourist, the lifestyle traveller and the lifestyle migrant are blurred. The sample for this research consists of relatively younger people. Most have travelled extensively, but have now determined to make Whistler their long-term home. Not to be confused with what Kannisto (2018) refers to as a group of young people who seek 'to travel like locals'. This group engages in market resistance to avoid tourism and want to connect with locals only. For this study's participants, the desire to be locals while avoiding tourism would be impossible in Whistler. This sample may also be confused with what Cohen (2011) refers to as lifestyle travellers, that is, people who travel for years on end. Both lifestyle travellers and lifestyle migrants are seeking to consume lifestyle. The difference between Cohen's sample and this sample is that the former seeks lifestyle through constant travel, while the latter believes their lifestyle is found by living in Whistler. The many styles of mobility serve to underscore that for young people today, mobility is viewed more as right or a given, rather than a privilege (Skrbis et al., 2014).

There are numerous typologies of lifestyle and amenity migrants. For example, in an analysis of ski industry towns in Colorado, Perdue (2004) claims that there are six types of migrants or locals. These include traditional ski bums, new ski bums, migrants (seasonal workers), trust fund babies, techies and entrepreneurs, all of whom he claims have significant impact on forming the nature and character of the ski industry town in Colorado. In their review of amenity migration in Canmore, Alberta, Robertson and Stark (2006) report the results of a focus group-style meeting with real estate agents. They conclude that there are five different types of people who purchase homes in the Canmore area: wealthy baby boomers over 40, valley workers buying their first home, investors seeking to speculate, 'lifestylers' who are usually from Alberta and second home owners.

Pavelka (2008) presents a typology of amenity migrants to the winter resort destination of Banff and Canmore, Alberta, also with five predominant types. The first consists of those fully transplanted individuals seeking a mountain recreation lifestyle. They need to work and knowingly sacrifice traditional success measures such as a career, home ownership and, at times, family, but are determined to make it work. The second is the same individual seeking a mountain recreation lifestyle and who must work, but at some point determines the costs are too great and leaves. The third is the fully transplanted individual who has worked through the initial years of struggle, found a suitable job or career and is raising a family much like their counterparts in urban settings. The fourth type is the long-term member of the community who cares less about mountain recreation and more about a strong social network. This type feels little to no conflict about living in a resort community and is generally found in the hospitality sector. The final person does not rely on the community for income and may be a second home owner, retiree, commuter or simply in a position where they are not required to work. This typology is based on the level of resistance that the different groups experience in relation to their aim of full-time residency, and the structural elements of place.

The sample of lifestyle migrants for this research can be found in the Pavelka (2008) typology to a certain degree. For example, the Whistler sample shares traits with the first and second group of fully transplanted migrants. They are seeking a mountain recreation lifestyle, rely on the community for employment and are working through the structural constraints. This group is mostly aware of the trade-offs that are required to move into the third group of settled migrants with a family, steady jobs and a career. The landed negotiation dynamic of lifestyle migrants refers to what they encounter upon arriving at their destination, and the ensuing negotiation to match expectation. Leisure Constraint Theory (Jackson *et al.*, 1993) postulates that people negotiate for their leisure through a series of three hierarchically ordered constraints in the form of intra-personal (personal values), inter-personal (significant others) and structural constraints (time, money, opportunity). Pavelka and Draper (2015) used the theory to explore the landed negotiation dynamic of lifestyle migrants to the Bow Valley. They concluded that the negotiation of structural constraints is the most important factor in determining whether migrants remain or leave. Structural components such as the economy, housing, roads, and health and educational infrastructure all contribute to the negotiation process (Robertson and Stark, 2006).

23.4 Methodology

Sixteen participants were recruited using a snowball method, the criteria was based on individuals who had the intention of living in Whistler indefinitely, have lived in Whistler for at least 2 years and had maintained winter employment in the resort community. Data collection involved a qualitative in-depth interview process based on four key questions: motivation for living in Whistler, challenges of life in Whistler, what is the difference between those who stay and leave, and their thoughts on the future. All interviews were recorded, transcribed and analysed for emergent themes. Transcription analysis was carried out using NVivo software whereby key themes and words were abstracted and over multiple analytical iterations, smaller clusters of themes settled. Only high-level themes are presented for the purpose of this chapter. The methodology closely follows that of Pavelka and Draper (2015) in their investigation of amenity migrants in Banff and Canmore, Alberta.

23.5 Results

23.5.1 Participant description

Table 23.1 presents a summary of the participants by age, length of time in Whistler, educational attainment, place of origin and gender. Of the 16 participants, the age range is from 20 to 34 years with a mean age of 29 years; the 2016 Whistler census reports the mean age to be 35.9 years. There are slightly more men than women – nine males to seven females, as shown in Whistler's reported population of 54% male and 46% female (Statistics Canada, 2016). The number of years each has resided in Whistler ranges from 2–12 years with a mean of 5.71 years. However, there are five participants (participants 4, 10, 13, 14, 15) who indicate that they have left Whistler during the summers for high-paying jobs elsewhere in order to earn enough money to return to work for the winter season at the ski school. This is not completely uncommon among lifestyle migrants (O'Reilly and Benson, 2016). All but three participants either work, or have worked, for Whistler Blackcomb Mountain at some point. Canada, the UK and Australia make up the places of origin, which appears homogeneous.

Table 23.1. Participant description.

Primary present occupation	Past or present ski hill employment	Age	Years in Whistler	Origin	Sex
1. Server	No	34	2	Ireland	F
2. Server	No	24	2	Ireland[a]	M
3. Bartender	No	20	2	Wales[a]	M
4. Ski operations	Yes	25	6 W	Canada	F
5. Server	Yes	21	5	Canada	F
6. Tourism	Yes	26	5	Canada	M
7. Ski school	Yes	27	5	England[a]	M
8. Server	Yes	32	12	Ireland	F
9. Server	Yes	30	8	England[a]	M
10. Ski school	Yes	27	6 W	England[a]	M
11. Tour guide	Yes	39	11	Canada	M
12. Construction	Yes	26	3.5	Canada	F
13. Ski school	Yes	30	8 W	Canada	F
14. Ski school	Yes	34	7 W	Australia[a]	M
15. Ski school	Yes	36	3 W	Australia[a]	F
16. Entrepreneur	Yes	33	6	England[a]	M
		29	5.71	UK 8 Can 6 Aus 2	M 9 F 7

[a]Either hold a Canadian passport or are currently applying for land immigrant status.
W indicates they leave Whistler for the summer to earn money in order to afford the winter teaching at ski school.

23.5.2　Motivation to live in Whistler

Participants were asked about their motivation for choosing Whistler as their long-term residence. All participants pursued a mountain recreation lifestyle variably defined, but consistently positioned in difference to one's previous place of residence. The most common theme is that participants sought an active mountain lifestyle involving a combination of mountain sports and touristic employment. The majority of participants arrived at Whistler via employment with the Whistler Blackcomb Mountain Snow School. Many (three-quarters) arrived with ski/snowboard experience from another resort in Europe, New Zealand or Canada, the others had no previous experience in ski/snowboard instruction.

Participants were asked why they chose Whistler specifically. Their response highlighted the reputation and stature of Whistler: 'Its Whistler, it's the biggest and best – of course I want to live in Whistler … everyone knows Whistler…' and 'if you're serious about a career in the ski industry you have to get to Whistler at some point'. The stature of Whistler within the world of snow sports makes it the place to be for those contemplating a career in the field. The relatively structured environment of snow school employment offers a reliable work schedule. For some, a residence-style accommodation was reported to provide a season of stability to get settled into the area, acquire a social network and learn of other opportunities.

The pursuit of an active mountain lifestyle invariably involves the pursuit of a like-minded social network that participants believed to be more likely in Whistler than in their previous place of residence. 'Your family's thousands of miles away and you meet a group of friends here that become your family' is a common sentiment regarding the strength of social pull. Just under half of the participants specifically noted the attraction of finding a cohort that they get to choose versus the one they grew up with in their hometown. 'I had great mates at home but they didn't share my values of the outdoors and skiing and just living well … here I can find people who share my values'.

During the course of the interviews, the importance of reinventing one's identity emerged among all participants in one way or another. The prospect of reinvention is common to all sorts of leisure migration including lifestyle migration (Nudrali and O'Reilly, 2016). Some participants spoke of reinvention in obvious ways such as, 'At home I was just another kid, but here I get to be and do the things I'm actually good at'. For others reinvention is subtler, whether it is to find a new group of friends or live an adventure-based lifestyle different from home that is considered to be exotic, relative to those of their old friends who were pursuing traditional paths. Two participants reported coming from strict religious households where life in Whistler represented an emancipation of sorts, where they could be whomever they choose.

Another theme is the attraction to living and identifying with a counter-culture lifestyle, but here the term counter-culture, which is prominent in lifestyle migration literature (Gosnell and Abrams, 2011), requires clarification. On one level it can be argued that there is little that is 'counter-culture' about Whistler, given that it exists as a commercial behemoth of tourism. On the other hand, choosing to live in Whistler compared with the hordes of tourists on holiday represents a commitment to a life of adventure and uncertainty that most are not willing to undertake. Their decision to reside in Whistler compared with the thousands who holiday there and return home makes this group of lifestyle migrants different. And being different is what subtly defines counter-culture. O'Reilly and Benson (2016) claim that working lifestyle migrants seek the renegotiation of work–life balance towards an ideal quality of life. This is true of the sample for this research as they all seek agency over their work–life balance.

23.5.3 Challenges of living in Whistler

Lifestyle migration literature recognizes many challenges to life once the migrant has landed. Depending on the context, there may be a new language to learn, making a new set of friends, local resentment, working odd jobs to subsidize life in the new destination or simply that expectations did not meet the reality. Alternatively, as O'Reilly and Benson (2016) state, '…reality bites once they have settled into their lives at the new destination' (p. 8). For this group of lifestyle migrants to Whistler, three themes emerged. The first theme is predictable and relates to the everyday negotiation of the structural elements of Whistler. The second is a rationalized repositioning of the idea of residency where they see themselves as a resident as opposed to a tourist. The third is the conflicted experience of outgrowing the place and gazing abroad.

Discourse on the challenges of living in Whistler can be heard in the cafes and pubs, and read in local newspapers and online chat rooms, it is simply hard to miss. The most profound challenge echoed by all participants is the negotiation of structural elements. These include the high cost of living, the scarcity of high-paying jobs, inconsistent or unreliable work, the lack of affordable accommodation requiring multiple jobs in order to afford rent and/or having to live with multiple roommates, poor transportation and not having access to relatively basic commercial goods. Securing accommodation is the most pressing of structural challenges and the one most likely to force a prospective employee to leave. All but two participants rent and two recently purchased a small townhouse in the town of Pemberton (80 km from Whistler) and commute to Whistler for work. Those who rent reported that despite their years in Whistler and the strength of their social networks, securing accommodation year over year remains a real concern. Four participants reported that it is not uncommon for new arrivals to spend half of their pay cheque on rent, which is not sustainable. Two reported living in crowded condominium units with seven other roommates, and another had just left a house with 11 roommates. They all reported that the first 2 years were the most difficult to negotiate accommodation because, as one participant noted, 'It takes time to get to know the place and the sleuthing to get a decent place to live and network to get a decent job … it's easy to live here and live like crap, but it's really hard to carve out a decent life if you're not totally rich here'.

Pavelka and Draper (2015) identify similar structural level concerns with amenity migrants in the Bow Valley, Banff and Canmore, Alberta. Working amenity migrants in the Bow Valley reported that the constant struggle with structural level constraints were the primary reason for leaving the area. Reeder and Brown (2005) claim that number of new jobs and earning potential generally increase with increased amenity migration development. Other researchers such as Nelson (2006) claim that in-migrants tend to outnumber jobs, and that the cost of living is a factor that causes many to leave their chosen communities. However in Whistler, all participants reported holding jobs. Though low-paying, they easily outnumber accommodations, evidenced by the number of 'Employees Wanted' signs on businesses, and reports of some businesses having to reduce hours of operation due to a lack of staffing.

For those who manage to work through the first 2 years and carve out a positive existence, their gaze may still shift to the outside world and a cognitive dissonance inevitably festers. All participants acknowledge that Whistler spawns a powerful bubble of reality with its own narrative and priorities; its exotic adventure dynamic can easily become the dominant narrative in one's own life. However, just under half of the participants and all those with undergraduate degrees reported that the inward focus on Whistler, and the relentless struggle with structural elements eventually palls, launching a consideration of other ways of living outside of Whistler. Participants also acknowledge that there are few career and educational upgrading opportunities. Even for supervisory levels, wages are far less than what is required to purchase a home in the area without significant external support. Retirees and second homeowners generally do not require employment at their new destination, which simplifies daily life. However, the sample for this research is at the front end of their career and life building, they must grapple with the limited opportunities within the community or leave. Of the 16 participants, ten reported that the challenge of negotiating Whistler's structural elements caused them to consider leaving the area altogether. Some reported that the prospect of leaving Whistler is a constant concern attached to the almost seasonal renegotiation of accommodations and jobs. The worry that one or the other will not fall into place makes an exit imminent. Participants were then asked what they perceived to be the differences between those come to Whistler with the aim of long-term residence and leave, and those who stay.

23.5.4 Why some stay and others leave

What do you do when you no longer want to teach skiing? Most participants came to Whistler to teach snow sports and move up in the ski industry. They teach skiing only to realize that it is not financially sustainable and upward mobility in the ski industry is a slow process. Many have taken on higher-paying hospitality jobs to increase their standard of living, but the choice is less appealing for the long term. This realization necessitates another reinvention, but again, the choices are to reinvent oneself within the constraints of the resources in the community, or leave. Participants discussed the underlying reasons why some people leave and others stay among those whose goal was to make Whistler their new long-term home.

When the costs of structural shortcomings overshadow the benefits of life in Whistler and an external option is presented, people leave. Perhaps for another resort community reputed to offer a better way of life, or back home where the prospects and limitations are at least familiar. Participants noted that the decision to leave is often precipitated by an event such as a physical injury that prevents them from working, creating a deficit in their finances. The decision to leave may be made when a close group of friends leave, or some are just not able to secure accommodations. Alternatively, as one participant noted, 'They realize the cost of this great new you [reinvention] is not worth sharing a house with ten other guys'.

People leave because they are forced into successive and unsatisfying reinventions, eventually concluding that to realize their potential, they must leave Whistler. A third of the participants reported that they or their partner were seriously considering leaving to further their education. That same group expressed concerns about staying and 'getting sucked into the Whistler vortex' whereby they are living a life with a higher-paying job, but that offers little meaning, other than allowing them to stay in

Whistler. Even so, the lure of simply staying is powerful, as one participant noted, 'If people are not chased out, they leave because they want to be an adult, others just want to stay in the bubble'. One participant summed up the struggle by stating, 'People come here to reinvent themselves whether they know it or not, and if they're successful they'll stay, if not – they won't'.

23.5.5 Thoughts on the future

Participants were asked to discuss their thoughts on the future of life in Whistler for working lifestyle migrants. There is no doubt that Whistler Blackcomb Mountain drives tourism for the resort municipality and that of the broader community, if not region. Vail's 2016 purchase of Whistler Blackcomb Mountain moved it into the stable of a massive ski resort conglomerate, making change inevitable. All the participants harboured cautionary views on the future of the 'hill' and 'village', and while some were more vocal than others, the theme was consistent. Common concerns are that Whistler is getting too big, too corporate and contains too many rules. Over half of the participants noted that Whistler Blackcomb Mountain is trying to get rid of day trippers, who identify as 'locals', for more lucrative overnight guests. Participants reported disappointment in learning that Vail's first significant capital development is to be a new chairlift, and not additional staff housing. They reported feeling underappreciated and fear it will erode the decades-old Whistler culture that made it a world-class resort.

The conclusion drawn by two-thirds of the participants is that despite the negative attention of the Vail Resorts Inc. acquisition, Whistler will continue to attract thousands of young people who will want to live the Whistler lifestyle. One-third offer a more pessimistic view that if a culture clash persists, it will eventually erode its reputation and attract only those who want to work a season and party, versus those who see it as a place to live and grow a career. However, this is not new, in their review of amenity migration in Whistler, Moore and Gill (2006) reported a transformation towards urbanization and a loss of character, declaring 'The traditional ski culture of Whistler is gradually giving way to a broader and more urban lifestyle'.

23.6 Discussion

The group of lifestyle migrants who are the object of this research follow a patterned course of events that frame their landed migrant experience. They are motivated to fashion an employment-based mountain recreation lifestyle within the backdrop of one of the most prominent winter resorts in North America. But the reality is that these people engage in multiple identity reinventions as they negotiate the realities of Whistler's structure, and extend their identity to places both planned and not. At some point, they either determine that they have carved something to their liking, continue to struggle or leave. This is the likely scenario for a large group of employment-based lifestyle migrants to resort communities. It places McIntyre's (2009; p. 230) characterization of lifestyle migration as 'a constant negotiating and re-negotiating of a path amidst the complex, chaotic and constantly changing socio-economic conditions … (into a lived context)'.

The challenge that participants face in negotiating the structural elements of the community is central to the lived experience of this group. These findings are not new, others have reported on similar findings for lifestyle migrants (Pavelka and Draper, 2015; Benson and O'Reilly, 2016). However, it is important to situate this group within the findings, and in relation to other types of lifestyle migrants. The participants are intent on establishing an indefinite residency in Whistler with demanding constraints. They need to find employment to support themselves in a resort community where employment is mostly touristic and wages are low. They hope to grow a career that will provide stability in a community with a high cost of living and where educational and related resources are scarce relative to a larger urban environment. It is a daunting task.

Other types of lifestyle migrants are likely to experience considerably less structural resistance (e.g. retirees, the independently wealthy and second home owners usually possess adequate resources and generally do not require employment). Short-term transients, gap year workers and visa permit-holders eventually and inevitably move on, but remain as resources in the area. Resort environments such as Whistler are structured by design to attract and host short-stay visitors, not long-term and poorly resourced lifestyle seekers. Consequently, the group that is the object of this research need to either aggressively negotiate a suitable place within a Whistler's touristic structure or leave.

Their plight can be dismissed as an experiment in privilege. However, it must also be viewed in light of the fact that as an important labour cohort, they represent a mid-level managerial layer. They also represent a force of social evolution for the destination, whereby their ideas influence the community as their tenure increases (Pavelka and Draper, 2015). Vail Resorts Inc. Whistler Blackcomb Mountain drives tourism and thus the structure of the community, and is at the crux of the landed dynamic of negotiation. When research participants were asked to comment on the future, they all acknowledged the central role of Vail Resorts Inc. and not the potential actions of the municipality, or trends in global tourism. Even prior to Vail's purchase, Whistler Blackcomb Mountain's growth strategies and management approaches were fixed on a pro-growth model of economic development (Gill and Williams, 2011). Vail's intention for the mountain operation is less clear, but this group of lifestyle migrants is concerned that Vail's culture will not fit in easily with the established Whistler community. This concern is echoed in numerous editorials in the local newspaper. Natalie Pearson (2018) specifically addressed the issue in the Bloomberg article, 'Is Vail Resorts Killing Whistler's Spirit?' If nothing else, the focus on Vail's takeover of Whistler Blackcomb Mountain is a case study that reflects the effect that a major attraction can have on the structure or on a destination.

23.7   Conclusions

The purpose of this research was to examine the landed dynamic of negotiation for a particular group of employment-based lifestyle migrants in Whistler, BC who are intent on permanent relocation. It was revealed that this group experiences structural resistance more comprehensively than other lifestyle migrant types less reliant on local structure. They are likely to experience multiple reinventions as part of the negotiation process and must determine if a satisfactory lifestyle is in reach or if they should leave. They are valuable to Whistler in many ways because they represent an important labour cohort of mid-level and potential future leaders of the community. They also represent an important element of the social evolution of the place. With their intent on indefinite residency, this group is more likely to see their ideas and views ripple throughout the community and thus alter the culture of the place. Other lifestyle migrants, such as second homeowners and seasonal workers, tend to have less connection with community (McNichol and Pavelka, 2014). This group of lifestyle migrants holds the possibility of altering the culture and direction of Whistler more than other clusters of residents.

References

Benson, M. and O'Reilly, K. (2009) Migration and the search for a better way of life: a critical exploration of lifestyle migration. *The Sociological Review* 57(4), 609–625.

Cohen, E. (1979) A phenomenology of tourist experiences. *Sociology* 13(2), 179–201.

Cohen, S.A. (2011) Lifestyle travellers: backpacking as a way of life. *Annals of Tourism Research* 38(4), 1535–1555.

Cohen, S.A., Duncan, T. and Thulemark, M. (2013) Lifestyle mobilities: the crossroads of travel, leisure and migration. *Mobilities* 10(1), 155–172. DOI:10.1080/17450101.2013.8264

Dupuis, B. (2015) Dismal staffing struggles worsen in Whistler. Available at: https://www.piquenewsmagazine.com/whistler/dismal-staffing-struggles-worsen-in-whistler/Content?oid=2667782 (accessed 31 January 2019).

Gartner, W.C. and Lime, D.W. (2000) *Trends in Outdoor Recreation, Leisure, and Tourism.* CAB International, Wallingford, UK.

Gill, A. and Williams, P. (2011) Rethinking resort growth: understanding evolving governance strategies in Whistler, British Columbia. *Journal of Sustainable Tourism* 19(4–5), 629–648.

Gill, A. and Williams P. (2006) Finding a pad in paradise: amenity migration effects on Whistler, British Columbia In: Moss, L. (ed.) *The Amenity Migrants: Seeking and Sustaining Mountains and their Cultures.* CAB International, Wallingford, UK, pp. 94–107.

Gosnell, H. and Abrams, J. (2011) Amenity migration: diverse conceptualizations of drivers, socioeconomic dimensions, and emerging challenges. *Geo Journal* 76(4), 303–322.

Gripton, S.V. (2009) The effects of amenity migration on the resort municipality of Whistler and its surrounding environs. *Environments* 37(1), 59–81.

Jackson, E.L., Crawford, D.W. and Godbey, G. (1993) Negotiation of leisure constraints. *Leisure Sciences* 15(1), 1–11.

Kannisto, P. (2018) Travelling like locals: market resistance in long term travel. *Tourism Management* 67, 297–306.

McIntyre, N. (2009) Re-thinking amenity migration: integrating mobility, lifestyle and social-ecological systems. *Die Erde* 140(3), 229–250.

Nudrali, O. and O'Reilly, K. (2016) Taking the risk: the British in Didim, Turkey. In: Benson, M. and O'Reilly, K. (eds) *Lifestyle Migration: Expectations, Aspirations and Experiences.* Routledge, London, pp. 137–152.

O'Reilly, K. and Benson, M. (2016) From lifestyle migration to lifestyle in migration: categories, concepts and ways of thinking. *Migration Studies* 4(1), 20–37.

Pavelka, J. (2008) Leisure negotiation and amenity migration for gateway communities. Available at: https://prism.ucalgary.ca/bitstream/handle/1880/46943/Pavelka.pdf?sequence=1&isAllowed=y (accessed 31 January 2019).

Pavelka, J. and Draper, D. (2015) Leisure negotiation within amenity migration. *Annals of Tourism Research* 50, 128–142.

Pearson, N.O. (2018) Is Vail Resorts killing Whistler's spirit? Available at: https://www.bloomberg.com/news/articles/2018-04-09/is-vail-resorts-killing-whistler-spirit (accessed 31 January 2019).

Perdue, R. (2004) Skiers, ski bums, trust fund babies, migrants, techies and entrepreneurs: the changing face of the Colorado ski industry. In: Weiermair, K. and Mathies, C. (eds) *The Tourism and Leisure Industry: Shaping the Future*. Haworth Hospitality Press, New York, pp. 209–226.

Reeder, R. and Brown, D. (2005) Rural areas benefit from recreation and tourism development. Available at: https://www.ers.usda.gov/amber-waves/2005/september/rural-areas-benefit-from-recreation-and-tourism-development (accessed 31 January 2019).

Resort Municipality of Whistler (2018) Economic development. Available at: https://www.whistler.ca/business/economic-development-whistler (accessed 31 January 2019).

Robertson, B. and Stark, C. (2006) Alberta's amenity rush. In: Moss, L. (ed.) *The Amenity Migrants: Seeking and Sustaining Mountains and their Cultures*. CAB International, Wallingford, UK, pp. 120–134.

Sherlock, K. (2001) Revisiting the concept of hosts and guests. *Tourist Studies* 1(3), 271–295.

Skrbis, Z., Woodward, I. and Bean, C. (2014) Seeds of cosmopolitan future? Young people and their aspirations for future mobility. *Journal of Youth Studies* 17(5), 614–625.

Statistics Canada (2016) 2016 Whistler census. Available at: https://www12.statcan.gc.ca/census-recensement/2016/dp-pd/prof/details/page.cfm?Lang=E&Geo1=POPC&Code1=1309&Geo2=PR&Code2=48&Data=Count&SearchText=Whistler&SearchType=Begins&SearchPR=01&B1=All&TABID=1 (accessed 31 January 2019).

Suvantola, J. (2002) *Tourist's Experience of Place*. Ashgate Publishing Company, Aldershot, UK.

Torkington, K. (2010) Defining lifestyle migration. *Dos Algarves* 19, 99–111.

Torkington, K. (2012) Place and lifestyle migration: the discursive construction of 'glocal' place-identity. *Mobilities* 7(1), 71–92.

Tourism Whistler (2018) Whistler's awards, ratings and recognition. Available at: https://www.whistler.com/about-whistler/awards (accessed 31 January 2019).

Vail Resorts Inc. (2018) Fact sheet. Available at: http://news.vailresorts.com/corporate/vailresorts/fact-sheet (accessed 31 January 2019).

Waltert, F. and Schlapher, F. (2007) The role of landscape amenities in regional development: a survey of migration, regional economic and hedonic pricing studies (Working Paper No. 0710). University of Zurich – Sozialökonomisches Institut, Zürich, Switzerland.

Williams, D.R. and McIntyre, N. (2002) Where heart and home reside: changing constructions of place and identity. In: Michigan State University (ed.) *Proceedings of the 5th Recreation and Tourism Trends Symposium East Lansing MI*. Department of Parks and Recreation and Tourism Resources, East Lansing, Michigan, pp. 392–403.

Part III Winter Tourism Development and Sustainability

24 Winter Tourism Development and Sustainability: Regional Development, Ownership and Infrastructure; Environmental Management and Sustainability; Historical and Future Perspectives, Trends and Implications

HAROLD RICHINS*

Faculty of Adventure, Culinary Arts and Tourism, Thompson Rivers University, Kamloops, BC, Canada

24.1 Introduction

As indicated within the numerous chapters of this book, tourism in winter has historically had significant challenges, created substantial socio-economic opportunities for communities and on a broader scale, provides for a significant, yet considerably uncertain future (Richins, and Hull, 2016; Musa, et al., 2015; Schmidt et al., 2016). To understand and address these uncertainties and opportunities, numerous approaches have been attempted and implemented over a significant period. Many have relevance to winter tourism, and have included: considerations of historical, present and futures thinking and perspectives; community and destination decision making, policy and planning; the provision of operational, governance, modelling, management practices (see Fig. 24.1) and structural change; and regional, national and international engagement, networks and collaborations of relevance (Inskeep, 1991; Gunn and Var, 2002; Weed and Bull, 2004; Kruk et al., 2007; Edgell et al., 2008; Richins, 2009, 2011; Musa et al., 2015; UNWTO, 2015; Hull and Richins, 2016a; Hellmeister and Richins, 2018). An exploration of these approaches in tourism shows a variety of solutions, as demonstrated through regional tourist destination governance, including integrated models, methods and theories; destination government policy and planning; focused development directives and procedures; communications and networks; and initiated partnerships and projects (Blank, 1989; Inskeep, 1991; Marien, 1992;

---

* E-mail: hrichins@tru.ca

Fig. 24.1. Early snowmaking to lengthen the winter sports season in British Columbia, Canada. (Photograph courtesy of Harold Richins.)

Dowling, 1993; Auyong, 1995; van Fossen and Lafferty, 2001; Gunn and Var, 2002; Hall and Richards, 2003; Neto, 2003; Singh *et al.*, 2003; Edgell *et al.*, 2008; Hall, 2008; George *et al.*, 2009; Ayman and Husam, 2010; Wray *et al.*, 2010; Laws *et al.*, 2011).

On a broader level and with meaningful consideration has been the instigation of a number of international initiatives to build awareness and strategic commitment on a global to local level. This has included various sustainable and stewardship goals and integrated implementation stratagems (Inskeep, 1991; Dowling, 1993; Hall and Richards, 2003; Neto, 2003; Edgell *et al.*, 2008; Wray *et al.*, 2010; Richins *et al.* 2011; UNWTO, 2015). An important priority developed through international significant collaborative effort has resulted in the long-range development framework stemming from the seven UN Millennium Development Goals, which have been enhanced to include 17 global Sustainable Development Goals (see Table 24.1) set by the United Nations General Assembly in 2015 (UNWTO, 2015).

As relevant to tourism, the United Nations World Tourism Organization indicated tourism's important role in the following statement: 'Building on the historic Millennium Development Goals (MDGs), the ambitious set of 17 Sustainable Development Goals and 169 associated targets is people-centred, transformative, universal and integrated. Tourism has the potential to contribute, directly or indirectly

Table 24.1. UN Sustainable Development Goals. (UN, n.d.)

UN Sustainable Development Goals	
Goal 1: No poverty	Goal 10: Reducing inequalities
Goal 2: Zero hunger	Goal 11: Sustainable cities and communities
Goal 3: Good health and well-being for people	Goal 12: Responsible consumption and production
Goal 4: Quality education	Goal 13: Climate action
Goal 5: Gender equality	Goal 14: Life below water
Goal 6: Clean water and sanitation	Goal 15: Life on land
Goal 7: Affordable and clean energy	Goal 16: Peace, justice and strong institutions
Goal 8: Decent work and economic growth	Goal 17: Partnerships for the goals
Goal 9: Industry, innovation and infrastructure	

to all of the goals.' This provides an important long-term strategic framework for tourism development and sustainability, and more specifically in addressing challenges regarding tourism within colder winter areas. Virtually all of the goals have particular relevance to tourism and particularly with winter tourism, including the following: Goal 3 (good health and well-being for people), Goal 4 (quality education), Goal 5 (gender equality), Goal 6 (clean water and sanitation), Goal 7 (affordable and clean energy), Goal 8 (decent work and economic growth), Goal 9 (industry, innovation and infrastructure), Goal 11 (sustainable cities and communities), Goal 12 (responsible consumption and production), Goal 13 (climate action) and Goal 17 (partnerships). A valuable document, entitled 'Tourism and the Sustainable Development Goals' outlined the relevance of tourism to each of these goals (UNWTO, 2015).

Illustrations of approaches relevant to winter tourism include: the International Centre for Integrated Mountain Development's outline of a strategic process to build capacity and achieve results in sensitive regions (Kruk *et al.*, 2007); the provision of a mountain tourism framework (Nepal and Chipeniuk, 2005), which offers a way of considering recreation and tourism issues in mountain regions; and the Sustainable Mountain Tourism Experience Model (SMTE; see Fig. 24.2), which adopts a management approach to the impact on place (or locale, which is relevant to the people within the place), and emphasizes a focus on practice of relevance to planning, management and governance of tourism within the regional area (or areas) that may be affected (Richins and Hull, 2016).

The chapters in Part III may provide further insight into understanding the critical and diverse challenges and opportunities pertinent to tourism with a dependence on winter activities and experiences (see Fig. 24.3). Though not all chapters in this section are consistent with the variety of these models and approaches acknowledged above, nor do they demonstrate wholly the UN Sustainable Development Goals, there is significance in gaining knowledge and understanding of tourism development and sustainability issues of relevance to tourism in winter settings. The following includes a summary of the chapters in Part III of this book.

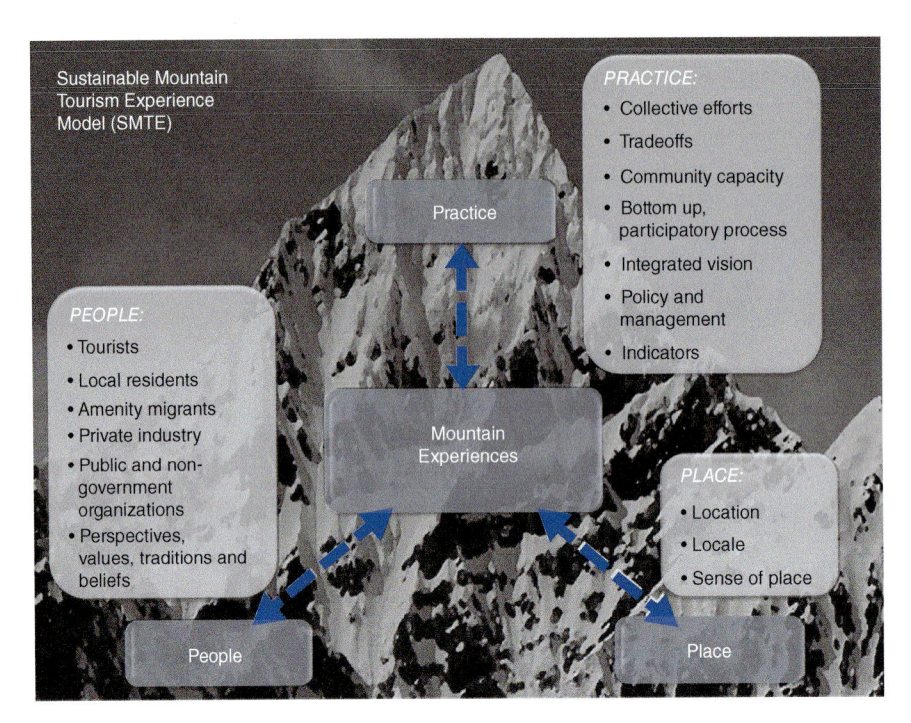

Fig. 24.2. Sustainable Mountain Tourism Experience Model. (From Richins and Hull, 2016.)

Fig. 24.3. Winter tourism at Sun Peaks Municipality, British Columbia, Canada. (Photograph courtesy of Harold Richins.)

24.2 Summary of Chapters in Part III: Winter Tourism Development and Sustainability

The chapters in Part III on winter tourism development and sustainability cover topics on historical features of ski activities, literature on ski and snow sports industry development and economic sustainability, writings on the challenges of sustainability of ski resort communities, and articulating significant changes in organizational ownership and its effect on ski resort development. Additionally this section provides meaningful literature on the transformation, diversification and future of the ski and snow sports industry, minimizing risk of winter alpine activity, and the challenges and progression of significant leadership, growth, success aspects and future sustainability of ski resorts. The chapters in this section are summarized further below:

24.2.1 Chapter 25. Development of Downhill Skiing Tourism in Sweden: Past, Present and Future

Authors: O. Cenk Demiroglu, Linda Lundmark and Magnus Strömgren

Perhaps the initiation of winter tourism began in Scandinavia with the introduction of the wooden ski for transportation in winter environments. Demiroglu, Lundmark and Strömgren provide a historical perspective with Chapter 25. From early beginnings (over 3000 years ago) in the use of skis for functional activity (hunting, combat, transport), ski use changed later for recreational, sports and tourism purposes, even becoming a symbol of aristocracy, royalty and eventually part of the national identity of Sweden. Ski use and the advent of mountain-oriented communities were shown to be a particular growth trend during the more peaceful periods after World War II due to cultural foundations and improvements in time, income, skills and access. The interest in winter downhill ski tourism saw long periods of growth in Sweden, primarily due to governmental policy changes in holiday provision, transportation improvements, uphill mountain access methods, active and increased leisure interest, and a focus on economic development within mountain environments. This also provided an impetus for a newer, less affluent type of sports tourist who participates in winter mountain experiences in the country. This, in turn, resulted in a substantial increase in visitor numbers as well as amenity migrants to these growing mountain communities.

According to the chapter, government planning and support, including public–private partnerships, as well as various diverse ownership, management and community structures, have provided on a regional and local scale, further influences on mountain tourism development within Sweden. In addition, with a very high percentage of the population showing interest and participation in winter resort areas, downhill skiing became the most prominent activity within winter tourism. After providing an understanding of the historical development of downhill ski tourism, the chapter concludes with a discussion of the numerous present and future changing economic and climate patterns that are expected to create a number of challenges in future local, regional vibrancy.

24.2.2 Chapter 26. The Challenges of Sustainability in the Management of Ski Resorts: The Experience of the Dolomites

Authors: Umberto Martini, Federica Buffa and Serena Lonardi

The chapter on sustainability in the management of ski resorts by Umberto Martini, Federica Buffa and Serena Lonardi provides new insight into addressing present and future challenges, which are significantly different from past circumstances. Chapter 26 acknowledges a traditional model of mountain tourism that has achieved substantial growth and prosperity; however, there is also an indication of external challenges and changing interests and needs of present and future customers, which may dramatically impact the balance of sustainability approaches and outcomes.

The chapter identifies nine pillars or drivers that have influenced the development and success of winter tourism within the Dolomite region including aspects of lift expansion, connections and collaboration of operations, snowmaking technology, additional innovation, accessibility and safety aspects, and the offering of diverse services. While acknowledging the international reputation and perceived model of good management and development practice of Dolomite mountain tourism, the authors indicate the challenges ahead within the context of future and diverse trends and effects. Concerns are expressed regarding continued development and long-term success within identified changing circumstances.

An integrated and innovative approach is suggested involving a number of unique and dynamic factors of relevance to better understanding and implementing strategic commitments regarding diverse market segments, climate change impacts and issues of seasonality, water and energy management techniques, mobility and transport approaches, and further natural and cultural resource management mechanisms. Due to the numerous indicated future challenges and an increasing diversity of market trends and customer interests and needs, the authors suggest this more integrated and strategic approach will ensure a greater possibility of viable and continued success.

24.2.3 Chapter 27. The Role of Cable Cars and Ski Lifts as Key Innovations in the Evolution of Winter Tourism

Author: Marius Mayer

Access to winter tourism has long been an important factor in its development, especially over the past five or six decades. Road and train systems and in particular mechanisms to get people into the higher mountain regions have allowed active participation within these challenging regions. Marius Mayer, in Chapter 27, discusses the historical and critical role that various uphill transportation devices have played in building and maintaining tourism destination success, principally within winter alpine regions where snow has been consistently prevalent.

From its early beginnings with very basic, often precarious and sometimes dangerous lift systems, to highly sophisticated and large capacity systems, the development of cable cars and ski lifts has enabled numerous innovations in winter tourism. Mayer discusses the important role that these lift systems, often interconnected, have played in greatly influencing the relatively rapid development of villages and resort towns that is prevalent today.

The author traces a historical perspective that first describes the importance of cable cars and ski lifts as basic innovations for ski and winter tourism, with most locations beginning as a single lift and many transforming over time into fully operational ski areas. At a later stage in uphill lift capacity, development commitments were made to increase accessibility of high alpine and glacier areas, providing for further innovations in the quality, speed and capacity of lifts. And based on increased capacity and financial viability, a number of regional areas built connecting lift access, thus expanding neighbouring ski areas and villages into large-scale ski destinations. This was successful, due in part, to the instigation of a number of complex partnerships including landowners, small ski lift operators, village leaders and numerous other stakeholders. The author provides a strong argument that uphill mountain transport was and is one of the key drivers of innovation, economic development, diffusion and change within winter alpine communities, and has also provided for further diversity of activity choice in the trend towards all-season alpine tourism experiences.

24.2.4 Chapter 28. Merging of Ski Resorts, Monopolization and Changes in Ownership Structures: The Case of Whistler

Author: Alison Gill

The chapter on North American resort acquisition, ownership and corporate culture by Alison Gill provides interesting insights into the historical foundation and changing nature of the ski resort industry over a number of decades. The nature of ownership and strategic management is for the most part significantly different from models found in Europe and elsewhere, where more network-oriented relationships and cooperation of diverse enterprises exist. In Chapter 28, a historical perspective is provided in both the broader aspects of ski resort corporate giants and in particular with Whistler Blackcomb as a case example. Starting from very diverse beginnings, various organizations have built, sold and acquired mainly stand-alone mountain resort properties over a 60-year period, with the recent two decades being the most dynamic.

The chapter provides a context and profile of corporate mountain resort ownership from seemingly humble beginnings to today's large companies with billions in asset value. In more recent times two large enterprises have emerged (Vail Resorts Inc. and Alterra Mountain Company), with ownership and control of 18 and 13 mountain resorts, respectively. As a case example of the changing patterns of development, competition, rivalry, ownership and management approaches, one of the very largest mountain resorts, Whistler Blackcomb (current name) is discussed in some detail. Of particular interest in the chapter is the changing nature of stakeholder and mountain community relationships and a discussion of both the dependencies, approaches and risks in the way in which larger mountain resort corporations engage within the communities in which they exist.

24.2.5 Chapter 29. How to Manage Ski Resorts in an Environmentally Friendly Way – Challenges and Lessons Learnt

Authors: Ulrike Pröbstl-Haider and Claudia Hödl

With a number of winter tourism destinations prioritizing environmental management as an important practice, a number of approaches have been taken to do so. Ulrike Pröbstl-Haider and Claudia Hödl, in Chapter 29, provide a comparison of two case studies of winter mountain resorts in Europe. They conducted an analysis of the differences and commonalities relative to motivation, circumstances and opportunities in the provision of environmental management certification programmes within the resorts. This included such aspects as the motivation from both management and employees to participate, significance to the enterprise for environmental improvement, perceived benefit to the organization of the commitment, and additional factors (external and internal to the organization) of relevance to the process and potential for success in the programme. Two quite different ski and mountain resorts were selected as part of the case study analysis including a relatively new mountain resort in the Pirin Mountain range in south-western Bulgaria (Bansko) and a more established mountain resort within the Austrian Alps (Schmitten).

The case study analysis supports both the direct and indirect benefits to participation including the establishment of environmental management systems within the mountain resort, building environmental monitoring for baseline and future data collection, the provision of improvement procedures and processes, and improved awareness and commitment to management and staff for environmental responsibility and implementation of practices. The findings of the Bansko and Schmitten mountain resort cases suggest that that significant environmental (as well as cost) improvements can be achieved despite differences in geographical, political and structural circumstances, and that improving the sustainability of winter mountain tourism resorts through a commitment to an environmental certification process is valuable.

24.2.6 Chapter 30. Tourism Diversification in the Development of French Ski Resorts

Authors: Coralie Achin and Emmanuelle George

Coralie Achin and Emmanuelle George provide a chapter on the changing direction over a few decades related to the broadening needs and challenges of French ski resorts. This focuses on diversification beyond uphill ski tourism to incorporate and integrate broader community needs and interests. With the acknowledgement of the changing nature of climate as well as the diversification of interests within mountain environments in France, strategies policies have been put in place to address these issues. Achin and George acknowledge the identification of two strategies of adaptation including a shorter-term approach in utilizing technologies for the extension of winter snow experiences and a longer-term strategy of expanding mountain tourism experience offerings, with, in turn, expansion to all-season and all-elevation tourism offerings.

The second more strategic approach mentioned above also involves the expanded nature of tourism governance models beyond the protection of specific uphill winter ski capacity. The chapter elaborates on various approaches and ramifications of this changing tourism governance strategy, which the authors suggest is leading to the diversification of communities, stakeholders and decision makers. Further in the chapter is the description of the significant differences of the private–public French ski and mountain resort model, and particularly the emphasis on the municipality leadership as a key part of leadership and decision making for resort development and management as compared with most other regions in Europe as well as within North America. In addition the extended resort model as is particular to France provides for either expanded mountain tourism activities and/or further emphasis on either traditional or non-traditional economic activity.

The unique governance model within these mountain communities, as articulated by the authors of the chapter, has led to the more connected nature of inter-municipalities that incorporate both higher mountain elevation resort communities and offerings and lower, more diverse mountain-related offerings and community developments. This has worked to strengthen the interconnected nature of tourism destination marketing and management. With newer destination development policies, there has been a further expansion and integration of lower-level alpine communities for diversification of tourism offerings through multi-seasons with an additional focus on natural and cultural tourism experiences. Achin and George, however, question the role of management in this newer governance model as well as the ability of the model to preserve the unique aspects of smaller winter mountain destinations.

24.2.7 Chapter 31. Preferences for Renewable Energy Sources Among Tourists in the European Alps

Authors: Alexandra Jiricka-Pürrer, Johannes Schmid and Ulrike Pröbstl-Haider

With the increased commitment to renewable energy and addressing climate change on the global stage, locations chosen for the construction of these alternative energy systems can be seen as an encroachment on the landscape aesthetics in alpine tourist destinations. Chapter 31 by Alexandra Jiricka-Pürrer, Johannes Schmid and Ulrike Pröbstl-Haider explores tourist's perceptions and potential for concern of potential installations within various locations in alpine regions of Austria.

The attraction of people to visit mountain regions has been discussed in the literature and provided visually through art and photography for over a century. And a component of importance has often included a significant interest in the natural landscape. This is of particular importance to tourists, who often seek out natural landscapes for their aesthetic and pristine qualities. With the increased use of solar and wind to generate renewable energy, the installations needed to do so may have a significant effect on the visual features and value that tourists see as essential.

The results of a study of over 2000 people was conducted in both winter and summer in four diverse regional alpine areas of Austria and compared and contrasted a variety of factors which may influence the adaptation and tolerance of renewable installations near or within tourism destinations. Though support for renewable energy has been steadily increasing, there are issues identified which suggest that more careful consideration would be useful in creating a balance between large visible installations and the aesthetic interests and attractive aspects that are important motivators for visitation to alpine winter and summer destinations.

24.2.8 Chapter 32. A Resort Community Without Residents? The Case of Jumbo Glacier Resort in the Purcell Mountains of British Columbia, Canada

Authors: Cameron E. Owens and Murray B. Rutherford

A case study chapter by Cameron E. Owens and Murray B. Rutherford discusses the decades-long process of a new ski resort development and describes in some detail a long-standing polarization and numerous challenges surrounding the decision approval process at the provincial and regional levels. This involves a case study of the Jumbo Glacier high alpine ski resort proposal, which is still in doubt since its inception in 1991. The description follows a series of attempts, challenges, oppositions, legal battles, approvals, lapses and highly contentious issues surrounding the application for an all-season uphill lift system and resort village development within a rather remote region of the southern BC Rockies. While proponents of the resort development project see it as an ideal development for the future of alpine winter and summer mountain experiences within a context of climate change and providing access to those seeking access to high alpine while enjoying developed village infrastructure, others see the proposal as disaster for the region, in particular that it may damage the fabric of wilderness and wildlife habitat and change forever the majestic and relatively pristine mountainous region.

The chapter discusses the historical perspectives and series of events and outcomes (or lack thereof), also the various steps and missteps, and the diversity of positions taken by various divided advocates in what is perhaps one of the longest decision making processes in BC to approve or disallow a tourism development of this type. Various milestones and requirements are shown with highly differing views and emotions expressed while the decision making process is seen as flawed, dragged out and incomplete. The case perhaps shows the need for significant refinement in both how and the extent to which diverse voices are heard and also regarding the importance of a straightforward, impartial and transparent approach to tourism resort development decision making. In addition the case provides further an example of the value in best matching the needs and interests of the regional community in which a development will sit, as well as aligning with the interests and needs of those involved in planning and implementing reasonable, viable, professional and sustainable tourism projects.

24.2.9 Chapter 33. Winter Tourism and Seasonality in Iceland

Authors: Þorvardur Árnason and Johannes T. Welling

The chapter by Árnason and Welling explores the growth of winter tourism within a country (Iceland), which has traditionally had a prevalence for tourism within the warmer summer months of June to August. Over the past decade there has been a growing interest in snow- and ice-based tourism within a country that has rather an iconic image related to adventurous activity within pristine Nordic environments. The authors discuss various perspectives on winter tourism with a particular emphasis on seasonality as a multi-faceted phenomenon and in reflecting variability and change. Other aspects in the conceptual description of winter tourism are acknowledged in the chapter as having relevance to winter sports tourism and involving a close connection to images of snow and holiday stereotypical ambiance.

Within the context of a regional area of Iceland Árnason and Welling indicate the reasons for significant growth and development of winter tourism. Key aspects include the uniqueness and substantive nature of glaciers in the regional area, which have perceived aesthetic, experiential and cultural values. Also of importance is the location of these natural assets, which are near prominent mountain ranges as well as being close to dramatic ocean settings.

The authors discuss the initial commercial tourism activities such as four-wheel vehicle access, snowmobiling and Nordic skiing tours onto the glacial areas, with later expansion to water-based tours and glacier hikes. With this development and interest in winter activities in the region has come a significant shift in the ratio of international tourism as well as an increase in small operators offering an increasing number of winter-based experiences. The chapter concludes with a discussion about the challenges in the further development of winter-based tourism within the regional area as well as more broadly regarding Iceland. These challenges have relevance to limited natural resource, access to natural activities within the winter season, issues of overcrowding (or perceived overcrowding) and particularly with the emergence of ice cave experiences, challenges are discussed regarding limitations of international awareness of unique winter-based tourism activities.

24.2.10   Chapter 34. Safety, Risk and Accidents – Experiences from the European Alps

Authors: Ulrike Pröbstl-Haider

With participation in winter tourism pursuits, there has been a long history of challenges faced by those engaged as participants in outdoor activities. Within more organized and controlled areas available for winter activity, mitigating risks has become an important commitment for winter sports operators. The chapter by Ulrike Pröbstl-Haider provides insight into the control, management and goal of minimization of risk, particularly with the focus on the winter alpine mountain sector.

Different regions in different countries have taken measures and made commitments either on a regulatory and legal basis, or on a voluntary basis, to mitigate risk through a variety of means. There is both a perception and reality that taking major steps in the development and implementation of safety measures will reduce significantly the chance of injury and harm. This chapter acknowledges important work conducted on risk, risk behaviour and the consequences of risk for winter tourism, the key links to success in the reduction of injury, and a discussion of safety measures available and taken in order to achieve the best outcomes for both participants and operators. An exploration of the diversity and profile of injuries in winter alpine areas provides for a more knowledge-based understanding of the present and future situation and its possibilities in risk and safety management practice as well as responsibilities taken by participants to prepare more readily for the potential risk factors to prevent accidents and injuries within winter alpine environments.

24.2.11   Chapter 35. Collaboration and Leadership as Success Factors of a Ski Resort – A Multiple Case Study from Finland

Authors: Raija Komppula and Emma Alegria

The chapter provides an account of the historical development regarding three of Finland's largest ski resorts including Levi, Ruka and Ylläs, and factors that have affected their different extent and rates of expansion over a number of years. The authors, Raija Komppula and Emma Alegria, explore perceptions of stakeholders of destination success factors in winter mountain resorts in Finland and in particular with these three most prominent resorts. These factors have relevance to aspects of collaboration and leadership differences that have influenced the longer-term development and outcomes of success with these destinations.

As discussed in the chapter within Finland, local governments and/or the provincial authorities provide the impetus, responsibility and governance facets of relevance to facilitating and monitoring development within local and regional areas. These significant decision making organizations may or may not have shared vision and strategy in terms of destination development, including adjacent communities, which may result in either fragmentation of development projects or success and clarity of direction and integration in future implementation and application.

The authors indicate the importance of functional and collaborative destination management and marketing organizations as critical to the success and progress of larger winter mountain destinations in Finland, as they are key drivers in facilitating effective and relevant leadership and development. An important part of winter mountain tourism, destination success includes determinants of location, accessibility, appealing product and service offering, excellence of visitor experiences and community support. The chapter provides a comparison of three case studies of three significant winter mountain resorts within Finland (namely, Levi, Ruka and Ylläs) describing a number of details of relevance to these determinants and to the collaboration and destination leadership of each resort in its past, present and future development success.

24.2.12 Chapter 36. Winter Tourism: Lost in Transition? The Process of Transformation and Inertia of the Ski Industry and Places in the French Alps

Author: Philippe Bourdeau

A second chapter of relevance to winter tourism in the Alps provides insight into the challenges that ski resort development faces moving forward and the potential clashes between the current industry emphasis on uphill winter ski and snowboard activities and its vulnerabilities in continuing to prioritize traditional approaches toward economic and enterprise development. The author, Philippe Bourdeau, suggests that 'the industry has been heavily criticized for an excessive standardization of what is on offer, as well as a chronic inability to adapt itself to evolving demands'. In addition, through a critical lens the author provides arguments about the significant challenges ahead if the ski resort industry in the Alps in particular, does not become far more aware of the threats to its long-term success while committing to holistic, innovative, adaptive and integrated approaches in dealing with the future.

The author suggests a transformative process within mountain tourism environments in reorienting activity, spaces, facilities, frameworks and priorities towards a much more diverse multi-seasonal, multi-activity and multi-experience model. This model strongly advocates for the future that living and working in the Alps may include aspects of 'four seasons' (winter, spring, summer, autumn), of 'four spaces' (resorts, villages, high mountain, market town centres), of 'four activities' (agriculture, crafts services, recreation, new information and communication technologies) and of 'four economies' (production, public, residential, social). This is perhaps best looked at as a transformative process in building frameworks for true sustainability in planning, development, engagement and involvement, and in doing so through the lens of a multitude of stakeholders including enterprises, communities and governments with a priority for building engaged and fruitful experiences and lifestyles of those affected over the long term.

References

Auyong, J. (1995) Tourism and conservation. In: Hotta, K. and Dutton, I. (eds) *Coastal Management in the Asia-Pacific Region: Issues and Approaches*. Japan International Marine Science and Technology Federation, Tokyo, Japan, pp. 95–116.

Ayman, I. and Husam, K. (2010) Whole life sustainability in the design of tourist resorts: a coastal alteration prediction model (CAP) using GIS and statistical tools. *Management of Environmental Quality: An International Journal* 21(1), 108–121.

Blank, U. (1989) *The Community Tourism Industry Imperative: The Necessity, the Opportunities, Its Potential*. Venture, State College, Pennsylvania.

Dowling, R.K. (1993) An environmentally-based planning model for regional tourism development. *Journal of Sustainable Tourism* 1(1), 17–37.

Edgell, D., Allen, M., Smith, G. and Swanson, J. (2008) *Tourism Policy and Planning: Yesterday, Today and Tomorrow*. Butterworth-Heinemann, Oxford, UK.

George, E.W., Mair, H. and Reid, D. (2009) *Rural Tourism Development: Localism and Cultural Change*. Channel View, Bristol, UK.

Gunn, C. and Var, T. (2002) *Tourism Planning: Basics, Concepts, Cases*. Routledge, London.

Hall, C.M. (2008) *Tourism Planning: Policies, Processes and Relationships*. Pearson/Prentice Hall, London.

Hall, D. and Richards, G. (2003) *Tourism and Sustainable Community Development*. Routledge, London.

Hellmeister, A. and Richins, H. (2018) Green to gold: beneficial impacts of sustainability certification and practice on tour enterprise performance. *Sustainability* 11(3), 709/1–17. DOI:10.3390/su11030709

Hull, J. and Richins, H. (2016a) Development, planning and governance in mountain tourism: overview, contextual development and areas of focus. In: Richins, H. and Hull, J.S. (eds) *Mountain Tourism: Experiences, Communities, Environments and Sustainable Futures*. CAB International, Wallingford, UK, pp. 290–298.

Hull, J.S. and Richins, H. (2016b) Mountain tourism: implications and sustainable futures. In: Richins, H. and Hull, J.S. (eds) *Mountain Tourism: Experiences, Communities, Environments and Sustainable Futures*. CAB International, Wallingford, UK, pp. 363–369.

Inskeep, E. (1991) *Tourism Planning: An Integrated and Sustainable Development Approach*. Van Nostrand Reinhold, New York, New York.

Kruk, E., Hummel, J. and Banskota, K. (2007) *Facilitating Sustainable Mountain Tourism, Volume 1. Resource Book*. ICIMOD, Kathmandu, Nepal.

Laws, E., Richins, H., Agrusa, J. and Scott, N. (2011) *Tourist Destination Governance: Practice, Theory and Issues*. CAB International, Wallingford, UK.

Marien, M. (1992) Environmental problems and sustainable futures: major literature from WCED to UNCED. *Futures* 248, 731–757.

Musa, G., Higham, J. and Thompson-Carr, A. (2015) *Mountaineering Tourism*. Routledge, London.

Nepal, S. and Chipeniuk, R. (2005) Mountain tourism: towards a conceptual framework. *Tourism Geographies* 7(3), 313–333.

Neto, F. (2003) A new approach to sustainable tourism development: moving beyond environmental protection. *Natural Resources Forum* 27(3), 212–222.

Richins, H. (2009) Environment, development and sustainability – a multidisciplinary approach to the theory and practice of sustainable development. *Environment, Development and Sustainability* 11(4), 271–282.

Richins, H. (2011) Issues and pressures on achieving effective community destination governance: a typology. In: Laws, E., Richins, H., Agrusa, J. and Scott, N. (eds) *Tourist Destination Governance: Practice, Theory and Issues*. CAB International, Wallingford, UK, pp. 51–65.

Richins, H. and Hull, J.S. (2016) *Mountain Tourism: Experiences, Communities, Environments and Sustainable Futures*. CAB International, Wallingford, UK.

Richins, H., Agrusa, J., Scott, N. and Laws, E. (2011) Tourist destination governance approaches and solutions: structural change, community engagement, networks and collaborations. In: Laws, E., Richins, H., Agrusa, J. and Scott, N. (eds) *Tourist Destination Governance: Practice, Theory and Issues*. CAB International, Wallingford, UK, pp. 137–143.

Schmidt, J., Werner, C. and Richins, H. (2016) Mountain tourism in Germany: challenges and opportunities in addressing seasonality at Garmisch-Partenkirchen. In: Richins, H. and Hull, J.S. (eds) *Mountain Tourism: Experiences, Communities, Environments and Sustainable Futures*. CAB International, Wallingford, UK, pp. 255–269.

Singh, S., Timothy, D. and Dowling, R. (2003) *Tourism in Destination Communities*. CAB International, Wallingford, UK.

UN (n.d.) About the Sustainable Development Goals. Available at: https://www.un.org/sustainabledevelopment/sustainable-development-goals/ (accessed 31 January 2019).

UNWTO (2015) Tourism and the Sustainable Development Goals. Available at: http://cf.cdn.unwto.org/sites/all/files/pdf/sustainable_development_goals_brochure.pdf (accessed 31 January 2019).

van Fossen, A. and Lafferty, G. (2001) Contrasting models of land use regulation: community, government and tourism development. *Community Development* 36(3), 198–211.

Weed, M. and Bull, C. (2004) *Sports Tourism: Participants, Policy and Providers*. Elsevier, Oxford, UK.

Wray, M., Dredge, D., Cox, C., Buultjens, J., Hollick, M. *et al.* (2010) Sustainable regional tourism destinations: best practice for the sustainable management, development and marketing of regional tourism destinations. STCRC, Gold Coast, Australia.

25 Development of Downhill Skiing Tourism in Sweden: Past, Present, and Future

O. CENK DEMIROGLU*, LINDA LUNDMARK AND MAGNUS STRÖMGREN

Department of Geography, Umeå University, Umeå, Sweden

25.1 Introduction

Skiing is an activity that has evolved throughout millennia since the prehistoric and the ancient times. Its cradle is asserted as northern Eurasia, extending from Japan to Scandinavia (Edlund and Yttergren, 2016). Artefacts and petroglyphs discovered in Scandinavia and China date the history of skiing back to 10,000 years ago (Lund, 1996, 2007; Kulberg, 2007; Zhaojian and Bo, 2011). However, throughout these ages, skiing was mainly practised as a means for transport, hunting and battling, and it was only during the past two centuries that it became an object of sports, recreation and tourism. A first major step towards such change was taken in Scandinavia as the public started to get more involved with skiing as a means of sports and entertainment, and this trend stretched to the Alps and North America following an outmigration trend from Scandinavia, of especially miners, by the end of the 19th century.

During post-World War II, in line with the general boom in tourism, ski tourism grew exponentially due to rising leisure time and disposable income, improved transportation and the return of millions of soldiers trained for skiing for battling reasons. In some countries, downhill skiing tourism was seen as a critical opportunity to boost socio-economic development in the peripheral mountain regions, thus receiving strong governmental support. Starting from the 1980s onwards, the industry faced some maturity especially at the conventional destinations such as North America, the Alps and Japan. Today, ski recreation and tourism are a major industry with around 6000 ski areas that attract 400 million annual skier visits (Hudson, 2000; Hudson and Hudson, 2015; Vanat, 2018), yet still facing the challenge of market stagnation, now coupled with the ever more-felt impacts of climate change. Likewise, in Sweden, the downhill skiing industry is one of the leading outdoor recreation and tourism sectors, requiring a thorough assessment of its trends and challenges embedded in the past and anticipated for the future.

This chapter is organized into two main sections. First, it highlights the major milestones in the development of downhill skiing tourism in Sweden from a supply perspective. Then an outlook on the future of the industry is portrayed with a special focus on major issues such as the changing markets and climates.

---

* E-mail: cenk.demiroglu@umu.se

25.2 The Past

As with the history of skiing in many other lands, the development of ski tourism in Sweden occurred in two distinct phases: the prehistoric and ancient times, and the period of industrialization – or, the 'utility period' and the 'sports period', as alternatively referred to by Edlund and Yttergren (2016).

25.2.1 Prehistoric and ancient times

Skiing in Sweden and its Nordic neighbours is at least as old as the region's indigenous people, the Sámi. These semi-nomadic people have for many millennia lived in the northern parts of Norway, Sweden and Finland and north-west Russia, all of which are characterized as regions with long and snowy winters. The Sámi have utilized skiing as a natural mode of transport for travelling, hunting and herding reasons. Ski artefacts found in Kalvträsk (see Fig. 25.1) in northern Sweden have been dated back to 3200 BC of the Neolithic Age. Likewise, rock carvings of skiers discovered in Alta, Rødøy and Bøla in Norway have dates as old as 3000 to 6000 years (Kulberg, 2007). Later, skiing has been adopted also by other peoples of the region, as evident on a

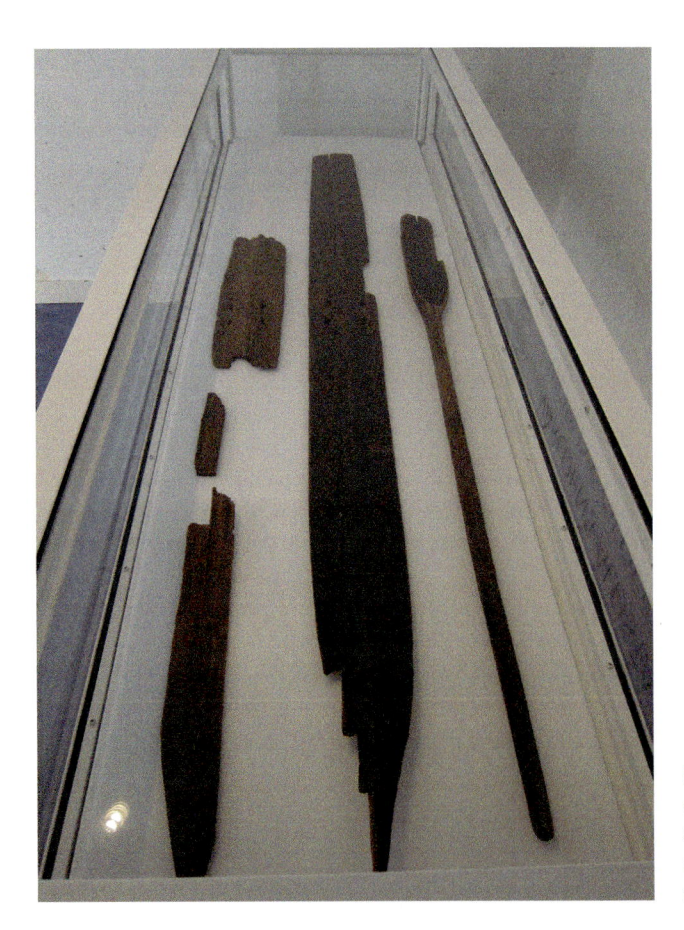

Fig. 25.1. The 5200-year-old 'Kalvträsk ski' exhibited at Västerbottens Museum (© Moralist, 2017; licensed under CC-BY-SA-3.0.)

Viking Age rune stone, found in Böksta and dating back to the 11th century AD. On the bottom left of the stone (see Fig. 25.2) one can observe the depiction of an archer on skis, who is considered to symbolize Ullr – a god in the Norse mythology. The mythological eddas identify the troll-goddess Skaði also with skiing, implying that skiing had also become a status symbol, besides a utility tool, within the Scandinavian cultures by the turn of the millennium. This soon was reflected into aristocracy with the royalty getting involved in skiing, which had then become an essential mode of battling and communications, and partly a competition sport, for many centuries in Sweden (Martinell, 1999; Edlund and Yttergren, 2016).

25.2.2 Period of industrialization

Skiing had its global evolution into an object of mass sports, recreation and tourism during the 19th and 20th centuries. In the mid-19th century in the Telemark region of Norway, then part of a royal union with Sweden, a special type of ski binding was developed enabling more people to enjoy skiing with an increased ease of turns, brakes, jumps and ascends. Public competitions regularly took place, especially around the city of Christiania (Oslo), and skiing grew around the idrett philosophy that promotes health and training and soon became a symbol of national identity for the Norwegians, who were to declare their independence from the union in 1905 (Bø, 1992; Lund, 1996). Meanwhile in Sweden, similar competition grounds were already established at various venues in cities and towns such as Stockholm, Gävle, Sundsvall and Jokkmokk by the end of the 19th century (Martinell, 1999). However, it could be said

Fig. 25.2. Ski-god 'Ullr' depicted on Böksta rune stone from the 11th century (bottom left). (© Berig, 2007; licensed under CC-BY-SA-3.0.)

that skiing became a popular recreational sport in the beginnings of the 20th century when the Swedish Tourist Federation (Svenska Turistföreningen) and the Outdoor Association (Friluftsfrämjandet) became more involved with the development of mountain areas and skiing. The Outdoor Association initially promoted skiing through the demonstrations of the King's Guard (of the United Kingdoms of Sweden and Norway), comprising Norwegian officers trained in skiing. Demand for skiing grew rapidly, as the sport was introduced to schools through courses and competitions and many school ski trips started to be organized. Moreover, following Norway's secession from Sweden, the rising patriotism among the Swedes, who had acknowledged the lead of Norway in nature-based tourism resources and development, is claimed to have triggered the domestic demand towards their own mountains (Martinell, 1999; Nilsson, 2003; Edlund and Yttergren, 2016).

While cross-country skiing had already grown into a popular sport by the 1920s, as evident in the Vasaloppet race that has attracted thousands of skiers each year since its inauguration in 1922, downhill skiing tourism started to take the lead during the winter seasons with the establishment of the first mountain resorts such as Åre, which was already a well-known tourist destination for its mountain climate during the non-winter seasons – a transformation pattern similarly observed for the Swiss Alps during the same periods. Following World War II, increasing disposable income and leisure time, with paid vacations already ensured by the Holiday Act in 1938, and the spreading of car ownership, in addition to the already well-established rail network into the mountains, triggered the involvement of urban populations, beyond the aristocracy and the elite, in addressing their recreational needs. Installation of ski lifts from the 1940s onwards eased uphill transportation for downhill skiing, making it a common sport for a larger mass of tourists, whom Nilsson (2003, p. 34) calls the 'lift people', who 'represented a social group where collective style, inspired by the working class, was mixed with an individual elite style'. Following opening of the first ski lifts in Åre, Storlien and Björkliden, the number grew into 180 by 1965 to respond to the increasing demand of this emerging market (Nilsson 2001, 2003; Hall *et al.*, 2008; Lundkvist and Gerremo, 2017).

Starting from the 1970s, the Swedish government started to become more involved in promoting the expansion and 'resortification' of downhill skiing tourism, especially since they acknowledged more the power of this type of tourism in fostering regional development at peripheral mountain regions (Hall *et al.*, 2008), resembling what the French government had already implemented for its mountain regions through the 'Snow Plan (Le plan Neige)' since the 1960s. Potential recreational areas of top priority were identified by the Leisure Commission to be located in the mountainous regions of Dalarna, Jämtland, Västerbotten and Norbotten counties (Nilsson, 2003). The first concrete outcomes of this impetus were reflected in the increasing quantity and quality of lifts installed. Following the construction of Sweden's first aerial lift, the Åre cable car, many more aerial chair- and gondola lifts were built throughout the Swedish mountains during the 1980s and the 1990s. The total number of lifts increased from 347 in 1974 to 684 in 1982 and further to 906 in 1986, reaching a peak of 1050 in 1992, and thereafter entering a decline trend down to 800s by the turn of the century (Lundkvist and Gerremo, 2017). Nonetheless, the share of the Swedish population that had made a visit to the mountain regions once during the periods 1980–1984 compared to 1995–2000 rose from 73% to 84%. A major increase occurred for Dalarna (22% to 34%) while the other popular county, Jämtland, had a small increase from 30% to 32% and the remaining two mountainous counties, Västerbotten and Norbotten, registered slight declines from 10% to 7% and 11% to 10%, respectively. Moreover, the major activity during those visits had become downhill skiing, with 36%, compared with the 22% in 1984, of the visitors being engaged, followed by hiking, with its share remaining at 32%, cross-country/backcountry skiing, with a slight decrease from 25% to 24%, and snowmobiling, with a major increase from 9% to 16% (Fredman and Heberlein, 2003; see also Fredman and Chekalina, Chapter 16 in this book).

During the last decade of the 20th century, major labour, amenity and lifestyle migration to ski destinations in the Swedish mountains have also been observed. Ski tourism development has not only provided jobs for the locals but also attracted labour inflows of especially young populations; thus acting as a partial remedy to the rural decline faced within the region due to a shift away from the once labour-intensive primary sectors. However, then it could be argued that new nodes of socio-economic density have been created in the rural landscapes by ski resorts (Lundmark, 2005, 2006; Müller, 2006; Hall *et al.*, 2008). Such pattern is also evident elsewhere in the world where 'the ski industry is not only designed for the use of visiting urban populations, it also generates a process of urbanization amidst a peripheral rural context', as noted by Lasanta *et al.* (2013, p. 104) in reference to the political ecological approach of Stoddart (2012) to skiing. In most extreme cases, one could even face the so-called 'Aspen effect', where the residents and incoming labour force cannot afford housing prices anymore and are displaced by the arrival of second home owners, and consequently peak-season traffic and off-season ghost towns are created (Clifford, 2002). In the case of Sweden, ski resorts have also become a major attraction for second home development. Lundmark and Marjavaara (2005) determined a significant positive relationship between proximity to ski lifts and the number of second homes by taking account of the 29,000 second homes located in mountain municipalities in 2001. Further studies show that ski and second home tourism development in the mountains brought mainly the urban rich (Müller, 2005), and a young labour force that is attracted not really by the job opportunities themselves but the lifestyle promised by the natural and built amenities of the mountain environment (Müller, 2006).

25.3 The Present

The global ski industry in the 21st century has been characterized by major challenges such as stagnation, hyper-competition and climate change. Many conventional ski destinations of the Alps, Nordic Europe, North America and Japan have been confronted with declining skier visits, while some rapidly emerging markets such as China have helped partly restore the global figure. Such decline is attributed to the changing demographics, such as the ageing populations, as well as increasing competition from other holiday and leisure activities (Vanat, 2018; National Ski Areas Association, 2018). Climate change, on the other hand, has its impacts felt ever more on ski resorts, resulting in seasonal shrinkages and variability and the consequent adaptive measures, such as snowmaking investments, by the industry and behavioural changes, such as spatial substitution, adopted by the consumers and even edging a competitive advantage for those relatively less exposed areas (Demiroglu *et al.*, 2013; Steiger *et al.*, 2019). A major survival response from the supply side has been a focus on expansion, extension and integration of ski resorts into mega attractions, diversified for a year-round offer and ensuring a stronger marketing and bargaining power. Such trends have been coupled with the rise of oligopolistic ski corporations, who have become the major players at the destinations, forming a destination organizational structure of what Flagestad and Hope (2001) have coined as the 'corporate model' that has been spreading from North America towards Europe since the late 1980s, following a need or opportunity for consolidation of the supply side over a mature market (Harbaugh, 1997; Hudson, 2000). Similarly, in Sweden, the financial crisis of the early 1990s had also set the stage for acquisitions over the ski resorts, and a few specialized industry giants had already evolved by the turn of the century (Nilsson, 2001, 2003; Nordin, 2007; Farsari, 2018).

Ski lift ticket revenues (see Fig. 25.3), along with many other relevant statistics (see Table 25.1), are a common performance indicator recorded by the Swedish Ski Areas Industry Association (SLAO, 2009, 2010, 2011, 2012, 2013, 2014, 2015, 2016, 2017, 2018). The revenues, in constant prices and net of the VAT, have had a jump start in the development phase of the 1980s with total sales increasing by 60% from 245 million SEK in the 1983–84 season to 390 million SEK in the 1987–88, followed by a stagnation period of the late 1980s and early 1990s. After a leap in 1994, a stagnation and development cycle recurred until the season of 2007–08 where the sales hit the record amount of 1 billion SEK for the first time in the industry's history.

SLAO reports include more detailed information about the past decade of the industry (see Table 25.1). Here, a striking growth is apparent for the past 5 years, after a period of undulation. Such a trend resembles that of the global ski industry, where a

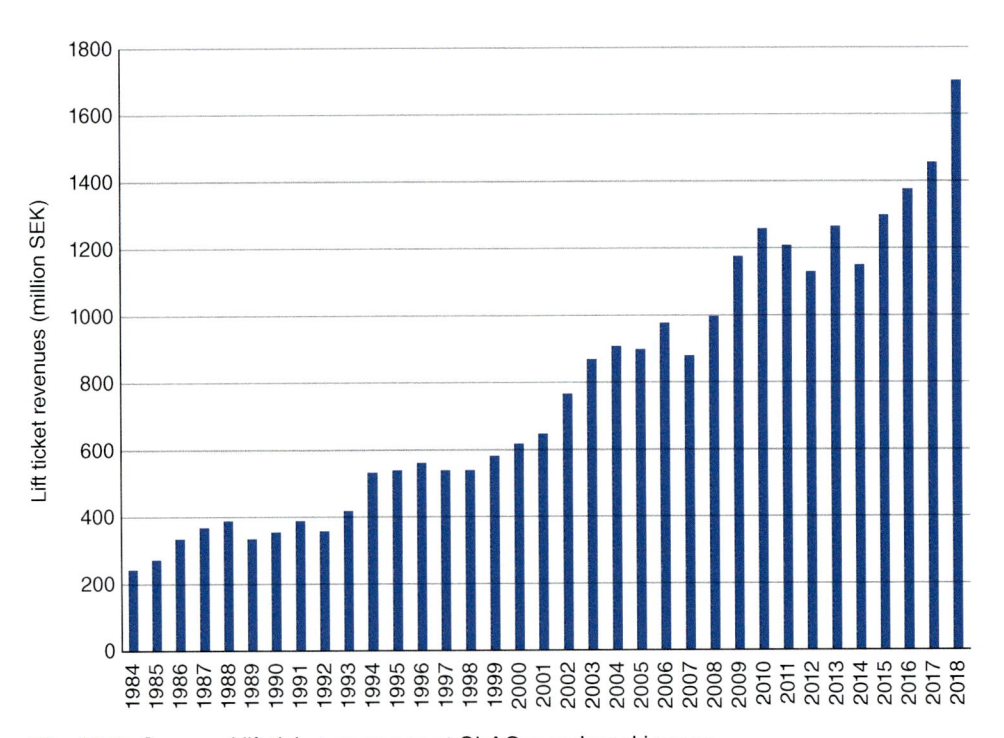

Fig. 25.3. Seasonal lift ticket revenues at SLAO member ski areas.

Table 25.1. Downhill skiing tourism indicators based on SLAO reports.

Indicator	2009	2010	2011	2012	2013	2014	2015	2016	2017	2018
1. Inventory										
1.1. Number of downhill ski areas	227	228	227	227	225	225	220	216	208	208
1.2. Number of downhill ski lifts[a]	820	820	800	800	800	800	800	840	NA	835
1.3. Ski area ownership (%)										
1.3.1. Private entity/company	33	33	38	47	49	33	33	30	33	NA
1.3.2. Municipality/foundation	29	29	31	30	34	47	47	28	25	NA
1.3.3. Association/organization/club	38	38	31	23	17	20	20	42	42	NA
1.4. Ski area operated by (%)										
1.4.1. Private entity/company	35	35	45	51	54	35	35	35	NA	NA
1.4.2. Municipality/foundation	12	12	11	14	15	19	19	12	NA	NA
1.4.3. Association/organization/club	53	53	44	35	31	46	46	53	NA	NA
2. Visitation[b]										
2.1. Skier visits (million)	NA	8.5	8.3	7.8	8.5	7.7	8.5	9.0	9.2	9.9
2.2. Skier visits at top 50 ski areas (million)	7.4	7.6	7.3	6.7	7.3	6.6	7.2	7.8	8.0	8.8
2.3. Skier visits at top 50 ski areas (%)	NA	89	88	86	86	86	85	87	87	89
3. Lift ticket revenues (million SEK)	1,180	1,260	1,212	1,132	1,267	1,152	1,300	1,380	1,460	1,704
3.1. Lift ticket price per skier visit (SEK)	NA	148	146	145	149	150	153	153	159	172
3.2. Counties (million SEK/%)										
3.2.1. Dalarna	543/46	567/45	521/43	498/44	545/43	530/46	572/44	593/43	613/42	716/42
3.2.2. Jämtland	401/34	416/33	388/32	396/35	418/33	438/38	455/35	483/35	511/35	596/35
3.2.3. Others	236/20	277/22	303/25	238/21	304/24	184/16	273/21	304/22	336/23	392/23
3.3. Top five companies/owners (million SEK/%)[c]	817/69	841/67	809/67	793/70	885/70	855/74	925/71	999/72	1,042/71	1,230/72
3.4. Top company (million SEK/%)	598/51	611/48	589/49	577/51	630/50	627/54	671/52	703/51	732/50	836/49
4. Investments										
4.1. Total investments (million SEK)	NA	NA	1,000	890	750	700	NA	644	425	275
4.2. Investments/prior season revenues (%)	N/A	N/A	79	73	66	55	N/A	50	31	19

[a]There are around 100 additional magic carpets.
[b]Updated figures from latest reports are considered.

recovery is observed following a long stagnation trend (Vanat, 2018). Moreover, from 2004 onwards, lift ticket prices have started to increase at a rate above that of the Consumer Price Index, despite the reduction in the rate of VAT from 12% to 6% since the 2006–07 season (SLAO, 2010). This increase is partly attributed to the increasing investments in snowmaking and lifts (Falk and Hagsten, 2016). Although not based on the original index set by Falk and Hagsten (2016), it could be observed that the prices are growing even more, as the lift ticket price per skier visit hit an all-time high of 172 SEK in the 2017–18 season. Investments, on the other hand, were as high as 79% of the prior season's lift ticket revenues in 2010–11. Breakdown of the investments in the past three seasons were 43%, 31% and 26% for lifts, snow management and accommodation, respectively, while 340 SEK million more investments are planned for the 2018–19 season (SLAO, 2016, 2017, 2018).

Fredman *et al.* (2012) determined the perceived value and cost of a downhill skiing trip in the Swedish mountains as 5290 SEK and 4710 SEK, respectively, yielding a net recreation value of 580 SEK per person during his/her stay in 2009 – compared with the 312 SEK surplus estimated for 1992 (Boonstra, 1993). On the other hand, ski visitation is not only limited to the tourists but also the local recreationists, spending that could be as low as one-seventh of the tourists', as in the case of the US (Fredman *et al.*, 2008, p. 46). When assessing the overall direct revenues from downhill skiing tourism and recreation in Sweden, the industry itself employs a rule of thumb that sets 1 SEK spent for a lift ticket to 10 SEK spent for the overall visits, including the expenditures on accommodation, food and beverages, equipment, etc. (SLAO, 2014, 2016). Taking account of the 2017–18 season, this approach yields a 17 billion SEK volume. Although such a figure may not constitute a significant share of the 5 trillion SEK GDP of Sweden, the spatial concentration of the industry reflects its importance in combating the socio-economic decline risk in rural and peripheral regions. A majority of the lift ticket revenues are generated in the two mountainous counties, Dalarna and Jämtland. Likewise, most of the skier visits are also paid to the ski areas within these counties (see Fig. 25.4). Also worthwhile noting, however, is the institutional accumulation of the revenue among very few players, with the top company leading the market by around 50% through its three large ski resorts and an urban ski area (see Table 25.1).

A study by Statistics Sweden (Moström and Rosenblom, 2014) determined the number of downhill skiing areas in Sweden as 370. As of 2018, SLAO figures relate to 208 ski areas. The difference between these two figures is partly due to the differences between the counting methods of the two organizations, such that two nearby facilities could be considered as one single area by one of the parties and vice versa, but also mostly because not all ski areas, especially the micro-sized ones, are members of SLAO. Therefore, 370 could be taken as a reliable count, and the total number of lifts, together with the 840 in SLAO's inventory, could be considered as around 1000, as also acknowledged by SLAO (2014, p. 18).

An attempt to map the distribution of all downhill skiing areas in Sweden in terms of their surface area (courtesy of Jerker Moström, Statistics Sweden) and the latest skier visits (SLAO, 2018) is displayed in Fig. 25.4. As a first step, the inventories of SLAO and Statistic Sweden are merged with each other, with the multiple entries created by the latter reduced down to the integrated ski resort level to conform to SLAO's registry of skier visits. As a result, 336 ski resorts and areas with a total surface area of 9471 ha, including slopes, lifts, accommodations and all relevant facilities, were

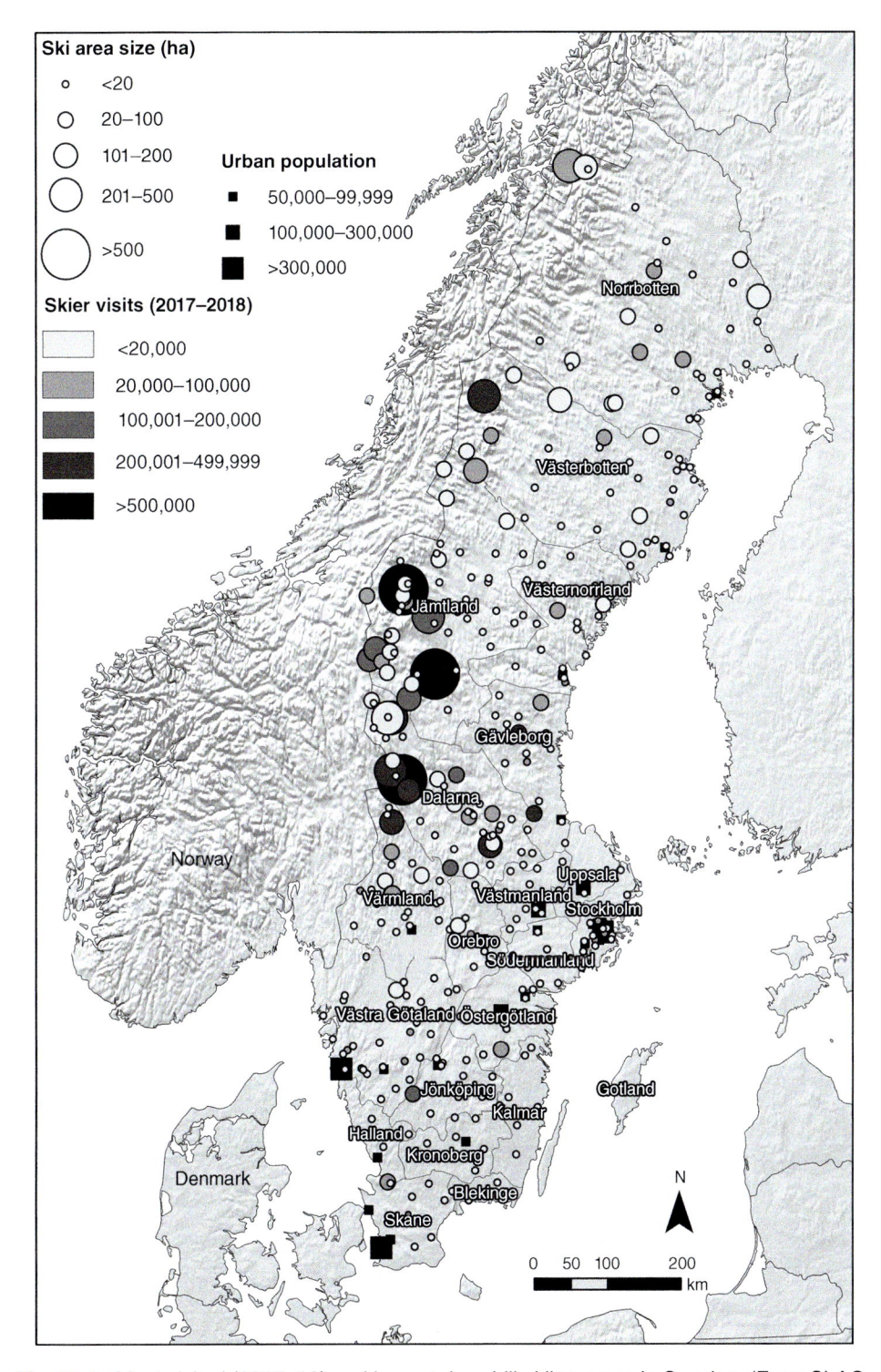

Fig. 25.4. Most visited (2017–18) and largest downhill skiing areas in Sweden. (From SLAO, 2018; courtesy of Jerker Moström, Statistics Sweden.)

determined. The agglomeration of the industry in the central inlands is in line with the changed decision of the Leisure Commission on treating proximity to densely populated areas as a main factor in prioritization of the destinations to be developed in the 1970s (Nilsson, 2003). This also partly holds true with what the sports space theory suggests as 'the natural resource base, rather than market access, will determine the locations where sport tourism takes place' (Hinch and Higham, 2004, p. 90). Therefore, it could be expected that recreational tourism will find its development spots in the peripheries as these are usually the regions rich in nature-based resources. However, the fact that the mountainous and colder, yet very sparsely populated, northern inlands of Sweden have a relatively limited skiing offer does provide a counterargument for this view, and the many micro- and small-sized establishments observed within and around the urban localities further highlight the contribution of the market proximity factor. What really is applicable to the arguments by Hinch and Higham (2004), based on Christaller (1966) and Bourdeau *et al.* (2002), on the other hand, is a hierarchy of the peripheral ski destinations over the urban ski areas, where the 'Big Three', which have attracted 37% of skier visits and half of the lift ticket revenues in 2018, form the high-order product that attracts a national, and partly international, clientele, followed by competitors that mainly cater for regional and local demand.

25.4 The Future

Whether or not the current economic success trend, at least in terms of the lift ticket sales, of the Swedish downhill skiing industry can be maintained in the future is a matter of various human and physical factors. On the human side, general demographic and ski-specific behavioural changes of the consumers (see also Fredman and Chekalina, Chapter 16), as well as investment plans on the supply side, play major roles. On the physical side, climate change imposes a direct threat on the global tourism industry, thus many destinations and businesses need to cope with this phenomenon by assessing their vulnerabilities correctly and building resilience accordingly (Steiger *et al.*, 2019).

25.4.1 Impact of socio-economic changes

As opposed to coastal mass tourism, ski tourism is mainly a domestic activity in many countries of the world (Vanat, 2018). While most European sunlust tourists need to travel to their Mediterranean neighbours or to exotic destinations such as South-east Asia and the Caribbean, ski tourists will usually find suitable places in their home countries or through convenient cross-border trips, the latter of which generate the main component of the so-called internationality of ski tourism. Moreover, generally in countries with a relative lack of snow and mountainous terrains, a snow sports culture is not well developed, hence no major international flows originating from these markets are recorded. An exception here is the British and the Dutch markets, where snow sports culture is historically strong but the natural base for developing ski tourism is limited for topographic and/or climatic reasons. Thus they, together with Germans and Russians, constitute an essential share of the incoming markets – mainly for the Alpine countries, who also have their own strong domestic bases.

In Sweden, the most recent market studies (SLAO, 2011, 2016, 2018) show that the Swedes dominate the client base by 88%, 86%, 89% and 87% of the total skiers in 2009, 2011, 2016 and 2018, respectively, while the composition of the international interest comes mostly from the neighbouring Norwegian and Danish snow sports enthusiasts. Thus, it could be concluded that currently ski tourism in Sweden is mostly domestic with some additional interest from its immediate neighbours. Therefore, future changes in the economy and the demography of the country would have major implications.

Future population changes for Sweden (see Fig. 25.5) are vital indicators of future trajectories in the domestic ski tourism market, as long as the current disposable income and leisure time levels are maintained or improved. As of 2011, 20% of the Swedish population, 1.9 million Swedes, were active visitors to Swedish ski areas and resorts. In 2018, 10% of the Swedish skiers were children aged between 0 and 7 years. This is considered as an advantage by the industry as the young skiers of today are expected to pass the torch to the next generation (SLAO, 2011, 2014, 2018). The demographic prognosis looks good with a constant increase in births, especially after 2030, and the consequent likelihood of newcomers to the ski market. Yet the competitiveness of skiing over other leisure, especially digital, activities, will remain in question, as has been the case among Generation X and Millennials in the US ski market (National Ski Areas Association, 2018), though a hybridization of mobile technologies with outdoor recreation in a way that mutually boosts the demand may also be on the rise (Svenska Camping and SLAO, 2013, p. 32). Likewise, any contribution from the future net positive immigration trend to the growth of the domestic ski market will be a matter of the origins of the immigrants and how they may be integrated into the market if they are unfamiliar with snow sports.

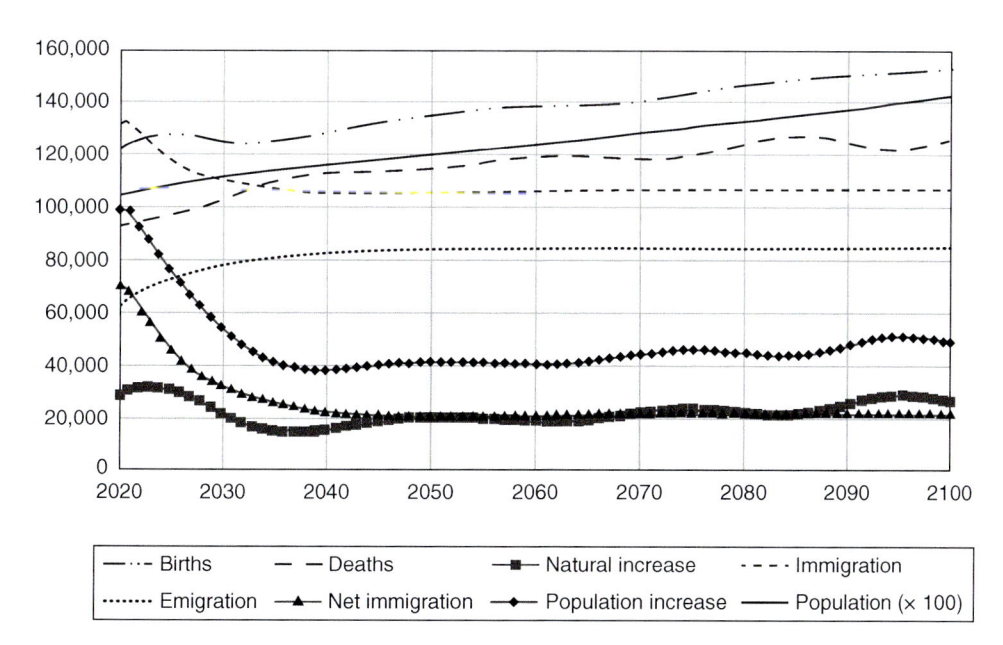

Fig. 25.5. Population projections for Sweden 2020–2100. (Data from Statistics Sweden, 2018.)

More than 5 billion SEK has been invested in Swedish ski tourism in the past decade (see Table 25.1). Despite a transfer of ski area proprietorship and management from associations, organizations and sports clubs to the private sector and then back to the non-profit organizations, via the municipalities and foundations, the influence of the corporate investors and operators is on the rise. This trend is often coupled with increased efforts for property development and sales, as evident through new and expanding resorts in the rural areas of Älvdalen, Umeå and Jokkmokk municipalities. While such projects may profit their investors and modify the regional socio-economic structure by boosting inflows of visitors, second home owners, labour and other entrepreneurs in the near future, they are also likely to fuel the debate on negative aspects of the corporate ski industry (Clifford, 2002), such as possible land use conflicts with the primary sector representatives.

In addition to the property investments, public–private initiatives on infrastructure and mega events are also worthwhile mentioning to get a better comprehension of the future of the Swedish ski industry. The two most striking developments in this respect are the Scandinavian Mountains Airport project and the Swedish Olympic Committee's recent attempt on a bid for the 2026 Winter Olympic Games. The airport, planned to open prior to the 2019–20 season, has been developed through the efforts of an industry-leading company, together with state and municipal support, and, through its location at Dalarna's Norwegian border, it is expected to ease accessibility of the area's mega resorts for the Danish and the wider British, Dutch, German and Russian markets, and provide the region with an even higher order on the Swedish ski landscape (see Fig. 25.4). Yet it also remains a paradoxical development that shall foster air travel and greenhouse gas emissions, and thereby lead to shorter ski seasons (Andersson and Ahlgren, 2017). The 2026 Olympics, on the other hand, was planned to be hosted by Stockholm and Åre, following Sweden's previous ambitious but never successful six bidding attempts from 1984 till 2002. While political and economic concerns remained over the costs and impacts of such a mega event, it could have eventually provided a major contribution to the internationalization of Swedish downhill skiing tourism, but the bid was lost to the Italian duo of Milan and Cortina d'Ampezzo.

25.4.2 Impact of climate change

The growth of downhill skiing tourism is an important input for regional development, especially in the sparsely populated rural and peripheral areas of Sweden. An early report by the Swedish government (Swedish Commission on Climate and Vulnerability, 2007) asserts that most ski areas, outside of the mountainous regions, may not be viable to operate, as their snow depths are projected to be <10 cm for more than half of the total number of days with snow cover by as early as the 2020s. The report stressed the importance of snowmaking for adaptation, yet also provided a reminder about the possible conflicts to come over the use of scarcer water resources of the future, especially in southern Sweden. Relocation to higher and north-facing altitudes was another adaptation suggestion, including even more radical ideas such as 'a structural shift of winter tourism towards areas that are more assured of having snow in the northernmost parts of the country' (p. 395). Moreover, a careful climate change impact assessment is also vital for the aforementioned Olympic bid in a future where the climatic suitability of even the once reliable previous hosts is under threat (Scott *et al.*, 2019).

The only scientific study on the impacts of climate change on Swedish downhill skiing tourism predicts an economic loss for the end of the 21 century, which is larger than the total lift ticket revenues at the time of the study (Moen and Fredman, 2007). Since this study used the snowfall variable, instead of the more relevant snow depth variable, to explain natural snow reliability (Steiger *et al.*, 2019), an alternative nationwide assessment (see Fig. 25.6) is made by the authors by mapping snow reliability indicators based on the snow cover projections available from the Swedish Meteorological and Hydrological Institute (SMHI, 2015).

The results displayed in Fig. 25.6 are based on values per catchment area, rather than ultra-high resolution grids, therefore should not be taken for granted at the ski area/resort scale, but could be used as guidelines for larger regional development decisions. Here the SMHI projections on the 'annual number of days with a minimum snow water equivalent (SWE) of 20 mm' are treated as a natural snow reliability indicator, as 20 mm of SWE roughly represents a snow depth of 50 cm, taking a snow density of 0.4 g/cm^3 as a reference for managed snow. This snow depth is considered as 'good' for downhill skiing (Witmer, 1986). The minimum number of days that meet this criterion are then further classified under various thresholds that indicate minimum viable season lengths for ski areas. Whereas the '100 days' rule is commonly applied worldwide (Abegg *et al.*, 2007), '60 days' is also sometimes utilized especially in the case of warmer and urban or peri-urban ski areas that could take advantage of denser days in terms of visitation (König, 1998). A 200-day zone is additionally examined here to identify the (potential) regions with the longest natural ski seasons. The reference period is based on the 1991–2013 average and the future projections cover the 2021–2050 and the 2069–2098 periods under a relatively business-as-usual (RCP 8.5) and a rather optimistic (RCP 4.5) scenario (van Vuuren *et al.*, 2011). Under both scenarios, major natural snow reliability issues emerge mainly around the coastal and southern parts by 2050. By the end of the century, almost all coastal ski areas, as well

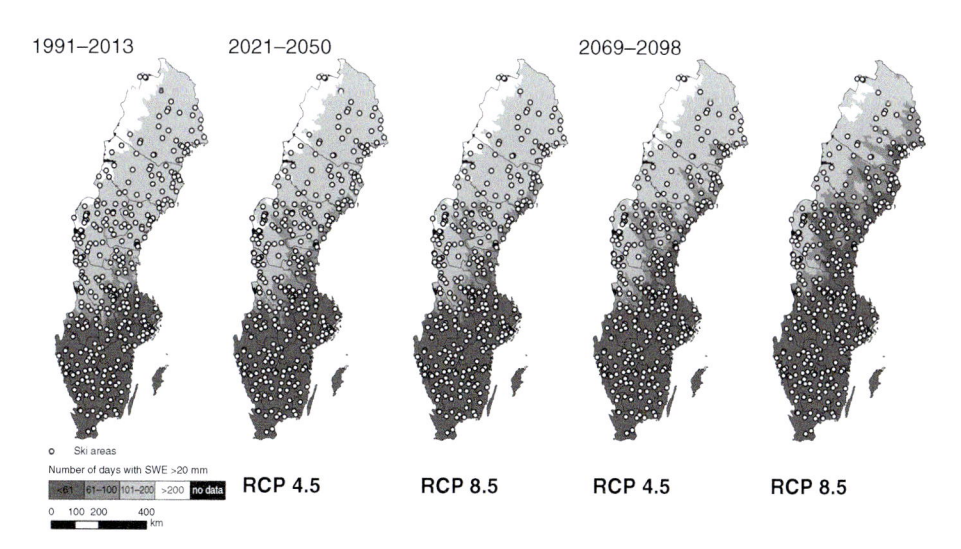

Fig. 25.6. Natural snow reliability conditions in Sweden under climate change. (Data from SMHI, 2015.)

as those in the eastern parts of Dalarna and Jämtland, enter a non-reliability zone where the number of naturally skiable days is 60 or less. Here, the most reliable regions remain in the extreme northern inlands along the Norwegian border, and especially in and around Sarek and the Kebnekaise Massif.

While the above picture casts a partial shadow on the future of Swedish downhill skiing tourism, in reality, adaptation to climate change is already in effect, and many ski areas make use of snowmaking systems for both adaptation and competition reasons. The once natural snow-dependent lift ticket sales have started to become more liberated since the late 1980s (Falk and Lin, 2018). Already by 2009, 149 of the 227 SLAO member ski areas had snowmaking systems established (SLAO, 2009). During 2016–2018, a total of 375 million SEK was invested for snowmaking and snow management, e.g. grooming (SLAO, 2016, 2017, 2018). However, contemporary snowmaking systems are also sensitive to climate change as they require cold and dry weather conditions to operate. Above a certain wet bulb temperature, snow production is not possible, and at the limits, operational costs rise. Besides, they extensively compete for the water resources, as mentioned in the governmental report above (Swedish Commission on Climate and Vulnerability, 2007). Therefore, other adaptation measures (Scott and McBoyle, 2007) should also be on the agenda.

Diversification through the introduction of year-round and non-ski products is another common adaptation method observed among the Swedish ski resorts. Investment in mountain bike trails has become a trending differentiation method in the past decade, especially because it is one of the few alternative activities that can commercially justify expensive lift investments. However, the extent of such conversion/diversification is questionable as the biker market size may not be equivalent to that of the downhill skiers. Focusing on property development, on the other hand, does secure cash inflows at an earlier stage of the deteriorating snow reliability, yet transfers the risk of any value loss to the consumers, who will mostly be second home owners.

Perhaps, one of the most interesting adaptation efforts at the policy level then is the idea of relocation to the relatively advantageous north (Swedish Commission on Climate and Vulnerability, 2007; Brouder and Lundmark, 2013). The northern inlands display superior future snow conditions and could benefit from any spatial substitution behaviour arising among ski tourists not satisfied with their favourite ski resorts in the future. In fact, some established resorts of the area have already been declared as the 'winners' (Brändström, 2008), but in order for a real structural shift to happen, other national and international resorts would need to become more exposed to climate change. The two promising regions, Sarek and Kebnekaise, on the other hand, are not as blessed by winter sunlight, due to their Arctic latitudes, as they are by snow reliability, therefore their potential needs to be assessed within a more comprehensive attractiveness index. Moreover, these places are already well-established nature-based tourism destinations valued for their preserved amenities, and a land use change for the sake of ski resort development could bring in new conflicts.

While the ski areas of the mountainous regions, particularly in the north, may seem to be more resilient to climate change, it is apparent that a major problem will arise among the southern and the coastal ski areas (Brouder and Lundmark, 2011). This should not, however, be perceived as a total advantage for the resilient resorts, as most of these micro- and small-sized areas cater for local needs of the urban populations, and are usually the first points of contact and retention venues for the development and sustainability of the ski tourism market. Therefore, a problem in the most vulnerable areas could mean a problem for the most resilient, as the latter are partly dependent on the former's performance in recruiting and maintaining a domestic skier base. Moreover, even outside these ski areas, a deterioration of the urban snow cover could reduce the so-called 'backyard effect' (Hamilton, 2007), resulting in an overall demotivation for ski trips. In the future, the industry as a whole, together with local and central governments, may need to contribute to the adaptive capacities of these vulnerable establishments, and even consider developing artificial ski areas at urban centres.

As opposed to the relatively inelastic position of ski tourism suppliers against climate change, the demand side could be highly elastic responding directly to the changing weather conditions. Moreover, some other rising trends within travel behaviour, such as climate friendliness (Demiroglu and Sahin, 2015) and hypermobility (Cohen and Gössling, 2015), could have their own effects on the Swedish downhill skiing industry. In response to the changing climate conditions, ski tourists may perform spatial or activity substitution. While the northern inlands could benefit from becoming an alternative to less snow reliable destinations, other regions in the country could lose much income due to such a spatial shift. Moreover, a study in Norway (Demiroglu *et al.*, 2018) shows that less snow reliability at designated resorts could lead the consumers to freely exploit the snowiest regions on Telemark or alpine tour skis. While such equipment provides the riders with a similar joy to downhill skiing, it liberates them from the need for lifts for uphill transport, thus putting the industry at risk of losing a significant revenue item. The rising climate friendliness, on the other hand, calls for 'staycations' that promote low-carbon, local recreation, and this is also reflected in policies favouring carbon tax on flights yet putting remote ski resorts at risk (Boström, 2017). A contrasting current is then the ever-increasing hypermobility, which may have further consequences for destination loyalty and substitution.

25.5 Conclusions

Since the use of the first skis for utility reasons millennia ago, Sweden has come a long way to the point where skiing has become a significant object of contemporary mass tourism. Following first the involvement of the state for regional development goals in the 1970s and then the rise of the corporate players in response to the financial crisis in the 1990s, today Swedish downhill skiing tourism portrays a steady growth, in contrast to many of its conventional competitors in the international market. However, as in many parts of the global ski domain, downhill skiing demand is predominantly domestic and partly regional for Sweden, and the future success depends on the recruitment of new skiers from a growing population in a fierce competition against other increasingly popular recreation and leisure activities. In this respect, comprehensive assessments on the vulnerabilities of existing ski areas are also essential in order to maintain the levels of first contact at the local bases as well as to suggest new regions to accommodate the domestic and the likely substituting international demand.

Acknowledgements

This study was supported by the Swedish Research Council for Sustainable Development, FORMAS, as part of the project Mobilising the Rural: Post-productivism and the New Economy. We thank Jerker Moström from Statistics Sweden for sharing their inventory of the downhill skiing areas in Sweden.

References

Abegg, B., Agrawala, S., Crick, F. and de Montfalcon, A. (2007) Climate change impacts and adaptation in winter tourism. In: Agrawala, S. (ed.) *Climate Change in the European Alps: Adapting Winter Tourism and Natural Hazards Management*. OECD, Paris, pp. 25–60.

Andersson, J. and Ahlgren, J. (2017) En flygplats i Sälen är ett steg mot mindre snö och kortare vintrar. Available at: https://www.freeride.se/en-flygplats-salen-ar-ett-steg-mot-mindre-sno-och-kortare-vintrar/ (accessed 17 July 2019).

Berig (2007) Böksta runestone. Available at: https://commons.wikimedia.org/wiki/File:U_855,_B%C3%B6ksta.jpg (accessed 26 August 2018).

Bø, O. (1992) *På ski gjennom historia*. Norske samlaget, Oslo, Norway.

Boonstra, F. (1993) *Valuation of Ski Recreation in Sweden: A Travel Cost Analysis*. Umeå University, Umeå, Sweden.

Boström, A. (2017) Tomma skidbackar med dyrare flyg. Available at: https://www.svensktnaringsliv.se/regioner/vasterbotten/tomma-skidbackar-med-dyrare-flyg_687063.html (accessed 12 November 2018).

Bourdeau, P., Corneloup, J. and Mao, P. (2002) Adventure sports and tourism in the French mountains: dynamics of change and challenges for sustainable development. *Current Issues in Tourism* 5(1), 22–32. DOI:10.1080/13683500208667905

Brändström, M. (2008) Skidturism tjänar på nytt klimat. Available at: https://www.svt.se/nyheter/lokalt/vasterbotten/skidturism-tjanar-pa-nytt-klimat (accessed 26 August 2018).

Brouder, P. and Lundmark, L. (2011) Climate change in northern Sweden: intra-regional perceptions of vulnerability among winter-oriented tourism businesses. *Journal of Sustainable Tourism* 19(8), 919–933. DOI:10.1080/09669582.2011.573073

Brouder, P. and Lundmark, L. (2013) A (ski) trip into the future. In: Müller, D.K., Lundmark, L. and Lemelin, R.H. (eds) *New Issues in Polar Tourism: Communities, Environments, Politics*. Springer, Dordrecht, The Netherlands, 149–161.

Christaller, W. (1966) *Central Places in Southern Germany* (translated by C.W. Baskin). Prentice-Hall, Englewood Cliffs, New Jersey.

Clifford, H. (2002) *Downhill Slide: Why the Corporate Ski Industry is Bad for Skiing, Ski Towns, and the Environment*. Sierra Club Books, San Francisco, California.

Cohen, S.A. and Gössling, S. (2015) A darker side of hypermobility. *Environment and Planning A* 47(8), 166–179. DOI:10.1177/0308518X15597124

Demiroglu, O.C. and Sahin, U. (2015) *Ski Community Activism on the Mitigation of Climate Change*. Istanbul Policy Center, Karakoy-Istanbul, Turkey.

Demiroglu, O.C., Dannevig, H. and Aall, C. (2013) The multidisciplinary literature of ski tourism and climate change. In: Kozak, M. and Kozak, N. (eds) *Tourism Research: An Interdisciplinary Perspective*. Cambridge Scholars Publishing, Newcastle upon Tyne, UK, pp. 223–237.

Demiroglu, O.C., Dannevig, H. and Aall, C. (2018) Climate change acknowledgement and responses of summer (glacier) ski tourists in Norway. *Scandinavian Journal of Hospitality and Tourism* 18(4), 418–438. DOI:10.1080/15022250.2018.1522721

Edlund L.-E. and Yttergren, L. (2016) Skiing. In: Olsson, M.-O., Backman, F., Golubev, A., Norlin, B., Ohlsson, L. *et al.* (eds) *Encyclopedia of the Barents Region: Vol. II, N-Y*. Pax Forlag, Oslo, pp. 321–324.

Falk, M. and Hagsten, E. (2016) Importance of early snowfall for Swedish ski resorts: evidence based on monthly data. *Tourism Management* 53, 61–73. DOI:10.1016/j.tourman.2015.09.002

Falk, M. and Lin, X. (2018) The declining dependence of ski lift operators on natural snow conditions. *Tourism Economics* 24(6), 662–676. DOI:10.1177/1354816618768321

Farsari, I. (2018) A structural approach to social representations of destination collaboration in Idre, Sweden. *Annals of Tourism Research* 71(1), 1–12. DOI:10.1016/j.annals.2018.02.006

Flagestad, A. and Hope, C.A. (2001) Strategic success in winter sports destinations: a sustainable value creation perspective. *Tourism Management* 22(5), 445–461. DOI:10.1016/S0261-5177(01)00010-3

Fredman, P. and Heberlein, T. (2003) Changes in skiing and snowmobiling in Swedish mountains. *Annals of Tourism Research* 30(2), 485–488. DOI:10.1016/S0160-7383(02)00110-X

Fredman, P., Boman, M., Lundmark, L. and Mattsson, L. (2008) *Friluftslivets ekonomiska värden: En översikt*. Friluftsliv i förändring, Östersund, Sweden.

Fredman, P., Boman, M., Lundmark, L. and Mattsson, L. (2012) Economic values in the Swedish nature-based recreation sector – a synthesis. *Tourism Economics* 18(4), 903–910. DOI:10.5367/te.2012.0149

Hall, C.M., Müller, D.K. and Saarinen, J. (2008) *Nordic Tourism: Issues and Cases*. Channel View Publications, Bristol, UK.

Hamilton, L.C., Brown, B.C. and Keim, B. (2007) Ski areas, weather and climate: time series models for integrated research. *International Journal of Climatology* 27(15), 2113–2124. DOI:10.1002/joc.1502

Harbaugh, J.A. (1997) Ski industry consolidation or financing 90s style? *Ski Area Management* 36(6), 51–52.

Hinch, T.D. and Higham, J.E. (2004) *Sport Tourism Development*. Channel View Publications, Clevedon, UK.

Hudson, S. (2000) *Snow Business: A Study of the International Ski Industry*. Cengage Learning EMEA, Boston, Massachusetts.

Hudson, S. and Hudson, L. (2015) *Winter Sport Tourism: Working in Winter Wonderlands*. Goodfellow Publishers, Oxford, UK.

König, U. (1998) *Tourism in a Warmer World: Implications of Climate Change due to Enhanced Greenhouse Effect for the Ski Industry in the Australian Alps*. University of Zurich, Zürich, Switzerland.

Kulberg, Ø. (2007) From rock carvings to carving skis. *Skiing Heritage* 19(2), 34–37.

Lasanta, T., Beltran, O. and Vaccaro, I. (2013) Socioeconomic and territorial impact of the ski industry in the Spanish Pyrenees: mountain development and leisure induced urbanization. *Pirineos: Journal of Mountain Ecology* 168, 103–128. DOI:10.3989/Pirineos.2013.168006

Lund, M. (1996) A short history of alpine skiing. *Skiing Heritage* 8(1), 5–19.

Lund, M. (2007) Norway: how it all started. *Skiing Heritage* 19(3), 8–13.

Lundkvist, S. and Gerremo, H. (2017) Liftens historia. Available at: http://slao.se/fakta/liftens-historia/ (accessed 17 July 2019).

Lundmark, L. (2005) Economic restructuring into tourism: the case of the Swedish mountain range. *Scandinavian Journal of Hospitality and Tourism* 5(1), 23–45. DOI:10.1080/15022250510014273

Lundmark, L. (2006) Mobility, migration and seasonal tourism employment. *Scandinavian Journal of Hospitality and Tourism* 6(1), 54–69. DOI:10.1080/15022250600866282

Lundmark, L. and Marjavaara, R. (2005) Second home localizations in the Swedish mountain range. *Tourism* 53(1), 3–16.

Martinell, V. (1999) *Skidsportens historia: Iängd 1800–1949*. V. Martinell, Järna, Sweden.

Moen, J. and Fredman, P. (2007) Effects of climate change on alpine skiing in Sweden. *Journal of Sustainable Tourism* 15(4), 418–437. DOI:10.2167/jost624.0

Moralist (2017) Kalvträskskidan at the ski museum in Umeå. Available at: https://commons.wikimedia.org/wiki/File:Skidmuseet_(02).jpg (accessed 26 August 2018).

Moström J. and Rosenblom, T. (2014) Skidbackarnas yta större än Täby. Available at: https://www.scb.se/sv_/Hitta-statistik/Artiklar/Skidbackarnas-yta-storre-an-Taby (accessed 26 August 2018).

Müller, D.K. (2005) Second home tourism in the Swedish mountain range. In: Hall, C.M. and Boyd, S. (eds) *Nature-based Tourism in Peripheral Areas: Development or Disaster?* Channel View Publications, Bristol, UK, pp. 133–148.

Müller, D.K. (2006) Amenity migration and tourism development in the Tärna mountains, Sweden. In: Moss, L. (ed.) *The Amenity Migrants: Seeking and Sustaining Mountains and their Cultures.* CAB International, Wallingford, UK, pp. 245–258.

National Ski Areas Association (2018) Model for growth. Available at: www.nsaa.org/growing-the-sport/model-for-growth (accessed 26 August 2018).

Nilsson, P.-A. (2001) Tourist destination development: the Åre Valley. *Scandinavian Journal of Hospitality and Tourism* 1(1), 54–67. DOI:10.1080/15022250127795

Nilsson, P.-A. (2003) *Åre Tourism: the Åre Valley as a Resort during the 19th and 20th Centuries.* Hammerdal Förlag, Hammerdal, Sweden.

Nordin, S. and Svensson, B. (2007) Innovative destination governance: the Swedish ski resort of Åre. *The International Journal of Entrepreneurship and Innovation* 8(1), 53–66. DOI:10.5367/000000007780007416

Scott, D. and McBoyle, G. (2007) Climate change adaptation in the ski industry. *Mitigation and Adaptation Strategies for Global Change* 12, 1411–1431.

Scott, D., Steiger, R., Rutty, M. and Fang, Y. (2019) The changing geography of the Winter Olympic and Paralympic Games in a warmer world. *Current Issues in Tourism* 22(11), 1301–1311. DOI:10.1080/13683500.2018.1436161

SLAO (2009) Skiddata Sverige 2008–2009. Available at: http://slao.se/content/uploads/2016/11/SLAOstatistik_09.pdf (accessed 26 August 2018).

SLAO (2010) Skiddata Sverige 2009–2010. Available at: http://slao.se/content/uploads/2016/11/SLAOstatistik_10.pdf (accessed 26 August 2018).

SLAO (2011) Skiddata Sverige 2010–11. Available at: http://slao.se/content/uploads/2016/11/SLAOstatistik_10.pdf (accessed 26 August 2018).

SLAO (2012) Skiddata Sverige 2011–12. Available at: http://slao.se/content/uploads/2016/11/SLAO_skiddata_2011-12_webb.pdf (accessed 26 August 2018).

SLAO (2013) Skiddata Sverige 2012–2013. Available at: http://slao.se/content/uploads/2016/11/SLAO_skiddata_2012-13_webb.pdf (accessed 26 August 2018).

SLAO (2014) 2014 Snörapporten: Svenska Skidanläggningars Brancshrapport. Available at: http://slao.se/content/uploads/2016/10/Branschrapport_2014_webb_sidor.pdf (accessed 26 August 2018).

SLAO (2015) 2014–2015 Skiddata för Vintern: Svenska Skidanläggningars Brancshrapport. Available at: http://slao.se/content/uploads/2016/10/SLAOBranschrapport2015_pages.pdf (accessed 26 August 2018).

SLAO (2016) Branschrapport 2015/2016. Available at: http://slao.se/content/uploads/2016/10/160916-Branschrapport-slutlig-2016.pdf (accessed 26 August 2018).

SLAO (2017) Branschrapport 2016 2017. Available at: http://slao.se/content/uploads/2017/07/Branschrapport-2017-l%C3%A5guppl%C3%B6st.pdf (accessed 26 August 2018).

SLAO (2018) SLAO Branschrapport 2017 2018. Available at: http://slao.se/content/uploads/2018/07/SLAO_2018_Branschrapport_klar_juli.pdf (accessed 26 August 2018).

SMHI (2015) Nerladdningstjänst för SCID. Available at: https://data.smhi.se/met/scenariodata/rcp/scid (accessed 26 August 2018).

Statistics Sweden (2018) Population changes by observations and year. Available at: www.statistikdatabasen.scb.se/pxweb/en/ssd/START__BE__BE0401__BE0401A/BefPrognosOversiktN/table/tableViewLayout1/?rxid=86abd797-7854-4564-9150-c9b06ae3ab07 (accessed 26 August 2018).

Steiger, R., Scott, D., Abegg, B., Pons, M. and Aall, C. (2019) A critical review of climate change risk for ski tourism. *Current Issues in Tourism* 22(11), 1343–1379. DOI:10.1080/13683500.2017.1410110

Stoddart, M.C.J. (2012) *Making Meaning out of Mountains: The Political Ecology of Skiing.* UBC Press, Vancouver, Canada.

Svenska Camping and SLAO (2013) Framtidens utomhusupplevelser. Available at: http://utomhusupplevelser.se/static-content/rapport2013/framtidens-utomhusupplevelser-2013.pdf (accessed 26 August 2018).

Swedish Commission on Climate and Vulnerability (2007) Sweden facing climate change – threats and opportunities. Available at: https://www.government.se/contentassets/5f22ceb87f0d433898c918c2260e51aa/sweden-facing-climate-change-preface-and-chapter-1-to-3-sou-200760 (accessed 26 August 2018).

Van Vuuren, D.P., Edmonds, J., Kainuma, M., Riahi, K., Thomson, A. *et al.* (2011) The representative concentration pathways: an overview. *Climatic Change* 109, 5–31.

Vanat, L. (2018) 2018 International report on snow and mountain tourism: overview of the key industry figures for ski resorts.

Witmer, U. (1986) *Geographica Bernensia: G25. Erfassung, Bearbeitung und Kartierung von Schneedaten in der Schweiz.* University of Bern, Bern, Switzerland.

Zhaojian, D. and Bo, W. (2011) *The Original Place of Skiing – Altay Prefecture of Xingjian, China.* People's Education Press, Beijing, China.

26 The Challenges of Sustainability in the Management of Ski Resorts: The Experience of the Dolomites

UMBERTO MARTINI[1], FEDERICA BUFFA[1]* AND SERENA LONARDI[2]

[1]*Department of Economics and Management, University of Trento, Trento, Italy;* [2]*DP Tourism and Leisure in Mountain Regions, University of Innsbruck, Innsbruck, Austria*

26.1 The Challenges Faced by Mature Skiing Areas: A Brief Overview

The Dolomite area, located in the eastern Italian Alps, has for over 50 years been one of the most important tourist areas in the alpine arc. Winter sports, and downhill skiing in particular, are some of the main tourist attractions. From the point of view of destination management, the Dolomite tourist areas are typical community destinations (Murphy, 1985; Kaspar, 1995; Bieger, 1996; Murphy and Murphy, 2004; Flagestad and Hope, 2001; Beritelli *et al.*, 2016) in that they are characterized by the presence of small and medium-sized hospitality enterprises (both hotels and other) side by side with territorial marketing organizations (regional destination management organizations – DMOs) and larger, corporate, cableway companies.

In recent years, this winter tourism model (centred on downhill skiing) has had to face not only market changes (globalization, new tourist demand trends, digitalization), but also the macro trend of sustainability, brought to particular prominence by climate change, which has affected the entire Dolomite area (Bonzanigo *et al.*, 2016).

Winter tourism in the Dolomites is at a turning point: the very practice of skiing – both as a sport and, more broadly, as a tourist product – needs to be re-evaluated. The ski sector is now mature, the boom years – a period in which skiing became a mass sport, with huge investments being made in infrastructure (lifts, slopes, programmed snow systems, etc.) and, inevitably, heavy impacts on the management of mountain territories – are over (Bausch and Unseld, 2018; Mauri and Turci, 2018).

The concept of mass skiing led to choices, which, although seen as justifiable while the sector was booming, reveal their limitations (which are also economic) when subjected to careful critical analysis. Global warming in particular is forcing the industry to reconsider its model, as snowfall decreases and retreats to ever-higher altitudes (Agrawala, 2007; Müller and Weber, 2008; Dawson and Scott, 2013; IPCC, 2015).

---

* E-mail: federica.buffa@unitn.it

Fig. 26.1. Dolomites landscape. (Photograph courtesy of Umberto Martini.)

The Dolomite area provides a typical example of the above development model, with alpine skiing becoming a pillar of the local economy, as indicated by the fact that the region's ski consortium (Dolomitisuperski) (www.dolomitisuperski.com/en) is the largest in the Alps.

The model of mass skiing, which enabled many of the Dolomite valleys to achieve very significant levels of economic and social development after World War II, is today being challenged by exogenous factors such as climate change, evolving tourist preferences and behaviours, and the general evolution of the global tourism market (Dwyer et al., 2009), all of which threaten to undermine its economic, environmental and social sustainability.

In this chapter we will discuss the pillars that have enabled the development of the Dolomite winter tourism offer, the limits of this model and the challenges that stakeholders in the sector are now facing. Our analysis is based on findings from fieldwork conducted in some of the Dolomites' main tourist destinations with key players in the winter tourism sector (the directors of the destination management organizations and ski lift companies), which aimed to discover whether – and if so, how – the concept of environmental sustainability is influencing the management of winter tourism offers.

26.2 Mass Ski in the Dolomites: The Pillars of the 'Model'

The key characteristics of the 'mass ski model' in the Dolomites that have determined its success can be summarized as follows:

1. *The quality of the lifts*: the ski resort or station is equipped with ski lifts that provide the highest appropriate hourly carrying capacity, thereby reducing queues and wait times; the old ski lifts have been replaced with more advanced, spacious cable cars that guarantee a quick and comfortable ride. The ratio between the number of skiers transported up to the slopes and the carrying capacities of the slopes themselves must be optimized in order to avoid overcrowding and its attendant risks and frustrations.
2. *Ski carousels*: the higher quality lift facilities then enable value to be added to the station through the creation of connections with other slopes and/or nearby areas, all accessible using a single ski pass. The skier can thus choose between a variety of itineraries, and a day's skiing becomes a 'journey through spaces' rather than a 'repetitive up–down activity'. The enlarging of a carousel can also provide a solution to the problem of overcrowded slopes.
3. *Programmed snow*: meteorological variability and unpredictability inevitably limit the availability of skiing as a tourist product. This problem has been solved by installing snow cannons that allow natural snow cover to be complemented by artificial, thus guaranteeing that slopes and carousels remain open. These programmed snow systems have also meant that the traditional winter tourism calendar (slopes opening at the beginning of December and closing in March) can be followed (except in exceptionally unfavourable conditions).
4. *The preparation of slopes and snow grooming*: the opening up of mass skiing to a growing number of tourists (not all of whom are proficient sportspeople), combined with the growing popularity of new equipment (such as carving skis) has led to the need to make the slopes easier, by widening them and eliminating any bumps and natural irregularities, a process that also increases the efficacy of the programmed snow

systems. The slopes thus become level strips of compact snow, and the ski industry develops equipment designed for speed and conductivity on this type of slope, where the snow is hard and the incline moderate.

5. *Innovation/novelty*: tourists' desire for novelty must constantly be satisfied: guests need to find something new each season – a new slope, a new route, a new lift, a new link, a new feature such as night skiing on floodlit slopes.

6. *Accessibility*: ski resorts must be easily and quickly reached – by private vehicle, in particular. Easy access allows 'snow commuters' – day trippers who live reasonably close to the destination – to join the resort's guests on the slopes. The road networks are prioritized, involving the building of fast roads and parking areas near the lifts (sometimes with an entry-point system, which means that the first lift functions as the entrance to the whole carousel). 'Information highways' are also vital to give potential commuters instant access to information on current weather and snow conditions on the slopes – a variety of communication channels, particularly websites and apps, serve this purpose.

7. *Safety, both active and passive*: since mass ski tourism naturally increases the number of skiers while simultaneously lowering average experience levels, certain restrictions have to be put in place, such as the regulation of access to the slopes and surrounding areas. To this end:

- a police service is being introduced onto the slopes in an increasing number of resorts/stations; their tasks are to ensure that skiers respect regulations around time and access to lifts and, sometimes, to breathalyse them (just as is done to vehicle drivers);
- off-piste skiing is forbidden, and severely sanctioned;
- areas reserved for snowboarding are being created, and, in general, an attempt is being made to manage the problems that result from the fact that traditional skis, carving skis and snowboards all involve different movements and slowing mechanisms;
- emergency and A&E services are permanently present on the slopes, and use of helicopters is increasing;
- safety regulations are being introduced, such as obligatory helmets and personal insurance against accidents, whether self-inflicted or caused by a third party.

8. *A variety of services and attractions on the slopes*: very few skiers now spend all day actually skiing, the expansion of the market means that high-altitude entertainments and on-piste bars and restaurants (offering such attractions as music, children's entertainment, a solarium) are highly valued.

9. *Coherence with the calendar of the tourist season*: although skiing is now a mass sport, it still has to follow the calendar of tourist activity upon which the tourist industry is based; this means that the season must begin at the end of November, to coincide with the World Cup races, and end either in March or at the beginning of April.

This framework has without question resulted in significant levels of economic growth, in terms of both companies' turnover and increased tourist arrivals and nights during the season. Nevertheless, as the following section will show, when the question of the model's sustainability is taken into account the situation becomes considerably more nuanced.

26.3 Innovative Ski Offers in the Dolomites: Is the 'Mass Model' Still Applicable?

The type of offer developed in the Dolomites has enabled this region to become an internationally recognized model of good practice in ski tourism. That said, it is necessary to analyse whether or not this model can be adapted to the future demands and new trends of the tourism market. The main issues that need to be investigated are, in order of importance:

1. the area's environment and climate;
2. trends in the tourism market and patterns of consumption;
3. the economic/financial sustainability of investments in infrastructure, and levels of risk;
4. analysis of the impact of the mass ski model on the local economy.

As already underlined, the Dolomites are an emblematic example of an alpine area in which these four issues represent the main challenges to be managed (Agrawala, 2007; Müller and Weber, 2008; Töglhofer *et al.*, 2011; Soboll and Dingeldey, 2012; Dawson and Scott, 2013; Duglio and Beltramo, 2016). In light of these studies, we observed that with regard to the first of these questions, analysis quickly reveals that the environmental sustainability of the mass ski model is, in some cases, seriously compromised. The issues of primary concern are the following:

1. The constant construction/enlarging of lifts and slopes has brought huge costs and opportunities in terms of environmental destruction and the degradation of landscapes, plant species threatened with extinction, disturbance to wildlife, altered microclimates – although these impacts are not immediately monetized, they represent an environmental cost, especially when their irreversibility is taken into account. Programmed snow systems, the modification of slopes and snow grooming (see Section 26.2) all involve high-impact engineering work, including at times the alteration of the landscape.
2. The anthropization of the mountain tops, which is occurring due to the increased transport capacity of the lifts and the on-piste entertainment offer, becomes an inevitable source of various forms of pollution, above all refuse, the disposal of which often appears to be a serious problem.
3. The increasing use of private vehicles and the concentration of tourism and daytrippers (from within a small or medium distance from the resort) means that heavy traffic is one of the main problems faced by tourists. This not only causes undoubted environmental damage but also growing dissatisfaction with (and at times even intolerance of) the inconveniences faced: tourists complain about both the difficulties in getting to their destination and, once there, a lack of adequate parking facilities (and the high costs in the areas where during the winter season tracts of land are turned into huge, and hugely expensive, car parks).

Increasing temperatures will – almost certainly – lead to the rising of the (natural) snowline in the near future (Beniston *et al.*, 2003; Agrawala, 2007; Gilaberte-Búrdalo *et al.*, 2014). Ski stations in the Dolomites at altitudes below 1200–1400 m are already finding it difficult to guarantee the viability of their slopes during the season, and it is predicted that within the next few years this problem will extend to stations up to 1800 m. Nor can the programmed snow systems, which themselves require certain temperature and humidity levels, be relied upon; moreover, huge quantities of (drinking) water go into the creation of snow, and the current pattern of decreasing precipitation (both in summer and winter) is leading to increasing water shortages.

Until now, the above concerns have not actually impacted negatively on the most important of the stations included in our 'model'. Trends in the tourism market, however, must also be taken into consideration (Unbehaun et al., 2008; Dawson et al., 2011; Cocolas et al., 2016). In the first place, a range of holiday choices that until very recently would have been unimaginable are available to the tourist of today. The growing costs of skiing (equipment, ski passes) and the decline that is an inevitable stage within the product's life cycle may thus combine to slow demand. Winter tourists are also skiing less and less, and increasingly demanding the availability of other activities on the snow (Skipass Panorama Turismo, 2017). The significance of these issues is further heightened when the economic aspect of the investments necessary to underpin the mass ski model is factored in. The substantial investments in the construction and maintenance of the lifts, slopes and programmed snow changed the character of the Dolomite ski stations. They no longer reflect the original tourist district model, which is marked by the flexibility inherent in a small business model. This flexibility within the industrial sector – the subject, over the years, of well-known (Italian and international) research (Boari and Lipparini, 1999; Becattini et al., 2009; van Gils and Zwart, 2009; Villa and Taurino, 2018) – can be attributed to:

- the reduced importance of the fixed cost component; and
- the direct involvement of the business owner and his/her family, which means that personal assets (capital) are available to augment those of the business itself, with frequent resource flows from one to the other, particularly at critical periods.

These factors allow businesses to operate in favourable break-even conditions, since they mean that costs can be adjusted even when there are variable (falling) demand flows. The size of the investments in infrastructure described above fundamentally changes this situation, making the offer of a ski station like that of any other 'big enterprises', which needs to be able to create a high, stable demand that allows it to deal with the economic and financial challenges that inevitably arise.

There is therefore a return to the principles of Fordism, which explain the notion of big business inflexibility, allowing us to accurately interpret the new conditions of the 'model' stations. An escalation of growth is triggered that also involves businesses in the accommodation sector (both hotels and others), who have to ensure that there is sufficient accommodation capacity to cope with the break-even requirements of the area, considered as a whole. The need to attract high tourist numbers creates, in turn, an inescapable escalation in which the new services on offer have to be aimed at ever broader market segments, or, indeed, at new emerging markets in which the Dolomite stations have to compete not only with similar offers made by other locations in the alpine arc, but also with different types of tourist destination (the sea, the big cities, lowland/hill itineraries).

These factors, moreover, give rise to a fundamental question in relation to the nature of the economic development that occurs with the mass ski model. The tourist areas of the Dolomites have always been guided by the spirit of endogenous development, with the local population being closely involved in tourism. The capital necessary for mass skiing, and the implications of this need for management and marketing, risk distorting the endogenous development model, and opening the door to a new, capitalist, logic that 'thinks big'. This would very probably lead to a change in how the added value generated by tourism is divided between the various local actors: the constant tendency towards growth within each sector can, in fact, lead to a change in the financial structure of the businesses that, in the medium term, can even lead to local firms moving out of the hands of local business people. The local economy would suffer serious damage, since the added value (although it would of course be created) would flow out and away, relegating local actors (who would not benefit from the proceeds of the station's activities) to the status of subordinate tools, with no say in the management of either the territory or its offer. The deployment of substantial public funds for local development, moreover, loses its meaning within such a context, with all the consequences this may have for levels of wellbeing and quality of life.

In conclusion, the mass ski model, which, it must be remembered, has allowed many of the Dolomite resorts and valleys to enjoy very significant economic and social development ever since the post-war period, is today challenged by exogenous factors such as climate change, evolving tourist preferences and behaviours and, more generally, the transformation of the global tourism market, which threatens to undermine its sustainability:

1. Economic: rising costs driven by required investment in both technology and marketing – now absolutely vital to give destinations international visibility.
2. Environmental: due to growing anthropization, environmental stress, the modification of landscapes, problems of water scarcity and use.
3. Social: residents risk losing control of businesses and capital, although previously they were always leaders in the tourist offer. The steady distancing of the new generation from their families' traditional activities is also an issue.

Within this framework, our research focuses on the issue of environmental sustainability, which is one of the most urgent challenges to be faced in order to ensure the survival of the model itself and, indeed, that of the communities of the Dolomite valleys, whose very existence – high in the mountains; far from the cities of the plains, the nerve centres of contemporary development – is predicated upon its continued success.

26.4 Innovative Ski Offers and Environmental Sustainability: The Dolomites' 'New' Approach

26.4.1 Research methodology

Our research focuses on the Dolomite area of Trentino (one of the three Italian regions included in the Dolomite area) and covers four key ski destinations (Val Rendena – Madonna di Campiglio, Val di Sole, Val di Fiemme, Val di Fassa). The choice of these areas was based on their historical and continuing importance for the development of the Dolomite winter offer, and, indeed, of the entire region, both in terms of demand flow and due to the size of the accommodation sector and the scale of their winter sport infrastructure. The information below gives a picture of the four destinations (ISPAT, 2016, 2017):

- In the winter season, these areas registered over seven million presences, more than 60 % of the total nights registered in Trentino.

- There are 660 hotels, with ~43,000 beds (just under half of all beds in Trentino).
- There are more than 32,000 non-hotel structures (including second homes), corresponding to ~167,000 beds.
- The ski areas are served by 143 lifts, capable of carrying a total of more than quarter of a million people an hour.
- In 2016 the lifts carried more than 56.4 million people (about 75% of all ski lift users in Trentino that year).

In the light of the importance that these Dolomite ski destinations attach to the development of their ski offer, our research investigates whether and to what extent the innovations – which these destinations have to make to remain competitive – are informed by, and address, issues of environmental sustainability. We conducted in depth personal interviews with two key groups of decision makers in the ski stations – the directors of the DMOs and representatives of the ski lift companies. We drew up a list of the sustainable business practices and behaviours engaged in by operators in the four areas, and analysed how aware of, and concerned by, environmental issues these key players are. This allowed us to ascertain the management choices made by the most influential and powerful actors involved in the definition of the areas' winter offers.

After a discussion of the main innovations in the ski offers of the past 5 years and the most important changes that have occurred in the winter tourism market, the semi-structured questionnaire used to interview the key players focused on six main areas:

1. *The satisfaction of new demand requirements for sustainable tourism offers and the existence of new forms shaped by the innovation of the offer*: particular attention was paid to identifying the profile of the current Dolomite winter tourists, examining whether, and to what extent, it explains the new demand trends – greater interest in winter sports other than downhill skiing and more awareness of environmental issues and landscape conservation.

2. *Climate change and the problem of snow reliability*: we considered the capacity of the ski areas to guarantee snow cover on the slopes throughout the winter season, revealing the extent to which investment has been focused on programmed snow systems.

3. *Water management and the problems of competing claims for water resources*: two topics are investigated – water availability in the ski areas and the analysis of water supplies for the production of artificial snow.

4. *Energy conservation and good environmental management practices (EMPs)*: we looked at the energy sources (traditional vs renewable) used to power the lifts and the snow grooming equipment, and at waste management policies.

5. *Alternative mobility*: given the serious traffic problems faced by the Dolomite areas, particularly during the winter season, we examined the (current and future) services available, and the availability and use of mobility cards, which allow tourists to reach the ski stations by public transport.

6. *Territorial and landscape management, natural and cultural resource management, and the integration of these into the traditional tourist product (which revolved almost entirely around skiing)*: the choices being made around the management of natural

resources and their valorization were key to our dialogue with the interviewees as we identified current challenges and opportunities for the development of the areas' ski offers and collaboration with local stakeholders.

The main findings from the interviews (held in the spring of 2018) with the key players in the Dolomite ski areas are presented in the next section.

26.4.2 Research findings

The ski areas' key players demonstrate a keen interest in the acquisition and modernizing of the most advanced programmed snow systems that enable the prompt, efficient creation and maintenance of artificial snow. It seems clear that the focus of the winter stations continues to be research into innovation of the offer in order to guarantee optimal conditions for tourist experiences on the snow.

Although the issue of sustainability is recognized, and acknowledged to be important, it still seems to be considered secondary to that of developing winter holiday offers that can generate the 'wow factor' expected by those tourists in search of 'Entertainment & Excitement'. Our main findings in support of this conclusion are summarized in Table 26.1 and are described below.

Table 26.1. Main research findings.

Focus	Results
New demand trends	Skiing is still the main pull factor. New emerging trends concern: quality of food, guided walks, bob sledding, wellness areas in hotels, *après ski*, increasing of the environmental awareness
Climate change and snow reliability	Awareness of declining snowfalls as a result of climate change. Investments in access to and/or management of water resources
Water management and competing claims for water resources	Concern about immediate availability of large quantities of water and subsequent creation of water reservoirs
	Sustainability: water used to produce artificial snow is seen as a 'loan'. Water reservoirs can prevent possible environmental problems
Good environmental management practices (EMPs)	New-generation machines that guarantee optimal performance and therefore are less polluting
	Waste management according to the norms
	Little use of alternative energy sources or hybrid snow grooming vehicles due to unfavourable conditions in the mountains
Alternative mobility	Numerous internal mobility services and private shuttle buses
	Ski-chauffeur services in some destinations, in order to obviate inefficiencies caused by the underuse of shuttle buses
Territorial management	Tendency to minimize the impact of the ski industry, even though everyone agrees the landscape of the Dolomites must be protected and respected
	Limitations accepted as an opportunity to invest in the quality of the offer

The satisfaction of new demand requirements for sustainable tourism offers and the existence of new forms shaped by the innovation of the offer

The main reason why tourists decide to holiday in the Dolomites is still to go skiing, although visitors are spending decreasing amounts of time actually on the slopes. Other activities and sports are of interest, but to a lesser extent than skiing.

With regard to the customer base, the search for alternative activities is more evident among the Italian target market, where the youngest segment appears to be disaffected with skiing. The foreign market (particularly tourists from Poland) is, in contrast, still very focused on downhill skiing, and spends the greater part of the day on the slopes. Foreign tourists are paying greater attention to the quality and provenance of the food they consume while on holiday, and prefer to eat Italian cuisine. This trend has encouraged investment in the Dolomite areas in the refurbishment of high-altitude restaurants and refuges, where gastronomy has become an added value in relation to other destinations.

New trends are also emerging with regard to the seasons and the ski destinations. In high season, Italian tourists are in the majority and there is a great demand for *après ski*/off-piste entertainment and activities, especially in the ski areas, which, in recent years, have launched plans to differentiate their winter offer by introducing alternatives to complement traditional downhill skiing – guided walks, with or without snow shoes; bob sledding on purpose-built slopes; wellness areas in hotels; and *après ski* in the refuges and bars, both near the slopes and in the valleys.

The environmental awareness of the target markets has increased (particularly among tourists who come in the summer season). This awareness is most acute among tourists from northern Europe (Holland, Germany, Scandinavia), as demonstrated by, for example, their more frequent use of ski buses and public transport in general. Tourists from Eastern Europe are the least concerned with environmental issues.

Climate change and the problem of snow reliability

Key players see declining snowfalls as the most obvious, and most challenging, result of climate change. Considerable investments have been made in programmed snow systems, in an attempt to adapt to, and overcome, inadequate snow cover. Access to and/or the management of water resources is the crucial factor in this regard, and the purchase of the machines and equipment required is a critical issue. The implications for water management and energy conservation lie at the centre of this issue.

Water management and the problems of competing claims for water resources

The availability of water for the production of artificial snow has not to date been perceived as a problem by operators in the sector; their main concern is the immediate availability of large quantities of stored and ready-to-use water. During the ski season (December–March), the ideal climatic conditions for the production of artificial snow occur surprisingly rarely. When they do, instant action is vital. Ski areas have therefore created water reservoirs that allow them to produce snow only when this can most effectively be done. This achieves two important goals: (i) the capacity to produce snow as soon as conditions allow, and (ii) reduced energy consumption, since the snow is only being created when climatic conditions are optimal.

Our research reveals that the operators are unanimously agreed that this technique is sustainable in terms of water use and conservation. The water taken from the reservoirs in winter returns to the aquifers when the snow melts in spring. Water use is thus seen as a 'loan', which in no way deprives the ski area of its water resources. The creation of the reservoirs is seen as having a positive environmental impact since they capture the – occasionally excessive – precipitation, thereby preventing possible environmental problems.

Energy conservation and good EMPs

There is little use of alternative energy sources in the ski areas. No station, in fact, produces its own energy, although many of them buy electricity from companies that draw upon green energy. Most of the key players are sceptical about the possibility of using alternative/renewable energy sources because conditions in the mountains are not considered to be favourable, and the use of electric or hybrid snow grooming vehicles is viewed with equal scepticism. The key players who are aware of these possibilities feel that, currently, such vehicles cannot be relied upon given the extreme winter temperatures at high altitude, which result in inadequate battery performance. The use of snow grooming vehicles also highlights the question of energy conservation. Large amounts of money have gone into the purchase and renewal of machinery and equipment because the ski areas are looking for new-generation vehicles which can guarantee optimal performance. Although the purchase of these vehicles is prompted by a search for such optimal performance, it nevertheless transpires that positive results are also gained in terms of emissions, since the new vehicles are less polluting than their predecessors.

The key players confirm that waste (whether ordinary or hazardous) management is an established practice in the ski stations and is implemented in accordance with the tight norms put in place by the local authorities. The ski areas use certified companies for the disposal of their waste.

Alternative mobility

The destinations have numerous internal mobility services. All the ski areas have policies in place to discourage the use of private vehicles; there are ski bus services to the slopes and a coordinated public transport service (tourists can purchase a mobility card). Some accommodation structures provide private shuttle buses that bring tourists from their hotel to the ski lifts. Although this service helps to discourage tourists from using their own cars, it often has limitations since, if not well managed, underuse of the service can lead to increased traffic and consequent CO_2 emissions. To obviate such inefficiencies, some ski areas have introduced ski-chauffeur services (a sort of 'on call' taxi), which only operate when actually requested.

Territorial and landscape management, natural and cultural resource management, and the integration of these into the traditional tourist product (which revolved almost entirely around skiing)

The landscape and environment of the Dolomites is confirmed as the most important pull factor in tourists' choice of its ski areas. The key players thus agree that these must be respected and protected as an integral part of their ski offer. Nevertheless, some operators are reluctant to accept restrictions on the use of the territory. In fact, while on the one hand our interviewees demonstrated interest in the conservation of natural resources and in the issues linked to environmental sustainability, on the other, they tended to minimize the environmental impact of the ski season and to view environmental protection as an obstacle to the development of the winter offer (particularly with regard to the extension of the areas where skiing is permitted). The presence of ski lifts is associated with greater security and environmental protection: where they exist, it is claimed, the local area is more attentively monitored and potential hydrogeological instability can be prevented.

On the other hand, some key players view strict urban planning instruments as a development opportunity for the destination, which should be investing in the content and quality of the offer (encouraging integration and collaboration between the various territorial actors), rather than focusing exclusively on the possible expansion of slopes and lifts.

26.5 Conclusions

Our research reveals the significant interest evinced by key players in the Dolomite ski areas in discovering ways to innovate their winter tourist offers. They are particularly keen to be able to guarantee optimal conditions for downhill skiing and are attempting to do so by investing heavily in programmed snow systems, both for the *production* of snow and its *management* on the slopes. There is also a growing interest in the introduction of innovative offers that diversify the winter sports experience and create opportunities for *après ski* entertainment.

The key players are, of course, aware of the issue of environmental sustainability, but do not prioritize it in their decision making when defining and organizing their winter offers. Local government restrictions on the use of natural resources are still not generally seen as necessary conditions for the preservation of the territory. The creation of new slopes is still seen – in some areas – as the most effective way to satisfy the target markets, and the risks linked to the development of an *unsustainable mass tourism* model (Weaver, 2000) are still not recognized. This attitude has very possibly been influenced by the key players' perception of winter tourists as being more interested in their skiing experience, the efficiency of the lifts, the quality of the entertainment offered, etc. than in the sustainability of their chosen holiday. Alternative mobility strategies, however, are being successfully adopted in many of the ski areas. Although driven by the need to make the ski stations more accessible (rather than by a desire to adopt any particular EMP), the ski areas have invested heavily in public transport services and the development of alternatives to the use of private vehicles.

Overall, our research has identified some signs that the ski areas are paying attention to the question of environmental sustainability, but this dimension is still peripheral when operators are designing their offers. The operators do not yet seem willing

Research question	• Is environmental sustainability influencing the management of winter tourism in the Dolomites?
Priority of key players	• Innovation in the 'snow system' to guarantee the 'wow effect'.
Main risk of the current 'mass model'	• Development of an unsustainable mass tourism model as described by Weaver (2000).
Main risk for winter tourism management	• Marketing myopia.
Main areas actually addressed by environmentally sustainable strategy	• Alternative mobility • Waste management • Territorial management

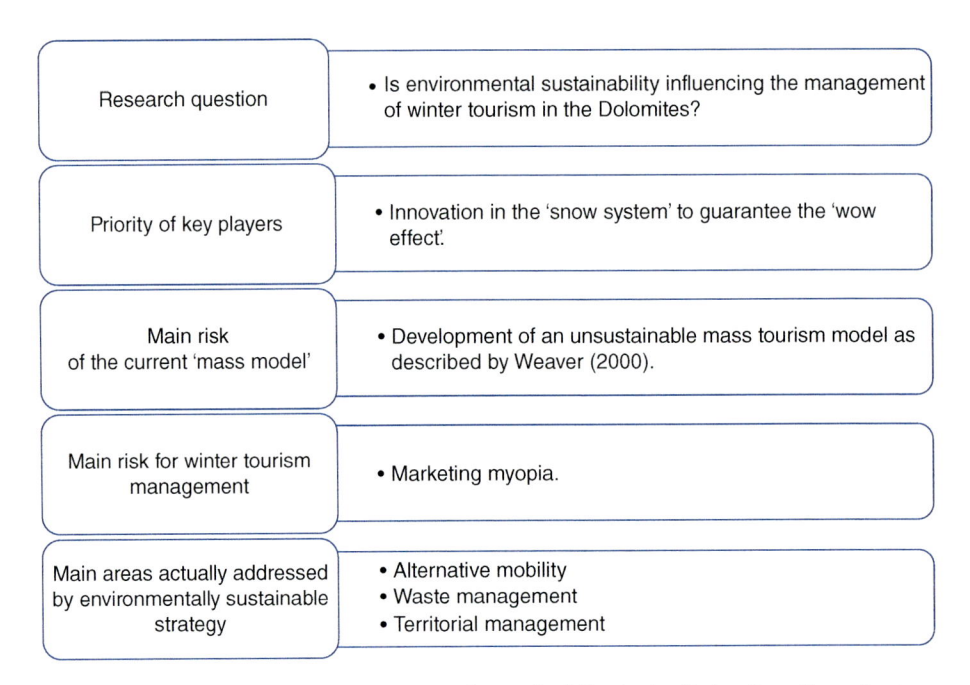

Fig. 26.2. Winter tourism and environmental sustainability in the Dolomites: the actual scenario.

to change the mass ski model that has traditionally served them so well, and propelled the Dolomites into the international winter sports market.

From a managerial perspective, the choices of the key players can be viewed as an example of marketing myopia, which is leading them to favour mass demand in their offer development strategies and to ignore the new trends driven by a growing variety of market segments (see Fig. 26.2). Although still limited, the signs emerging seem to indicate a growing trend. There is, in fact, no doubt that the number of winter tourists who spend less – or even no – time on the slopes (*slons* tourists – snow lovers not skiers) is increasing, as is the awareness of the issue of environmental sustainability among the summer visitors to the Dolomites (this increased awareness is recognized by operators). It is to be hoped that these factors will cause operators to question the viability of the mass ski model, at least in the medium to long term. Inevitably, the choices made with regard to the exploitation of natural resources (land, water) and the building of infrastructure in the definition of a resort's winter offer will impact on the landscape and environment, which are the key *pull factors* for the tourists who choose to holiday in the Dolomites.

References

Agrawala, S. (2007) *Climate Change in the European Alps*. OECD, Paris, France.
Bausch, T. and Unseld, C. (2018) Winter tourism in Germany is much more than skiing! Consumer motives and implications to Alpine destination marketing. *Journal of Vacation Marketing* 24(3), 203–217. DOI:10.1177/1356766717691806

Becattini, G., Bellandi, M. and De Propris, L. (2009) *A Handbook of Industrial Districts*. Edward Elgar Publishing, Cheltenham, UK.

Beniston, M., Keller, F., Koffi, B. and Goyette, S. (2003) Estimates of snow accumulation and volume in the Swiss Alps under changing climatic conditions. *Theoretical and Applied Climatology* 76(3–4), 125–140. DOI:10.1007/s00704-003-0016-5

Beritelli, P., Buffa, F. and Martini, U. (2016) Logics and interlocking directorships in a multi-stakeholder system. *Journal of Destination Marketing and Management* 5(2), 107–116. DOI:10.1016/j.jdmm.2015.11.005

Bieger, T. (1996) *Management von Destinationen*. Oldenbourg, Munich, Germany.

Boari, C. and Lipparini, A. (1999) Networks within industrial districts: organising knowledge creation and transfer by means of moderate hierarchies. *Journal of Management and Governance* 3(4), 339–360. DOI:10.1023/A:1009989028605

Bonzanigo, L., Giupponi, C. and Balbi, S. (2016) Sustainable tourism planning and climate change adaptation in the Alps: a case study of winter tourism in mountain communities in the Dolomites. *Journal of Sustainable Tourism* 24(4), 637–652. DOI:10.1080/09669582.2015.1122013

Cocolas, N., Walters, G. and Ruhanen, L. (2016) Behavioural adaptation to climate change among winter alpine tourists: an analysis of tourist motivations and leisure substitutability. *Journal of Sustainable Tourism* 24(6), 846–865. DOI:10.1080/09669582.2015.1088860

Dawson J. and Scott, D. (2013) Managing for climate change in the alpine ski sector. *Tourism Management* 35, 244–254. DOI:10.1016/j.tourman.2012.07.009

Dawson, J., Havitz, M. and Scott, D. (2011) Behavioural adaptation of alpine skiers to climate change: examining activity involvement and place loyalty. *Journal of Travel and Tourism Marketing* 28(4), 388–404. DOI:10.1080/10548408.2011.571573

Duglio, S. and Beltramo, R. (2016) Environmental management and sustainable labels in the ski industry: a critical review. *Sustainability* 8(9), 851/1–13. DOI:10.3390/su8090851

Dwyer, L., Edwards, D., Mistilis, N., Roman, C. and Scott, N. (2009) Destination and enterprise management for a tourism future. *Tourism Management* 30(1), 63–74. DOI:10.1016/j.tourman.2008.04.002

Flagestad, A. and Hope, C.A. (2001) Strategic success in winter sports destinations: a sustainable value creation perspective. *Tourism Management* 22(5), 445–461. DOI:10.1016/S0261-5177(01)00010-3

Gilaberte-Búrdalo, M., López-Martín, F., Pino-Otín, M.R. and López-Moreno, J.I. (2014) Impacts of climate change on ski industry. *Environmental Science and Policy* 44, 51–61. DOI:10.1016/j.envsci.2014.07.003

IPCC (2015) *Climate Change 2014. Synthesis Report*. Contribution of Working Groups I, II and III to the Fifth Assessment Report of the Intergovernmental Panel on Climate Change [Core Writing Team, Pachauri, R.K. and Meyer, L.A. (eds)]. IPCC, Geneva, Switzerland.

ISPAT – Istituto di Statistica della Provincia di Trento (2016) Annuario statistico 2016. Available at: www.statweb.provincia.tn.it/incpage.asp?p=annuari.asp&t=annstat (accessed 10 July 2018).

ISPAT – Istituto di Statistica della Provincia di Trento (2017) Annuario online. Available at: www.statweb.provincia.tn.it/annuario (accessed 10 July 2018).

Kaspar, C. (1995) *Management im Tourismus*. Haupt, Bern, Switzerland.

Mauri, C. and Turci, L. (2018) From ski to snow: rethinking package holidays in a winter mountain destination. *Worldwide Hospitality and Tourism Themes* 10(2), 201–210. DOI:10.1108/WHATT-12-2017-0076

Müller, H. and Weber, F. (2008) Climate change and tourism – scenario analysis for the Bernese Oberland in 2030. *Tourism Review* 63(3), 57–71. DOI:10.1108/16605370810901580

Murphy, P.E. (1985) *Tourism: A Community Approach*. Methuen, New York.

Murphy, P.E. and Murphy, A.E. (2004) *Strategic Management for Tourism Communities: Bridging the Gaps*. Channel View Publications, Bristol, UK.

Skipass Panorama Turismo (2017) Skipass Panorama Turismo. Osservatorio Italiano del Turismo Montano. *Situazione congiunturale Montagna Bianca Italiana. Inverno 2017-2018. Previsioni e Tendenze*. Modena Fiere – JFC, Modena, Italy.

Soboll, A. and Dingeldey, A. (2012) The future impact of climate change on Alpine winter tourism: a high-resolution simulation system in the German and Austrian Alps. *Journal of Sustainable Tourism* 20(1), 101–120. DOI:10.1080/09669582.2011.610895

Töglhofer, C., Eigner, F. and Prettenthaler, F. (2011) Impacts of snow conditions on tourism demand in Austrian ski areas. *Climate Research* 46(1), 1–14. DOI:10.3354/cr00939

Unbehaun, W., Pröbstl, U. and Haider, W. (2008) Trends in winter sport tourism: challenges for the future. *Tourism Review* 63(1), 36–47. DOI:10.1108/16605370810861035

van Gils, A. and Zwart, P.S. (2009) Alliance formation motives in SMEs: an explorative conjoint analysis study. *International Small Business Journal* 27(5), 5–37. DOI:10.1177/0266242608098345

Villa, A. and Taurino, T. (2018) From industrial districts to SME collaboration frames. *International Journal of Production Research* 56(1–2), 974–982. DOI:10.1080/00207543.2017.1401244

Weaver, D.B. (2000) A broad context model of destination development scenarios. *Tourism Management* 21(3), 217–222. DOI:10.1016/S0261-5177(99)00054-0

27 The Role of Cable Cars and Ski Lifts as Key Innovations in the Evolution of Winter Tourism

Marius Mayer*

Universität Greifswald, Greifswald, Germany

27.1 Introduction

The following quotations illustrate that cable cars and surface lifts[1] (CCSLs) are among the most crucial innovations for winter and ski tourism (Jülg, 1999, 2007; Denning, 2014).

- 'There is no winter tourism without ropeways!' (Leitner, 1984, p. 99).
- 'Mountain transportation, but especially the ski areas developed with its help, are the true motors of mountain tourism' (Bieger, 1999, p. 155).
- 'The utilisation of mechanical uphill transportation was an inevitable precondition for the development of skiing to a popular mass sport' (König, 2000, p. 195).
- 'After the 1960s a winter sport destination without ropeways was beyond imagination' (Jülg, 2007, p. 254.).
- 'Cableways are at the core of alpine tourism transport system and without them a well-developed tourism industry could not exist in the alpine area with the inevitably negative impact on tourism related jobs in the surrounding alpine valleys and villages' (Brida *et al.*, 2014, p. 2).
- 'Without ropeway enterprises willing to invest, the enormous frequencies of ski tourism in alpine destinations would not be possible' (Luger and Rest, 2017, p. 28).
- 'The importance of the ropeway industry for the Austrian winter tourism is beyond doubt. Without the technical development of the Alps for skiing, there would only be a small fraction of guest arrivals and overnight stays in the winter season' (Hartl, 2017, p. 408).

Without uphill lifts, there would be of course ski touring as a small niche, but most likely downhill skiing as mass tourism would never have emerged (Pfund, 1984; Hartl, 2017; Wieser, 2017). Imagining that CCSLs were never invented and skiers would still have to climb up themselves, what would the Alps look like today?[2] (especially the higher altitude levels where ski tourism is spatially concentrated; Bätzing, 2017). The quick development from peripheral, poor mountain villages characterized by depopulation to affluent, dynamic globally known winter sport destinations with in-migration – often within just one generation – would not have happened (Jülg, 1999). Also summer tourism would have developed much less dynamically, as attraction points to enjoy panoramic views would not be accessible for the masses (Bieger, 1999; Keller, 2003) and

---

* E-Mail: marius.mayer@uni-greifswald.de

would be less stable, as the second season would be absent that provides the necessary utilization to pay off investments and keep trained staff (Jülg, 1966, 2007; Leitner, 1984).

Today's skiing industry would most likely not exist if it were not for mechanical uphill transportation. However, besides being the crucial basic innovation for ski tourism, the technological progress through innovations in CCSLs also has had an important influence on the further development of ski tourism. The main aim of this chapter is to illustrate these influences in different development stages. Interestingly, this topic is not covered extensively in the literature, as also noted by Wieser (2017), possibly due to its middle position between technical history, transportation and tourism research; maybe also because the data about CCSLs are surprisingly scarce and require extensive research efforts (see Mayer, 2008, 2009; Job *et al.*, 2014). Therefore, the chapter will frame CCSLs as innovations in tourism and then present in more detail five developments of ski tourism as consequences of technological change. The final section sheds a light on the economic relevance of CCSLs.

27.2 Cable Cars and Ski Lifts as Innovations in Tourism

Bieger *et al.* (2005) classify cable car companies as location-bound attractions that offer recreational experiences to their customers and are part of the service sector. Two main drivers of CCSL innovation can be identified that influence the operators: (i) the propagation of technological improvements by the manufacturers, which plays a decisive role not only in the emergence of innovations but also as active propagators of their diffusion,[3] and (ii) customer requirements (Bieger *et al.*, 2005; Mayer, 2009). Thus, the demand side of CCSLs can be differentiated between the business-to-business (b2b) customers of CCSL technology, the ski area operators and the final consumers – the snow sport participants. Improvements for the latter target group can be called consumer innovations, while the first are firm (or operator/organizational) innovations. These firm innovations can be explained as technological innovations that were not realized for the benefit of guests, but for the purpose of saving costs for the operators (e.g. the so-called direct drive for chairlifts and gondolas is a motor that saves considerable amounts of electric energy and costs for the operators, but visitors would not notice any difference). Some innovations, however, offer benefits to both guests and the operators. In general, the operators' main focus lies in adding value for their guests. As expected, the preferences of these two target groups can vary considerably. For instance, from the cost perspective a reversible aerial tramway is preferable to detachable gondolas with smaller cabin sizes, but the latter's transport comfort is much higher (seats, not standing densely face-to-face with strangers) and waiting time is much lower due to usually much higher capacities. Operators need to assess carefully whether costly up-to-date CCSL infrastructures really pay off by creating customer added value (e.g. seat heating) (Mayer, 2008, 2009). Table 27.1 provides an overview of the different innovation types CCSLs can take, shows in which innovation typologies they can be grouped, and distinguishes between front and back stage innovations, i.e. whether innovations are directly visible by skiers (front), only by the operators (back) or both. Often, these typologies differentiate between the scope and impact of innovations, as radical and incremental innovations do not match the importance of basic innovations. If the CCSLs as such constitute the necessary basic innovation for ski tourism (see Section 27.3.1), then the introduction of detachable high-speed and

Table 27.1. Cable car and ski lifts as innovations in tourism. (Adapted from Mayer, 2009, 2014; based on the references cited in the table.)

Typology	Innovation types	Examples
Emergence of new combinations of means of production (Schumpeter, 1939; Hjalager, 2002)	Product innovation (front stage)	Glass-bottom gondola for ropeways; weather protection bubble for chairlifts
	Process innovation (front and back stage)	Direct drive of ropeways/chairlifts
	Organizational innovation (back stage)	Vertical integration through take-over of accommodation by CCSL operating companies
	Institutional innovation (back stage)	Introduction of a new technological norm (e.g. safety requirements)
	Marketing innovation (front and back stage)	Customer loyalty programmes, social media marketing
Impact and range (Mensch, 1972; Koschatzky, 2001)	Basic innovation	Ski lifts as means of transportation
	Radical innovation	Detachable chairlifts as express ski lifts
	Incremental innovation	Introduction of the eight-seater chairlift
Source/initiator/point of origin (Koschatzky, 2001)	Technology – push	Seat heating for chairlifts/gondolas
	Need – pull/demand – push	Introduction of high-capacity ski lifts reduces waiting time
Target group (Brown, 1981)	Consumer innovation	Seat heating for chairlifts/gondolas
	Firm innovation	Direct drive for ropeways/chairlifts
Effect on established patterns of consumption (Robertson, 1971)	Continuous innovation	Development from eight-seater to ten-seater gondola
	Dynamically continuous innovation	Development of detachable small-sized gondolas with seats
	Discontinuous innovation	Introduction of cable cars and ski lifts themselves
Dimension/scope (Christensen, 2003)	Sustaining innovation	Ski lifts with self-service t-bars
	Disruptive innovation	Detachable chairlifts

high-capacity chairlifts replacing surface lifts is a radical innovation, while the slightly larger eight-seater chairlift is only an incremental step forward from six-seater lifts. The typologies by Robertson (1971) and Christensen (2003) contain similar nuances.

Figures 27.1 and 27.2 show examples of different CCSL types.

27.3 The Nexus Between Ski Tourism and Lifts: Five Theses

This section presents the nexus between ski tourism and CCSLs based on five theses, which refer mostly to the Alps.

27.3.1 Cable cars and ski lifts as basic innovations for ski and winter tourism

The first step in the technical development of mountains for tourism included railways, which reached the Alps from the 1850s onwards. In the late 19th century also side

Fig. 27.1. Photo tableau of traditional CCSL types. First line from left: cog railway, reversible aerial tramway; second line: one-seater chairlift (fixed-grip), surface lift (t-bar). (Photographs courtesy of Marius Mayer.)

valleys were linked and with the help of the cog and pinion technology, mountain destinations like Zermatt in Switzerland were reached. The following step extended these railways up on the actual mountains to access panoramic views (see Fig. 27.1, first line left), which was the typical form of alpine tourism then (Bätzing, 2015). Examples from Switzerland include Rigi (1871), Gornergrat (1898) or Jungfraujoch (1912) (König, 2000).

Around the same time, skiing was first practised in the Alps, adapted in technique to the downhill runs and gained fast popularity. Skiing was remarkably different from today: it was an adventurous activity including strenuous uphill hikes followed by only one downhill run (Jülg, 1999; Denning, 2014). The decisive step was then to use the existing mountain railways also in winter to do repeated runs and avoid the uphill hike.[4] As these winter operations turned out to be highly successful, the first lifts were built, which were explicitly targeted to the skiers, with the Parsenn funicular in Davos, Switzerland (1931) being the most prominent. In the 1930s the crucial innovation of the surface/drag lifts followed (see Fig. 27.1, second line right). They were the first means of transportation targeting skiers only, and were much cheaper compared with

Fig. 27.2. Photo tableau of modern CCSL types. First line from left: double-seater chairlift (fixed-grip), four-seater mono-cable gondola detachable; second line: six-seater detachable chairlift, doubled surface lift on glacier; third line: funitel, tricable gondola detachable. (Photographs courtesy of Marius Mayer.)

cog railways, funiculars or aerial tramways (for operators and skiers alike) but had even higher transport capacities (Hannss and Schröder, 1985). The first modern surface lift was built in Davos in 1934 (König, 2000) and in the same year Sestriere was founded in the Italian Alps, the first ex-nihilo ski destination (Denning, 2014). Although interrupted by World War II, the post-war ski boom actually began during this period, which is underlined by the example of Switzerland where the first chairlifts were built during the war (König, 2000). After 1945, no new cog railways and only a few funiculars were built. The 'ski boom' coinciding with the German 'Wirtschaftswunder', the

French 'trente glorieuses' or the Italian 'miracolo economico' was driven by aerial tramways, one-seater chairlifts (see Fig. 27.1, second line left) and, above all, the surface lifts.

Thus, CCSLs emerged as the basic innovation for ski tourism in the sense of Kondratieff and Schumpeter's theory of long waves (Bathelt and Glückler, 2018): skiing in the Alps shifted nearly completely to downhill skiing and became a mass market with destinations profiting from even one CCSL. Denning (2014) argues that there was a very strong relationship between the development of CCSLs and skiing as a significant leisure activity. Due to the development of uphill transport, which made several ski runs a day possible for the first time (and also increased the horizontal and vertical distances covered), the nature of skiing changed over time from an elitist, adventurous 'fight with nature' to a commodified, speed-driven sport activity that became increasingly open to a diversity of social groups and to nearly everyone who could afford lift tickets. In this way, CCSLs democratized skiing as a leisure activity (Jülg, 1999, 2007).

Jülg provided empirical evidence for the crucial role of CCSLs for the take-off of winter tourism after World War II as early as 1966. The presence of CCSLs leads to a dynamic development of winter tourism. This is shown by significant literature about tourism development in alpine valleys (Jülg, 1999; see Rainer, 2005 as an example). Figure 27.3

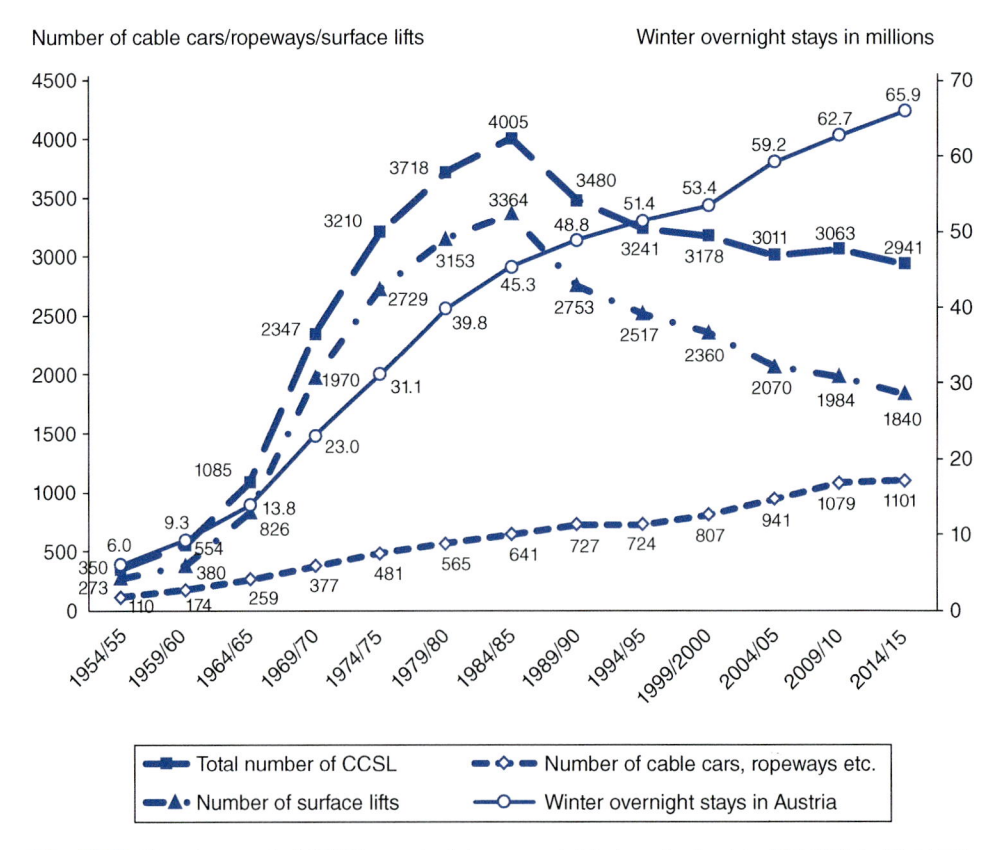

Fig. 27.3. Development of CCSLs and winter overnight stays in Austria 1954/55 to 2014/15. (Own figure based on Jülg, 1999, 2001; BMVIT, 2018; Statistik Austria, 2018.)

illustrates a nearly perfect correlation (Pearson R 0.989***) between the development of the winter overnight stays in Austria and the total number of CCSLs for the 1954/55 to 1984/85 period. That means, the more CCSLs that were built (the total number of CCSLs rose from 350 to 4005 in this period, +946%), and the more ski areas were developed, the higher the number of winter overnight stays rose on parallel (from 6.0 to 45.3 million, +652%). Since the mid-1980s the total number of CCSLs is decreasing due to the replacement of surface lifts and their closing down in isolated and low-altitude locations even though the overall transport capacities are still rising. This reduces the correlation strength to 0.794** for the complete period, while the still-increasing number of all lifts without surface lifts correlates nearly perfectly with the overnight stays in the winter season (0.986***) – winter overnight stays increased by 994% from 1954/55 to 2014/15, the number of all lifts without surface lifts by 901% (with their capacities even stronger rising). This indicates, that winter tourism in Austria (except for urban tourism in cities like Vienna or Salzburg) is strongly linked to the development of cable car and ski lift infrastructure and that surface lifts lost their crucial role to larger, higher performing, more expensive and more comfortable CCSL types (see Section 27.3.4). Brida *et al.* (2014) show equally high correlations between the monthly overnight stays and cableway passengers for South Tyrol between 2007 and 2010.

This crucial nexus between CCSLs and winter tourism is further exemplified by a comparison of winter tourism in municipalities with and without CCSLs in the German Alps: Table 27.2 shows that the ski destinations are larger with more accommodation, guest beds and winter overnight stays and higher tourism intensity. However, there is of course no determinism, i.e. CCSLs were not always the starting point of the tourism development but were added as attractions by already established spa towns like Bad Gastein in the Hohe Tauern, Salzburg, Austria or Bad Reichenhall in the German Alps or summer destinations like Mayrhofen in the Tyrolean Zillertal, Austria (Jülg, 1966, 1999; Wieser, 2017). This lack of determinism also means that the presence of CCSL is no guarantee for a dynamic development of ski/winter tourism as there are many examples of closed and dismantled ski areas (Falk, 2013 for Austria; Mayer and Steiger, 2013 for the German Alps).

Table 27.2. Tourism data of municipalities with and without ski areas in the German Alps. (Adapted from Mayer and Steiger, 2013.)

	Municipalities with ski areas ($n = 32$)	Municipalities without ski areas ($n = 69$)	T value
Number of accommodations (annual mean 2011)	69.2	25.4	−3.236**, $p < 0.01$
Guest beds (annual mean 2011)	2191.3	977.6	−3.043**, $p < 0.01$
Winter overnight stays in commercial accommodations 2011/12	117,951	42,247	−2.849**, $p < 0.01$
Tourism intensity 2011/12 (guest beds per 1000 inhabitants)	543.4	242.0	−2.565*, $p < 0.02$
Occupancy rate (winter 2011/12 average) in per cent	27.0	25.8	−0.507, n.s.

The starting point for winter tourism was most often the construction of the first CCSLs for which the local tourism pioneers took high financial risks and had to overcome huge resistance, both from sceptical peers in their villages and the regional/national politics and administration (Leitner, 1984; Rainer, 2005; Wieser, 2017). These risks were lower for already established summer destinations where the CCSLs were intended to either serve primarily as further attractions for the summer season and where the winter/ski season developed rather unintentionally but often quickly overtook the summer frequentation, or where the winter was consciously intended to be developed as a second season by setting up a ski area (Leitner, 1984; Jülg, 2007).

27.3.2 From single lifts to ski areas

While the sheer presence of CCSLs initiated winter tourism in many destinations, the further development of ski tourism would not have been possible without the formation of ski areas, often through the connection of single lifts to networks of increasing size and complexity to fulfil skiers' quickly rising demand for more variety. It is evident that the boom phase of ski tourism in the Alps (late 1950s to mid-1980s) goes hand-in-hand with the increased development of new and advanced equipment of existing ski areas (Jülg, 1999, 2007; Denning, 2014). The fast increase in guest frequentation and overnight stays ensured the profitability of the initial investments and allowed for continued improvement in projects, to link the initial lifts to interconnected ski areas ('Ski-Schaukel') – most often by connecting the CCSLs of neighbouring municipalities sharing two sides of the same mountain and finally the emergence of large-scale ski areas, at least in the Alps. This latest trend is covered in Section 27.3.5.

A constant problem was the lack of transport capacity especially of feeders in the morning leading to long queues (see Pause, 1970 for examples). Destinations often reacted by setting up another ski area on the neighbouring mountain to satisfy the strong demand (and often driven by competing interests of actors). At that time, the leading destinations in ski tourism were Davos-Klosters and St. Moritz, Grisons, Switzerland, each with several decentralized ski areas (Davos: five, St. Moritz: seven), which are nowadays an inconvenience given the trend for large-scale ski areas. These structures are inconvenient as economies of scale (e.g. one large artificial lake for snowmaking instead of several smaller lakes) are harder to realize for the operators (only in the case of connections that are more difficult to get permissions for in Switzerland due to restrictions). For skiers, these structures mean that they have to use their cars or uncomfortable buses to access all parts of the ski area or to move between the mountains as their offer is often not attractive enough to spend a whole day there compared with larger, connected ski areas.

With the invention and diffusion of innovative CCSLs (which were almost always linked to higher transport capacities), an ongoing concentration process began, as the new lifts provided much higher capacities from the bottom stations, which, in combination with the lifts on the mountain, increased the carrying capacity of the ski areas tremendously but required high investments and large guest bed capacities to provide the necessary utilization (Jülg, 1999, 2007).

Empirical evidence from the western Austrian Alps and the German Alps shows the strong correlations between the number of CCSLs, respectively their transport capacity and the number of guest arrivals/overnight stays. That means, the more CCSLs, the more important winter tourism (Mayer, 2009; Mayer and Steiger, 2013).

27.3.3 Accessibility of high-alpine and glacier areas

CCSLs as such prolong the ski season by providing access to higher mountain areas with their higher natural snow reliability. From the 1960s onwards, innovative ropeway technology allowed the developing of high-alpine and glacier ski areas, which guaranteed nearly year-round snow reliability and extended the season considerably (Mayer, 2012; Mayer et al., 2018). Especially important was the invention of surface lifts situated on the moving ice masses of glaciers in 1964 (Zermatt) and 1967 (Kitzsteinhorn) (Fig. 27.2, second line right), while more primitive mobile lifts on glaciers had already been developed in Cervinia/Plateau Rosa (Italy and Switzerland) and on Passo Stelvio/Stilfserjoch (Italy) as early as the mid-1950s. Other related innovations were high-capacity underground funiculars, which were also positive in terms of landscape aesthetics (Kitzsteinhorn 1974, Pitztal 1983, Saas-Fee 1984, Tignes 1993, Mölltal 1997). In the late 1980s/early 1990s extremely wind-stable double cable ropeways like the DMC, DLM or the funitel (see Fig. 27.2, third line left) were developed by the manufacturers in close cooperation with the operators to provide weather-proof access in combination with high capacity (Josserand and Piard, 1993; Wieser, 2017). In the 2000s detachable mono-cable gondolas (MGDs) with extremely long rope spans and only a few towers required were introduced, which allowed the crossing of larger ice fields and thus important upgrades in capacity and comfort (8-MGD Tiefenbachferner, Sölden, Austria in 2000). Thus, glacier ski areas often served as focal points of CCSL innovation due to the extreme geographical conditions (Mayer, 2008).

27.3.4 Lift innovation as quality upgrade

Innovative CCSLs enable important quality upgrades of transportation in ski tourism. The most crucial innovation was most likely the detachable chairlift (see Fig. 27.2, second line left) coming up in its current specification in the 1970s and taking off in terms of spatial diffusion between the mid-1980s and 1990s (Mayer, 2008). In particular the four- and six-seater express chairlifts provided enough transport capacity to replace even doubled surface lifts deemed increasingly uncomfortable by skiers. They reduced waiting and transport time, increased skiing time considerably and offered comfort features like smooth upholstery, weather protection bubbles, conveyor belts at the entrances or seat heating. In terms of feeder lifts, MGD with six, eight and ten seats replaced the reversible aerial tramways or double-seater chairlifts. This reduced queues in the morning, and improved accessibility for pedestrians and logistics for restaurants and huts alike. As a result of this innovation-driven restructuring of CCSL systems, the overall number of CCSLs has been decreasing since the mid-1980s, the number of surface lifts is strongly decreasing (in a kind of vicious cycle the decreasing number reduces the capabilities of skiers to use them), while the number of express lifts is increasing (Mayer 2008, 2009; Mayer and Steiger, 2013; see Fig. 27.3).

Correlation analyses show that the innovativeness of the CCSL system is positively related to the size and success of ski destinations measured in the number of winter overnight stays. In destinations with more winter overnight stays the share of express lifts is higher, the mean CCSL age is reduced, the share of surface lifts is reduced, and the mean capacity per lift is higher. However, the causality is ambiguous: does the innovativeness of the CCSL system determine success in ski tourism or do successful destinations lead to costly lift innovations (Mayer, 2008, 2009; Mayer and Steiger, 2013)? Bieger noted already in 1999 that the costs of replacing a surface lift with a detachable chairlift are between four and six times higher than the initial investment, which contributes to the difficult financial situation of many operators (Falk and Steiger, 2018).

27.3.5 Connection of neighbouring ski areas to large-scale ski destinations

In the past two decades there has been a trend in the Alps to join neighbouring ski areas to large-scale ski destinations (Bätzing, 2015; Linseisen, 2016; Falk, 2017; Hartl, 2017). The main argument is usually the competitive edge gained through the relatively large extension of the available ski areas often by only adding a few connecting lifts. In many cases, these connections were only made possible by innovative lift technology like the crossing of deep valleys with high-capacity lifts. Since 2003/04, the 200-person reversible aerial tramway Vanoise Express has linked the two French ski areas La Plagne and Les Arcs to form one of the biggest resorts in the Alps (and around the globe) with 425 km of ski runs. Similarly, since 2004/05 a 3.6-km tricable gondola detachable (TGD) links the two formerly separate parts of the Kitzbühel ski area in Austria, which doubles the accessible ski area and, in addition, provides a unique transport experience more than 400 m above the ground made visible through glass bottoms in some gondolas (Mountain Manager, 2005; Mayer, 2009). According to the operator, the ongoing connection project between the Kitzsteinhorn glacier ski area and the town of Kaprun is also only feasible with the TGD technology (Salzburg. Orf.at, 2018), which unites the advantages of reversible aerial tramways with those of detachable gondola lifts (see Fig. 27.2, third line right). These connections are usually successful in economic terms, which is shown in the empirical studies by Linseisen, 2016 and Falk, 2017. However, as the overall number of skiers and first entries (in Austria) is merely constant, it might be argued that these connections only foster the concentration processes of ski tourism to the detriment of smaller destinations and a regionally balanced development (Hartl, 2017).

27.4 Economic Relevance of Cable Cars and Ski Lifts

Without CCSLs the economic relevance of ski tourism would be much smaller, as it would never have developed into the mass market we have today (see above) in terms of frequentation, and as the expenditures would be much lower (see Mayer and Kraus, Chapter 10). Skiers would not spend a considerable proportion of their travel budget on lift passes, which, in combination with their further skiing-related spending, generates important economic impact (€7.9 billion gross turnover lead to €3.6–4.3 billion direct and indirect economic impact of CCSL users in Austria; Manova, 2016). The increased spending also creates direct employment at the operating companies (7,050 year-round and 10,250 seasonal jobs directly from the Austrian CCSL industry; Manova, 2016), and indirect employment in accommodation, gastronomy, retail, services in the destinations, and ski service and retail in the source areas (81,930 job equivalents in forward- and backward industries in Austria; Manova, 2016) (see also Luger and Rest, 2017; Wieser, 2017). Studies by Manova (2016) for Austria and the Deutsches Wirtschaftswissenschaftliches Institut für Fremdenverkehr e.V. an der Universität München (DWIF, 2013) for Germany underline these considerable multiplier effects of CCSLs. In Austria, these multipliers vary between 5.3 (gross) and 7.1 (net value added). In other words, €1 spent at CCSLs leads to €5.3 to 7.1 total value added in Austria (Manova, 2016). Also the highly qualified manufacturing and R&D jobs with ropeway suppliers and their forward- and backward-linkages would only exist on a very limited level. Doppelmayr, one of the leading CCSL manufacturers, generates an annual gross turnover of €0.8 billion and has 2,720 employees in total, among them 1,398 in Austria and 384 in Switzerland (Doppelmayr, 2018). In the same vein the snowmaking business would not exist, as it is unlikely that these innovations would have been developed to ensure the snow reliability of ski touring slopes or Nordic ski tracks. Thus, the whole ski industry as we know it today would not be in place if it were not for CCSLs, which therefore can be regarded as the fundamental basic innovation of ski tourism.

Given this economic key function of CCSLs for the ski tourism economy, it makes sense to speak of these companies as focal enterprises (Luger and Rest, 2017). This also explains why these companies do not necessarily need to be profitable on their own because they pay off indirectly by detour profitability (Jülg, 1966) stressing the regional economic functions of lifts (Keller, 2003). The destination of Ischgl (Austria) is the best example of this strategy, where allegedly not 1 cent of dividend has been paid to the shareholders (mostly local tourism entrepreneurs) since its founding in 1961 and all profits have been reinvested to create one of the best-equipped and most modern ski areas of the world. The shareholders profit indirectly by high utilization of their own hotels, restaurants and bars filled with visitors attracted by the very competitive ski area (Wieser, 2017).

27.5 Conclusions

Technological advances in mountain transport technology are among the major drivers of industry change in ski tourism. CCSLs are the crucial basic innovation without which ski tourism would never have emerged as mass tourism including its economic relevance. CCSL innovations made it possible to develop both high-alpine/glacier ski areas and large-scale ski destinations. The resulting increase in transport quality and comfort, the reduction of waiting time and the accessibility of higher regions (although there is a decrease of CCSLs in absolute numbers; Wieser, 2017; also see Fig. 27.3) contributed decisively to the competitiveness of winter tourism, but are contrasted by rising costs for operators and guests alike. The connections of ski areas due to innovative CCSLs are mostly successful, but increase the spatial concentration of winter tourism, which might not be desirable when it comes to a balanced regional development (Bätzing, 2017). However, it may be argued that the skiers' pursuit of more extended ski areas is partly fuelled by the diffusion of high-speed/high-capacity lifts. Although the empirical test might be difficult, it is only the fast transportation and the reduced waiting time that enables skiers to discover much larger ski areas. Earlier, they spent much more time queuing or riding the lifts so larger ski areas were neither possible to ski for the average guest nor necessary. In this way, skiers nowadays can experience many more ski runs in the same time, which corresponds to the time/space compression noted by Denning (2014) for the introduction of CCSLs compared with ski touring.

Lifts are also very important for mountain tourism in summer. They serve as important attractions in themselves but also provide access to important attraction points and panoramic views (see also Brida *et al.*, 2014). The lifts to the most prominent locations can be highly profitable as they have no costs for ski run grooming, snowmaking, etc. but charge nearly the same or even higher prices compared with the lift passes in winter (e.g. Jungfraujoch and Titlis in Switzerland, or Zugspitze in Germany). This does not work for all lifts operating in summer of course.

What are the future prospects of CCSLs, especially in light of the challenges brought about by climate change and a relatively flat growth path for skier visits due to mature and ageing source markets (Steiger, 2012)? As the importance of the role of CCSLs for the summer season and pedestrians shows, transportation by CCSLs will continue to play an important role for mountain tourism in the future (Wieser, 2017). Depending on the individual vulnerability of destinations to global warming impacts, the seasons not depending on snow will become more important. Concerning skiers' transportation, the ongoing concentration process, quality upgrades and the replacement of existing lifts instead of new developments will most likely continue in the future. No-frills skiing concepts with simple and low-cost CCSLs (in combination with no snowmaking) implying low ticket rates for less affluent skiers do not seem to be viable on a large scale at the moment, but in specific niches definitely. Finally, the CCSL manufacturers have already started to diversify and to tap into new markets like urban transportation, however, of course not with surface lifts, but with high-capacity gondolas, which are much more cost-effective compared with underground metros.

Notes

[1] This combined term encompasses all mechanical means of transporting people up- (and down-) hill on mountains like cog railways, funiculars, aerial tramways, ropeways (gondola lifts, chairlifts) and surface/drag lifts. Unfortunately, there is no overarching English term that encompasses all means of mountain uphill person transport as does the German 'mechanische Aufstiegshilfen', the French 'remontées mécaniques' or the Italian 'impianti di risalita'.

[2] Leitner (1984) compares deserted valleys in the western Alps without tourism with the vibrant development of valleys in the Austrian federal state of Salzburg with tourism. He also describes the case of Thomatal, a municipality in the Lungau region of Salzburg, which he deems 'a real victim of the modern ski development' (p. 78) because the slopes ideally suited to skiing have not been equipped with CCSLs so far, while it was highly frequented during the ski touring era. Jülg (1999) also mentions Mürzzuschlag am Semmering (Styria, Austria) as an early hot spot of skiing, which is nowadays nearly completely forgotten.

[3] Technical abilities of skiers had improved so much that the downhill run took less and less time. This fact fostered the demand for uphill transportation to improve the relationship between up- and downhill movement again (Denning, 2014).

[4] In the western Austrian federal states of Vorarlberg, Tyrol and Salzburg, the correlation between winter overnight stays and the size of ski areas is very strong (Pearson R 0.890***), which fits well to the high importance of ski tourism there (Mayer, 2009).

[5] As indicator for the ski area size, transport capacity correlates highly significantly with the winter overnight stays in commercial accommodations (Pearson R 0.719***) (Mayer and Steiger, 2013).

[6] Correlation between overnight stays in the winter season 2007/08 in Vorarlberg, Tyrol and Salzburg (all Austria) with the innovativeness ranking: Spearman Rho −0.509***, with the mean transport capacity per cable car (2007/08): Pearson R 0.468*** (Mayer, 2009). For the German Alps (winter season 2010/11) these values are −0.216 (n.s.), respectively, 0.345* (Mayer and Steiger, 2013).

References

Bathelt, H. and Glückler, J. (2018) *Wirtschaftsgeographie*, 4th edn. UTB, Stuttgart, Germany.

Bätzing, W. (2015) *Die Alpen*, 3rd edn. Beck, Munich, Germany.

Bätzing, W. (2017) Orte guten Lebens. Visionen für einen Alpentourismus zwischen Wildnis und Freizeitpark. In: Luger, K. and Rest, F. (eds) *Alpenreisen. Erlebnis. Raumtransformationen. Imagination*. Studien Verlag, Innsbruck, Austria, pp. 215–236.

Bieger, T. (1999) Bergbahnen und Skigebiete auf dem Weg vom individualisierten Kleingewerbe zu konsolidierten Grosskonzernen? Erfahrungen und Tendenzen aus Nordamerika und ihre Wirkungen auf die Schweiz. *Jahrbuch der Schweizerischen Tourismuswirtschaft* 1998/99, 155–169.

Bieger, T., Laesser, C. and Romer, D. (2005) The relevance of revealed preferences in market oriented innovations. In: Keller, P. and Bieger, T. (eds) *Innovation in Tourism – Creating Customer Value* (Publication of the AIEST 47). AIEST, St. Gallen, Switzerland, pp. 31–48.

BMVIT (Bundesministerium für Verkehr, Innovation und Technologie) (2018) Anzahl der Seilbahnanlagen 1999/2000, 2004/05, 2009/10, 2014/15. Unpublished documents requested in personal communication. BMVIT, Vienna, Austria.

Brida, J.G., Deidda, M. and Pulina, M. (2014) Tourism and transport systems in mountain environments: analysis of the economic efficiency of cableways in South Tyrol. *Journal of Transport Geography* 36, 1–11. DOI:10.1016/j.jtrangeo.2014.02.004

Brown, L.A. (1981) *Innovation Diffusion. A New Perspective*. Methuen, London.

Christensen, C.M. (2003) *The Innovator's Dilemma*. Harper, London.

Denning, A. (2014) From sublime landscapes to "White Gold": how skiing transformed the Alps after 1930. *Environmental History* 19(1), 78–108. DOI:10.1093/envhis/emt105

Doppelmayr (2018) *Zahlen, Daten, Fakten*. Available at: https://www.doppelmayr.com/unternehmen/zahlen-daten-fakten/ (accessed 5 October 2018).

DWIF (Deutsches Wirtschaftswissenschaftliches Institut für Fremdenverkehr e.V. an der Universität München) (2013) Wirtschaftliche Effekte durch Seilbahnen im Winter in Bayern. Available at: https://docplayer.org/35866402-Wirtschaftliche-effekte-durch-seilbahnen-im-winter-in-deutschland.html (accessed 1 June 2018).

Falk, M. (2013) A survival analysis of ski lift companies. *Tourism Management* 36, 377–390. DOI: 10.1016/j.tourman.2012.10.005

Falk, M. (2017) Gains from horizontal collaboration among ski areas. *Tourism Management* 60, 92–104. DOI:10.1016/j.tourman.2016.11.008

Falk, M. and Steiger, R. (2018) An exploration of the debt ratio of ski lift operators. *Sustainability* 10(9), 2985. DOI:10.3390/su10092985

Hannss, C. and Schröder, P. (1985) Touristische Transportanlagen in den Alpen. Bedeutung, Merkmale und räumliche Verteilung der mechanischen Aufstiegshilfen. *disP – The Planning Review* 21(79), 19–25.

Hartl, F. (2017) Alpentourismus im Wandel. Überlegungen zur wirtschaftlichen Entwicklung einer Branche. In: Luger, K. and Rest, F. (eds) *Alpenreisen. Erlebnis. Raumtransformationen. Imagination*. Studien Verlag, Innsbruck, Austria, pp. 401–420.

Hjalager, A.-M. (2002) Repairing innovation defectiveness in tourism. *Tourism Management* 23(5), 465–474. DOI:10.1016/S0261-5177(02)00013-4

Job, H., Mayer, M. and Kraus, F. (2014) Die beste Idee, die Bayern je hatte: der Alpenplan. Raumplanung mit Weitblick. *GAIA* 23(4), 335-345. DOI:10.14512/gaia.23.4.9

Josserand, P. and Piard, J.-F. (1993) Le Funitel de Val Thorens. *Internationale Seilbahn-Rundschau* ISR 3/1993, 20–22.

Jülg, F. (1966) *Die Seilbahnen Österreichs und ihre Auswirkungen auf die Wirtschaft*. Österreichisches Institut für Raumplanung, Vienna, Austria.

Jülg, F. (1999) Faszination Schnee – Der Wintertourismus im Gebirge. Historische Entwicklung. In: Isenberg, W. (ed.) *Der Winter als Erlebnis – Zurück zur Natur oder Fun, Action und Mega-Events? Neue Orientierungen im Schnee-Tourismus* (Bensberger Protokolle 94). Thomas-Morus-Akademie, Bergisch-Gladbach, Germany, pp. 9–38.

Jülg, F. (2001) *Österreich. Zentrum und Peripherie im Herzen Europas*. Klett-Perthes, Gotha/Stuttgart, Germany.

Jülg, F. (2007) Wintersporttourismus. In: Becker, C., Hopfinger, H. and Steinecke, A. (eds) *Geographie der Freizeit und des Tourismus. Bilanz und Ausblick*, 3rd edn. Oldenbourg, Munich, Germany, pp. 249–258.

Keller, P. (2003) Perspektiven der Seilbahnwirtschaft. *Jahrbuch der Schweizerischen Tourismuswirtschaft* 2002/03, 187–205.

König, W. (2000) *Bahnen und Berge. Verkehrstechnik, Tourismus und Naturschutz in den Schweizer Alpen 1870–1939*. Campus Verlag, Frankfurt/Main, Germany.

Koschatzky, K. (2001) *Räumliche Aspekte im Innovationsprozess. Ein Beitrag zur neuen Wirtschaftsgeographie aus Sicht der regionalen Innovationsforschung* (Wirtschaftsgeographie 19). LIT, Münster, Germany.

Leitner, W. (1984) *Winterfremdenverkehr. Entwicklung, Erfahrungen, Kritik, Anregungen. Bundesland Salzburg 1955/56–1980/81*. Amt der Salzburger Landesregierung, Salzburg, Austria.

Linseisen, A. (2016) Touristische Entwicklungspfade österreichischer Alpengemeinden. Eine vergleichende Analyse der Effekte von Skigebietszusammenschlüssen und sanften Tourismuskonzepten aus evolutionärer Perspektive. MSc Thesis, University of Greifswald, Greifswald, Germany.

Luger, K. and Rest, F. (2017) Alpenreisen-Alpentourismus. Eine Standortbestimmung mit Rück- und Fernblick. In: Luger, K. and Rest, F. (eds) *Alpenreisen. Erlebnis. Raumtransformationen. Imagination*. Studien Verlag, Innsbruck, Austria, pp. 15–38.

Manova (2016) *Wertschöpfung durch österreichische Seilbahnen. Wertschöpfung im Winter. Endbericht Oktober 2016*. Available at: https://www.wko.at/branchen/transport-verkehr/seilbahnen/Wertschoepfung-durch-Oesterreichische-Seilbahnen.pdf (accessed 25 August 2018).

Mayer, M. (2008) Schneller, höher, weiter. Raumzeitliche Diffusionsmuster und wirtschaftliche Bedeutung innovativer Seilbahnanlagen in Westösterreich. *Mitteilungen der Geographischen Gesellschaft in München* 90, 151–187.

Mayer, M. (2009) Innovation as a success factor in tourism: empirical evidence from western Austrian cable-car companies. *Erdkunde* 63(2), 123–139. DOI:10.3112/erdkunde.2009.02.02

Mayer, M. (2012) Summer ski areas in the Alps: first victims of climate change? In: Kagermeier, A. and Saarinen, J. (eds) *Transforming and Managing Destinations: Tourism and Leisure in a Time of Global Change and Risks* (Studien zur Freizeit- und Tourismusforschung 7). MetaGIS, Mannheim, Germany, pp. 27–35.

Mayer, M. (2014) Tourism and innovation, innovation in tourism or tourism innovation? – Conceptions and approaches. In: Küblböck, S. and Thiele, F. (eds) *Tourismus und Innovation* (Studien zur Freizeit- und Tourismusforschung 10). MetaGIS, Mannheim, Germany, pp. 11–29.

Mayer, M. and Steiger, R. (2013) Skitourismus in den Bayerischen Alpen – Entwicklung und Zukunftsperspektiven. In: Job, H. and Mayer, M. (eds) *Tourismus und Regionalentwicklung in Bayern* (Arbeitsberichte der ARL 9). ARL, Hannover, Germany, pp. 164–212.

Mayer, M., Demiroglu, O.C. and Ozcelebi, O. (2018) Microclimatic volatility and elasticity of glacier skiing demand. *Sustainability* 10(10), 3536/1–14. DOI:10.3390/su10103536

Mensch, G. (1972) Basisinnovationen und Verbesserungsinnovationen. *Zeitschrift für Betriebswirtschaft* 42(4), 291–297.

Mountain Manager (2005) Spektakuläre 3 S-Bahn in Kitzbühel. Eine große Vision wurde Wirklichkeit. *Mountain Manager* 1/2005, 64–65.

Pause, W. (1970) *Münchner Skiberge*. BLV, Munich, Germany.

Pfund, C. (1984) Die Bergbahnen als Motor der touristischen Entwicklung. In: Brugger, E., Furrer, G., Messerli, B. and Messerli, P. (eds) *Umbruch im Berggebiet. Die Entwicklung des schweizerischen Berggebietes zwischen Eigenständigkeit und Abhängigkeit aus ökonomischer und ökologischer Sicht*. Haupt, Bern, Switzerland, pp. 391–405.

Rainer, K.J. (2005) *Eine Seilbahn verändert ein Tal*. Rainer Thomas & Co. KG, Kurzras/Schnals, Italy.

Robertson, T.S. (1971) *Innovative Behaviour and Communication*. Holt McDougal, New York.

Salzburg.Orf.at (2018) Kaprun baut längste Seilbahn der Ostalpen. Available at: https://salzburg.orf.at/news/stories/2931552 (accessed 9 October 2018).

Schumpeter, J.A. (1939) *Business Cycles: a Theoretical, Historical, and Statistical Analysis of the Capitalist Process*. McGraw-Hill, New York.

Statistik Austria (2018) Winter overnight stays in Austria 1999/2000, 2004/05, 2009/10, 2014/15. Database retrieval. Available at: http://statcube.at/statistik.at/ext/statcube/jsf/tableView/tableView.xhtml (accessed 4 October 2018).

Steiger, R. (2012) Scenarios for skiing tourism in Austria: integrating demographics with an analysis of climate change. *Journal of Sustainable Tourism* 20(6), 867–882. DOI:10.1080/09669582.2012.680464

Wieser, K. (2017) Die Erfindung des 'Halbschuh-Touristen'. Seilbahnen als Rückgrat im Bergtourismus und Alpha-Tiere der wirtschaftlichen Entwicklung in den Alpenregionen. In: Luger, K. and Rest, F. (eds) *Alpenreisen. Erlebnis. Raumtransformationen. Imagination*. Studien Verlag, Innsbruck, Austria, pp. 193–212.

28 Merging of Ski Resorts, Monopolization and Changes in Ownership Structures: The Case of Whistler

ALISON M. GILL*

Department of Geography and School of Resource and Environmental Management, Simon Fraser University, Burnaby, BC, Canada

28.1 Introduction

In October 2016, Vail Resorts, a Colorado-based corporation, purchased the Canadian resort operations of Whistler Blackcomb, a very successful mountain resort that for many years has been recognized as North America's premier mountain sports destination (Barrett, 2016). At a cost of CA$1.4 billion, this purchase represented the most expensive acquisition for a mountain resort company, which since 2002 had been rapidly expanding its corporate portfolio. Since 2016, Vail Resorts has acquired several resort properties in North America and, as of July 2018, had 15 resorts in its portfolio with another four mountain resorts having been acquired since August 2018. However, Alterra, a recently emerging mountain resort corporation is now challenging Vail Resorts' dominance in North America. In this chapter, a historic profile of corporate ownership of mountain resorts in North America is discussed before focusing on the changing ownership structure of Whistler's mountain operations. Reports in the media are then drawn upon, including perspectives from representatives of the Whistler community and Vail Resorts' corporate managers, to trace reactions to the impact of Whistler Blackcomb's change in ownership. The discussion addresses the challenges of 'corporate–community relations' with a particular focus on the influence of new corporate culture on Whistler's long-standing record of excellent corporate–community engagement.

28.2 Evolving Corporate Ownership of North American Mountain Resorts

The rapid rise of corporate ownership of North American ski resorts by publically traded companies began in the early 1990s with the expansion of the 'Big Three' companies – Vail Resorts Incorporated, Intrawest Corporation and the American Skiing Company (Clifford, 2002). As Clifford (2002, p. 5) observes, the success and expansion

---

* E-mail: agill@sfu.ca

Table 28.1. Acquisitions by the 'Big Three' mountain resort corporations 1986–2002. (From Gill and Williams, 2006, p. 28.)

Intrawest Corporation	Vail Resorts Inc.	American Skiing Co.
Whistler Blackcomb, BC (1986)	Vail, CO (1962)	Sunday River, MA (1980)
Tremblant, Que (1991)	Beaver Creek, CO (1980)	Attitash, NH (1995)
Panorama, BC (1993)	Keystone, CO (1997)	Sugarloaf, MA (1996)
Stratton Mountain, VT (1994)	Breckenridge, CO (1998)	Killington, VT (1996)
Snowshoe, WV (1995)	Heavenly, CA/NV (2002)	Mt Snow, VT (1996)
Copper Mountain, CO (1996)		Steamboat, CO (1997)
Mont Ste. Marie, Que (1997)		The Canyons, UT (1997)
Mammoth, CA (1997)		
Blue Mtn, Ont (1998)		
Mountain Creek, NJ (1998)		
Winter Park, CO (2002)		

of these three companies 'is anchored by their exploitation of public lands – principally lands managed by the United States Forest Service'.

Table 28.1 displays the ownership of resorts by the Big Three up to 2002. These 23 companies dominated the North American market with acquisitions peaking in the late 1990s. Vail Resorts, which already owned the very successful Vail and Beaver Creek resorts in Colorado, was the least aggressive during this period but did expand to Breckenridge in Colorado and Heavenly on the California/Nevada border. Intrawest Corporation, the most rapidly expanding company in the 1990s, acquired resorts across Canada and in both eastern and western regions of the United States. American Skiing Company focused more on eastern US locations but expanded its holdings to the western US with the purchase of Steamboat, Colorado and The Canyons, Utah. Harbaugh (1998) identifies the driving forces of these leading corporate mergers and consolidations as seeking to improve resort operations by integrating investments in on-mountain improvements with the development of real estate, especially four-season resort villages, and associated interests such as retail stores, hotels, travel and tour operations. Commenting on Vail Resorts' strategies Clifford (2002, p. 7) suggests 'it intends to get its corporate fingers into a lot of businesses in the neighbourhood'. Intrawest was a leading innovator in developing this resort village model, which served as the template for developing all of Intrawest's properties.

In the new millennium, the landscape of corporate ownership of mountain resorts changed quite dramatically. American Skiing Company experienced financial difficulties and having sold Heavenly to Vail Resorts in 2002, it sold Steamboat to Intrawest in 2006. With the sale in 2008 of its final property, The Canyons, the company was dissolved. Intrawest's rapid expansion was fuelled by the financial wealth of its new owner, Fortress Investment Group, a private New York-based investment company, which had bought Intrawest in October, 2006 for $2.8 billion (Moore and Spain, 2006). However, the global economic crisis of 2008 resulted in financial problems for Fortress, and they divested their interests in a number of resort properties, including Whistler Blackcomb. Intrawest properties still continued to operate successful mountain resort destinations in the United States, but in May 2017, after its acquisition by the newly formed partnership of Henry Crown and Company (the owners of Aspen

Ski Company) and an investment firm, KSL Capital Partners, it was announced that Intrawest would no longer exist as a public company (Blevins, 2017).

Between 2010 and 2018 Vail Resorts embarked on a rapid expansion plan, acquiring 13 new mountain resorts including Whistler Blackcomb, with a strategy of expanding the geographical range of their properties in part to hedge against variable regional snow conditions (see Table 28.2). In the west their acquisitions, as well as building on their existing Colorado strength, included expanding into Utah with the purchase of Canyons Resort, followed soon after by the hostile takeover of its neighbour, Park City Mountain Resort. Recently several eastern resorts including Stowe, Vermont have extended Vail Resorts' incursion into the eastern US market.

Table 28.2. Vail Resorts' acquisitions 1996–2018. (From Vail Resorts – Wikipedia contributors, 2018.)

Name	Location	Date opened	Date acquired
Vail Ski Resort	Eagle County, Colorado	1962	N/A
Beaver Creek Resort	Near Avon, Colorado	1980	N/A
Breckenridge Ski Resort	Breckenridge, Colorado	1961	1996
Keystone Resort	Keystone, Colorado	1970	1996
Heavenly Mountain Resort	Lake Tahoe, California/Nevada	1955	2002
Northstar California	Placer County, California	1972	2010
Kirkwood Mountain Resort	Kirkwood, California	1972	2012
Afton Alps	Denmark Township, Minnesota	1963	2012
Mount Brighton	Brighton, Michigan	1960	2012
Canyons Resort	Park City, Utah	1968	2013
Park City Mountain Resort	Park City, Utah	1963	2014
Perisher Ski Resort	Perisher Valley, Australia	1951	2015
Wilmot Mountain	Kenosha County, Wisconsin	1938	2016
Whistler Blackcomb	Whistler, British Columbia, Canada	1966	2016
Stowe Mountain Resort	Stowe, Vermont	1933	2017
Mount Sunapee Resort	Newbury, New Hampshire	1948	2018
Okemo Mountain Resort	Ludlow, Vermont	1955	2018
Crested Butte	Crested Butte, Colorado	1962	2018
Stevens Pass	Leavenworth, Washington	1937	2018

Table 28.3. Alterra resorts, 2018. (From Alterra Mountain Company, 2018.)

Number	Name
1	Steamboat, Colorado[a]
2	Winter Park, Colorado[a]
3	Squaw Valley – Alpine Meadows, California
4	Mammoth Mountain, California[a]
5	June Mountain, California
6	Big Bear Mountain, California
7	Stratton, Vermont[a]
8	Snowshoe, West Virginia[a]
9	Tremblant, Quebec[a]
10	Blue Mountain, Ontario[a]
11	Deer Valley, Utah
12	CMHC Heli-Skiing & Summer Adventure, British Columbia
13	Solitude Mountain, Utah
14	Crystal Mountain Resort, Washington

[a]Previously Intrawest properties.

The rapid growth of the new mountain resort corporation, Alterra, created in 2017, has been described as 'an emerging Denver-based ski industry giant' (Rubino, 2018). Alterra Mountain Company comprises 14 mountain destinations spread throughout six states and three Canadian provinces (see Table 28.3). Seven of these resorts had been previously owned and developed by Intrawest.

While market expansion strategies by both Vail Resorts and Alterra reflect similar patterns of acquisition and capital improvements of geographically dispersed properties, their approaches differ. Whereas Vail Resorts prominently brands its corporate identity at all of its resorts, Alterra prefers not to, as their website states 'we honour each destinations' unique character and authenticity' (Alterra, 2018). This distinction is also reflected in competition around the two companies' season passes. Vail Resorts' Epic Pass has been operating for the past 10 years and its market share has expanded across 18 resorts with the acquisition of new properties. Alterra's Ikon Pass was modelled on Vail Resorts' successful Epic Pass and in July 2018 was accessible to 27 destinations. Although, there are only 14 resorts under Alterra ownership, pass holders have access (with some limitations) to partner resorts that are independently owned. These include major ski destinations across North America including Aspen-Snowmass in Colorado (independently owned by the Crown family); Jackson Hole, Wyoming; and Snowbird, Utah. A partnership in June 2018 with Thredbo, Australia also introduced direct market competition for passes with nearby Vail Resorts' Perisher property in the Snowy Mountains. Alterra's success in getting independent resorts to join the Ikon pass is attributed to past good relationships with the resorts (Steiner, 2018).

28.3 Whistler: Changes in Ownership of Mountain Operations

The origins of Whistler's resort development lie in the bid by a group of Vancouver businessmen known as the Garibaldi Olympic Development Association (GODA) to host the 1968 Olympic Games. The proposed site on Whistler Mountain (see Fig. 28.1)

Fig. 28.1. Inukshuk on the peak of Whistler Mountain. (Photograph courtesy of Harold Richins.)

was located 120 km from Vancouver, along a gravel road with no infrastructure development or services. Although the bid failed, it raised interest in the potential for ski development on the mountain. Consequently, from 1962 to 1965 Garibaldi Lifts Limited, a sister organization to GODA, raised funds and began the development of the ski area with lifts and a gondola, with skiing officially opening on Whistler Mountain in 1966 (Caputo, 2015). This attracted avid skiers, many of whom constructed A-frame cabins near the base. Recognizing the potential for developing tourism in the area, the provincial government paved the road. In 1971, 5 years after operations began on Whistler Mountain, the board of directors of Garibaldi Lifts phased out the shareholders and an investment company from Toronto bought out the remaining shares. Still dreaming of hosting a Winter Olympics, local visionaries began talking about how to create a world-class summer and winter resort. In 1975, the Resort Municipality of Whistler (RMOW) was incorporated as the first designated resort municipality in Canada (Gill, 2000). Whistler Village was developed, not at the original base on the south side of Whistler Mountain, but on the north side where it intersected with Blackcomb Mountain. Separate companies on the two mountains undertook infrastructural development for ski development during the construction phase of the Village. In 1980 Hastings West, a group of Vancouver-based investors, purchased Garibaldi Lift Company and subsequently, the name changed to Whistler Mountain Ski Corporation (Morrison, 2014).

Meanwhile on Blackcomb Mountain a call for bids was issued in 1978 to develop Blackcomb for skiing. The bidding to develop Blackcomb was contested by two companies, the Aspen Skiing Company, and the newly formed Blackcomb Skiing Enterprises. Aspen, having recently developed the Fortress Mountain Resort in Alberta, won the contest. A new company, Fortress Mountain Resorts, was formed with a 50–50 partnership between Aspen and the Business Development Bank of Canada. The new competition, paid for partially by tax dollars, was not initially appreciated by Whistler residents (Morrison, 2014). As a result of this foundational work, Whistler Village (see Figs 28.2 and 28.3), Blackcomb Mountain and the north side of Whistler Mountain opened for business in December 1980.

Fig. 28.2. View of Whistler Village from Whistler Mountain. (Photograph courtesy of Allison Gill.)

Fig. 28.3. Community of Whistler. (Photograph courtesy of Harold Richins.)

The opening of Blackcomb led to a period of intense rivalry between the two mountain operations. The character of the mountains and their target markets were distinctive. As Caputo (2015) observes, Whistler Mountains operations were large and quite traditional, reflecting the views of its Canadian and European visionaries, and the Vancouver-based Hastings West Group that took over Garibaldi Lifts Limited was new to the business of skiing. In contrast, Blackcomb was aimed at a younger market, US-dominated and half controlled by the Aspen Corporation, already experienced in the ski business. During the 1980s and 1990s, there was an unprecedented level of constant upgrades and improvements not seen at other resorts. In 1986, Blackcomb's assets and real estate rights were bought by Intrawest, a fledgling Vancouver-based real estate developer. Intrawest was an early developer of timeshare and condominium listings and saw the potential in developing real estate in the ski resort.

In 1998, Intrawest bought its rival, the Whistler Mountain Ski Corporation, and immediately began major infrastructure upgrades on Whistler Mountain. It also acquired Whistler Mountain Ski Corporation's valuable future real estate development rights known as 'bed units'. These had been allotted to the company by the RMOW as incentives during the early development stages in a 'lands for lifts' agreement (Gill, 2007). In the following decade, Intrawest with its combined operations on the two mountains achieved great success to become consistently ranked as North America's premier mountain resort. At its peak of success, Intrawest was purchased in 2006 by the alternative asset management firm, Fortress Investment Group. However, in the wake of the 2008 global recession and 3 weeks before the opening of the 2010 Winter

Olympic Games (co-hosted by Vancouver and Whistler) Fortress failed to make payment on its loan used to buy out Intrawest (Ferreras, 2010a). In order to reduce Fortress' debt load, Intrawest was forced to divest itself of several of its resort holdings, including a partial sale of Whistler Blackcomb. This was achieved in 2010 through a public offering of shares of a new independent company, Whistler Blackcomb Holdings, on the Toronto Stock Exchange. The net outcome of the reorganization was that Whistler Blackcomb Holdings became the managing partner with control of 75% of the partnership with Nippon Cable continuing to own the remaining 25%. With this transaction Whistler Blackcomb severed its connection to Fortress and most of its ties to Intrawest, although some senior Intrawest representatives remained on the Board of Whistler Blackcomb Holdings, along with some other local representatives (Ferreras, 2010b). Intrawest sold its remaining 24% stake in Whistler Blackcomb to KSL Capital Partners in 2012. As discussed in detail in the next section, Vail Resorts bought Whistler Blackcomb, in October, 2016, with Nippon Cable retaining its long-standing 25% share in the company (CNW, 2016).

28.4 Corporate–Community Relations

There is increasing recognition in mountain resorts of what Rothman (1998) terms the 'corporatisation of place' and growing stakeholder concern regarding the social and environmental impacts of corporate influence. As Gill and Williams (2006, p. 26) have observed, '[t]he degree to which places are transformed is in part a function of the nature of the relationship between the corporation and the community especially with respect to issues of power'. Flagestad and Hope (2001, p. 452) in observing Vail Resorts' and Intrawest's company reports from the late 1990s, concluded that 'ski corporations have a dominant influence on how the destination is operated as a strategic business unit as well as strong political power in the community-related development of the destination'. However, mountain resort operators have demonstrated for some time a growing awareness of the need for stronger alliances with the communities in which they operate (Sherman and Neslin, 1996). The importance of these alliances seems now to be a standard acknowledgement by corporate spokespersons to the media on the acquisitions of new mountain operations. In this section, I first consider past institutional factors that have influenced corporate–community relationships in Whistler. I then use the lens of various local and national media and websites to examine the reactions of Whistler's local residents and stakeholders and the opinions of corporate spokespeople to the acquisition of Whistler Blackcomb by Vail Resorts.

28.4.1 Past factors influencing corporate–community relations in Whistler

Over the past 50 years of organized ski development in Whistler, there have been a number of significant changes in ownership driven by global market factors and North American competition among resort developers. However, these transitions of ownership have on the whole been friendly takeovers, even if in the early stages change causes some dissenting voices. Despite its international recognition as North America's premier mountain resort that attracts global as well as regional and local visitors, there has always been a perception among locals that Whistler is fundamentally

Canadian, and indeed in some peoples' minds, locally controlled and managed. The financial ownership perspective described above perhaps reveals a rather different picture. For example, at an early stage the involvement of Aspen Skiing Company is evident in the financing and operation of Blackcomb. However, the acquisition by Intrawest in 1986 was perceived as establishing local ownership, as the company began as a Vancouver real estate development company and its CEO, Joe Houssian, owned a home in Whistler and was known to many. With the subsequent merger with the locally run Whistler Mountain Ski Corporation in 1997, and attainment of increasing recognition and success, Whistler enjoyed a period of corporate stability. However, the purchase in 2006 by Fortress, a US global investment and asset management firm, and the subsequent stepping down of Houssian as CEO signalled an era of corporate and financial uncertainty for Intrawest, who despite having expanded their holdings to other Canadian and US resorts, regarded Whistler as their flagship operation.

Whistler (RMOW) was created under a new Resort Municipality Act of 1975 that specifically distinguishes it from other municipal designations by recognizing it as a 'resort community'. The ski companies, although major stakeholders in the power structure of the resort, were required under the Act to comply with local land use development regulations and also coordinate their marketing strategies with all other commercial enterprises in the RMOW. However, in 1982 under the edicts of a newly crafted provincial Commercial Alpine Ski Policy, these ski lift companies were also granted participation in an innovative 'lands for lifts' programme that enabled them to acquire future development rights on specific Whistler land in return for their investment in mountain infrastructure. This policy proved to be a significant positive influence on the level and rate of corporate real estate development that took place in the ensuing years. From a corporate perspective it is also notable that Intrawest's real estate development strategy became a widely emulated model at other Intrawest resorts.

Gill and Williams (2011) argue that Whistler's growth dependent path was determined by a political and regulatory system established at its inception that locked the resort community's development into a defined land base and planning strategy that promoted controlled growth. Although over time political changes occurred, power remained with three primary decision making groups: the municipality, the mountain operator(s) and the provincial government, all of whom remained committed to continued growth up to an agreed upon limit.

The success of a mountain resort operation depends not only on the level of investment in infrastructural and facility development but also in more intangible aspects (Gill, 2000). For example, the relationship between the community and corporate interests changed in 1997 when Intrawest acquired the Whistler Mountain Skiing Company. The emergence of a monopoly by Intrawest initially caused concern among some residents, who envisaged problems common to 'single-industry towns' with respect to issues of power and decision making. Fortunately, Intrawest recognized the importance of good community relations to their success in Whistler and sought to establish a 'social license to operate' (Williams et al., 2007; Williams et al., 2012). The company strived to inform and engage community stakeholders in a variety of its environmental initiatives with the intention of reducing its future development transaction costs with local decision makers.

In 2000, when Whistler approached its established growth capacity limit rather faster than anticipated, the stakeholders embarked on an alternative governance model centred on an innovative integrated comprehensive sustainability strategy that was based on principles of 'The Natural Step', an international not-for-profit research, educational and advisory organization. Whistler engaged in an aggressive public engagement process between 2002 and 2004 that culminated in the development of the sustainability plan known as *Whistler2020*, which provided a consensus-based vision, strategic direction and a set of ambitious steps to navigate towards a sustainable future (Gill and Williams, 2008). With the forthcoming Winter Olympic Games in 2010, there was strong support not only by the community but also by Intrawest to embrace a sustainability path (Gill and Williams, 2011). From a corporate perspective, pursuing innovations that resulted in the company receiving 28 national and international awards between 1998 and 2010 for outstanding environmental management and social performance greatly enhanced Intrawest's reputational capital at Whistler Blackcomb (Whistler Blackcomb, 2018).

28.4.2 Reactions to Vail Resorts' acquisition of Whistler Blackcomb

In August 2016, the announcement of Vail Resorts intention to purchase Whistler Blackcomb 'sent shock waves through the resort' (Ogilvie, 2016). The article continues: 'For years we have been writing about how the resort, and indeed Whistler Blackcomb (WB), does not want to be Vail, how Vail gets things wrong, and how we can improve on our nature-based product and our community by not doing what Vail does'.

The purchase of Whistler Blackcomb was by far the largest addition to the growing collection of Vail Resorts' acquisitions and the one with the greatest number of visitors (approximately 2 million per annum). It also offered the most reliable snow conditions of any of the resorts (Plummer, 2016). Whistler Blackcomb's well-established, growing summertime tourism attractions and visitors were also a feature that was seen as offering valuable lessons for the development of Vail's other resorts (Plummer, 2016).

While Vail's acquisition is seen to provide opportunities for further growth in tourism numbers and businesses in Whistler, this also means further challenges for attracting and housing a growing workforce and managing increasing traffic problems. Issues raised by Council and other stakeholders in the early stages concerned the degree to which Vail Resorts would be contributing to solutions to these broader community concerns. In response, Vail Resorts publically stated their commitment to Whistler Blackcomb's success by supporting the following initiatives: the Master Development Agreements with the local First Nations; continuing principally local Canadian leadership; maintenance of local employment; and, substantial investment in Whistler Blackcomb's infrastructure and growth plans, including the extensive Renaissance Plan that had been recently developed; and commitment to community and environmental sustainability (PR Newswire, 2016).

An advantage that the RMOW has compared with many other mountain resorts is its well-established track record of controlled community growth regulated by policy and bylaws that apply to all community stakeholders including the mountain corporation. However, some voiced concern that despite the hope of economic stability, the corporate takeover could lead to Whistler losing the unique appeal that has made it an internationally sought after destination (Plummer, 2016). While reassuring to investors, statements such as that made by Katz, Vail Resorts CEO, who said 'The connection with Vancouver [international airport] sets Whistler Blackcomb up for great growth with China and Southeast Asia' (Plummer, 2016), can give rise to anxiety for some community residents who have had confidence over the past two decades in a restricted municipal growth management programme.

Vail Resorts' acquisition of Whistler Blackcomb was finalized in a $1.4 billion friendly takeover in October 2016, making it the 14th North American resort in the collection. As Vail Resorts' CEO Rob Katz commented: 'Whistler Blackcomb is one of the most iconic mountain resorts in the world and we are tremendously excited to welcome the resort and talented team who work there to the Vail Resorts family' (Barrett, 2016). He went on to assure employees that the vast majority of Whistler Blackcomb staff would stay on, including the Whistler Blackcomb CEO, Dave Brownlie, who under Vail Resorts ownership became Whistler Blackcomb's chief operating officer (COO). Acknowledging the tight relationship between the resort and the community and its unique brand and Canadian identity, he added, 'We look forward to working with the Whistler Blackcomb team to ensure the long-term success of the resort and community'. A month later, 60 employees were laid off primarily in the IT, finance and marketing departments, including the senior VP in marketing and sales and the chief financial officer. The reason given was redundancies as the result of jobs already being done at the corporate offices in Colorado (Dupuis, 2016a). Dave Brownlie (COO) left the company within 8 months to be replaced by a new COO, Pete Sonntag, a veteran mountain resort manager from the United States.

By September 2017, after a winter season of excellent snow conditions at Whistler Blackcomb and a related boom in visitor levels, there were community concerns over tourist overcrowding, a lack of affordable housing, a shortage of employees, escalating cost of living and, more generally, Vail Resorts' takeover of Whistler Blackcomb (Barrett, 2017). With the new COO at the helm there were many start-up problems relating to switching to Vail Resorts corporate computer system and a recruiting model driven from the Colorado headquarters. Despite these concerns, in December 2017 Vail Resorts announced a major $66 million investment in infrastructure development at Whistler Blackcomb, which represented not only the largest single-year capital investment in Whistler Blackcomb's history but also the largest in any Vail Resorts mountain operations (Barde, 2017). This development plan replaced the Renaissance Plan, which had been proposed by the previous owners as an ambitious, phased, long-term plan aimed as a hedge against climate change. It had focused on developing indoor facilities such as a water park and other indoor amenities that would also appeal to non-skiers. While controversial with some residents, concerned about 'Disneyfication' of the resort (Barde, 2017), the Renaissance Plan was initially supported by Vail Resorts (Dupuis, 2016b). While some long-term investment items such as real estate and housing development may be pursued in the future, all of Vail Resorts' current plans relate to mountain upgrades including new gondolas aimed at improving the visitor experience especially for novice skiers. Vail Resorts, CEO, Rob Katz announced in a call to investors that 'We're obviously trying to open up new markets in Whistler, especially at the high end, both in Asia and the United States and Europe' (Barde, 2017). While Vail Resorts' new development plan was supported by the mayor and various long-term Whistler Blackcomb managers (Barde, 2017), others have voiced concern that Vail Resorts is only interested in the high-end destination visitor at the expense of the local and regional market that has sustained the resort's success for decades (Maxwell, 2017).

By 2018, corporate–community relations seemed to have taken a further step in the wrong direction. This was evidenced in an April article from the internationally recognized media outlet, *Bloomberg*, which carried a story entitled, 'Is Vail Resorts

Killing Whistler's Spirit' (Pearson, 2018). Locals were very upset by the introduction of the 'Epic Pass', a highly marketed benefit of being part of Vail Resorts. This season pass was sold at a cost of $899 and gives holders access to the company's 15 or more resorts in North America and Australia. However, it must be purchased before the season opens. For those people, including many locals who have neither the time nor the money to benefit from a season pass, the daily cost of a lift ticket is high. Vail Resorts argues that getting people to commit before the season opens is in response to the increasing variability of weather due to climate change and that such a business strategy is necessary for business security (*Pique* staff, 2018). At the same time previously discounted passes for local residents were discontinued although, following negative feedback from locals, some consideration of future discounted passes for some groups may occur including perhaps a pass for 5 days of free access to elementary school children. In a media interview, responding to the question, 'What efforts are you taking, if any, to preserve and promote Whistler's distinct culture?' Vail Resorts' CEO Robert Katz's evasive response was essentially that Whistler's importance to Vail Resorts is its uniqueness and 'that's a community conversation that the resort needs to be very much a part of' (*Pique* staff, 2018).

Although, from a corporate perspective, the acquisition of Whistler Blackcomb was seen as a success due to a very successful 2017–18 winter season that attracted 8% of the corporation's Epic Pass holders to Whistler Blackcomb – due in large part to poor snow conditions in other US Vail Resorts properties. As a consequence visitor numbers in Whistler set a record for the third straight year (Pearson, 2018). However, local skiers from Whistler and regionally from the Lower Mainland Region of BC were less than happy, especially as Whistler Blackcomb tickets are priced with a base rate in US dollars, which fluctuates daily against Canada's poorly performing dollar. An article in *Macleans*, an established Canadian current affairs and news magazine entitled 'Why a lot of B.C. skiers are kissing Whistler goodbye' reinforces the cost-related reasons that British Columbians are choosing from other excellent ski resorts in BC (Tanner, 2018).

Whistler has been proud not only of its outstanding skiing terrain but also of the culture that it has created over its relatively short history. They built arguably the world's best ski resort and feel a sense of ownership. Claire Ogilvie observed in an article in the local *Pique Newsmagazine* in April that, although residents realized there would be a change, 'we didn't realise, well … how American Vail Resorts really is' (Ogilvie, 2018). The concern over Vail Resorts' growth plans to attract the high spenders is shared by many residents, who are increasingly seeing the local retail and business sector being taken over by external, often corporate interests (Wongkee and Gill, 2019).

In response to the bad press surrounding the discontentment of locals, Whistler Blackcomb's COO, Pete Sonntag, engaged in a major public relations campaign. In the local *Pique Newsmagazine* the title of an article states 'We acknowledge that we made some mistakes' (Barrett, 2018a). The main message was that the company is committed to 'making things right'. Corporate issues ranged from embarrassing delays in accessing passes for opening day due to computer glitches, to minor annoyances such as initially listing mountain weather conditions in degrees Fahrenheit rather than Celsius (as used in Canada), and using American rather than Canadian spelling. Sonntag stressed the importance of communications observing, '[i]f we were to do one thing differently, it would be to come in with full awareness that this is an issue and it's something we need to pay attention to, and the details do matter' (Barrett, 2018b).

However, the biggest and most critical gap in Whistler Blackcomb's extensive development plans is the provision of housing for seasonal staff. While Whistler has done better than most resorts with respect to supporting affordable housing for permanent employees, seasonal workers have been the company's responsibility. Although Whistler Blackcomb built housing for workers 20 years ago it is inadequate given the recent explosion of visitors, resulting in staff shortages and reduced service (Maxwell, 2018). Despite promises of a new housing project, it was not included in the major development plan and by July 2018 no details had been announced. Katz's responses to questions concerning the looming crisis of provision of seasonal employee housing have been vague (*Pique* staff, 2018), although this possibly may have to do with regulatory issues within the municipality.

Until its recent acquisition by Vail Resorts, Whistler, unlike many mountain resorts in the United States, has been relatively sheltered from the effects of changing corporate ownership. Even during the past decade when Intrawest underwent considerable financial restructuring the reputational image of Whistler Blackcomb as North America's leading mountain resort was not affected. The stabilizing effect that Intrawest played over a period of more than three decades is significant. Whistler Blackcomb was Intrawest's flagship resort and, despite Intrawest's rapid corporate expansion across North America in the 1990s, it was considered by residents of Whistler to be a 'local' company. Importantly, Intrawest and the RMOW developed a good collaborative relationship that was guided by the legislation established at Whistler's inception. The challenges presented by the recent takeover of Whistler Blackcomb by Vail Resorts represent a disruption of corporate–community relations that in part represent the effects of cultural distinctions between Canada and the United States. Rebuilding trust among the community and the new corporate owners will be the major challenge facing the resort.

In conclusion, competition between the key corporate owners of North American mountain resorts over the past 30 years has been aggressive, resulting in shifting ownership patterns that reflect the influence of both local and global circumstances on the vulnerabilities of mountain resort operations. As competition for rapidly emerging global markets grows, especially from China and elsewhere in Asia, the two North American corporate mountain resort giants, Vail Resorts and Alterra, will compete to acquire and develop new and existing resort properties to accommodate both changing market demands and the spectre of impending climate change. To achieve success in the face of these impending changes, the importance of building good corporate–community relationships cannot be overstated.

References

Alterra (2018) About. Available at: https://www.alterramtnco.com/about (accessed 8 July 2018).
Barde, J. (2017) Vail Resorts reimagines Whistler Blackcomb's future. Available at: https://www.piquenewsmagazine.com/whistler/vail-resorts-reimagines-whistler-blackcombs-future/Content?oid=6005156 (accessed 8 July 2018).
Barrett, B. (2016) Vail Resorts completes acquisition of Whistler Blackcomb. Available at: https://www.piquenewsmagazine.com/whistler/vail-resorts-completes-acquisition-of-whistler-blackcomb/Content?oid=2806390 (accessed 8 July 2018).
Barrett, B. (2017) Vail Resorts looks towards Whistler's future. Available at: https://www.piquenewsmagazine.com/whistler/vail-resorts-looks-towards-whistlers-future/Content?oid=4657288 (accessed 8 July 2018).

Barrett, B. (2018a) We acknowledge that we made some mistakes. Available at: https://www.piquenewsmagazine.com/whistler/we-acknowledge-that-we-made-some-mistakes/Content?oid=8208305 (accessed 8 July 2018).

Barrett, B. (2018b) Vail Resorts sees strong quarter despite poor snow season in U.S. Available at: https://www.piquenewsmagazine.com/whistler/vail-resorts-sees-strong-quarter-despite-poor-snow-season-in-us/Content?oid=9235327 (accessed 8 July 2018).

Blevins, J. (2017) $1.5 billion deal rocks Colorado ski industry as Aspen Skiing Co. acquires Steamboat and operator of Winter Park resort. Available at: https://www.denverpost.com/2017/04/10/steamboat-winter-park-ski-resorts-acquired/ (accessed 18 July 2019).

Caputo, D. (2015) The history of Whistler's lifts. Whistler Museum. Available at: https://blog.whistlermuseum.org/2015/04/04/the-history-of-whistlers-lifts (accessed 8 July 2018).

Clifford, H. (2002) *Downhill Slide: Why the Corporate Ski Industry is Bad for Skiing, Ski Towns and the Environment*. Sierra Club Books, San Francisco, California.

CNW (2016) Vail Resorts and Whistler Blackcomb agree to strategic combination. Available at: https://www.newswire.ca/news-releases/vail-resorts-and-whistler-blackcomb-agree-to-strategic-combination-589455381.html (accessed 19 November 2018).

Dupuis, B. (2016a) Vail Resorts lays off 60 people at Whistler Blackcomb. Available at: https://www.piquenewsmagazine.com/whistler/vail-resorts-lays-off-60-people-at-whistler-blackcomb/Content?oid=2836638 (accessed 8 July 2018).

Dupuis, B. (2016b) Brownlie talks Vail resorts, Renaissance and more. Available at: https://www.piquenewsmagazine.com/whistler/brownlie-talks-vail-resorts-renaissance-and-more-at-chamber-luncheon/Content?oid=2872062 (accessed 8 July 2018).

Ferreras, J. (2010a) Intrawest misses loan payment. Available at: https://www.piquenewsmagazine.com/whistler/intrawest-misses-loan-payment/Content?oid=2166834 (accessed 10 July 2018).

Ferreras, J. (2010b) Whistler Blackcomb completes public offering. Available at: https://www.piquenewsmagazine.com/whistler/whistler-blackcomb-completes-public-offering/Content?oid=2169390 (accessed 10 July 2018).

Flagestad, A., and Hope, C.A. (2001) Strategic success in winter sports destinations: a sustainable value creation perspective. *Tourism Management* 22(5), 445–461.

Gill, A.M. (2000) From growth machine to growth management: the dynamics of resort development in Whistler, British Columbia. *Environment and Planning A: Economy and Space* 32(6), 1083–1103. DOI:10.1068/a32160

Gill, A.M. (2007) The politics of bed units: the case of Whistler, British Columbia. In: Coles, T. and Church, A. (eds) *Tourism, Politics and Place*. Routledge, London, pp. 125–159.

Gill, A. M. and Williams, P.W. (2006) Corporate responsibility and place: the case of Whistler, British Columbia. In: Clark, T., Gill, A.M. and Hartmann, R. (eds) *Mountain Resort Planning and Development in an Era of Globalization*. Cognisant Communication, Elmsford, NY, pp. 26–40.

Gill, A.M. and Williams, P.W. (2008) From 'guiding fiction' to action: applying 'The Natural Step' to sustainability planning in the resort of Whistler, British Columbia. In: McCool, S.F. and Moisey, R.N. (eds) *Tourism, Recreation and Sustainability: Linking Culture and Environment*, 2nd edn. CAB International, Wallingford, UK, pp. 121–130.

Gill. A.M. and Williams, P.W. (2011) Rethinking resort growth: understanding evolving governance strategies in Whistler, British Columbia. *Journal of Sustainable Tourism* 19(4–5), 629–648. DOI:10.1080/09669582.2011.558626

Harbaugh, J. (1998) It's all in your prospectus: IPO's are giving the ski industry a different image and, for the short term, a different valuation. *Ski Area Management* 37(1), 67–68.

Maxwell, G.D. (2017) Resistance is futile. Available at: https://www.piquenewsmagazine.com/whistler/resistance-is-futile/Content?oid=5291778 (accessed 8 July 2018).

Maxwell, G.D. (2018) We are Burger King all the way. Available at: https://www.piquenewsmagazine.com/whistler/we-are-burger-king-all-the-way/Content?oid=6805649 (accessed 8 July 2018).

Moore, A. and Spain, W. (2006) Intrawest agrees to $2.8 billion buyout. Available at: www.marketwatch.com/story/resort-operator-intrawest-agrees-to-28-billion-buyout (accessed 7 May 2019).

Morrison, J.L. (2014) Envisioning Whistler. Available at: https://www.piquenewsmagazine.com/whistler/envisioning-whistler/Content?oid=2552202 (accessed 1 July 2018).

Ogilvie, C. (2016) You're so Vail. Available at: https://www.piquenewsmagazine.com/whistler/youre-so-vail/Content?oid=2799449 (accessed 8 July 2018).

Ogilvie, C. (2018) Looking for answers. Available at: https://www.piquenewsmagazine.com/whistler/looking-for-answers/Content?oid=8208623 (accessed 8 July 2018).

Pearson, N.O. (2018) Is Vail Resorts killing Whistler's spirit? Available at: https://www.bloomberg.com/news/articles/2018-04-09/is-vail-resorts-killing-whistler-spirit (accessed 8 July 2018).

Pique staff (2018) A Q&A with Vail Resorts CEO Rob Katz. Available at: https://www.piquenewsmagazine.com/whistler/a-qanda-with-vail-resorts-ceo-rob-katz/Content?oid=8962701 (accessed 8 July 2018).

Plummer, E. (2016) A new beginning. Available at: https://www.piquenewsmagazine.com/whistler/a-new-beginning/Content?oid=2872970 (accessed 8 July 2018).

PR Newswire (2016) Vail Resorts and Whistler Blackcomb agree to strategic combination. Available at: https://www.prnewswire.com/news-releases/vail-resorts-and-whistler-blackcomb-agree-to-strategic-combination-300310250.html (accessed 8 July 2018).

Rothman, H. (1998) *Devil's Bargains: Tourism in the Twentieth-Century American West*. University Press of Kansas, Lawrence, Kansas.

Rubino, J. (2018) Denver's Alterra Mountain Co. to buy Utah's Solitude Mountain Resort. Available at: https://www.denverpost.com/2018/06/20/alterra-mountain-co-buys-solitude-mountain-resort/ (accessed 18 July 2019).

Sherman, H.D. and Neslin, D.S. (1996) Environmental regulation – its future. *Ski Area Management* 35(3), 57–58, 83–84.

Steiner, C. (2018) Alterra's Ikon Pass gives skiers a real rival to Vail's Epic Pass. Available at: https://www.usatoday.com/story/travel/destinations/2018/01/26/alterras-ikon-pass-gives-skiers-real-rival-vails-epic-pass/1070807001 (accessed 8 July 2018).

Tanner, A. (2018) Why a lot of B.C. skiers are kissing Whistler goodbye. Available at: https://www.macleans.ca/news/canada/why-a-lot-of-b-c-skiers-are-kissing-whistler-goodbye/ (accessed 18 July 2019).

Vail Resorts – Wikipedia (2018) Vail Resorts. Available at: https://en.wikipedia.org/wiki/Vail_Resorts (accessed 10 July 2018).

Whistler Blackcomb (2018) Whistler Blackcomb List of Sustainability Awards. Available at: https://www.whistlerblackcomb.com/explore-the-resort/about-the-resort/environment/environmental-awards.aspx (accessed 8 July 2018).

Williams, P.W., Gill, A.M. and Ponsford, I. (2007) Corporate social responsibility at tourism destinations: toward a social license to operate. *Tourism Review International* 11(2), 133–144. DOI:10.3727/154427207783948883

Williams, P.W., Gill, A.M., Marcoux, J. and Xu, N. (2012) Nurturing 'social license to operate' through corporate-civil society relationships in tourism destinations. In: Hsu, C. and Gartner, W. (eds) *The Routledge Handbook of Tourism Research*. Routledge, London, pp. 196–214.

Wongkee, S. and Gill, A.M. (2019) Resort retail resilience: the contested spaces of retailing in Whistler, Canada. In: Saarinen, J. and Gill, A.M. (eds) *Resilient Destinations and Tourism: Governance Strategies in the Transition towards Sustainability in Tourism*. Routledge, London, pp. 135–152.

29 How to Manage Ski Resorts in an Environmentally Friendly Way – Challenges and Lessons Learnt

ULRIKE PRÖBSTL-HAIDER AND CLAUDIA HÖDL*

Institute of Landscape Development, Recreation and Conservation Planning, University of Natural Resources and Life Sciences, Vienna, Austria

29.1 Introduction

Many winter tourism destinations have started to promote their commitment to the environment. Some highlight already accomplished achievements (e.g. Ski Lifts Lech in Austria[1]), while others present high-flying visions (e.g. the Laax winter destination in Switzerland[2]). Studies conducted by the German Sport University Cologne (Roth *et al.*, 2018) have shown that environmental aspects of a ski resort are important to tourists. Moreover, ecological certification has long been recognized as a valuable tool to influence markets and has become increasingly important in tourism (Font, 2001; Buckley, 2002). This way, environmental aspects can be used to sharpen a resort's profile and to identify and attract its respective target group(s) with ever-improving precision. However, as a result tourists are confronted with an increasing number of terms, labels and classification systems addressing so-called 'green' concerns, such as environmentally friendly management or sustainability.

Aside from differentiation and marketing aspects, certification systems are also used as a tool to enhance the sustainable development of ski resorts. As such, these certifications play a key role in sustainable tourism management (Font, 2002; Honey, 2002; Bien, 2007). Honey and Rome (2001) define certification as a voluntary procedure which assesses, audits and provides a written assurance that a facility, product, process or service meets specific standards. In addition, it awards a marketable logo to those enterprises that meet or exceed baseline standards. Ideally, the certification clearly demarcates sustainable from unsustainable organizations (Font and Harris, 2004). It is, therefore, considered an important tool to ensure competitiveness and differentiation, as it helps build consumer confidence (Sloan *et al.*, 2011).

In general, there are three different categories of certificates (Sloan *et al.*, 2011; SustainableTourism.net, 2014):

- individual concepts;
- generic environmental certifications on an international or European level (International Organization for Standardization (ISO): ISO 14001 and ISO 14004, Eco-Management and Audit Scheme (EMAS)); and

---

* E-mail: claudia.hoedl@boku.ac.at

- certification by governmental initiatives (e.g. 'Das Österreichische Umweltzeichen'/ 'The Austrian Ecolabel').

By now, a large number of individual standards have emerged and many companies have elected to adopt them (see World Tourism Organization (WTO), 2002; Sloan *et al.*, 2011). Thereby, they make use of the varied certifying programmes in existence and ensure compliance with their sustainability standards. Overall, all credible certifications are defined by three crucial components:

1. Setting of environmental standards.
2. Third-party certification of these standards.
3. Value-added marketing or environmental communication.

In addition to the various individual concepts, the ISO has developed more generic environmental certifications that do not apply to one industry in particular (e.g. ISO 14001, which specifies the requirements for an environmental management system, and ISO 14004, which provides general guidelines for the establishment, implementation, maintenance and improvement of an environmental management system). In Europe, the EMAS also serves as an environmental benchmark and plays an important role in various economic branches (Pröbstl and Jiricka, 2009; Pröbstl-Haider *et al.*, 2019).

However, the application of EMAS in winter tourism is still very limited. As of December 2018, only one large cable car enterprise in the Alps, namely the Schmittenhöhebahn AG in Austria, has applied this instrument. Therefore, this chapter aims to encourage cableway operators and ski area managers to introduce environmental management systems (EMSs) in their organizations by presenting different experiences and applications. To this end, we will outline key aspects in different settings by describing two separate case study areas and presenting the experiences and insights gained in each of them. With this comparison, we hope to contribute to an exchange process enabling different organizations in the industry to learn from one another.

29.1.1 Basic principles and requirements of ISO 14001 and EMAS

In the following, we focus on two international certification frameworks. They are both characterized by rules and standards and have the same goals but differ in their development histories, their areas of application and – to a minor extent – in their requirements (Pröbstl-Haider *et al.*, 2019):

- The international standard for environmental management, ISO 14001, lays down the criteria for an environmental management system and is part of a larger group of standards. It was first developed in 1996 as 14001:1996. The current version of ISO 14001 came into effect in September 2015 as ISO 14001:2015.
- EMAS stands for 'Eco-Management and Audit Scheme'. It is a voluntary system in which businesses (as well as other organizations and institutions within EU member states) can participate. The regulation has been in effect since April 1995 and has been revised twice already. EMAS III has been in force since 11 January 2010 (Regulation (EC) No 1221/2009). With this revision, it became possible for organizations outside of the EU to participate. The general aim of the regulation (as with ISO 14001) is to promote continuous improvement of organizations' environmental performance.

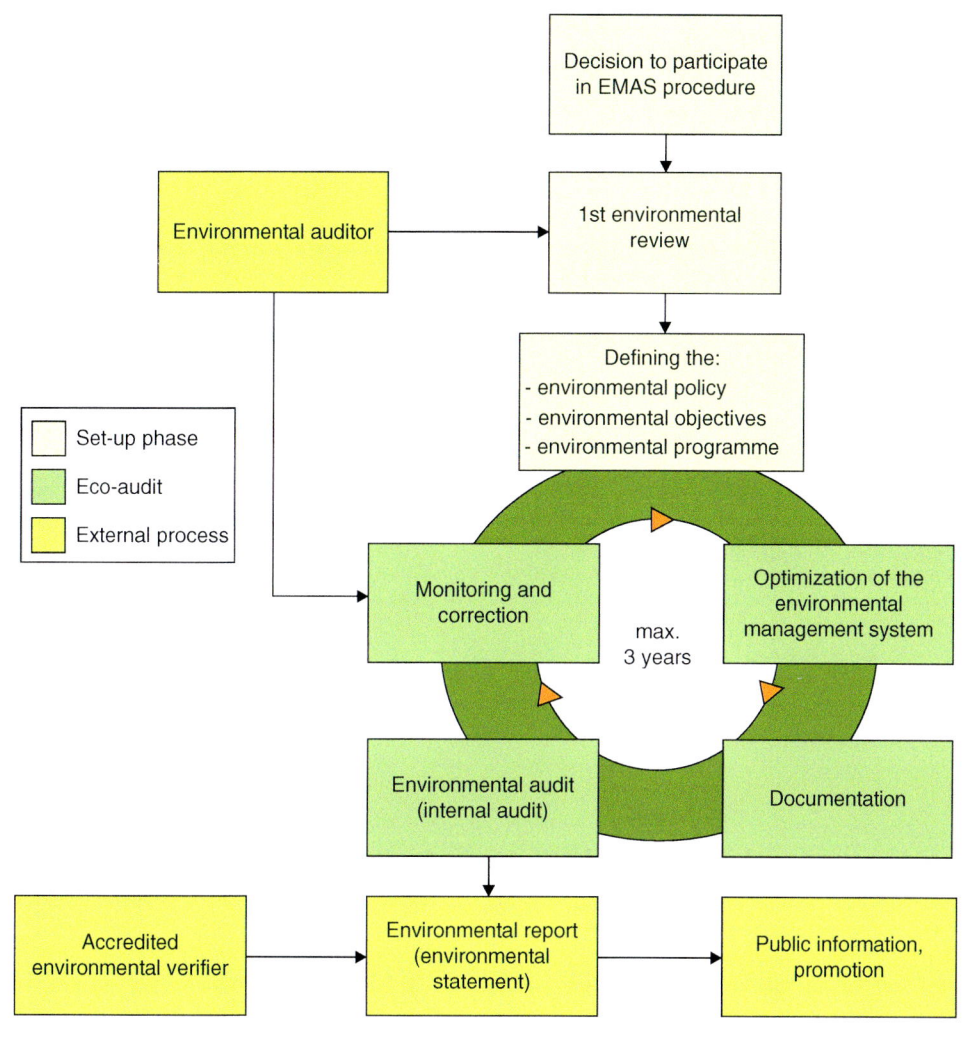

Fig. 29.1. Basic principles of environmental management according to EMAS. (Translated from Salak, 2008; original figure based on Pröbstl *et al.*, 2003.)

Both concepts follow the same basic principles, as illustrated in Fig. 29.1. Crucial to these schemes are the continuous improvement of EMSs and their external evaluation.

The table below gives an overview of the areas in which ISO 14001 and EMAS differ. This chapter will mainly concentrate on EMAS, since it is the more far-reaching instrument, especially when it comes to communication or to the consideration of direct and indirect impacts. Comparisons and differences are shown below (see Table 29.1).

Many businesses make use of the extensive similarities between the requirements of the two systems. They register for both ISO 14001 and EMAS certification, since this does not require much greater internal effort than meeting the requirements of just one of the two (this was, for instance, the strategy pursued by Ski Lifts Lech in Austria from 1999 until 2006).

Table 29.1. Comparison of features and requirements of ISO 14001 and EMAS. (From Pröbstl-Haider et al., 2019.)

Features	ISO 14001	EMAS	Differences
Decision on implementation and definition of area of application	+	+	
Definition of environmental policy	+	+	
Procedure for assessing, monitoring, documenting and implementing measures relevant to significant environmental aspects	+	++	In the case of EMAS: consideration of direct and indirect environmental aspects, completion of the first environmental review
Procedure for assessing legal requirements	+	+	
Compliance with requirements of environmental law	+	++	In the case of EMAS: also an assessment of compliance with relevant regulatory requirements by environmental verifiers
Improvement of environmental performance	+	++	Emphasized more by EMAS, e.g. through a mandatory selection of core indicators
Measures for realization and implementation in the organization	+	+	
Training, awareness-raising and participation	++	++	In the case of ISO 14001: particular focus on environmental training. In the case of EMAS: particular focus on participation of personnel and flow of information. Long-term, process-oriented participation
Communication	+	++	In the case of EMAS: open dialogue with interested parties, environmental statement is publicly available, EMAS logo
Documentation, internal observation	+	+	

Businesses and organizations often wish to manage various areas 'systematically'. By using an EMS, they can monitor the quality (of products and/or services), environmental protection, work safety, and health and safety of their customers in an integrated manner.

Simultaneous implementation of ISO 14001 and EMAS is mostly chosen in cases in which the two systems are expected to appeal to different target groups (e.g. to address both customers from within the EU, as well as customers from outside who are not familiar with EMAS). Alternatively, companies may choose to register for both systems in order to thoroughly document and communicate the extensive level of examination they undergo.

29.2 Methodological Approach

In order to analyse typical challenges and environmental problems that may occur when EMAS is implemented, we selected one representative destination in the Alps with a long tradition in winter tourism and one Eastern European mountain resort representing the development of new, upcoming ski resorts.

In both ski resorts, we supported the process over a period of 2 years from the first decision in favour of establishing an EMS to the final external evaluation. We contributed to a standardized process of data collection as well as the evaluation of the collected data, and helped the respective resorts to develop first implementation measures. The similar degree of involvement in both cases allowed us to conduct action research, which is a key instrument to (i) alleviate an immediate problematic situation, and (ii) to generate new knowledge about system processes (Reason and Bradbury, 2007).

For this study, action research was chosen as the most suitable method, because this participatory approach enabled us:

- to understand the circumstances influencing practitioners' decision making;
- to become acquainted with a common language, which in turn allowed us to join the conversation and take part in critical exchanges within the respective working groups, such as the marketing or the technical team of the respective ski resort;
- to learn more about typical internal networking and communication systems; and
- to create the right social climate for an open and critical exchange.

The aim of the applied action research approach was to help build appropriate structures for the EMS from the very outset of the planning and certification process, to set up the necessary system and competencies, and to modify the relationship of the system to its respective environment.

By forming joint collaborations within mutually acceptable ethical frameworks, action research aims to address the practical concerns of people dealing with an acute, problematic situation, as well as to contribute to the goals of social science (Reason and Bradbury, 2007). In the case of ski resort management, it is crucial to establish an understanding of how particular actors define their present situation and to reach a consensus on these starting points, so that planned actions can produce their intended outcomes.

In this chapter, we analyse the differences and commonalities between the two case studies in relation to the following aspects:

- Motivation to participate in an auditing scheme.
- Relevance and objects of environmental improvement.
- Information, marketing purposes and target groups.
- Relevance for internal management and motivation of the employees.
- Relevance of additional/external factors such as climate change.

The overall goal was to identify and analyse significant differences, which we expected to occur due to the different cultural–discursive, material–economic and social–political circumstances and arrangements in each resort. These findings can be addressed in promotional material for EMAS or considered in future fieldwork.

29.3 Description of the Case Study Areas

29.3.1 The Alps mountain resort

The ski and hiking area Schmittenhöhe, also known simply as 'Schmitten', is located in the mid-western part of Austria about 90 km from the city of Salzburg. It is named after the Schmittenhöhe Mountain at the edge of the Kitzbühel Alps with its peak reaching over 1900 m. At its foot lies the town of Zell am See, which has been connected to the mountain via cable car since 1927, making it the first cable car in the province of Salzburg and only the fifth in Austria at the time. Today, it is equipped with gondola cabins created by Porsche Design that offer a panoramic view of the surrounding Alps, including some peaks over 3000 m. The ski area itself lies between an altitude of 945 m in the valley and almost 2000 m at the summit station. In winter, 27 different lifts are operative and 77 km of marked ski runs are available. Additionally, the offer includes various attractions such as a 'fun-slope', a snow park for free skiers and snowboarders, a night-slope that is open several times a week and a snow park for children. The resort, moreover, makes an effort to engage the tech-enthusiasts among its guests by providing a free of charge GoPro rental service, a ski movie-slope, where each run can be filmed for subsequent analysis, and offering performance statistics to be accessed through a guest's ski pass number (including the vertical metres and kilometres of slopes covered and the number of lift rides completed throughout the day). The area also features a variety of restaurants, guesthouses, mountain huts, cafés and bars catering for visitors.

A number of cable cars operate outside of the winter season as well, making the area popular with hikers. There is a wide range of hiking trails for various skill levels, and special offers include group hikes with trained guides as well as workshops (e.g. for yodelling or yoga). Additionally, there are more than 30 objects and large-scale sculptures installed throughout the area under the motto 'art on the mountain', providing further points of attraction for hikers.

The theme of 'ecology' features prominently on the ski resort's website and the cable car company stresses that they 'treasure nature as the underlying foundation for ski sports and hiking in the mountains' (Schmittenhöhebahn AG, n.d.). They also describe the efforts they undertake to increase energy efficiency and to operate sustainably. Plans to expand the ski area were initially approved by the province of Salzburg but have been put on hold since 2011 due to appeals made by environmental organizations and a local initiative. Following several legal proceedings, the decision concerning the project's Environmental Impact Assessment (EIA) was amended and ultimately approved by court in April 2018 (Umweltbundesamt, 2018).

29.3.2 The Eastern European mountain resort

Bansko is a ski and mountain resort located in the south-western part of Bulgaria. It lies on the banks of the Glazne River at the foot of the Pirin Mountains, directly below their highest part. The town is situated about 6 km from Razlog and 150 km from Sofia, the capital of Bulgaria. The Pirin Mountains are an alpine type mountain range, its highest peak, called Vihren, reaching over 2900 m. The town of Bansko is located at 925 m above sea level, while the ski resort lies at an altitude of 990–2600 m. The area features excellent skiing and snowboarding conditions and provides all the expected infrastructure including several mountain huts and shops, a rich history, and a mix of old and new architecture. Many hotels of various standards are available and cater to different budgets. Regarding après ski activities, the resort offers a number of bars and traditional restaurants called 'Mehana'. In the past decade, significant investments to modernize and expand existing amenities have been made by Yulen AD, the company running the ski area. Additionally, numerous new luxury hotels and other facilities were constructed around the gondola lift station in town. The ski resort attracts guests in all seasons, but its busiest time is during the winter months. Thanks to the features described above, Bansko is said to be one of Bulgaria's best winter resorts, boasting the longest ski runs (there are 75 km of marked ski runs in total) and the richest cultural history. It has even been voted Bulgaria's best ski resort for six consecutive years (2013–2018) at the World Ski Awards ceremony (World Media and Events Limited, 2018).

However, Bansko ski resort has also sparked heavy criticism due to it being partially located within the Pirin National Park, which is both a World Heritage site selected by the United Nations Educational, Scientific and Cultural Organization (UNESCO) and part of the European Union's Natura 2000 network. Environmental non-governmental organizations (NGOs) claim that the construction of the ski area has already caused irreversible damage to nature. Moreover, a draft of the park's new management plan as well as amendments made to the current plan are feared to pave the way for a significant expansion of the existing ski infrastructure and for extensive logging activity, which would cause further deterioration to the park's ecosystem (Dalberg Advisors, 2018). In April 2018, the Bulgarian government's decision to forego a Strategic Environmental Assessment (SEA) for the new management plan was revoked in the first instance (Stojanovski, 2018). The amendments to the current management plan were also revoked, as they were found to violate several environmental laws (Decision 10238/27.07.18)[3] (BNT, 2018).

29.4 Results

29.4.1 Motivation to participate in an auditing scheme

The situation in the Alps mountain resort

There are several reasons why the Schmittenhöhebahn AG cable car enterprise would participate in EMAS certification. First of all, its biggest shareholder is part of the automobile industry (the Porsche GesmbH). For its management, applying an auditing system is a standard procedure to ensure product quality and to deal with legal and safety issues. In the automobile sector, this is even a prerequisite for many suppliers and subcontracting companies. However, the main motivation stems from the cable car enterprise's self-perception and self-image. The company sees itself as a front-runner within the industry, as an enterprise that goes beyond the minimum standards and manages all environmental issues in an exemplary manner to meet the requirements of a 'top-class ski resort'. In addition, marketing aspects and the desire to stand out from other resorts with a 'green image' certainly play a significant role as well.

Aside from these arguments, the enterprise also strongly emphasizes efficiency in its management. The auditing process is expected to enhance overall efficiency and save money without lowering any existing standards. The implementation of renewable energy facilities is an important aspect in this context.

The situation in the Eastern European mountain resort

In the case of Bansko, it was not an internal process that led to EMAS certification but an impulse that came from the outside. The public discussion on environmental standards of ski runs hosting international competitions prompted the FIS (Fédération Internationale de Ski/International Ski Federation) to place these aspects under greater scrutiny. Following complaints issued by the local administration and environmental NGOs, the cable car enterprise in Bansko, which (like the Schmittenhöhebahn AG) is part of a bigger consortium, decided to improve the environmental situation and apply European-wide standards including an external evaluation.

It was hoped that the application of EMAS would meet with approval at the FIS and eventually allow the resort to host annual ski racing events as part of the Alpine Skiing World Cup. Meanwhile, the significant growth of the destination – with an increasing number of accommodation options and second homes, and the construction of accompanying infrastructure – has led to changes in the guest structure. There has been a noticeable increase in Western European arrivals, which has in turn altered the guest expectations the ski resort has had to fulfil, including environmental issues and standards. Therefore, the decision in favour of EMAS was also influenced by the internationalization of guests and the need to meet the demand of future target groups and international standards.

29.4.2 Relevance and objects of environmental improvement

The situation in the Alps mountain resort

As mentioned before, the EMAS process for the Austrian resort was not initiated in order to improve its current environmental standards, but to confirm and communicate through an external review the high level of environmental responsibility the company had already achieved. The resort's main ski runs were created many years ago. For the few adaptations added in the recent past, the most cutting-edge technology available was used, including restoration measures to combat adverse effects on the environment through construction work. The overall condition of the local vegetation was found to be very positive, containing all typical semi-natural vegetation types as well as areas of a high to very high degree of naturalness.

Nevertheless, a closer look revealed certain environmental problems that still need to be resolved. One of them is the increase in cycling tourism across the main chain of the Alps. Biking is forbidden on the Schmittenhöhe Mountain (see Fig. 29.2) and local farmers, forest owners and hunters have been strongly opposed to the provision of any kind of infrastructure for this potential touristic target group.

However, as Fig. 29.3 shows, bikers still use the hiking trails on the mountain despite clear signage. In the picture, the two hikers try to avoid a conflict by walking at the edge of, or even off, the trail. This example demonstrates that the cable car enterprise has to monitor its summer tourists in order to minimize negative impacts caused by trampling or illegal activities such as mountain biking (see Fig. 29.4). Environmental

Fig. 29.2. In order to avoid conflicts with hikers in summer and autumn, mountain biking is not allowed on the Schmittenhöhe Mountain. Signposts alongside hiking trails call attention to this rule, which was established in agreement with local landowners. (Photograph courtesy of Ulrike Pröbstl-Haider.)

Fig. 29.3. Although biking is forbidden, the two hikers have to walk off-trail to avoid a conflict. (Photograph courtesy of Ulrike Pröbstl-Haider.)

Fig. 29.4. Widening a trail often leads to increasing erosion and further affects nearby vegetation. (Photograph courtesy of Ulrike Pröbstl-Haider.)

impacts were mainly detected in areas with overlapping use, e.g. areas where different summer tourism activities take place, areas that are used in winter as well as summer and on slopes that are used for cattle grazing outside of the winter season.

A second field leading to increasing problems is the adaptation to ongoing land use changes in the Alps. In many cases, the willingness of farmers to manage areas located in ski resorts is decreasing. The steep terrain, the danger of plastic contamination in their livestock's fodder and the comparatively low yield of hay all contribute to this trend. Only areas for cattle grazing are still requested by farmers. However, the inventory showed that the areas dedicated to hay production were characterized by particularly high biodiversity and outstanding beauty (see Fig. 29.5). Maintaining this quality as a part of the tourism product in summer was one of the key challenges and had implications for the overall summer management.

The requirement to adapt overall land use (see Fig. 29.6) and to compensate for changes in agricultural management represents a common challenge many ski resorts face in the Alps.

The situation in the Eastern European mountain resort

In contrast to the Alps mountain resort analysed above, most of the slopes in Bansko have only been developed in recent years. In Bansko, there is a shortage of experienced

Fig. 29.5. This picture shows one of the highly valuable meadows of the Schmittenhöhe ski resort. (Photograph courtesy of AVEGA.)

Fig. 29.6. This picture was taken in an area where the current management approach (mulching) needs to be reconsidered in order to maintain the outstanding diversity of the aforementioned meadows. (Photograph courtesy of Ulrike Pröbstl-Haider.)

firms and enterprises specializing in mountain resort development, as well as a lack of knowledge transfer between science and the wider public. Still, the technical equipment is of excellent quality and the safety standards for skiers and personnel are the same here as they are in Western Europe. However, knowledge about vegetation, soil conditions and the management of water on slopes is lagging behind. There is also little local history and traditional know-how available on how to construct and maintain stable and attractive ski runs. Consequently, the review and auditing process

Fig. 29.7. This picture shows the construction of a double 'Krainerwand' to stabilize the flank of a steep slope. (Photograph courtesy of Ivan Hadjiev.)

focused first on significant improvements to slope stability and on the prevention of further erosion (see Fig. 29.7). Second, it addressed the regeneration of local vegetation, and, third, it attended to the required improvements in water management.

The recultivation and regeneration of many slopes were achieved by adapting the seed mixture used and by improving the measures to reduce erosion. The following pictures provided by the enterprise managing the Bansko mountain resort show the differences between the situation before and after this intervention, and underline the effectiveness of the auditing process (see Fig. 29.8 and Fig. 29.9).

Thanks to an efficient knowledge transfer process and the substantial involvement of the local team, significant improvements could be achieved. Nevertheless, it will take at least another 20 years to reach semi-natural conditions, provided that the initiated management measures (tailor-made to suit Bansko's specific conditions) will be continued.

29.4.3 Information, marketing purposes and target groups

The situation in the Alps mountain resort

Given its main motivation, as laid out in Section 29.4.1, it comes as no surprise that the cable car enterprise running the Austrian resort has been targeting the media from the very start, presenting their new measures as the result of their long-term commitment to environmental responsibility as a 'green business'. Press conferences with guided tours were organized and complemented by a brochure and additional information made available online. The enterprise developed information material addressing tourists and

Fig. 29.8. A recultivation area next to a ski lift, picture taken on 29 June 2011. (Photograph courtesy of Ivan Hadjiev.)

other interested members of the public – thereby complying with a stipulation by EMAS, but making additional efforts to attractively design and regularly update the provided information. The enterprise has even received an award for the quality of their publicly available environmental statement.[4] This award was used, in turn, to communicate the company's environmental achievements and commitment to the public.

The marketing concept of the resort is based on the message that skiing there does not harm the environment, since, throughout its entire management system, measures are taken to protect the local environment as best possible, as well as to minimize the impact on endangered species or even to improve their situation (mainly concerning plants, insects and birds). Therefore, the enterprise tends to present the certification directly to its clients. In this context it is important to note that the majority of the resort's clients come from German-speaking countries and that they are known to care about environmental aspects in ski resorts (Roth *et al.*, 2018).

The situation in the Eastern European mountain resort

In the Eastern European mountain resort, marketing the auditing process first and foremost targets administrative bodies and institutions, such as the Pirin National Park, the National Ministry of Environment and Water (MOEW) and environmental

Fig. 29.9. The same area showing the result of successful recultivation efforts only 4 months later, picture taken on 25 October 2011. (Photograph courtesy of Ivan Hadjiev.)

NGOs based in Bulgaria. The developed measures are intended to showcase the efforts that were made to protect the local environment and to enhance the revitalization of slopes and areas below ski lifts.

The auditing process, and the significant financial and personnel efforts connected to it, are also emphasized and communicated to international sports associations such as the FIS. In so doing, the resort's operators hope that their environmental engagement will enhance the likelihood of the destination being selected to host future sporting events.

In contrast to the Alps mountain resort, the Bulgarian ski resort addresses institutional target groups, as mentioned above, rather than its guests who mainly come from Russia, Eastern Europe and the UK. The reason for this difference might be that tourists from these countries are not generally known for their interest in sustainable tourism offers, unlike their German counterparts (TUI AG, 2017).

29.4.4 Relevance for internal management and the employees' motivation

The situation in the Alps mountain resort

As mentioned in the introductory section, EMAS is characterized by processes aimed at enhancing education, training, awareness-raising and participation. In many modern cable car enterprises in the Alps, such as Schmittenhöhebahn AG, participatory processes have already been incorporated into the existing management practice. However, the involvement of personnel in the auditing process still uncovered several misunderstandings and a certain degree of miscommunication between the various divisions of the enterprise. The participatory approach increased awareness of communication problems and was a precondition for introducing new modes of cooperation. Participation is also crucial for the employees' motivation and identification with the enterprise, supports the development and implementation of innovative ideas, and leads to a higher level of self-responsibility among individuals, teams and divisions within the enterprise.

The situation in the Eastern European mountain resort

In the case of the Bulgarian ski resort, we found that an organized participatory process supported by a translator was not a common practice, and was therefore difficult to initiate. Nevertheless, the procedure also resulted in positive outcomes, such as an increase in trust and a stronger identification of employees with the enterprise.

We found the participatory approach here to be an important instrument to improve communication patterns between various divisions, to boost motivation among personnel and to strengthen their commitment. Employees felt that their opinion was important to us as well as to the enterprise, which seemed to be a new experience for them. Overall, participation and exchange were especially important for communication, but were less relevant for innovation and self-responsibility.

29.4.5 Relevance of climate change and CO_2 emissions

The situation in the Alps mountain resort

Exposure to climate change and the resulting vulnerability of Austrian ski resorts were seen as important issues that were discussed intensively. The auditing process even included a specific calculation of prospective climatic scenarios that also addressed existing and future options for artificial snowmaking. Furthermore, the enterprise has invested in an energy concept, as well as in photovoltaic and alternative heating systems for new buildings. Both the current rate of energy consumption and the company's responsibility for the future were diligently considered whenever measures for the upcoming years were decided on.

The situation in the Eastern European mountain resort

The impact of climate change on a ski resort characterized by continental climate conditions was considered to be less severe than for the Alps. Therefore, this issue was of little interest for the participants in the Eastern European mountain resort. Aside from the (presently) good natural snow conditions, the resort pointed out that the cold temperatures it experienced in winter were also suitable for artificial snowmaking. The challenges they faced in reducing erosion and fostering renaturalization and restoration of slopes, alongside the administrative and legal requirements they had to meet, seemed to represent more pressing concerns in their eyes, so that climate change and CO_2 emissions were not yet considered an urgent issue.

29.5 Discussion

29.5.1 Methodological approach

Action research is often criticized for not being sufficiently detached, neutral or independent. However, the implementation of an auditing process following EMAS or ISO 14001 necessitates a certain degree of involvement and identification with the organization concerned. The success of an action research approach hinges on an in-depth understanding of the values relevant actors prioritize, since these values guide the selection of means and goals when solving specific problems, and further steer actors' commitment to a particular solution (Susman and Evered, 1978; Kemmis et al., 2014). In our case, the historical background of the ski resorts also played an important role and was much more significant than expected. The role of participatory processes and the involvement of employees in the Alps mountain resort certainly differed from our experience in the Eastern European mountain resort, which featured much more hierarchical structures. These structures also defined the individual employee's understanding of their own role within the enterprise. There is simply no way of experiencing, analysing and describing these differences without becoming involved in the process. Applying action research can be one of the most effective ways of rendering the theoretical or practical knowledge the researcher possesses truly useful for practitioners and to cultivate greater openness and acceptance among them. Moreover, not only do we gain important, practically relevant knowledge from involving researchers in real-life situations, but the situation itself simultaneously evolves into a product of knowledge transfer, causing a learning process on both sides.

29.5.2 Advantages for the enterprise

After drafting a joint auditing report and organizing an internal audit process, we asked both enterprises whether they were satisfied with the experience and whether they would repeat it. Both enterprises answered in the affirmative, even though the Eastern European mountain resort in 2017 was still awaiting its official national acceptance (despite a positive external evaluation).

Further discussions supported the arguments stated below, highlighting the direct and indirect advantages of participating in EMAS. These arguments have been well-documented in various other publications (e.g. Pröbstl and Jiricka, 2009).

- Establishment and qualification of an EMS through analysis, evaluation, identification of deficiencies and risk analysis (including safety and legal risks).
- Development of a GIS-based environmental monitoring system as a by-product (a form of environmental data collection that can be continued in the future).

- Establishment and step-by-step improvement of the internal environmental monitoring system, including risk management.
- Increasing awareness for ecological responsibility among the organization's management and staff.
- Improvement of the profit and market economy situation (more relevant in the case of the Alps mountain resort than in the Eastern European mountain resort).
- Recognition all over Europe and by international associations.

29.6 Conclusions

This chapter summarizes the insights gained from integrated, transnational assessment procedures applied in two different contexts. Based on the principles of an EMS prescribed by international rules and standards (EMAS), the aim in both ski resorts was to define key preconditions and to provide data and recommendations for an efficient implementation. Due to the multitude of European directives that have to be taken into account, e.g. the 'Environmental Liability Directive' (Directive 2004/35/CE of the European Parliament and of the Council), the 'Birds Directive' (Directive 2009/147/EC of the European Parliament and of the Council) and the 'Habitats Directive' (Council Directive 92/43/EEC), environmental management in ski areas has gained significant importance, especially in the Alps and in other European winter sports destinations. Our findings show that significant environmental improvements could be achieved in both areas despite their different geographical, political and structural conditions. In both cases, the enterprises were able to save money in the long run and to improve their tourism offers. However, the expectation that an auditing process will facilitate future planning processes or foster the expansion of a ski resort is wrong. Therefore, this should not be used as an argument to promote environmental certification. Nevertheless, drawing on extensive action research, our study has shown that the idea of improving the sustainability of an organization by entering into a certification process is still valid.

Notes

[1] The company has established an EMS and embraces environmental protection as part of their business policy. Further details can be found under the header 'sustainability' on the homepage of Lech-Zürs Tourism. Available at: https://www.lechzuers.com/en/service/sustainability/ (accessed 16 July 2019).

[2] Laax states that it wants to become the 'world's first self-sufficient winter sport resort'. They have started an initiative called 'Greenstyle' and published several videos about their visions and aims on their website. Available at: https://www.laax.com/en/info/greenstyle (accessed 12 July 2018).

[3] The court ruling is available in full online (in Bulgarian) at: www.sac.government.bg/court22.nsf/d038edcf49190344c2256b7600367606/967828fa6df6795dc22582ac0023c479?OpenDocument (accessed 6 September 2018).

[4] The 'Schmitten' cable car enterprise received an EMAS award for their 2016 environmental statement from the Austrian Federal Ministry of Agriculture, Forestry, Environment and Water Management (BMLFUW). Available at: https://www.schmitten.at/de/service/presse/pressetexte/nachhaltig-erfolgreich-die-schmitten-in-zell-am-see_p3152 (accessed 4 September 2018).

References

Bien, A. (2007) *A simple User's Guide for sustainable Tourism and Ecotourism*, 3rd edn. Center on Ecotourism and Sustainable Development (CESD), Washington, DC.

BNT (Bulgarian National Television) (2018) Court overruled the changes to Pirin National Park Management Plan. Available at: https://www.bnt.bg/en/a/court-overruled-the-changes-to-pirin-national-park-management-plan (accessed 6 September 2018).

Buckley, R. (2002) Tourism ecolabels. *Annals of Tourism Research* 29(1), 183–208. DOI:10.1016/S0160-7383(01)00035-4

Council Directive 92/43/EEC of 21 May 1992 on the conservation of natural habitats and of wild fauna and flora. Available at: https://eur-lex.europa.eu/legal-content/EN/TXT/?uri=CELEX:31992L0043 (accessed 4 September 2018).

Dalberg Advisors (2018) *Slippery Slopes: Protecting Pirin from Unsustainable Ski Expansion and Logging*. WWF – World Wide Fund for Nature, Gland, Switzerland.

Directive 2004/35/CE of the European Parliament and of the Council of 21 April 2004 on environmental liability with regard to the prevention and remedying of environmental damage. Available at: https://eur-lex.europa.eu/legal-content/EN/TXT/?uri=celex:32004L0035 (accessed 4 September 2018).

Directive 2009/147/EC of the European Parliament and of the Council of 30 November 2009 on the conservation of wild birds. Available at: https://eur-lex.europa.eu/legal-content/EN/TXT/?qid=1536062433597&uri=CELEX:32009L0147 (accessed 4 September 2018).

Font, X. (2001) Regulating the green message: the players in ecolabelling. In: Font, X. and Buckley, R. (eds) *Tourism Ecolabelling: Certification and Promotion of Sustainable Management*. CAB International, Wallingford, UK, pp. 1–18.

Font, X. (2002) Environmental certification in tourism and hospitality: progress, process and prospects. *Tourism Management* 23(3), 197–205. DOI:10.1016/S0261-5177(01)00084-X

Font, X. and Harris, C. (2004) Rethinking standards from green to sustainable. *Annals of Tourism Research* 31(4), 986–1007. DOI:10.1016/j.annals.2004.04.001

Honey, M. (2002) *Ecotourism and Certification: Setting Standards in Practice*. Island Press, Washington, DC.

Honey, M. and Rome, A. (2001) *Protecting Paradise: Certification Programs for Sustainable Tourism and Ecotourism*. Institute for Policy Studies, Washington, DC.

Kemmis, S., McTaggart, R. and Nixon, R. (2014) *The Action Research Planner: Doing Critical Participatory Action Research*. Springer, Singapore.

Pröbstl, U. and Jiricka, A. (2009) Das Europäische Eco-Management and Audit Scheme (EMAS) als Instrument für einen nachhaltigen Betrieb von Skigebieten. In: Bieger, T., Laesser, C. and Beritelli, P. (eds) *Trends, Instrumente und Strategien im alpinen Tourismus*. Erich Schmidt Verlag, Berlin, pp. 35–42.

Pröbstl, U., Roth, R., Schlegel, H. and Staub, R. (2003) *Auditing in Skigebieten. Leitfaden zur ökologischen Aufwertung*. Stiftung pro natura – pro ski, Vaduz, Liechtenstein.

Pröbstl-Haider, U., Brom, M., Dorsch, C. and Jiricka-Pürrer, A. (2019) *Environmental Management in Ski Areas: Procedure – Requirements – Exemplary Solutions*. Springer, Berlin. DOI:10.1007/978-3-319-75061-3

Reason, P. and Bradbury, H. (2006) *Handbook of Action Research*. Sage, London.

Roth, R., Krämer, A. and Severiens, J. (2018) *Zweite Nationale Grundlagenstudie Wintersport Deutschland 2018*. Stiftung Sicherheit im Skisport (SIS), Planegg, Germany.

Salak, B. (2008) Grundlage für ein nachhaltiges Schutzgebietsmanagement im Rahmen der EMAS II-Verordnung, illustriert am Beispiel des Nationalparks Gesäuse. MSc Thesis, University of Natural Resources and Life Sciences Vienna, Vienna.

Schmittenhöhebahn AG (n.d.) Sustainable values at the Schmittenhöhebahn. Available at: https://www.schmitten.at/en/service/company/ecology (accessed 21 September 2018).

Sloan, P., Legrand, W. and Chen, J.S. (2011) *Sustainability in the Hospitality Industry: Principles of Sustainable Operations*. Routledge, London.

Stojanovski, F. (2018) Bulgarian environmental activists score important court victory in struggle to #SavePirin National Park. Available at: https://globalvoices.org/2018/05/02/bulgarian-environmental-activists-score-an-important-court-victory-in-struggle-to-savepirin-national-park/ (accessed 16 July 2019).

Susman, G.I. and Evered, R.D. (1978) An assessment of the scientific merits of action research. *Administrative Science Quarterly* 23(4), 582–603.

SustainableTourism.net (2014) Tourism accreditation and certification. Available at: https://sustainabletourism.net/sustainable-tourism/sustainable-tourism-resource/tourism-accreditation-and-certification/ (accessed 16 July 2019).

TUI AG (2017) TUI global survey: Sustainable tourism most popular among German and French tourists. Available at: https://www.tuigroup.com/en-en/media/press-releases/2017/2017-03-07-tui-survey-sustainable-tourism (accessed 19 December 2018).

Umweltbundesamt (2018) Online-Abfrage UVP-Genehmigungsverfahren. Vorhaben-Titel: Schigebietserweiterung Hochsonnberg Piesendorf. Available at: www.umweltbundesamt.at/umweltsituation/uvpsup/uvpoesterreich1/uvpdatenbank/uvp_online/?cgiproxy_url=http%3A%2F%2Fwww5.umweltbundesamt.at%2Fuvpdb%2Fpz21schema.pl%3Ftiny%3D1%26session%3DDUyYhQXHNACKlhzuG0N3SI1I%26set%3D2 (accessed 7 September 2018).

World Media and Events Limited (2018) 6th Annual World Ski Awards Winners. Available at: https://worldskiawards.com/winners/2018 (accessed 18 December 2018).

World Tourism Organization (WTO) (2002) *Voluntary Initiatives for Sustainable Tourism: Worldwide Inventory and Comparative Analysis of 104 Eco-labels, Awards and Self-commitments*. World Tourism Organization, Madrid, Spain.

30 Tourism Diversification in the Development of French Ski Resorts

CORALIE ACHIN* AND EMMANUELLE GEORGE

University of Grenoble-Alpes, Irstea-LESSEM, Grenoble, France

30.1 Introduction

Since the 1930s and particularly after World War II, many mountain territories have been structured around resorts and downhill ski areas. This progressive establishment of ski resorts has provided important economic resources for the respective mountain territories (Lasanta *et al.*, 2007). In addition to purchasing ski passes, tourists need to rent accommodation and possibly ski equipment as well as buy food, etc. Finally, operating a tourist destination involves several services, which sustain local employment and help maintain permanent – or semi-permanent – population levels in these remote and disadvantaged places. Thus, ski resorts play a role in land use planning.

However, since the creation of these resorts, the context has evolved. Global change has not spared mountain areas, which now face both climate change (e.g. François *et al.*, 2014) and societal development (Frochot, 2016). This has resulted in the inevitable adaptation of the tourism sector. In particular, the current – and future – increase in temperatures has reduced snow cover and restricted the ability of ski resorts to stay focused on downhill skiing. Nevertheless, climate change does not affect all resorts in the same way. Low- and mid-elevation ski resorts, more than others, face difficult winters, and the Intergovernmental Panel on Climate Change predicts (IPCC, 2014) the disappearance of many alpine ski resorts in the next 50 years. Furthermore, ski resorts are also affected by changes in leisure behaviour. Until the 1980s, the clientele of ski resorts came for skiing, whereas today they expect other activities to be on offer (Atout France, 2011). Faced with these changes, ski resorts need to adapt themselves.

Two main strategies of adaptation have been identified. The first is mitigation, e.g. with the development of snowmaking equipment or the creation of artificial water reservoirs (Dawson and Scott, 2007; Spandre *et al.*, 2015). The second strategy is aimed at diversifying the tourism offerings. More specifically, it aims at making available other activities based on the natural and cultural heritage of the area. Naturally, these resources are not always located next to the ski resorts, but more often in the valleys and/or the villages. Thus, the diversification of tourism involves expanding the areas comprising tourism destinations, depending on the territorial amenities available (Achin and George-Marcelpoil, 2016).

---

* E-mail: coralie.achin@irstea.fr

At the same time, French municipalities experienced changes in the national administrative organization. The New Territorial Organization of the Republic law (NOTRe law, proclaimed on 7 August 2015) aims to simplify the current territorial complexity, in particular by reducing the number of regions (Nuts 2) and by strengthening the role of municipality groups or 'inter-municipalities'. Among the significant changes introduced, these inter-municipalities instead of the municipalities are now taking over the organization of tourism. This has led to the creation of an inter-municipal tourism office that aims to promote this new territory. Thus, these transformations have had an impact on tourism destinations, which were originally not structured at this scale.

In this chapter, we address the developments in tourism governance, along with the characteristics and processes that define tourism governance. In particular, we aim (i) to understand, in the French Alps context, how the organization of tourism destinations will evolve, due to both the diversification of tourism and institutional reform, and (ii) to identify the drivers of these changes. Furthermore, we show how public policies dedicated to ski resorts can help ski resorts and their territories in regenerating tourism governance. To address these questions, we used semi-structured interviews conducted with different nature stakeholders between February and October 2017 in the different mountain areas or massifs[1] (see Fig. 30.1). In particular, we met with both political and socio economic stakeholders involved in tourism development and with citizens, mostly members of associations created to contribute to local tourism (e.g. associations for heritage valorization). Through the questions asked, we tried to understand stakeholders' perceptions of tourism, the strategies they want to develop and the relationships between the stakeholders (nature, intensity, etc.) involved in the functioning of the tourism destination. We complemented the data from these 42 interviews with several tourist planning reports and contracts related to public policies adopted from the 2000s, the latest of which were signed between 2015 and 2017.

First, we show how the research of ski resorts has evolved (see Section 30.2). The focus on the bilateral relationship between the municipalities and the ski lift operators has shifted, and the scene has become more complex as it now integrates the various public and private stakeholders, which have become even more important once the diversification of ski resorts began. Recently, this organization was questioned by French territorial reform, creating new territories to manage tourism skills (see Section 30.3). In the last part of this chapter, we show that this development (and in particular the renewed governance imposed by the territorial reform) was anticipated by the dedicated public policies (see Section 30.3).

30.2 From Ski Resort Governance to a Diversification of Tourism Governance

The great expansion of French ski areas during the 1960s and 1970s entailed the creation of more than 300 ski resorts, which were initially led by the mayor and the ski lift operator. However, the increasing uncertainties faced by the resorts and the directive to implement tourism diversification have led to a renewed analysis of ski resort governance that includes more stakeholders on an extended territorial scale.

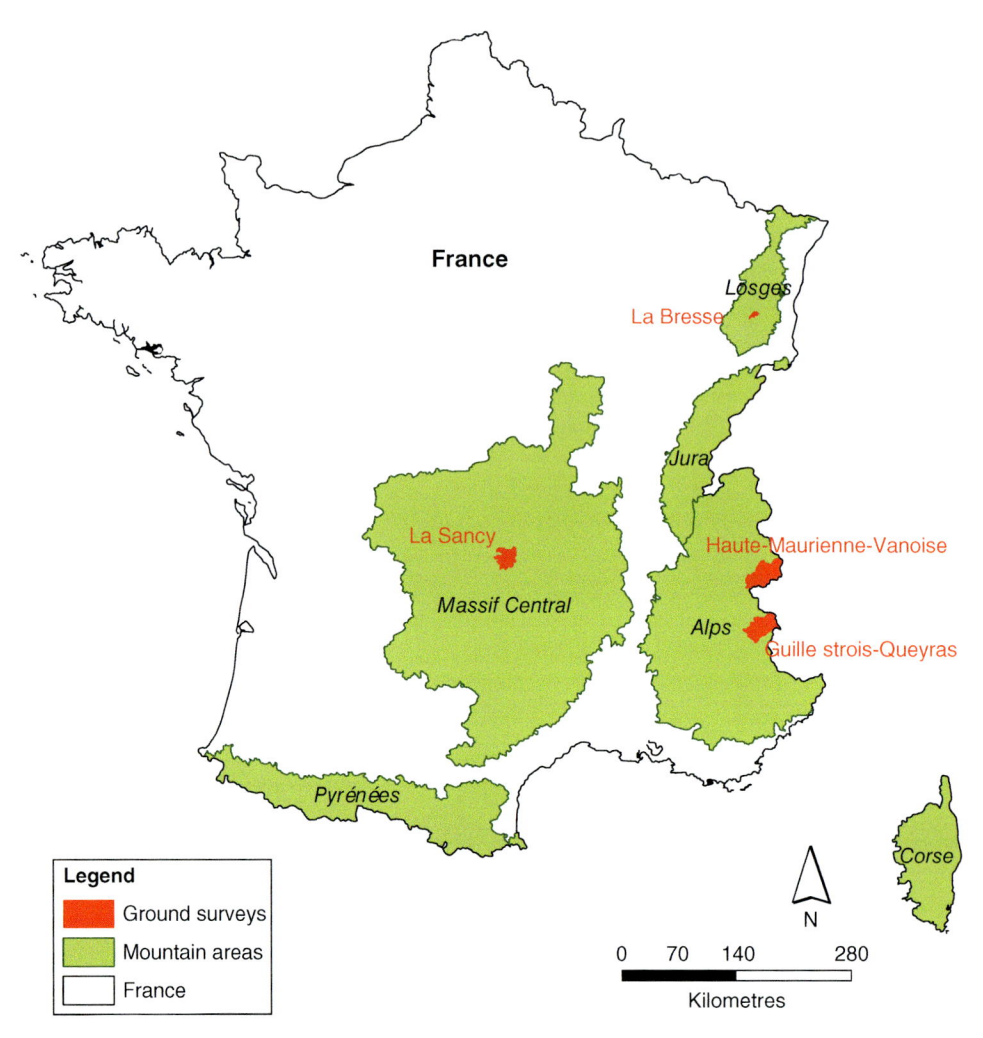

Fig 30.1. Location of the French massifs and ground surveys. (Own figure based on IGN Bd Carto®, 2016; Decree n°2004-69 of 16 January 2004 on the delimitation of the massifs.)

30.2.1 A ski resort governance marked by a central role of public actors

Ski resorts are usually perceived as a unified tourism destination, whose functioning, however, relies on multiple actors. The diversity of stakeholders involved has been the subject of many articles (Bodega *et al.*, 2004; Nordin and Svensson, 2007; Gill and Williams, 2011; Clivaz and George-Marcelpoil, 2016). These stakeholders maintain several differing relationships that contribute towards defining the type of governance followed. Thus, the corporate and community models of Flagestad and Hope (2001) are used as reference for several analyses of governance. They discuss case studies that have foundations in international governance approaches, which vary from an economic-centred model found mainly in North America to a more public–private model, which is found in European ski resorts. The governance of French ski resorts, however, does not have an equivalent model internationally. It derives mainly from the Mountain Law enacted on 9 January 1985: articles 42 and 46 of the law specify the control of tourist activities by the municipality. Seen as a public service, ski lifts and their exploitation are subject to a contract between the mayor and the ski lift operator.[2] Besides the mayor, the ski resort governance system involves the various economic players, mainly the ski lift operators but also the hoteliers, the ski equipment rental companies or the restaurateurs located next to the ski resort (Gerbaux and Marcelpoil, 2006). Most often, the leadership of these ski resort areas will define the type of governance: their diversity characterizes the diversity of French ski resort governance, which involves models that are similar to the community model, where a lot of independent and various stakeholders (politics, economics) are involved in the functioning of the ski resort. Thus, a strong leadership of the mayor in the ski resorts can resemble the community model, while the strong leadership of the ski lift operator in the ski resort is not unlike the corporate model. To summarize, the initial governance of French ski resorts (since the 1980s) was implemented at the scale of the municipality giving the mayor a specific role in the leadership of the tourist destination (see Fig. 30.2). We call this pioneer organization 'mountain tourism destination 1' (MTD 1).

30.2.2 Tourism diversification governance: the inclusion of new actors for a renewed destination

After focusing on snow and winter season, the diversification of tourism meant that the emphasis of ski resorts was not placed only on the winter season. This does not imply that the resorts turned their backs on the winter season, but that they aimed to enhance other activities that would not be dependent on the climate and on meteorological parameters. The diversification of tourism can take two main forms. First, it

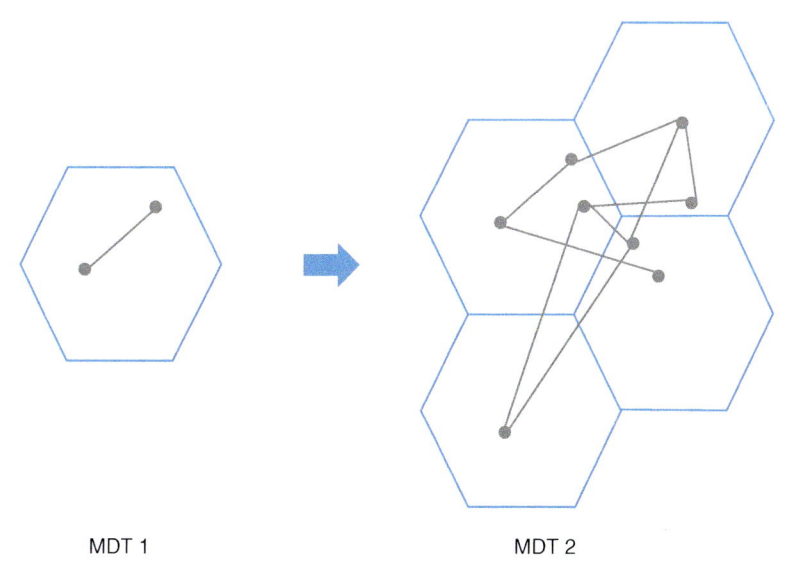

Fig. 30.2. Evolution of local governance: from a MDT 1 to a MDT 2.

can lead to the development of other activities, during winter or in an all-year-round tourism. Here, tourism remains the main economic focus. The second option is to develop other economic sectors, either traditional, e.g. agriculture or industry, or non-traditional, e.g. creating tourism products like farm visits or textile industry routes. The development of new products aims to provide a 'specific tourism offering', as opposed to downhill skiing, which can be defined as a 'generic tourism offering' (Achin and George-Marcelpoil, 2016). This change in the tourism offering has in turn led to a change in the tourism scale of development: from a focus on ski resorts to a diversification of the tourism territory. This spatial extension is necessary because the new activities and resources are not necessarily, and rarely, located next to the ski area.

Consequently, a definition of the new territory is needed, according to the location of the new resources being offered. However, this change is accompanied by the necessary change in local tourism governance. Indeed, these new tourism products assume the inclusion of all providers into the network. In addition, because of the extension of the tourism reference area, the managers of other services such as real estate, restaurants or convenience stores located outside the ski resort (considered as the place of concentration of the real estate and the ski slopes) in the new territory are included in the redefined network. This arrival of new actors (i.e. tourism operators) with different statuses involves a regeneration of current tourism governance, with a possible redefinition of the leadership roles.

Other elements are needed for the transformation of a tourism destination to the new tourism scale. The most important is certainly to transmit a feeling of belonging to the new tourism destination among the stakeholders (Achin and George-Marcelpoil, 2016). This entails at least two changes. The first is related to the capacity of the actors to face competition and be able to develop complementary products and tourism offers. The second is mostly related to the promotion of this new tourism destination (Achin and George-Marcelpoil, 2016). To date, the name of the ski resort has benefited from an established, often international, reputation. However, the challenges in this context are to characterize the new tourism area (MDT 2; see Fig. 30.2) that will be organized and promoted as part of the tourism diversification plan where several ski resorts can co-exist. This set-up is based on communication between local and existing brands and on new communication support of the destination.

In practice, different strategies have been observed, among which we present two opposite approaches to tourism diversification. The first example is the ski resort of La Bresse, in the Vosges Mountains.[3] This ski resort represents the main tourism activity of the territory and is similar to a corporate model where the cable car CEO owns the lifts, restaurants, real estate and ski-rental store. Tourism diversification was introduced by both the ski resort and the tourism office of the municipality but did not lead to a renewal in local governance. Indeed, although several activities were added to the tourist brochure, this was not accompanied by a commonly defined tourism strategy. On the contrary, these new tourism interests were not allowed to take part in decision making by the existing tourist office members. Here, the destination promoted was larger than the ski resort, while local governance had not changed. In the 'Massif du Sancy' (Massif Central), the situation was very different. From 2000, the elected officials decided to group together in a new inter-municipality dedicated to tourism organization. This led to the creation of an inter-municipality tourist office and the development of a tourism strategy on this scale. Even if the new local governance is led by the ski resorts' mayors, most of the tourism stakeholders are included.

30.3 The French Territorial Reform and its Consequences on Local Tourism Organization

30.3.1 Short presentation of the law

The territorial reform related to the recent adoption of the NOTRe law in 2015 has led to important organizational and institutional changes. We present two of the measures: the systematization of the inter-municipalities (LAU 1) and the attempt to rationalize the distribution of powers between the different institutions.

The development of the inter-municipality aims to include all municipalities within a broader group, considered important for streamlining and pooling of local public expenditure. The size of these inter-municipalities has increased and set a minimum of 15,000 inhabitants, except for mountain municipalities,[4] for which a lower number is allocated (5000 inhabitants). Even if this small size is met, however, the number of inter-municipalities in the Alps has decreased by almost 35% since 2015. As proposed by the prefects of the 'Department' (Nuts 3), the inter-municipal map has led to numerous mergers of existing inter-municipalities, de facto questioning the place of tourism in the new institutional perimeters. Indeed, tourism exists in many parts of the Alps and contributes greatly towards boosting the local economy but this does not mean that the entire territory is touristic. For example, the direct and indirect revenues generated by winter tourism represent 50% of the Savoie department's GDP (where the larger ski resorts are located).[5] Therefore, some rural and touristic areas now need to organize themselves with non-touristic and bigger municipalities: are the different municipalities not concerned by tourism activity willing to pay for expensive tourism infrastructure while the benefits primarily go to the tourism stakeholders?

The second contribution of the law that we mention here is the strengthened role of the inter-municipalities concerning tourism. So far, the municipalities had been charged with this responsibility. They could decide to create a tourist office based on the legal form that they had chosen. In addition to the mandatory missions (welcoming tourists, providing information and coordinating stakeholders), they could also be in charge of creating the local tourism policy, of realizing tourism studies, of organizing cultural events or of commercializing tourism benefits. The creation of an inter-municipality tourist office was left to the decision of the municipalities concerned, and depended on the nature of the skills to be transferred. Flexibility was the norm. With the NOTRe law, the competence of skill creation by tourist offices now lay with the inter-municipalities. This measure was met by strong opposition from elected officials of different tourism associations.[6] Consequently, derogations were granted to tourist municipalities,[7] to preserve the skill of tourism promotion, including the creation of tourism offices. Therefore, in mountain territories inter-municipality tourist offices co-exist with some municipality tourist offices, intending to promote (and to preserve) the ski resort's brand, which is more highly recognized than the inter-municipality tourism brand, as said by both tourism operators and elected people (source interviews).

30.3.2 Impacts of the NOTRe Law for mountain tourism destinations

As pointed out earlier, all the municipalities in the mountain tourism regions now are included in an inter-municipality. The boundaries of the inter-municipalities were designed by department prefects (given this responsibility by the state). Thus, the decision did not belong to the local stakeholders. This has resulted in important distinctions between the inter-municipalities responsible for tourism diversification (described as MDT 2) and the new inter-municipalities that have 'lawful authority' to organize tourism.

One example can be found in the 'Haute-Maurienne' valley. Until the reform, this territory was structured in two different inter-municipalities: the inter-municipality of 'Haute-Maurienne-Vanoise' and the inter-municipality of 'Terra-Modana' (see Fig. 30.3). The first is located at the top of the valley and has three middle-sized downhill ski resorts. Tourism is the most important component of the local economy, with agriculture in a less important role (source interviews). An inter-municipality tourist office was created in 2010 to promote the 'Haute-Maurienne-Vanoise'[8] tourism destination. Since then, the stakeholders have created a tourism organization at this territorial scale. The Terra-Modana inter-municipality, for its part, is located further down the valley. It was developed around two main economic sectors: industry and tourism.

The industrialization of Modane, the main city, started in the early 20th century (Chabert, 1978). After the crisis in industry, tourism was developed with the creation of three middle-sized ski resorts in this inter-municipality. Unlike the Haute-Maurienne-Vanoise inter-municipality, tourism organization was maintained at the municipality level. Three tourism offices were created in the three municipalities with ski resorts. Despite the different organization of tourism between the inter-municipalities of Terra-Modana and Haute-Maurienne-Vanoise, the diversification of tourism in both cases is implemented at the scale of the inter-municipalities, under the management of the public actors. Indeed, the elected stakeholders (and the authorities of the two

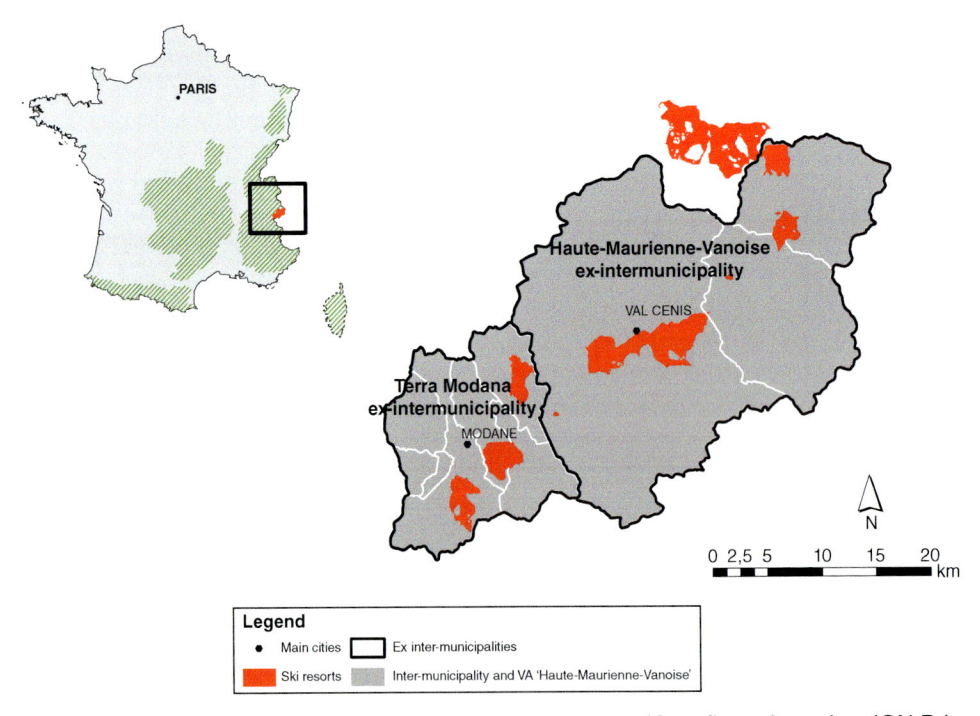

Fig. 30.3. The Haute-Maurienne-Vanoise inter-municipality. (Own figure based on IGN Bd Carto®, 2016; IRSTEA Bd Stations, 2017; IRSTEA Bd EV, 2018.)

inter-municipalities) sought harmonization, with the development of a tourism strategy in each of the two inter-municipalities, corresponding to the MDT 2. In 2017, the implementation of the NOTRe law led to a merger of the two inter-municipalities. Today, tourism skills have been transferred to the new inter-municipality with the main consequence being the creation of a unique tourist office at the scale of the new inter-municipality, which became the MDT 3. Thus, the work initiated for the diversification of tourism has to be continued at this new scale with, inevitably, some tensions between stakeholders. First, the role of tourism in the economy and the efforts deployed for its development differed between the two inter-municipalities. Then, the replacement of the municipal tourist offices by an inter-municipality tourist office led to opposition by some stakeholders, who used to be organized at an infra-territorial scale. In this mountain territory, the institutional reorganization surely made sense in terms of tourism destination and was facilitated by the intermediary creation of the MDT 2 especially in Haute-Maurienne-Vanoise (which introduced an inter-municipality function).

30.4 Public Policies to Accompany the Mountain Territories and Their Development

During the 1960s, the French state supported the creation of ski resorts. Twenty years later, with the succession of three snow-free winters, public policies were adopted to support these ski resorts. After targeting the management of ski resorts, dedicated public policies focused on tourism diversification of the resorts.

30.4.1 Three generations of public policies dedicated to ski resorts and mountain territories

Tourism development has been a responsibility of public actors for a long time. Since the introduction of annual paid leave, the state has helped create the third-generation ski resorts,[9] while other institutions have supported the creation of access roads. After this initial creation period, the ski resorts moved to a management phase. In the 1970s, they started facing difficulties, such as poor sales of real estate, market saturation or the well-known three snow-free winters at the end of the 1980s. In reaction, the public authorities, and especially the regions and departments,[10] adopted public tourism policies dedicated to ski resorts. First, the policy adopted by the ex-Rhône-Alpes region (1995–2000) aimed to support ski resorts in strengthening their management to implement an enterprise organization, by 'fostering the transfer of its methods and organisations or by fostering the grouping of the numerous stakeholders' (Conseil Régional Rhône-Alpes, 1995). In addition, these policies helped improve the reliability of snow cover with the funding of snowmaking installations.

The renewal of this policy from 2006 to 2012 marked an important turning point in defining the future of 'mid-elevation ski resorts' (George and Achin, n.d.). Tourism diversification, which constituted a minor objective in the past, became the most important goal. To this end, only inter-municipality territories, natural and regional parks, or other groupings of municipalities could be candidates. This represented a major development in policy, with aid not focused only on the ski resorts; candidates had to additionally develop a long-term tourism strategy. This led to the labelling of 27 'valley areas' (VA). In the northern Alps region where this policy was confined, the VAs were mixed up with MTD 2, corresponding to the tourism diversification territory. The policy's requirements for forward planning provided the territory with a framework in which to organize their future tourism. Indeed, one of the main difficulties for tourism stakeholders was to move beyond the short-term management, which corresponds to a limited management to current or urgent business. The requirement to establish a tourism strategy (without which the territory is not eligible for the financial support) required moving beyond the arguments of lack of time, lack of competences and/or vision for the future of tourism. The VAs public policy acted as a support for the renewal of the local governance of tourism, proposing a framework in which to collectively imagine and elaborate on an alternative to the snow-focused tourism offerings.

Current public policy (2014–2020) is aimed at both the imperative of tourism diversification and the inter-municipal dimension of the projects. First, while tourism diversification was seen to encompass all tourism activities not related to downhill skiing, it is now considered as the tourism valorization of natural and cultural heritage. For example, this has led to the creation of hiking trails and chapels or artisan roads. The second aspect of the policy is related to the territories admitted as candidates for public funding. The previous policies had introduced the inter-municipalities approach, and the current policies pursue this approach by further developing it. After the initial experiences, some VA mergers and extensions were proposed by the policy representatives. The underlying idea was to define more relevant and especially larger tourism territories. The boundaries of these new VAs have taken into account the still temporary outlines of the inter-municipalities resulting from the NOTRe law.

30.4.2 A tourism governance renewal supported by the Valley Areas' public policies

In Haute-Maurienne-Vanoise, territorial reform has led – as we have seen – to the merger of the two inter-municipalities, which previously organized tourism activity. Here, it is important to underline the significance of the public policies dedicated to mountain tourism, and especially the current policies. Indeed, by encouraging the two inter-municipalities to unite as one candidate, the policy leaders have anticipated the legal obligation to merge the inter-municipalities. To elaborate on a common strategy, they decided to gather together the tourism projects from all the municipalities. Subsequently, they categorized and prioritized these projects to achieve a shared tourism strategy, validated by the policy leaders. During this process, the various actors became acquainted and learnt to work together. In addition, tourism planning helped to win the stakeholders' acceptance of the creation of a common tourist office. With the definition of a common strategy and a shared tourism destination brand, there has not been a desire to preserve local tourist offices.

In the 'Guillestrois-Queyras' VA (see Fig. 30.1), the situation is rather different. Here too, two VAs were created in 2006, one in the 'Guillestrois' and the other in the Queyras Regional Nature Park. At the request of the public authorities and to prepare for territorial reform, these two VAs merged when public policy was renewed. In January 2017, the two inter-municipalities (corresponding to the two ex-VAs) also merged. After 1 1/2 years of existence, a distinction remains between the two territories. The head of tourism notes in particular the preservation of the two tourism destinations and the struggle to initiate a common tourism organization. Although an inter-municipality tourist office has been created, two of the ski resorts have decided to preserve their municipality tourist office.[11] Elaboration of the tourism strategy and the related action plan have facilitated the common work of all the local elected officials. However, the reduction in financial resources has led to a demobilization of these stakeholders and a loss of the networking aims pursued by the public policy.

30.5 Conclusions

To conclude, ongoing studies confirm the diversity of the governance models of French ski resorts. Indeed, the directive for tourism diversification, related to climate change, has forced ski resorts to renew their organizational dynamics. Thus, these current dynamics still range between the original tourism governance focused on the ski resort, the winter season and the ski lift operator, and, since the 2000s, a tourism diversification governance that aimed at creating a new tourism destination larger than the ski resort, involving more stakeholders and with the perspective of all-year-round tourism.

These different dynamics also highlight the important factors that are needed for tourism diversification and more generally for the future of ski resorts. First, the stakeholder networks and their expansion with 'new' stakeholders questions the future of the leaders in place, their nature but also their renewal. The second point highlights the limits of the tourism destination. Questions regarding this include: How to define a good territorial balance to preserve the unity of the destination? How to achieve a structural dimension that can be extended beyond the ski resorts? And how to preserve tourism's interests over a large area, where potentially the mountain (and its tourism stakes) is marginal, compared with cities included in the same inter-municipality?

Acknowledgements

The findings in this chapter are based on a project (EValoscope) financed by the European Union with the cooperation of the Regional European Development Fund, under Strategic Objective 1 of the Interregional Operational Programme 2014–2020 for the Alps Mountains.

Notes

[1] Unless otherwise specified in the text, the term 'Alps' refers to the French part of the Alps.
[2] These contracts are only needed in the case of private exploitation of the lifts; the municipality can choose to directly manage this activity.
[3] France has five 'massifs' on its mainland territory: the Alps, the Jura, the Massif Central, the Pyrenees and the Vosges. They have been defined by the Mountain Law of 1985 and include mountainous municipalities that have significant disadvantages involving more difficult living conditions and restricting the exercise of certain economic activities.
[4] This specific size also concerns other inter-municipalities, with a low population density.

[5] Le Tourisme en Savoie. Available at: www.observatoire.savoie.equipement-agriculture.gouv.fr/Atlas/5-tourisme.htm (accessed 1 February 2019).

[6] See for instance Laurent Wauquier, President of the National Association of Mountain Elected (ANEM) keynote address during the 31th Congress of the Association (15–16 October 2015). Available at: www.anem.fr/upload/pdf/Discours_ouverture_de_Laurent_WAUQUIEZ__President_de_I__ANEM__depute_de_la_Haute_Loire_20151126112222_31eme_Congres_Discours_ouverture_LW.pdf (accessed 10 October 2018).

[7] Ranking in tourism municipalities is realized by prefectural order.

[8] 'Vanoise' refers to the Vanoise National Park, which is partly in the territory of the inter-municipality.

[9] The third generation of ski resorts was created in the 1960s *ex nihilo* with the support of the French state, in optimal places for downhill skiing. Their construction optimized tourism by creating a snow industry: real estate was vertical and was located with all the services at the convergence point of lifts and slopes (Cumin, 1970).

[10] The 1982 laws on decentralization gave local authorities new prerogatives and greater resources. Among them, the departments and regions (Nuts 2 and 3) henceforth had a capacity in town and country planning.

[11] By way of exception, the NOTRe law allows the tourism-classified municipalities and resorts to maintain their tourist office.

References

Achin, C. and George-Marcelpoil, E. (2016) The tourism diversification in French ski resorts: what are effective drivers for sustainable tourism in mountain resorts? In: Lira, S., Mano, A., Pinheiro, C. and Amoêda, R. (eds) *Tourism 2016: International Conference on Global Tourism and Sustainability*. Green Lines Institute for Sustainable Development, Barcelos, Portugal, pp. 11.

Atout France (2011) *Carnet de route de la montagne: Pour un développement touristique durable des territoires de montagne*. Collection Marketing touristique. Atout France, Paris.

Bodega, D., Cioccarelli, G. and Denicolai, S. (2004) New inter-organizational forms: evolution of relationship structures in mountain tourism. *Tourism Review* 59(3), 13–19. DOI:10.1108/eb058437

Chabert, L. (1978) Vallées montagnardes et industrie: le cas des Alpes françaises du nord (Mountain valleys and industry: the example of the northern French Alps). *Bulletin de l'Association de Géographes Français* 55(453), 187–191. DOI:10.3406/bagf.1978.5030

Clivaz, C. and George-Marcelpoil, E. (2016) Moutain tourism development between the political and administrative context and local governance: a French-Swiss comparison. In: Dissart, J.-C., Dehez, J. and Marsat, J.B. (eds) *Tourism, Recreation and Regional Development. Perspectives from France and Abroad*. Routledge, Abingdon, UK, pp. 93–106.

Conseil Régional Rhône-Alpes (1995) Charte 'entreprise-station' 1995–2000. Conseil Régional Rhône-Alpes, Lyon, France.

Cumin, G. (1970) Les stations intégrées. *Urbanisme* 116, 50–53.

Dawson, J. and Scott, D. (2007) Climate change vulnerability of the Vermont ski tourism industry (USA). *Annals of Leisure Research* 10(3–4), 550–572. DOI:10.1080/11745398.2007.9686781

Flagestad, A. and Hope, C.A. (2001) Strategic success in winter sports destinations: a sustainable value creation perspective. *Tourism Management* 22(5), 445–461. DOI:10.1016/S0261-5177(01)00010-3

François, H., Morin, S., Lafaysse, M. and George-Marcelpoil, E. (2014) Crossing numerical simulations of snow conditions with a spatially-resolved socio-economic database of ski resorts: a proof of concept in the French Alps. *Cold regions science and technology* 108, 98–112. DOI:10.1016/j.coldregions.2014.08.005

Frochot, I. (2016) Consumer co-construction and auto-construction mechanisms in the tourist experience: applications to the resort model at a destination scale. In: Dissart, J.-C., Dehez, J. and Marsat, J.B. (eds) *Tourism, Recreation and Regional Development. Perspectives from France and Abroad*. Routledge, Abingdon, UK, pp. 123–138.

George, E. and Achin, C. (n.d.) Implementation of tourism diversification in ski resorts in the French Alps: a history of territorializing tourism. In: Dissart, J.-C. and Seigneuret, N. (eds) *Local Resources and Well-being: a Multidisciplinary Perspective* (provisional title). Accepted for publication.

Gerbaux, F. and Marcelpoil, E. (2006) Gouvernance des stations de montagne en France: les spécificités du partenariat public-privé. *Revue de géographie alpine* 94(1), 9–19. DOI:10.3406/rga.2006.2380

Gill, A.M. and Williams, P.W. (2011) Rethinking resort growth: understanding evolving governance strategies in Whistler, British Columbia. *Journal of Sustainable Tourism* 19(4–5), 629–648. DOI:10.1080/09669582.2011.558626

IPCC (2014) *Climate Change 2014 – Impacts, Adaptation, and Vulnerability. Part A: Global and Sectoral Aspects. Contribution of Working Group II to the Fifth Assessment Report of the Intergovernmental Panel on Climate Change*. Cambridge University Press, Cambridge, UK.

Lasanta, T., Laguna, M. and Vicente-Serrano, S.M. (2007) Do tourism-based ski resorts contribute to the homogeneous development of the Mediterranean mountains? A case study in the Central Spanish Pyrenees. *Tourism Management* 28(5), 1326–1339. DOI:10.1016/j.tourman.2007.01.003

Nordin, S. and Svensson, B. (2007) Innovative destination governance: the Swedish ski resort of Åre. *The International Journal of Entrepreneurship and Innovation* 8(1), 53–66. DOI:10.5367/000000007780007416

Spandre, P., François, H., Morin, S. and George-Marcelpoil, E. (2015) Snowmaking in the French Alps. *Journal of Alpine Research – Revue de géographie alpine* 103(2), 1–17. DOI:10.4000/rga.2913

31 Preferences for Renewable Energy Sources Among Tourists in the European Alps

ALEXANDRA JIRICKA-PÜRRER*, JOHANNES SCHMIED AND ULRIKE PRÖBSTL-HAIDER

Institute of Landscape Development, Recreation and Conservation Planning, University of Natural Resources and Life Sciences, Vienna, Austria

31.1 Introduction

Regarding the mitigation of climate change, the use of renewable energy sources is considered the most important factor in national and international strategies. Many alpine communities are accordingly implementing renewable energy installations. In winter tourism destinations, the production of renewable energy gains further importance in connection with the increased dependence on artificial snowmaking. In alpine skiing areas the percentage of ski slopes that are now being covered with artificial snow has significantly increased over the past 5 years. Major skiing resorts in Austria and Switzerland rely on artificial snowmaking for 80–100% of their snow cover (Zegg *et al.*, 2010).

While the use of renewable energy is beneficial overall with regard to climate mitigation targets, it might create conflicts with ongoing efforts to foster multi-seasonal tourism offers. Many studies have shown that summer tourists consider the natural landscape in alpine regions as one of the most important factors for their choice of holidays (Österreich Werbung, 2009, 2012). The multitude of studies dealing with different groups of holidaymakers including climbers, hikers and random samples of holiday seekers, etc. support this aspect (Muhar *et al.*, 2006; Pröbstl, 2010). The way landscapes are perceived, however, varies between different socio-demographic groups (Howley, 2011), as well as different nationalities (Bell *et al.*, 2008).

A decrease in seasonality – as currently pursued by winter tourism destinations due to the effect of climate change – requires an infrastructure that suits the preferences of summer, as well as winter guests (TAC, 2011). Hence, it will become increasingly important for tourist destinations to maintain their landscapes' appeal for visitors all year round. Consequently, the production of renewable energy in these regions will also have to comply with this goal.

The use of renewable energy could, however, also be a competitive advantage with regard to criticism concerning artificial snowmaking (as a measure skiing areas apply to adapt to the effects of climate change).

---

* E-mail: alexandra.jiricka@boku.ac.at

Against this background, we were interested in the tourists' reaction to the development of renewable energy installations in the alpine area. In this chapter, we want to discuss the following questions:

- Which of the available infrastructure facilities used to generate renewable energy finds the greatest degree of acceptance among tourists?
- Which of these renewable energy installations could have an impact on further tourism development?
- Is there a difference between summer tourists' and winter tourists' acceptance of renewable energy?
- Could local production of renewable energy lead to a competitive advantage for tourist destinations and how important is the supply of renewable energy for tourists' choice of destination?

Five main hypotheses derived from these considerations:

1. The particular holiday season (winter/summer) has a significant influence on tourists' preferences for renewable energy sources.
2. Socio-demographics of tourists (especially age and nationality) have a considerable influence on the acceptance of renewable energy.
3. Energy supply by means of renewable energy is important for tourists' choice of destination.
4. Local production of renewable energy could create a competitive advantage for destinations.
5. Tourists assess renewable energy facilities that are attached to existing structures (including buildings, existing infrastructure) more positively than systems that are set up independently.

31.2 Background

So far, only a small number of studies have explicitly focused on the attitudes of tourists towards renewable energy production. Most of the available literature is in the field of wind energy studies (see, for example, BWEA, 2006; Davidson, 2010; Lilley et al., 2010; Frantál and Kunc, 2011). Many of the existing studies specifically focus on offshore wind farms (Ladenburg, 2010; Swofford and Slattery, 2010; Waldo, 2012; Westerberg et al., 2013).

Ladenburg (2010) conducted a survey with 1082 respondents including both residents and local day visitors to beaches close to offshore wind parks. The respondents' attitudes were generally very positive towards the farms, although frequent walkers on the beach – representing those with a stronger connection to the area – displayed lower acceptance than 'non-frequent' (occasional) walkers. Ladenburg also suggests that demographics have an influence on the perception of the power plants – especially age. Other studies have shown that offshore wind parks even tend to have positive effects on tourism by attracting interested recreation seekers (Devine-Wright, 2005). BWEA (2006) also found that suitable marketing measures could substantially boost a region's income.

Yet other studies argue that wind turbines have a negative impact on tourists' perception of their destination's landscape. In a presentation of their research on a Finnish wind park project, Tyrväinen *et al.* (2012) point out that tourists considered the wind turbines to have a negative impact on the landscape. Their mixed-method approach encompassed quantitative and qualitative methods such as picture samples that were evaluated by international, as well as domestic tourists. While locals engaging in recreational activities in the area perceived the wind turbines more positively, foreigners were more critical of the project. These opposing views held by locals versus non-local tourists have also been observed by Waldo *et al.* (2013). Lilley *et al.* (2010) came to similar conclusions in their study, as almost a quarter of their 1076 respondents found the effects of 'turbines on the appearance of landscape' to be negative or very negative. In both studies – Tyrväinen *et al.* (2012) and Lilley *et al.* (2010) – the tourists' attitudes towards the specific projects in question did not correlate with their general attitudes towards wind energy. Only when they were confronted by a project located, or to be located in their favourite holiday destination, did they experience wind energy as disturbing. In a qualitative survey, Waldo (2012) addressed the correlation between preferred activities and the acceptance of offshore wind energy production. He observed that the majority of stakeholders were against two new sites for offshore wind parks installed in the area. General attitude concerning the efficiency of wind energy was found to have a strong influence on this point of view. Yet it was the aesthetic value of wind turbines that was judged most negatively. While discussing their attitudes towards installations for wind energy, activities such as 'watching the sunset, relaxing and feeling free and [being] close to nature' were mentioned as having been negatively impacted. These aspects seem to be essential in the assessment of renewable energy in touristic regions, especially since the abovementioned 'activities' constitute typical motivations in the choice of a holiday destination.

Many statements made by residents interviewed in Waldo's study reflect the aesthetic problem of large renewable energy projects: 'They're not noisy or anything – but when you turn around and suddenly see them, they make you stop and think. It's like you're not in the countryside anymore, you're at an industrial site. They take so much space that you find that you're perhaps not thinking about the landscape, like you did before. We used to have an almost unbroken horizon' (private citizen, interview 39, Waldo 2012, p. 697).

While Broekel and Alfken (2015) confirm the negative impact, in particular by offshore wind turbines for German tourists, Landry *et al.* (2012) previously revealed a more differentiated picture by a revealed preference (RP) and stated preference (SP) approach. Westerberg *et al.* (2013) also investigated the contradictory effects of offshore wind farms with regard to different tourist segments. This study highlighted two major points: First, it concluded that holiday activity, age, nationality and loyalty towards holiday destination each have a direct influence on tourists' perception of renewable energy production. Second, the distance of the energy production site to the place of observation was shown to have a major effect – an aspect that will also be highly relevant in the discussion concerning alpine areas. In contrast to the constellation onshore/offshore, mountainous areas provide a variety of different angles from which to observe the landscape that do not allow for a simple restriction of vantage points. Furthermore, the high degree of mobility increases the different visual perceptions alpine tourists experience over the course of their holiday. Nevertheless, offshore wind parks, wind parks in coastal areas and wind parks in open – less diversified (heterogeneous) – landscapes are seen differently in comparison with wind energy constructions in highly diversified touristic landscapes such as landlocked mountainous regions in Central Europe. Frantál and Kunc (2011) examined tourists' and entrepreneurs' acceptance of wind energy in two selected regions of the Czech Republic. The number of respondents in favour of wind turbines – stating that turbines could be used effectively to support further development of tourism – equalled the number of respondents against wind turbines. Yet it seems surprising that 90% of visitors did not see their future visits to the area affected by new wind parks. Still, more than 20% of tourists stated that wind turbines had a relatively negative impact on their holiday experience. This seems to indicate somewhat ambivalent views as well as a capacity to adapt to new infrastructure projects at the preferred holiday destination.

In contrast, a handful of studies from Australia, including Dalton *et al.* (2008) and Lothian (2008), deal with the valorization of renewable energies as criteria for the choice of sustainable holiday options. Dalton *et al.* (2008) asked hotel guests at four different Australian locations about their attitude towards micro-generation renewable energy supply (RES) implemented in the hotels they were staying at. Face-to-face interviews, as well as distributed questionnaires, were used to survey a total of 280 respondents. The collected data revealed that more than 80% of the respondents considered it important for accommodations to utilize renewable energy sources. However, less than half were willing to pay more for RES. In contrast to Ladenburg's findings (2010), age played only a minor role in the degree of acceptance of renewable energy, though acceptance varied between different nationalities.

Kelly *et al.* (2007) support these findings on tourists' preference for a resort that uses renewable energy over one that does not, arguing that day tourists, especially, consider it as a means of increasing eco-efficiency. On the other hand, tourists staying on a weekly basis took a more ambivalent stance. With regard to destination choice, a study carried out by Needham and Little (2013) found that only a small number of tourists (12–13% of their respondents) preferred a destination that used renewable energy sources and made efforts to reduce its energy consumption.

In the alpine context, there is, however, a distinct lack of in-depth studies adopting a comprehensive approach that takes the diverse effects caused by renewable energies into account and compares summer and winter tourists' perceptions. The on-site survey in the four large-scale skiing destinations both in winter and in summer provided an opportunity to survey the perception of alpine tourists who are both familiar with the landscape and were just experiencing it while responding to the questionnaire. Although the study was carried out 7 years ago research about renewable energies in alpine skiing destination is still scarce.

31.3 Method

An extensive survey was conducted in four large Austrian skiing destinations in the winter season of 2010/11, leading to a sample size of 1165 participants. A questionnaire was developed within the Alps research project ADAPT, which deals with efficient and highly accepted RES systems for winter sports destinations. This survey was carried out in the destinations Lech am Arlberg, Schladming, Zell am See and Silvretta Montafon, which to a large extent, each rely on artificial snow coverage. The characteristics of each of these skiing regions are presented in Table 31.1. These resorts cover the existing range of Austrian skiing regions with regard to their geographical

Table 31.1. Main characteristics of the four study areas across Austria.

Characteristics	Lech am Arlberg	Schladming	Zell am See	Silvretta Montafon
Federal state	Vorarlberg	Styria	Salzburg	Vorarlberg
Size	279 km (Lech/Zürs)	126 km (Planai-Hochwurzen)	77 km	158 km
Altitude	1480 m	680–2100 m	750–2000 m	700–2300 m
Major target groups	High performers/intermediate and advanced	Family oriented, World Cup	International, fun oriented	Various target groups
Artificial snow coverage	100%	95%	100%	Approx. 55%
Environmental Policy (online)	Environmental declaration (ISO 14001, former EMAS)	Brief information included in the overall policy	Environmental declaration (EMAS certification since 2017)	No information available
Price level (2010/11)	Per day €44.50	Per day €42	Per day €42	Per day €40.50

distribution in the main winter sport regions in Austria. Each, moreover, differs in their target groups, altitude, access to the area and size. Larger resorts (i.e. medium to large in comparison with the Austrian 'average') were chosen because of their potential financial and management capacity to introduce and integrate renewable energies into their overall energy concept.

In order to allow a comparison between winter and summer guests, the survey was repeated during the summer season of 2012. The questionnaire was, again, available in two languages. In total, the summer survey included 1016 respondents from the four different regions.

At the beginning of the questionnaire, tourists were asked about the most common summer activities in alpine holiday areas in Austria. These were sourced by cross-reading relevant studies concerned with activities in mountainous regions (such as Weiermair, 1999; Latu et al., 2010), sports tourism (Ritchie and Adair, 2004), as well as studies on general activities in Austrian summer tourism (Österreich Werbung, 2012), thereby compiling a suitable and compact list of activities to choose from. Multiple answers were possible.

The study is characterized by a very high response rate in summer and winter compared with other studies in outdoor recreation and tourism research. Table 31.2 describes both the winter (WS) and summer surveys (S1) in detail, including sample size, gender distribution, age distribution, type of visit according to duration of stay, nationality and main activities carried out within the region.

Table 31.2 shows similarities and differences between the two samples. Germany and Austria are the main countries of origin among the respondents. Summer tourists are slightly older than those surveyed during the winter season. In winter, we also had more male respondents. These differences are still reflective of the current conditions in each season and are in line with Austrian tourism statistics (Österreich Werbung, 2012).

Table 31.2. Sample description.

	Winter study (WS)	Summer study (S1)
Response rate	70%	87%
Sample size (*n*)	1165	1016
Sample size per tourist area (*n*)	Schladming: 188 Zell am See: 228 Lech: 206 Silvretta/Montafon: 543	Schladming: 257 Zell am See: 260 Lech: 234 Silvretta/Montafon: 265
Time of survey	Mostly weekdays 2010/2011	Mostly weekdays July 2012
Gender distribution	35.4% female 60.7% male 3.9% no value	45.7% female 46.9% male 7.5% no value
Type of visitor	79% week tourists 13% day tourists 4% locals 2% skiing instructors/ travel guides 2% others	74% week tourists 17% day tourists 3% locals 2% seasonal workers/ travel guides 3% others 1% no value
Age distribution	8.7% (age 14–17) 8.3% (age 18–24) 7.4% (age 25–29) 16.9% (age 30–39) 38.7% (age 40–49) 11.7% (age 50–59) 5.3% (age 60+)	5.2% (age 14–17) 7.8% (age 18–24) 7.2% (age 25–29) 12.9% (age 30–39) 20.4% (age 40–49) 20.1% (age 50–59) 22.4% (age 60+) 4.0% (no value)
Nationality of visitors	27.8% Austria 54.2% Germany 7.3% Netherlands 2.7% Switzerland 7.8% others	17.6% Austria 45.0% Germany 5.5% Netherlands 4.8% Switzerland 5.0% Great Britain 4.8% Scandinavia 6.4% Slavic countries + Hungary 2.7% Arab countries + India 2.0% no value
Main activity	87% skiing 12% snowboarding 1% others (single choice only)	60.8% relaxation 13.5% cultural activities 73.5% hiking 13.3% bicycle riding 7% climbing 11.9% socializing 63% experiencing nature 6.4% others (multiple answers possible)

31.3.1 Data collection

The sampling method for both surveys included data collection conducted in cooperation with cable car enterprises and at main tourist areas, such as market places, tourist offices and in pedestrian zones at the respective resorts. In each case, the selected areas had been chosen on the basis of recommendations by cable car management in an effort to maximize the number of guests participating in the study. Questionnaires and pens were handed out to tourists at the base stations. They were asked to fill in the questionnaires during their cable car ride, after which the sheets were collected at the mountain top either by local staff or by our team. The data collection at other places was handled in the same manner, by distributing printed questionnaires to several people simultaneously and collecting them after completion.

In this particular survey, the applied technique of on-site self-completion had two major advantages. First, the possibility of approaching a large number of people who might otherwise be rather unwilling to interrupt their current activities to answer questions; second, no bias occurs in contrast to face-to-face interview situations, in which respondents are confronted with an interviewer. However, respondents may be influenced by other guests sharing the same cable car or other people at a restaurant table. Overall, 3 days were spent collecting data in each holiday destination.

31.3.2 Survey design

The quantitative questionnaires consisted of 14 predominantly closed questions (apart from minor exceptions). For most questions, a high degree of comparability could be maintained between the winter questionnaire and the questionnaire adapted for the summer season. The surveyed independent variables concerned the respective visitor group, holiday activities, country of origin, age and gender. The remaining questions relevant for this study assessed tourists' evaluation of different types of renewable energy production in terms of their impact on the landscape, environment and emissions, as well as tourists' perception of destinations that use different strategies for energy production.

In order to ask tourists about RES, we first had to explain the possible options. Several studies, including Dalton *et al.* (2007) and Tyrväinen *et al.* (2012), used pictures of possible production facilities and asked respondents to rate them in order to ensure they were aware of the impact the plants would have on the landscape. To avoid a potential bias, we decided not to use such photographs or drawings. Using visual aids would have required four different sets of pictures – one set for each region accounting for differences in the landscape – which would have compromised comparability between the regions. Had we only used one set of images, on the other hand, the regions' differences in landscape, cityscape, etc. would not have been reflected.

The selection of RES facilities was based on the possibilities currently on offer and in use in alpine ski resorts and cable car enterprises (Zegg *et al.*, 2010).

We tried to describe the potential size and location as clearly as possible and presented the following options (hereafter described as categories of energy production):

- small compact wind turbines (max. 5 m high) at suitable sites;
- small compact wind turbines next to facility sites/parking lots;
- tall efficient wind turbines in exposed places;

- modification of existing water reservoirs for the implementation of hydroelectric power stations;
- hydroelectric power generated by damming of local rivers;
- photovoltaic or solar systems installed on south-orientated slopes;
- photovoltaic or solar systems installed on buildings;
- large, efficient biogas plants;
- small biogas plants that are integrated into the landscape; and
- geothermal energy used to heat buildings.

These ten different options were evaluated by tourists participating in the survey in relation to their possible impacts: first, on the environment; second, on landscape aesthetics; and third, regarding possible emissions. Furthermore, the importance of environmental aspects – including the share of renewable energy in the overall energy supply, as well as the reduction of energy consumption – were evaluated as to their role in the selection of a holiday destination.

31.3.3 Data analysis

SPSS 18.0 was used to record and evaluate the collected data. Mean values, frequencies, one factorial ANOVA, as well as Chi-Square were the main statistical tools applied throughout the study. Yet, after detailed analysis including testing skewness, as well as kurtosis of the data and applying quick-tests (Miles and Shevlin, 2001), it was decided that Chi-Square was better suited than ANOVA or a possible t-test. This decision was made in order to achieve a more accurate understanding of each individual distinctness, rather than assessing only mean value distributions.

For the tests, a significance level of 95% ($\alpha = 0.05$) was accepted. This means that differences between the results of the winter and the summer study, as well as independent data's influence on perceptions of renewable energy, were each required to have p values of $p < 0.05$. The null hypotheses that were generated with the applied test were subsequently analysed in order to re-evaluate the outcome of the study's research questions and hypotheses. The main test used for assessment is indicated in the figures' labelling. The use of $p < 0.05$ or $p < 0.01$ is additionally indicated within the charts with either one star (*) or two stars (**), respectively.

Previously, the distribution of the sample group (SG) has been displayed. To ensure the study's comparability with existing tourism research as well as to ensure a higher degree of transparency, 'week tourists' (WT) were analysed separately. This step entailed an exclusion of the following groups: 'day tourists', 'locals', 'skiing instructors', 'seasonal workers', 'others' and 'no value', in order to distinguish the group of WT from other visitor groups. However, a comparison between cross-tabulations of perceptions among WT and SG revealed that both categories generated very similar results. This study will, therefore, focus on the larger sample size (SG).

31.4 Results

Tourists were asked to rank criteria for the selection of a holiday destination according to their relevance to their personal decision making process (see Table 31.3 for a comparison between summer and winter study). The criteria were ranked according to their importance

Table 31.3. Criteria set for the summer and winter survey and related mean values (1 = very important to 5 = unimportant).

Winter study	Mean value	Summer study	Mean value
Quality of slopes	1.46	Well expanded cable car offer	2.41
Snow security	1.45	Predictable climate/weather	2.38
Price performance ratio	1.66	Price performance ratio	1.88
Accessibility	1.82	Accessibility/location	2.00
Size of the ski area	1.89	Sport facilities	2.60
Atmosphere	1.90	Atmosphere	1.69
Landscape aesthetics	1.96	Landscape aesthetics	1.32
Maintenance of attractive landscape	1.98	Maintenance of attractive landscape	1.64
Low impact on nature	2.02	Low impact on nature	1.88
Family-friendliness	2.27	Family-friendliness	2.19
Number of huts	2.35	Cultural experience	2.66
Ecological slope preparation	2.49	Choice of gastronomy	2.31
Ecologically friendly management	2.61	Energy friendly management	2.56
Use of renewable energy	2.75	Use of renewable energy	2.70
Après ski/party	3.19	Party scene	3.94
Environmentally friendly accessibility	2.89	Eco-friendly access to the area	2.70
		Appearance of the village	1.99
		Ecological preservation	1.98

for the selection of a holiday destination using the following system: 1 = very important, 2 = important, 3 = neutral, 4 = rather unimportant, 5 = unimportant. The selection criteria were compiled on the basis of surveys, such as Ritchie and Adair (2004), Latu *et al.* (2010) or Österreich Werbung (2012), combined with environmental aspects most relevant to alpine tourist destinations (Österreichischer Seilbahnverband, 2012).

The comparison between the criteria for choosing a holiday destination in the summer study and the winter study revealed several major differences (see Fig. 31.1). On the one hand, winter tourists evaluated the 'price performance ratio' as more important, as well as aspects related directly to the performance of their sport activities (such as the quality and length of slopes). On the other hand, summer guests rated the criteria 'atmosphere' and 'maintenance of attractive landscape' significantly higher than the guests included in the winter survey. Especially the criterion 'beauty of the landscape' showed striking differences. Around 80% of S1 rated this aspect as very important, almost doubling the percentage derived from the winter survey (around 40%).

31.4.1 Perception of renewable energies

To survey tourists' perception of the possible impact of renewable energies, three categories of effects were considered:

- effects on landscape;
- effects on the environment; and
- possible effects of emissions.

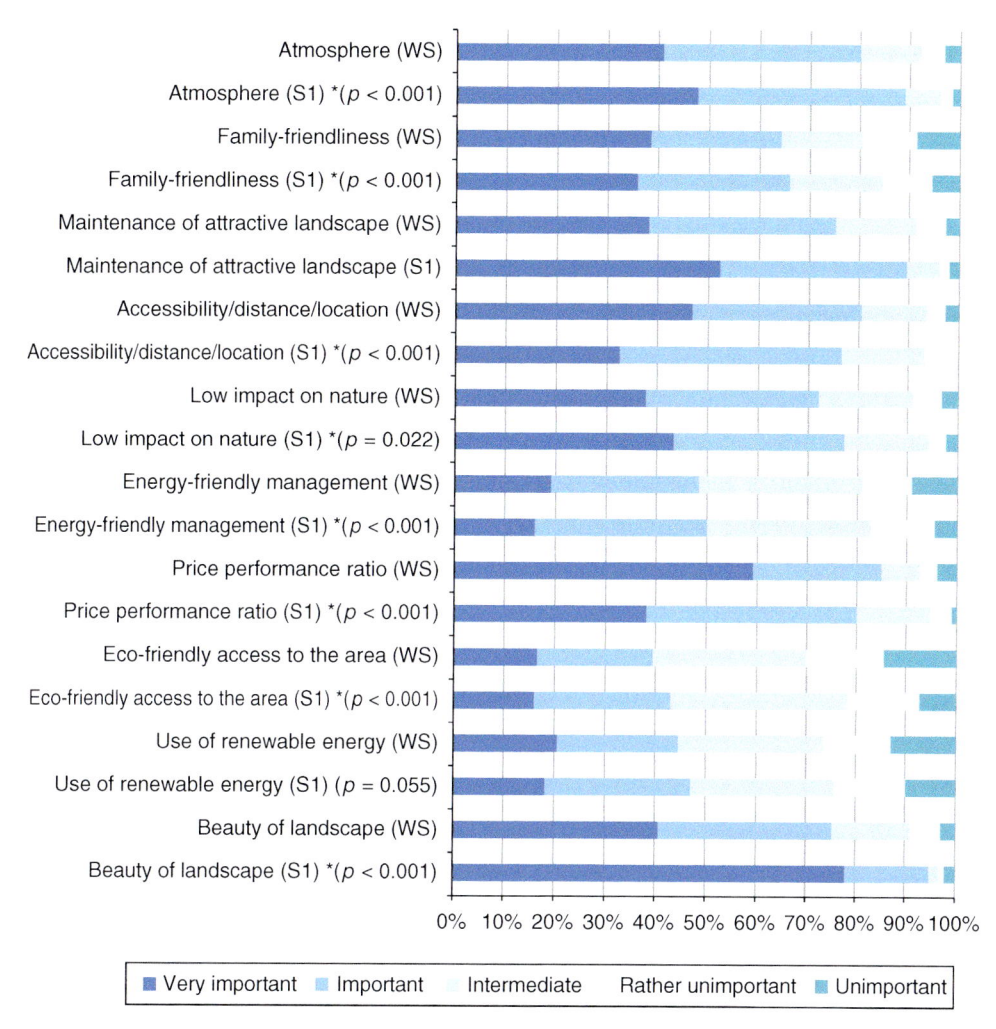

Fig. 31.1. Comparison of WS and S1 regarding the importance of different criteria for the selection of a holiday destination (chi²: α = 0.05, *p < 0.05).

In general, renewable energy plants that are added to existing infrastructure – like solar panels on buildings or hydroelectric power plants linked to existing water reservoirs – were rated significantly better than free-standing energy plants, such as tall wind turbines or solar systems close to slopes. Comparing the three aforementioned aspects (effects on the landscape/environment; emissions), the perception of renewable energy production differed the most between these types (i.e. attached vs. free-standing) with regard to their effects on the landscape.

When comparing the perception of 'possible effects of renewable energy on landscape' a significant difference between the summer and winter survey was observed for four types of renewable energy production (see Fig. 31.2). Both types of photovoltaic systems – namely 'photovoltaic or solar systems on south orientated slopes' and 'photovoltaic or solar systems on buildings' – were preferred by tourists in the winter study. 'Small compact wind turbines at suitable sites', as well as 'geothermal energy for

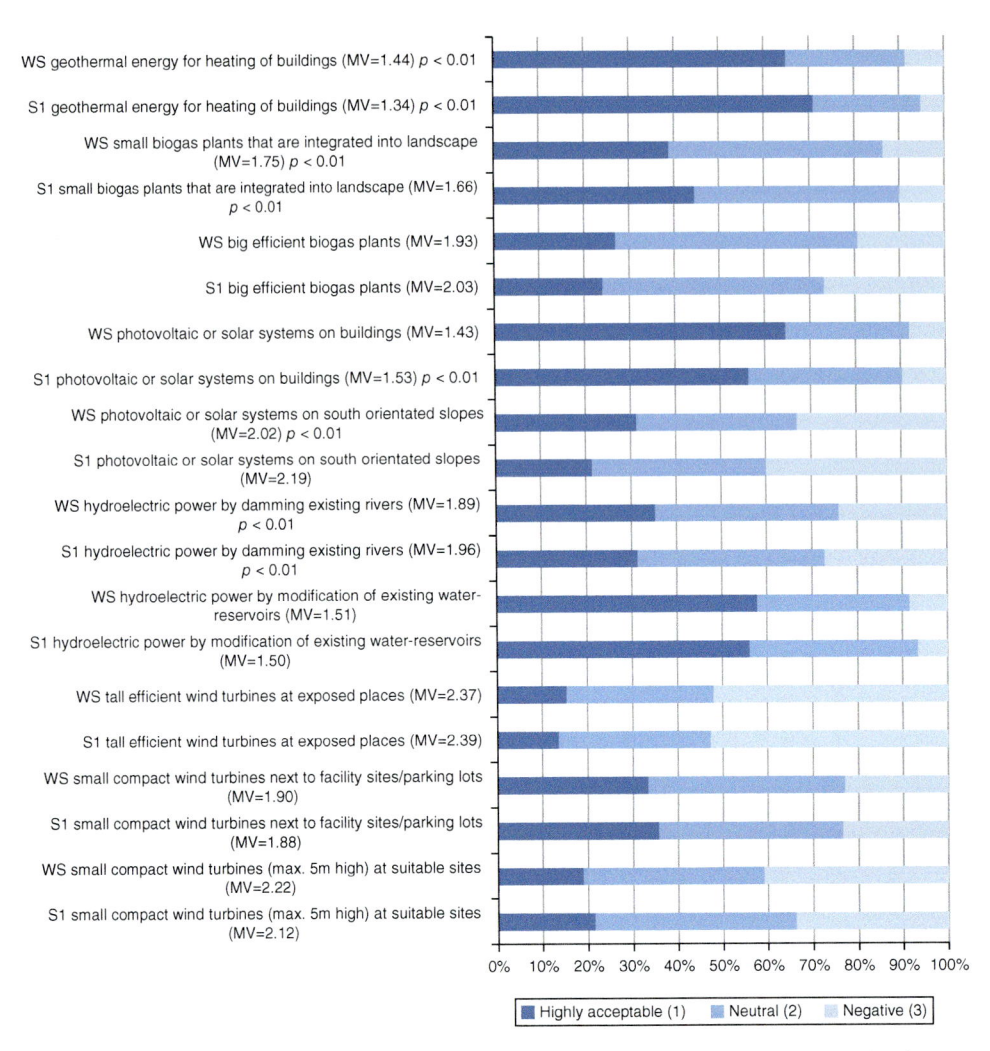

Fig. 31.2. Comparison of S1 and WS on possible effects of renewable energy on landscape (mean value (MV): 1 = highly acceptable, 2 = neutral, 3 = negative).

heating of buildings' found more support among summer tourists. Also, fewer respondents described their impact on the landscape as 'negative' in the summer sample.

On the other hand, the assessment of 'effects on the environment' followed along similar lines in both the winter and the summer study. The only category displaying a significant difference was 'geothermal energy for heating of buildings'. This aspect was assessed more positively in the summer study than in the winter study.

The influence of nationality

There is clear evidence that nationality has an influence on the evaluation of different types of renewable energy. Twelve out of 30 cases showed significant results, which demonstrated that tourists from different countries evaluated the given categories of renewable energy production differently.

Overall, Germans took the most negative view of renewable energy productions' impact on landscapes. In addition, people from 'Slavic countries + Hungary' and The Netherlands were relatively critical of this aspect. These three nationalities evaluated the environmental impact of plants the most negatively. Swiss guests showed an affinity for biogas plants and, overall, they seemed to evaluate the environmental impact of renewable energy more positively. Austrian and British nationals were mostly in between, with Austrians showing a slightly more positive attitude than the British in most cases.

Figures 31.3 and 31.4 show a strong concern among German tourists regarding wind energy and its impacts on the landscape. This negative perception of the impact of renewable energy production on the landscape articulated by German tourists was also evident in all other categories. A total of 63% of Germans assessed 'tall efficient wind turbines at exposed places' as 'bad', while 50.6% held the same opinion of 'photovoltaic or solar systems on south orientated slopes'. A little over 30% of German respondents were against 'large efficient biogas plants', showing a slightly more positive attitude in comparison with their reaction to wind and solar energy.

Figure 31.5 depicts the way different nationalities evaluate the impact of 'photovoltaic or solar systems on south orientated slopes' on the landscape. Scandinavians assessed this type of energy most positively. This is interesting, since solar fields are less common in Scandinavian countries, because of their limited efficiency due to local weather conditions and solar radiation. However, overall, this kind of energy production was viewed rather negatively.

'Large efficient biogas plants' were assessed less negatively than the photovoltaic systems mentioned above. A total of 54.5% of Swiss guests rated their impact on the

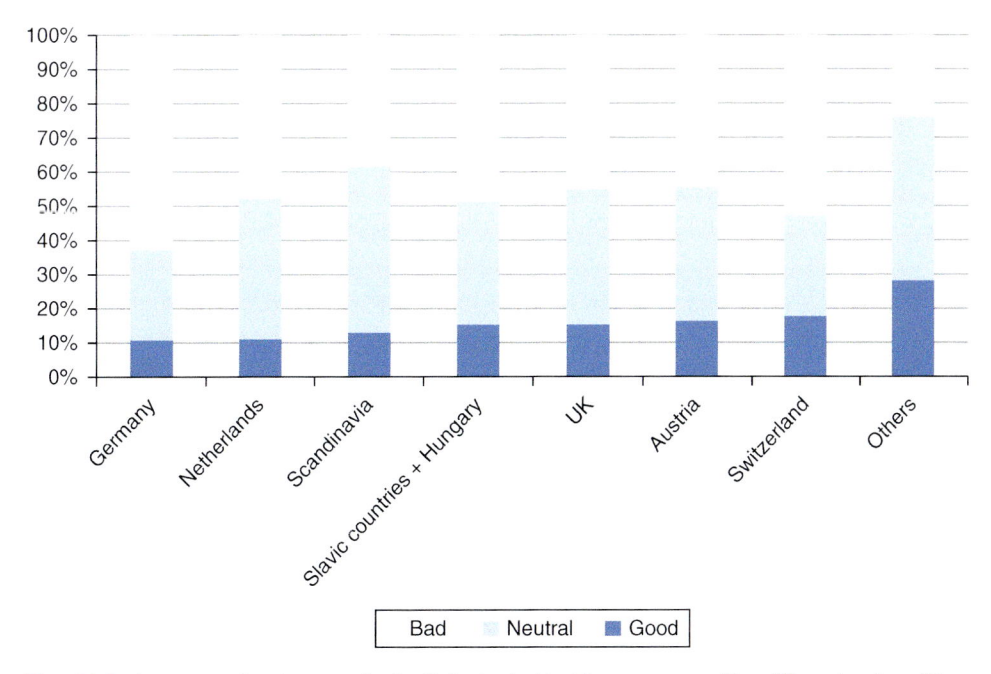

Fig. 31.3. Impact on landscape of tall efficient wind turbines assessed by different nationalities (ANOVA: $F = 5.300$, $\alpha = 0.05$, $p < 0.001$; $chi^2 = 43.348$, $\alpha = 0.05$, $p < 0.001$).

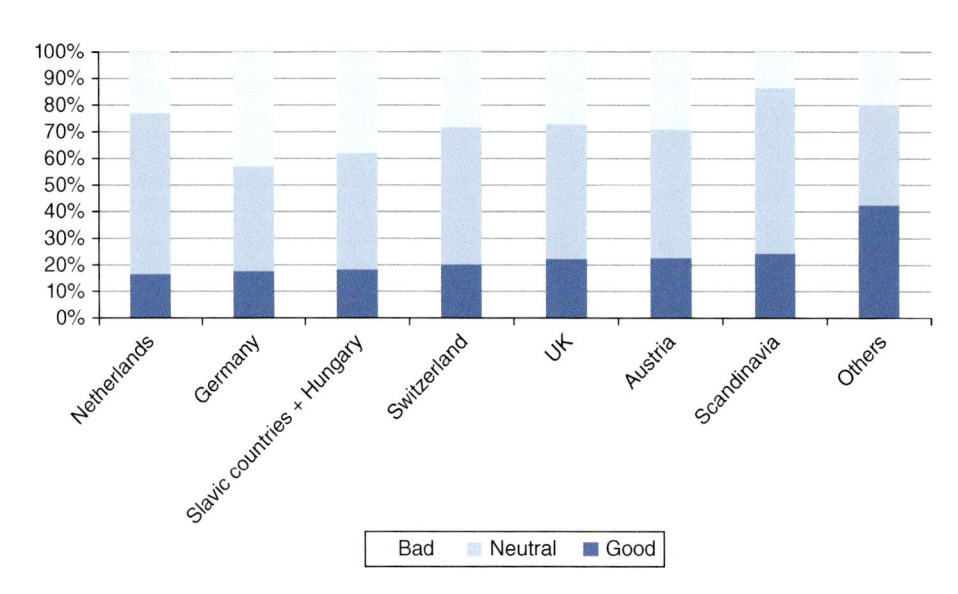

Fig. 31.4. Impact on landscape of small compact wind turbines as assessed by different nationalities (ANOVA: $F = 4.682$, $\alpha = 0.05$, $p < 0.001$; $chi^2 = 46.606$, $\alpha = 0.05$, $p < 0.001$).

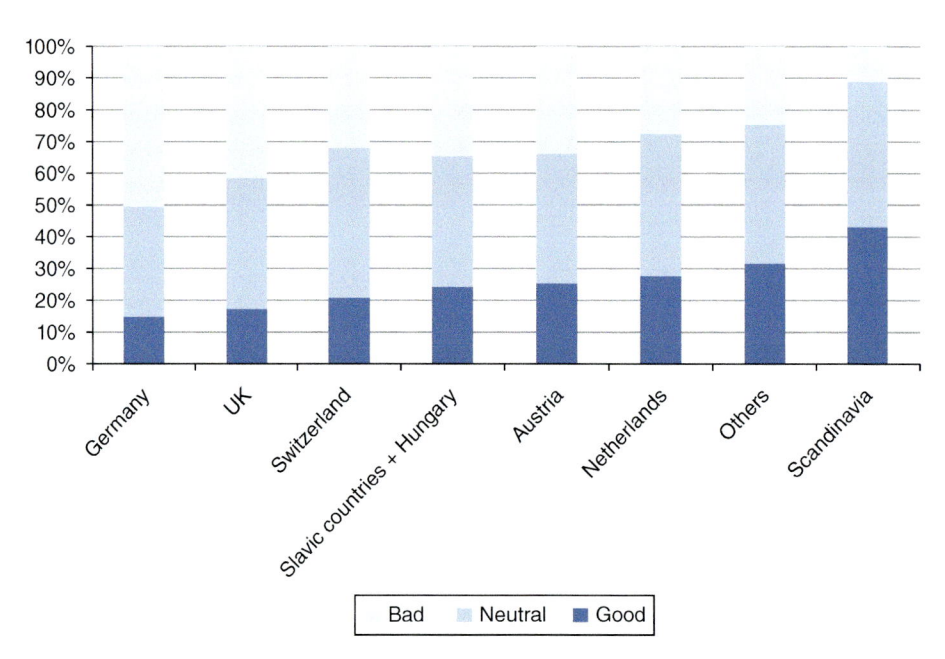

Fig. 31.5. Impact on landscape of photovoltaic or solar systems as assessed by different nationalities (ANOVA: $F = 4.682$, $\alpha = 0.05$, $p < 0.001$; $chi^2 = 46.606$, $\alpha = 0.05$, $p < 0.001$).

landscape as 'good'. Acceptance was relatively high among Austrian guests as well. However, the percentage of Austrian respondents categorizing their impact as positive was below 30%. As previously stated, Germans were again most critical of their impact on the landscape.

Results of the summer study are in line with those of the winter study. In general, German guests were more critical than Austrian tourists. Only hydroelectric power reversed this trend, as Austrian tourists were more critical of this particular form of renewable energy production.

The influence of age

There were nine categories within the summer study in which different age cohorts displayed significant differences in their perceptions of renewable energy in a holiday destination. Five of them concerned wind energy and showed marked differences between the age groups regarding their views on its impact on the environment. Differences were particularly pronounced between the age group '25–29' and the over 60s.

Moreover, it became clearly evident that the age group '60 and older' was the most critical. This category was persistently among the age groups that evaluated the given examples most negatively, with the notable exception of geothermal energy. Among the other two 'older' age groups, including 40–59-year-olds, the acceptance rates were similar, though not quite as negative.

The younger age groups, including 25–39-year-olds, were, on the whole, more positively inclined towards all types of renewable energy plants. They were also among the groups that rated wind energy the most positively.

The 18–24-year-olds were not located in the most extreme ranges of the results and could be described as taking a rather more positive stance than other groups. The results of the age group '14–17' fluctuated the most, thereby indicating that formation of opinion within this age group is still ongoing and is particularly susceptible to outside influences.

Regarding the perceived effect on the environment, all of the three wind energy categories – 'small compact wind turbines at suitable sites', 'small compact wind turbines next to facility sites/parking lots' and 'tall efficient wind turbines in exposed places' – achieved the highest acceptance rates from the age group '25–29' (see Fig. 31.6).

Finally the impact of 'tall efficient wind turbines at exposed places' on the landscape showed highly significant differences among the age groups (see Fig. 31.7). Again, the two oldest age groups were most critical ('60 and older', and '50–59'). In these age groups, more than 50% of the participants stated that wind turbines would have a negative impact on the landscape. The younger tourists, once more, rated wind energy more positively than older age groups. The 14–17-year-olds, closely followed by 25–29-year-olds, assessed this production facility the most positively.

Figure 31.8 shows 'photovoltaic or solar systems on south orientated slopes' as assessed by different age groups. The age group '30–39' (58.9%) evaluated the solar systems as 'good' most of the time. They were followed by the age group '14–17'. Again, it was the group '60 and older' who ranked this energy category the worst in comparison with other age groups. However, even in this age group, the majority viewed solar systems on slopes as having a 'good' rather than a 'bad' impact.

The impact of emissions caused by 'tall efficient wind turbines at exposed places' was the only included example that triggered significantly different responses among the various age groups when looking at emissions, as illustrated in Fig. 31.9. The three oldest age groups, '60 and older', '40–49' and '50–59', rated emissions of tall wind turbines the worst, whereas the age group of '25–29', again, took the least negative stance, followed by 18–24-year-olds and the age group '30–39'.

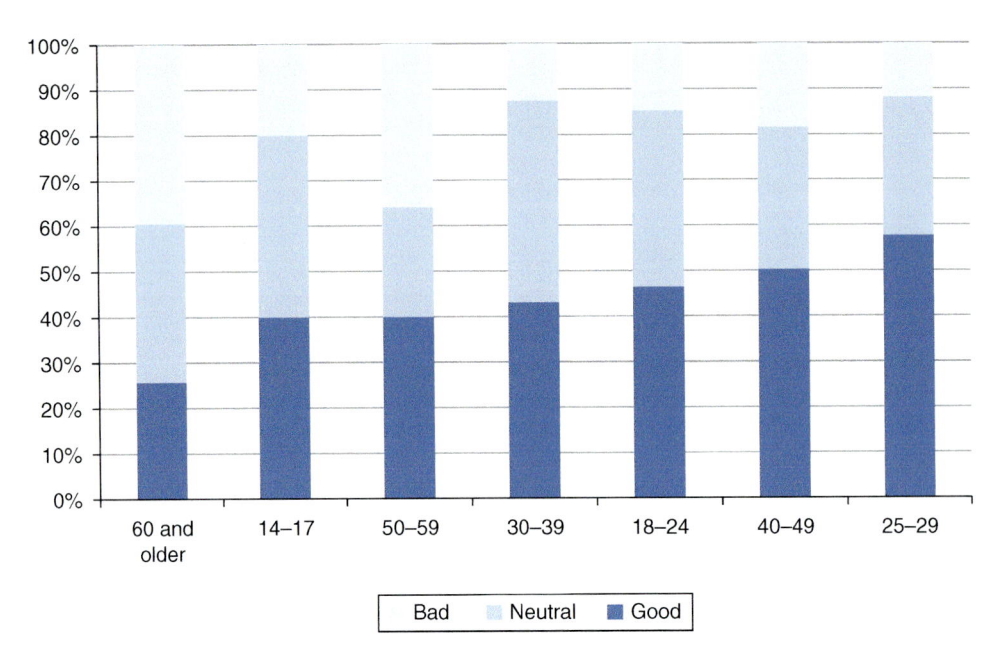

Fig. 31.6. Impact on environment of tall efficient wind turbines as assessed by different age groups (ANOVA: $F = 7.532$, $\alpha = 0.05$, $p < 0.001$; chi^2 = 61.798, $\alpha = 0.05$, $p < 0.01$).

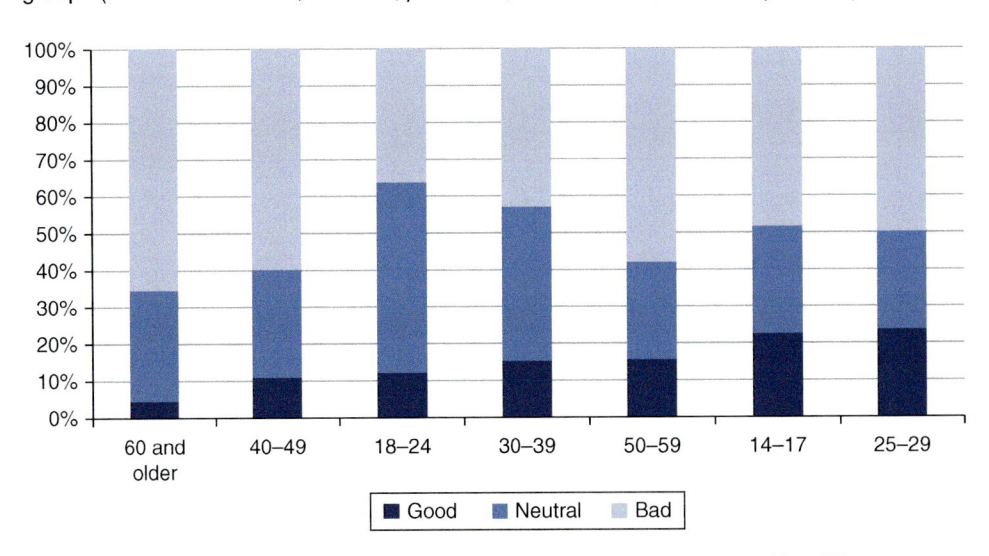

Fig. 31.7. Impact on landscape of tall efficient wind turbines as assessed by different age groups (ANOVA: $F = 2.850$, $\alpha = 0.05$, $p = 0.010$; chi^2 = 28.215, $\alpha = 0.05$, $p = 0.005$).

31.4.2 The importance of renewable energy production in the region

Figure 31.10 shows how many tourists would 'prefer a holiday destination which produces its own energy'. About 60% of all summer guests replied either 'absolutely' or 'yes' when asked if they would prefer local energy production, while only 43.8% of winter tourists (who answered the question) shared this positive view.

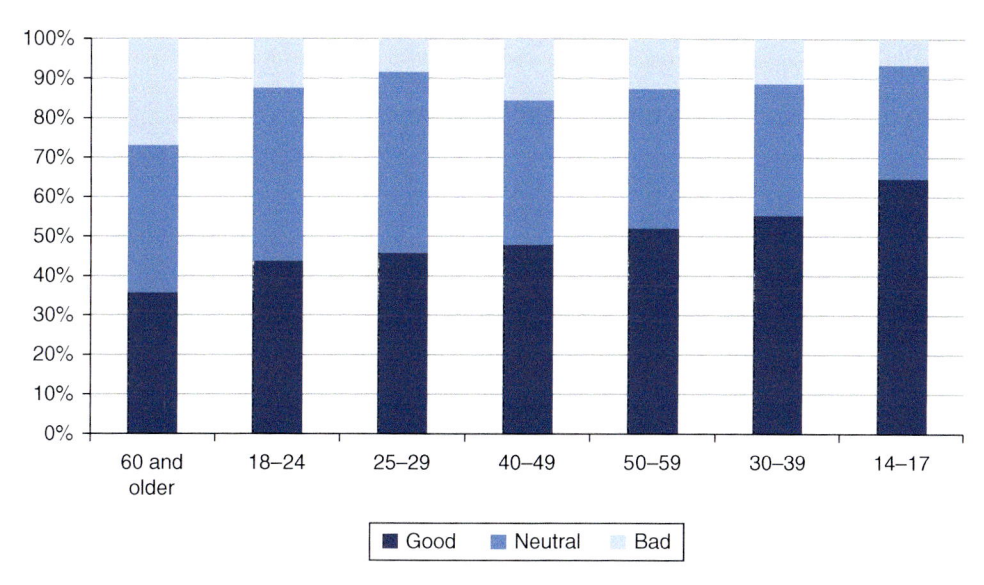

Fig. 31.8. Impact on environment of photovoltaic or solar systems as assessed by different age groups (ANOVA: $F = 2.639$, $\alpha = 0.05$, $p = 0.015$; chi^2 = 28.245, $\alpha = 0.05$, $p = 0.005$).

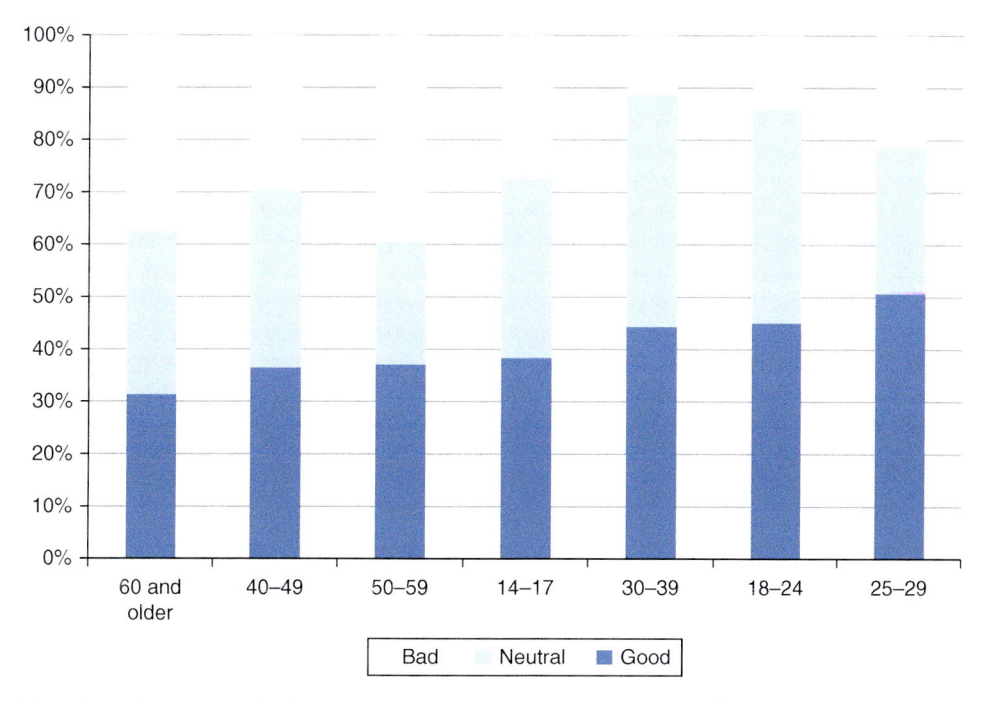

Fig. 31.9. Emissions of tall efficient wind turbines as assessed by different age groups (ANOVA: $F = 4.521$, $\alpha = 0.05$, $p < 0.001$; chi^2 = 45.994, $\alpha = 0.05$, $p < 0.001$).

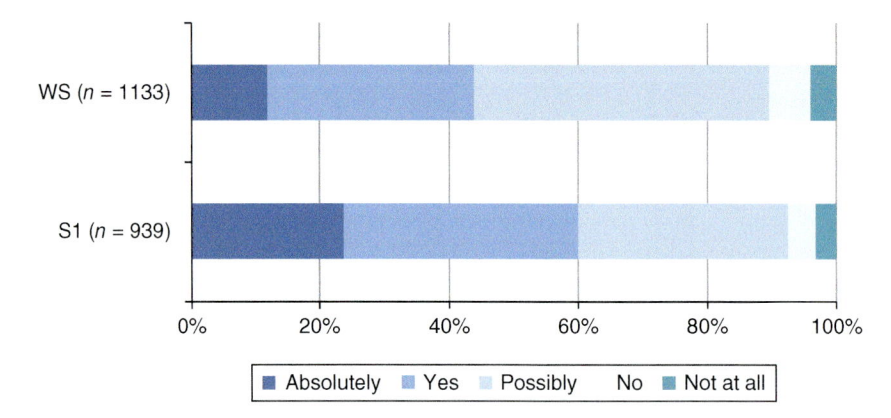

Fig. 31.10. Comparison of S1 and WS regarding preference for a destination that produces its own energy (chi²: α = 0.05, $p < 0.001$).

31.5 Discussion

The presented study was designed to gain a better understanding of tourists' preferences concerning the use of renewable energy in Austrian alpine tourist destinations. Upfront, the primary assumption had been that both winter and summer tourists would display different attitudes towards different types of locally produced renewable energy. The results show that this assumption was correct.

A set of variables was tested to find out if they had any influence on the perception of renewable energy in tourist destinations. One such variable was the summer tourists' main holiday activity. This category shows little evidence of correlation with any particular preference for renewable energy. Socio-demographic differences, specifically nationality and age, on the other hand, appear to be convincingly linked to varying attitudes towards renewable energy. For example, Germans and older age groups – both primary target groups for Austrian tourism – are very critical of various types of local energy production.

Furthermore, this survey investigated to what extent local production of renewable energy is a factor in tourists' choice of a holiday destination. Even if it does not represent a primary criterion for tourists' choices, it can be noted that tourists are becoming more and more aware of the importance of a reasonable and appropriate energy supply for their holiday destinations.

In the following section, the study's findings will be discussed with respect to their implications for the initial hypotheses.

31.5.1 Importance of local production of renewable energy for the choice of destination

As previously stated, findings suggest that several other criteria are more important for tourists' destination choice than local production of renewable energy. Summer tourists rank criteria such as 'beauty of landscape', 'maintenance of this landscape', 'accessibility' and 'atmosphere', much higher on their list of priorities than the use of renewable energy. This is in line with other studies (Österreich Werbung, 2009, 2012) that came to similar conclusions concerning both summer and winter guests. They place the above criteria among the most important for the choice of a holiday destination. In addition, this study has shown that there is a significant difference between summer and winter holiday selection regarding price–performance ratio, which plays a major role in the selection of a winter holiday but has only minor importance for the selection of a summer holiday.

Through a further line of questioning, this study has also found that renewable energy production is relatively unimportant for the selection process in comparison with other environmental criteria. So far, the results point towards the conclusion that renewable energy production plays no significant role in tourists' choice of destination. However, when asked directly about the importance of renewable energy production in a tourism destination, a high proportion of both winter and summer guests considered it 'preferable' or even 'absolutely preferable'. Furthermore, tourists rate a destination that uses renewable energy produced in the region far better than a destination that uses imported renewable energy, while a destination using predominantly conventional energy sources fares worst. Critical voices may argue that these responses are the result of leading questions; however, they can still be seen as proof that tourists – particularly summer tourists – are aware of the increasing need for more sustainable energy sources.

In summary, similar to findings by Westerberg *et al.* (2013), only a very small percentage of tourists classify local production of renewable energy as a primary factor in their choice of a holiday destination. Several other criteria, including beauty of landscape, maintenance of landscape, price and atmosphere, are considered more important. However, the first two criteria mentioned raise a note of caution when it comes to investing in renewable energy sources especially with regard to summer guests. As our results have shown, tourists perceive some sources of renewable energy as far more disruptive to the environment and landscape than others. Those perceived as most detrimental could prevent tourists from choosing a particular destination. Voltaire *et al.* (2017) confirm this risk and warn of welfare loss due to displacement of tourists because of wind farms. Their results of a revealed and SP analysis refer to the Catalonian coast with mountainous areas near scenic beaches. The hypotheses '(H3): Local production of renewable energy is important for the tourists' destination choice' and '(H4): Local production of renewable energy could lead to a competitive advantage for destinations' should, therefore, not be entirely rejected. Nevertheless, a full confirmation of H3 is also not possible, as results show that renewable energy is, for the most part, not actively considered in tourists' destination choices.

31.5.2 Tourists' perception of renewable energy production in alpine destinations

The study has proven that both summer and winter tourists clearly differentiate between distinct types of renewable energy production in touristic regions. The results have shown that alpine tourists have a clear preference for smaller plants over larger facilities. Furthermore, tourists rate renewable energy installations connected to existing structures (including buildings, existing lakes, existing infrastructure) more positively than systems constructed on natural sites (i.e. standalone structures).

Several studies (see, for example, Gordon, 2001) highlight the importance of designing plants that fit into the existing landscape.

Accordingly, the study could verify the hypothesis '(H5): Tourists evaluate renewable energy constructions that are attached to existing structures (including buildings, existing lakes, existing infrastructure) better than standalone models installed on natural sites'.

Verification of H5 does not come as a surprise, since the use of existing structures carries several objective advantages. These include a reduction of resource use, less damage to natural landscapes and less impact on natural scenery. However, constructions that are attached to existing structures also require careful planning. According to Gabel (2004), renewable energy installations can also harm the appearance of existing structures and cultural sites. Yet, there are national, as well as local policies that have the potential to prevent possible harm. Building codes, as published in Alpbach (Pikkemaat *et al.*, 2006; European Forum Alpbach, 2010), and the spatial planning laws of the federal state of Vorarlberg that make Environmental Impact Assessments obligatory (County Government of Vorarlberg, 2007) are two examples. The existence of such regulatory policies further supports the focus on construction of renewable energy plants attached or adjacent to existing structures, wherever possible.

The study's respondents were clearly able to distinguish between the impact of renewable energy production on the local landscape and its impact on the environment and potential emissions. These results perfectly demonstrate that renewable energy production's impact on landscapes is assessed more critically than other impacts. When it comes to climate change adaptation, alpine destinations need to keep the different sensibilities of summer and winter tourists in mind, particularly with respect to the preservation of a landscape's beauty and their efforts to decrease seasonality.

31.5.3 Variables with influence on tourists' attitudes towards renewable energy

A number of variables were tested as to whether they had any impact on summer tourists' perception of renewable energy.

In contrast to Westerberg *et al.* (2013), who examined tourists' main holiday activities, this study did not find any clear evidence that holiday activities had any influence on the perception of different types of energy sources. Definitive proof would have benefited tourist destinations by establishing a first indication of their target groups' specific preferences for renewable energy. Yet the number of statistically significant results is insufficient to allow such conclusions. This topic, nevertheless, merits further research, not least because a better understanding of its target group would enable destination management to make informed decisions in relation to renewable energy provision. In order to achieve more conclusive results on this issue, a different approach may be better suited, namely the use of single-choice answers rather than the multiple answers that were available in our study's questionnaire.

Another assumption we put forth was that summer tourists' age and nationality influence their acceptance of renewable energy. As previously discussed, Ladenburg (2010) observed that age substantially influenced the perception of wind parks. The study presented here also found age to influence the acceptance of different types of renewable energy production. Older age groups were particularly critical towards most of the categories.

This finding becomes especially relevant for alpine destinations with regard to seasonality – considering that many summer destinations strongly rely on hiking tourists with a high percentage of mature guests. A cross-tabulation also shows that Germans – the largest guest group in the summer survey – make up a comparatively large share of the three oldest tourist groups. This leads us to another central aspect: the influence of nationality. Perceptions have been shown to vary according to respondents' countries of origin. However, there seem to be similarities between the responses of German guests and those of older age groups. It has been established that both groups individually comprise a large percentage of the SG. Further studies will need to clarify if these two variables reinforce each other or function independently.

Nevertheless, there is some evidence in support of the theory that the country of origin plays a crucial role in perceptions of renewable energy. As mentioned, German nationals were shown to be very critical of wind as well as solar power. Germany is one of the world's leaders in these two types of renewable energy production (Jacobsson and Lauber, 2004; Gross, 2007; Fried et al., 2011; VEND, 2012). On the contrary, geothermal energy is in its infancy in Germany, though it has recently received a boost in support and is widely regarded as holding unique potential for Germany's future energy production (Bürgermeister, 2008; Purkus and Barth, 2010). Have Germans seen enough of wind and solar power? Are they eager to see other means of renewable energy production at their holiday destination? Does this provide an explanation of the study's results and conclusive proof of the influence of nationality on the way renewable energy is perceived? Broekel and Alfken (2015) confirm the negative perception of large-scale wind turbines by Germans. In their home country German tourists tend to displace from their favourite villages and shoreline if the number of wind turbines increases. Recently Langer and Wooliscroft (2018) surveyed lower acceptance by Germans for wind energy production as well in the cross-country comparison between Germany and New Zealand.

In conclusion, hypothesis (H2) can be verified: 'Socio-demographics (especially age) and nationality have an influence on the acceptance of different types of renewable energy production'. Evaluation of the age variable indicates a growing acceptance of renewable energy sources, as younger age groups detected only minor negative impacts. The nationality variable remains controversial and could not definitively establish a positive effect of 'habituation' (i.e. a constant exposure in the home country). Frequent exposure to renewable energy constructions may have the potential to influence individual perception. Yet further research is required to find out to what extent it influences acceptance levels. As of now, certain values attributed to different forms of energy supply appear more likely to influence attitudes, as argued by Westerberg et al. (2013) in their comparison of guests from northern and southern European countries.

31.5.4 The influence of holiday season on tourists' preferences for renewable energy

As publications by Scott et al. (2009), TAC (2011) and many others have shown, it will be of immense importance for tourist destinations to overcome seasonality. These studies also highlight the need to create an infrastructure that suits the demands of both summer and winter guests. Only then can a balance be achieved that supports sustainable development in tourist regions. The production of renewable energy in tourist regions will also have to meet these requirements and find acceptance among both winter and summer tourists.

A comparison between winter and summer tourists has shown that in most cases perceptions of renewable energy's impacts are quite similar. The only divergences have been observed in the fields of solar energy and geothermal energy. The former found more favour among winter tourists, the latter among summer tourists. Furthermore, summer tourists were more inclined to support local production of renewable energy. However, this study has also shown that diverging responses among winter and summer guests are likely linked to differences in socio-demographic variables. In light of this, the hypothesis '(H1): The holiday season (winter/summer) has a significant influence on tourists' preferences for renewable energy' cannot be fully confirmed. The observed differences in perceptions of energy infrastructure between the two seasons were not significant enough to warrant such a conclusion, since both winter and summer tourists agreed in their preference for renewable energy installations close to existing infrastructure over large and exposed infrastructure. Yet one more aspect needs to be considered in this discussion: summer tourists rate the importance of (a pristine) landscape highly in their choice of destination. Deviating from key priorities cited by winter tourists, this aspect constitutes one of the three most important criteria when choosing an alpine holiday experience in the summer. Regarding the aim of multi-seasonality, it is important to keep this difference in mind.

31.6 Conclusions and Outlook

The aim of this study was to gain further, in-depth knowledge of tourists' perceptions of renewable energy production in alpine tourist destinations. The study shows that tourists who visit the alpine regions generally have a positive view of local production of renewable energy. However, they perceive some plants as having a more negative impact than others. Especially the impact of constructions on local landscapes has the potential to deter some tourist segments. Therefore, investments in alpine destinations should be carefully planned, particularly regarding type and location. The aim should be to install energy systems that are suitable for the region in a number of ways. Not only should they be well integrated into existing structures and landscapes, they should also be designed to find approval among different touristic target groups. In particular, larger, starkly visible facilities and systems that are not attached to existing structures are more likely to trigger a negative response. In view of the study's results, future designs for RES in touristic alpine regions may need to consider doing without tall wind turbines in exposed sites.

Furthermore, it has become clear that constructions of photovoltaic systems on meadows, large biogas plants and hydroelectric power produced by dams in natural rivers are highly sensitive issues. On the other hand, geothermal energy, photovoltaic and solar thermal systems attached to pre-existing buildings and hydroelectric power generated by modification of existing water reservoirs are, in general, assessed rather positively.

It was also shown that renewable energy production and other environmental criteria are not yet priorities in the choice of a holiday destination. Scenery, atmosphere and price–performance ratio still constitute the main incentives. Renewable energy plants that strongly interfere with the alpine landscape could, therefore, place a destination at a competitive disadvantage.

Nevertheless, tourists generally take a positive view of local renewable energy production. It appears that the majority also prefers a holiday destination that produces its own energy in comparison with imported renewable energy or conventional energy. This is in line with the direction in which responsible tourism development has been going in recent years. Numerous studies (see, for example, Kaae, 2001; Dalton *et al.*, 2008; Needham and Little, 2013) confirm an increasing interest in environmentally friendly tourism. They, moreover, underline the need for destinations to implement measures reducing the impact of tourism on the environment. De Sousa *et al.* (2015) address the potential to market wind energy production as 'green tourism'. Frantál and Urbánková (2017) even point out the potential of renewables as a touristic attraction themselves.

Constructions of additional infrastructure for renewable energy production can help mitigate negative environmental effects including CO_2 emissions, which are a main driver of climate change. This objective also requires alpine skiing destinations to establish independence from external energy suppliers – an important aspect considering the increased energy demand linked to climate change adaptation as well as efforts to remain competitive in terms of pricing.

In conclusion, when planning an investment in renewable energy production, destinations should take additional aspects into account. One major concern should be the different attitudes adopted by summer and winter guests. Even though it was shown that attitudes are, to a certain degree, guided by socio-demographic characteristics, the study could still detect a higher demand for an intact landscape among summer tourists. It has been widely acknowledged that bad infrastructural decisions can have a severe impact on the landscape, particularly in areas that are already overloaded with winter sport infrastructure. Consequently, this situation could further aggravate summer tourists' apprehension regarding new renewable energy plants. At the same time, summer tourism is said to become more and more important in alpine areas in relation to intensified efforts to counteract seasonality. In particular in the context of climate change adaptation a shift from winter to summer tourism is desired by several alpine destinations (Abegg and Steiger, 2011; Pröbstl-Haider *et al.*, 2015; Steiger *et al.*, 2016).

Research in the fields of sustainable rural development and RES, as well as studies on the role of environmental criteria in destination choice, have created an awareness of the topic. Educating and raising awareness may not see quick and direct results, but in the long run, these measures could prove to be vital. In this context, the strategies alpine destinations choose to build awareness among their guests are crucial. Though the study was conducted more than 5 years ago the situation in Austrian skiing areas is still comparable. Many of them struggle between the aim to provide a more climate-friendly tourism product and the fear of negative impacts of large-scale energy infrastructure. The way they approach their customers on the topic of RES could have a substantial influence on their perceptions and acceptance though in the future.

References

Abegg, B. and Steiger, R. (2011) Will Alpine summer tourism benefit from climate change? A review. *IGF-Forschungsberichte* 4, 268–277.

Bell, S., Simpson, M., Tyrväinen, L., Sievänen, T. and Pröbstl, U. (2008) *European Forest Recreation and Tourism*. Taylor & Francis, London.

Broekel, T. and Alfken, C. (2015) Gone with the wind? The impact of wind turbines on tourism demand. *Energy Policy* 86(C), 506–519. DOI:10.1016/j.tourman.2009.11.005

Bürgermeister, J. (2008) Geothermal electricity booming in Germany. Available at: https://www.renewableenergyworld.com/articles/2008/06/geothermal-electricity-booming-in-germany-52588.html (accessed 16 July 2019).

BWEA (British Wind Energy Association) (2006) The impact of wind farms on the tourist industry in the UK. Available at: www.oddzialywaniawiatrakow.pl/upload/File/BWEA%20krajobraz.pdf (accessed 8 February 2019).

County Government of Vorarlberg (2007) Leitbild 2010+ Tourismus Vorarlberg. Available at: https://vorarlberg.at/web/land-vorarlberg/contentdetailseite/-/asset_publisher/qA6AJ38txu0k/content/tourismusleitbild-des-landes?article_id=140833 (accessed 30 January 2019).

Dalton, G.J., Lockington, D.A. and Baldock, T.E. (2008) A survey of tourist attitudes to renewable energy supply in Australian hotel accommodation. *Renewable Energy* 33(10), 2174–2185. DOI:10.1016/j.renene.2007.12.016

Davidson, M. (2010) Impact of wind farms on tourism in Skamania county. Available at: https://topslide.net/view-doc.html?utm_source=impact-of-wind-farms-on-tourism-in-skamania-county-washington-prepared-by-michael-davidson-june (accessed 8 February 2019).

De Sousa, A.J.G. and Kastenholz, E. (2015) Wind farms and the rural tourism experience – problem or possible productive integration? The views of visitors and residents of a Portuguese village. *Journal of Sustainable Tourism* 23(8–9), 1236–1256. DOI:10.1080/09669582.2015.1008499

Devine-Wright, P. (2005) Beyond NIMBYism: towards an integrated framework for understanding public perceptions of wind energy. *Wind Energy* 8(2), 125–139. DOI:10.1002/we.124

European Forum Alpbach (2010) Built Environment Symposium: 3–4 September 2010. Available at: https://www.alpbach.org/en/event/baukulturgespreche-2 (accessed 5 February 2019).

Frantál, B. and Kunc, J. (2011) Wind turbines in tourism landscapes Czech Experience. *Annals of Tourism Research* 38(2), 499–519. DOI:10.1016/j.annals.2010.10.007

Frantál, B. and Urbánková, R. (2017) Energy tourism: an emerging field of study. *Current Issues in Tourism* 20(13), 1395–1412. DOI:10.1080/13683500.2014.987734

Fried, L., Shukla, S. and Sawyer, S. (2011) *Global Wind Report*. GWEC Global Wind Energy Council, Brussels, Belgium.

Gabel, G. (2004) Beeinträchtigungen des Landschaftsbilds durch Windenergieanlagen–Kompensation durch Ersatzzahlung? *Natur und Landschaft* 79(11), 507–510.

Gordon, G. (2001) Wind energy, landscape: reconciling nature and technology. *Philosophy and Geography* 4(2), 169–184. DOI:10.1080/10903770124626

Gross, M. (2007) Germany goes for solar. *Current Biology* 17(16), 616–617. DOI:10.1016/j.cub.2007.07.053

Howley, P. (2011) Landscape aesthetics: assessing the general publics' preferences towards rural landscapes. *Ecological Economics* 72, 161–169. DOI:10.1016/j.ecolecon.2011.09.026

Jacobsson, S. and Lauber, V. (2004) The politics and policy of energy system transformation – explaining the German diffusion of renewable energy technology. *Energy Policy* 34(3), 256–276. DOI:10.1016/j.enpol.2004.08.029

Kaae, B.C. (2001) The perceptions of tourists and residents of sustainable tourism principles and environmental initiatives. In: McCool, S.F. and Moisey, R.N. (eds) *Tourism, Recreation and Sustainability: Linking Culture and the Environment*. CAB International, Wallingford, UK, pp. 289–313.

Kelly, J., Haider, W., Williams, P.W. and Englund, K. (2007) Stated preferences of tourists for eco-efficient destination planning options. *Tourism Management* 28(2), 377–390. DOI:10.1016/j.tourman.2006.04.015

Ladenburg, J. (2010) Attitudes towards offshore wind farms – the role of beach visits on attitude and demographic and attitude relations. *Energy Policy* 38(3), 1297–1304. DOI:10.1016/j.enpol.2009.11.005

Landry, C.E., Allen, T., Cherry, T. and Whitehead, J.C. (2012) Wind turbines and coastal recreation demand. *Resource and Energy Economics* 34(1), 93–111. DOI:10.1016/j.reseneeco.2011.10.001

Langer, K. and Wooliscroft, B. (2018) The acceptance of wind energy in a leading country and low deployment country of wind energy: a cross-national comparative analysis. *Renewable Energy Focus* 27, 111–119. DOI:10.1016/j.ref.2018.09.003

Latu, C., Boghinciuc, M., Coca, A., Ibánescu and Munteanu, A. (2010) Preliminary study of active tourism stages. In: Dornelor Basin, Romania, Proceedings of the 5th WSEAS International Conference on Economy and Management Transformation. vol. 1, 24–26 October 2010, West University of Timisoara, Timisoara, Romania.

Lilley, M.B., Firestone, J. and Kempton, W. (2010) The effect of wind power installations on coastal tourism. *Energies* 3(1), 1–22. DOI:10.3390/en3010001

Lothian, A. (2008) Scenic perceptions of the visual effects of wind farms on South Australian landscapes. *Geographical Research* 46(2), 196–207. DOI:10.1111/j.1745-5871.2008.00510.x

Miles, J. and Shevlin, M. (2001) *Applying Regression and Correlation – a Guide for Students and Researchers*. Sage, London.

Muhar, A., Schauppenlehner, T., Brandenburg, C. and Arnberger, A. (2006) *Trends und Handlungsbedarf im Sommer-Bergtourismus*. University of Natural Resources and Life Sciences, Vienna.

Needham, M.D. and Little, C.M. (2013) Voluntary environmental programs at an alpine ski area: visitor perceptions, attachment, value orientations, and specialization. *Tourism Management* 35, 70–81. DOI:10.1016/j.tourman.2012.06.001

Österreich Werbung (2009) T-Mona (Tourism Monitor Austria): Urlauber in Österreich Winter 2008/2009. Österreich Werbung, Vienna.

Österreich Werbung (2012) T-Mona (Tourism Monitor Austria): Urlauber in Österreich Sommer 2011. Österreich Werbung, Vienna.

Pikkemaat, B., Peters, M. and Weiermair, K. (2006) *Innovationen im Tourismus*. Erich Schmidt Verlag, Berlin.

Pröbstl, U. (2010) Natura 2000, Sport und Tourismus in Europa – Herausforderungen, Optimierungspotenziale und beispielhafte Lösungen – Natura 2000, sports, and tourism in Europe – challenges, potential for optimisation, and examples of solutions. *Natur und Landschaft* 85(9/10), 402–407. DOI:10.17433/9.2010.50153043.402-407

Pröbstl-Haider, U., Haider, W., Wirth, V. and Beardmore, B. (2015) Will climate change increase the attractiveness of summer destinations in the European Alps? A survey of German tourists. *Journal of Outdoor Recreation and Tourism* 11, 44–57. DOI:10.1016/j.jort.2015.07.003

Purkus, A. and Barth, V. (2010) Geothermal power production in future electricity markets – a scenario analysis for Germany. *Energy Policy* 39(1), 349–357. DOI:10.1016/j.enpol.2010.10.003

Ritchie, B.W. and Adair, D. (2004) *Sport Tourism: Interrelationships, Impacts and Issues*. Channel View Publications, Bristol, UK.

Scott, D., de Freitas, C.R. and Matzarakis, A. (2009) Adaptation in the tourism and recreation sector. In: Ebi, K.L., Burton, I. and McGregor, G.R. (eds) *Biometeorology for Adaptation to Climate Variability and Change*. Springer, Dordrecht, The Netherlands, pp. 171–194.

Steiger, R., Abegg, B. and Jänicke, L. (2016) Rain, rain, go away, come again another day. Weather preferences of summer tourists in mountain environments. *Atmosphere* 7(63), 1–12. DOI:10.3390/atmos7050063

Swofford, J. and Slattery, M. (2010) Public attitudes of wind energy in Texas: local communities in close proximity to wind farms and their effect on decision-making. *Energy Policy* 38(5), 2508–2519. DOI:doi.org/10.1016/j.enpol.2009.12.046

TAC (Tourism Advisory Committee) (2011) Annual tourism report 2010: Austria. Available at: https://ec.europa.eu/docsroom/documents/11658/attachments/1/translations/en/renditions/pdf (accessed 7 May 2019).

Tyrväinen, L., Järviluoma, J., Nikkola, K. and Silvennoinen, H. (2012) *Selvitys matkailijoiden suhtautumisesta Mielmukkavaaran tuulipuistohankkeeseen. Metlan työraportteja 237.* METLA, Vantaa, Finland.

VEND consulting GmbH (2012) Summary: Photovoltaikstudie Österreich/Deutschland. VEND, Nürnberg, Germany.

Voltaire, L., Loureiro, M.L., Knudsen, C. and Nunes, P.A.L.D. (2017) The impact of offshore wind farms on beach recreation demand: policy intake from an economic study on the Catalan coast. *Marine Policy* 81, 116–123. DOI:10.1016/j.marpol.2017.03.019

Waldo, Å. (2012) Offshore wind power in Sweden – a qualitative analysis of attitudes with particular focus on opponents. *Energy Policy* 41, 692–702. DOI:10.1016/j.enpol.2011.11.033

Waldo, Å., Johansson, M., Ek, K. and Persson, L. (2013) Wind power in open landscape, forest, mountain and sea – an interdisciplinary study. In: Swedish EPA (ed.) Book of Abstracts Conference on Wind Power and Environmental Impacts, Stockholm, 5–7 February, Report 6546. Swedish EPA, Stockholm, pp. 102–104.

Weiermair, K. (1999) The tourism practices of city-dwellers in the Alps. *Revue de géographie alpine* 87(1), 119–130.

Westerberg, V., Bredahl Jacobsen, J. and Lifran, R. (2013) The case for offshore wind farms, artificial reefs and sustainable tourism in the French Mediterranean. *Tourism Management* 34, 172–183. DOI:10.1016/j.tourman.2012.04.008

Zegg, R., Küng, T. and Grossrieder, R. (2010) *Energiemanagement Bergbahnen – Studie und Handbuch 2010.* Seilbahnen Schweiz, Bern, Switzerland.

32 A Resort Municipality Without Residents? The Case of Jumbo Glacier Resort in the Purcell Mountains of British Columbia, Canada

CAMERON E. OWENS[1] AND MURRAY B. RUTHERFORD[2]*

[1]*Department of Geography, University of Victoria, Victoria, BC, Canada;*
[2]*School of Resource and Environmental Management, Simon Fraser University, Burnaby, BC, Canada*

> In the end, everything in politics turns on the distribution of spaces… It is always a matter of knowing who is qualified to say what a particular place is and what is done in it.
> (Rancière, 2003, p. 201)

In a remote valley in the mountainous south-east of the province of British Columbia (BC), Canada, there is a tourist resort town unlike any other in the world. Jumbo Glacier Mountain Resort Municipality has a mayor and councillors, bylaws and a tax revenue stream from the provincial government, but it has no buildings or infrastructure and nobody lives there. The town legally exists, but for all practical purposes it is make-believe, incorporated on paper as a 'Mountain Resort Municipality' by the provincial government in 2012 in an extraordinary attempt to move forward a developer's stalled application for an all-seasons resort project. Since first being proposed in 1991, Jumbo Glacier Resort had stumbled through a variety of government review processes, pushed by a growth-oriented coalition of business and government supporters, and opposed at every step by equally determined Indigenous and non-Indigenous community members and other government officials (Owens, 2011).

The move by the BC provincial government to create a Mountain Resort Municipality, which largely removed the development from the jurisdiction of the existing regional government, arose out of concerns about the trajectory of the review process. Despite receiving a provincial environmental assessment (EA) approval certificate in 2004 after more than a decade of review, a number of regulatory requirements remained. In particular, the land for the development needed to be rezoned by the local regional district (BC's rough equivalent of a county or regional government area), which would require a local public hearing (Metcalfe, 2009). Supporters of the resort feared that, due to the high level of opposition among local people, the probable result of a public hearing would be further delays or, worse, that the rezoning application would be rejected and the project would not be able to proceed (Owens, 2011).

---

* E-mail: murray_rutherford@sfu.ca

In order to bypass the requirement for rezoning and local public review, and to finally enable construction to begin, provincial government officials acted by amending and invoking a rarely used law to impose a new local government – a Mountain Resort Municipality – in the location of the proposed resort, with a mayor and councillors appointed by the provincial government, but no other voters. The strategy was successful, but the developer subsequently encountered other difficulties and in 2015 the BC Minister of Environment ruled that the EA approval for the resort had expired due to insufficient progress on construction (BC MOE, 2015). The developer successfully challenged that ruling in court and the government filed an appeal to the BC Court of Appeal (Ditson, 2018). The hearing of the appeal is expected to take place in 2019. Meanwhile, none of the proposed buildings have been constructed and the 'town' remains empty, 27 years after the proposal for the resort was first submitted.

What follows is the story of this decades-long struggle over the Jumbo Valley. The story is set in BC, which has its own peculiar colonial historical geography, but it is a story that should be of interest to a broader audience, as it explores the complexities and contradictions of tourism development and governance in pursuit of the idealized but contested goal of sustainability. Like many other struggles over resource development, this one is rooted in different images, values and visions for a particular place. The EA and other regulatory reviews of the proposed Jumbo Glacier Resort faced the challenging task of understanding and weighing the conflicting perspectives and claims about this place, evaluating the scientific evidence and determining the public interest. Or, as the 1996 BC *Environmental Assessment Act* described the goal, 'to promote sustainability by protecting the environment and fostering a sound economy and social well-being' (RSBC 1996, chapter 119, s. 2(a)).

The contested place that is the setting for this story is a spectacularly beautiful alpine region: a valley 1700 m above sea level, rimmed by glacier-clad mountain peaks reaching to more than 3000 m. Proponents of the Jumbo Glacier Resort see this place as an ideal location for a unique year-round tourism development in an area of Canada that is legendary for skiing and other winter sports; with exhilarating scenery, favourable climate and deep powdery snow conditions. In their view the proposed resort, with more than 5000 beds and as many as 3000 visitors per day (Jumbo Glacier Resort, 2015), would provide tremendous benefits that easily outweigh the social and environmental costs, which they believe could be mitigated. Environmentalists and wilderness advocates, however, see this same place as part of the wild Purcells, a majestic and largely uninhabited mountainous region that includes the protected Purcell Wilderness Conservancy, located just to the south of Jumbo Valley, and the fabled Lake of the Hanging Glaciers, in the drainage adjacent to Jumbo (Owens, 2011). They value the region for its wildness, its contribution to local 'sense of place' and its unusual diversity of large mammals and other wildlife. Local conservation groups call it the 'Serengeti of North America' (Hurtak, 2015). In their view, the Jumbo area should be kept wild. Another group of firm opponents of the project, the Ktunaxa First Nation – Indigenous people who have lived in the region for thousands of years – have their own unique perspective. For them, the area where the Jumbo Resort is proposed is Qat'muk, imperfectly translated as the place where the Grizzly Bear Spirit was born, goes to heal itself, and returns to the spirit world. Qat'muk is highly sacred to the Ktunaxa, and they believe that its spiritual value would be destroyed by the construction of the resort (Ktunaxa Nation, 2010; and see *Ktunaxa Nation v. British Columbia (Forests, Lands and Natural Resource Operations)*, 2017).

32.1 Jumbo Glacier Resort and the Promise of Sustainability

Oberto Oberti, the mastermind behind Jumbo Glacier Resort, grew up skiing in the Italian Alps. When he immigrated to Canada and established an architecture and design practice in Vancouver, he never lost his passion for skiing. In the 1980s, he became inspired to develop a proposal for a year-round ski resort in the interior mountains of BC. Oberti joined forces with a Japanese company and in 1991 submitted a proposal for the ultimate ski resort in the Purcell Mountains, to be reviewed under BC's Commercial Alpine Ski Policy (CASP). This policy had been conceived in the early 1980s in recognition that the provincially owned land base with its many snow-covered mountains presented fantastic opportunities for alpine tourism and recreational development.[1] After widespread consultation with the tourism industry, the BC government developed CASP, which established an incremental process designed to promote carefully planned, well-balanced, environmentally sensitive tourism (BC MLPH, 1982). By subjecting proposals to a detailed review by government agencies, along with input from the public and First Nations, CASP was intended to ensure that developments would serve the public interest. In practice, however, the public interest would prove highly contested and elusive to define.

The CASP initiative was part of a larger shift in BC government policy at the time – a move away from encouraging rapid exploitation of the province's natural resources, towards a more sustainable approach to development. During the 1980s, mounting concerns about the environmental impacts of resource exploitation in BC, and particularly concerns about the clear-cutting of old-growth forests, had culminated in protests, civil disobedience, blockades and other conflicts. These protests sometimes aligned with the concurrent efforts of First Nations to slow or stop industrial resource exploitation in areas they claimed as traditional territories. National, even international, attention was drawn to a 'war in the woods' in BC that disrupted industry and confounded land use governance. Even more troubling, the conflicts exposed unresolved issues related to colonial occupation of Indigenous lands (Wilson, 1999; Braun, 2002).

Sustainable development, which was emerging at the time as a prominent vision in global discourse, offered hope for a more peaceful and prosperous future, and was mobilized by the left-of-centre New Democratic Party (NDP) government that swept into power in BC in 1991 (Owens, 2011). Sustainable development aligned perfectly with the province's motto, *Splendor Sine Occasu* – Splendour Without Diminishment. In the spirit of the Brundtland Commission's sustainable development report (WCED, 1987), provincial decision makers relished the promise that economic growth could continue, but, with careful management and new technologies, could be aligned with environmental protection and social goals to meet the needs of present and future generations. Tourism and recreation development were seen as vital elements of BC's sustainable development strategy (Owens, 2011). Branded in tourism ads as 'Super-Natural BC', the province could capitalize (without diminishment) on its impressive forested and mountainous landscape in less extractive, if no less colonial, ways.

The proposal for the Jumbo Glacier Resort appeared to fit well with this buoyant *zeitgeist*. The project would feature lift-accessed skiing and a sightseeing gondola on four magnificent glaciers; a resort featuring hotels and condominium units; and supportive commercial services, restaurants and shops. Along with unparalleled skiing and other recreational opportunities and the accompanying economic benefits, Jumbo would take social and environmental goals into consideration. The project represented a major investment in the economically stalled East Kootenay region of BC, which was suffering due to declines in the resource-extraction industries; it featured targeted employment opportunities and other benefits for First Nations; and it would attempt to minimize ecological impacts through conscientious design, a compact footprint, state of the art technologies and a comprehensive environmental management system (Pheidias Project Management Corp., 2010).

However, despite the promise of sustainable development, relentless opposition dogged Jumbo Glacier Resort from the beginning. Opponents raised concerns ranging from threats to wilderness values, grizzly bears and community sense of place, to dubious economic feasibility and the social burden on infrastructure for nearby communities (Owens, 2011). They asserted that the project was more about real estate than recreation, and that it represented an alienation of public land for private benefit. Ultimately, they argued that it had no 'social license' to operate. The editor of a local paper colourfully observed that the resort represented a 'farcical billion dollar or so project, based on rapidly melting glaciers, catering to dwindling numbers of skiers who can't afford to play on sinking established hills, let alone what would be an elite rich person's playground' (I. Cobb, 2014, personal communication).

The three main Indigenous groups potentially affected by the resort diverged in their positions on the development (Owens, 2011). The Ktunaxa Nation objected to the Jumbo proposal, seeing this as yet another incursion into its unceded traditional territory. As noted earlier, the valley and adjacent mountains are recognized by Ktunaxa as Qat'muk, considered profoundly sacred as the home of Kławła Tukłułak?is – the Grizzly Bear Spirit. In contrast, the Kinbasket-Shuswap First Nation supported the project and entered into an impact benefit agreement with the developer, setting out specific economic (and possibly other) benefits to be provided to the Kinbasket-Shuswap (*Ktunaxa Nation v. British Columbia (Forests, Lands and Natural Resource Operations)*, 2014). A third Indigenous group, the Sinixt people, opposed the Jumbo Resort, which would be established in territory that they also claim. However, the Sinixt had no formal status in the EA review, because in the 1950s the Canadian government had ruled that the Sinixt were officially extinct in Canada, since ostensibly all the remaining Sinixt people lived in the United States.[2]

32.2 Searching for Firm Foundations for Decision Making

In this context of conflict over the future of the Jumbo Valley, the government review process for the resort proposal sought to escape politics, parse out the facts of the case and deliver an objective, technical evaluation of the merits of the development. However, the dream of an uncontested, technical, apolitical way forward proved untenable. To the extent that a project review involves grappling with competing visions of what a place is and what should be done there, it is inescapably political (Rancière, 2003). It is about assumptions, values, ethics and aspirations – questions for which science is ill-suited. Technical studies can be commissioned to predict the impact of a project such as Jumbo on grizzly bear habitat, for example, but science cannot determine how many grizzly bears we, as a society, would be willing to forego. Science cannot dictate how to evaluate concerns about more abstract but important elements such as sense of place. Science cannot evaluate how the Jumbo Resort would impact the sacredness of a valley or how that impact should be weighed. As one government decision maker involved with the Jumbo review noted: 'it's really as much art as science. We hope we get a better decision by involving a lot of different people. In the end, it's an informed judgment call' (anonymous, 2009, personal communication).

As noted earlier, the Jumbo Resort proposal was accepted for review through the provincial government's CASP process in 1991. However, the proposal came at a time of great change in land use governance in the province. As part of the new NDP government's commitment to sustainable development, a major regional land use planning effort – the Commission on Resources and Environment (CORE) – was launched in 1992. The ambitious intention of CORE was to conduct large-scale planning exercises, involving extensive public and stakeholder engagement, to determine what values should prevail and guide land use in each watershed in the province. While that broad scope was never fully realized, planning negotiations among stakeholders facilitated by CORE took place in four particularly contentious regions in the province, including the East Kootenay region where Jumbo was to be sited (Owens, 2011).

Given the considerable controversy surrounding the Jumbo project, the province suspended the CASP review of Jumbo pending the outcome of the CORE planning process for the East Kootenay region. But if government officials hoped that some clear direction for decision making about the Jumbo Resort would emerge from this planning exercise, they were to be disappointed. The outcome of the CORE process was ultimately inconclusive for the Jumbo proposal. The East Kootenay Land Use Plan, prepared by CORE officials based on stakeholder negotiations, designated the Jumbo and Upper Horsethief Valley watersheds as a 'Special Management Area' – meaning the following: 'enhanced levels of management are required to address sensitive values such as fish and wildlife habitat, visual quality, recreation, and cultural/heritage features. The management intent is to maintain these values in the areas while allowing compatible human use and development to occur' (BC CORE, 1994, p. 103). The precise implications of this designation for a resort development of the type and scale proposed by Jumbo were not entirely clear and have been debated fiercely since (Owens, 2011). The regional plan stated that while the Special Management Area designation does not automatically preclude resort development, the Jumbo 'site-specific proposal is far too detailed to be addressed' at the regional planning level (p. 110). Instead, the plan recommended that:

> The approval process for a resort development in Jumbo Creek include an environmental assessment under the provincial *Environmental Assessment Act*. This assessment should identify potential impacts and mitigative measures to address impacts prior to development approval. The process should also include public involvement to ensure that all values and perspectives are fully considered in a final decision.
> (BC CORE, 1994, p. 110)

Supporters of the Jumbo Resort proposal asserted that this CORE recommendation vindicated the project, and that so long as the 'technical' EA review approved the proposal, Jumbo Resort could be interpreted as aligning with the designation in the East Kootenay Land Use Plan. Opponents of the project argued that the CORE negotiations about this issue were actually inconclusive, and certainly did not sanction a resort development of the scale of Jumbo (Owens, 2011).

Importantly, the Ktunaxa Nation was not a party in the CORE negotiations. The Ktunaxa elected to observe but not participate, taking the position that their nation is a separate government rather than an interest group and that the provincial government should negotiate directly with the Ktunaxa about land claims and a potential treaty before conducting land use planning processes such as CORE (Owens, 2011).

The result of the CORE process for Jumbo, then, was that the ultimate decision on the fate of the project was deferred. The Jumbo proposal was swept up as one of the first projects to be reviewed under the new provincial *Environmental Assessment Act*, which came into force in 1995. Under this legislation, EAs were mandated to identify and mitigate adverse environmental, economic, social, cultural, heritage and health effects of major development proposals in order to foster sustainability. Environmental assessment in BC is proponent-driven, in that the project proponent and its consultants conduct the studies of potential impacts and mitigation measures, and prepare an assessment report for review by the provincial Environmental Assessment Office, which then makes a recommendation to provincial cabinet ministers about whether or not the project should be approved, and with what conditions (Rutherford, 2009). Decision making in the EA review is informed by the proponent's commissioned scientific studies along with public and First Nations' input. The history of EAs in BC reveals that these reviews almost never result in the rejection of a project (Boyd, 2003; Haddock, 2010), but going through the process should lead to improvements in design.

For the Jumbo proposal, the EA review that started in 1995 took almost 10 years to complete. During that time, a new, right-of-centre Liberal government was elected in BC on a platform that emphasized deregulation and governmental efficiency. In 2002, this new government passed a redesigned and substantially streamlined *Environmental Assessment Act* (Rutherford, 2016). The BC Environmental Assessment Office then issued a transition order, transferring the Jumbo proposal once again into a new EA process. Finally, in 2004 the EA for Jumbo was completed and the province issued an EA certificate approving the project. But the EA approval did little to reduce the controversy over Jumbo Glacier Resort (Owens, 2011).

32.3 The Politicization of Assessment

Environmental assessment is often represented as a technical, neutral and apolitical process, but both opponents and supporters of the Jumbo proposal denounced its EA as anything but that. Opponents decried the EA process as a 'rubber stamp' for business as usual, with pre-determined decisions merely being afforded legitimacy by the review (Owens, 2011). They complained that grizzly bears and mountain goats were being sentenced to death by 'back-room decision-makers on an island somewhere in the Pacific Ocean' (referring to the location of the provincial capital, Victoria), while 'global warming is rapidly rendering the Jumbo four-season ski resort an impossible dream' (Campsall, 2003). They felt that the proposal had been pushed through the regulatory process by a growth-oriented coalition of business leaders and supportive provincial and local government officials, including a high-profile provincial cabinet minister. Even more insidious, in their view, when they showed up at public open houses during the EA they were surprised to find government officials and proponents both distributing promotional material and addressing questions, to the extent that, 'you couldn't tell who was who' (Owens, 2011).

Opponents of the Jumbo project were particularly frustrated by the narrow scope of the review. Scoping in EA involves determining which aspects of a project will be evaluated and which potential impacts will be included in the assessment (Hanna, 2016). Essentially, this establishes the required information that the proponent must provide and evaluate in its scientific studies and assessment report. In determining the scope of an EA, the BC Environmental Assessment Office draws on guidance documents, international best practices and experience. Opportunities are provided for public review and comment on scoping decisions, and the proponent and government officials are expected to consult with affected First Nations (Rutherford, 2016). But inevitably, scoping involves discretion and professional judgement. Trade-offs must be made between thoroughness and efficiency, and these trade-offs are made in the context of budgetary and staffing concerns, workload pressures, institutional and political culture, and governmental mandates.

For Jumbo's opponents, a particularly egregious omission was that the implications of climate change were largely 'scoped out' of the EA review (Owens, 2011). Given that the resort would rely on glaciers that were arguably melting, and that the project would presumably be a major international tourist draw with associated greenhouse gas emissions, it would seem that climate change should be a central consideration. However, to the frustration of resort opponents, this concern was almost completely excluded from the review process. The rationale provided by the EA reviewers was threefold. First, they argued that climate change was an area of 'much uncertainty' (BC EAO, 1998, section C.1). Second, they were also unsure about 'how any information which the proponent could provide would be evaluated' (BC EAO, 1998, section C.1) Finally, they accepted the proponent's argument that climate change would not affect Jumbo as significantly as it would affect other resorts in the province. Indeed, the proponent remarkably mobilized climate change as an argument in favour of the resort. The provincial reviewers specifically referred to this perceived advantage in their report recommending approval of the project: 'Given its elevation (1,700 to 3,419 m), the Project is at less risk from the potential effects of climate change than most other ski resorts' (BCEAO, 2004, p. ix). A sceptic might wonder whether, even if there were still enough snow in the future to ski at Jumbo, the ski industry would continue to be viable when the rest of the resorts had closed, but the EA reviewers were satisfied with the proponent's argument. For critics of the EA, the decision to almost completely exclude from the review an element as important as climate change was a clear indication of the dysfunction and politicization of the process (Owens, 2011).

Opponents of the resort also argued that politicization of the EA process was evident in the assessment of those factors that *were* included in the scope of the review. Environmental assessments are supposed to evaluate the extent to which the adverse effects of a project are 'significant'. While such reviews involve science, they also are inescapably discretionary and ultimately about beliefs, values and judgement (Wolfe, 1987; Beattie, 1995). The review of the potential impacts of the Jumbo project on grizzly bears clearly illustrates this point.

From the outset, impacts on grizzly bears were among the primary concerns about the proposed Jumbo development (Owens, 2011). In BC, grizzlies are considered valuable in ethical, ecological and cultural terms: important in their own right, but also as umbrella or keystone species[3] and charismatic symbols. The BC government's 1995 *Grizzly Bear Conservation Strategy* states that the bear is 'perhaps the greatest symbol of the wilderness' and 'its survival will be the greatest testimony to our environmental commitment' (BC MOELP, 1995, p. vii). In the Jumbo EA, the study of impacts on grizzlies began with research to estimate the status of the local grizzly bear population, after which the proponent hired a consultant to model the potential impacts of the project on grizzlies. The consultant concluded that the impacts on grizzly bears would be substantial, but that he could not judge whether these impacts should be considered significant because the province had not established criteria for significance (Apps, 2003). However, he said that studies of grizzly bears in other regions had treated impacts of this magnitude as significant. He also determined that the impacts could not be fully mitigated within the Jumbo Valley itself, but could possibly be mitigated by restricting further access by motorized vehicles to neighbouring watersheds: 'Through partial or total motorised access closures throughout the analysis area, a "no net impact" standard can theoretically be attained' (Apps, 2003, p. 33). Note that in the absence of specific provincial criteria for significance, the consultant chose to use a standard of 'no net impact' on the grizzly bear population. This choice aligns with the Canadian federal *Guide on Biodiversity and Environmental Assessment* (CEAA, 1996, p. 3), which states that one of the principles in assessing effects on biodiversity is 'no "net loss" of the ecosystem, species populations or genetic diversity'.

In April 2004, the BC Ministry of Environment's large carnivore specialist weighed in on the grizzly bear issue for Jumbo, agreeing that it might be possible 'to achieve the "no net impact" objective over the short term' but that it would be difficult and expensive (Austin, 2004, p. 10). He argued that:

> In the absence of extraordinary measures to ensure indefinite implementation of mitigation measures ... it can be assumed that there will be a substantial impact to grizzly bear habitat effectiveness, mortality risk and, most importantly, the fragmentation of grizzly bear distribution in the Purcell Mountains over the long-term as a result of the project.
> (Austin, 2004, p. 11)

This provincial expert was also sceptical about whether the BC government would actually be able to allocate the resources that would be required to impose, enforce and monitor the mitigation regime over the long term to ensure its effectiveness.[4] Furthermore, he recognized that the mitigation option of restricting motorized access to adjacent drainages would prove decidedly unpopular. Essentially, the local public would be restricted from accessing treasured recreation areas to offset the impacts of a resort that many of them did not want in the first place.

So, at this point (in April 2004) there was clearly much concern about potential impacts on grizzly bears. The proponent's own consultant had predicted that the resort would have substantial impacts in the immediate valley, although he believed that these impacts could be mitigated by restricting motorized access in adjacent watersheds. However, this mitigation option would be highly unpopular. The province's grizzly bear expert had expressed considerable concern about the project and was dubious about his own government's capacity to institute the extraordinary measures required to mitigate, enforce and monitor effectively.

It is difficult to ascertain exactly what happened next. But, with a procedural deadline looming in the EA review, the province's large carnivore specialist was reassigned and a new Ministry of Environment official, who had no previous involvement in the case, took over the file (Haddock, 2010). On 2 July 2004, this new official sent an e-mail to the director in charge of the Jumbo EA with a remarkably altered assessment of the significance of impacts on grizzly bears:

> In review of available information, including the CEA [the cumulative effects assessment on grizzly bears undertaken by the proponent's consultant], it has been determined that there is a low risk that the JGR project would result in a reduction of the grizzly bear population of such significance that the population in the Central Purcells GPBU [Grizzly Bear Population Unit] would become threatened. This determination considers that ... mitigation programs set forth by the proponent for the area within and immediately adjacent to the CRA [Controlled Recreation Area] are fully applied ... and ... the proponent will ... maintain their proposed monitoring program, and will adjust their mitigation programs to the fullest extent when resort-related impacts to grizzly bear populations or habitat use are evident.
>
> (Stewart, 2004)

Note that this new assessment relies heavily on the proponent's monitoring and mitigation programmes, and does not appear to take into account the province's own limited capacity and poor record of monitoring and enforcement, which were of concern to Austin (2004; see also Auditor General of British Columbia, 2011). Moreover, the threshold for judging significance has shifted from 'no net impact' to a far less onerous standard: that the regional population would become threatened. Under BC wildlife policy, 'threatened' status generally means 'likely to become endangered if limiting factors are not reversed' (BC, 2018a).

When the Environmental Assessment Office recommended approval of the Jumbo project later in 2004, the summary paragraph explaining why the impacts on grizzly bears were not considered significant stated that there was a low risk that the project would impact bears to the extent that the population of the Central Purcells would become threatened (BC EAO, 2004). The wording was copied verbatim from the e-mail of 2 July 2004 quoted above. Notably, the contentious proposal to restrict motorized access to other drainages to offset loss of habitat in the Jumbo Valley was not even mentioned, although the proponent's own consultant had advised that effective mitigation would require something that drastic. Of course, that was when 'no net impact' was the standard for judgement.[5]

Concerns about politicization of the EA process were not restricted to the opponents of Jumbo Resort. The proponent and other supporters of Jumbo also complained about the review process. However, they saw the politicization not in terms of government–industry collusion, but rather as 'clearly favouring environmental protection', 'frustratingly labyrinthine', involving 'too much confusion, giving too much time to outlandish claims' and 'hijacked by the radical green agenda' (Owens, 2011, p. 172). The proponent described the committee appointed by the EA Office to oversee the review as 'a highly opinionated jury ... including a majority of people who had a declared agenda to stop the project based on an erroneous summary of its content' (Oberti, quoted in Owens, 2011, p. 173). Perhaps the most damning evidence of possible political interference in this direction was revealed in documents obtained by the proponent under a *Freedom of Information and Protection of Privacy Act* request to the provincial government in 1996, during the early stages of the review. The request turned up e-mail correspondence among staff within the BC Ministry of Environment that suggested that some of them might have been working surreptitiously to stifle the application. The strategies discussed in these e-mails included using the proponent's funds to work on ensuring that the development did not proceed, being slow to produce requested documentation (thereby delaying the review), using further studies as a stalling technique and collecting information specifically to stop the development (Pheidias Project Management Corp., 2010). Other e-mails included inaccurate descriptions of the project, such as calling the proposed Jumbo Resort 'a village the size of Banff' (Banff has more than 8000 permanent residents).

The proponent was particularly frustrated by the amount of attention given in the EA review to the objections of a small local population that opposed the project, which the proponent discounted as parochial 'NIMBYism' (not in my backyard). For example, the exasperated vice-president of Jumbo argued:

> Too much emphasis on the local can stymie larger scale beneficial policies. We never would have built the nationally vital Canadian Pacific Railway if we had local people deciding everything. How can you manage the province if every local voice is heard? The province is the proper scale for dealing with these matters.
>
> (G. Costello, 2009, personal communication)

Another supporter of the project, the provincially appointed mayor of Jumbo Glacier Mountain Resort Municipality, accused the opposition of 'shopping around for a jurisdiction'. Resort opponents were allegedly 'only interested in defining the context of this case as the local region because that scale supports their position. What if the province was skeptical and most local people wanted the resort? Would they still want to keep the decision local?' (G. Deck, 2009, personal communication).

The eventual decision by the provincial government to bypass the existing local government and create a Resort Municipality can thus be seen in the context of a range of moves by both sides, working in cooperation with various allies within the process, each side trying to advance its own particular interest and to frame that interest as representing the broader public interest. The move to avoid a local rezoning hearing fit with the efforts of supporters to define the public interest at the larger, provincial, scale. Of course, opponents of the move were quick to retort that local stewardship of local places should be considered as embodying the larger scale public interest.

The complexity of this issue of local versus provincial is further illustrated by the fact that in 2009 the elected council of the local regional district actually passed a resolution by a narrow margin (eight to seven) asking the province to create the new Resort Municipality and take the issue out of the regional district's hands (Pynn, 2009). Apparently, local councillors who voted for this resolution felt that the project 'was too large for the local government to handle' (CBC News, 2009). However, four of the five councillors representing areas closest to the proposed Jumbo development voted against the resolution. As one local politician observed about the rationale for asking the province to intervene: 'That is a bunch of baloney. The project at this stage would be nothing more than a land-zoning question – it's what the Regional District was set up to do. They should resign if they can't do it. Regional districts all over the province handle big projects' (quoted in Metcalfe, 2009).

32.4 The Home of the Grizzly Bear Spirit

The EA reviewers who evaluated the Jumbo Resort proposal also had the responsibility of determining the potential effects of the project on Aboriginal (Indigenous) rights (see Rutherford, Chapter 4, for a more detailed discussion of Indigenous rights and resort development in BC). Canadian courts have ruled that the federal and provincial governments have a constitutionally mandated duty to consult with potentially affected Aboriginal people, including First Nations, before making any decision that may infringe on Aboriginal rights. Governments may also be required to provide accommodation for such infringements. This duty to 'consult and accommodate' was clearly triggered by the application for approval of the Jumbo Glacier Resort (*Ktunaxa Nation v. British Columbia (Forests, Lands and Natural Resource Operations)*, 2017).

The rights and beliefs of the Ktunaxa First Nation were a critical issue in the EA. In the earlier stages of the review, the Ktunaxa joined with the Shuswap Nation to participate in public hearings about the project and to engage in initial consultations with the proponent and the provincial government. After the Shuswap First Nation elected to support the project, the Ktunaxa continued on its own in negotiations with the proponent and the province. The proponent made some substantial changes to the proposed project in response to the concerns of the Ktunaxa and others, but the Ktunaxa asserted throughout the review that Jumbo Valley had special spiritual value to them. The full extent of that spiritual value was not revealed until 2009, when Ktunaxa representatives informed the province that the valley was exceptionally sacred and that construction of any permanent structures in the area would destroy this spiritual value (*Ktunaxa Nation v. British Columbia (Forests, Lands and Natural Resource Operations)*, 2017). A BC Supreme Court judge described the Ktunaxa position as follows:

> The Ktunaxa say that to allow the proposed resort in Qat'muk would desecrate this sacred site and cause the Grizzly Bear Spirit to leave. If the Grizzly Bear Spirit leaves Qat'muk, the Ktunaxa say they will no longer be able to receive physical or spiritual assistance and guidance from that spirit. Their rituals and songs about the Grizzly Bear Spirit will lose all meaning and efficacy.
> (*Ktunaxa Nation v. British Columbia (Forests, Lands and Natural Resource Operations)*, 2014, p. 8)

No accommodation would realistically be sufficient for such a loss. In 2010, the Ktunaxa issued the 'Qat'muk Declaration' confirming that Qat'muk is the home of the Grizzly Bear Spirit, and unilaterally proclaiming a refuge area 'consisting of the upper part of the Jumbo valley' and a buffer area 'consisting of the remainder of the Jumbo watershed … so that the Grizzly Bear Spirit, as well as grizzly bears, can thrive within and around Qat'muk' (Ktunaxa Nation, 2010).

In spite of this declaration, the provincial minister responsible for the Jumbo development decided in 2012 that the project could proceed, and stated that the consultation and accommodation measures that had been taken by the province for the infringement on Ktunaxa rights were sufficient. The Ktunaxa challenged this decision in court and, after losing the initial case, appealed all the way to the Supreme Court of Canada. In addition to arguing that they had not been adequately consulted and accommodated, the Ktunaxa asserted that the approval of this resort in the home of the Grizzly Bear Spirit violated their constitutionally protected right of freedom of religion (*Ktunaxa Nation v. British Columbia (Forests, Lands and Natural Resource Operations)*, 2017). In November 2017, the Supreme Court issued a judgment upholding the BC minister's decision about Jumbo. The court ruled that the state's constitutional duty to protect freedom of religion

> is not to protect the object of beliefs, such as Grizzly Bear Spirit. Rather, the state's duty is to protect everyone's freedom to hold such beliefs and to manifest them in worship and

practice or by teaching and dissemination. In short, the [constitution] protects the freedom to worship, but does not protect the spiritual focal point of worship.
(*Ktunaxa Nation v. British Columbia (Forests, Lands and Natural Resource Operations)*, 2017, paragraph 71)

The court also ruled that the BC Minister's decision about the adequacy of provincial consultation and accommodation of the Ktunaxa was reasonable. The court emphasized that the Ktunaxa had negotiated with the province and the proponent for several years about possible benefits to be provided to the Ktunaxa from the project before the Ktunaxa declared in 2009 that the project could not go forward at all because it would destroy the spiritual value of the place (*Ktunaxa Nation v. British Columbia (Forests, Lands and Natural Resource Operations)*, 2017). The Ktunaxa, however, argued that the knowledge of the true spiritual value of the place was not disclosed earlier because that specific knowledge was held only by a few Ktunaxa knowledge keepers and that Ktunaxa beliefs prevented them from sharing this knowledge more broadly except in extremely dire circumstances (*Ktunaxa Nation v. British Columbia (Forests, Lands and Natural Resource Operations)*, 2017, Appellant's Factum).

Thus, for the Ktunaxa the problems with the Jumbo review went well beyond politicization, and involved fundamental questions about whether the state institutions that conducted and oversaw the EA and approved the project were capable or even appropriate to deal with the norms, traditions and values of an Indigenous culture in which respect for, and secrecy of, sacred places is paramount (see Dhillon, 2017).[6]

32.5 Towards a Conclusion: Repoliticizing and Democratizing Review

The Jumbo story described above unfolded in BC, with its unique institutions, colonial legacies and oppositional politics. However, the story affords broader lessons, particularly about the myth that a simple, technical, apolitical evaluation can determine whether a contested proposal in a contested setting will meet the standards of sustainability and sustainable development. In this story we touched on four main themes:

1. The inescapability of politics and values in the purportedly scientific and technical field of environmental assessment. Although some of the questions asked in reviews of major development projects invite scientific analysis, in the end the overarching questions of what a place is and what is done there are about assumptions, values, beliefs and ethics, and thus outside of the realm of science. In the Jumbo case, the developer's dream of an awe-inspiring tourism destination in the wilds of Canada encountered the reality of the fervent opposition of many people who lived in the region, who perceived and valued the Jumbo Valley in other, vastly different, ways. Finding the common good in the face of such conflicting perspectives and claims is a problem of political decision making (governance) not science.
2. The challenge of identifying and advancing the common good at different spatial and temporal scales (local, regional, national, short-term, long-term). For winter tourism development, this issue may surface in conflicts between state-level desires for economic development and increased tourism, versus local concerns about the effects of development on a particular place and the people who live there now and in the future.

3. The additional challenge of assessing and managing the cumulative effects of one development proposal in combination with other existing and future projects and activities. In the Jumbo case, the initially proposed mitigation measure of restricting future motorized access to other watersheds in order to allow the Jumbo Resort to proceed was not adopted in the final assessment recommendations, probably because it was likely to be unacceptable to stakeholders as a constraint on their future activities in the region.
4. The conflicts between the institutions and asserted authority of a post-colonial state government and the authority, rights and perspectives of Indigenous people who have lived and governed themselves in a particular place for millennia before the arrival of colonial 'settlers'. In the Jumbo case, it is quite possible that the valley in which the resort is proposed has been sacred to the Ktunaxa people for more than 400 generations. In our view such deeply rooted claims need to be met affirmatively with humility and respect.

Considering the extent of the conflict and insidious manoeuvring associated with the Jumbo review and the extraordinary length of time involved, it is tempting to submit that the review process needs to be depoliticized. However, reviews of projects like this can never really be apolitical (Beattie, 1995). Questions of trade-offs, of reconciling social, ecological and economic priorities, of evaluating claims about sense of place and sacredness, and of determining what scale is most appropriate for decision making about the public interest – none of these lend themselves to technical apolitical analysis. Rather than attempting to depoliticize the review, we need to repoliticize review processes in more transparent and deeply democratic ways.[7]

Ultimately, decision making will inescapably be set in the context of competing values and beliefs, and we need to explicitly recognize it as such. We can then reject nefarious attempts to 'escape from the conversation' (Bernstein, 1983, p. 199); for example, by establishing a make-believe resort municipality or working behind the scenes to hinder or delay a proposal. Embracing the political, we are invited to imagine more deeply democratic forms of decision making that recognize the value but also the limitations of science and afford space for diverse voices to argue the merits of their claims about what sustainability means, and the strength of their qualifications to determine what a place is and what is done in it.

Notes

[1] Most of the land base in British Columbia is considered provincial 'Crown land', meaning that it is owned by the BC government (approximately 88.7 million ha, or 94% of the province), although much of this tenure is contested by First Nations.

[2] The claims of the Sinixt to legal status in Canada have recently become stronger, due to a BC Supreme Court ruling in 2017 that a Sinixt descendant living in the United States is entitled to Aboriginal (Indigenous) rights in Canada under the Canadian constitution (*R. v Desautel*, 2017).

[3] The BC Ministry of Environment's Ecological Restoration Guidelines (BC MOE, 2001, p. 70) define an umbrella species as 'a species that requires large areas of habitat, and if managed for, will encompass the needs of some other species as well'. A keystone species is defined as 'a species that affects the survival and abundance of many other species, and if removed will result in a relatively significant shift in the composition of the ecological community' (BC MOE, 2001, p. 68).

4 This scepticism appears to have been justified, as subsequent evaluations of the EA process in BC have identified major shortcomings in the province's monitoring and enforcement programmes (Haddock, 2010; Auditor General of British Columbia, 2011). For example, the Auditor General of BC (2011, p. 5) determined that 'the Environmental Assessment Office cannot assure British Columbians that mitigation efforts are having the intended effects because adequate monitoring is not occurring and follow-up evaluations are not being conducted'.

5 Three years later, a comprehensive DNA study of grizzly bears conducted for the BC Ministry of Environment (Proctor et al., 2007) found that there were far fewer grizzlies in the Central Purcell Population Unit than the government's previous habitat-based estimates used in the Jumbo EA had indicated. The new research estimated that there were 87 grizzly bears rather than 150. Yet the EA approval for Jumbo was not modified as a result of this new research, and the Jumbo Glacier Resort Master Plan issued in 2010 (Pheidias Project Management Corp., 2010) still quoted the higher numbers used in the 2004 EA report.

6 During the period of time that the Ktunaxa case challenging the approval of the Jumbo Resort was working its way through the courts, Oberto Oberti finalized plans for another large all-season resort in BC, approximately 500 km north of the Jumbo Valley, near the mountain community of Valemount. The contrast between the history of the Valemount Glacier Resort proposal and the Jumbo case is striking. In Valemount, the Simpcw First Nation, in whose traditional territory the resort will be constructed, supported the project (Oberti Resort Design and Pheidias Group, 2016). According to Simpcw Chief Nathan Matthew, 'We were in at the very beginning of the planning' (quoted in Ebner, 2017). The developer signed a Memorandum of Understanding and an Impact and Benefits Agreement with the Simpkw, under which the First Nation will receive property within the resort village and revenues from the project (BC, 2017; Matthews, 2017). As partial compensation for the resort development, the BC government transferred Crown land to the Simpkw in another area of Simpkw traditional territory (CBC News, 2018). The Village of Valemount also supported the project. According to the proponent, it was the mayor and council of Valemount who first contacted Oberti about the possibility of developing the resort, and community members were involved early in the planning process, including in the decisions about the location and scope of the project (Oberti Resort Design and Pheidias Group, 2016).

7 At the time of writing this chapter, BC has just passed legislation creating a new *Environmental Assessment Act*, which should come into force in late 2019 (BC, 2018b). The province has not yet finalized and released regulations and policies specifying the details of the EA process under the new legislation, but the early promotional material at least offers some hope that the new process will begin to address problems revealed in the Jumbo case. The three stated goals of the revisions to the EA process are as follows:

> Enhancing public confidence by ensuring impacted First Nations, local communities and governments and the broader public can meaningfully participate in all
> stages of environmental assessment through a process that is robust,
> transparent, timely and predictable;
> Advancing reconciliation with First Nations; and
> Protecting the environment while offering clear pathways to sustainable project
> approvals by providing certainty of process and clarity of regulatory considerations including opportunities for early indications of the likelihood of success.
>
> (BC, 2018b)

There is a decided emphasis in the new legislation on early engagement 'to identify interests, issues and concerns of Indigenous nations, stakeholders, and the public, ... including identifying serious issues with the project proceeding through an EA' (BC, 2018c, p. 5). Also emphasized is a commitment to government-to-government negotiations and a 'clearly defined process for seeking consensus with participating Indigenous nations, including a number of opportunities identified throughout the process that aim to secure consent on decisions'

(BC, 2018c, p. 5). It is less clear whether the current BC government has the appetite for a renewed commitment to broadly participatory, comprehensive regional land use planning. However, by building on past experiences with consensus-based planning in the province, supported by regional cumulative effects assessment, and combined with a genuine commitment to reconciliation with First Nations, the provincial government could establish a better mechanism for working out competing land use values. Environmental assessment could then be deployed more narrowly to assess potential impacts of specific projects.

References

Apps, C.D. (2003) A cartographic model-based cumulative effects assessment of JGR on grizzly bears in the Central Purcell Mountains, British Columbia. ENKON Environmental and Pheidias Project Management, Aspen Wildlife Research, Calgary, Canada.

Auditor General of British Columbia (2011) An audit of the Environmental Assessment Office's oversight of certified projects. Office of the Auditor General of British Columbia, Victoria, Canada.

Austin, M. (2004) A review of the project application for the proposed Jumbo Glacier Alpine Resort based on the potential impacts to grizzly bears. Prepared on behalf of the Environmental Stewardship Division, Ministry of Water, Land and Air Protection. BC MWLAP, Victoria, Canada.

BC (British Columbia) (2017) Province approves new all-season mountain resort in Valemount. Available at: https://news.gov.bc.ca/releases/2017FLNR0045-000865 (accessed 1 October 2018).

BC (British Columbia) (2018a) Glossary for species and ecosystems at risk. Available at: https://www2.gov.bc.ca/gov/content/environment/plants-animals-ecosystems/conservation-data-centre/explore-cdc-data/glossary-for-species-ecosystems-at-risk (accessed 12 December 2018).

BC (British Columbia) (2018b) Environmental assessment revitalization. Available at: https://www2.gov.bc.ca/gov/content/environment/natural-resource-stewardship/environmental-assessments/environmental-assessment-revitalization (accessed 3 January 2019).

BC (British Columbia) (2018c) Environmental assessment revitalization intentions paper. Available at: https://www2.gov.bc.ca/assets/gov/environment/natural-resource-stewardship/environmental-assessments/environmental-assessment-revitalization/documents/ea_revitalization_intentions_paper.pdf (accessed 3 January 2019).

BC CORE (British Columbia Commission on Resources and Environment) (1994) East Kootenay Land Use Plan. BC Commission on Resources and Environment, Victoria, Canada.

BC EAO (British Columbia Environmental Assessment Office) (1998) Proposed Jumbo Glacier Alpine Resort project, Glacier Resorts Ltd: final project report specifications. BC Environmental Assessment Office, Victoria, Canada.

BC EAO (British Columbia Environmental Assessment Office) (2004) Jumbo Glacier Resort project assessment report. BC Environmental Assessment Office, Victoria, Canada.

BC MLPH (British Columbia Ministry of Lands, Parks and Housing) (1982) Commercial alpine ski policy. BC Ministry of Lands, Parks and Housing, Victoria, Canada.

BC MOE (British Columbia Ministry of Environment) (2001) Ecological restoration guidelines for British Columbia. Available at: www.env.gov.bc.ca/fia/documents/TERP_eco_rest_guidelines/glossary/index.html (accessed 1 August 2018).

BC MOE (British Columbia Ministry of Environment) (2015) Information bulletin: Jumbo Glacier Resort project not substantially started. 18 June. Available at: https://www.projects.eao.gov.bc.ca/news (accessed 1 August 2018).

BC MOELP (British Columbia Ministry of Environment, Lands and Parks) (1995) A future for the grizzly: British Columbia grizzly bear conservation strategy. BC Ministry of Environment, Lands and Parks, Victoria, Canada.

Beattie, R.B. (1995) Everything you already know about EIA (but don't often admit). *Environmental Impact Assessment Review* 15(2), 109–114. DOI:10.1016/0195-9255(95)00001-U

Bernstein, R. (1983) *Beyond Objectivism and Relativism: Science, Hermeneutics and Praxis*. University of Pennsylvania Press, Philadelphia, Pennsylvania.

Boyd, D. (2003) *Unnatural Law: Rethinking Canadian Environmental Law and Policy*. UBC Press, Vancouver, Canada.

Braun, B. (2002) *The Intemperate Rainforest: Nature, Culture, and Power on Canada's West Coast*. University of Minnesota Press, Minneapolis, Minnesota.

Campsall, B. (2003) Letter to the editor, 24 December 2003. *The Invermere Valley Echo*, Invermere, Canada.

CBC News (2009) Jumbo Glacier Resort plan shifts to province. Available at: https://www.cbc.ca/news/canada/british-columbia/jumbo-glacier-resort-plan-shifts-to-province-1.791499 (accessed 3 August 2018).

CBC News (2018) Crown land transferred to First Nation as part of B.C. resort deal. Available at: https://www.cbc.ca/news/canada/british-columbia/valemount-resort-land-transfer-simpcw-first-nation-1.4567416 (accessed 26 September 2018).

CEAA (Canadian Environmental Assessment Agency) (1996) A guide on biodiversity and environmental assessment. Minister of Supply and Services Canada, Ottawa, Canada.

Dhillon, S. (2017) B.C. First Nation officials see Jumbo Glacier ski resort ruling as failing of top court. Available at: https://www.theglobeandmail.com/news/british-columbia/bc-first-nation-officials-depict-jumbo-ski-resort-ruling-as-failing-of-top-court/article36823211/ (accessed 3 August 2018).

Ditson, D. (2018) Jumbo's legal boondoggle continues. Available at: https://www.columbiavalleypioneer.com/news/jumbos-legal-boondoggle-continues/ (accessed 18 July 2019).

Ebner, D. (2017) Vancouver man's proposed ski resort garners support from government, First Nations. Available at: https://www.theglobeandmail.com/news/british-columbia/vancouver-mans-proposed-ski-resort-garners-support-from-government-first-nations/article36035800/ (accessed 3 August 2018).

Haddock, M. (2010) *Environmental Assessment in British Columbia*. University of Victoria Environmental Law Centre, Victoria, Canada.

Hanna, K.S. (2016) *Environmental Impact Assessment: Practice and Participation*, 3rd edn. Oxford University Press, Don Mills, Canada.

Hurtak, F. (2015) The vanishing 'Serengati of North America'. Available at: https://www.cranbrooktownsman.com/news/the-vanishing-serengeti-of-north-america/ (accessed 3 August 2018).

Jumbo Glacier Resort (2015) About the project. Available at: http://jumboglacierresort.com/about (accessed 1 August 2018).

Ktunaxa Nation (2010) Qat'muk declaration. Available at: www.ktunaxa.org/who-we-are/qatmuk-declaration (accessed 1 August 2018).

Matthews, E. (2017) Valemount resort opening pushed back again: Oberti. Available at: https://www.therockymountaingoat.com/2017/06/valemount-resort-opening-pushed-back-again-oberti (accessed 1 August 2018).

Metcalfe, B. (2009) Jumbo Ski Resort carves new legal tracks. Available at: https://thetyee.ca/News/2009/10/26/JumboSkiMunicipality (accessed 3 August 2018).

Oberti Resort Design and Pheidias Group (2016) Valemount Glacier Destination master plan. Valemount Glacier Destinations Ltd. and Pheidias Project Management Corporation. Available at: http://valemountglaciers.com/master-plan (accessed 4 January 2019).

Owens, C.E. (2011) Contesting sustainability in the Valley of the Grizzly Spirit: models of justice in environmental conflict and assessment. PhD Thesis, Simon Fraser University, Burnaby, Canada.

Pheidias Project Management Corp. (2010) Jumbo Glacier Resort master plan. Glacier Resorts Ltd. and Pheidias Project Management Corporation, Vancouver, Canada.

Proctor, M., Boulager, J., Nielsen, S., Servheen, C., Kasworm, W. *et al.* (2007) Abundance and density of Central Purcell, South Purcell, Yahk, and south Selkirk Grizzly Bear Population Units in southeast British Columbia. BC Ministry of Environment, Nelson and Victoria, Canada.

Pynn, L. (2009) Province urged to give Jumbo project resort municipality status; regional district vote called 'stab in the back' by environmentalists. Available at: https://vancouversun.newspapers.com/search/#query=Province+urged+to+give+Jumbo+project+resort+municipality+status%3B+Regional+District+vote+called+%27stab+in+the+back%27+by+environmentalists (accessed 3 August 2018).

Rancière, J. (2003) Politics and aesthetics: an interview. *Angelaki: Journal of Theoretical Humanities* 8(2), 191–211. DOI:10.1080/0969725032000162657

Rutherford, M.B. (2009) Impact assessment under British Columbia's Environmental Impact Assessment Act. In: Hanna, K.S. (ed.) *Environmental Impact Assessment: Practice and Participation*, 2nd edn. Oxford University Press, Don Mills, Canada, pp. 298–317.

Rutherford, M.B. (2016) Impact assessment in British Columbia. In: Hanna, K.S. (ed.) *Environmental Impact Assessment: Practice and Participation*, 3rd edn. Oxford University Press, Don Mills, Canada, pp. 238–254.

Stewart, R. (2004) E-mail to Martyn Glassman (EAO), Re: Jumbo Glacier Resorts – grizzly bears. 2 July 2004.

WCED (World Commission on Environment and Development) (1987) *Our Common Future*. Oxford University Press, New York.

Wilson, J. (1999) *Talk and Log: Wilderness Politics in British Columbia*. UBC Press, Vancouver, Canada.

Wolfe, L.D.S. (1987) Methods for scoping environmental impact assessments, a review of literature and experience. Prepared for the Federal Environmental Assessment Review Office. Larry Wolfe Associates, Vancouver, Canada.

Legal Cases Cited

Ktunaxa Nation v. British Columbia (Forests, Lands and Natural Resource Operations), 2014 BCSC 568.

Ktunaxa Nation v. British Columbia (Forests, Lands and Natural Resource Operations), 2017 SCC 54.

R. v, Desautel, 2017 BCSC 2389.

33 Winter Tourism and Seasonality in Iceland

Þorvardur Árnason[1]* and Johannes T. Welling[2]

[1]*Hornafjordur Research Center, University of Iceland, Hornafjordur, Iceland;* [2]*Department of Geography and Tourism Studies, University of Iceland, Reykjavík, Iceland*

33.1 Introduction

Winter tourism is a relatively recent phenomena in most of Iceland, a northern country traditionally characterized by a high degree of seasonality with regard to foreign visitor numbers, especially in the rural regions (Árnason, 2013; Þórhallsdóttir and Ólafsson, 2017; Gil-Alana and Huijbens, 2018). Until recently, the large majority of foreign tourists visited Iceland during the high season (June–August). The relative importance of the nine remaining low-season months (i.e. January–May and September–December) has, however, been growing. More foreign tourists now visit Iceland during these months, taken as a whole, than during the summer. The increase of foreign visitation during the winter season (January–March and November–December) has been particularly rapid, with a 32.3% average annual increase since winter 2010–2011, when this trend first became apparent. This chapter will present an overview of how tourism seasonality in Iceland has changed in recent years, with particular emphasis on a case study area, Hornafjörður municipality, in rural south Iceland. This area was chosen because of the rapid development of winter tourism there over the past 7 years. As limited research on tourism seasonality has so far been conducted in Iceland, this chapter will mainly make use of existing data from various external sources,[1] but also present findings from primary research. Certain observations on the case study area, furthermore, rely on unpublished information from various national or regional institutions, or are based on knowledge gained through the authors' research efforts in Hornafjörður. This chapter is thus a 'bricolage' of sorts, piecing together available data from many and somewhat disparate sources, in order to build up a description of how winter tourism currently stands in Hornafjörður in relation to the situation at the national and regional levels in Iceland. Following this, we present some thoughts on how winter tourism took root in the case study area, and whether or not this novel development there is likely to be sustained in the future.

33.2 Reflections on 'Seasonality' and 'Winter Tourism'

Tourism seasonality is a well-documented phenomena encountered worldwide, in different contexts and to varying extents (BarOn, 1975; Butler, 1994; Baum and Lundtorp,

---

* E-mail: thorvarn@hi.is

2001; Koenig-Lewis and Bischoff, 2005). BarOn (1975) provides an early description of seasonality in tourism:

> Most forms of human activity are affected by the seasons of the year. There are considerable variations in the climate throughout each year, in the hours of daylight and of sunshine, the minimum and maximum temperatures, rainfall, snow etc. These affect many business and leisure activities in particular months, in a similar manner each year. (...) Apart from this "natural seasonality", there is "institutionalised seasonality" due to holidays and other events at specific times of the year, e.g. Christmas and the summer vacations of schools, universities and many places of work.
>
> (BarOn, 1975, p. 2)

BarOn furthermore mentions 'sociological and economic reasons' for seasonality, such as 'differential prices for tourism services and air fares in different seasons' (BarOn, 1975, p. 2). Butler (1994, p. 332) refers to tourism seasonality as a 'temporal imbalance in the phenomenon of tourism', which can be expressed by such elements as 'numbers of visitors, expenditure of visitors, traffic on highways and other forms of transportation, employment, and admissions to attractions'. Butler furthermore adds a fifth cause of seasonality to BarOn's list, that of 'inertia or tradition': 'There can be little doubt that many people take holidays at what are peak seasons because they have always done so, and old habits tend to die hard' (Butler, 1994, p. 333).

Taken together, BarOn's (1975) and Butler's (1994) descriptions of tourism seasonality present a multi-facetted phenomenon that has diverse and possibly interactive causes, the outcome of which can be evidenced by different sets of data, reflecting patterns of variability and change over a given period of time. The timeframe of analysis is crucial and should, arguably, reflect a period of at least 5–10 years – otherwise the changes observed might be mere short-term 'perturbations' in the normal ebb and flow of tourism in the study area. To paraphrase Butler, tourism seasonality initially requires a relatively 'permanent imbalance' in one or more elements for true 'seasons' – in tourism terms – to emerge. Change over time is furthermore to be expected, perhaps revealing fairly stable long-term trends, which then lead to a state of 'lower' or 'higher' seasonality in a given area. Another critical factor is the unit of analysis, which may in practice be dictated by available data, rather than based upon observed spatio-temporal tourism patterns. As an example, tourism statistics in Iceland are commonly presented either as national or regional data, although data on other spatial levels can also be found. Data on the national level tend to obscure variability within a given country, whereas smaller-scale data may be irrelevant in tourism contexts as the units in question (e.g. municipalities) are defined by socio-political or historical considerations, which do not necessarily have any bearing for foreign visitors.

Winter tourism can either be defined broadly as the sum total of all tourism activities taking place in a given destination over the course of the winter season, however its timeframe is defined, or more narrowly as tourism activities taking place during the winter and *only* being available during that time period, due to natural and/or societal conditions. Much of the available literature on winter tourism concerns winter sports tourism, such as downhill or cross-country skiing (e.g. Steiger *et al.*, 2019), which – being predicated on the presence of snow – meets the criteria for the narrower definition, even if this definition is not articulated as such. A quite different form of winter tourism, which nonetheless reflects its close connection to seasonal characteristics, is the extensive 'Christmas' tourism evidenced in northern Finland, in particular in Rovaniemi, marketed as the 'headquarters of Santa Claus' (e.g. Tervo-Kankare *et al.*, 2013). Here the most important seasonal characteristic is socio-cultural, rather than natural, but still intimately connected to the winter. The broader and more inclusive definition is not without its merits; however, as characteristic winter activities interact with a range of other tourism services, such as accommodation, catering and transport, which are not exclusive to the winter. Furthermore, tourist activities that are offered on a whole-year basis can provide very different experiences when practised in winter as compared with other seasons.

Another aspect of 'winter tourism' requiring further clarification concerns the timeframe referred to – i.e. both the time of year and length of period – as well as the total number of defined seasons. As an example, sources of tourism statistics in Iceland tend to present the 'winter' in terms of a single calendar year, most commonly January–March and November–December. This approach may not present a problem for long-term comparisons of annual tourist numbers but in a highly dynamic tourism environment, its validity is more suspect as it joins together what are effectively two different winter periods. A more precise approach would be to define the winter as, e.g. November–December of year n and January–March of year $n + 1$. The number of 'seasons' in a given calendar year is also open to conjecture. The traditional four seasons approach may be valid in many circumstances, but does not necessarily reflect the reality of the processes underlying tourism seasonality in the study area. As an example of an alternative approach, Þórhallsdóttir and Ólafsson (2017) identified seven tourist seasons at Skaftafell, a popular whole-year tourist destination within Hornafjörður municipality. In this instance, physical data (i.e. statistical patterns observed in data from vehicle counters) were used to define the number and duration of tourist seasons at a given destination, with the aim of defining seasons that were uniform with regard to target groups and travel behaviour. Three of their seven seasons more or less correspond to spring, summer and autumn as commonly defined, but the remaining four are defined as 'early winter', 'winter', 'late winter' and 'end of winter'. Furthermore, the season 'winter' as defined by Þórhallsdóttir and Ólafsson overlaps adjacent calendar years, lasting from mid-October to mid-February.

It is not our intention to try to resolve the issues outlined above, as these have arisen largely through reflections relating to work on the existing datasets on tourism seasonality and winter tourism currently available for Iceland. Our own chapter is thus 'beset' by several of these conceptual and/or methodological issues, which we raise mainly for consideration in future, more in-depth, research concerning winter tourism development and its relations to changes in tourism seasonality.

33.3 Tourism Development and Seasonality in Iceland

33.3.1 Tourism seasonality on the national level

Foreign tourism in Iceland has increased enormously over the past 7 years. Historically, the annual growth in foreign visitation was, on average, between 6 and 7% per year. This situation changed dramatically as of 2011 – since then, foreign tourism growth in Iceland has been measured in double-digit figures every year, reaching a maximum high of 39% annual growth between 2015 and 2016. The mean annual growth in foreign visitation between 2010 and 2017 was 24.3% (Icelandic Tourism Board, 2018a). This prolonged period of increase also coincides with a period of transition from predominantly summer tourism to whole-year tourism, where there has been relatively much greater growth in the winter, spring and autumn seasons than over the summer (see Fig. 33.1). Thus, in 2017, the winter season as defined by the Icelandic Tourism Board (i.e. January–March and November–December) accounted for 33.3% of foreign visits to Iceland, the spring season (April–May) for 13.6% and the autumn (September–October) for 17.6% – the combined share of the low-season months was therefore 64.6% (Icelandic Tourism Board, 2018a). This represented a substantial change from previous years: in 2010 for example, the low season in total amounted to 50.5% of that year's foreign visitation. These ratios, furthermore, do not do justice to the increase in absolute numbers of tourists – the number of foreign visitors during the winter season thus increased seven-fold (from 105,521 to 732,029 visitors) from 2010 to 2017 (Icelandic Tourism Board, 2018b).

These statistics must be qualified with a number of observations. First, tourism in Iceland is not geographically homogeneous – there exist large-scale differences between the city of Reykjavík and its surrounding urban municipalities (collectively referred to as the 'capital area') and the more rural regions elsewhere in Iceland (see Fig. 33.2). Tourism seasonality has historically been much less pronounced in the capital area than in the rural regions (Árnason, 2013). Furthermore, tourists' modes of transportation in Iceland have exhibited a large-scale change over the years, with ever-increasing numbers of foreign visitors opting to use rental cars during their stay in Iceland, rather than travel with tour buses or public transport. Thus, during summer 2017 (June–August), 68% of foreign tourists in Iceland used rental cars, compared with 36% in 2003 and 21% in 1996 (Guðmundsson, 2018a). During the winter of 2017–2018, 44% of all foreign visitors to Iceland used rental cars as their main form

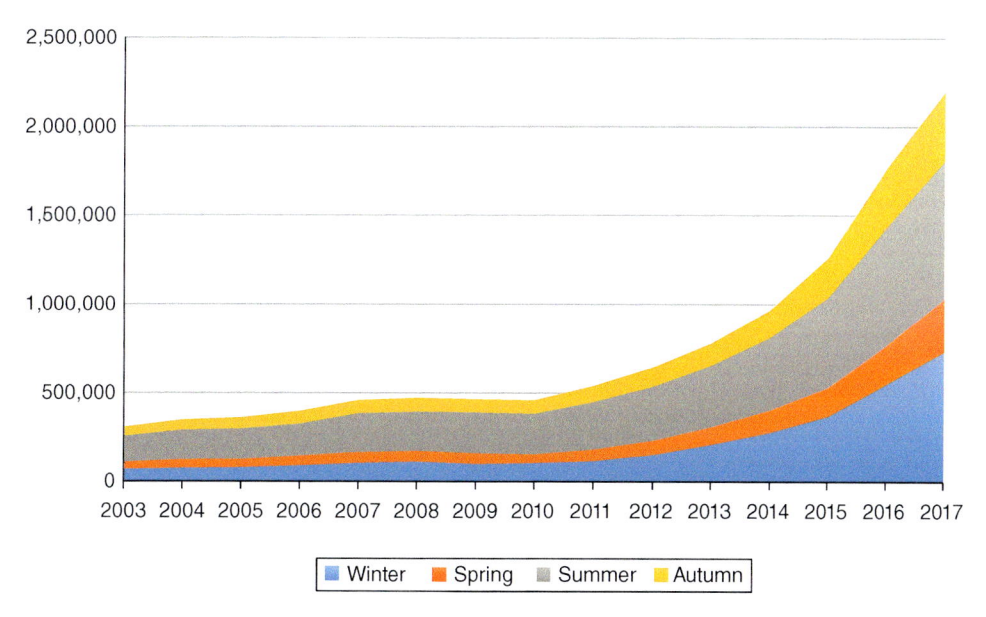

Fig. 33.1. Number of foreign visitors departing from Keflavík Airport 2003–2017, showing seasonal differences between winter (January–March and November–December), spring (April–May), summer (June–August) and autumn (September–October) of each calendar year. (Own figure based on Icelandic Tourism Board, 2018b.)

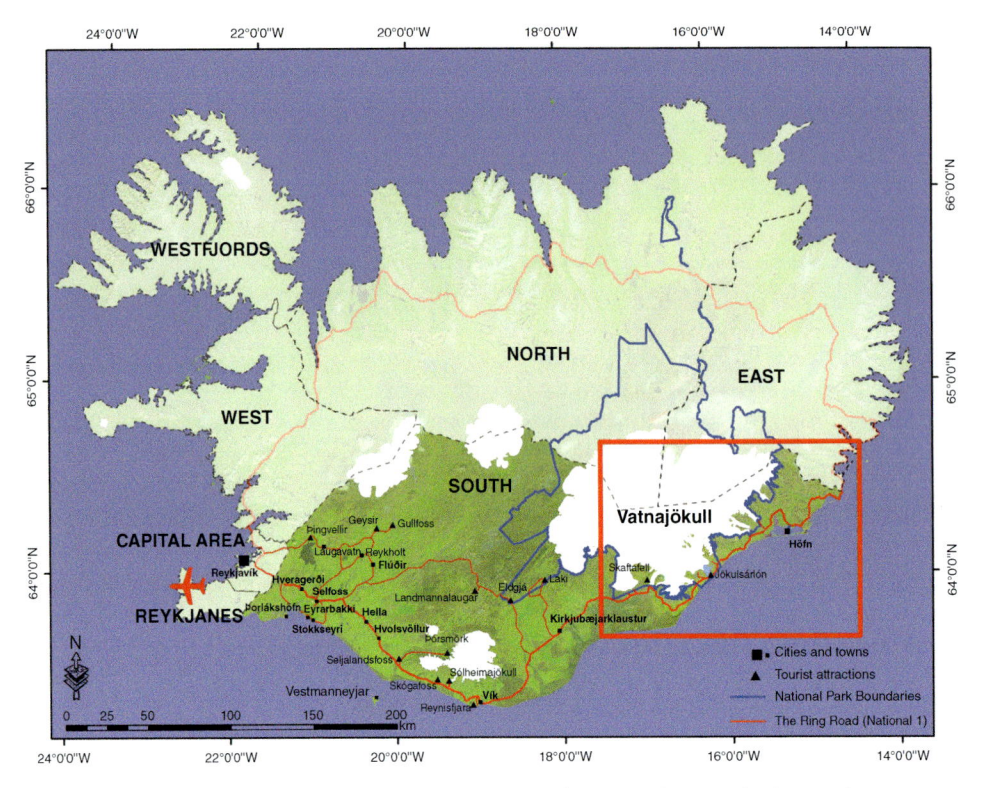

Fig. 33.2. Map of Iceland, showing: (a) the seven defined tourism marketing regions, Keflavík International Airport and the Ring Road; (b) the main towns, scenic sites and tourist routes in south Iceland. (Figure courtesy of Snævarr Guðmundsson, Þorvarður Árnason and Johannes Welling.)

of transport during their stay (Guðmundsson, 2018a). The distances travelled by foreign tourists in rental cars during the winter are considerably shorter than during the summer – the average total travelling distance was thus 1000 km during winter 2017 as compared with 2050 km during the summer (Guðmundsson, 2018a). These figures suggest that tourists' travel patterns may undergo considerable seasonal changes, dependent on a number of potential causes, such as shorter duration of visits, more difficult driving conditions, different choices of scenic sites to visit and activities to undertake, and, in general, different personal motivations for visiting Iceland in winter vis-à-vis summer.

An important factor underlying the growth of winter tourism in Iceland is likely to be the large increase in the availability of flights during the wintertime. Thus, in 2016, Keflavík Airport was connected to a total of 90 foreign destinations (ISAVIA, 2017). In 2017, 12 airlines flew to and from Iceland on a whole-year basis, or almost half of the 27 airlines operating regular flights during the summertime (ISAVIA, 2018). Another factor may be the growing popularity of Northern Lights tours, which started to be systematically marketed by Icelandair in autumn 2008 and became a very popular tourist activity during the low season shortly thereafter (Heimtun *et al.*, 2014). It is also probable that there are one or more 'common denominators' contributing both to the overall annual growth in tourism and the relatively more pronounced increase of winter tourism. One such factor may be the large-scale devaluation of the national currency (the Icelandic króna), resulting from the financial crisis, which started in late 2008 (Jóhannesson and Huijbens, 2010). Another such common factor may involve the increased presence of Iceland in the global media following the volcanic eruption in Eyjafjallajökull in 2010 (Benediktsson *et al.*, 2010). Finally, mention should be made of government-sponsored tourism marketing campaigns, which were intensified in the aftermath of the 2008 financial crisis. In 2011, a new tourism policy for Iceland was approved by the Icelandic Parliament (Alþingi, 2011). This policy was the first in Iceland to specifically target tourism seasonality and define measures to reduce this. The Icelandic government subsequently increased funding for marketing campaigns intended to attract foreign visitors to Iceland during the low season.

33.3.2 Tourism seasonality on the regional level

The growth of low-season tourism in Iceland in recent years has led to somewhat decreased seasonality in rural regions. Official statistics on spatial tourist distribution between July 2017 and May 2018 illustrate the current situation (Tourism Task Force, 2018). The spatial scheme for analysing this distribution is based on the seven defined tourism marketing regions in Iceland (see Fig. 33.2). During the period July 2017 to May 2018, the capital area was visited by around 94% of all foreign tourists. This percentage remained nearly constant throughout the period, clearly demonstrating the very low seasonality of this marketing region (see Fig. 33.3). At the other end of the spectrum, the Westfjords received almost no foreign visitors during the winter. In north, east and west Iceland, tourist numbers dropped sharply in late autumn and

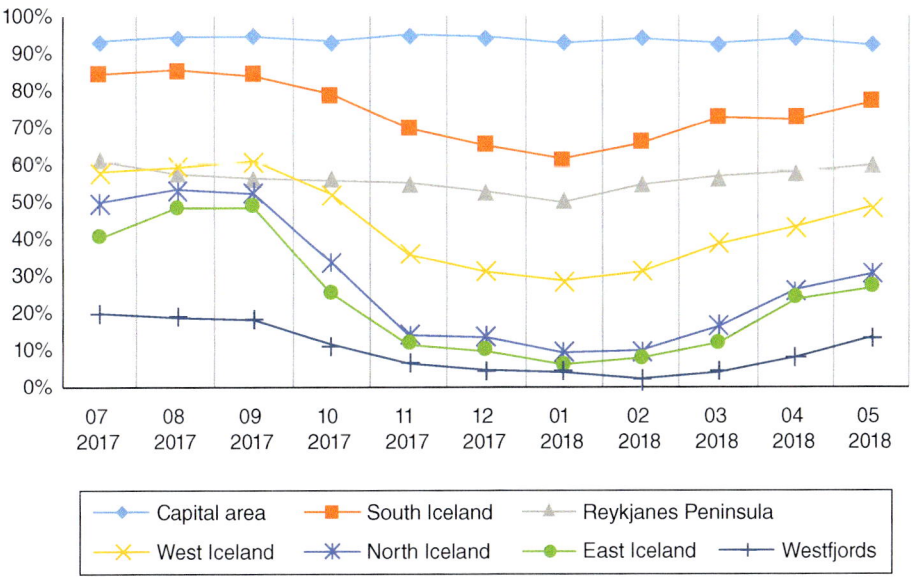

Fig. 33.3. Ratio of foreign tourists in each of the seven tourism marketing areas, relative to the total number of foreign visitors in Iceland per month, July 2017–May 2018. (Own figure based on Tourism Task Force, 2018.)

remained low throughout the winter. Tourist numbers in the Reykjanes peninsula were quite steady (50–60%) throughout the year, perhaps not unexpectedly as this region is very close to the capital area. South Iceland was the only peripheral rural area that received substantial tourist numbers during the winter, even if somewhat lower than in the summer.

Again, these results must be qualified. 'South Iceland', as defined for tourism marketing purposes, covers a very large region, stretching from the town of Þorlákshöfn in the west to the town of Höfn in the east, a distance of 429 km by road (see Fig. 33.2). The region is very diverse and includes both lowland and highland areas. National road nr. 1 – the 'Ring Road' – runs through the lowland, connecting the towns there one to another. Many scenic sites, accessible all year round, can furthermore be found within walking distance from the Ring Road. The duration of visits by foreign guests is, on average, shorter during the winter than during the summer. Thus, the average length of a visit to Iceland was 9.3 days in August 2017 as compared with 5.0 days in December (Tourism Task Force, 2018). As previously noted, fewer tourists use rental cars during the winter than during the summer and those that do tend to drive shorter distances than their counterparts during the summer. As almost all foreign tourists enter and leave the country at Keflavík Airport, the interplay of these factors places the more peripheral regions at a certain disadvantage.

33.4 Case Study Area: Hornafjörður Municipality

33.4.1 General description

Hornafjörður is the third largest municipality in Iceland, stretching roughly 200 km by road from west to east and covering an area of 6280 km^2 (see Fig. 33.4). About 62% of this area is now managed by Vatnajökull National Park. The national park, established in 2008, covers an area of about 14,400 km^2, most of which is managed as an International Union for Conservation of Nature (IUCN) Category II protected area. The park includes the whole Vatnajökull icecap and all of its numerous outlet glaciers, covering around 7800 km^2 in total. The area of the park located within Hornafjörður municipality consists almost entirely of diverse glacier landscapes, most prominently the south-eastern quarter of Vatnajökull icecap and its outlet glaciers. The glaciers and pro-glacial landscapes of Hornafjörður have been the subject of natural science studies for over 80 years (e.g. Evans, 2016; Björnsson, 2017). More recently, these glaciers have also begun to be studied in terms of their aesthetic, experiential and cultural values (e.g. Jóhannesdóttir, 2015; Jackson, 2019).

In Fig. 33.4, several important characteristics of Hornafjörður municipality are readily apparent: the omnipresence of the glacier icecap, the extensive mountain ranges, and the limited arable land available between the glacier and the sea. The Ring Road runs through the lowland, connecting the numerous scenic sites together, like beads on a necklace. Höfn, the only town in this area, owes its origins to a natural harbour that allowed for the establishment of a fishing industry there. Hornafjörður is the easternmost municipality in south Iceland. The road distance from Reykjavík to Höfn is 450 km. Skaftafell and Jökulsárlón are the most heavily visited scenic sites in the municipality. Vatnajökull National Park operates a visitors' centre at Skaftafell, which also functions as a meeting point for tourists embarking on commercial tours to nearby

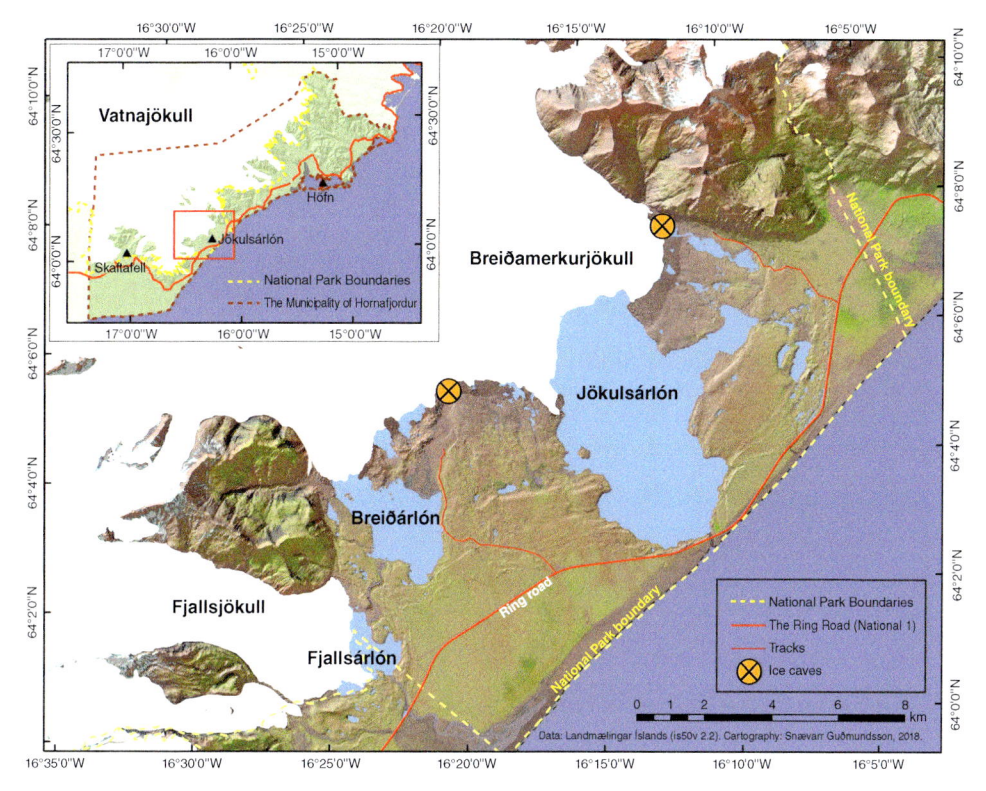

Fig. 33.4. Map showing: the borders of Hornafjörður municipality (insert, top left), and the Breiðamerkursandur area, with national park boundaries, jeep tracks and approximate locations of ice caves indicated. Glacier margins based on data from 2017. (Figure courtesy of Snævarr Guðmundsson, Þorvarður Árnason and Johannes Welling.)

glacier tongues, most commonly glacier hikes. Jökulsárlón lies roughly in the middle of Breiðamerkursandur, right beside the Ring Road. This area, i.e. the pro-glacial lake and its surroundings, was added to Vatnajökull National Park in July 2017. Jökulsárlón is the largest pro-glacial lake in Iceland and grows ever larger, due to the rapid recession of Breiðamerkurjökull, which calves into it from the north (Guðmundsson *et al.*, 2017). During the winter, Jökulsárlón (see Fig. 33.5) is commonly used as the starting point for commercial tours to the natural ice caves, which are found in the terminus of Breiðamerkurjökull, both west and east of the pro-glacial lake.

33.4.2 Tourism development in Hornafjörður

Hornafjörður has a long history of tourism. An important milestone in this regard was the establishment of Skaftafell National Park in 1967, along with the visitor's centre and camping site developed there; this area was merged into Vatnajökull National Park in 2008. Hornafjörður offers a wide range of recreational opportunities, with various forms of glacier tourism being the most prominent, due to the proximity of Vatnajökull and its many outlet glaciers and pro-glacial lagoons. The character and development of glacier tourism in Hornafjörður has been discussed by the authors in

Fig. 33.5. Jökulsárlón, the most heavily visited tourism destination in the case study area, in January 2012. (Photograph courtesy of Þorvarður Árnason.)

a previous paper (Welling and Árnason, 2016), as well as findings from research on glacier tourism elsewhere (Welling, *et al.*, 2015). The first commercial glacier tourism activities to be developed in Hornafjörður were super-jeep, snowmobiling and cross-country skiing tours on Vatnajökull icecap, followed by boat tours on Jökulsárlón and glacier hikes on Skaftafellsjökull and Svínafellsjökull. Until recently, such activities were only available during the summertime, with tour companies closing their doors to tourists in late autumn, even though many forms of glacier tourism can be undertaken all year round, e.g. 'blue ice hiking' on glacier tongues or motorized tours on Vatnajökull icecap. Important milestones in the development of winter tourism in the area concern the whole-year service supplied in Skaftafell and Jökulsárlón as of winter 2009–2010. The single most important factor in this regard, however, was the development of commercial tours to natural ice caves which, after some preliminary attempts in earlier years, started to be marketed by local entrepreneurs in 2010 (E.R. Sigurðsson, Hofsnes, 2018, personal communication).

Seasonality has traditionally been quite pronounced in Hornafjörður – in 2010, foreign visitation during the low season thus amounted to only 18.8% of the annual total, whereas in 2017 this ratio had risen to 53.7% (Guðmundsson, 2018b). The only long-term data currently available on tourist numbers in Hornafjörður are based on a visitors' survey that has been administered at Keflavík Airport since 1974. Figure 33.6 shows the results of this survey for the period 2010–2017. These results demonstrate a similar trend to the one presented earlier for the development of seasonality in Iceland as a whole (see Fig. 33.1). Tourism has been growing relatively faster in winter, spring and autumn than during the summer, leading to lower seasonality over time.

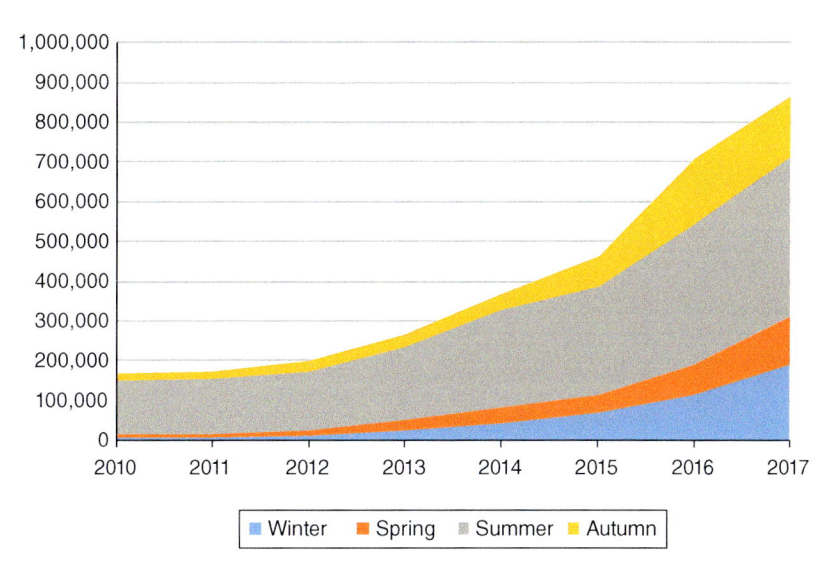

Fig. 33.6. Number of foreign tourists visiting Hornafjörður municipality 2010–2017, showing seasonal differences between winter (January–March and November–December), spring (April–May), summer (June–August) and autumn (September–October) of each calendar year. (Own figure based on Guðmundsson, 2018b.)

Winter is by far the fastest growing season; in 2010 only 3.8% of all tourists visited Hornafjörður during the wintertime while in 2017 this share had increased to 21.8%. In absolute numbers, this reflects an increase from 6500 visitors to 188,000 visitors during this period – an almost 30-fold increase. If we compare this with the situation on the national level, then during this same period the relative share of the winter season grew from 23.0% to 33.5% – a substantial increase, but still an order of magnitude lower than the developments in Hornafjörður.

Figure 33.7 shows the relative spatial distribution within Hornafjörður municipality of foreign tourists throughout the year 2017, based on self-reported visits to the three main tourism sites within the area (Guðmundsson, 2018b). A large majority (83–95%) of all tourists travelling to Hornafjörður visited Jökulsárlón. Visitation at Skaftafell was also relatively high during the summer months, but considerably lower during the winter. Seasonality was most pronounced in Höfn, which was visited by 67.6% of all tourists travelling to the municipality in June 2017 but only by 29.7% of such visitors in January 2017.

33.5 Winter Tourism in Hornafjörður

33.5.1 Winter activities

Natural ice cave tours have in recent years become the quintessential winter tourism activity in Hornafjörður. Such tours are only available during the winter, i.e. from early November to late March, as entering the caves at other times of the year can either be impossible or extremely dangerous. Ice caves are not unique to Hornafjörður, these can also be found in glaciers elsewhere in Iceland but not in the same

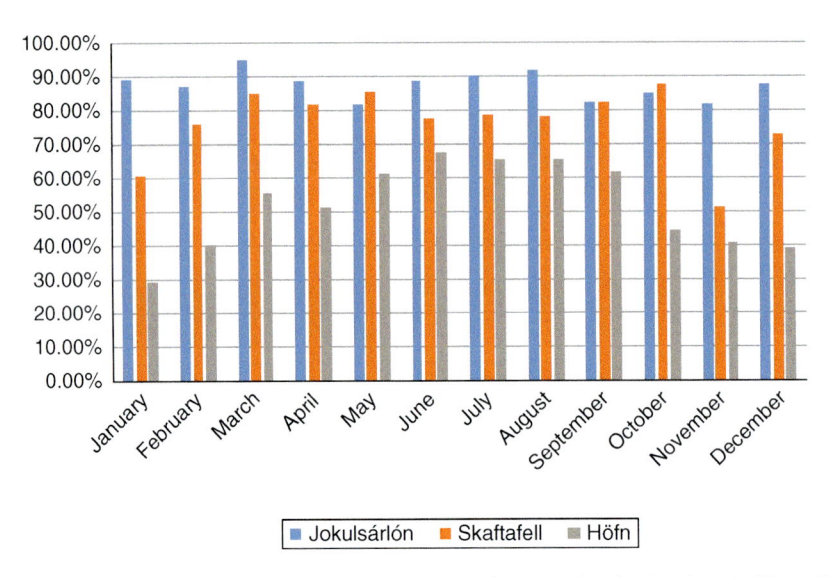

Fig. 33.7. Ratio of foreign visitors by month in 2017 at three tourist destinations in Hornafjörður, relative to the total number of visitors to the municipality. (Own figure based on Guðmundsson, 2018b.)

numbers, nor with the same ease of access. A typical ice cave tour starts with a rendezvous at Jökulsárlón, after which the customers climb on board a super-jeep or similar vehicle that transports them to the terminus of the glacier where the ice caves are to be found.

The ice caves utilized for commercial tours in Hornafjörður are primarily subglacial tunnels, formed by flow of summer meltwater rivers, which – when they dry up during the winter – can reveal cavernous openings and large vaults or hollows, often interspaced with moulins that allow light to penetrate deep into the interior of the tunnel (see Fig. 33.8). These tunnels are always dangerous to enter, due to the omnipresent risk of falling ice blocks or even large-scale collapses, but least so during the coldest part of the year. The ice caves have an unusual and strong visual appeal, as the following description by Jackson (2019) demonstrates:

> Today, the ice caves in Iceland are among the most photographed places in the country, pictures of unbelievable hues of sapphire, bubble-waved walls of sheer blue resembling underwater worlds, of time-stopped frozen waterfalls, ice tunnels, ice stalagmites, incandescent sublimation crystals and jagged icicles, low winter light pouring through blue ice caves filtering flickering blue-golden glows.
>
> (Jackson, 2019, p. 191)

33.5.2 Supply-side dynamics

The importance of the tourism sector to Hornafjörður is clearly reflected in the number of tourism businesses based in the municipality; a rural community with around 2300 permanent inhabitants. In 2017, these companies numbered around 180 in total (B. Freysteinsson, Höfn, 2018, personal communication) and 30 companies thereof offered commercial tour activities of various sorts (H. Arinbjarnarson,

Fig. 33.8. Opening of natural ice cave ('Crystal Cave') in Breiðamerkurjökull glacier, December 2015. (Photograph courtesy of Þorvarður Árnason.)

Reykjavík, 2018, personal communication). Most of these businesses are family-run microenterprises. The importance of glaciers is evidenced by the activity descriptions of local tour operators, as reported to the Icelandic Tourism Board (see Fig. 33.9). The close ties to glacier tourism are also evident in the names chosen for these local companies, e.g. Iceguide, Ice Explorers, Glacier Adventure, Glacier Trips, Glacier Journey, Glacier Guides, Arctic Guides and Blue Iceland.

The impact of growing winter tourism can furthermore be inferred from these figures, as most of the local glacier tourism companies that have commenced operations in the past few years rely heavily on ice cave tours for their income. The local tour operators are, however, not alone in utilizing the 'frozen assets' of Vatnajökull National Park. A large number of non-local companies conduct tours in these same glacial landscapes, many of these with home bases in foreign countries. No fee is required for entrance into the park and neither the number of companies operating within the park nor the extent of their operations is accurately known. As a result, the national park has no means by which to regulate the number of visitors, except by closing off vulnerable areas for specific types of travel or even all forms of visitation (Vatnajökull National Park, 2013).

When it became apparent that new and potentially dangerous forms of commercial tourism activities – namely natural ice cave tours – had become established within the national park's boundaries, a post was established during winter 2016–2017 on the eastern side of Breiðamerkursandur to monitor traffic going to the ice caves there. The monitoring period started in late December and lasted for 3 months and thus covered about two-thirds of the operating period (H. Árnadóttir, Höfn, 2017, personal communication). Park rangers recorded the number of vehicles, number of passengers

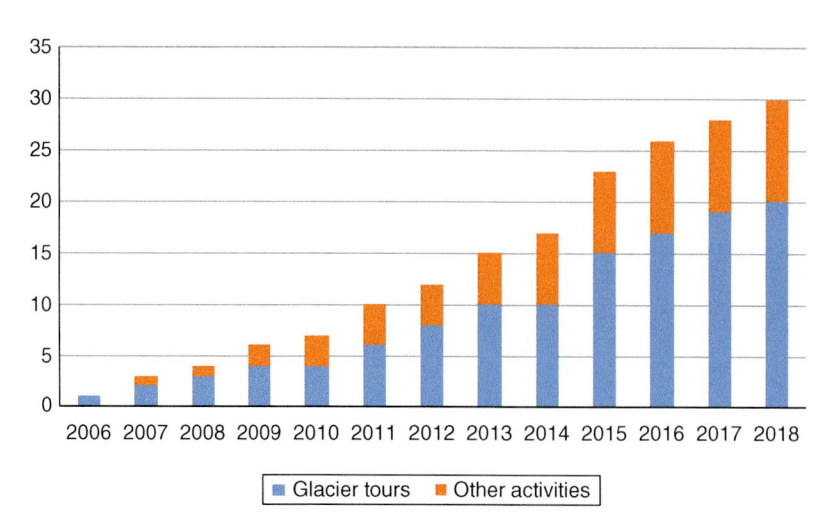

Fig. 33.9. Cumulative number of tour operator licences, issued to companies in Hornafjörður municipality, from January 2006 to June 2018. (Own figure based on Icelandic Tourism Board, 2018c.)

and the name of the company providing the tour. In total, 35 companies conducted tours to this area, 12 thereof on a daily basis, most of which offered multiple tours per day. The large majority (~75%) of the latter were local companies. Based on passenger counts and supplementary information received from tour companies, the park estimated that around 41,500 tourists had visited these ice caves during the 5-month operating period. This is more likely to be a conservative estimate than vice-versa as information was not forthcoming from all companies.

33.5.3 Demand-side dynamics

In 2010–2011, the Hornafjordur Research Center carried out a study to probe the feasibility of developing increased winter tourism in the adjacent municipalities of Hornafjörður and Skaftárhreppur (Árnason, 2013). At that point in time, winter tourists in the study area were still very few (see Fig. 33.6) and it was therefore decided to gauge summer tourist's perceptions of the Icelandic winter, their willingness to visit Iceland during this season and their preferences concerning winter activities. Almost 70% of the foreign participants in the survey stated that they were interested in visiting Iceland during the winter. Presented with a list of potential winter activities, the five highest scoring preferences were for Northern Lights tours (70%), bathing in hot pools (60%), walking tours (43%), photography (42%) and glacier hikes (38%). Natural ice cave tours were not included as an optional winter activity in this survey, as they had not yet been widely promoted.

In 2016, this line of research was continued with an exploratory study concerning the motivations, opinions and behaviours of foreign tourists visiting Hornafjörður during the winter (Welling and Árnason, 2019). This study was in two parts: the first phase qualitative (15 semi-structured interviews) and the second quantitative (139 completed surveys). Both phases of the study were carried out in February 2016. The majority of respondents were young adults (age 24–35 years) or 50+ adults living in

Western Europe or the USA. Most of them were travelling as couples or in small groups and stayed just 1–2 days in Hornafjörður; 38% did not overnight in the municipality. Most of the respondents (59%) organized their visits to glacier sites themselves, using social media or websites. The glacier sites in Hornafjörður were seen as an important or very important decision making factor for visiting the area by just over half of the respondents (56%). Around half of the respondents (52%) were first-time visitors to a glacier site. Presented with a list of potential winter activities, the highest scoring preferences were for ice cave tours (72%), sightseeing (70%), photography (67%), Northern Lights tours (60%) and glacier hikes (57%). Respondents were also asked about the glacier activities they had actually undertaken during their visit to the area (Fig. 39.10). Almost all respondents (99%) had undertaken at least one activity on the list; the average number of activities was 2.5. A large proportion (40%) of all reported activities were commercial offers.

Figure 33.10 shows the activities undertaken by the respondents during their visit to Hornafjörður. These results can, arguably, be taken as strong indication of the high importance of natural ice cave tours in the case study area, as these were undertaken by 45% of the survey's respondents. These results may not, however, correctly represent the situation in other periods of the winter season, nor during the winter as a whole, as the time frame of the survey coincided with what is usually the busiest time of year for ice cave tour operators.

Another study, using most of the same survey items, was conducted in Hornafjörður during summer 2015 (Welling and Árnason, 2019). A comparison between the two surveys reveals a number of differences between winter and summer visitors (see Table 33.1).

Winter visitors were on average almost 4 years older than summer visitors and their visits to the area were shorter. Winter visitors spent less time at the glacier sites than the summer visitors and had different interests concerning the activities on offer, most notably with regard to snowmobiling. Visitation to different glacier sites also differed, thus

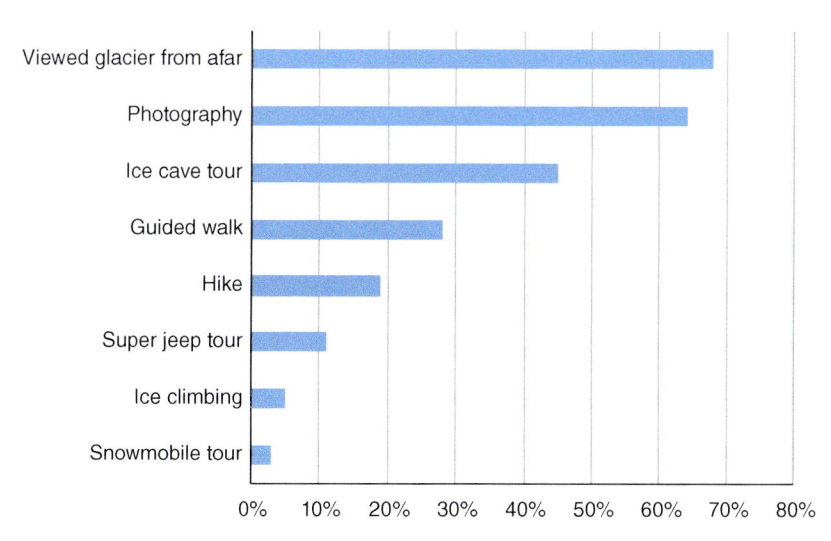

Fig. 33.10. Activities undertaken by survey respondents (*n* = 138) at glacier sites in Hornafjörður in February 2016. (Own figure based on data from Welling and Árnason, 2019.)

Table 33.1. Significant differences between summer and winter visitors to Hornafjörður, based on t-tests and Chi Square tests on a 1% significance level.

Question topics		Summer	Winter
Age of respondents (years)	Average	33.1	37.0
	41 years and older	22.3%	30.9%
Time spent at glacier site(s) during trip (h)	Average	6.3	4.5
Duration of stay in the region	<2 days	21.0%	38.0%
Activities interested in doing during trip	Hiking	83.1%	34.0%
	Snowmobiling[a]	17.2%	34.5%
	Mountaineering[a]	21.6%	12.9%
	Swimming/bathing	37.5%	20.9%
Visited glacier sites	Svínafellsjökull	37.7%	25.9%
	Fjallsárlón	14.9%	4.3%
	Breiðamerkurjökull	7.4%	17.3%
Motives to visit glacier site(s)[b]	To see a glacier in real life	4.2	4.6

[a]Difference between summer and winter on 0.05 significance level; [b]Measured on 5-point Likert scale (1 = not important at all; 5 = very important).

Fig. 33.11. Photographer inside natural ice cave ('Treasure Island Cave') in Breiðamerkurjökull glacier, January 2018. (Photograph courtesy of Þorvarður Árnason.)

a much higher proportion of tourists visited Breiðamerkurjökull during the winter. Finally, there were significant differences between summer and winter visitors with regard to their motivation to visit glacier sites. The motivation 'to see a glacier or ice cave in real life' had a significantly higher average score among the winter visitors than among the summer visitors, while the opposite was true of the motivation 'to be close to nature'.

This last result can be interpreted as an indication that winter tourists travel to the area to experience specific glacier environments to a greater extent than summer visitors.

33.6 Discussion and Conclusions

Although still incomplete, the 'composite picture' of tourism seasonality that emerges from the data described above is one of multiple interacting factors, stemming from diverse causes, both natural and socio-cultural, and being expressed as a variety of elements, such as changes in visitor numbers over time and seasonal differences in travel patterns and recreational activities. Tourism seasonality in Iceland is furthermore expressed at multiple spatial levels – national, regional and municipal – and while there are important differences between these, it seems clear that there are certain factors (or constraints) underlying the potential for change on all levels, e.g. the single access point into the country at Keflavík Airport and the structure of the national road system, in particular the layout of the Ring Road. Understanding these factors and their interactions requires in-depth knowledge about, e.g. the motivations of foreign visitors travelling to Iceland during the winter, their patterns of mobility, and their choices of activities, which is currently beyond our grasp. Nonetheless, some reflections may still be hazarded.

Winter tourism can be seen as the 'polar opposite' of summer tourism and thus – all other things being equal – the tourism season least likely to develop in Iceland, given that it should be most distinct from the historically dominant summer season. Outside the capital area, winter tourism was almost non-existent in Iceland until winter 2010–2011 and still remains very limited in most rural regions of Iceland (see Fig. 33.3). Growing winter tourism in the south region of Iceland is the main exception to this rule and this is therefore the region where the clearest evidence of distinct winter tourism characteristics might be found, if indeed these exist. As Hornafjörður is the most peripheral part of south Iceland, relative to the capital area and international airport, the authors considered this to be an interesting area to study, especially as the growth of tourism during the winter has been very rapid there.

There are two main reasons to assume that foreign visits to Hornafjörður – in particular the area around Jökulsárlón – during the winter may involve factors that are specifically related to the winter season. First, such visits provide access to glacier tourism activities that are most commonly found in this area, some of which are furthermore only available during the winter. Second, many of these activities are commercial in nature, requiring substantial payment to undertake them, unlike visits to most other scenic sites in south Iceland frequented by tourists during the winter. Viewed in this light, natural ice cave tours are quintessential winter tourism activities, as they are only available from early November to late March and are almost exclusively accessed through guided commercial tours. It therefore does not seem unreasonable to assume that a large number of foreign visitors travelling during the winter to Hornafjörður do so specifically in order to undertake commercial activities that are not available to them during other seasons. The results of our 2016 survey support this conclusion as ice cave tours were the most preferred potential activity indicated by the respondents (72%) and a large proportion of respondents (45%) had actually undertaken such activities (see Fig. 33.10).

The strongest indication of the importance of ice cave tours for winter tourism in Hornafjörður is probably found in the large number of visitors to the caves during winter 2016–2017, recorded on-site by Vatnajökull National Park. Another indication is the growing number of companies, both local and non-local, offering commercial tours to these ice caves. Probing these issues further will require extensive research on whole-year basis, in Hornafjörður and other parts of south Iceland.

Whatever its ultimate cause(s) may be, the 30-fold increase of winter tourism in Hornafjörður over the past 7 years has had widespread effects, not only on the glacier tour operators, but on the local tourism sector as a whole. Hotels, guesthouses and restaurants that used to close for the winter are now open all year round and many of them enjoy very brisk business during the former low season. The transition to whole-year tourism is, arguably, vital to these companies, not just in terms of increased annual sales but in offering a new and much improved way of running their business operations. The local community has benefited as well, both in economic terms and through the influx of new community members, both of Icelandic and foreign origin.

Whether this development can be sustained remains unclear, however, as the natural ice caves are 'volatile' attractions in several ways. First, the number of ice caves suitable for tourism is likely to be limited to two to three main areas in any given winter. Second, there is no way to guarantee the accessibility of any natural ice cave, as the glacier tongues and subglacial tunnels change from year to year. Third, the growing number of tour companies utilizing this limited resource has led to overcrowding of the most accessible caves. Fourth, the emergence and growing popularity of ice cave tours is unlikely to be traced to conventional marketing, as such tours – unlike e.g. Northern Lights tours – have not been the subject of large-scale marketing campaigns. Instead, the increasing interest in such tours appears to stem primarily from customers' 'word-of-mouth' activities on social media. Any negative turn of such social media exposure – e.g. due to overcrowding of caves or overall diminishing quality of tours – could have quite severe repercussions for winter tourism in Hornafjörður.

As this chapter has demonstrated, tourism seasonality has decreased on the national level in Iceland in recent years. However, south Iceland is the only rural region where winter tourism has gained a substantial foothold. The development of extensive winter tourism in Hornafjörður, the most peripheral area of this region, would seem unlikely unless new opportunities for tourism activities, distinct from those available during the summer, had emerged during this period of growth. Natural ice cave tours are only on offer during the wintertime and there is considerable evidence to suggest that the commercialization of such tours had been the most important driving force behind the recent emergence of winter tourism in Hornafjörður. Sustaining winter tourism in the future will require increased attention to quality issues by tour operators (e.g. limiting the number of customers per tour), greater diversification of commercial tour products (thus lessening the overwhelming importance of ice caves), and more control of commercial winter activities by national park and municipal authorities (to ensure the safety of foreign guests visiting the ice caves or hiking on the glaciers). At the time of writing, it is not clear whether the above-mentioned considerations will be attended to in the near future.

Acknowledgements

The authors wish to thank Snævarr Guðmundsson for his assistance in designing Fig. 33.2 and Fig. 33.4.

Note

[1] The use of multiple datasets was required as there is currently no single source available in Iceland that provides up-to-date and/or long-term information about the various facets of tourism seasonality and winter tourism discussed in this chapter.

References

Alþingi (2011) Tillaga til þingsályktunar um ferðamálaáætlun 2011–2020. Available at: https://www.althingi.is/altext/139/s/pdf/0758.pdf (accessed 18 July 2019).

Árnason, Þ. (2013) Vetrarferðamennska í Skaftafellssýslum – þróun og framtíðarmöguleikar. University of Iceland – Hornafjordur Research Center, Höfn, Iceland.

BarOn, R.R.V. (1975) *Seasonality in Tourism*. Economist Intelligence Unit, London.

Baum, T. and Lundtorp, S. (2001) *Tourism Seasonality*. Pergamon, Amsterdam, The Netherlands.

Benediktsson, K., Lund, K.A. and Huijbens, E.H. (2011) Inspired by eruptions? Eyjafjallajökull and Icelandic tourism. *Mobilities* 6(1), 77–84. DOI:10.1080/17450101.2011.532654

Björnsson, H. (2017) *The Glaciers of Iceland. A Historical, Cultural and Scientific Overview*. Springer, New York.

Butler, R.W. (1994) Seasonality in tourism: issues and problems. In: Seaton, A.V. (ed.) *Tourism: The State of the Art*. Wiley, Chichester, UK, pp. 332–339.

Evans, D.J.A. (2016) *Vatnajökull National Park (Southern Region): Guide to a Glacial Landscape Legacy*. Vatnajökull National Park, Reykjavík.

Gil-Alana, L.A. and Huijbens, E.H. (2018) Tourism in Iceland: persistence and seasonality. *Annals of Tourism Research* 68, 20–29. DOI:10.1016/j.annals.2017.11.002

Guðmundsson, R. (2018a) Erlendir vetrarferðamenn, vegir og þjónusta 2017–2018. Rannsóknir og ráðgjöf ferðaþjónustunnar, Hafnarfjörður, Iceland. Available at: www.vegagerdin.is/upplysingar-og-utgafa/rannsoknarskyrslur/umferd/annad/ (accessed 1 June 2018).

Guðmundsson, R. (2018b) Erlendir ferðamenn í Austur-Skaftafellssýslu og að þremur stöðum þar, 2004–2017. Rannsóknir og ráðgjöf ferðaþjónustunnar, Hafnarfjörður, Iceland.

Guðmundsson, S., Björnsson, H. and Pálsson, F. (2017) Changes of Breiðamerkurjökull glacier, SE-Iceland, from its late nineteenth century maximum to the present. *Geografiska Annaler: Series A, Physical Geography* 99(4), 338–352. DOI:10.1080/04353676.2017.1355216

Heimtun, B., Jóhannesson, G.Þ. and Tuulentie, S. (2014) *Northern Lights Tourism in Iceland, Norway and Finland*. The Arctic University of Norway, Tromsø, Norway. DOI:10.7557/7.3266

Icelandic Tourism Board (2018a) Tourism in Iceland in figures 2018. Available at: https://www.ferdamalastofa.is/static/files/ferdamalastofa/Frettamyndir/2018/oktober/tourism-in-iceland-2018.pdf (accessed 1 June 2018).

Icelandic Tourism Board (2018b) Visitors to Iceland through Keflavik Airport, 2003–2018. Available at: https://www.ferdamalastofa.is/en/recearch-and-statistics/numbers-of-foreign-visitors (accessed 1 June 2018).

Icelandic Tourism Board (2018c) Útgefin leyfi – ferðaskipuleggjendur (issued licenses – tour operators). Available at: https://www.ferdamalastofa.is/is/leyfi-og-loggjof/ferdaskipuleggjendur-2006-2018/utgefin-leyfi-ferdaskipuleggjendur (accessed 6 February 2019).

ISAVIA (2017) Annual and CSR report 2016. Available at: https://www.isavia.is/media/1/ars--og-samfelagsskyrsla-2016---enska_x3_m_breytingum_web_x2_230817-.pdf (accessed 1 June 2018).

ISAVIA (2018) Árs- og samfélagsskýrsla 2017. Available at: https://www.isavia.is/media/1/ars-og-samfelagsskyrsla-2017-spreads-v02.pdf (accessed 1 June 2018).

Jackson, M. (2019) *The Secret Lives of Glaciers*. Green Writers Press, Brattleboro, VT.

Jóhannesdóttir, G.R. (2015) Icelandic landscapes: beauty and the aesthetic in environmental decision-making. PhD Thesis, The University of Iceland, Reykjavík, Iceland.

Jóhannesson, G.T. and Huijbens, E.H. (2010) Tourism in times of crisis: exploring the discourse of tourism development in Iceland. *Current Issues in Tourism* 13(5), 419–434. DOI:10.1080/13683500.2010.491897

Koenig-Lewis, N. and Bischoff, E.E. (2005) Seasonality research: the state of the art. *International Journal of Tourism Research* 7, 201–219. DOI:10.1002/jtr.531

Steiger, R., Scott, D., Abegg, B., Pons, M. and Aall, C. (2019) A critical review of climate change risk for ski tourism. *Current Issues in Tourism* 22(11), 1343–1379. DOI:10.1080/13683500.2017.1410110

Tervo-Kankare, K., Hall, C.M. and Saarinen, J. (2013) Christmas tourists' perceptions to climate change in Rovaniemi, Finland. *Tourism Geographies* 15(2), 292–317. DOI:10.1080/14616688.2012.726265

Þórhallsdóttir, G. and Ólafsson, R. (2017) A method to analyse seasonality in the distribution of tourists in Iceland. *Journal of Outdoor Recreation and Tourism* 19, 17–24. DOI:10.1016/j.jort.2017.05.001

Tourism Task Force (2018) *Mælaborð ferðaþjónustunnar* [on-line tourism metrics]. Available at: http://stjornstodin.is/maelabord-ferdathjonustunnar (accessed 1 June 2018).

Vatnajökull National Park (2013) *Stjórnunar- og verndaráætlun*. Available at: https://www.vatnajokulsthjodgardur.is/is/um-thjodgardinn/stjornunar-og-verndaraaetlun (accessed 1 June 2018).

Welling, J. and Árnason, T. (2016) External and internal challenges of glacier tourism development in Iceland. In: Richins, H. and Hull, J.S. (eds) *Mountain Tourism: Experiences, Communities, Environments and Sustainable Futures*. CAB International, Wallingford, UK, pp. 174–183.

Welling, J. and Árnason, Þ. (2019) *Vetrarferðamennska í Ríki Vatnajökuls*. University of Iceland – Hornafjordur Research Center, Höfn, Iceland.

Welling, J.T., Árnason, Þ. and Ólafsdottír, R. (2015) Glacier tourism: a scoping review. *Tourism Geographies* 17(5), 635–662. DOI:10.1080/14616688.2015.1084529

34 Safety, Risk and Accidents – Experiences from the European Alps

ULRIKE PRÖBSTL-HAIDER*

Institute of Landscape Development, Recreation and Conservation Planning, University of Natural Resources and Life Sciences, Vienna, Austria

34.1 Introduction

Alpine skiing is the most popular winter sport discipline in Germany and is performed recreationally by more than 4 million people. Compared with other sporting activities, however, the injury rate in alpine skiing is perceived to be quite high.

Many Austrian regions have made it obligatory for children up to 15 years old to wear a helmet. Parents and supervisors are held responsible and have to ensure compliance with the rule. However, no ski resort has implemented controls or fines for those ignoring this legal requirement. They state that in the case of an accident involving children who are not wearing a helmet it is likely that the insurance company may pay less or nothing towards the necessary treatment. Similar regulations are in place in other countries, such as Slovenia, Croatia and Italy. In Italy, the obligation to wear a helmet for under 14-year-olds is monitored by the police, who are also responsible for mountain rescue on slopes. Children without a helmet lose their ski pass and have to pay a fine of about €200. Switzerland, Germany, France, Sweden, the US and Canada have not made it obligatory to wear a helmet, but have instead opted to invest in campaigns to increase risk awareness among both children and adults.

Recent research findings by Dickson *et al.* (2017), however, explored associations between helmet use and head injuries in snow sports by investigating reported snow sport injuries in western Canada from 2008–2009 to 2012–2013. The key finding was that increased helmet use (from 69% to 80%) was not associated with a reduction in reported head injuries.

The way risks are perceived is also influenced by court decisions. The Higher Regional Court in Munich decided that an injured couple who were not themselves responsible for the accident but had not been wearing helmets were, nevertheless, up to 50% liable (OLG München, 2012). The head judge justified this decision by arguing that skiing cannot be compared with cycling. Skiing is an outdoor recreational activity that is known to be risky and dangerous. Therefore, the joint liability is justified.

However, risk is also a significant motivation drawing people to skiing and snowboarding. This strong emotional component can be described as a 'rush' (a single

---

* E-mail: ulrike.proebstl@boku.ac.at

tangible experience) or the experience of flow and thrill. Experiences that offer such a rush are often risky, but it is this rush rather than the risk it involves that creates the attraction. Rush is addictive and never guaranteed, but the prospect of experiencing a rush is sufficient motivation to participate in an outdoor recreational activity that is known to be risky (Buckley, 2012). However, the role of risk in outdoor recreation is much more complex. Therefore, this chapter will analyse the role of risk and danger in outdoor recreation with a special focus on winter tourism and will then present recent findings on accidents and injuries when practising winter sport activities. Finally, this chapter will provide recommendations to reduce the number of accidents and related injuries in the future, focusing on the European Alps.

34.2 Safety and Risk in Outdoor Recreation

Risk, risk behaviour and the consequences of risk for tourism have been the subject of studies across various disciplines including sociology, psychology, tourism and sports sciences (Aufmuth, 1986; Cube, 1990; Apter, 1992; Le Breton, 1995; Allmer, 1998; Csikszentmihalyi and Jackson, 2000; Haegeli and Pröbstl-Haider, 2016; Stewart-Patterson, 2016). Pröbstl-Haider *et al.* (2016) clarify key terms in this context and summarize main findings on risk and risk-related behaviour in tourism across different research fields. 'Risk' is defined as a consequence of individual decision making, while 'danger' occurs due to specific environmental events and conditions, such as thunderstorms, rock fall or avalanches (Luhmann, 1991). 'Objective risks' relate to natural hazards that cannot be affected by users (such as rock fall), while 'subjective risks' denote a situation in which a person does not accurately judge their ability or fitness according to the challenge lying ahead. The former represents an objectively quantifiable risk relating to the occurrence of dangerous situations or events (Opaschowski, 2000). However, research in the field of psychology has found that there is no such thing as an objective risk (Krimsky and Golding, 1992; Slovic, 1992; Wynne, 1992; Weber, 2001; Slovic and Weber, 2002; and many others). From the psychological point of view, even probabilistic risk estimations by natural scientists are perceived as subjective and assumption-laden, because inputs in theoretic models and concepts also depend on individual judgements, such as the selection of indicators and weighting of parameters. This perspective proposes that research should focus on how people subjectively transform objective risk information and how this transformed information influences their decision making and lives, more generally. This highlights the importance of improving our understanding of people's perception of risks.

Research on risk awareness shows that it is strongly linked to experience and information (Cube, 1990; Luhmann, 1991; Örley, 2014). Therefore, research on outdoor recreational activities focuses a great deal on the influence of experience, skill and self-assessment of an individual's own competence (Dustin *et al.*, 1986; Ewert and Hollenhorst, 1989). Many authors in outdoor recreation research explain behavioural patterns based on individuals' experience and/or commitment to their activity of choice (Dustin *et al.*, 1986; Grant *et al.*, 1995). A distinction is often made between an introductory, a development and a high-commitment stage. Those pursuing recreational activities at the introductory stage have basic skill levels, often prefer to participate in group and/or guided activities and typically delegate risk management concerns to a group leader. Individuals at this stage typically perceive risk as a discomfort. Individuals at the development stage commonly exercise a degree of individual control over their activity, whether they are guided by leaders or are in the presence of similarly experienced peers (Grant *et al.*, 1996). At this stage, the handling of a manageable degree of risk becomes an important part of the overall experience. At the high-commitment stage, recreational activities are pursued by experienced individuals who typically possess higher skill levels and who may participate in activities in more hazardous environments (Keyes, 1985). The risk awareness in this group is high, but risk is also perceived as a (positive) stimulant (Robinson, 1992; Ewert, 1994; Buckley, 2012). Further research has also shown the influence of other factors on risk perception including the frequency of participation; locus of control and motivational factors; the setting and environmental conditions; environmental and social orientation; as well as the individual's risk perception (Ewert and Hollenhorst, 1989). Furthermore, individuals are not consistently risk-seeking or risk-averse across all domains and situations, even when the same assessment method is applied (Schoemaker, 1990; Weber *et al.*, 2002). Risk-taking is not simply a personal attitude but is the result of a trade-off decision in any given situation (Weber *et al.*, 2002).

A cross-cutting meta-analysis (Byrnes *et al.*, 1999) also revealed significant gender differences indicating that, overall, men display more risk-taking behaviour – but again demonstrating significant differences across various domains. Women and families with children tend to take fewer risks and their risk awareness is higher (Weber *et al.*, 1998; Glaeßer, 2005).

Psychological research on risk has focused on how humans process information about dangerous situations and possible risks and how they make judgements or arrive at decisions (Epstein, 1994; Sloman, 1996; Chaiken and Trope, 1999; Slovic *et al.*, 2002). Slovic and Weber (2002) describe two fundamentally different modes of decision making:

- The association- and affect-driven process, which is intuitive, automatic and fast.
- The rule- and reason-based process, which is based on knowledge and prior experiences.

Risk perception is influenced by association- and affect-driven processes as much as – or more than – by rule- and reason-based processes (Loewenstein *et al.*, 2001). In cases in which the two processing systems generate diverging outcomes, the association- and affect-driven processes usually prevail. Slovic and Weber (2002) underline that the relationship and interplay between the two processing models are further complicated by the way they seem to depend on how people receive information about the magnitude and likelihood of possible events. The authors highlight that the challenge people are faced with when managing risks is to conquer the complex interplay between the more emotional association- and affect-driven and the rule- and reason-based processes.

New tourism offers use this complex interplay under the umbrella of 'adventure', avoiding the terms risk and danger, but emphasizing the flow feeling (Swarbrooke *et al.*, 2003; Williams and Soutar, 2009; Csikszentmihalyi, 2017). According to Humphreys (2014) adventure is a state of mind, a spirit of trying something new and leaving your comfort zone. Adventure tourism offers present themselves in the context of enthusiasm, ambition, open-mindedness and curiosity. Winter tourism destinations face the challenging task to fulfil these adventurous dreams while providing a safe environment.

34.3 Safety Concepts in Winter Tourism Resorts

The development of detailed safety concepts have become standard practice in well-managed winter tourism businesses worldwide. A resort's management is expected to keep skiers safe from so-called objective risks such as avalanches and to reduce subjective risks by monitoring the slopes, providing its guests with relevant information, ensuring adequate sign posting and safety precautions, and by fencing off dangerous areas. However, the legal obligations to maintain safety measures in organized skiing space significantly differ from those in free skiing space (see Table 34.1). In Europe, the so-called 'organized skiing areas' consist of all marked ski pistes and/or routes, but do not include additional alternative opportunities. Outside of this organized skiing space in the so-called 'free skiing space', any risk is generally considered a question of the skier's personal responsibility. Furthermore, safety issues are linked to environmental conditions and the danger they are perceived to cause, as well as the skier's respective personal responsibility. Regarding the legal obligation to maintain safety on ski slopes, typical and atypical hazards are differentiated. Typical hazards usually include obstacles inherent in the terrain, moguls, individual spots clear of snow and variable snow conditions, but also marking rods and signposts.

From the point of view of environmental management, operators must either eliminate potential atypical hazards or give sufficient warning (Dambeck and Wagner, 2007). Hazards are considered atypical if a skier cannot be expected to anticipate them, given the appearance and designated difficulty level of the piste. These include obstacles such as concrete blocks, ditches, stones or boulders. They are only considered atypical, however, if they are not visible from a distance (Dambeck and Wagner, 2007). National legislations need to be considered because different countries often vary in these points, also regarding the personal responsibility of the skier.

In legal disputes, judgements usually consider the extent of the hazard, the degree of perceptibility, the reasonability of security measures and the capability of those responsible for ensuring safety, as well as the type of measures in place (e.g. warnings, protective measures, removal or fencing off). If operators consider a hazard's degree of perceptibility to be low and prefer to remove it rather than to rely on warnings or protective measures, such actions may have environmental effects. Moreover, the legal obligation to maintain safety standards is limited to the operating times of lifts and usually ends with the control run. This aspect is also significant in relation to environmental management. A clear marking of the piste edge is especially important in this

Table 34.1. Legal obligation to maintain safety in a ski area in the European Alps. (After Pröbstl-Haider *et al.*, 2019.)

Organized skiing space		Free skiing space
Piste	Ski route	Alternative route
Marked	Marked	Unmarked
Graded with sufficient width	No defined width	Not graded
Mostly groomed	Ungroomed	Ungroomed
Controlled	Not controlled	Not controlled
Secured against atypical and alpine hazards	Secured against avalanches	Not secured against alpine hazards

regard. Narrow sections, piste crossings, as well as crossings with footpaths or roads, tow lifts and facilities for piste grooming need to be clearly flagged by warning signs, if they constitute a potential hazard. The legal obligation to maintain safety also pertains to areas away from the slopes, e.g. paths leading to parking areas, toilets or transportation facilities. The question of liability is also influenced by publicized codes of conduct (e.g. the International Ski Federation (FIS) rules) and other information that has a positive effect on self-protection.

The risk of an accident involving another skier or snowboarder on the slope is often underestimated. Here, ski resorts try to influence their customers' behaviour and decision making by promoting rules of conduct, risk avoidance and asking them to be mindful of other guests. However, these efforts to enhance rule- and reason-based decision making and behaviour have certain limitations. 'Too much' signposting can be disadvantageous, however, because it still needs to be effective in varying snow and weather conditions. What is more, extensive signposting can create the subjective impression that no hazards need be observed wherever warning signs are absent.

34.4 Accidents and Injuries Related to Alpine Skiing

The following paragraphs will present an overview and discussion of prevalent accidents and injuries over the past 30 years. Analyses of accidents and injuries help us to understand the circumstances and reasons behind risk-related behaviour, such as speed or choosing a steep slope.

34.4.1 Methodological approach

The presented data of a long-term monitoring conducted since 1979/80 are based on information provided by skiers who were involved in an accident. When claiming their insurance, they were asked to fill in a questionnaire and explain the circumstances surrounding their accident and the related injuries. This database is, therefore, based on information given voluntarily and collected by the respective insurance company. The database, moreover, covers 38 years, which allows for an analysis of long-term trends, as well as an understanding of the influence of new equipment such as carving skis. The database only includes skiers from Germany. However, since German skiers account for around 50–60% of guests in alpine winter sport destinations in Austria, Bavaria, South Tyrol and certain destinations in Switzerland, the findings are highly relevant for all alpine destinations and most likely representative of key problems. The data presented here use 4.2 million active skiers as a baseline for calculation. In this study, only those injuries were included that required treatment by a medical doctor.

34.4.2 Current situation and trends

Based on the data collected in 2017 and 2018, the number of injured skiers is currently ~41,000 to 43,000 per year. These figures have not changed much over the past 5–10 years. However, compared with the first recorded statistics in the season of 1979/80, there has been a significant reduction in the percentage of injured skiers in relation to the total amount of skiers. If the season of 1979/80 is set as the baseline at 100%, the reduction is around 58% (see Fig. 34.1).

In the last season included in this database (winter season 2017/18) about 7400 to 7600 skiers needed in-patient treatment in hospital (Schulz, 2018). In addition, Fig. 34.2 shows that the number of severe injuries is continuously declining. However, this piece of good news is not only the result of a decline in major injuries but

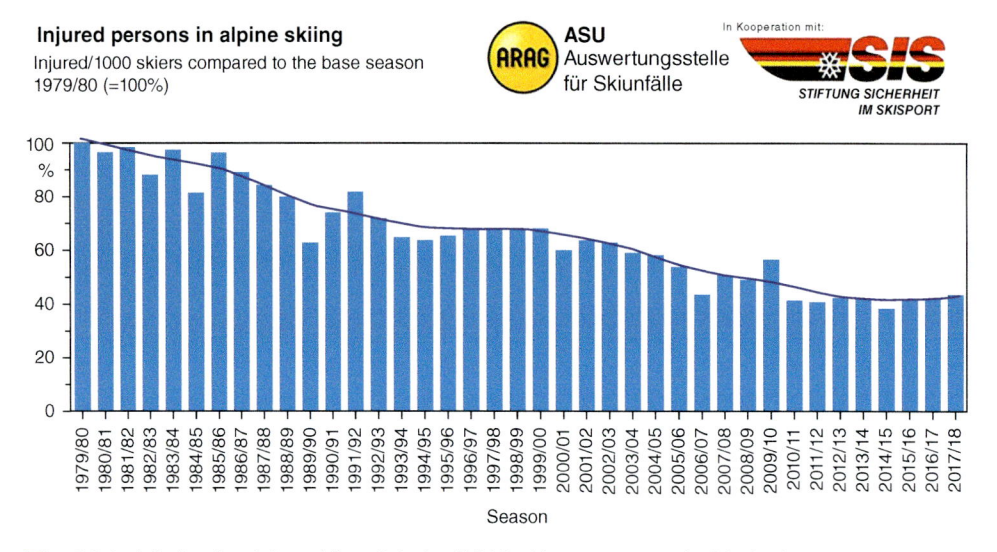

Fig. 34.1. Injuries in alpine skiing, injuries/1000 skiers compared with the base season 1979/80 (= 100%). (Figure courtesy of ARAG, Evaluation centre for ski accidents – in cooperation with the Safety in Ski Sport Foundation; translated from Schulz, 2018.)

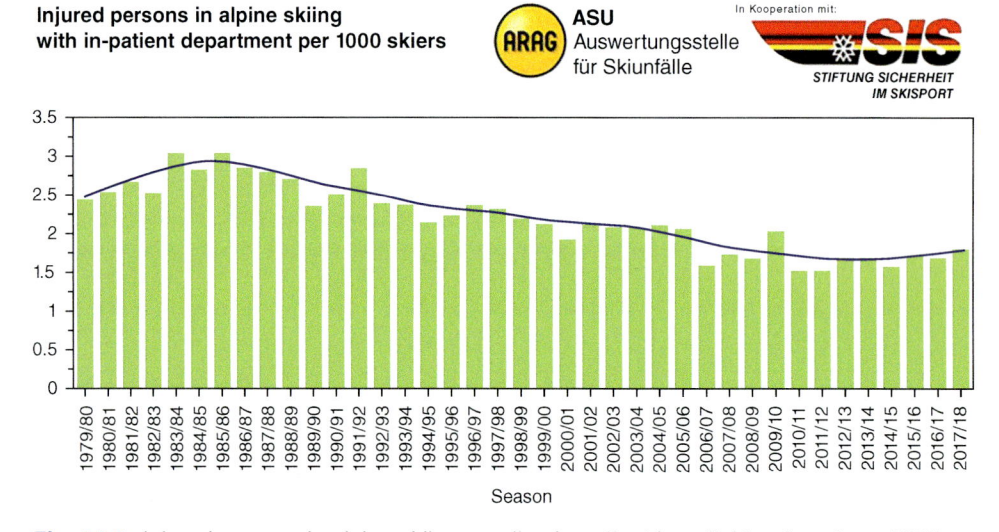

Fig. 34.2. Injured persons in alpine skiing needing in-patient hospital treatment per 1000 skiers. (Figure courtesy of ARAG, Evaluation centre for ski accidents – in cooperation with the Safety in Ski Sport Foundation; translated from Schulz, 2018.)

is also linked to the advancement of different medical treatments that do not require a long hospital stay anymore.

34.4.3 Injury profile

Figure 34.3 provides a simple overview of the parts of the body most often affected by injuries. Contrary to the illustration shown in Section 34.4.2 (see Fig. 34.1), however, it does not allow us to detect the degree of risk involved, as there is no corresponding reference value. The inclusion of gender as a category of analysis has proven to be worthwhile, as there are significant differences in injury distribution between men and women. Knee and shoulder injuries are the most common injuries.

Injury localization for adults over 15 years of age

Head injuries accounted for 10.8% of all injuries. Men are significantly more often affected by head injuries than women (11.1% vs. 10.2%). The proportion of shoulder injuries, however, decreased by 2% for men and by 3% for women compared with the previous season (2016/17). Nevertheless, the difference between the sexes is still significant, since men are twice as often affected by shoulder injuries as women.

Fig. 34.3. Injured body areas of skiers. (Figure courtesy of ARAG, Evaluation centre for ski accidents – in cooperation with the Safety in Ski Sport Foundation; adapted from Schulz, 2018.)

The percentage of torso injuries presents a similar picture, though it should be noted that injuries in this part of the body occur more than three times as often in men as in women (11.8% vs. 3.3%).

Almost one-third of all skiing injuries affect the knees. The percentage of female skiers suffering knee injuries has remained significantly higher than that of male skiers (42.9% vs. 26.4%). It should be noted that the percentage of knee injuries among men has also slightly increased compared with the previous season 2016/17 (23.4%) (Schulz, 2018). Hence, the knees are still the most frequently injured parts of the body in alpine skiing.

Development of injury localization

Similar to the rise in previous years, the risk of suffering a knee injury while skiing has slightly increased from 2.7 to 2.89 per 1000 skiers (comparing 2016/17 with 2017/18). This increase demonstrates once again that, despite an overall decline in the risk of knee injuries, it is still a major problem in skiing.

A look at other parts of the body at risk of injury reveals that the risk of shoulder injuries has slightly risen compared with the previous season (from 2.44 to 2.46 per 1000 skiers). The risk of injury in the torso/hip/thigh area has also increased from 1.78 to 1.91 per 1000 skiers (Schulz, 2017, 2018). Compared with the previous year's data, the risk of injury of the forearm and hand, head and neck, or feet and lower leg has slightly decreased (Schulz, 2018). Over the long term, head and neck injuries have approximately halved since 1979/80 (see Fig. 34.4). With regard to head injuries, it should again be mentioned that, according to scientific studies, the use of ski helmets has more influence on the severity of head injuries than on their number (Dickson et al., 2017; Milan et al., 2017).

Collision accidents

Compared with the previous season, the risk of collision accidents has slightly increased. In addition to obvious collisions, cases of lighter collision and impediment are also included in this calculation whenever the injured skiers indicated that they were responsible for the accident. It must be emphasized that the proportion of accidents caused by collisions is unacceptably high, accounting for 16% (Schulz, 2018).

Overall, the data collected previously and the data from the last winter season (2016/17) show that the overall risk could be significantly reduced. Especially the widespread use of helmets has reduced the amount of severe head injuries. However, the risk of a shoulder or knee injury is slowly increasing. One reason behind this development can be found in improved technology and the introduction of the carving ski, which enables skiers to move at faster speeds. The study also revealed significant differences between men and women. Knee injuries are more common in women, while shoulder injuries more often occur in male skiers.

Studies assume that women are more likely not to practise other sports and, therefore, cannot absorb the extra strain on the thigh muscles which in turn impacts the knee. The prevalence of shoulder injuries in men has been linked to higher speeds, which can contribute to shoulder injuries in the event of a fall.

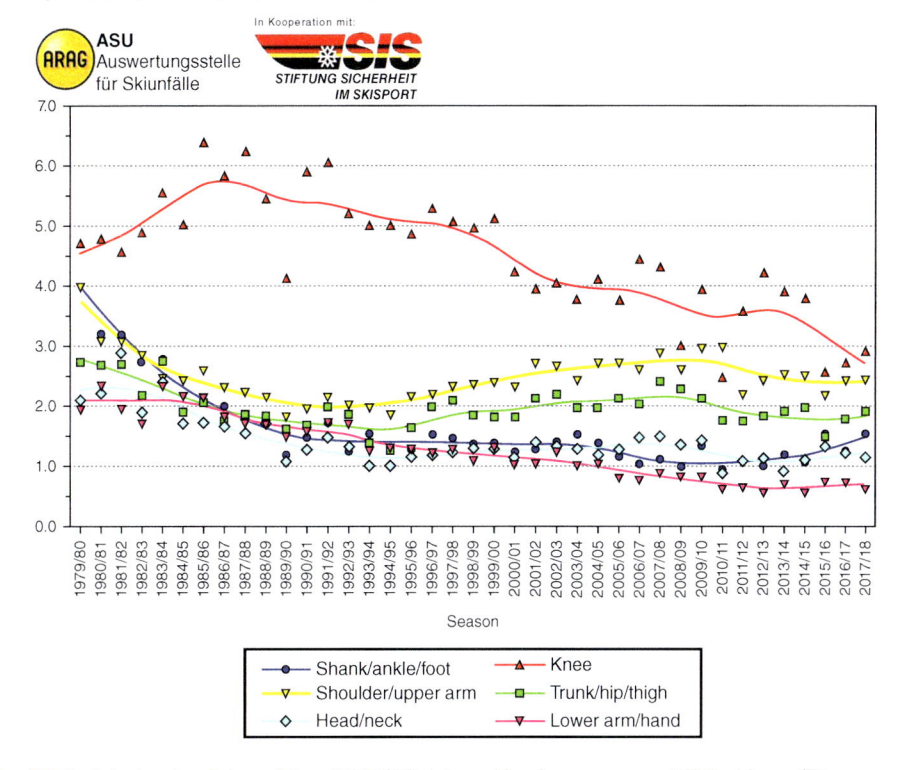

Fig. 34.4. Injuries in alpine skiing 2017/18, injured body areas per 1000 skiers. (Figure courtesy of ARAG, Evaluation centre for ski accidents – in cooperation with the Safety in Ski Sport Foundation; translated from Schulz, 2018.)

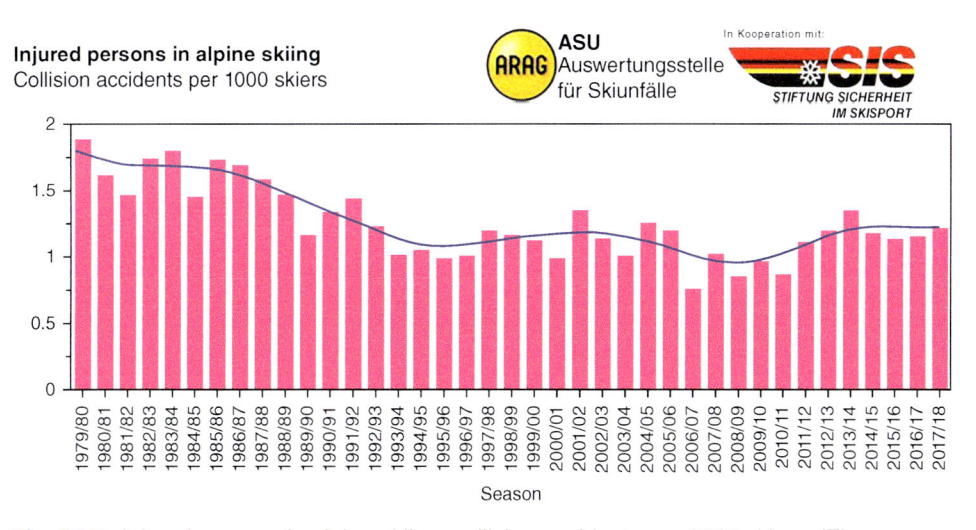

Fig. 34.5. Injured persons in alpine skiing, collision accidents per 1000 skiers. (Figure courtesy of ARAG, Evaluation centre for ski accidents – in cooperation with the Safety in Ski Sport Foundation; translated from Schulz, 2018.)

Table 34.2. Ranking of sport activities presenting the percentage of injured active sportsmen for Austria. (From Bässler, 2002; Steiner and Bauer, 2002, as cited in Kisser, 2002.)

Ranking	Activity	Population	Injured	Risk
1	Football	700,000	38,000	5.4
2	Volleyball	700,000	12,000	1.7
3	Snowboarding	1,000,000	12,000	1.2
4	Downhill skiing	2,800,000	26,000	0.9
5	Cycling	3,800,000	21,000	0.6
6	Ice skating, ice hockey	1,300,000	8,000	0.6
7	Inline skating	1,000,000	6,000	0.6
8	Tennis	1,000,000	5,000	0.5
9	Running	1,900,000	6,000	0.3
10	Hiking, mountaineering	3,200,000	7,000	0.2

Studies have also shown that the risk of a collision accident is on the increase. A total of 16% of all injuries are currently caused by collisions. Collisions are, therefore, still one of the most significant causes of accidents. The skiing industry may consider this issue a good starting point for their efforts to reduce injuries on slopes and adopt suitable measures to remedy the high number of collisions.

However, a conclusive comparison with other outdoor recreational activities sports seems difficult. To determine whether or not skiing is a risky sport is not an easy task as the statistical compilations of injuries and injury risk are two different matters.

Further factors to consider range from the number of sports hours performed (accidents with a doctor's visit per 1000 h of sport) (Bässler, 2002) to accidents per 1000 days of sport's practice and the number of accident victims in relation to the number of people performing the sport in question (Schulz, 2017). The ranking of sport activities showing the relation between the number of active sportsman and the amount of injured persons indicates that overall the risk of getting injured when skiing is considerably lower than the risk for football or volleyball (see Table 34.2).

34.5 Recommendations

34.5.1 Recommendations for ski resort management

In light of the analyses of ski accidents representative for the European Alps over the past decades, it is obvious that safety measures set up by enterprises alone are not enough to reduce accidents and severe injuries. However, an enterprise can help reduce accidents, especially in relation to injuries caused by collisions. Recommendations to improve safety-related aspects in ski areas (during winter use) include:

- the provision of overview maps for orientation concerning all forms of use, including a guidance system and section overviews demarcating difficulty levels and currently closed-off areas;
- information about potential hazards (e.g. avalanches, snow conditions, change of weather);

- clearly marked piste edges, particularly at crossings, exits and in areas with increased hazards located outside of the slopes;
- marking of hazard areas;
- securing atypical hazard areas;
- securing piste edges with atypical hazards;
- publicizing a code of conduct;
- providing a point of contact for security issues within the business; and
- publicizing emergency facilities (e.g. mountain rescue service).

So-called safety plans, including a consultation with experts during a piste inspection, have often proven valuable for businesses during the environmental management process. Experts in North America (CSSSO, 2009), further, recommend regular speed reading. Measures to manage the number of skiers allowed on slopes, e.g. by limiting the number of lift tickets sold, is difficult since the number alone has no influence on the overall spatial distribution and the respective distribution during the day. Many collisions occur at the end of the day on those pistes leading to the exit or the main transportation means. If the ski area is also used for summer tourism, there are a number of additional aspects that need to be considered (Seilbahnen Schweiz, 2011).

Further measures to reduce accidents and severe injuries need to target skiers themselves in order to promote behavioural changes. In order to avoid knee injuries, for example, appropriate preparation is essential, ideally to be undertaken throughout the year. Speed should not only be adapted to the particular slope conditions, but also to one's own ability. In order to raise awareness for these aspects, ski lifts can implement the following measures:

- Providing information at lifts, especially in the waiting area, concerning proper conduct and the importance of warming up. It would also be important to use videos instead of blackboards to communicate rules of behaviour or to motivate people to warm up.
- The design of facilities can encourage skiers to warm up. Ski resorts are currently missing an opportunity in this regard, as ski areas are increasingly accessed via escalators.
- Off-piste dangers should also be better communicated with the help of videos. This information should also take the interests of local wildlife into account.[1]
- An app has been launched to promote special training regimes for skiers, which demonstrates simple exercises that can be incorporated in everyday life. This (or similar) applications could be adopted by operators and promoted in the spirit of good customer relations, including featured promotion on their own websites.
- A new type of safety training represents the most recent addition to this discussion. It uses specialized eyeglasses to show the speed at which the skier is travelling and how long it would take him/her to stop at this speed. This technology could provide a valuable teaching experience for young people in particular and could lead to new insights. However, there are no known examples of a practical application of such technologies or related research findings, as yet.

34.5.2 Recommendations for skiing enthusiasts

While thrill, rush and the excitement generated by high speeds may lead to dangerous behaviour, the figures presented here show that severe injuries are often the result of a lack of exercise throughout the year, rather than the activity itself.

A closer look at the gendered breakdown of different types of injuries reveals that the knee is significantly more often injured in the female segment compared with the male. One reason for this 'typical female injury' is the fact that many women are not physically active during the summer season. For example, the important hamstring muscles (the medial hamstring contributes to medial rotation of the leg at the flexed knee joint, while the lateral hamstring contributes to lateral rotation) are not sufficiently exercised and, consequently, cannot adequately support the knee. New trends – such as ski associations promoting a training app and other awareness raising campaigns – play a crucial role in encouraging all-year-round activities aimed at strengthening the leg muscles. However, these findings also hold true for other tourists who are not adequately prepared for their winter tourism activities. Regular visits to fitness studios, Nordic walking or specially developed workouts for skiers are, therefore, highly recommended. Appropriate and well-maintained equipment also contributes to greater safety in skiing (BFU, 2018).

Shoulder and arm injuries more often affect men. Medical experts point to high or disproportionate speed as the main causes for such injuries in men. In this case, effective recommendations are much more difficult to formulate. However, statistics show that most accidents occur in the afternoon and on the third day of the holiday. Experts believe that the main reason for this phenomenon can be found in decreasing concentration levels in the afternoon and after several days. Therefore, since speed requires high levels of concentration as well as skiers' vigilance, recommendations emphasize the need for sensible planning, such as taking regular breaks during a day of skiing and incorporating other activities into the holiday, such as half a day of recuperation at a spa or enjoying the winter landscape in a horse-drawn sleigh.

Note

[1] See for example the following campaign video published by the Alpine Network of Protected Areas, available at: https://www.youtube.com/watch?v=Y2-n4wUEm3g (accessed 6 February 2019).

References

Allmer, H. (1998) 'No risk – no fun' – Zur psychologischen Erklärung von Extrem- und Risikosport. In: Allmer, H. and Schulz, N. (eds) *Erlebnissport - Erlebnis Sport*. Brennpunkte der Sportwissenschaft, Academia Verlag, St. Augustin, Germany, pp. 60–90.
Apter, M.J. (1992) *The Dangerous Edge: the Psychology of Excitement*. Free Press, New York.
Aufmuth, U. (1986) Risikosport und Identitätsbegehren. Überlegungen am Beispiel des Extremalpinismus. In: Hortleder, G. and Gebauer, G. (eds) *Sport – Eros – Tod*. Suhrkamp, Frankfurt, Germany, pp. 188–215.
Bässler, R (2002) Unfallrisiko im Sport. Quantifizierung des Unfallrisikos beim Sporttreiben. Report prepared for 'Institut Sicher Leben', Vienna, Austria.
BFU (Beratungsstelle für Unfallverhütung) (2018) Ratgeber Unfallverhütung, Sport und Bewegung, Skifahren. Available at: https://www.bfu.ch/de/ratgeber/ratgeber-unfallverh%C3%BCtung/sport-und-bewegung/wintersport/skifahren/skifahren-tipps (accessed 22 December 2018).

Buckley, R. (2012) Rush as a key motivation in skilled adventure tourism: resolving the risk recreation paradox. *Tourism Management* 33(4), 961–970. DOI:10.1016/j.tourman.2011.10.002

Byrnes, J.P., Miller, D.C. and Schafer, W.D. (1999) Gender differences in risk taking: a meta-analysis. *Psychological Bulletin* 125(3), 367–383. DOI:10.1037/0033-2909.125.3.367

Chaiken, S. and Trope, Y. (1999) *Dual-Process Theories in Social Psychology*. Guilford Press, New York.

Csikszentmihalyi, M. (2017) *Flow: Das Geheimnis des Glücks*. Klett-Cotta, Stuttgart, Germany.

Csikszentmihalyi, M. and Jackson, S. (2000) *Flow im Sport: der Schlüssel zur optimalen Erfahrung und Leistung*. BLV, Munich, Germany.

CSSSO (California Ski and Snowboard Safety Organization) (2009) Ski resorts celebrate national safety awareness week while keeping patrons in the dark about safety plans. Press release, 16 January 2009.

Cube, F. (1990) *Gefährliche Sicherheit. Die Verhaltensbiologie des Risikos*. Piper, Munich, Germany.

Dambeck, G. and Wagner, H. (2007) *Recht und Sicherheit im organisierten Skiraum*. Interski Vermittlungs-, Reise- und Verlags-GmbH, Planegg, Germany.

Dickson, T.J., Trathen, S., Terwiel, F.A., Waddington, G. and Adams, R. (2017) Head injury trends and helmet use in skiers and snowboarders in Western Canada, 2008–2009 to 2012–2013: an ecological study. *Scandinavian Journal of Medicine and Science in Sports* 27(2), 236–244. DOI:10.1111/sms.12642.

Dustin, D.L., McAvoy, L.H. and Beck, L.A. (1986) Promoting recreationist self-sufficiency. *Journal of Park and Recreation Administration* 4(4), 43–52.

Epstein, S. (1994) Integration of the cognitive and the psychodynamic unconscious. *American Psychologist* 49(8), 709–724. DOI:10.1037//0003-066X.49.8.709

Ewert, A. (1994) Playing the edge: motivation and risk taking in a high-altitude wilderness like environment. *Environment and Behavior* 26(1), 3–24. DOI:10.7771/2327-2937.1016

Ewert, A. and Hollenhorst, S. (1989) Testing the adventure recreation model: empirical support for a model of risk recreation participation. *Journal of Leisure Research* 21(2), 124–139. DOI:10.1080/00222216.1989.11969794

Glaeßer, D. (2005) *Handbuch Krisenmanagement im Tourismus: Erfolgreiches Entscheiden in schwierigen Situationen*. Erich Schmidt, Berlin.

Grant, B.C., Thompson, S.M. and Boyes, M. (1996) Risk and responsibility in outdoor recreation. *Journal of Physical Education, Recreation and Dance* 67(7), 34–36. DOI:10.1080/07303084.1996.10604817

Haegeli, P. and Pröbstl-Haider, U. (2016) Research on personal risk in outdoor recreation and nature-based tourism. *Journal of Outdoor Recreation and Tourism* 13, 1–9. DOI:10.1016/j.jort.2016.02.001

Humphreys, A. (2014) *Microadventures: Local Discoveries for Great Escapes*. HarperCollins, New York.

Keyes, R. (1985) *Chancing It: Why We Take Risks*. Little Brown, Boston, Massachusetts.

Kisser, R. (2002) Epidemiologie des Verletzungsgeschehens. Wie gefährlich ist Sport? – ein Vergleich von Daten aus Deutschland, Österreich und der Schweiz. In: Kuratorium für Schutz und Sicherheit (ed.) *Mit Sicherheit mehr Sport*. Kuratorium für Schutz und Sicherheit, Vienna, pp. 49–61.

Krimsky, S. and Golding, D. (1992) *Social Theories of Risk*. Praeger, Westport, Connecticut.

Le Breton, D. (1995) *Lust am Risiko: von Bungee-jumping, U-Bahn-surfen und anderen Arten, das Schicksal herauszufordern*. Dipa, Frankfurt, Germany.

Loewenstein, G.F., Weber, E.U., Hsee, C.K. and Welch, N. (2001) Risk as feelings. *Psychological Bulletin* 127(2), 267–286. DOI:10.1037/0033-2909.127.2.267

Luhmann, N. (1991) *Soziologie des Risikos*. De Gruyter, Berlin.

Milan, M., Jhajj, S., Stewart, C., Pyle, L. and Moulton, S. (2017) Helmet use and injury severity among pediatric skiers and snowboarders in Colorado. *Journal of Pediatric Surgery* 52(2), 349–353. DOI:10.1016/j.jpedsurg.2016.11.001

OLG München (2012) Court decision from 22.03.2012, Az.: 8 U 3652/11. Schadensminderung wegen Mitverschuldens des Geschädigten aufgrund der Nichtbenutzung eines Ski-Helmes. Available at: https://research.wolterskluwer-online.de/document/70a16a15-a49b-41dc-9da0-fbcfae3e6306 (accessed 16 July 2019).

Opaschowski, H.W. (2000) *Xtrem: Der kalkulierte Wahnsinn. Extremsport als Zeitphänomen.* Germa Press, Hamburg, Germany.

Örley, F. (2014) *Die Lust am Risiko: warum Extremsportler ihr Leben für den Sport riskieren.* Disserta Verlag, Hamburg, Germany.

Pröbstl-Haider, U., Brom, M., Dorsch, C. and Jiricka-Pürrer, A. (2019) *Environmental Management in Ski Areas: Procedure – Requirements – Exemplary Solutions*. Springer, Berlin. DOI:10.1007/978-3-319-75061-3

Pröbstl-Haider, U., Dabrowska, K. and Haider, W. (2016) Risk perception and preferences of mountain tourists in light of glacial retreat and permafrost degradation in the Austrian Alps. *Journal of Outdoor Recreation and Tourism* 13, 66–78. DOI:10.1016/j.jort.2016.02.002

Robinson, D.W. (1992) A descriptive model of enduring risk recreation involvement. *Journal of Leisure Research* 24(1), 52–63. DOI:10.1080/00222216.1992.11969871

Schoemaker, P.J.H. (1990) Are risk-attitudes related across domains and response modes? *Management Science* 36(12), 1451–1463. DOI:10.1287/mnsc.36.12.1451

Schulz, D. (2017) Unfälle und Verletzungen im alpinen Skisport, Zahlen und Trends der Saison 2016/2017. ARAG, Düsseldorf, Germany. Available at: https://www.ski-online.de/files/dsv-aktiv/PDF/Projekte/ASU-Unfallanalyse-2016-2017.pdf (accessed 10 June 2018).

Schulz, D. (2018) Unfälle und Verletzungen im alpinen Skisport, Zahlen und Trends der Saison 2017/2018. ARAG, Düsseldorf, Germany. Available at: https://www.deutscherskiverband.de/datei.php?system_id=1362846 (accessed 10 January 2019).

Seilbahnen Schweiz (2011) Checkliste Verkehrssicherungspflicht für Sommeraktivitäten, Arbeitsgruppe Sommeraktivitäten von Seilbahnen Schweiz. Seilbahn Schweiz, Bern, Switzerland.

Sloman, S.A. (1996) The empirical case for two systems of reasoning. *Psychological Bulletin* 119(1), 3–22. DOI:10.1037/0033-2909.119.1.3

Slovic, P. (1992) Perception of risk: reflections on the psychometric paradigm. In: Krimsky, S. and Golding, D. (eds) *Social Theories of Risk*. Praeger, Westport, Connecticut, pp. 117–152.

Slovic, P. and Weber, U.E. (2002) Perception of risk posed by extreme events (prepared for discussion at 'The Conference on Risk Management Strategies in an Uncertain World', Palisades, New York, 12–13 April 2002). Available at: wws.princeton.edu/system/files/research/documents/Perception%20of%20risk_2013_Regulation%20of%20Toxic%20Substances%20and%20Hazardous%20Waste_Slovic.pdf (accessed 6 February 2019).

Slovic, P., Finucane, M.L., Peters, E. and MacGregor, D.G. (2002) The affect heuristic. In: Gilovich, T., Griffin, D. and Kahneman, D. (eds) *Heuristics and Biases: The Psychology of Intuitive Judgment*. Cambridge University Press, New York, pp. 397–420.

Stewart-Patterson, I. (2016) Measuring decision expertise in commercial ski guiding in a more meaningful way. *Journal of Outdoor Recreation and Tourism* 13, 44–48. DOI:10.1016/j.jort.2015.11.009

Swarbrooke, J., Beard, C., Leckie, S. and Pomfret, G. (2003) *Adventure Tourism: the New Frontier*. Butterworth Heinemann, Oxford, UK.

Weber, E.U. (2001) Personality and risk taking. In: Smelser, N.J. and Baltes, P.B. (eds) *International Encyclopedia of the Social and Behavioral Sciences*. Elsevier Science Limited, Oxford, UK, pp. 11274–11276.

Weber, E.U., Hsee, C.K. and Sokolowska, J. (1998) What folklore tells us about risk and risk taking: cross-cultural comparisons of American, German, and Chinese proverbs. *Organizational Behavior and Human Decision Processes* 75(2), 170–186. DOI:10.1006/obhd.1998.2788

Weber, E.U., Blais, A.-R. and Betz, N.E. (2002) A domain-specific risk-attitude scale: measuring risk perceptions and risk behaviors. *Journal of Behavioral Decision Making* 15(4), 263–290. DOI:10.1002/bdm.414

Williams, P. and Soutar, G.N. (2009) Value, satisfaction and behavioural intentions in an adventure tourism context. *Annals of Tourism Research* 36(3), 413–443.

Wynne, B. (1992) Risk and social learning: reification to engagement. In: Krimsky, S. and Golding, D. (eds) *Social Theories of Risk*. Praeger, Westport, Connecticut, pp. 275–300.

35 Collaboration and Leadership as Success Factors of a Ski Resort – A Multiple Case Study from Finland

Raija Komppula* and Emma Alegria

Business School, University of Eastern Finland, Joensuu, Finland

35.1 Introduction

The aim of this chapter is to investigate stakeholders' perceptions of the factors affecting the success of a destination, in this case the three biggest ski resorts in Finland. This study does not try to explain the success or failure. Instead, it introduces stakeholders' perceptions of the contribution of different kinds of stakeholders to the growth and success of the ski resorts in question. Success in this case is measured by growth in overnights and turnover of ski pass ticket purchases, following Bornhorst *et al.* (2010). Their study is a rare example of research discussing in-depth determinants of destination success, particularly those that can be affected by the tourism enterprises and other local actors. Bornhorst *et al.* (2010) state that achieving success in tourism is challenging and still not very well understood. This study is an attempt to fill this gap in knowledge.

There are around 100 ski resorts in Finland, the smallest of them having only one lift and two slopes, while the largest resort, Levi, has 43 slopes and 28 lifts and 230 km of cross-country tracks (Finnish Ski Area Association, 2018). There are approximately half a million active downhill skiers in Finland, and some 1.3 million active cross-country skiers – 'active' meaning that the person has been doing the activity during the ongoing season (Finnish Ski Area Association, 2014, 2016). A Finnish skier spends an average of 9 days downhill skiing per year, but would prefer to ski 16 days. A total of 27% of the Finnish downhill skiers are loyal to one ski resort, but more than half of the skiers visit several domestic ski resorts during a season (Finnish Ski Area Association, 2016). The most important ski resorts are located in the Finnish Lapland, in a distance of 800–1100 km from the main domestic market, i.e. the capital area. Domestic skiers comprise the most important target market for all the Finnish ski resorts, and especially those located in Lapland attract ski tourists from all parts of Finland.

This chapter presents a multiple case study from northern Finland, comparing the three biggest ski resorts (measured by ski lift turnover), namely Levi, Ruka and Ylläs. Measured by value of ski pass turnover, during the 1996/97 season both Ylläs and

---

* E-mail: raija.komppula@uef.fi

Levi had a turnover of around €2.2 million, with Ruka having a turnover of almost €3.5 million. Over the next 10 years Levi caught up with Ruka, and in the 2006/07 season both had a turnover of around €6.5 million, and Ylläs less at €3.9 million. Similar kinds of development can be seen from the overnight statistics, particularly after the year 2008, when the overnights in Ylläs started to decrease and those in Levi and Ruka increased rapidly. The growth in the number of available beds in these resorts has been quite steady in all the resorts, as has the fluctuation of room occupation rates. Based on these facts it can be argued that Levi and Ruka have been able to increase significantly their popularity among tourists, while the growth of Ylläs has been much slower. Nevertheless, if we compare the natural resources of Ylläs, measured by highest elevation in the slopes, length of the slopes or number of slopes, or even the amount of cross-country skiing tracks, Ylläs would be the number one.

According to previous studies, the most important attributes affecting consumers' ski destination choice are price (e.g. Richards, 1996), snow quality and diversity of the ski terrain (e.g. Godfrey, 1999) and the overall destination image (e.g. Ferrand and Vecciatini, 2002). As it can be argued that the market, as well as snow and weather conditions are more or less the same for Levi, Ylläs and Ruka, all of them being located in northern Finland, the attractiveness to the customers appears to be related to the perceived image of the resort, and dependent on the activities of the stakeholders in the resort (Komppula and Laukkanen, 2016). Komppula's (2014) findings in a Finnish rural destination emphasize the importance of different stakeholders, especially entrepreneurs and municipalities, in the development and success of a destination. As several studies (Bregoli and Del Chiappa, 2013; Komppula, 2014; Pforr *et al.*, 2014; Zehrer *et al.*, 2014) demonstrate the importance of coordination of activities, and collaboration between the stakeholders in destination success, this chapter focuses on collaboration and leadership in the destination.

35.2 Collaboration and Leadership as Determinants of Destination Success

Pike and Paige (2014) raise the question of 'who' should take the responsibility for the planning and marketing of a destination. This is relevant in community-type destinations, in which there is typically not one single organization that has the power or the acceptance to control other destination stakeholders (Volgger and Pechlaner, 2014). Unique characteristics of the destination affect the way in which cooperation and leadership form and establish in a destination (Beritelli *et al.* 2007; Timur and Getz, 2008; Kozak *et al.* 2014; Tuohino and Konu, 2014).

In Finland, it is the local governments and/or the provincial authorities that carry the responsibility of tourism destination policy making. If these decision making organizations do not have a common vision and strategy in terms of destination development, it can lead to competing development projects and fragmented marketing projects executed by neighbouring municipalities, particularly, if there are no destination marketing organizations in the region (Komppula, 2014). The interviewees in Komppula's (2014) study considered that municipalities should not take care of operative marketing but rather provide the basis for it by giving financial support to the destination marketing organization's (DMO) marketing activities. Another role that the public sector could have is to enforce stakeholder engagement. The public sector should create a favourable entrepreneurial climate that supports entrepreneurs' actions and attracts investments to a destination (Komppula, 2014). The findings of Presenza and Cipollina (2010) from Italy suggest that the firms may regard the public sector, such as tourism bureaus and regional governments, as even more significant for their management and marketing undertakings than private stakeholders (Presenza and Cipollina, 2010). This may also apply to Finland, which has no uniform structure of organizations involved in the tourist industry, but regional- and local-level structures differ between regions, meaning that in some rural tourism destinations no DMOs even exist (Tuohino and Konu, 2014).

DMOs are often regarded as having the coordinating role in destinations (Beritelli *et al.*, 2015). Although the coordinating role of the DMO is widely emphasized in destination marketing and management literature (Komppula, 2014), Franch *et al.* (2010) suggest that there is not one actor responsible for the destination management but rather a destination is regarded as a network of actors affecting each other. Several authors highlight that a DMO's role as a destination coordinator is dependent on the roles of the individuals that are affiliated to it (e.g. Strobl and Peters, 2013; Beritelli *et al.*, 2015; Komppula, 2016), Beritelli *et al.* (2015) calling them a destination's elite network. In other words, it is the actors linked to the DMO that drive the coordination in a destination, and a DMO is an organization that constitutes these actors (Beritelli *et al.*, 2015). This would mean that the DMO itself is not the focal point but rather the people that operate in it.

Pechlaner *et al.* (2014) emphasize that understanding destination leadership is crucial for any tourism destination. While destination governance focuses on destination structures and norms, destination leadership has more to do with individual actors, their visions, capability to influence other actors and capability to create relationships (Beritelli and Bieger, 2014). Several authors (Hankinson, 2012; Strobl and Peters, 2013; Beritelli and Bieger, 2014; Komppula, 2014, 2016) state that destination leadership is accredited to individuals within a destination. A lack of creative, committed and risk-taking entrepreneurs (Russell and Faulkner, 1999, 2004; Komppula, 2014) or municipality officials or politicians (Komppula, 2016) can inhibit a destination's overall development. Destination leaders are often charismatic individuals, described as passionate, intuitive, visionary and creative, and often able to predict future market trends and product opportunities (McCarthy, 2003; Komppula, 2016).

Destination leaders need to be able to motivate and inspire other destination stakeholders to strive for the common goals of a destination (Pechlaner *et al.*, 2014) and build trust among stakeholders (Beritelli and Bieger, 2014). According to Beritelli and Bieger (2014), it is essential that leadership stems from the destination or region itself and a common objective of pulling all the actors together should, therefore, be the success of the destination. Kozak *et al.* (2014) note that destination leadership is strongly impacted by locality, i.e. being local. They suggest that destination leadership should be personalized to each destination to better serve its purpose and to be more successful, by respecting the local networks as well as the history of the networks.

To sum up, according to the literature, the determinants of destination success seem to be location, accessibility, attractive product and service offering, quality visitor experiences and community support, the latter referring to collaboration and leadership in the destination. Location as well as attractions based on nature and culture are more or less given, and regarded as comparative advantage, but the other determinants may be influenced by the activities of the actors in the destination.

Hence, in this study stakeholders in the three biggest ski resorts in Finland are interviewed in order to explore their perceptions of the determinants of success in these particular destinations. The literature discussion above will guide the data analysis.

35.3 Case Descriptions

35.3.1 Levi

Levi ski resort is located in the village of Sirkka in the municipality of Kittilä. The first steps towards organized tourism activity were taken in 1964, when the municipality of Kittilä purchased some land near the Levi fell. The mayor of the municipality in 1963 had a clear vision of how to turn Levi into a veritable holiday town. When the land had been purchased, investments were made in the first ski lifts and a valley station. In 1976, two local entrepreneurs and representatives of the municipality of Kittilä established a ski lift company to maintain and develop the ski slopes. The mayor also had a decisive role in the process of persuading a large Finnish trade union to build its holiday venue, a hotel, at Levi in 1981. Due to its challenging traffic connections and remote location, building an airport in Kittilä became one of the key issues in the development of tourism at Levi. Collaboration among the mayor, local tourism entrepreneurs and trade unions led to the opening of an airport in Kittilä in February 1983.

The municipality of Kittilä launched a 3-year tourism development project in 1987. It aimed to create an all-year programme service centre in Levi to bring together the disordered services. One of the key results achieved by the development project was a general land use plan for the Levi area. The area could be developed based on this plan. Levin Matkailu Oy, a tourism company owned by tourism and accommodation industry entrepreneurs, representatives of other businesses and the municipality of Kittilä, was established in 1989.

Finland's first gondola lift opened at Levi in the early 2000s. In 2000, Levi hosted the men's European Cup Alpine skiing competition in slalom and giant slalom. After this competition, Levi was permanently added to the European Cup calendar. In November 2006, Levi hosted the opening competitions of the women's and men's slalom season, and after this event, Levi was named as the opening venue of the World Cup until 2013. The slope company invested a total of €12.5 million in a new service building and two new lifts during the 2007/08 season. Congress and Exhibition Centre Levi Summit opened in 2007. Over the years, Levi has grown into a full-service tourist destination that is open all year round, with more than 200 companies being active in Levi.

35.3.2 Ruka

Ruka is located in the municipality of Kuusamo and is the second largest ski resort in Finland measured by the number of ski lift tickets sold. The Ruka-Kuusamo area has approximately 600 km of snowmobile routes, 160 km of hiking routes and 350 km of canoeing routes. Around 1 million tourists visit the Ruka-Kuusamo area each year. The municipality of Kuusamo is also one of the most popular second-home sites in Finland, with almost 7000 holiday homes. Furthermore, the region is home to the Oulanka National Park, with some 200,000 visitors a year (Metsähallitus, 2018).

The beginning of the story of Ruka ski resort dates back to 1954 when some 20 people interested in winter sports started clearing the slopes of the fell at Ruka, and the first Finnish championships in alpine skiing were organized in Ruka in 1956. Important actions for the development of Ruka were implemented in the 1970s, when entrepreneurs in Ruka and the municipality started to make systematic investments to generate a competitive edge and to develop Ruka into a versatile, top-class ski resort. The cooperation between the Ruka destination and the municipality of Kuusamo was especially important in the early 1980s when land use plans that would remodel the entire area were made at Ruka. At the end of the 1980s, an international airport was constructed in Kuusamo. The first Freestyle Ski World Cup was arranged at Ruka in 2005. Since late November 2005, Ruka has hosted Ruka Nordic, the season's first World Cup event in cross-country skiing, ski jumping and Nordic combined.

The conscious branding of Ruka started in the 1980s, based on the skiing product, meaning that Ruka ski resort can be considered the first real tourism brand in Finland. The ski lift company owned the brand logo and the other companies paid their share of the marketing expenses to the lift company's bank account. In 1999 the municipality and the companies of Ruka started joint marketing with a desire to generate more powerful marketing communications by combining the investments in marketing the summer offering of Kuusamo and the winter offering of Ruka. Hence, the concept of destination was broadened to contain the whole municipality of Kuusamo including the Ruka resort. In 2002, the largest tourism enterprises in the region joined forces with the municipality of Kuusamo to establish the Ruka-Kuusamo Tourism Association, aiming at promoting year-round tourism activities under a joint brand of Ruka-Kuusamo. The demand for incentive travel collapsed in 2008, after which some of the companies in Ruka were obliged to find new target markets. During 2014, reorganization of the board of the tourism association occurred, and a renewal of the Ruka-Kuusamo brand logo was presented. The change back to a brand logo focusing on Ruka caused some disagreement with the Ruka area tourism industry and other fields of industries as well as with the municipality.

35.3.3 Ylläs

Ylläs fell is located in the northern part of Kolari municipality in Lapland, Finland. The Ylläs ski resort area entails the villages of Äkäslompolo and Ylläsjärvi, which are located on opposite sides of the fell. Ylläs is located near to the Pallas-Yllästunturi national park, which is, based on the number of visitors, the most popular national park in Finland, with some half a million visitors per a year (Metsähallitus, 2018). There are two ski lift companies on opposite sides of Ylläs fell, which together comprise 63 ski slopes and 28 ski lifts. The longest slope in Ylläs fell is 3 km long and the elevation in the slopes reaches 464 m at the highest point.

Tourism in Ylläs has its roots in the 1930s when local people started accommodating tourists in their homes. The first actual hotel in Äkäslompolo, Hotelli Humina, was built in the 1950s. The first ever ski lift was built on the Ylläs fell in the 1950s by the municipality on the Äkäslompolo side of the fell. Later, in the 1960s and 1970s Yllärjärvi residents played a major part in building the first lift on the Ylläsjärvi side of the fell, and at the beginning of the 1980s the villagers established their own ski lift company in Ylläsjärvi. In 1985 two private entrepreneurs, from outside the region, bought 60% of the shares of the ski lift company in Ylläsjärvi, and later also bought the rest of the shares. The owners started investing strongly in new slopes and ski lifts until the beginning of the 1990s. On the other side of the fell, the ski lift company had moved from the hands of the municipality to a private company, which experienced a bankruptcy during the 1990s recession. The ski resort on the Ylläsjärvi side tried to buy the bankrupt company but the offer was not accepted. Until the year 2000, the Äkäslompolo ski resort was owned by a property management company. The new rise of the Äkäslompolo ski resort started when the current owner, a hotel chain, made major investments in the facilities during 2007 and 2008. For the customer, the fell has been one ski resort from 1984, when the companies on the opposite sides of the fell agreed to offer a joint ski ticket.

In 1987 the first joint marketing and centralized booking office was established in Ylläs with 150 shareholders. In the 1990s, another central booking office was established by a private entrepreneur, creating the setting of two central booking offices in the area. Later on, the joint marketing fell apart and the marketing of the area was externalized to a provincial party (Lapland Tourism Marketing organization). The situation changed again in 2003 when the new joint marketing organization (Ylläs Tourism Association) was established in Ylläs as an effort to pull together the marketing and event planning of the area as well as the maintenance of the ski tracks. Before this development, the villages, for instance, had their own separate systems for the maintenance of the tracks. In 2015, the collaboration was reorganized into two separate units: the Ylläs Marketing limited company having its focus on the marketing of the destination and the other (association) focusing, for instance, on the maintenance of the skiing tracks.

The accessibility of Ylläs experienced major enhancements in the 1980s when the airline and train connections to the area were established. At the beginning of the 1990s, Ylläs was strongly growing and it was ahead of Ruka and Levi in its popularity. The recession in the 1990s, however, slowed down all investments in Ylläs. During that time, Levi and Ruka jumped ahead of Ylläs in their development and popularity. The beginning of the new century was, again, a time of growth until the economic downturn in 2008 put a stop to it once again. The recovery since then has been, to some extent, slow in comparison with Levi and Ruka.

35.4 Images and Facts

According to a study on the images of Levi, Ruka and Ylläs by Komppula and Laukkanen (2016), Levi and Ruka attract particularly downhill skiers and social life seekers, who value good restaurants and social life activities. Families are also an important target group for both Levi and Ruka. Ylläs attracts all age groups, but particularly the elderly and cross-country skiers. According to Komppula and Laukkanen (2016), Levi and Ruka have favoured young people and children in their promotional material pictures. In the marketing materials of Ylläs, adults and families seem to be the focus. Hence, the image of Ruka and Levi seems to attract youngsters, families and party seekers, whereas Ylläs seems to be more for cross-country skiers and elderly active sports seekers. According to Konu *et al.* (2011) the socio-demographic development among Finnish customers may have a major role in the development of the Finnish ski industry in the future, as many Finnish downhill skiers start cross-country skiing in middle age and are then active in both.

Table 35.1 demonstrates that out of the three destinations, Ylläs and its natural surroundings seem to offer the most prominent settings for different skiing activities.

Figure 35.1 demonstrates the development of overnight stays and Fig. 35.2 the development of number of beds in registered accommodation establishments in

Table 35.1. Facts and figures of the case resorts Levi, Ruka and Ylläs.

	Levi	Ruka	Ylläs
Lifts	28	22	28
Slopes	43	35	63
Beds (information based on the website of the resort)	24,000	12,000[a]	23,000
Longest slope (m)	2,500	1,300	3,000
Highest elevation in the slopes (m)	325	201	463
Nordic skiing tracks (2018) (km)	230	108	330
Establishment of collaborative marketing organization (year)	1989	2002	1987
The first ski lift (year)	1964	1957	1957
The first hotel (year)	1981	1963	1945
Distance to the airport (km)[b]	14	27	40–55
Distance to the capital area of Finland by car (km)	980	830	970

[a]6900 additional second homes, approx. one-third in commercial use.
[b]Levi and Ylläs are served by the same airport, Kittilä.

Fig. 35.1. Registered overnights 1995–2016. (Figure by Art-Travel Ltd, based on data from Statistics Finland.)

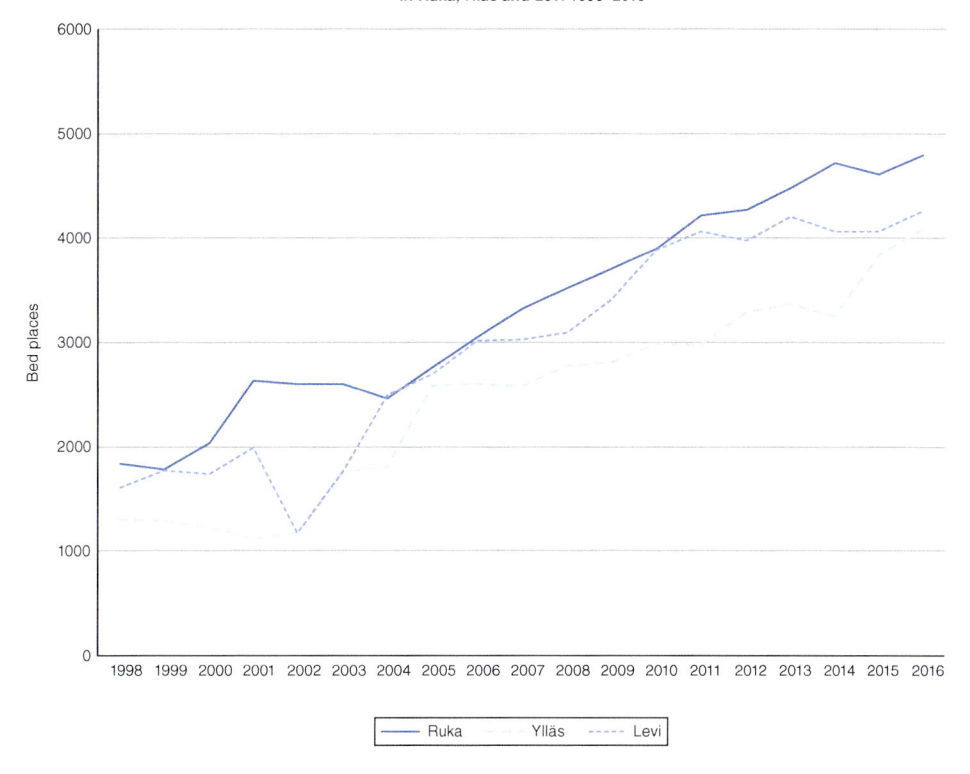

Fig. 35.2. Number of beds in registered accommodation. (Figure by Art-Travel Ltd, based on data from Statistics Finland.)

the case resorts. Fig. 35.3 presents the value of ski pass turnover in each of these resorts.

As can be seen from these three figures, the development of Ylläs has been on a lower level than its counterparts Levi and Ruka. The market conditions are more or less the same for all. From the resource point of view, Ylläs could be seen as most competitive in terms of comparative advantage.

35.5 Method and Data

Each of the cases have been studied as an intensive case study in which the goal has been to build a comprehensive and holistic understanding of the unique history and surroundings of the case, bringing forward the distinctive aspects of each (Eriksson and Kovalainen, 2008). In each case the informants were chosen by utilizing a snowball sampling method, in which the first interviewee suggests to the researcher who could be interviewed next (Eriksson and Kovalainen, 2008). It was taken into consideration that representatives from all stakeholder groups (entrepreneurs, DMO, municipality), should be included in each sample. A description of the interviewed stakeholders is presented in Table 35.2. The first interviewee in each case was chosen

Value of ski pass turnover incl. VAT (€1000), 1996/97–2016/17

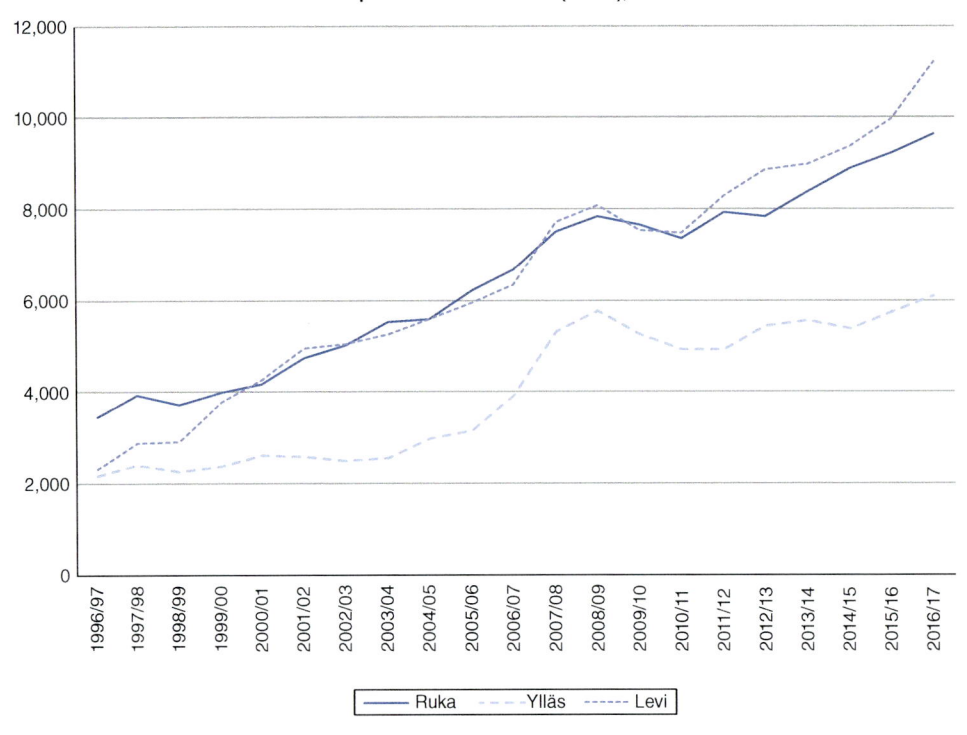

Fig. 35.3. Value of ski pass turnover. (Figure by Art-Travel Ltd, based on data from Suomen hiihtokeskusyhdistys ry.)

Table 35.2. Interviewees' background.

	Levi	Ruka	Ylläs
Representatives of the destination organization	2	2	1
Entrepreneurs	3	6	7[b]
Managers of tourism companies	3	5	1
Municipality representatives	1	1	2
Politicians	1[a]	1	1[a]
Event organizers	0	1	0
Interviewees	9	16	11

[a]The politician is also an entrepreneur.
[b]One of the interviewed entrepreneurs at Levi also had experience from Ylläs.

to represent either the DMO or the municipality, a person who knew the history of the area well and, therefore, was able to provide information on who else could have valuable knowledge and insights on the topic.

The interviewees were asked to relate their own history at the resort, and their contribution to the development and leadership of the resort, to discuss the key events and turning points in development of the resort and, finally, to evaluate the contribution of different stakeholders (DMO, municipality, enterprises, politicians, etc.) in the development of the resort.

Table 35.3. Sources of secondary data.

Levi	Ruka	Ylläs
- Newspaper clippings obtained from the Kittilä library - Archives of Levin Matkailu Ltd - A chronicle of Levi - A chronicle of Levin Matkailukeskus Ltd - www.levi.fi	- A chronicle of Ruka - Newspaper clippings from the local newspaper - Tourism strategy, statistics and master plan from the municipality of Kuusamo - Earlier research on Ruka development by Naturpolis Ltd - www.ruka.fi	- Newspaper clippings obtained from the local newspaper - A chronicle of Äkäslompolo village association - Archives of one municipality officer - www.yllas.fi

In the interviews of Ruka and Levi, the interviewees were not directly asked to compare the three resorts, but many interviewees did make comparisons, particularly between Ruka and Levi, but also commented on the success of Ylläs. In the interviews at Ylläs, as the final question the interviewees were shown the figures concerning the growth in overnights and ski pass turnover in the three resorts, and the interviewees were asked to comment on the figures.

Important sources of information in each case study were newspaper clippings, which were available in local libraries and/or local newspaper archives. Additionally, different kinds of chronicles, earlier studies and the webpages of the respective ski resorts were utilized. The secondary data were collected in each case by Master's students, who also conducted some of the interviews and transcribed all the interview data. The sources of secondary data are presented in Table 35.3.

35.6 Findings

35.6.1 Levi

According to the interviewees, one of the key issues behind the success of Levi is the long-term plans upon which local development has been based. The municipality's land use planning policy has been carefully thought out, facilitating start-ups and expansion of businesses. The main leader of the development projects has been a public utility in the municipality of Kittilä. Systematic construction of the close-knit Levi village centre was one of the key issues that allowed Levi to stand out from the competition. The local residents have had a decisive role when they selected for the municipal council people who wanted to develop tourism in Levi.

The mayor of Kittilä during the early years of the development of Levi was mentioned as integral in the early development of Levi. The success and the major role of the lift company is deemed to be based on its long-term managing director, who has been also a long-time chairperson of the board of directors of the Levi DMO. The interviewees believed that, since he was a local resident, he had a powerful motivation to turn both the lift company and the entire tourist destination into a successful business. The largest hotel, owned by the trade unions, also had a major role in the development of the Levi brand in the 1990s when it offered its services all year round, thus allowing the tourist destination to be open all year round. At present, there are several hotels and a large selection of other accommodation services in Levi, which has reduced the significance of individual actors.

The DMO has been handling joint marketing since 1987. The interviewees had strong faith in the ability of the DMO to plan and implement the marketing. According to the interviewees, systematic development of the Levi brand started when the DMO was established, and the organization's success and significance are based on its long history. Literature often sees the management and development of a tourist destination as a process where the key responsibility is borne by a DMO (Pike and Page, 2014). The findings of the Levi case are partially congruent with this assumption. The board of directors of the DMO was compared by the interviewees to a team where each player has their own role and their own views about issues. This finding seems to indicate that, in the case of Levi, the managing director of the DMO does not carry the principal responsibility for the generation of the key elements; instead, the policies are determined by the board of directors. Cooperation between internal stakeholders is deemed an important issue in Levi, even though certain people have had a key role. The cooperation between the parties has created an atmosphere that encourages investments and construction and also attracts customers.

The interviewees did not share any clear idea about the Levi brand identity. Nevertheless, they stated that cooperation between the actors is important for the brand. Images of good location and accessibility, concrete versatility of services, cooperation within the area, active operations and being an industry pioneer are issues that have been linked to the Levi brand. Some of the interviewees were of the opinion that Levi's image as a party place is genuine and describes Levi well, and has been created based on the Levi brand identity. Many of the interviewees were of the opinion that the image of Levi had been created by the joint marketing efforts and marketing plans, but some of the interviewees thought that the party image was created by a couple of individuals alone. They believe a dominant image as a party venue is harmful for the area and did not wish to promote it further in the marketing communication. The local entrepreneurs have participated in the changing of the image by expanding and redeveloping their services to, for instance, make Levi a more child-friendly tourist destination.

35.6.2 Ruka

All of the interviewees in the case of Ruka listed as one of Ruka's strengths the excellent, close-knit and persistent cooperation between the key entrepreneurs and business managers. The cooperation between the companies continued for decades without any official organization, shaping mutual trust. The Ruka-Kuusamo Tourism Association was established as late as 2002 to continue the joint marketing. All of the interviewees were clearly of the opinion that people who are able to work together are the key to successful cooperation. According to them, the secret of a successful and growing destination lies in innovative and enthusiastic entrepreneurs and leaders as well as having someone who knows how to coordinate the activities. The interviewees mention three key entrepreneurs that can be seen as drivers of development in Ruka.

The roles of entrepreneurs, municipal officials and politicians have changed in the course of Ruka's life cycle. The role of the municipality was especially important in the early 1980s when land use plans that would remodel the entire area were made in Ruka. The interviewees also note that in the 1980s and right up to 1997, the mayor of the municipality was the personage who exerted marked influence on the development of tourism, together with the key entrepreneurs. Favourable attitudes of the municipal decision makers and comprehensive networks consisting of decision makers in the Helsinki Metropolitan Region were also needed.[1]

35.6.3 Ylläs

The Ylläs area is geographically divided into two separate villages on opposite sides of Ylläs, which creates a unique local setting to the destination. According to the interviewees from Ylläs, as well as some of the interviewees from Ruka and Levi, this setting has affected the development of the area significantly. Three of the interviewees from Ylläs regard it as a strength, while others consider the setting to have caused fragmentation in the cooperation and overall development of the area throughout the years. The situation has created a competitive setting between the villages, which, again, has affected their ability to cooperate well and make decisions together. The situation has also created a setting in which locals identify themselves with their own village rather than identifying themselves with Ylläs. This brings challenges to effective cooperation and leadership. On the positive side, the new road between the villages (opened in 2005), shortening the distance from 31 km to 15 km, was believed to have diminished the competition between the villages and brought them a little closer to each other.

The local setting of being divided into two villages also surfaces from how the destination marketing and cooperation have developed in Ylläs. Creating a joint marketing organization and conducting effective cooperation have been challenging in the area. There has been no collective vision among destination stakeholders. The marketing organization has tried to placate the desires and interests of all of its members, causing the effectiveness of marketing practises to suffer and the development to become slower. This has also had a negative effect on trust among stakeholders. Trying to please everyone has led to a situation where there is no focus on who should be the target customers. Over the years, there has also been a dichotomy between cross-country and downhill skiing, causing fragmentation in the marketing practises. However, nature as the focus of marketing has nowadays gained consensus among the stakeholders.

The municipality's role in the joint marketing and cooperation has been insignificant in the past. The interviewees had consistent views on how the municipality has related to tourism in the Ylläs area in the past. Instead of tourism, the focus has rather been on the mining industry. The role of the municipality in the joint marketing of Ylläs has also so far been insignificant.

The findings of Ylläs suggest that the cooperation has not been working effectively, mainly due to disagreements among entrepreneurs, lack of collective vision and trust, and difficulties in committing to joint efforts. The DMO has been to some extent ineffective in its operations and the municipality has not been supporting tourism development. No definitive leader is present in guiding the cooperation and the local tourism entrepreneurs or other tourism actors are not keen to attain this position.

The Ylläs area is considered to lack strong tourism personalities that would lead the destination cooperation and development of the entire area.

35.7 Comparison of the Cases and Discussion

The comparison of the three cases is summarized in Table 35.4. When comparing the three cases, Ruka and Levi have had no political pressures preventing their focus on developing central villages in the resort, whereas Ylläs has had from the very beginning a unique setting, with the area being divided into two separate centres. This has over the years overemphasized the topic of local context and affected the way cooperation and leadership have formed in Ylläs. Though the interviewees of Levi and Ruka have emphasized the crucial role of the municipality in long-term planning, active land ownership and land use policy, the municipality of Kolari has not had this kind of role. This may be due to the fact that the local setting causes political rivalry between the villages across all kinds of municipality policies and decision making. Hence, the strong role of the municipality particularly in the early stages of the development of the resorts, with the help of political support from the residents, has made it possible for Levi and Ruka to have favourable circumstances for growth and success.

In the early years of the development of Ruka and Levi their home municipalities had committed, visionary, charismatic and active mayors, and/or other municipality officers, who used their personal networks and charisma when negotiating with potential investors and other stakeholders in order to enhance the development of the resorts. Interviewees from both Levi and Ruka also emphasized the role of charismatic entrepreneurs and managers of the core companies as key success factors of the resorts. Their enthusiasm has encouraged new entrepreneurs to start new businesses and grow. In Ylläs resort, there seem to be some visible and strong personalities who often have opposing approaches to each other when trying to make decisions together. In Levi all the key personnel in the destination development mentioned by the interviewees were originally local people. This was also the case in Ruka, although the 'father' of Ruka originally came from the capital area of Finland.

Based on these three case studies, the core factor enhancing the success of the ski resorts seems to be successful collaboration between the private and public sector

Table 35.4. Comparison of the cases.

	Levi	Ruka	Ylläs
Common vision and support for tourism among the residents	Yes	Yes	No
Role of the municipality in tourism development	Active	Active	Passive
Charismatic and enthusiastic tourism actors	Several	Several	Few
Leadership	Based on DMO	Based on individuals	No leadership
Collaboration and trust among tourism actors	Strong	Strong	Weak
Consensus about the identity	None	None	None

stakeholders and particularly between the entrepreneurs. The Ruka case is an example of a destination that succeeded in growing and developing even without a formal collaborative organization. On the other hand, Levi has had a well-functioning DMO from the early years of its success story. In Ylläs, two separate villages and disagreements among entrepreneurs, together with actors with strong opposing views, were regarded to be noteworthy factors causing difficulties in cooperating and conducting joint marketing decisions. Finally, collaboration requires leadership, and based on the findings of our three case studies, leadership seems to be based on charismatic, collaborative personalities, not on organizations.

There was one issue that was common for all cases, namely lack of consensus about the ski resort brand identity. In Levi and Ruka there was some disagreement between the stakeholders about the positioning of the resort in the market. Although the 'party image' seems to bring profits, particularly to restaurants, it may be harmful in the family segment. In Ylläs, the disagreements were about the contradiction between ski slopes and pure nature. Nevertheless, all the resorts have been able to find a consensus about the core message of the marketing communication.

35.8 Conclusions

This study suggests that effective collaboration and leadership are key facilitators to the success of a destination. The findings support the notion of Beritelli and Bieger (2014), who suggest that the leadership in a destination is attributed to individuals, not necessarily to organizations. As Komppula (2016) notes,

> charismatic entrepreneurs and business managers, committed and visionary municipality officials and influential politicians may take control of leadership in the destination, being those individual people who are the primary stakeholders in tourism development.
>
> (Komppula, 2016, p. 73)

This notion is also supported by Franch *et al.* (2010). Characteristics of charismatic entrepreneurs (McCarthy, 2003) are typical for these key actors: intuitive, visionary and creative.

It can be argued that a strong role of local people may be a strength for a destination, enhancing the sense of identity with the place and facilitating a cooperative atmosphere among the actors, supporting the findings of Hallak *et al.* (2012), Czernek (2013), Kennedy and Augustyn (2014), Kozak *et al.* (2014) and Åberg (2014). Being 'local' does not necessarily need to refer to being born in the region, or being a permanent resident of the region, but may also refer to a long-term commitment to the region in a form of business ownership and active presence in the daily operations, as is shown in the Ruka case (Komppula, 2016). Nevertheless, strong local identity in two separate villages in Ylläs has affected cooperation negatively throughout the years of joint marketing, confirming Komppula's (2014) findings from a rural destination in Finland, which emphasize that geographical fragmentation can create a barrier to effective cooperation.

Community-type destinations, like all these ski resorts, are often built on networks in which a variety of stakeholders interact with each other and affect each other (Beritelli *et al.*, 2007; Franch *et al.* 2010). This study shows that the leadership role of the DMO as a forum for collaboration for stakeholders may be fruitful, as in the case of

Levi. On the other hand, in Ruka, the DMO was not seen as the leader of the collaboration. A DMO could take the role of creating a cooperative atmosphere and interacting with destination stakeholders (Bornhorst *et al.*, 2010), which could be possible in the case of Ylläs, if it had an external manager, neutral to both villages, and capable of building trust among the stakeholders. Bornhorst *et al.* (2010) suggest that stakeholders can either provide coordination, increasing success, or cause fragmentation, which reduces success. According to them, this choice is important for every single stakeholder and is highly influenced by the leadership style of the DMO and the degree to which it is stakeholder-oriented.

Acknowledgements

Päivi Pahkamaa, MSc (University of Lapland), Miikka Pohjola, MSc, and his supervisor Saila Saraniemi, PhD (University of Oulu), are gratefully acknowledged for their contribution in data collection and the initial phase of the data analysis in the cases of Levi and Ruka.

Note

[1] For more detailed information about the Ruka case, see Komppula (2016) and Saraniemi and Komppula (2019).

References

Åberg, K.G. (2014) The importance of being local: prioritizing knowledge in recruitment for destination development. *Tourism Review* 69(3), 229–243. DOI:10.1108/TR-06-2013-0026

Beritelli, P. and Bieger, T. (2014) From destination governance to destination leadership – defining and exploring the significance with the help of a systemic perspective. *Tourism Review* 69(1), 25–46. DOI:10.1108/TR-07-2013-0043

Beritelli, P., Buffa, F. and Martini, U. (2015) The coordinating DMO or coordinators in the DMO? – an alternative perspective with the help of network analysis. *Tourism Review* 70(1), 24–42. DOI:10.1108/TR-04-2014-0018

Beritelli, P., Bieger, T. and Laesser, C. (2007) Destination governance: using corporate governance theories as a foundation for effective destination management. *Journal of Travel Research* 46(1), 96–107. DOI:10.1177/0047287507302385

Bornhorst, T., Ritchie, B.J.R. and Sheehan, L. (2010) Determinants of tourism success for DMO's and destinations: an empirical examination of stakeholders' perspectives. *Tourism Management* 31(5), 572–589. DOI:10.1016/j.tourman.2009.06.008

Bregoli, I. and Del Chiappa, G. (2013) Coordinating relationships among destination stakeholders: evidence from Edinburgh (UK). *Tourism Analysis* 18(2), 145–155. DOI:10.3727/108354213X13645733247657

Czernek, K. (2013) Determinants of cooperation in a tourist region. *Annals of Tourism Research* 1(40), 83–104. DOI:10.1016/j.annals.2012.09.003

Eriksson, A. and Kovalainen, P. (2008) *Qualitative Methods in Business Research*. Sage, London.

Ferrand, A. and Vecciatini, D. (2002) The effect of service performance and ski resort image on skiers' satisfaction. *European Journal of Sport Science* 2(2), 1–17. DOI:10.1080/17461390200072207

Finnish Ski Area Association (2014) SHKY Hiihto- ja laskettelututkimus 2014. TNS. Available at: www.ski.fi (accessed 18 May 2018).

Finnish Ski Area Association (2016) SHKY Laskettelijatutkimus – Toukokuu 2016. Available at: www.ski.fi (accessed 18 May 2018).

Finnish Ski Area Association (2018) Kaikki laskettelusta, lumilautailusta ja Suomen hiihtokeskuksista. Available at: www.ski.fi (accessed 18 May 2018).

Franch, M., Martini, U. and Buffa, F. (2010) Roles and opinions of primary and secondary stakeholders within community-type destinations. *Tourism Review* 65(4), 74–85. DOI:10.1108/16605371011093881

Godfrey, K.B. (1999) Attributes of destination choice: British skiing in Canada. *Journal of Vacation Marketing* 5(1), 225–234. DOI:10.1177%2F135676679900500103

Hallak, R., Assaker, G. and Lee, C. (2013) Tourism entrepreneurship performance: the effects of place identity, self-efficacy, and gender. *Journal of Travel Research* 54(1), 36–51. DOI: 10.1177%2F0047287513513170

Hankinson, G. (2012) The measurement of brand orientation, its performance impact, and the role of leadership in the context of destination branding: an exploratory study. *Journal of Marketing Management* 28(7–8), 974–999. DOI:10.1080/0267257X.2011.565727

Kennedy, V. and Augustyn, M.M. (2014) Stakeholder power and engagement in an English seaside context: implications for destination leadership. *Tourism Review* 69(3), 187–201. DOI:10.1108/TR-06-2013-0030

Komppula, R. (2014) The role of individual entrepreneurs in the development of competitiveness for a rural tourism destination: a case study. *Tourism Management* 40, 361–371. DOI:10.1016/j.tourman.2013.07.007

Komppula, R. (2016) The role of different stakeholders in destination development. *Tourism Review* 71(1), 67–76. DOI:10.1108/TR-06-2015-0030

Komppula, R. and Laukkanen, T. (2016) Comparing perceived images with projected images – a case study on Finnish ski destinations. *European Journal of Tourism Research* 12, 41–53.

Konu, H., Laukkanen, T. and Komppula, R. (2011) Using ski destination criteria to segment Finnish ski resort customers. *Tourism Management* 32(5), 1096–1105. DOI:10.1016/j.tourman.2010.09.010

Kozak, M., Volgger, M. and Pechlaner, H. (2014) Destination leadership: leadership for territorial development. *Tourism Review* 69(3), 169–172. DOI:10.1108/TR-05-2014-0021

McCarthy, B. (2003) Strategy is personality-driven, strategy is crisis-driven: insights from entrepreneurial firms. *Management Decision* 41(4), 327–339. DOI:10.1108/00251740310468081

Metsähallitus (2018) Kansallispuistojen, valtion retkeilyalueiden ja muiden virkistyskäytöllisesti merkittävimpien Metsähallituksen hallinnoimien suojelualueiden ja retkeilykohteiden käyntimäärät vuonna 2017. Available at: www.metsa.fi/documents/10739/3335805/kayntimaarat2017.pdf/d4414a36-b10d-428c-aa90-c5b50f25e4e5 (accessed 8 June 2018).

Pechlaner, H., Kozak, M. and Volgger, M. (2014) Destination leadership: a new paradigm for tourist destinations? *Tourism Review* 69(1), 1–9. DOI:10.1108/TR-09-2013-0053

Pforr, C., Pechlaner, H., Volgger, M. and Thompson, G. (2014) Overcoming the limits to change and adapting to future challenges: governing the transformation of destination networks in Western Australia. *Journal of Travel Research* 53(6), 760–777. DOI:10.1177/0047287514538837

Pike, S. and Paige, S.J. (2014) Destination marketing organizations and destination marketing: a narrative analysis of the literature. *Tourism Management* 41(1), 202–227. DOI:10.1016/j.tourman.2013.09.009

Presenza, A. and Cipollina, M. (2010) Analysing tourism stakeholder networks. *Tourism Review* 65(4), 17–30. DOI:10.1108/16605371011093845

Richards, G. (1996) Skilled consumption and UK ski holidays. *Tourism Management* 17(1), 25–34. DOI:10.1016/0261-5177(96)00097-0

Russell, R. and Faulkner, B. (1999) Movers and shakers: chaos makers in tourism development. *Tourism Management* 20(4), 411–423. DOI:10.1016/S0261-5177(99)00014-X

Russell, R. and Faulkner, B. (2004) Entrepreneurship, chaos and the tourism area lifecycle. *Annals of Tourism Research* 31(3), 556–579. DOI:10.1016/j.annals.2004.01.008

Saraniemi, S. and Komppula, R. (2019) The development of a destination brand identity: a story of stakeholder collaboration. *Current Issues in Tourism* 22(9), 1116–1132. DOI:10.1080/13683500.2017.1369496

Strobl, A. and Peters, M. (2013) Entrepreneurial reputation in destination networks. *Annals of Tourism Research* 40, 59–82. DOI:10.1016/j.annals.2012.08.005

Timur, S. and Getz, D. (2008) A network perspective on managing stakeholders for sustainable urban tourism. *International Journal of Contemporary Hospitality Management* 20(4), 445–461. DOI:10.1108/09596110810873543

Tuohino, A. and Konu, H. (2014) Local stakeholders' views about destination management: who are leading tourism development? *Tourism Review* 69(3), 202–215. DOI:10.1108/TR-06-2013-0033

Volgger, M. and Pechlaner, H. (2014) Requirements for destination management organizations in destination governance: understanding DMO success. *Tourism Management* 41(1), 64–75. DOI:10.1016/j.tourman.2013.09.001

Zehrer, A., Raich, F., Siller, H. and Tschiderer, F. (2014) Leadership networks in destinations. *Tourism Review* 69(1), 59–73. DOI:10.1108/TR-06-2013-0037

36 Winter Tourism: Lost in Transition? The Process of Transformation and Inertia of the Ski Industry and Places in the French Alps

PHILIPPE BOURDEAU*

UMR PACTE CNRS, LabEx ITEM, University of Grenoble-Alpes, Grenoble, France

36.1 Introduction

After many years as a lever of economic development during the 20th century, alpine winter tourism has encountered many uncertainties and factors of structural, sectoral and global change. These factors include a decrease in the numbers of skiers, rising competition between resorts, the emergence of new recreational activities and an ageing skiing population. Climate change both reveals and accelerates these transformations by highlighting the contradictions and vulnerabilities of a system whose development from a localized bricolage of ski stations to a globalized industry in just a few decades seems to have lost its knack, as well as the ability to face future obstacles (Bourdeau, 2009a).

French ski resorts are a classic case study of these issues as they are built on a significantly large infrastructure of tourism based upon a principle of monoactivity centred around alpine skiing and the tourist property market. Over the past 30 years, the industry has been heavily criticized for excessive standardization of offerings, as well as a chronic inability to adapt itself to evolving demands. The end of the first-degree touristic equation: 'winter sports = uniqueness (skiing) + uniformity (resorts) + repetitiveness (annual holiday)' (Chevallier, 1996) has meant a rupture that is particularly difficult to grasp for resorts. As a recent parliamentary report points out, 'Those French ski resorts resulting from the snow plan are often criticised for offering standard activities that do not give the consumer the possibility to broaden their range of activities and discover new ones' (Masson-Maret and Vairetto, 2014).

Numerous scientific studies conducted over the past 10 years document the conditions in which the winter tourism sector in the Alps and the Pyrenees is more or less voluntarily – and very slowly – giving way to conditions imposed by socio-cultural change and touristic demand, environmental and economic sustainability and the impact of climate change (Gauchon, 2010; Achin and George, 2013; Clivaz et al., 2015)

---

* E-mail: philippe.bourdeau@univ-grenoble-alpes.frs

in order to conceive and put into place policies of adaptability of destinations that go beyond new developmental models.

On a larger scale, this sectoral perspective can of course be replaced within the wider Anthropocene framework (Steffen *et al.*, 2015), in which tourism is clearly identified as fully contributing to the 'peak everything' (Heinberg, 2010). The tourism sector is confronted with transformation requirements that involve reorientations and redefinitions characteristic of transitional situations, in which previously legitimate activities of the sector can no longer be maintained, creating strong uncertainties and potential future crises. In that respect, the following text refers to long-term observations and research carried out in different touristic environments in the French Alps over the past 30 years. Focusing on dilemmas and challenges of tourism policy and engineering facing climate and cultural change, it examines and discusses the processes and conditions in which the sustainable winter sports transition operates and does not operate. Indeed, on the territorial and professional levels, both very creative dynamics and logic of inertia and (mis)adaptations can be observed at the price of strong functional contradictions and strategic tensions. This contribution to the book attempts to show that the challenge of this tension between creativity and inertia is the exploration and affirmation of new development models that are better suited to local and global changing context. Beyond a necessary proof effect based on sourced data and facts, it includes a speculative dimension motivated by an attempt to contribute to the debate on the transformation of mountain economies and identities in contemporary societies.

36.2 Climate Change as Accelerator of Contradictions

As a key variable in the evolution of winter tourism, climate change accelerates structural contradictions and increases the amount of threats for the winter season as it is understood today. In the 20th century, the economy of winter sports was structured around particular times in the year when skiers would gather at the bottom of the ski lift ready for the snow season. Climate change has meant that the synchronization of these events and social rhythms and norms (holidays), heavy infrastructure (equipment and services), as well as environmental resources available in stock and flow (water, snow, energy) has become more and more complex and costly. It is indeed why we have seen, since the 1990s, the development of artificial snow production in response to the incertitude of natural snowfall and thus the winter tourism economy's exposure to the hazards presented by climate change. In France, 30% of the slopes are fitted with snow guns, as opposed to 48% in Switzerland, 60% in Austria and 70% in Italy. This means that we now must create €3/m^3 of snow[1] that used to fall without any cost. Not only is this snow-covered area likely to increase (15% of French skiing areas in 2007, 30% in 2018 and 70–80% estimated for 2030 according to the operators' forecasts), but the cost of production will increase in parallel to the price of energy and the need to produce snow in above-freezing temperatures. Without mentioning the increasing tensions surrounding water and energy resources, the fact that the winter sports system is running at increasing costs means it will have an impact on the economic model of resorts. Indeed, this extra cost is partly due to the upscaling of winter sports, reducing the demographic scale of participants to offer more niche sports. Only 8% of French people go skiing at least once every 2 years (Hoibian, 2010), a participation rate that has been stagnating for several decades, and is lower than other alpine countries like Switzerland and Austria, where more than 20% of the population participate in skiing (Vanat, 2018). The consequence of this niche is further emphasized if we consider that 2–3% of skiers consume nearly 80% of skier days (Berlioz, 2006). In so doing, we are moving further and further away from the 'skiing for all' utopia, a government policy implemented in the 1960s and 1970s to democratize the access to winter sports, to socially justify the developments of ski resorts in France, which doesn't prevent the apparent fully open access to winter sports from prevailing in some cities close to the Alps and in media discourse.

As ski resorts gradually lose national, regional and even local visitors, they are forced to look much further to find a new international clientele. This approach also comes with an increasing advertising cost at a time of growing competition between resorts given the stagnation of the ski market and the fact that ski destinations covet the same clients – notably those coming from the two major European markets: Germany and the UK (Vanat, 2016). This leads many observers and actors in the field of winter sports to suggest that resorts 'run the risk of running out of skiers before running out of snow'. We can assign the non-renewal and abandonment by skiers to a combination of several factors:

- Demographic: the ageing European population limits the number of practitioners of the sport, despite the continuation of a minority of the most passionate skiers.
- Social and economic: the increase in costs and the upscaling of ski resorts excludes a growing number of former skiers and population, including young people and residents of mountain areas not able to afford tourist stays, ski equipment and passes.
- Cultural: the charming aspect of winter sports is no longer as noticeable as in the 1960s to 1970s, led by novelty and properties of social distinction. The already existing weak skiing culture in France is eroding little by little with public interest shifting towards less sporting destinations and activities, more focused on wellbeing, culture and heritage.
- The media: according to our repeated observations (Bourdeau *et al.*, 2007) the media publish less and less material about winter sports, or rather deal with the more problematic aspects in the sector, such as climate change or the controversy surrounding development projects of snow culture.

In this context, winter sports resorts are likely to be seen more and more as emblems of the excesses of the 20th century: culturally lagging behind and out of touch with issues surrounding sustainability. This is likely to emphasize those controversies linked to development projects and the constant large-scale financial support from communities and the state, further weakening – including at the local level – the longheld general consensus on this subject (Bourdeau *et al.*, 2007). At the same time, the ideal of upscaling resorts with a focus on luxury tourism is mostly contradicted by the development of budget winter sports packages driven by tour operators who negotiate discount prices with the resorts, further weakening their economic model.

As the work of Bonnemains (2015) shows, the current bias of an almost exclusive investment in 'large-scale artificially produced snow' has negative long-term effects by reinforcing tourist monoactivity based on snow sports: industrially produced snow increases the short-term resilience of the alpine winter economy yet decreases it in the long term by reducing its ability to adapt to a diversified economy, giving the illusion of a perfect and definitive solution that prevents the investment of ideas and money in alternative projects. Much like the desalination of seawater in littoral zones, artificially produced snow can be understood as maladaptation (Barnett and O'Neill, 2010). We can also consider an extractivism analysis (Burchardt and Dietz, 2014), insofar as the exploitation of the snow resource is pushed to its maximum, at the price of growing cost of energy and tensions surrounding the water supply. Here we can find the idea of a 'temptation of immunity' (Garcia, 2015) designed to ensure the continuity of a system through seeking exoneration from adapting to change. The snow resource then appears as a socio-technical lock-in (Liebowitz and Margolis, 1995) fundamental for winter tourism.

Considering that the amplification of ski lift equipment and artificial snow might slow down the decline of winter sports seems to be a risky calculation taking into account the investments to be made and the increase in the costs it entails, notwithstanding the demand for more diversified leisure activities by the public, and the sensitivity of natural environments to the impacts of human activities and climate change. These projects seem primarily related to communication issues between resorts within the context of increased competition, shown in a report by the French Senate: 'There is a general trend over oversized tourism projects or their aberrant distribution, most often within a spirit of competition as opposed to complementarity' (Masson-Maret and Vairetto, 2014). In France, the giant cableway project intending to link the resorts of l'Alpe d'Huez and Les Deux Alpes illustrates what some observers consider as a 'leap forward', which has more to do with a communication operation than a development strategy.

Moreover, this policy of overdevelopment seems to neglect the long-term rebalancing of the seasonal, geographical and economic distribution of tourist numbers to the mountains, a large number of whom favour the summer and areas located outside of ski resorts. For the French clientele, summer has become the most significant period for mountain tourism with 51% of overnight stays representing 45% of touristic expenditure, as opposed to only 33% of overnight stays and 40% of touristic expenditure in winter. Summer is also ahead of winter in the proportion of overnight stays in commercial accommodation (45% versus 39%) and for the duration of stays (7.2 days versus 5.3). In addition, 74% of summer overnight stays and 49% of winter overnight stays take place outside of ski resorts. We can forecast that this evolution will be exacerbated by the lengthening of the summer season due to climate change, while winter will become shorter. In addition, the sharp decline in the amount of French families taking part in winter sports (down 17% between 2008 and 2013) is threefold in ski resorts as opposed to trips outside of these regions (ATOUT France, 2016).

36.3 Between Creative Dynamics and Inertia of Alpine Winter Tourism

Mountain tourism in winter is both destabilized and stimulated by a series of interacting changes whose climatic, cultural, technological and economic factors are not easily separated. In this mutation under the constraint of uncertainties and threats, the logics of adaptation observable in various destinations, sectors and trades are incredibly variable and often contradictory. Multiple change signals and transition indicators can be found in practices and experiments undertaken in the field, while at the same time strong inertia and resistance illustrate the difficulty of changing models.

36.3.1 Transformative practices at the heart of the tourism system

Transition dynamics are active at different geographic and social scales. They operate first within tourism and sports practices themselves. Special attention can be paid to mobile kinds of sport tourism that re-examine the 'fixity' of the polarized development model on tourist resorts (in both winter and summer). This is the case for hiking, trail running, Nordic walking, snowshoeing and back-country skiing, but also for cycling (Pechlaner et al., 2015). These practices constitute powerful leverage for the transformation of mountain tourism by reorienting the activity of tourist destinations, by reorganizing tourist spaces from very limited and widespread facilities and equipment, and by extending the constricted seasonal framework, which seemed to be a given. This is also the case for a growing number of forms of 'nomadic skiing': alpine and Nordic ski touring, snowshoeing, snow-kiting and skijoring. This vagabond, opportunistic and frugal ski experience develops outside the equipped areas almost without any infrastructure, and allows strong spatial and temporal reactivity with snow fluctuations. It is a revival of the spirit of early skiing as a means of movement and ascent, and it is developing in a completely unexpected way to meet the needs of skiers in a context of both cultural and climate change.

This creative act then operates within professional sectors where various experimentations with new ways of living and working on a daily basis appear through a profusion of initiatives. In doing so on an individual, through couples or on a collective scale, people experience work and life projects marked by ethical voluntarism and a search for existential coherence, in phase with a set of values of environmental and social responsibility. The common characteristics shared by these professionals are self-limitation of income intended to privilege the search for an art of living over economic success; a tendency to go beyond categories by crossing sectors such as sport, heritage, art, literature, agriculture, manual or intellectual work; a priority given to the quality of relationships with both people and the environment; and the combination of strong local roots with external networks (Corneloup and Bourdeau, 2015). In this model, innovation is a form of daily deviance on the part of 'ordinary' people who transgress rules or codes to achieve objectives that are not legitimate or expected, and can thus contribute to an inversion of norms (Alter, 2000).

At a crucial moment of transition of sporting activities, individual initiatives, and professional and territorial sectors, the case of Nordic skiing is exemplary. Its development in secondary massifs and low-lying sites exposes it to the full impact of climate change, while its weak economic base does not allow for heavy investment in artificial snow installations. However, it is currently undergoing change by redefining its geographical, seasonal and sport parameters. By promoting various local initiatives, as well as in peripheral massifs, it has also incorporated practices such as Nordic hiking, snowshoeing, ski-hok (a hybrid of snowshoeing and Nordic skiing) and biathlon, not to mention winter trails, fat bike, Nordic walking and roller skiing. These activities are easily adapted to snow cover variations either directly (trail, fat bike, etc.), or by offering the possibility to 'switch' between practices such as dog sledding/cani-hiking, Nordic skiing/Nordic walking. They are ideal for very attractive off-piste enjoyment, and their multiple combinations allow seasonal overlaps, or even an almost continuous practice during the year. Sporting events that may otherwise be cancelled because there is not enough snow can go ahead anyway, regardless of the conditions. The development of roller skiing has led to the opening of a summer ski school, employing several instructors in Corrençon in the Vercors massif, with the slogan 'a world where skiing never stops' (Vercors Tourisme, n.d.).

These creative processes, largely neglected or unthought of by tourism engineering, perfectly illustrate alternative models for innovation: innovation based on culture (KEA, 2009) and uses (Parsons and Rose, 2009), niche innovation (Schot, 1998), innovation under constraints (Caniëls and Rietzschel, 2015), frugal innovation, reverse innovation (periphery – centre) and innovation through subtraction of resources (snow) or equipment (ski lifts, snow guns). Through establishing 'bridges' connecting activities and certain periods during the year, these processes contribute to a welcome seasonal adjustment of tourism in the face of uncertainties regarding the climate. Their emergence is at the crossroads of a strong cultural autonomy of practitioners, the competence and abundant inspiration of the professionals in the field, as well as geographical and cultural contexts favourable for experimentation. All of these factors provide the perfect environment for recreative laboratories (Falaix and Corneloup, 2017), all of which are not tied in to habitual marketing and communication practices. Areas outside resorts, such as in mountain passes and refuges, which for a long time have been considered as mere transit points, are now becoming fully fledged tourist destinations driven by the increasing convergence of half-organized, near-spontaneous practices, in both winter and summer. These include access to the first snowfall, snow-kiting, ski hiking, tobogganing, trail running, contemplation, cycle tourism, nature education, scientific tourism and artistic residencies.

36.3.2 Inertia and maladaptive rational

'Ski bashing' has become commonplace in the media over the past few years with titles such as: 'at skiing you hardly ski any more'; 'there's more to life than skiing'; 'Is transporting snow by helicopter really acceptable?'; 'skiing or drinking water: will we soon have to choose between the two?'; 'too posh to be green ... they chose to boycott skiing'; 'stop going on about skiing'.[2] Often presented by the media as 'addicts' or as those clinging on to a supposedly waning tourist model, winter sports actors freely express their distress and irritation when it comes to the misunderstandings they are faced with. Yet there is nothing illogical or illegitimate about their wait-and-see policy, resistance to change or conservatism given a number of economic, cultural and political factors. It should first be noted that key sectors of the winter economy such as real estate, ski education, and some shops and accommodation continue to enjoy comfortable economic income through upscaling, driven by the import of foreign customers with high purchasing power. At the local level, we can also see the determining political weight of operators (shops, accommodation, special services, etc.) who are anchored by an income-driven economic model – in both land and property – that is often inherited and therefore can withstand seasonal climate and economic threats. Field observations show that they are therefore resilient during bad seasons and do not feel the need to change their business operations. On the other hand, more recent operators whose presence is less anchored locally and who are often driven by innovative projects find themselves much more vulnerable to similar threats.

If most of the professionals working in winter sports resorts freely express the difficulty they face in terms of 'mourning the snow', they go on to say that despite the difficulties they are driven by passion. Winter sports bear a certain social and cultural responsibility that is rather distinctive, as well as rewarding, particularly with strong identities attached to professions such as the ski instructor, the ski patrol rescuer or the snow groomer driver. This charm is also manifested in a strong symbolic attachment to winter sports resorts as emblems of modernity and the attractiveness of the mountains of which these regions have long been deprived. This often goes hand-in-hand with a strong developmental mythology based on our faith in technology: ski lifts, snow ploughs or artificial snow production. This powerful image continues to fuel the epic tale of 'the resort which saves the mountain'. During the past 60 years, winter sports are usually considered to have been a decisive engine for the economy and mountain societies. Largely based on the property sector and the tourism of ski resorts, this industrially designed model has occupied the entire physical, economic and symbolic aspects of alpine massifs. Faced with the threat of change, professionals and local elected officials tend to reason in terms of 'total substitution or nothing'. According to field observations and interviews, we can point out that since no diversification activity available to date can offer an economic model comparable with winter sports, they are only able to see the lack of a credible complete replacement model. They therefore feel that they are being asked to accept an even more uncertain future, which largely fuels a 'There Is No Alternative' (TINA) syndrome: 'If there's no skiing, there's nothing' (Place Gre'net, 2015).

In this context, it is enough to enjoy a particularly prosperous year every 3–4 years –and, if possible, an Olympic medal! Our long-term observations show that this restocks the coffers of the resorts, as well as encourages operators not to give up on snow tourism as long as they can persuade local officials and the banks to continue to support ambitious plans to revive the industry. This process is not only played out on the local level, but also often results from the weight given by corporate and sector lobbies (National Union of Ski Instructors, National Association of Ski Resort Mayors) to maintain the status quo. It is under their influence that the tourism policies of the Auvergne-Rhône-Alpes and Provence-Alpes-Côte d'Azur regions have shifted their focus in massive support of winter sports resorts, thanks to changes in the political situation in 2016. In Auvergne-Rhône-Alpes, it was the president of the National Union of French Ski Instructors, Gilles Chabert, nicknamed 'the most powerful man above 1,000 m', who is responsible for coordinating mountain policy. At the launch of the 'Plan-neige station' campaign in May 2016, he said: 'In this region, the words "snow" and "snow guns" aren't known at all; I will make sure this changes'. While addressing the president of the region, Laurent Wauquiez, he also said: 'You should know that we will need a lot of money'. In addition to the abandonment of the previous 'Mountain 2040' plan, which sought to effectuate a real transition, Mr Chabert took a 'turn back 50 years' at the time of the 'Pompidou snow plan' because 'it worked like a dream'. He concluded by saying: 'All we want to do is ski; the rest is some blah blah blah' (Shahshahani, 2016).

In the prevailing cultural and political context, many initiatives promoting alternatives are largely ignored or even invisible, and local development practice continues to be obsessed with winter sports. For example, in Villard-de-Lans, in the Vercors Massif, a rescue archaeology company was discreetly set up in the commune employing around 37 people, exceeding the amount of year-round jobs of the skiing industry by 17, with the latter still considered as the main – or even the only – employer of the region. We can also observe many residential transitions in metropolitan areas, where the economic weight of year-round residents is more and more significant in the sports tourism sector (Bachimon *et al.*, 2014). We can also see a clear lack of attention paid to the fact that the summer season is taking over the winter season in terms of tourist numbers and financial figures. Because global warming is lengthening the summer season while it shortens the winter season, we might observe a larger polarization in a small number of resorts. More generally, field experience shows that all forms of tourism that are flourishing outside of resorts are most often neglected or misunderstood.

In many ways, these positions are echoed in what Banergee and Duflo (2012) show in their analysis of maldevelopment in the form of three toxic 'I's', reinforcing each other in the maintaining of a biased relationship to the 'real': ideology, ignorance and inertia. While the concern for mountain territories was that there would be a move away from skiing altogether in the 1990s, making way for snowboarding or snowshoes, then moving entirely away from snow-related activities in 2000s and finally abandoning all tourism in 2010, we might consider that they have somewhat fallen behind in this cultural and economic reorientation model. This is highlighted by the report of the French National Audit Office published early in 2018, noting that the rationalization and diversification recommendations it had previously issued in an audit in 2011 for the resorts were not really heard, highlighting the increasing vulnerability of ski resorts in the northern Alps due to global warming, and pointing out the inadequate responses of their managers (Cour des Comptes, 2018).

36.4 Discussion: 'Practices Change More Quickly Than the Climate'[3]

Should we perfect the past or prepare for the future? Faced with challenges maintaining employment in the mountains, the use of industrial snow is undoubtedly an indispensable tool for overcoming the shortage of snow caused by climate change, as long as the long-term plan over the next 20 years also creates favourable conditions for practices and tourist models able to do without the snow. However, industrial snow seems to be considered as the definitive solution to the effects of climate change, preventing real diversification policies. Similar to the risk of a decreasing number of older skiers due to the development of niche practices, resort managers are hoping to see the imminent arrival of rich Indian and Chinese tourists, justifying the optimistic drive of considerable investments in the ski industry.

We often come across the notion of 'accelerated inertia' (Rosa, 2015), which is illustrated by privileging technological innovation and marketing to the detriment of entirely unthinkable social innovation. However, change in winter tourism is 'already there'. It operates visibly or discreetly in the interstices and on the periphery of the system, where sectors, destinations, organizations and individual operators reposition themselves in niches more conducive to multi-seasonal continuities. At the very heart of the winter tourism system, skiing is no longer as central as in the past: despite its own contradictions, it has long been the real estate sector that carries a major part of the economy, and a feeling of imagination linked to the wellbeing and festive practices slowly taking over from a traditional, especially sporty, mountain holiday concept.

Moreover, if resorts remain at the heart of the tourist landscape, a less polarized model at the geographical, temporal and economic levels reinforces the development of tourism outside of resorts; that is, where the strength of legitimate models diminishes, and where a disengagement of dominant norms stimulates the ability to find arrangements, make exceptions and experiment with alternatives to overcome structural and functional handicaps. Field observations show that this creativity relies less on amenities than on the skill and passion of professionals and amateurs who take a new look at the environmental resources and the cultural codes of recreational practices, including relying on new materials. We can therefore observe the phenomena of games related to the slope in terms of inversions between descent and climb. The celebration of the 'up-hill flow' allows a rehabilitation of the climb, which takes place both in winter thanks to the craze for ski touring, and the summer thanks to the electric assistance bike. Inventiveness also relies on the creative potential of counter-cultures and recreational resistance (Bourdeau and Lebreton, 2013) that bypass, divert or return the norms and standardization of the recreational experience programmed by the facilities and the tourist industry: off-piste, 'DIY' of materials and spaces, nocturnal and experimental practices. It also makes the most of its environmental responsibility to bring (back) more localized practices and alternative modes of mobility. The NGO Mountain Wilderness has championed a 'change of approach' campaign since 2007 finding new ways for people to access mountain tourist destinations without a car.[4] Still within the mode of 'already existing', the 'amenity migration' phenomenon (Bourdeau, 2009b; Perlik, 2011) is quietly contributing to the rise of a residential economy (Segessemann and Crevoisier, 2015), which decisively complements the conventional tourist economy.

In many mountain communities, tourism actors and local sportspeople work more and more with 'new' inhabitants and their families or visiting friends. The notions of residential tourism or visiting friends and relatives tourism (Griffin, 2013) continually express this largely unthought of, ignored or repressed diversification process. In many local contexts, an observation of the actual degree of the 'already existing' transition would be very useful, not only to measure these phenomena, but also to work to update dominant representations that are out of step with social and economic reality. The respective weights often now reversed between the summer and winter seasons could also be highlighted, while the usual representation is that in the mountains 'during the winter we work, and in the summer we make our pocket money'.[5] Beyond the strategic debates about the future of winter tourism, it is on the ground that a confrontation of wishful thinking and certain visions of the future takes place. It has sparked controversy over numerous developments, the linking of resorts and projects of expansion of the ski areas. Although the opposition coming often from urban nature protection organizations is standard, the novelty is that disputes also come more and more often from inhabitants, elected and local professionals, traditionally favourable to the facilities. The local collectives where they gather generate numerous petitions, legal action and press articles, as well as important demonstrations, on skis, on foot or on snowshoes. We can see the example of a meeting against the extension of the ski resort of Chamrousse (Isère) in the Vans sector, in March 2016, which brought together more than 600 people, and led – at least temporarily – to the abandonment of the project; or even the example at the Ratti Pass, which gathered nearly 700 hikers in January 2017 to denounce the project of a connection between the ski areas of Roc d'Enfer and Mont Chéry, in the resort of Gets (Haute-Savoie).

In other cases, there is also a mobilization of local collectives around participatory funding to allow associative management of small ski lifts that can be dismantled in order to maintain popular winter sports practice. But local mobilization also takes place to defend a resort threatened with closure, including challenging 'after ski' projects.

The most representative case in France concerns the resort of Abondance (Haute-Savoie) whose closure in 2007 and the project of conversion to heritage and cultural tourism sparked strong local tensions, leading to the organization of a demonstration 'For skiing … against pseudo-cultural development' (Suchet and Raspaud, 2010). More than just an employment issue – which was not really threatened – the main fears expressed concern the loss of a local identity built around 50 years of skiing and the resulting sense of 'symbolic death', as well as on a negative vision of heritage – 'Heritage is something for the elderly' – and a doubt about its economic potential, including the fear of a collapse of property prices of secondary residents.

It is also at the local level that we find the very sensitive question in France of the central role of public funding of winter sports – whether this is in the form of direct or indirect subsidies, or by property tax exemption. A rational reorientation of this policy of quasi-permanent support would make it possible to make considerable room to manoeuvre in terms of jobs. This is exemplified by the opponents of the Hauteville-Valromey (Ain) plateau's citizens' collective,[6] who objected to an industrial snow production equipment project: 'and you, companies and inhabitants of the Hauteville/Valromey plateau, with €1 million, how many jobs are you going to create?' (Descamps and Ortillon, 2016). In a context of dwindling public funds, and at a time when we are beginning to imagine that it will be necessary to subsidize ski passes to mitigate their price inflation (Clivaz et al., 2015), the political question of financial support from public authorities will therefore be increasingly important. And even if mountain officials are rightly paralysed by the question of maintaining jobs, they will be less and less able to avoid the debate that is widespread in the very heart of the territories concerned.

36.5 Conclusion: 'Reinventing' Winter Tourism?

Following the themes of 'reconquest' in the 1990s and 're-enchantment' in the 2000s, 'reinvention' is today a leitmotif when expressing the needs and aspirations for change in a context of climate, energy and economic crises against a backdrop of technological revolution. This adaptive injunction resonates all the more strongly in winter tourism as the system of winter sports inherited from the second half of the 20th century is an exhausted model, subjected to a peak of contradictions and destined for real reconstruction. Yet how can we consider models that are more flexible, diversified, creative and sustainable in the face of the triple challenge of the climate, energy and economic crises? This transition project involves an intellectual, strategic and political investment, avoiding any generalization to clearly distinguish the very different situations in which the mountain territories are located.

If we fast forward a few decades, we can begin to sketch out the scenario of an alpine skiing sanctuary in very large mountain resorts, suitable for communications and infrastructural investments, such as widespread artificial snow production, ski lifts, recreational resources, as well as prestigious commercial and festive facilities. The predominately international clientele will also redirect some of the economic activity around shopping and clubbing. This is while a growing number of small and medium-sized resorts near major cities will have converted to residential functions throughout the year, which in some cases will allow the continuation of the winter sports activity dedicated to local clientele, in a double process of amenity migrations and post-tourism.

We can then imagine that winter tourism will continue as a recreational niche for a minority of the population, while the mountain becomes an attractive residential area: we will therefore live more in the mountains, but there will be less tourism, even if residential and 'relatives and friends' tourism will develop. The closest and most connected stations to the alpine metropolises could experience the strongest development while the more distant and less well-connected would decrease. It can also be imagined that small and micro stations based on minimal infrastructures will be maintained thanks to their ability to withstand the intermittences of exploitation related to snow cover variations, by relying on close attendance of a large public.

The more the winter atmosphere is altered by climate change, the more the aesthetic, symbolic and recreational attractiveness of snowy landscapes can be expected to become important to visitors' expectations. A legitimate concern of operators and observers of winter tourism is the weakening of the imagination of the 'pure white' mountain, which may reduce the desire to take part in winter sports. Indeed, we can assume that 'guaranteeing the winter atmosphere' will be more and more difficult in the future because it is not a purely snowy one. The artificial snow production is adapted to the practice of skiing, but not (except at exorbitant costs) to the simulation of a winter atmosphere in the streets and the landscape of the resorts. The notion of a winter atmosphere must therefore be valued both in the case of snow, but also considered in its possible or probable absence. For low-altitude destinations, a radical repositioning of the rural mountain atmosphere 'little snow' or 'completely snowless' will be designed. The cultural heritage and traditions (Christmas, light festivals, bonfires, songs, shows, local crafts, woodwork, etc.) can be an aesthetic and experiential support for this atmosphere, playing on symbols associated with snow, even if it is missing. In addition, we need not overlook climate change: first because the milder and less snowy winters could allow for other activities as opposed to traditional winter sports, attracting urban populations for whom the snow is potentially dissuasive or has negative connotations; second, because – paradoxically – the adaptive injunction of climate change may enable some mountain regions to engage in a transition that provides alternative solutions and innovation. Finally, if the impact of climate change will be mostly negative for the winter season (lack of snow, extra cost of artificial snow production, loss of winter atmosphere), it may be positive for the summer season, which will be extended from April to October, offering visitors and inhabitants of the mountains increased climatic comfort compared with urban areas.

The highly speculative nature of this prospective vision of the future does not claim any certainties. At the risk of exaggerating for the purposes of demonstration, it is possible to express these uncertainties in the form of questions relating to the recreational nature of the mountain regions: A quest for peace and harmony or a bidding war? Contemplative or over-active mode? Immersion in nature or shopping and amusement parks? Intimate craft design or prestigious equipment? Celebrating heritage or unbridled clubbing? Family-friendly gatherings or raucous celebrations? Human mediation or digital technology? Digital detox or wi-fi everywhere? Luxury or social tourism? Ski tours or heli-skiing? Of course, these oppositions are not new but do carry with them the cultural universes and values under strain that underlie the multiple contradictory injunctions of contemporary societies: Should we go faster or slow down? Innovation or precaution? High-tech or low-tech? 'Bigger is better' or 'small is beautiful'? Growth or degrowth? Hyper-connection or disconnection?

The contours of an undecided dilemma are then drawn around contemporary societies, between those who refer to a 'consumerist' norm (Ballesta et al., 2016) and those who refer to a 'pro-environment' norm (Félonneau and Becker, 2008).

The recreational transition (Corneloup, 2017) appears to be a reorganization under tension (Vlès and Bouneau, 2016), which gives pride to hesitations and controversies over the legitimate ways to design the future of tourism and recreation in a changing world. The central challenge is to deploy a coherent set of approaches and actions through which practices and the tourism economy are transformed in a climate-compatible way, integrating cultural change and mastering technological change. In fact, if very rational criteria help to explain the inertia of tourist operators, one of the major problems of transition is above all a lack of representation of the future as a possible and desirable future. How to relay the force of the modern myth of the ski resort as a utopia 'that has proved itself and its time' (Knafou, 1991)? How to get out of a snow socio-technical lock-in that forces winter tourism operators to pursue unachievable goals while other achievable goals are neglected? It is the challenge of designing and implementing transition pathways (Geels and Schot, 2007) that propose reorientation, bifurcation and conversion patterns oriented towards low-carbon tourism practices and new tourism offerings (local tourism, residential tourism, leisure migration, staycation) but also redeployed in space (villages and sites away from resorts) and in time (to go away for longer, take it more slowly, or even less often?). In a transition approach, the role of niche innovations, like in the Nordic sector for example, is to propose alternative solutions that seem less and less marginal and radical as they contribute to structuring a new development model, or to deeply restructuring the existing model (Boulanger, 2015).

The first half of the 20th century witnessed a space–time revolution in tourism: the sea became the dominant summer destination while mountains established themselves as the most popular winter destinations; that is to say, a complete reversal of geographical and seasonal polarity with regard to the initial situation in the 18th and 19th centuries. This overturning of habits, which is linked to essentially geo-cultural factors (increase in heliotropism, evolution of our relationship with our body, development of skiing, mass recreation, etc.), has of course made great demands on the capacity to adapt for tourist operators and destinations. While it is at the origin of contemporary tourism, it is obvious that this geo-seasonal balance cannot be considered as an immutable fact. The current climatic shift, acting as a catalyst in the structural mutations of tourism, could eventually lead to a new space–time repolarization (Bourdeau, 2008). We would therefore witness a sort of 'back to square one' of tourism with summer flow turned towards the mountains as a natural 'climatized zone', and winter flow drained by the coasts offering a large selection of various swimming, sailing and wellness activities.

A phenomenon of this type occurring over several decades throws considerable light on the impression of uncertainty that has been hitting mountain tourism for the past 20 years. Itself a vector of an economy of substitution with respect to agriculture and mountain industry, from now on the tourist sector finds itself facing the limits of its own stability; indeed, of its durability. Without losing sight of the diversity of regional tourist topologies and destinations, or of the multiplicity of variables that influence the future of this sector, it therefore seems urgent to advance beyond a number of certitudes. This 'step to the side' cannot be satisfied with a simple tactical aggiornamento, in terms of marketing and communication, for example, but it must constitute an authentic turnaround in strategy. The preoccupation with diversification linked to the weakening effects of climate change does not therefore rest only on an offer of new recreational activities – of which a very rich variety already exists – but also on the interest shown in new spaces, new publics, new times and new meanings. This is thanks to the assertion of the legitimacy of a multiplicity of protagonists and operators, of working methods, of choices of professional life, of everyday life and recreational models. By going beyond the initial models of all-skiing, all-snowing and all-tourism, the living Alps can hope to assert themselves in the future as mountains of the 'four seasons' (winter, spring, summer, autumn), of the 'four spaces' (resorts, villages, high mountain, market town centres), of the 'four activities' (agriculture, crafts services, recreation, new information and communication technologies) and of the 'four economies': production, public, residential, social. The objective of such a highly speculative vision is to outline the project for a more diversified mountain economy and greater resilience to the uncertainties of the future. Empirical research must of course document the wide range of experiments and creative initiatives that fuel transformative transition paths as trajectories of diversification, reorientation or conversion of mountain economies and ways of living and working.

Acknowledgements

Several research projects valued in this text have been financially supported by the LabEx 'Innovation and Mountain Territories' (Université Grenoble-Alpes, Agence Nationale de la Recherche).

Notes

[1] According to the DGEDD (2009), artificial snow cost in 2009 €2.5–3 per m^3, of which about half in energy cost, i.e. a consumption of 0.6 kWh/m^3 excluding pumping of the water, which accounted for 5–10% of the package price, with equipment amortized in 20–30 years.

[2] The titles were found on various news websites: www.slate.fr, www.letemps.ch, www.franceinter.fr, www.la-croix.com, www.lemonde.fr, www.nouvelobs.com/rue89.

[3] Quoted during an interview with Bruno Gardent, a mountain leader and ski instructor in Grave, Haute-Alpes, France.

[4] For more information, see the campaign's website. Available at: https://www.changerdapproche.org (accessed 7 February 2019).

[5] Bernard Lagarrigue (1986) Editorial. *Aménagement et montagne* 52, 5. Available at: https://data.bnf.fr/en/34418707/amenagement_et_montagne__grenoble_/#relations (accessed 14 May 2019).

[6] For more information on the citizens' collective, see their website. Available at: http://hautevillevalromey.wixsite.com/collectif-citoyen (accessed 7 February 2019).

References

Achin, C. and George, E. (2013) Sorties de piste pour la performance touristique des stations de sports d'hiver. *Tourisme and Territoires* 3, 67–92.

Alter, N. (2000) *L'innovation ordinaire*. Presses Universitaires de France, Paris.

Atout France (2016) Le poids du tourisme dans les Alpes: étude factuelle et chiffrée. Presented by Berthier, M.J. at the Symposium 'Le tourisme dans le massif alpin: bilans et perspectives', 5 February 2016, Grenoble, France.

Bachimon, P., Bourdeau, P., Corneloup, J. and Bessy, O. (2014) Du tourisme à l'après-tourisme, le tournant d'une station de moyenne montagne: St-Nizier-du-Moucherotte (Isère). Available at: http://geoconfluences.ens-lyon.fr/informations-scientifiques/dossiers-thematiques/les-nouvelles-dynamiques-du-tourisme-dans-le-monde/articles-scientifiques/du-tourisme-a-l-apres-tourisme (accessed 31 January 2019).

Ballesta, O., Carimentrand, A., Causse, E., Delerue, F., Felonneau, M.L. et al. (2016) L'adoption de comportements écologiques face au déclassement social: éléments préliminaires. In: Bourg, D., Dartiguepeyrou, C., Gervais, C. and Perrin, O. (eds.) *Les Nouveaux Modes De Vie Durables. S'engager Autrement*. Le Bord de l'eau, Lormont, France, pp. 107–112.

Banerjee, A. and Duflo, E. (2012) *Poor Economics: Barefoot Hedge-fund Managers, DIY Doctors and the Surprising Truth About Life on less than $1 a Day*. Penguin, London.

Barnett, J. and O'Neill, S.J. (2010) Maladaptation. *Global Environmental Change* 20(2), 211–213. DOI:10.1016/j.gloenvcha.2009.11.004

Berlioz, F. (2006) Les données de base de la connaissance: analyse des évolutions, impact sur le devenir du tourisme en montagne. Direction des études et de l'aménagement touristique de la montagne/Observation, développement et ingénierie touristiques (DEATM-ODIT), Challes-Les-Eaux, France.

Bonnemains, A. (2015) Vulnérabilité et résilience d'un modèle de développement alpin. Trajectoire territoriale des stations de haute altitude de Tarentaise. PhD Thesis, Université Grenoble Alpes, Grenoble, France.

Boulanger, P.-M. (2015) Transition. In: Bourg, D. and Papaux, A. (eds) *Dictionnaire de la pensée écologique*. PUF, Paris, pp. 1011–1015.

Bourdeau, P. (2008) The Alps in the age of new style tourism: between diversification and post-tourism? In: Borsdorf, A., Stötter, J. and Veuillet, E. (eds) *Managing Alpine Future*. Austrian Academy of Science Press, Vienna, pp. 81–86.

Bourdeau, P. (2009a) From après-ski to après-tourism: the Alps in transition? Reflections based on the French situation. *Journal of Alpine Research* 97(3), 1–11. DOI:10.4000/rga.1054

Bourdeau P. (2009b) Amenity migration as an indicator of post-tourism; a geo-cultural approach to the Alpine case. In: Moss, L.A.G., Glorioso, R.S. and Krause, A. (eds) *Mountain Culture*. Banff Centre, Banff, Canada, pp. 25–32.

Bourdeau, P. and Lebreton, F. (2013) Les dissidences récréatives en nature: entre jeu et transgression. Available at: www.espacestemps.net/articles/les-dissidences-recreatives-en-nature-entre-jeu-et-transgression (accessed 31 January 2019).

Bourdeau, P., Adamkiewicz, E., Apilli, E., Boudieres, V. and Boulogne, A. (2007) *Sports d'hiver en mutation*. Hermès-Lavoisier, Paris.

Burchardt, H. and Dietz, K. (2014) (Neo)-extractivism. A new challenge for development theory from Latin America. *Third World Quarterly* 35(3), 468–486. DOI:10.1080/01436597.2014.893488

Caniëls, M. and Rietzschel, E. (2015) Organizing Creativity: Creativity and Innovation under Constraints. *Creativity and Innovation Management* 24(2), 184–196. DOI: 24. 10.1111/caim.12123.

Chevallier, M. (1996) Paroles de modernités. Pour une relecture culturelle de la station de sports d'hiver moderne. *Revue de Géographie Alpine* 84(3), 29–39. DOI:10.3406/rga.1996.3868

Clivaz, C., Gonseth, C. and Matasci, C. (2015) *Tourisme d'hiver. Le défi climatique*. Presses Polytechniques et Universitaires Romandes, Lausanne, Switzerland.

Corneloup, J. (2017) Transition récréative et écologie corporelle. *Juristourisme* 195, 17–20.

Corneloup, J. and Bourdeau, P. (2015) Changement culturel et effets générationnels dans les métiers sportifs de la montagne. In: Attali, M. (ed.) *L'ENSA à la conquête des sommets.*

La montagne sur les voies de l'excellence. Presses Universitaires de Grenoble, Grenoble, France, pp. 171–194.

Cour des Comptes (2018) Les stations de ski des Alpes du nord face au réchauffement climatique: une vulnérabilité croissante, le besoin d'un nouveau modèle de développement. Rapport public annuel 2018. Available at: https://www.ccomptes.fr/sites/default/files/2018-01/14-stations-ski-Alpes-nord-face-rechauffement-climatique-Tome-2.pdf (accessed 7 February 2019).

Descamps, P. and Ortillon, P. (2016) Hauteville-Lompnes – Le collectif contre les canons à neige lance une pétition. Available at: https://www.lavoixdelain.fr/actualite-23919-hauteville-lompnes-le-collectif-contre-les-canons-a-neige-lance-une-petition?page=post (accessed 7 February 2019).

DGEDD (2009) Rapport du Conseil Général de l'Environnement et du Développement Durable n° 006332-01. Available at: http://cgedd.documentation.developpement-durable.gouv.fr/documents/cgedd/006332-01_rapport.pdf (accessed 7 February 2019).

Falaix, L. and Corneloup, J. (2017) Habitabilité et renouveau paradigmatique de l'action territoriale: l'exemple des laboratoires récréatifs. *L'Information géographique* 81(4), 78–102.

Félonneau, M.-L. and Becker, M. (2008) Pro-environmental attitudes and behavior: revealing perceived social desirability. *Revue internationale de psychologie sociale* 21(4), 25–53.

Garcia, P.-O. (2015) Sous l'adaptation, l'immunité: étude sur le discours de l'adaptation au changement climatique. PhD Thesis, Université Grenoble-Alpes, Grenoble, France. Available at: https://tel.archives-ouvertes.fr/tel-01470390/document (accessed 9 May 2019).

Gauchon, C. (2010) Sports d'hiver et tourisme durable: mythes et réalités. In: Marcelpoil E., Bensahel-Perrin, L. and François, H. (eds) *Les stations de sports d'hiver face au développement durable*. L'Harmattan, Paris, pp. 63–72.

Geels, F.W. and Schot, J. (2007) Typology of sociotechnical transition pathways. *Research Policy* 36(3), 399–417. DOI:10.1016/j.respol.2007.01.003

Griffin, T. (2013) Visiting friends and relatives tourism and implications for community capital. *Journal of Policy Research in Tourism, Leisure and Events* 5(3), 233–251. DOI:10.1080/19407963.2013.776370

Heinberg, R. (2010) *Peak Everything: Waking Up to the Century of Declines*. New Society Publishers, Gabriola Island, Canada.

Hoibian, S. (2010) Un désir de renouveau des vacances d'hiver. Rapport réalisé à la demande de la Direction Générale de la Compétitivité, de l'Industrie et des Services (DGCIS). CRÉDOC, Paris.

KEA (2009) The impact of culture on creativity. Study prepared for the European Commission. Available at: www.keanet.eu/docs/impactculturecreativityfull.pdf (accessed 31 January 2019).

Knafou, R. (1991) La crise du tourisme dans les montagnes françaises. Un système qui a fait ses preuves et son temps. *Les Dossiers de la Revue de Géographie Alpine* 6, 13–21.

Liebowitz, S.J. and Margolis S.E. (1995) Path dependence, lock-in and history. *Journal of Law, Economics, and Organization* 11(1), 205–226. DOI:10.2139/ssrn.1706450

Masson-Maret, H. and Vairetto, A. (2014) Rapport d'information au Sénat n° 384. Available at: https://www.senat.fr/rap/r13-384/r13-3841.pdf (accessed 7 February 2019).

Parsons, M. and Rose, M. (2009) Lead User Innovation and the UK outdoor Trade Since 1850. Lancaster University Management School, Working paper 2009/028. Available at: http://eprints.lancs.ac.uk/48970/1/Document.pdf (accessed 9 May 2019).

Pechlaner, H., Demetz, M. and Scuttari, A. (2015) Alpine biking tourism. The Future of Cycle Tourism in the Alps. Available at: https://www.alp-net.eu/wp-content/uploads/2018/07/theALPS-Bike-Study-2015.pdf (accessed 31 January 2019).

Perlik, M. (2011) Alpine gentrification: the mountain village as a metropolitan neighbourhood. *Journal of Alpine Research* 99(1), 1–16. DOI:10.4000/rga.1370

Place Gre'net (2015) L. Reynaud:'s'il n'y a pas le ski, il n'y a rien'. Available at: https://www.placegrenet.fr/2015/01/17/laurent-reynaud-sil-ny-pas-ski-il-ny-rien/48161 (accessed 7 February 2019).

Rosa, H. (2015) *Social Acceleration. A New Theory of Modernity*. Columbia University Press, New York.

Schot, J.W. (1998) The usefulness of evolutionary models for explaining innovation. *History of Technology* 14(3), 173–200. DOI:10.1080/07341519808581928

Segessemann, A. and Crevoisier, A. (2015) Beyond economic base theory: the role of the residential economy in attracting income to Swiss regions. *Regional Studies* 50(8), 1388–1403. DOI:10.1080/00343404.2015.1018882.

Shahshahani, L. (2016) Laurent Wauquiez: 'La neige de culture est la base de notre politique montagne'. Available at: https://www.montagnes-magazine.com/actus-laurent-wauquiez-neige-culture-base-politique-montagne (accessed 7 February 2019).

Steffen, W., Broadgate, W., Deutsch, L., Gaffney, O. and Ludwig, C. (2015) The trajectory of the Anthropocene: the great acceleration. *The Anthropocene Review* 2(1), 81–98. DOI:10.1177/2053019614564785

Suchet, A. and Raspaud, M. (2010) A case of local rejection of a heritage tourism policy: tourism and dynamics of change in Abondance, French Alps. *International Journal of Heritage Studies* 16(6), 449–463. DOI:10.1080/13527258.2010.505038

Vanat, L. (2016) Bilan de la saison 2015–2016. Fréquentation des domaines skiables. Available at: www.vanat.ch/RM-CH-palmares-JS2016-R-F-Laurent%20Vanat.pdf (accessed 31 January 2019).

Vanat, L. (2018) 2018 International report on snow and mountain tourism: overview of the key industry figures for ski resorts. Available at: https://vanat.ch/RM-world-report-2018.pdf (accessed 31 January 2019).

Vercors Tourisme (n.d.) Un monde où … le ski ne s'arrête jamais. Available at: http://skiroue.vercors.fr/files/2015/07/vercors-campagne-ski-105x148.jpg (accessed 7 February 2019).

Vlès, V. and Bouneau, C. (2016) *Stations en tension*. Peter Lang, Bern, Switzerland.

Index

Note: Page numbers in **bold** type refer to **figures**
Page numbers in *italic* type refer to *tables*
Page numbers followed by 'n' refer to notes

Abondance 502
Aboriginal peoples 36, 39
Aboriginal rights 40–41, 434–436
Aboriginal Title and Rights 36, 37, 38–39
    Canadian Constitution 39–40
accelerated inertia 500
access roads 395
accessibility 54–55, 57, 239, 240, 261, 296, 349
    disabled 54, 55
    glaciers 297, 347
    high-Alpine areas 347
    ski resorts 327
Accident & Emergency services 327
accidents 301, 461–462
    collision 468, **469**, 470, 471
    skiing 465–470
accommodation 3, 20, 57, 329
    affordable 118, 282
    carbon dioxide emissions 69
    and climate change 18, 87
    eco-friendly 86
    energy efficient 88, 89
accountability 129
achievement 241–242
action research 372, 384
activities, winter 9
adaptation 3, 47
    strategy 4
        SWOT analysis 95–97, 101
added value 330, 333, 340
adventure camps 141, **141**
adventure tourism 463
adventure-based lifestyle 281
advertising
    ski resorts 495
    word-of-mouth 132, 149
aerial tramways 340
affluent tourists 189
agriculture 3, 392, 504
air travel 316
    and climate change 87
    energy consumption 82, 83
    greenhouse gas emissions 83, 88
airports 57, 216, 277, 363, 450, 457

all-season destinations 19
all-season tourism 12, 298
Alpenplan *see* Alpine Plan
alpine communities, lower-level 299
Alpine Convention 92, 100, 161
Alpine Plan (Alpenplan) 15, 26–28, 31, 32
alpine ski resorts
    gross income 117
    pricing strategies 20, 116–137
alpine skiing 20, 103, 189, 461
alpine (winter) tourism 64, 496–500
    supply and demand 124
    value chain 259, **259**
Alps 9, 493
    alternative outdoor activities 236–245
    artificial snowmaking 65, 70
    Australian 16, 36
    Austrian 25, 346
    Carpathian 10
    climate change 17, 64–72
    Convention on the Protection of the Alps
        (2013) 161
    French 302–303, 493–508
    German 92, 345, *345*
    glaciers 64
    hotel prices 113n1
    land use changes 378
    product development 266–271
    snow coverage 64
    Swiss 308
    temperatures 64
    transport 70
    Tyrolian 9, 31, 118
    water resources 64
    see also Bavarian Alps; European Alps
alternative mobility 331, 332, 334, 335
alternative outdoor activities 179–180
    Alps 236–245, *239*
alternative winter sports activities 237, 238, *242*
    Tyrol 236–245
amenity migration 277, 278–279, 282, 501, 502
    Banff 282
    Canmore 278–279, 282
    Sweden 295, 309

American Dream 278
American Skiing Company 354–357, *355*
Amsterdam, ecological footprint 83
Anthropocene 494
anthropogenic climate change 85
après ski 105
    Bansko 375
    Dolomites 333, 335
archaeology 499
Argentina, Bariloche 36
art on the mountain 374
artificial ski areas, Sweden 319
artificial snowmaking 2, 11, 12, 49, 57, 93, 96, 98, 99, 383, 400, 403–404, *404*, 494–496, 503
    Alps 65, 70
    cost-revenue analysis 129–130
    costs 3–4, 116, 120, 505n1
Aspen effect 309
Aspen Skiing Company 359, 360, 362
auditing 3, 373, 375–376, 385
Australia, ski resort managers 77
Australian Alps 16, 36
Australians 276
Austria
    Alpbach-Seenland 83–89
    Alpbach-Tal-Seenland 18
    biodiversity 65
    cable cars 104
    carbon dioxide emissions 69
    destination selection 407–408, *408*, **409**, 416–417
    expenditure behaviour 104
    Hohe Tauern National Park 30, **31**
    Ischgl 349
    Kaprun 348
    Kitzbühel 348
    Kitzsteinhorn 348
    Lech am Arlberg **12**, 403–404, *404*
    Malfontal 9, **10**
    mountaineering villages 30
    nature experience programmes 67–68, **68**
    overnight stays 64, **65**, 344–345, **344**
    renewable energy 403–421, *405*, 406
    Salzburg 55–56, 64
    Schladming 403–404, *404*
    Silvretta Montafon 403–404, *404*
    ski lifts 104
    snowmaking facilities 65–66
    stay duration 69
    summer activities 404
    Thomatal 350
    transportation 68–69
    Zell am See 403–404, *404*
    see also Tyrol
Austrian Alps 25, 346
Austrian Ecolabel 370
Austrian Tourism Bank 66

authentic products 54
authenticity 58, 357
auto-mobility 89
autumn tourism 56
Avalanche Canada 150
avalanches 21, 153, 252, 464
    skills training courses 149–150, 152
aviation 82

backcountry
    ethics 152
    huts 230
    skiing 229, 232, 237, 243, 309
    tours 149
backpacking 75, 105
backyard effect 319
Banff (Canada) 279, 434
Bansko 298, 374–375, 376
    accommodation 118
    après ski 375
    cable cars 376
    carbon dioxide emissions 383–384
    climate change 383–384
    environmental improvement 378–390
    guest structure 376
    internal management 383
    marketing 381–382
    recultivation 380, **381**, **382**
    Strategic Environmental Assessment (SEA) 375
Bariloche 36
Bavaria 15
    Alpine Plan 26–28, 31, 32
    SnowBavaria 58
    spatial planning 27–28, **27**
Bavarian Alps 9, 31, 32, 92
    cable cars 27, 28
    climate change adaptation 19, 92–102
    development 27–28
    global warming 13
    infrastructure 26, 100
    landscape protection areas 30
    multifarious product 92–93
    overnight stays 28
    ski lifts 27, 28
    transport infrastructure 26
    winter sport resorts 92
    zoning 26
behaviour
    consumers 158, 161, 167, 169
    environment 158
    leisure 388
    risk 301
    sustainable 157
    see also expenditure behaviour
behavioural change 18, 87, 471
behavioural research 1

best practices 5
bikes, rental 87
biking 12–13, **13**, 16, 77, 87, 96, 376–377
    mountain 75, 80, 318
biodiversity 65, 432
biogas plants 407, 411, 420
biomechanics 236
biotopes 13, 96, 99
Birds Directive 385
Black Forest 20
Black Forest National Park, expenditure behaviour 110–112, *111*
blue ice hiking 450
bob sledding 333
bookings 128
    Internet 55, 260
branding
    destinations 12
    identity 485, 489
    regional 58
Brazil 273
British Columbia 10, 15–16
    Adventure Tourism – Land use Operational Policy 150
    Central Purcells 433
    Commercial Alpine Ski Policy (CASP) 427, 429
    commercial snowmobile offers 14
    Commission on Resources and Environment (CORE) 429, 430
    Crown Land 437n1
    Environmental Assessment Act (2019) 438n7
    First Nations planning 35–46
    government policy 427
    Grizzly Bear Conservation Strategy (1995) 431–432
    indigenous rights 35–46
    Jumbo Valley 36, 42, 426, 436
    Melvin Creek Valley 35–36, 42
    Ministry of Environment, Ecological Restoration Guidelines (2001) 437n3
    Park Act (2006) 43
    protected areas 42–43
    Purcell Mountains 36, 299–300, 426, 427
    Purcell Wilderness Conservancy 426
    resource exploitation 427
    snowmaking **292**
    snowmobiling 21–22
    Sun Peaks Municipality **294**
    Sun Peaks Ski Resort 15, 35
    sustainable development policy 427
    Tod Mountain 35
    Valemount Glacier Destination Resort 44, 438n6
    see also Jumbo Glacier Resort; Whistler; Whistler Blackcomb
British Columbia Commercial Snowmobile Operators Association (BCCSOA) 152
British Columbia Rockies 300
British Columbia Snowmobile Federation (BCSF) 148
British North America Act (1867) 39
Brundtland Commission 427
Buckelwiesen 95
Buddhism 266
budgeting 228
buffer zones 15, 26, 253
building codes 418
Bulgaria
    Pirin Mountains 298
    Pirin National Park 375, 381
    ski resorts 57
    see also Bansko
Bürger Pass 130
buses 221
    ski 88, 333, 334
business 10, 44, 50
    carbon footprint 80
    green 380
    sustainability 18
business model 3, 4, 20, 77, 118–121
business-led tourism promotion, subsidies 66

cabin tours 146, 149
cable cars 3, 25, 57, 58, 128
    Åre 308
    Austria 104
    Bavarian Alps 27, 28
    capacity utilization 54
    carbon footprint 66
    economic relevance 348–349
    enterprises 20, 119, 131, 340
        digital future 127–128
    as innovation 341–346, *341*
    investment 113
    role 296–297, 339–353
    Tatra Mountains 248, 249
cable cars and surface lifts (CCSLs) 339–353, *341*, **342**, **343**, 350n1
    Austrian overnight stays 344–345, **344**
    multiplier effect 349
cableways 324, 339
camping 75
camps, adventure 141, **141**
Canada
    Banff 279, 434
    Bow Valley 279, 282
    Canmore 278–279, 282
    Constitution 38, 39–40
    federal and provincial governments 37
    Guide on Biodiversity and Environmental Assessment 432
    Jasper National Park 44
    ski resorts 36, 158

Canada (*continued*)
    Vancouver International Airport 277, 363
    see also British Columbia
Canadian Council of Snowmobile Organizations 148
capacity 54, 155, 156, 293
carbon
    footprint 80, 82, 83, 84, 86, **86**
    offsetting 83
carbon dioxide emissions 11, 17, 56, 82, 88, 334, 383–384, 421
    accommodation 69
    Austria 69
    stakeholders 77–78
    transportation 69
caribou closures 151–152
Carpathian Alps 10
Carpathian Mountains 32, 246, 250, 254
cars 88, 89, 207
    electric 18
    greenhouse gas emissions 89
    private 13
    rental 221, 445, 446
    self-owned 197, 308
Caucasus 32
caving, Tatra National Park 249, 250
Central Purcell Mountains 433
certification 369–370
    environmental 298
chairlifts 340, 343, 347, 348
    Hoher Kranzberg 98
    Mittenwald 95
challenges 9–23, 53–56, **53**
    common 2–3, **2**
    economic 13–14
    spatial and socio-cultural 9–11
Chambers of Commerce 77
change 187–188
chapels 396
child care 11
children 97, 120, 142, 200
    health 142–143
    skiing 94, 461
    winter sports 14
China
    culture 263, 265
    landscape loss 267
    market 4, 181, 265, 266, 272, 273
    National Level Scenic and Historic Interest Areas 267
    nature 266–268, 272
    population growth 267
    skiing 268
    urbanization 267
    wilderness 267
    World Heritage Sites 267
China Inbound Service 258–266, 268
    value chain 264–266, **264**

Chinese guests 3
    activities 263–264, **263**
    cultural values 268
    customer experiences 261–263, **262**
    expectations 260, 266
    food 262, 263, 264, 265
    management consequences 264–266
    satisfaction 260–261, **261**
    Switzerland 176, 181, 257–275
    travel motivations 259
    typical 260
Chinese speaking staff 265
Chinese students, nature and landscape perception 266–271
Christmas tourism 47, 56, 443–444
citizens 389
cleanliness 261
climate 125, 319
    mitigation targets 400
climate change 1, 11, 49, 76, 80, 298, 503
    and accommodation 18, 87
    adaptation 2, 11–13, 17, 47, 49–50, 59, 67–69, 76–77
        Bavarian Alps 19, 92–102
        bottom-up 99
        cultural differences 207–208
        mountain areas 9
        stakeholders 99
        top-down 99
        trains 207–208
    and air travel 87
    Alps 17, 64–72
    anthropogenic 85
    and communication strategies 66–67
    contradictions 494–496
    current strategies 65–67
    Dolomites 324
    and downhill ski tourism 316–319
    European Alps 12
    impact assessments 316
    local impacts 76
    mitigation 59, 77–78
    perceptions 12, 17–18, 73–81, 197
        Western Maine 12, 73–81
    policy 51
    public planning 50, 53
    resident perceptions and behaviours 78–79
    and ski resorts 4, 388
    skiing 184, 309
    and snow reliability 331, 332, 333
    and summer tourism 503
    survey 84–89, **85**
    and sustainability factors 55–56
    technical solutions 11, 12, 17, 65
    tourist perceptions 13
    and transportation 85, 87
    and travel mobility 18, 82–91

Climate and Energy Model 89
climbing, Tatra National Park 248, 249
coaches 13, 88, 89
cog railways 343
collaboration 3, 77, 301–302
    Finland 476–492
collision accidents 468, **469**, 470, 471
colonization 37
Colorado, ski industry 278
Commercial Alpine Ski Policy 362
common development plans 119
common good 436
communication 11, 125, 373, 383, 504
    climate change 66–67
    environmental 370
    target groups 205
community 10, 156, 298, 300, 324, 363, 501
    involvement, Whistler 167, 168
compensation 10
competition 54, 56, 100–101, 248, 366, 392, 495
conference tourism 16
conflict
    interpersonal 228, 233, 234
    publics 228–229
    recreation 229
    resolution 25
    social values 1, 229, 233, 234
Confucianism 266, 268
conservancies 43
conservation
    energy 331, 332, 334
    landscape 331
    nature 15, 19, 95–96, 99, 253–254, 267
conservationists 24, 32
construction 65, 376
consumers
    behaviour 158, 161, 167, 169
    interest 158, 167, 168–169
convenience 241–242
Convention on the Protection of the Alps (2013) 161
cooperation 20, 53, 152, 383
    nature conservation 253–254
corporate model 310
corporate–community relations, Whistler 354, 361–366
corporations 297, 310, 357
    North American mountain resorts 354–357
corporatization, place 361
cost
    artificial snowmaking 3–4, 116, 120, 505n1
    efficiency 2
    energy 116, 129, 188, 496
    living 276, 282
    operating 105
    snowmobiling 153
    see also price; pricing
counter-culture lifestyle 281–282

counter-urban movement 278
cross-continental differences 193
cross-country skiing 11, 94, 237, 239, 308, 476
    changes in participation 186, **186**, 187
    cultural differences 196, 197
    Sweden 177, 186–187, **186**, 309
cross-cultural differences 193
crowdfunding 20, 124
Crown Land 38, 437n1
cruise ship industry 19, 20, 94, 130
culinary tourism 16
cultural differences 3
    climate change adaptation 207–208
    cross- 193
    destination choice 193
    online surveys 194, 195
    overcrowding 223
    skiing 178, 192–211
cultural events 11, 93
cultural experiences 193, 199
cultural features 267
cultural heritage 388, 396, 503
cultural identity, landscape 272
cultural landscapes 27
cultural practices 35
cultural products 17
cultural programmes 67
cultural resource management 296, 331–332, 335
cultural responsibility 498–499
cultural sites 418
cultural tourism 299, 502
cultural values 268, 448
culture 16, 58, 286, 365, 495
    China 263, 265
    definition 192–193
    destination choice 178
    hospitality 58
    Indigenous 436
    marketization 58
    preservation 161
    snow sports 314
    sports 193
customer-centric products 55
customers
    added value 340
    current and future 14
    loyalty 20, 131–133
    needs 175
    research 55
    value 58
customized products 14, 258
customized services 258
cycling *see* biking

Dalarna 55, 308, 312, 316
Davos 342, 343

day trippers 20, 58, 92, 94, 147, 284
    expenditure behaviour 105, 106, 107, 110
decision making 66, 192, 298, 335, 373
    Jumbo Glacier Resort 428–430
    organizations 302, 362
    public interest 437
    risk 463
deforestation 100
demand 2, 4, 16, 49, 117, 324
    changing 53, 54–55, 57
    diversity 3
    international 4
    and supply 55, 58
destination 1
    all-season 2, 19
    branding 12
    choice 175–176, 207
        Austria 407–408, *408*, **409**, 416–417
        cultural differences 178, 193
    community 324
    coordinators 478
    development 299, 302, 477
    management 13, 302
    new 392
    policy and planning 13, 291
    success 476–492
        collaboration 477–479, 489
        determinants 478
        leadership 477–479, 489
    sustainability 155–172
        Europe 158, 160–161
Destination Competitiveness Model 158, **159**
destination management organizations (DMOs) 49, 95, 324, 477–478, 485–487, 489–490
    directors 326, 331
    semi-public 51
developers 24
development 1, 2, 4, 158, 291–304
    Bavarian Alps 27–28
    concepts 3–4
    destination 299, 302, 477
    economic 25–26
    environmental aspects 24–25
    environmental goals 176
    EU funds 57
    Europe 53–56
    European Alps 9, 15
    Hornafjödur 449–451
    incremental 4
    investors 57
    limits 15, 24–26
    pseudo-cultural 502
    public actors 395
    regional 48, 51
    resort towns 296
    rural 3
    ski resorts 30, 302
    urban 4
    villages 296, 297
    zones 15
    see also economic development; products, development; sustainable development
Diemtigtal
    expenditure behaviour 106–110, *106*, *107*, *109*
    nature-based tourism 106–110
differences *see* cultural differences
digitalization (digital technology) 127, 134n6, 324
disabled 54, 55, 97
discrete choice experiment 194–196, **196**, 205–207
Disneyfication 364
disposable income 188, 308
disputes 501
diversification 2, 16–17, 67, 189, 500, 505
    French ski resorts 298–299, 388–399
    products 59, 77
    ski resorts 177
    Sweden 318
dog sledding 243
Dolomites 296, 328–330, 333
    après ski 333, 335
    climate change 324
    environmental destruction 328
    environmental sustainability 336, **336**
    landscape **325**
    mass ski model 326–327
    new approach 330–335, *332*
    new demand trends 331, *332*, 333
    public transport 333, 335
    ski consortium 325
    sustainability 324–338
    temperature 328–329
downhill skiing 55, 314–319
    changes in participation **186**
    climate change impact 316–319
    costs 312
    expansion 308
    Finland 476
    indicators 310, *311*, 312
    socio-economic changes 314–316
    Sweden 177, 185, **186**, 295, 305–323, 312, *313*, 314
dynamic pricing, SkiArena Andermatt-Sedrun 126–127, **126**, **127**, 134n5

e-cars 87, 89
e-mobility 13, 89
Eastern Europe, ski resorts 118
eco-friendly mobility 18
Eco-Management and Audit Scheme (EMAS) 369, 370, 373, 375, 376, 382, 384, 385
    basic principles 370–372, **371**, *372*
ecological footprint 83

ecological responsibility 385
ecology 374
economic benefits 11
economic challenges 1, 9, 13–14
economic change 187–188
economic development 3, 73
    mass ski model 329–330
    mountain areas 3
    pro-growth model 285
    regional 103
    Sweden 295
    tourism development 25–26
economic factors 54
economic growth 56, 59, 327, 427
economic migration 277
economic sustainability 167, 330
economical guests 129
economy 95, 395
    global 16, 53
    local 104, 328, 330
    mountain 505
    regional 53
    sharing 87, 89
    tourism 504
    winter 498
ecosystems 432
educational trips 17, 253
efficiency 375–376
elderly 54, 59, 64, 97, 120
electric cars 18
electric energy 340
elevations 2
emergency facilities 471
emissions
    noise 29
    renewable energy 408, 409, 410, 413
    wind turbines **415**
    see also carbon dioxide emissions; greenhouse gas emissions
employees 384
    motivation 373, 382–383
employment 54, 68, 116, 176–177, 184, 285, 349
    local 388
endogenous development model 329–330
energy 66, 82, 296, 494
    conservation 331, 332, 334
    consumption 66, 69, 69, 383
        air travel 82, 83
        New Zealand 82
        reduction 84, 86, **86**, 88
        transport 17
    costs 116, 129, 188, 496
    efficiency 56, 128
    electric 340
    geothermal 407, 409, 413
    photovoltaic 407
    solar 77, 299, 407, 409, 411, 413, 419

    wind 299, 409, 411, 417, 419, 421
    see also renewable energy
engagement
    investors 4
    stakeholders 362–363
    vertical 130–131
entrepreneurs 54, 488, 489
environment 331
    awareness 180
    behaviour 158
    certification 370
    change 187–188
    communication 370
    consciousness 54, 59
    construction 376
    destruction 328
    goals 176, 428
    monitoring 298
    NGOs 100, 375, 376, 381–382
    protection 164, 335, 427, 433
    renewable energy 408, 409, 410, 413
    responsibility 497
    ski resorts 297–298
    standards 370
Environmental Assessment Act (BC, 1996) 426, 430
environmental assessment (EA) 430–434, 436
environmental certification 298
environmental change 187–188
Environmental Impact Assessments (EIAs) 418
environmental impacts 3, 24–25, 222, 222
environmental improvement 373, 376–390
Environmental Liability Directive (2004) 385
environmental management practices (EMPs) 331, 332, 334
environmental management systems (EMSs) 370, 384
environmental sustainability 330
    Dolomites **336**
    innovative ski offers 330–335
environmentalists 25, 103
environmentally friendly management, ski resorts 369–387
environmentally friendly tourism 421
equipment, technology 251
erosion 222, 376, **378**, 380, 383
Europe
    destination sustainability 158, 160–161
    development trends 53–56
    Eastern 118
European Alps 19
    climate change 12
    development 9, 15
    German tourists 21
    renewable energy 299
    sustainability 157, 167, 168
European regional tourism strategies, comparison 16–17
European tourism Research Institute 184

European Union (EU) 54, 57, 385
expenditure
    seasonal 103, 104, 113
    snowmobiling 147, *148*
    studies 104–106
expenditure behaviour 14
    Austria 104
    average 104
    Black Forest National Park 110–112, *111*
    day trippers 105, 106, 107, 110
    nature-based tourism 107, *108*, 109, *109*
    overnight stays 105, 107, 110
    Switzerland 104
    winter season 105–106
    winter sport activities 19–20, 103–115
experience-led tourism 19, 20, 133
experiences, regional 205
extreme conditions 64

Facebook 162
family-friendliness 239
farm visits 392
farmers 25, 378
Fellhorn 69, *69*
financial crisis
    global (2007–2010) 213
    Iceland (2008) 447
    Sweden (1990s) 310, 319
financial tools 49
Finland
    collaboration 476–492
    cross-country skiing 476
    downhill skiing 476
    gondolas 479
    leadership 476–492
    ski resorts 301–302, 476–492
    skiing tunnels 11
Finnish Lapland 55, 57, 476
First Nations 10, 37, 363, 427, 428, 430, 431, 435
    historical context 38–39
    Land Management Act (1999) 41–42
    planning 15–16, 41–43
        British Columbia 35–46
        territorial and rights 43–44
fishing 39, 243
fitness 232–233, *233*, 243
flexibility 121
flexibilization 67, 68
flights 56, 94, 446
focal enterprises 349
food 58, 181
    Chinese guests 262, 263, 264, 265
footprint
    carbon 80, 82, 83, 84, 86, **86**
    ecological 83
Fordism 329

foreign independent tourist (FIT) 259, 260, 266, 273
foreign tourism
    Iceland 444–445, **445–455**
fossil fuel 56
France
    Abondance 502
    Auverge-Rhône-Alpes 49, 499
    Chamrousse 501
    Guillestrois-Queyras VA **390**, 396–397
    Haute-Maurienne-Vanoise inter-municipality 394, **394**, 395, 396
    Hauteville-Valromey 502
    La Bresse 392
    La Plagne 116, 348
    massifs 389, **390**, 397n3
        Massif Central 392
    Modane 394
    Provence-Alpes-Côte d'Azur 54, 499
    Queyras National Park 396–397
    ski lifts 391
    territorial reform 393–395, 396
    Vanoise National Park 30, 398n8
    Villard-de-Lans 499
    see also French ski resorts; Mountain Law
Frau Holle Guarantee 67
free skiing space 464
free-riders 237
Freestyle Ski World Cup 480
French Alps 302–303, 493–508
French ski resorts 398n9, 493–508
    Chamonix/Les Houches 116
    diversification 298–299, 388–399
    Les Arcs 348
    private–public 298
    Ratti Pass 501
    stakeholders 391
    Val Thorens 116
frost days, Germany 93
funding 20, 124
    public 502
funiculars 343, 347

Garibaldi Lifts Limited 358, 359, 360
Garibaldi Olympic Development Association (GODA) 357, 358
Gastings West Group 360
gastronomy 333
gender
    and injuries 472
    and risk 463
generally suitable zones 26
Generation X 315
geothermal energy 407, 409, 413
German Alps 92, 345, *345*
German Cable Car Association 104
German Sport University Cologne 21, 117

Germans 21, 197
Germany 139
    Black Forest 20, 110–112, *111*
    Fellhorn 69, *69*
    frost days 93
    ice days 93, *93*
    Munich 92
    North Rhine-Westphalia 21
    schools 21, 139
    snow sports 138
    see also Bavaria
Geysir 220, 221, **223**
Gibson's principles 156
glaciers 49, 212, 431, 448, 449–450, 453, 455, 456
    accessibility 297, 347
    activities 455–456, **455**
    Alps 64
    Iceland 300
    Lake of the Hanging Glaciers 425
    melting 64
    Valemount Glacier Destination Resort 44, 438n6
    see also Jumbo Glacier Resort
global financial crisis (2007–2010) 213
global tourism market 2, 326
global travel 189
global warming 2, 13, 47, 49, 56, 324, 500
globalization 1, 324
goats 430
gondolas 248, 340, 350, 364, 479
governance
    local **391**, 392
    regional destination 291
    tourism 298, 389–392
GPS-based equipment 188
green business 380
green concerns 369
green image 375
green labels 164
green marketing 78
green movement 158
green tourism 421
greener products 157
greenhouse gas emissions 73, 316
    air travel 83, 88
    cars 89
    reduction 49, 88
    slope management 66
    Whistler 82
Grizzly Bear Spirit 36, 426, 428, 434–436
grizzly bears 428, 430, 431–433, 438n5
groomed pistes 250, 251
growth
    community 363
    economic 56, 59, 327, 427
guests 1, 129
    see also Chinese guests
guided tours 21

guides 146, 272
    availability 152
    licensing 14
    training 14, 21–22
    wages 153
    see also snowmobile guiding; snowmobiling
Gulf States 181, 258, 273
gymnastics, ski 140

habitats 9, 13, 433
Habitats Directive (1992) 385
hay production 378, **379**
hazards 464, 470
    management 21, 153, 471
health 54, 59, 130, 237, 240
    children 142–143
helmets 461
heritage 495, 502
    cultural 388, 396, 503
    natural 388, 396
high altitudes, construction projects 65
high-Alpine areas, accessibility 347
hiking 16, 27, 32, 75, 94–95, 374, 376–**377**
    blue ice 450
    buses 88
    cultural differences 196, 197
    Sweden 309
    Tatra National Park 248, 250
    trails 67, 396
Hohe Tauern National Park 30, **31**
Holiday Act (UK, 1938) 308
horse sledges 11, 251
hospitality 54, 58, 279, 283
hotels 119, 485–486
    Iceland 216–217, **218**, 221
    prices, Alps 113n1
    renewable energy supply (RES) 403
    Trentino 331
housing 57, 276, 363, 366
hybrid visitors 112, 179, 228–235
hydroelectric power 407, 409, 420
hypermobility 319

ice 47
    caps 212
    caves 301, 450, 451–452, **453**, 456, **456**
        tours 453–454, 455, 457–458
    days
        Germany 93, *93*
    rinks 67
    see also glaciers
Iceland
    all-season tourism 178
    buses 221
    climate 212–213

Iceland (*continued*)
    currency 447
    daylight 212–213
    financial crisis (2008) 447
    flights 446
    foreign tourism 444–445, **445**
    Geysir 220, 221, **223**
    glaciers 300
    Höfn 451
    hotels 216–217, **218**, 221
    infrastructure 220
    international arrivals 214, **214**, 215, **215**
    international visitors 217, **218**, 219, 221
    Jökulsárlón 221, 449, 450, **450**, 451, 457
    Keflavík Airport 216, 450, 457
    landscapes 226
    map **446**
    marketing areas 447–448, **447**
    nature destinations 178–179, 212–227, **219**
    overcrowding 179, 213, 222–224, 223, **224**, 225, **225**, 301
    overnight stays 216
    parking 222
    rental cars 221, 445, 446
    Reykjavík 216, 217, 224, 445
    seasonality 213, 300–301, 442–460, **445**
        on regional level 447–448, **447**
    Skaftafell National Park 449, 451
    stay duration 448
    transportation 445–446
    travel 221
    Vatnajökull 213
    Vatnajökull National Park 448, 449, 453–454, 458
    visitors
        motivations 217
        nationality by season 216, **217**
    whole-year tourism 458
    see also Hornafjörður
Icelandic Tourist Board 217, 219–226, **220**, 453
identity 278, 281, 283
    branding 485, 489
    corporate 357
    cultural 272
    local 502
ideology 500
ignorance 500
image, green 375
impact benefit agreements 10, 44
income 117, 188, 308
incremental development 4
incremental model 3
India 181, 258, 273
Indian reserves 38
indicative planning 49
Indigenous Community and Conserved Areas, definition 42

Indigenous culture 436
Indigenous lands 427
Indigenous peoples 40, 437
Indigenous Protected and Conserved Areas, definition 42
indigenous rights 15–16, 434–436
    British Columbia 35–46
indoor ski slopes 140
industrial snow 500
industrialization 394
industry 392
    ski 278, 302–303, 309, 493–508
    textile 392
inertia 494, 498–500
information 181, 263, 327
infrastructure 3, 56–58, 97–98, 272, 360, 364
    all-season 225
    Bavarian Alps 26, 100
    constructed 249–250, 336
    costs 116
    Iceland 220
    investment 324, 328, 329
    marketing 16
    public–private partnerships 316
    renewable energy 401
    ski tourism 25
    Valais 57
    villages 300
infrastructure-based tourism 20, 25, 31
injuries 236
    and gender 472
    localization 467–468, **467**
    reduction 301
    skiing **457**, 461, 465–470, **466**, **469**
innovation 327, 383, 498, 503
    Dolomites 328–330
    environmental sustainability 330–335
insight travelling 258
institutionalized seasonality 443
institutions, power 393
insurance 49, 249
inter-municipalities 299, 389, 392, 393, 394, 395, 396
inter-municipality tourist office 393, 394, 397
international market 2
International Organization for Standardization (ISO) 369
International Ski Federation (FIS) 376, 382, 465
International Union for Conservation of Nature (IUCN) 30, 42, 246, 448
Internet 55
    bookings 55, 260
interpersonal conflict 228, 233, 234
Intrawest Corporation 354–357, 355, 360, 361, 362, 363, 366
inventiveness 501
investment
    cable cars 113

infrastructure 324, 328, 329
    mass ski model 329
    ski lifts 312
    snowmaking 113, 309, 312, 318
    Swedish ski tourism 316
investors, engagement 4
Ischgl 349
ISO 14001 Certification, basic principles 370–372, 372, 384
Italians, winter sports activities 197
Italy
    Aosta Valley 56, 57, 58
    Piedmont 58
    Stelvio National Park 30
    Trentino 330–335
    see also Dolomites; Sexten
iterative planning 19

jobs 3, 4, 10, 44
    hospitality 283
    snowmobiling 148
    training 10, 44
Jumbo Glacier Resort 36, 44, 299–300, 425–441
    climate change 431
    decision making 428–430
    environmental assessment (EA) 425, 426
    sustainability 427–428
Jumbo Valley 36, 42, 426, 436, 438

keystone species 437n3
Kinbasket-Shuswap first nation 428
Kitzbühel 348
Kitzsteinhorn 348
knowledge
    behavioural change 87
    local 21, 265
KSL Capital Partners 356, 361
Ktunaxa First Nation 36, 42, 426, 428, 429–430, 435, 436, 437
Ktunaxa Nation v. British Columbia
    (2014) 428
    (2017) 426, 435, 436

Laax 369, 385n2
labels, green 164
labour
    cohorts 276
    migration, Sweden 309
lakes 11, 94–95
land 42, 100, 161, 297, 430, 498
    Indigenous 427
    public 355
    regulation 37
    rights 38, 40
    sacred 37
    tenure 150
        snowmobiling 21, 22
    transfers 44
land tour operator (LTO) 265
land use 30, 51
    agricultural 3
    balanced 25–26
    changes 378
    planning 16, 41, 42, 429, 430
        Levi 485
        ski resorts 388
lands for lifts agreements 360, 362
landscape 197, 198, 205, 208, 400
    beauty 1, 299, 408
    conservation 331
    cultural identity 272
    Iceland 226
    loss 267
    natural 299
    perception 181
        Shanghai tourism students 268, *269, 270, 271*
    protection areas 29, 30
    renewable energy 408, 409, 410, **410**, 411, **411**
    seasonal 225
    snowy 503
    solar systems 411, **412**
    territorial and landscape management 331–332, *332*, 335
    wind turbines 411, **411, 412, 414**
Lapland 318
    Finnish 55, 57, 476, 480–481
    summer tourism 58
Lapland Tourism Marketing Organization 481
leadership 301–302
    destination success 477–479, 489
    ski resorts, Finland 476–492
leisure 278, 308, 388
    time 133
Leisure Constraint Theory 279
liability 465
lifestyle migration 181–182, 276–287, 309
    definition 277
    landed negotiation dynamic 279
    motivations 281–282
    participant description 280, *280*
    push and pull framework 278
    Sweden 309
lifestyle tourism 20, 133
lifestyle travellers 278
lifts *see* chairlifts; ski lifts
Likert scale 194, 221, 238
Lil'wat Nation 42
linguistic barriers 265–266
living costs 276, 282

local communities 156
local economy 330
    mass ski model 328
local employment 388
local governance, evolution **391**, 392
local identity 502
local knowledge 21, 265
local mobilization 501–502
local needs 22, 156
local planning 53
long-distance markets 258
long-haul flights 94
long-term planning 155

Maine *see* Western Maine
maldevelopment 500
Malfontal 9, **10**
Māori people 36
Mapuche people 36
market 83, 155
    Chinese 4, 181, 265, 266, 272, 273
    global 2, 326
    long-distance 258
    mountain tourism 32
    realism 206
    ski 183
marketing 3, 20, 58, 119, 178, 193, 380–382, 504
    direct 125
    green 78
    Iceland 447–448, **447**
    infrastructure 16
    Internet 55
    joint 130
    myopia 336
    organizations 302
    value added 370
marketization 58
mass ski model 324, 326–327, 336
    Dolomites 326–327
    economic development 329–330
    investment 328
    local economy 328
Massif Central 392
Master Development Agreements 363
meadows 95, 378, **379**
meaningful leisure time 133
media 380, 495
    social 272, 458
meetings, incentives, conferences and exhibitions (MICE) 58
mega-events 315
mega-trends 19, 184, 187
Memorandum of Understanding (MoU) 44
microclimates 328

microenterprises 453
migration
    amenity 277, 278–279, 309, 501, 502
    economic 277
    labour 309
    see also lifestyle migration
Millennials 14, 22, 315
    sustainability 155, 157–158, 162, 164–167, *166*
    sustainable mountain practices 164–165
mitigation 49, 388
mobility 13, 89, 278, 402
    alternative 331, *332*, 334, 335
    eco-friendly 18
    sustainable 18
mobilization, local 501–502
Modane, industrialization 394
mono-cable gondolas (MGDs) 347
monopoly 362
motivation theory 228
motivations 240–242, *241*, 243
motorized visitors 179, 228–235
Mountain Law, France
    (1985) 391
    NOTRe Law (2015) 393–395
mountain rescue 252, 471
Mountain Resort Municipality 425, 426
mountain resorts 362, 366
    alpine 20, 116–137
    see also North American mountain resorts; ski resorts
mountain tourism 32, 293, 296, 504
    summer 350
    Sweden 295
    transformation 302–303, 497
Mountain Wilderness 501
mountaineering 16, 30
mountains
    access 501
    anthropization 328
    areas 3, 9, 14, 16
    biking 12–13, 75, 80, 318
    communities 501
    economy 505
    huts 95, 240, 250
    industry 504
    public policy 395–397
    railways 341–342
    recreation lifestyle 279, 281
    regions 503
        peripheral valleys 113
    sustainability 161
    transportation 339
multi-seasonal tourism 400
multi-stage planning 19
multiplier effect 116

National Association of Ski Resort Mayors 499
National Ministry of Environment and Water
        (MOEW) 381
national parks 30, 44, 176
    conservation plans 247
    goals 248
    ticket prices 249
national planning 53
National Union of Ski Instructors 499
nationality, and renewable energy 410–413, **411**,
        416, 418–419
natural heritage 388, 396
natural landscape, summer tourism 400
natural resources 155, 331–332, 335
    exploitation 16, 36, 336
natural seasonality 443
Natural Step, The 363
natural tourism 299
nature 54, 59, 197, 198
    Chinese 266–268, 272
    conservation 19, 95–96, 99, 180, 267
        cooperation 253–254
        Tatra National Park 246
        Tyrol 15
    destinations
        Iceland 178–179, 212–227, **219**
        satisfaction 221–222, *222*
    experiences 12, 17, 199, 237, 240
        Austria 67–68, **68**
    preservation 161
    protection 24, 32, 249, 267
        Tatra National Park 253–254
    reserves 68, 176, 199
    stakeholders 389
    Styria 56
nature-based activities 104–195
nature-based tourism 20, 30, 308
    affluent tourists 189
    climate change risk perceptions 17, 18, 73, 81
    drivers 187
    expenditure behaviour 107, *108*, 109, *109*
    recreation users 73, 75
    stakeholders 73, 75, 76, 77
needs
    customers 175
    guests 1
    local 22, 156
    regional community 300
Neskonlith peoples 35
networking 20, 130–131, 373
networks
    rail 308
    redefined 392
    road 327
    social 279, 281, 282
    stakeholder 397
New Zealand 16, 82, 276

night-time activities 239, 240
NIMBYism 434
Nippon Cable 361
noise
    emissions 29
    pollution 229, 234
nomadic skiing 497
non-governmental organizations (NGOs),
        environmental 100, 375, 376, 381–382
non-motorized visitors 179, 228–235
non-skiers 58, 97
Nordic skiing 140, 497
North American mountain resorts
    Alterra 297, 354, 357, *357*
    Aspen 309, 359, 360, 362
    corporate ownership 354–357
    see also Vail entries
North Rhine-Westphalia
    schools 21, 139
    snow sport school trips 138–145, **141**
Northern Lights tours 221, *221*, 446, 454, 455, 458
Norway 54, 319
    Telemark 307, 319
    Vestlandet 51, 58
NOTRe Law (2015) 389, 393, 395, 398n11
novelty 327

objective risks 462
offshore wind parks 401, 402
Olympic Games 277, 357
    see also Winter Olympics
on-site mobility, eco-friendly 88
on-site surveys 230–231, 406
online bookings 55, 260
online surveys 185, 189, 194, 195, 230–231, 238
operating costs 105
operators, tourism 392
outdoor activities
    motivations 236–237
    social aspects 237
    see also alternative outdoor activities
Outdoor Association 308
outdoor recreation 462–463
overcrowding
    cultural differences 223
    Iceland 179, 213, 222–224, *223*, **224**, 225,
        225, 301
    perception 222–224, *223*, **223**, **224**, 225,
        225, 364
    Tatra National Park 251
overdevelopment 496
overnight stays 28, 106, 147, 216
    Austria 25, 64, **65**, 344–345, **344**, 350n4–6
    Tyrol 30, 64, 84
    expenditure behaviour 105, 107, 110
oversized tourism projects 496

overtourism 258
ownership, diversity 3–4

Para-Olympics 277
parking 98, 222, 239, 240
parks 75, 247, 381
    national 176, 396–397, 448, 449, 451, 453–454, 458
partnerships 48, 316
passes *see* ski passes
pastures 27
peace and quiet 241–242
photovoltaic systems 407, 409, 411, **412**, 413, **415**, 420
physical security 261
physiological health 142–143
picknickers 237
Pirin Mountains 298
Pirin National Park 375, 381
pistes 66, 250, 251
place 425, 428
    corporatization 361
planning 49–50, 158
    community involvement 157, 161, 164
    definition 48
    First Nations 35–46
    indicative 49
    iterative 19
    land use 16
    local 53
    long-term 155
    multi-stage 19
    national 53
    OECD countries 48
    raison d'être 48–49
    regional 1, 16, 17, 47–64
    resorts 14
    spatial 9, 15, 24–34
    statutory 49
    strategic 16, 49, 50
    territorial 15
    see also destination planning; tourism planning
pleasure seekers 243
Poland
    Białka Valley 250
    Kuźnice 250, 251, **252**
    Morskie Oko 250, 251
    see also Tatra Mountains; Tatra National Park
police service 327
policy 11, 16, 228
    climate change 51
    destination development 299
    public 48, 395–397
    regional 17
    sustainability 51
    tourism 161

Polish Nature Conservation Act (2004) 248
Polish Olympic Committee 253
politics
    environmental assessment (EA) 436
    stakeholders 389
pollution 267, 328
    noise 229, 234
post-tourism 502
postal surveys 184, 185
power, institutions 393
preferences 11, 175, 192
    cultural differences 178
    guests 1
    ski resorts 199–203
price
    alpine hotels 113n1
    dumping 131–133
    sensitivity 14, 121
        winter tourists 117–118
price performance ratio 408, 417
pricing 1, 3, 14, 118–121
    alpine ski resorts 20, 116–137
    business model 20
    critical evaluation 128–129
    flexible 131
    see also cost
primary production, decline 54
private–public ski resorts 298
products
    adaptation need 93–94
    authentic 54
    cultural 17
    customer-centric 55
    customized 258
        lifestyle-oriented 14
    development 16, 19, 58, 68, 70, 264, 265, 266–271
    diversification 59, 77
    greener 157
    new 11, 12, 128, 392
    preferences 181
    regional 59
programmed snow 326, 328–329, 332
Project Approval Certificates 36
property 4, 498, 499
protected areas 9, 15, 24–34, 68, 100, 176, 247, 253, 267, 448
    British Columbia 42–43
    management 254
    rules 249
    social functions 249
    Sweden 183
protected zones 26–27
Provence-Alpes-Côte d'Azur 54, 499
pseudo-cultural development 502
public funding, winter sports 502
public interest, decision making 437

public land, exploitation 355
public participation, Hoher Kranzberg 99–100
public planning, climate change 50, 53
public policy
    definition 48
    mountain territories 395–397
    ski resorts 395–396
    valley areas 396–397
public transport 18, 56, 87, 88–89, 199, 207, 239, 240, 261
    Dolomites 333, 335
publics, conflict 228–229
public–private partnerships 48, 316
Pyrenees 493

Qat'muk 426, 428
Qat'Muk Declaration (2010) 36, 42, 435
quality of life 330
Queyras National Park 396–397
quiet areas 15, 28, 29–30, 32

railways 308, 341–342
    cog 343
recreation 228, 229
    off the beaten track 250–251
Recreation Experience Preference (REP) scales 228
recreationist motivations 179, 228–235
recultivation, Bansko 380, **381**, **382**
recycling 78
redundancies 364
referral notices 43
regional brands 58
regional community needs 300
regional destination governance 291
regional development 48, 51
regional economy 53, 103
regional experiences 205
regional planning and policy documents 1, 16, 17, 47–64
regional products 59
regional stakeholders 16, 53
regional strategy and policy documents 52
regions 11, 51
religion, freedom of 435–436
relocation 318
Renaissance Plan 363, 364
renewable energy 18, 67, 77, 80, 164, 400–424
    age 413, **414**, 416, 418–419
    Austria 403–421, *405*
    emissions 408, 409, 410, 413
    environment 408, 409, 410, 413
    European Alps 299
    holiday seasons 419–420, 421
    infrastructure 401
    installations 401, 417–418, 420
    landscape 408, 409, 410, **410**, 411, **411**
    local population 401, 414, 416–417, **416**, 421
    nationality 410–413, **411**, 416, 418–419
    and perception 408–414
    tourist attitudes 401–403
    tourist perceptions 417–419
    valorization 403
renewable energy supply (RES) 403, 406, 421
rental bikes 87
rental cars 221, 445, 446
rescue services 225
research
    action 373, 384
    behavioural 1
    customer 55
    ski resorts 389
reservoirs 66, 334, 388, 407, 409
residents 79, 120
Resort Municipality Act (1975) 362
Resort Municipality of Whistler (RMOW) 156–157, 158, 359, 360, 362, 363
resortification 308
resorts
    community 362
    development 296
    planning 14
    village model 355
    see also mountain resorts; ski resorts
resources
    exploitation 427
    management, cultural 296, 331–332, 335
    regulation 37
responsibility, cultural 498–499
restaurants 119, 160, 199, 208
restrooms 222, 225
rights 10
    Aboriginal 36, 37, 38–41, 434–436
    First Nations 43–44
    fishing 39
    indigenous 15–16, 35–46, 434–436
    land 38, 40
risk 146, 236, 301, 461–462
    awareness 462, 463
    decision making 463
    definition 462
    gender 463
    management 385, 462
    objective 462
    outdoor recreation 462–463
    perceptions 75, 463
    skiing 461
    snowboarding 461
    subjective 462
    Tatra National Park 252–253
roads 29, 225, 296, 327, 395
roller skiing 497–498
ropeways 339, 347, 349

Ruhegebiete (quiet areas) 15, 29–30
rural development 3
rush 146, 461–462, 471

Saas Valley 125
sacred land 37
safety 1, 54, 188, 251, 261, 268, 272, 296, 301, 461–462, 471
    concepts 464–465
    outdoor recreation 462–463
    regulations 327
    ski resort management 470–471
    skiing 327, 464–465, *464*, 471–472
    slopes 3
    snowmobiling 148, 152
    Tatra National Park 252–253
Salzburg 55–56, 64
Sami people 16, 36
satisfaction, alternative outdoor activities 239–242, *240*
Scandinavia 12
Scandinavian Mountains Airport project 316
Schladming 403–404, *404*
schools 117
    alternative disciplines 142, **142**
    Germany 139
        North Rhine-Westphalia 21
    scientific studies 144
    ski 3, 119, 139, 160
    snow sports 21, 138–145, **141**
        instructors 142, 143
        trip barriers 141
    sports 94
season passes 118, 120, *121*, 131, 132, 357
seasonal workers 176, 286
seasonality 67, 296, 442–444
    Iceland 213, 300–301, 442–460, **445**
    institutionalized 443
    natural 443
seasons, tourism 327
second homeowners 16, 57, 286, 309
security 4, 261
Secwepemc Nation 35
Seilbahn-und Skigebietsprogramm 15, 26, 28
self-completion surveys 220
self-drive 216
services
    adaptation 264
    customized 258
    delivery 228
    diverse 296
    expansion 11
    providers 259, 265
    rescue 225
Shanghai tourism students, landscape perception 268, *269*, *270*, *271*

sharing economy 87, 89
shopping 264
Shuswap First nation 435
Silvretta Montafon 403–404, *404*
Simpkw First Nation 44, 438n6
Sinixt First Nation 428, 437n2
sites, cultural or environmental importance 10
Skaftafell National Park 449, 451
ski areas 346–347, 348, 349
ski bashing 498
ski boom 343–344, 346
ski buses 88, 333, 334
ski carousels 326
ski chauffeur services 334
ski competitions 248
ski consortiums, Dolomites 325
ski gymnastics 140
ski huts 199
ski industry 309
    Colorado 278
    French Alps 493–508
    inertia 498–500
    transformation 302–303
ski lifts 25, 134, 471, 496
    Austria 104
        Tyrol 29
    Bavarian Alps 27, 28
    certification 161
    companies 326, 331, 362
    economic relevance 348–349
    expansion 296
    France 391
    as innovation 341–346, *341*
    innovation 347–348
    investment 312
    operators 297, 389
    passes 105, 112, 348
    quality 326
    role 296, 339–353
    and ski tourism 341–348
    Sweden 308
    Tatra National Park 248
    ticket revenues 310, **310**, 312, 314
    tickets 118, 120
    Trentino 331
    see also chairlifts
ski market 183
ski operators 50
ski passes 118, 124, 207, 502
ski racing events 376
ski resorts 1, 195, 302, 476
    accessibility 327
    advertising 495
    alpine 20, 116–137
    Alps, location within 200, **202**
    Australia 77
    Bavaria 57

brand identity 489
Canada 158
and climate change 4, 388
collaboration 476–492
competition 495
costs 195
development 30, 302
diversification 177
Eastern Europe 118
Finland 301–302, 476–492
and global warming 500
governance 389–392
    community model 391
    corporate model 391
    public actors 390–391
Italian target group **204**
land use planning 388
leadership 476–492
management 373
    environmental 297–298, 369–387
    safety measures 470–471
management sustainability 296
as mega attractions 310
merging 354–368
mid-elevation 395
ownership 297, 354–368
preferences 199–203
private–public 298
public policy 395–396
research 389
selection criteria 198–199, **199**, 203, 205, 477
size 50, 206–207
stakeholders 395
sustainability 324–338, 369
Swedish 315
Swiss 121, **122**
tickets 120
    daily 131–132, 207
train access 200, **201**
turnover 116
websites 50
year-round 427
see also French ski resorts
ski schools 3, 119, 139, 160
ski touring 32, 240, 243
    Kasprowy Wierch 251, **252**
    Kuznice 251, **252**
    motivations 237
    off trail 251
    Tatra National Park 246–247, 248, 249, 250
ski tourism 328
    climate change 184
    development 25
    employment 184
    environmental impacts 24–25
    industrialization period 307–309
    infrastructure 25

prehistoric and ancient times 306–307
present 309–314
and ski lifts 341–348
spatial planning **27**
ski-boom 26
skiers
    behavioural change 471
    as members 14
    snowmobile-assisted 229, 232
    technical ability 350n3
skiing
    accidents 465–470
    for all utopia 495
    alpine 20, 103, 189, 461
    areas 324–326
        organized 464
    backcountry 237, 243, 309
    cat 151
    children 94, 461
    China 268
    and climate change 309
    code of conduct 471
    competitions 307
    costs 329, 495
    cultural differences 178, 192–211
    day trippers 92
    decline 188–189
    expenditure 117
    free 464
    and global warming 324
    heli 151
    history 305
    injuries **457**, 461, 465–470, **466**, **469**
    mass 324, 326–327
    mechanized 151
    nature of 344
    nomadic 497
    Nordic 497
    pistes 66, 250, 251
    risk 461
    roller 497–498
    safety 327, 464–465, 464, 471–472
    schools 139
    social aspects 198, 203
    teaching 182, 283
    ticket prices 118, **123**
    tunnels 11
    see also cross-country skiing; downhill skiing
Skinow 127
Skwelkwek'welt Protection Centre 35
sledges, horse 11, 251
slopes 57, 67, 195, 327
    greenhouse gas emissions 66
    indoor 140
    preparation 326–327
    quality 20
    safety 3

slopes (*continued*)
    security 4
    solar systems 409
    stability 380, **380**
small business tourism, economic role 50
small to medium-sized enterprises (SMEs) 54
smartphones 188
snow 47, 49, 67, 75, 225, 298, 318, 496, 500
    commuters 327
    coverage 64, 175–176
    days 316, 317
    depth 316, 317
    grooming 326–327, 328, 334
    guarantee 134
    guns 494
    industrial 500
    insecurity 55, 57
    insurances 49
    Norway 319
    powder 251
        untouched 147, **147**, 149, **149**
    programmed 326, 328–329, 332
    reliability 84, 103
        and climate change 331, 332, 333
    security 20, 93, 96, 130
    Sweden 317–318, **317**
    see also snowmaking
Snow Plan 308
snow sports
    culture 314
    Germany 138
    lessons 264
    schools 21, 138–145, **141**
snowboarding 140, 198, 327, 461, 500
snowmaking 66–67, 77, 184, 296
    Austria 65–66
    British Columbia **292**
    capacity 189
    equipment 25, 388
    investment 113, 309, 312, 318
    see also artificial snowmaking
snowmobile guiding 21–22
    caribou closures 151–152
    certification 152–154
    conflict with other user groups 151
    guides' availability 152
    and land tenure 150
    and local communities 146–154
snowmobile-assisted skiers 229, 232
snowmobiling 14, 75, 78, **147**, **153**, 179, 189, 229, 232
    British Columbia 14, 21–22, 150
    changes in participation 187, **187**
    costs 153
    day trippers 147
    growth 147–148
    guides 148–150
    jobs 148
    land tenure 21, 22
    overnight stays 147
    push and pull motivations 146–147
    safety 148, 152
    spending 147, *148*
    Sweden 177
snowshoeing 78, 103, 140, 227, 239, 500
sociability 241–242
social change 187–188
social conflicts 1
social goals 428
social interaction 232–233, *233*
social media 272, 458
social networks 279, 281, 282
social responsibility 497, 498
social sustainability 167, 330
social values conflict 229, 233, 234
socio-cultural conditions 1, 14
socio-psychological health 142–143
socioeconomic stakeholders 389
soft-tourism 30
soil conditions 379
solar energy 77, 299, 407, 409, 411, 413, **415**
    landscape 411, **412**
    slopes 409
solar power 419
solitude 232–233, *233*
Sound of Snow 67
South Tyrol 178, 192–211
spaces, distribution 425
spas 11, 93
spatial management 128
spatial planning 9, 15, 418
    Bavaria **27**
    ski tourism **27**
    Tyrol **27**, 28
    winter sport destinations 24–34
    winter sport tourism 26–30
spatial and socio-cultural challenges 9–11
Special Management Area 429
species
    keystone 437n3
    umbrella 437n3
spending *see* expenditure
sports 67, 93, 176, 314
    culture 193
    see also winter sports
sports space theory 314
stakeholders 25, 50, 101, 297, 298, 303, 392
    and carbon dioxide emissions 77–78
    and climate change
        adaptation 99
        mitigation 77–78
        perceptions 17–18, 73, 76–78, 79–80
    collaboration 489–490
    demobilization 397

engagement 362–363
French ski resorts 391
nature 389
nature-based tourism 73, 75, 76, 77
networks 397
political 389
regional 16, 53
Sexten 205
ski resorts 395
socioeconomic 389
standards 370
standby tourists 121
Startclim 67
St'át'imc Nation 35–36
Statistic Sweden 312
statutory planning 49
stay duration 69, 83, 448
staycations 319
Stelvio National Park 30
Stockholm 316
strategic planning 16, 49, 50
students 120
Styria 56
subjective risks 462
subsidies 66, 80, 502
summer tourism 12, 56, 339
    Austria 404
    climate change 503
    Lapland 58
    natural landscape 400
    winter sports destinations 11–12
supply 49
    and demand 55, 58
surface lifts 342–343, 345, 347, 348
surveys
    choice experiments 205
    on-site 230–231, 406
    online 185, 189, 194, 230–231, 238
    postal 184, 185
    response rates 189
    self-completion 220
sustainability 28, 101, 125, 155–172, 291–304, 370
    at home 163, *163*
    business 18
    and climate change 55–56
    destinations 155–172
    Dolomites 324–338
    economic 167, 330
    environmental 330–335, **336**
    European Alps 157
    on holiday 163, *163*
    Jumbo Glacier Resort 427–428
    Millennials 155, 157–158, 162, 164–167, *166*
    mobility 18
    mountain 161
    policy 51
    ski resorts 324–338
    social 167, 330
    valuing 164, 165
sustainability-profitability-gap 112
sustainable development 3, 5, 11, 14, 22, 155, 161, 419
    goals 1, 4
    ski resorts 369
Sustainable Mountain Tourism Experience Model (SMTE) 293, **294**
sustainable practices
    affordability 164–166, *164*
    European Alps 167, 168
    Millennials 164–165
Sweden 183, 188, 295, 318
    amenity migration 295, 309
    Åre 308, 316
    artificial ski areas 319
    backcountry skiing 309
    cross-country skiing 186–187, **186**, 309
    Dalarna 55, 308, 312, 316
    downhill skiing 185, **186**, 295, 305–323, 310, *311*, 312, **313**, 314
    economic development 295
    expanding resorts 316
    financial crisis (1990s) 310, 319
    foreign tourist consumption 189
    hiking 309
    Idre 36
    Jämtland 308–309, 312
    Jämtland Härjedalen 56
    Jokkmokk 307, 316
    Kebnekaise 318
    labour migration 309
    lifestyle migration 309
    mountain bike trails 318
    mountain tourism development 295
    Norbotten 309
    Olympic Committee 316
    population projections 315, **315**
    protected areas 183
    Sami people 16
    Sarek 318
    second homeowners 309
    ski lift ticket revenues 310, **310**, 312, 314
    ski resorts 315
    snow 316, 317–318, **317**
    snowmaking investment 318
    survey methodologies 184–185, *185*
    temperature 188
    Västerbotten 308, 309
    winter recreation trends 177–178, 183–191
Swedish Agency for Economic and Regional Growth 189
Swedish Environmental Protection Agency 184
Swedish Ski Areas Industry Association 310, 312
Swedish Tourist Federation 308
swimming 75, 95, 264

Swiss Alps 308
Swiss ski resorts, decline in visits 121, **122**
Switzerland 58
    Canton of Grisons 54, 55, 56, 57, 58, 257–258
    Canton of Valais 16, 57, 104
    Chinese guests 176, 181, 257–275
    crowdfunding model 20
    Davos 342, 343
    economic difficulties 54
    expenditure behaviour 104
    Laax 369, 385n2
    landscape perception 181
    Myclimate'Cause We Care' 134n4
    product preferences 181
    Saas Valley 125
    Saas-Fee 129–134, 134
    SkiArena Andermatt – Sedrun 126–127, **126**, **127**, 134n5
SWOT analysis 19
    adaptation strategy 95–97, 101

t-test 407
Taoism 266
Tatra Mountain Rescue Service 251
Tatra Mountains 246, 248, 249, 250
    Kasprowy Wierch 248, 250, 251, 252, **252**
    Kościeliska Valley 251
Tatra National Park
    caving 249, 250
    climbing 248, 249
    constructed infrastructure 249–250
    designated areas 246, **247**
    educational trips 253
    hiking 248, 250
    management 180–181, 246–256
    nature conservation 246, 253–254
    outdoor recreation activities **248**
    overcrowding 251
    risk 252–253
    safety 252–253
    ski lifts 248
    ski touring 246–247, 248, 249, 250
    user conflicts 251–252
    visitor monitoring 249–251, 254
technological change 187–188
technology 49, 187–188, 251, 296
    digital 127, 134n6, 324
Telemark 307, 319
temperature 49, 56, 64, 75, 79, 188, 328–329
territorial and landscape management 331–332, 332, 335
territorial reform, France 393–395, 396
territories 10, 15–16
textile industry 392
thematic analysis 51

Thomatal 350n2
thrill 462, 471
Ticketcorner 126, 127
tickets
    online 126
    prices 129
        skiing 118, **123**
    ski
        lifts 118, 120, 310, **310**, 312, 314
        resorts 120, 131–132, 207
Tla-oh-qui-aht Nation 42
tobogganing 99, 140, 243
Tod Mountain 35
touring *see* ski touring
tourism
    annual growth rate 257
    associations 119
    expansion 32
    multiplier effect 104
Tourism Monitor Switzerland 104
Tourism Naturally Conference (2018) 1
touristic value chain 258–259
tours
    backcountry 149
    cabin 146, 149
    guided 21
    Northern Lights 221, *221*, 446, 454, 455, 458
traffic 328, 363
trails, widening 376, **378**
trains 13, 88, 89, 197, 200, 296
    climate change adaptation 207–208
tramways, aerial 340
transformation 497–498
    French Alps 302–303
transition 494, 504, 505
transparency 129
transport 57, 163, 197
    Alps 70
    Austria 68–69
    Bavarian Alps 26
    buses 88, 221, 333, 334
    capacity 346, 347
    carbon dioxide emissions 69
    climate change 85, 87
    eco-friendly 84, 86, 87, **87**
    energy consumption 17
    Iceland 445–446
    low energy 83
    mountain 339
    networks 16
    quality 349
    urban 350
    see also public transport; trains
transportation, uphill 296, 308, 339, 340, 344, 350n1
travel 1, 86, 88

agencies 140
and climate change 18, 82–91
climate friendly 83
eco-friendly 89
global 189
Iceland 221
long-distance 67
packages 207
travellers, lifestyle 278
Trentino 330–335
tribal parks 42
tricable gondola detachable (TGD) 348
TripAdvisor 260
tropical nights 64
Tsilhqot'in Nation v. British Columbia (2014) 40
Tsilhqot'in Nations 42
two-year tourists 276–287
Tyrol 15, 58
  alternative winter activities 180, 236–245
  cable car and ski resort programme 28–29
  climate strategy 55
  hospitality culture 58
  Landscape Plan 29
  nature conservation law 15
  overnight stays 30, 64
  quiet areas 29–30, 32
  Seilbahn-und Skigebietsprogramm 15, 26, 28
  ski lifts 29
  South *see* Sexten
  spatial planning **27**, 28
Tyrolean Nature Conservation Act (1975) 29
Tyrolian Alps 9, 31, 118

umbrella species 437n3
Union of British Columbia Indian Chiefs 37
United Nations Declaration on the Rights of Indigenous Peoples (UNDRIP) 40–41, 44
United Nations Educational, Scientific and Cultural Organization (UNESCO) 375
United Nations (UN)
  Millennium Development Goals (MDGs) 292
  Sustainable Development Goals (SDGs) 292–293, *293*
United States of America (USA)
  Colorado 278
  National Forests 105
  see also North American mountain resorts; Western Maine
United States Forest Service 355
universities, role 143
uphill transportation 296, 308, 339, 340, 344, 350n1
  see also cable cars and surface lifts (CCSLs)
Urals 32
urban development 4
urban transportation 350
urbanization 267, 284, 309

Vail Pass Winter Recreation Area (VPWRA) 179, 229–234, **231**
  motivations 232–233, *232*, *233*
Vail Resorts Inc. 4, 22, 118, 167, 277, 284, 285, 297, 354, 361
  acquisitions 356
  Epic Pass 122–123, 131, 132, 357, 365
  pricing 128
  redundancies 364
  revenues 118, **119**
  Whistler Blackcomb 363–366
valleys 14, 113, 388, 396–397
value added 17, 258
  marketing 370
value chains 258–259
  alpine tourism 259, **259**
  China Inbound Service 264–266, **264**
values, cultural 268, 448
Vancouver International Airport 277, 363
Vanoise Express 348
Vanoise National Park 30, 398n8
Vatnajökull National Park 448, 449, 453–454, 458
vegetation 379, 380
vertical engagement 130–131
villages 296, 297, 300, 388
visitor
  expectations 251
  monitoring, Tatra National Park 249–251, 254
Visitor Monitoring Systems 177, 180
Vosges Mountains 392

wages 276, 282, 283, 285
walkers 20
warm winter destinations 94
waste management 334
water 11, 64, 494, 496
  claims 333–334
  management 57, 296, 331, 332, 333–334, 379, 380
weather conditions 2
wellbeing 130, 330, 495
wellness 11, 16, 58, 67, 93, 333
Western Maine 17–18
  climate change 12
    risk perceptions 73–81
  outdoor activities 75, 80
    frequencies 78, **78**
  recreation behaviour 79
  resident profile and recreational behaviour 78
  visitors 74
Whistler 277, 354–368
  community 156, **156**, 360
    involvement 167, 168
  corporate–community relations 354, 361–366
  culture 286, 365
  development 158, *160*, 161

Whistler (*continued*)
    energy consumption 82
    greenhouse gas emissions 82
    housing 363
    lifestyle migration 181–182, 276–287
    mountain operations ownership 357–361
    pricing 128
    residency challenges 282–283
    resort development 357
    Resort Municipality of (RMOW) 156–157, 158, 359, 360, 362, 363
    restaurants 160
    ski resort 118–119
    ski schools 160
    snowmobiling 150
    social sustainability 167
    structural elements 282–283, 285
    sustainability 155–172
    sustainable development 22
    traffic 363
    2020 Plan 156, 157, 158, 167, 168, 363
    urbanization 284
    Village 359, **359**
Whistler Blackcomb 156, 157, **168**, 276–277, 284, 354, 355, 359, 361
    day trippers 284
    gondolas 364
    housing 366
    infrastructure 364
    overcrowding 364
    ownership 297
    Snow School 281
    Vail Resorts Inc. 363–366
Whistler Mountain 277, 357–359, **358**, 360
White River National Forest (WRNF) 229, 230
whole-year tourism, Iceland 458
WiFi 198, 203
wilderness 21, 151, 267, 300
wildlife 12, 251, 300, 328
wind
    energy 299, 411, 421
    farms 417
    power 419
    turbines 401–402, 403, 406, 409, 411, 413, **414**, 419
        emissions **415**
        landscape 411, **411**, **412**, **414**

Winter Olympics 359
    (2006) 58
    (2010) 277, 360–361, 363
    (2022) 253, 268, 272
    (2026) 316
winter sports 58, 175, 331, 443, 498–499
    access 495
    Austrians 197
    Bavarian Alps 92
    children 14
    cultural factors 495
    destinations 11–12, 15, 24–34
    ecological footprint 112
    economic relevance 103–115
    expenditure behaviour 19–20, 103–115
    Germans 197
    Italians 197
    media 495
    motivations 197–198, **198**
    public funding 502
    schools 94
    spatial planning 26–30
    see also biking; hiking; ski entries; skiing; snow sports; snowmobiling;
winter tourism
    experiences 175–182
    reflections 442–444
    reinvention 502–505
    timeframe 444
winter tourists, price sensitivity 117–118
WinterCard (Saas-Fee) 123–125, 129, 130–132, 133, 134n3
    Gold 125, **125**, 132, 133
word-of-mouth advertising 132, 149
workers, seasonal 176, 286
World Heritage Sites (WHS) 267, 375

year-round ski resorts 427
year-round tourism 19, 49, 54, 59, 67, 426

zoning 9, **10**, 14, 176, 229, 234
    Bavarian Alps 26
    recreation 247–249
    VPWRA 230, **231**, 233

CABI – who we are and what we do

This book is published by **CABI**, an international not-for-profit organisation that improves people's lives worldwide by providing information and applying scientific expertise to solve problems in agriculture and the environment.

CABI is also a global publisher producing key scientific publications, including world renowned databases, as well as compendia, books, ebooks and full text electronic resources. We publish content in a wide range of subject areas including: agriculture and crop science / animal and veterinary sciences / ecology and conservation / environmental science / horticulture and plant sciences / human health, food science and nutrition / international development / leisure and tourism.

The profits from CABI's publishing activities enable us to work with farming communities around the world, supporting them as they battle with poor soil, invasive species and pests and diseases, to improve their livelihoods and help provide food for an ever growing population.

CABI is an international intergovernmental organisation, and we gratefully acknowledge the core financial support from our member countries (and lead agencies) including:

UKaid from the British people | Ministry of Agriculture People's Republic of China | Australian Government Australian Centre for International Agricultural Research | Agriculture and Agri-Food Canada | Ministry of Foreign Affairs of the Netherlands | Schweizerische Eidgenossenschaft Confédération suisse Confederazione Svizzera Confederaziun svizra — Swiss Agency for Development and Cooperation SDC

Discover more

To read more about CABI's work, please visit: **www.cabi.org**

Browse our books at: **www.cabi.org/bookshop**, or explore our online products at: **www.cabi.org/publishing-products**

Interested in writing for CABI? Find our author guidelines here: **www.cabi.org/publishing-products/information-for-authors/**